Politics of the Poor

The world is richer today than ever before. Yet, ever fewer people share in those riches, even in democracies, where people are promised a share in political participation. What does living in a democracy mean for its impoverished populations, people who simultaneously confront persistent deprivations and increasing inequalities? Do they absorb the universalistic ideas associated with democracy? Alternatively, do their precarious lives overwhelm them so much so that they cannot act beyond particularistic concerns? These questions motivated this study.

Drawing on diverse sorts of data, particularly fieldwork in India, the author argues that poor people neither assimilate into the universal values associated with democracy nor do they maintain their difference vis-à-vis democracy. Rather, they *negotiate* with democracy in multi-faceted ways. These practices outlast electoral cycles and participation in protest movements. They involve provisional transactions between contingent collectives of poor people on the one hand and politicians, bureaucrats and members of the dominant classes on the other. The political thoughts and practices entailed in such practices reveal the entanglements between universal values and particularistic ideas. In investigating these entanglements, the author draws on critical political theorists to elaborate an agonistic approach to studying democracy. Such an approach helps him to conceptualize democracy beyond the liberal normativity that suffuses most writings on the topic.

The book's contributions are threefold. Empirically, the book offers a rich and nuanced account of the multifaceted negotiations that constitute the 'politics of the poor'. Analytically, it outlines and elaborates the 'political spaces' that shape and are shaped by poor people's politics. Theoretically, *Politics of the Poor* contributes to developing an 'agonistic' approach to studying democracy. The author urges researchers of democracy to step beyond either enthusiastic narratives of the inevitability of democracy or apocalyptic accounts of democracy's impending death.

This book will interest academic researchers in the fields of democratic politics, Indian politics, and poverty, inequality and social class. It will also be valuable to graduate and postgraduate students studying politics and South Asia studies.

Indrajit Roy teaches at the Department of Politics, University of York and is Junior Research Fellow at Wolfson College, University of Oxford. He studies democratic deepening and societal transitions in the Global South. His specific research interests are studying citizenship in emerging markets, the connections between political change and social transformation, and South Asian politics.

SOUTH ASIA IN THE SOCIAL SCIENCES

South Asia has become a laboratory for devising new institutions and practices of modern social life. Forms of capitalist enterprise, providing welfare and social services, the public role of religion, the management of ethnic conflict, popular culture and mass democracy in the countries of the region have shown a marked divergence from known patterns in other parts of the world. South Asia is now being studied for its relevance to the general theoretical understanding of modernity itself.

South Asia in the Social Sciences will feature books that offer innovative research on contemporary South Asia. It will focus on the place of the region in the various global disciplines of the social sciences and highlight research that uses unconventional sources of information and novel research methods. While recognizing that most current research is focussed on the larger countries, the series will attempt to showcase research on the smaller countries of the region.

General Editor
Partha Chatterjee
Columbia University

Editorial Board
Pranab Bardhan
University of California at Berkeley

Stuart Coleridge
Durham University

Christophe Jaffrelot
Centre d'etudes et de recherches internationales, Paris

Other books in the series:
Government as Practice: Democratic Left in a Transforming India
by Dwaipayan Bhattacharyya
Courting the People: Public Interest Litigation in Post-Emergency India
by Anuj Bhuwania
Development after Statism: Industrial Firms and the Political Economy of South Asia by Adnan Naseemullah

Politics of the Poor

Negotiating Democracy in Contemporary India

Indrajit Roy

CAMBRIDGE
UNIVERSITY PRESS

CAMBRIDGE
UNIVERSITY PRESS

University Printing House, Cambridge CB2 8BS, United Kingdom

One Liberty Plaza, 20th Floor, New York, NY 10006, USA

477 Williamstown Road, Port Melbourne, vic 3207, Australia

314 to 321, 3rd Floor, Plot No.3, Splendor Forum, Jasola District Centre, New Delhi – 110025, India

79 Anson Road, #06–04/06, Singapore 079906

Cambridge University Press is part of the University of Cambridge.

It furthers the University's mission by disseminating knowledge in the pursuit of education, learning and research at the highest international levels of excellence.

www.cambridge.org
Information on this title: www.cambridge.org/9781107117181

First published 2018

Printed in India by Thomson Press (India) Ltd.

A catalogue record for this publication is available from the British Library.

Library of Congress Cataloging-in-Publication Data

Names: Roy, Indrajit, author.
Title: Politics of the poor : negotiating democracy in contemporary India /
    Indrajit Roy.
Description: Delhi, India : Cambridge University Press, 2016. | Includes
    bibliographical references and index.
Identifiers: LCCN 2016013218 | ISBN 9781107117181 (hardback)
Subjects: LCSH: Poor--Political activity--India. | Democracy--Social
    aspects--India. | Marginality, Social--Political aspects--India. |
    Political participation--India.
Classification: LCC HC440.P6 R685 2016 | DDC 320.954086/942--dc23 LC record available at
https://lccn.loc.gov/2016013218

ISBN 978-1-107-11718-1 Hardback

Contents

List of Tables, Maps, Figures and Charts

MAPS, FIGURES AND CHARTS

Acknowledgements

This book would not have been possible without the involvement and contributions of many people, although it goes without saying that errors are all mine!

Foremost among the people to whom I owe the most debt are my hosts and interlocutors in the four villages where I conducted ethnographic fieldwork. Given their misgivings about making their names public, they must remain anonymous. Nonetheless, I would like to place on record my gratitude to them for allowing me to live in their midst, hang out with them, and to be privy to the stories, gossip and scandals that they shared with one another. Besides providing me with food and accommodation, they cared for me when I was sick, helped me make sense of the going-ons in their neighbourhoods, and showered me with generosity and magnanimity of which I was perhaps not so deserving. For all these, and for everything else, I will always be indebted.

The book began life as a doctoral project, supported from a scholarship provided by the Queen Elizabeth House (QEH). My doctoral supervisors Nandini Gooptu and Sabina Alkire welcomed me to Oxford and back to academic life. I am grateful for the patience with which they answered my questions and clarified my doubts as well as for their advice and insights into developing my thesis. But above all, I am grateful for the friendship they offered me, the generous doses of wit and humour that made the thesis bearable, and the confidence they reposed in me despite my often bizarre ideas. My thesis examiners Frances Stewart and Stuart Corbridge offered important suggestions to clarify my argument. Barbara Harriss-White remains a critical interlocutor: 36 Victoria Road provided a cosy locale for the ideas in this book to develop. Diego Sanchez-Ancochea prodded me to get on with writing the book at a time when I was easily swayed by other projects. Jonathan Pattenden, Rosanna Pinheiro-Macado and Lucia Michelutti offered advice on portions of chapters, for which I am very thankful. Jocelyn Alexander, Nikita Sud and Abdul Raufu Mustapha provided invaluable insights from time to time, without which neither my doctoral thesis nor my book would have come to fruition. I deeply appreciate Biju Rao nudging me to undertake fieldwork in the areas that I eventually did.

Indeed, the intellectual debts I have accumulated are too many to recount. I want to particularly thank Kanchan Chandra, David Gellner, Shaibal Gupta, John Harriss, David Hulme, Surinder Jodhka and James Manor for their willingness to share their time and perspectives, which shaped my own thoughts on the subject. I am also grateful to Crispin Bates, Lawrence Cohen, Olle Frodin, Thomas Blom Hansen and Swagato Sarkar for hosting me at different workshops where I had the opportunity to develop the ideas that eventually form the basis for this book. Kunal Sen, Suman Seth, Stephanie Tawa-Lama-Rewal, Vamsichandran Vakulabharanam and his students AP Sreeraj and Debolina Biswas generously shared their insights and data, for which I can never thank them enough.

Many of the arguments developed in this book were based on discussions with students over the 'Politics of the Poor' module that I convened at QEH in Michaelmas Terms 2013–16. Amogh Sharma, Kat Eghdamian, Karine Yuki, Johanna Wallin, Lennart Bolliger, Ankita Pandey, Giulia Gonzales, Srujana Katta, Gerardo Torres Contreras, Vail Miller, Lealem Abebe, Carols Quembo, Ozlem Akkurt, Cristina Amrein Esnaola, Alexandra Bridges, Katie Rickard, Emilia Pool Illsley, Ahsan Minhas, Laura Stacey, Mary-Jean Chan, Anders Moller, Paulo Singer, Timothy Abel, Junko Asano, Moctar Kane, Natasha Maru, Rachael Midlen, Nicole Sparks, Charles-Alexis Couvreur, Saeed Hussaini, Cassandra Cardiff, Henrice Stoebesand, Kayla Svoboda, Sudheesh Ramapurath, Kwaku Abrefa Busia, Aban Haq, Cannelle Gueguen-Teil, Jayesha Koushik, Sana Moyeen, Kelly Casey and Aisha Ahmad: massive thanks to each one of you for engaging with my ideas and challenging them from time to time.

No research is possible without on-the-ground support. Manoj Rai at Society for Participatory Research in Asia (PRIA) and Biraj Patnaik at the Right to Food Campaign in India provided crucial practical advice without which I would have been completely lost. Indrani Bhattacharya at Child in Need Institute (CINI) and Rupesh at Koshish Charitable Trust have provided me with incredible support for which I will ever be grateful. This research would simply not have taken the shape it did had it not been for the tireless efforts of colleagues at Maldah Sahajogita Samiti (MSS) as well as Mahila Jagran Kendra (MJK). I am particularly grateful to Biswajit Bose and Najima di at MSS and Rajendra Poddar and Khagesh Srivastava at MJK for their unstinting support to this project and for helping me see this through.

At Cambridge University Press, I cannot thank Debjani Mazumder, Qudsiya Ahmed and their colleagues enough for their unstinting support in seeing this project through. It is a matter of honour that the editors of the South Asia in the Social Sciences series agreed to include this volume in their series. Comments from three anonymous reviewers were enormously helpful in the shaping of the argument in this book. The bibliography was an utter mess before Alex Lowe intervened and disciplined it.

It is overwhelming for me to recount debts to friends. Matthew McCartney, Nicolas Jaoul, Suryakant Waghmore, Thomas Goodfellow, Manali Desai, Oliver Owen, Sumeet Mhaskar, Uday Chandra, Diego Maiorano, Prashant Sharma and Subhasis Dey: I cannot thank you fellows enough for making this journey a cheerful one. To friends at QEH, I owe immense gratitude for not allowing my academic endeavours to degenerate into solitary confinement. Abby Hardgrove, Narae Choe, Elise Klein, S. J. Cooper-Knock, Elizabeth Chatterjee, Neil Howard, Sofia Donoso, Asha Amirali, James Morrissey, Jamie Furniss, Muhammad Ali Jan, Nadya Figuero, Shrochis Karki and Paul Kadetz: thanks people for making 'The Loft' such a wonderful place, a home away from home where wisdom and whiskey were ever flowing. Abhinav Mukerji, Shruti Narayan, Prasun Chatterjee, Ambar Chakrabarty, Ashwani Sinha and Abhijat Kanade: all I can say is, thanks for everything. The staff at QEH have made it as warm a working space as one can ever hope. To them, especially to Gary Jones and Penelope Rogers, my heartiest cheers.

The Roy Family remains a constant pillar of support for my endeavours. My parents Rita and Ovijit Roy and brother Prithvijit Roy have been generous with wisdom, entertainment and good cheer. The terrace at my in-laws' home in Kathmandu, from which one could watch the mighty Himalayas play hide-and-seek behind the clouds, offered a scenic locale where the initial thoughts for this book were penned. I am thankful to them all for accepting my idiosyncrasies, including the decision to give up my career as a development professional and return to the precarities of academe. To Uma, my wife, I will remain forever in debt not only because she tolerated my inconstant presence, but because she has constantly challenged me to refine my argument. Without her encouragement, neither the PhD nor the book would have been possible. Our daughter, Tia has taught me much about reading, writing and living. To her I dedicate this book.

Glossary

Aadmi	Hindi/ Maithili: Person (Literally: man, but often used as generic term to describe people).
Adivasi	Hindi/ Bangla: Indigenous. A reference to members of tribal communities and communities listed as Scheduled Tribe.
Ajuktipurna	Bangla: unreasonable.
Aman	Bangla: See Kharif crop.
Anyay	Hindi/ Maithili/ Bangla: Injustice.
Ashphorda	Bangla: Audacity.
Atyachaar	Hindi/ Maithili/ Bangla: Oppression.
Babu	Hindi/ Maithili/ Bangla: Gentleman.
Backward or Backward caste	Bihar: Terms to describe members of caste groups classified as OBC or EBC.- see Shudra, Other Backward Class and Extremely Backward Class below.
Bichar	Bangla: Reasoned deliberation.
Boro	See Rabi.
Bhadralok	Gentleman (Literally: civil man).
Bodolok	Influential person (Literally: 'Big Man').
Brahman	A community traditionally associated with priestly functions. Members consider themselves at the apex of the ritual Hindu hierarchy.
Chamar	A Scheduled Caste group, traditionally associated with leather work.
Chai	Hot beverage, comprising tea leaves, milk, sugar and local herbs.
Chasi	Bangla: Peasant
Chengras	Bangla dialect: Young boys, "chap".
Chhotolok	Person with limited social and economic resources (Literally: small person).
Chillam	A long tubular device typically used for smoking marijuana
Da	Bangla: elder brother/ a term of endearment for men.
Dabang	Hindi/ Mathili: Dominant.
Dalit	(Literally: broken people) Marathi: oppressed. Now in use all over India to describe ex-'untouchables'.
Dashavali	Literally: Committee of Ten. Unelected deliberative body among the Desiyas in Maldah.
Desiya	Self-description of the Rajbansi caste in north-central Bengal, literally "of this country".

Devi	Literally: Goddess. Suffixed with names of women to show respect.
Devta	God/ male deity.
Dom	A Scheduled Caste Group, traditionally associated with basket-weaving, drummers in village festivals and sometimes work at cremation grounds.
Doya	Bangla: pity, mercy.
Dusadh	A Scheduled Caste group, traditionally associated with patrolling the village.
Ek Sho deener kaaj	Bangla: colloquial to refer to the 100 days of work under the NREGA. See NREGA below.
Extremely Backward Class (EBC)	Bihar: An administrative classification by the Bihar Government of communities historically stigmatized as 'low caste' and confronting acute deprivations. Members of communities enumerated as EBC are eligible for protective discrimination and affirmative action in public education and government employment. A total of 108 communities from among intermediate status caste groups are classified in Bihar as EBC.
Forwards	Bihar: Term to describe members of General Castes. See General Caste below.
Gangot	A caste listed as EBC, whose members claimed to have descended from the river Ganfa.
Garib/ Gorib	Hindi/ Maithili/ Thaithi/ Bangla: Poor.
General Caste	Members of self-styled 'high castes', who are not classified for protective discrimination or affirmative action. Typically refers to Brahmans, Kayasths and Rajputs in eastern India but the specific community inclusions vary across India.
Gherao	A tactic of protest to surround those against who the protest is organized and heckle him or her.
Gram Panchayat	An elected council tasked with local government responsibilities.
Grihasth	Householder
High caste	See General Caste
Indira Awas Yojana	Subsidised housing scheme in rural India, named after former Prime Minister Indira Gandhi.
Izzat/ ijjat	Hindi/ Urdu/ Maithili: Honor.
Janata	Hindi/ Bangla: Populace.
Jati	Sub-caste. The empirical unit around which caste is structured.
Ji	Hindi: Form of respect.
Juktipurna	Bangla: reasonable.

Kaka	Bangla: Uncle.
Karma	Sanskrit: (Literally: deeds) In Hindu cosmology, a person's karma allegedly determines which caste s/he is born into in the next life. Very few of my respondents (only those of the self-styled 'high' castes) took this notion seriously.
Kayasth	A General Caste group, with ambiguous origins and, consequently, low ritual status but high social and economic status.
Kevat	A community listed as EBC, traditionally associated with boatmen.
Kharif	Urdu: the rainfed cropping season. The crop is sown during the monsoon (July/ August) and harvested in the winter (November/ December).
Khomota	Bangla: power/ influence/ ability.
Khomotashali	Bangla: Powerful.
Kisan	Hindi/ Maithili: Peasant.
Kotha	Bangla: Talk.
Kunjra	A Muslim caste listed as OBC. Traditionally associated with vegetable vendors.
Machan	A covered bamboo platform built by home-owners to entertain guests. Poorer households or communities often have community *machans*, where people can gather to chat. Also used as a safety platform up on trees by hunters.
Mahadalit	An administrative category designed by the Bihar State Government to target assistance to the most deprived communities among the Scheduled Castes. Political exigencies have, however, led to all Scheduled Caste groups being classified as Mahadalit as of 2015!
Majdur	Hindi/ Maithili: Labourer
Majhi Haraam	Customary headman of different Adivasi communities.
Majur	Bangla: Labourer
Manush	Bangla: Person.
Mukhya	Bihar: Elected President of the Gram Panchayat
Musahar	A Scheduled Caste communities whose members are believed to have been so imposerished that they survived by consuming the meat of rodents. Community members dismissed this as a 'myth' perpetuated by the self-styled 'high' castes. An alternative interpretation is that the name derived from the practice among them to dig out the burrows of rodents, and consume the foodgrain (aahar) stocked by rodents, not the rodents (musa) themselves

Naya Neta	Hindi/ Thaithi: Emergent political mediator, a fixer or a broker.
Nyayusangat	Hindi/ Maithili: Just, pertaining to justice.
Nyayjyo	Bangla: Just, pertaining to justice.
Other Backward Class (OBC)	All India: An administrative classification by the Indian Government of communities historically stigmatized as 'low caste'. Members of communities enumerated as OBC are eligible for protective discrimination and affirmative action in public education and government employment.
Pablik	Hindi/ Maithili: colloquial reference to 'public'
Padas	Bangla: Neighborhoods
Pandit	Hindi/ Bangla: priest. Sometimes used as a derogatory term to refer to the so-called 'high castes'
Pradhan	West Bengal: Elected President of the Gram Panchayat.
Qanoon	Hindi/ Urdu/ Maithili: law. The more popular term for what is called 'neeti' in Sanskrit
Rabi	The summer crop: Sown in November to February and harvesting time is March to June
Rajput	A self-styled 'high caste', noted for its social and economic dominance
Rozgar Sevak	A quasi-government employee responsible for the implementation of the NREGS
Rupee (₹)	Indian currency. In terms of PPP, US$ 1= ₹ 17.2
Sahajyo	Bangla: help
Santal/ Santhal/ Saotal	A community enumerated as Scheduled Tribe.
Scheduled Caste	All India: An administrative classification by the Indian Government of communities historically stigmatized as 'untouchable'. Members of communities enumerated as Scheduled Caste are eligible for protective discrimination and affirmative action in public education and government employment.
Scheduled Tribe	All India: An administrative classification by the Indian Government of communities historically stigmatized as 'primitive'. Members of communities enumerated as Scheduled Caste are eligible for protective discrimination and affirmative action in public education and government employment.
Shamaj	Bangla: Social organization of Sheikh Muslims (Literally: society)

Shamaj Sardar	Chieftain of a *shamaj*, selected on the basis of deliberations among community members.
Sheikh	A Muslim community, who claim descent from Arab settlers or Brahman priests.
Shershabadiyas	A Muslim community, whose members are believed to be descendants of the Afghan troops of the north Indian ruler Sher Shah Suri.
Shotheek	Bangla: Correct, fair
Shudra	Ritually impure (but not 'untouchable') castes. Primarily agriculturalists.
Tola	Hamlet
Untouchable	Ritually polluting caste, whose touch was alleged to be polluting. Categorized by post-colonial Indian Government as Scheduled Caste
Upkar	Favor
Upper caste	See General Caste
Ward	Administrative unit subsidiary to Panchayat
Ward Member	Elected representative of the Ward
Yadav	An OBC caste group
Zamindar	Literally: Landholders. In Bihar & West Bengal, the term is usually associated to describe the absentee landlord and his sub-feudaries created by the Permanent Settlement, 1793

Acronyms

APL	Above Poverty Line
BDO	Block Development Officer
BJP	Bharatiya Janata Party
BPL	Below Poverty Line
CPI(M)	Communist Party of India (Marxist)
CPI (ML-L)	Communist Party of India (Marxist Leninist - Liberation)
EBC	Extremely Backward Class
ICDS	Integrated Child Development Scheme
IRDP	Integrated Rural Development Programme
JD(U)	Janata Dal (United)
MDR	Major District Road
MPI	Mult-dimensional Poverty Index
NDA	National Democratic Alliance
MGNREGA	Mahatma Gandhi National Rural Employment Guarantee Act
MRP	Mixed Reference Period
NREGA	National Rural Employment Guarantee Act
OBC	Other Backward Class
OPHI	Oxford Poverty and Human Development Initiative
PDS	Public Distribution System
PRI	Panchayati Raj Institutions
PUCL	People's Union for Civil Liberties
RJD	Rashtriya Janata Dal
SC	Scheduled Caste
ST	Scheduled Tribe
TMC	Trinamul Congress
UN	United Nations
UPA	United Progressive Alliance
URP	Uniform Reference Period
VEC	Village Education Committee

Against False Binaries

> What we may be witnessing is not just the end of the Cold War, or the passing of a particular period of postwar history, but the end of history as such: that is, the end point of mankind's ideological evolution and the universalization of Western liberal democracy as the final form of human government.
>
> Francis Fukuyama, 1989

> People with a culture of poverty have very little sense of history. They are a marginal people who know only their own troubles, their own local conditions, their own neighborhood, their own way of life. Usually, they have neither the knowledge, the vision nor the ideology to see the similarities between their problems and those of others like themselves elsewhere in the world.
>
> Oscar Lewis, 1971

The problem

The world is richer today than it has been at any time in recorded history. 1 per cent of its richest people own over half its wealth, while 80 per cent of the global population shares less than 5 per cent of this wealth.[1] Such inequalities and the poverty they underpin[2] sit awkwardly with the fact that more people inhabit democracies than ever before, where they elect their governments and are a promised a share in political participation.[3] Indeed, of the over 1.6 billion people estimated to be living in poverty,[4] close to a billion inhabit democracies.[5] Their very existence challenges a long-dominant assumption in academia and beyond that poor people are incapable of, and therefore unsuited for, democracy.[6] The scepticism about democracy surviving in a socio-economic environment marked by poverty and inequality was particularly challenged at the turn of the century, when scholars gushed that democracy was on the ascendance.[7] Since then, however, fears that democracy is 'in recession'[8] have steadily gained ground. Geopolitical events from around the world, economic recession in capitalist democracies, and widening inequalities[9] across the globe have sobered the enthusiasm for democracy on display at the turn of the century.[10] The gnawing realization that processes labelled as democratization have been concomitant with widening inequalities of wealth and income has led observers to worry whether democracy is a luxury that people facing deprivations and disparities can afford.

The research question

That poverty and inequality cohabit with democracy provides the starting point for the themes explored in this monograph. What does living in a democracy mean for the world's billion-plus poor, people who simultaneously confront deprivations and disparities? This is the central question that motivates this monograph. One response to this question has been that poor people absorb the ideas and identities encompassed in notions associated with democracy, of citizenship, rights, improvement, and modernity. Seen from this perspective, the poor consent to democracy. Scholars who hold this view suggest that poor people seek *assimilation* into the 'universalistic' ideals associated with democracy?[11] Another response to this question is that the poor are so overwhelmed by the precariousness of their livelihoods that they remain immune to the charmed promises of democracy. Their everyday vulnerabilities compel them to seek recourse to clientelistic practices, communitarian vocabularies, preservation of the lifestyles with which they are familiar, and the comfort of their traditions. This point of view suggests that poor people are in conflict with democracy. Scholars who propound this view hold that poor people's 'particularistic' ideas and identities, which stem from their insecure lives, lead to the perpetuation of their *difference* vis-à-vis democracy.[12]

This way of approaching the problem maps on to what some social scientists have called the 'universalism/particularism conundrum' (Beiner, 1995, 12). This conundrum refers to the alleged dichotomy between universalistic and particularistic approaches to conceptualizing political life. Scholars who endorse the importance of universalistic relationships assume that the march of democracy connects ever-greater numbers of people with each other by engaging them in common practice through institutionalized elections and government by discussion. They expect the establishment of democracy to expedite the withering away of particularistic relationships. In their hopeful narratives, the poor seek assimilation into the universalism promised by democracy. They vote, make appeals, form associations, and adhere to the rule of law. Such scholars assume that, like others in society, poor people's political horizons would eventually be shaped by liberal ideas of individual autonomy and freedom unencumbered by primordialist collectives.[13] By contrast, scholars who endorse the importance of particularistic relationships lament the march of universalized ideas and celebrate the limits to their advancement. These authors document the ways in which the poor draw on their cultural traditions and communal networks to stake claims. In their accounts, people in poverty fall back on ethnic solidarities and traditional idioms to press their demands. Their very real constraints restrict their political horizons to making particularistic demands.[14]

Critical political theorists interrogate the binary between the universal and the particular. Ernesto Laclau (1992), for instance, is emphatic that the mutual exclusion between universalistic and particularistic approaches does not hold either conceptually or empirically. The issue at stake for him is to identify the struggle over the principles upon which the universal is constituted, rather than to pit a false binary between the universal and the particular. Likewise, Iris Marion Young (1989) tells us that the particularistic demands by oppressed social groups are not intended to shatter the political community as such but to facilitate their inclusion *as equals* in it. Historical sociologists reveal the ways in which the values that are today commonly associated with European universalism were actually built on a variety of quite particular achievements, such as the initiatives of the Black slave rebels in eighteenth century Haiti (Truillot, 1995) or the popular associations of thirteenth century England's pastoral regions (Somers, 1993). These insights render the putative divide between the universal and the particular unsustainable. In fact, universalist ideals appear to be forged on the crucible of quite particularistic practices. Entanglements, rather than neat dichotomies, characterize the relationship between the universal and the particular. The political practices readers will encounter in this book illustrate these entanglements. This book contributes to challenging the binary that often drawn between the universal and the particular, a binary which – as the title of this introductory chapter suggests – is false.

The arguments

In this monograph, I contribute to the growing body of literature which demonstrates that poor people neither seek assimilation into the universalistic premises of democracy nor aim to perpetuate their difference. Rather, I propose an alternative perspective.[15] By focussing on the manifold practices of people in poverty, as well as the ambivalent ideas and heterogeneous identities that impinge on such practices, I direct attention to their multifaceted *negotiations* in and with democracy. Such negotiations refer to provisional transactions between transient collectives of poor people with politicians, bureaucrats, employers and with one another. A key argument I make in this book is that these heterogeneous negotiations comprise a crucial repertoire in poor people's politics. These negotiations combine cooperation with conflict. They are not necessarily conducted within formal or official institutions. Nor are they always convened by organizations of the poor on the basis of their shared class or communal identities. They outlast electoral cycles, indicating that poor people do not quietly adapt themselves to the authority of elected representatives. They, thus, reflect neither assimilation into nor difference vis-à-vis democracy. Rather, they approximate what political theorists have referred to as an 'agonistic' approach to democracy.[16] That poor people's politics is a politics of agonistic negotiations is another key argument of this monograph.

Although poor people everywhere are subjected to quite specific oppressive social relationships, democracies offer unique opportunity structures for them to participate in the life of the political community. In this monograph, I depart from analysts who privilege either the opportunity structures offered by democracy[17] or the social relationships of power that prevail in society[18] as analytic units for studying the politics of the poor. Rather, I draw attention to the political spaces generated by the interaction between institutional opportunity structures and social relations of power. Thus, the third key argument of this book is that such political spaces shape poor people's politics and are shaped by them.[19]

Poor people's agonistic negotiations provide a clue to the familiar paradox of democracy: how are universalistic ideals to be forged by people if not from the standpoint of particularistic positions? While much of the literature on democracy produced by political scientists[20] continues to elucidate its macro-structural and institutional political-economic aspects, sociologists and anthropologists have begun to ethnographically study democracy and locate it in its social and cultural settings. One strand of this scholarship investigates the impact of democracy on social and cultural and settings.[21] Another strand examines the impact of social and cultural settings on democracy.[22] In this monograph, I draw on the perspectives offered by all three bodies of scholarship to contribute to an understanding of the entanglements between democracy, its socio-cultural contexts and structural-institutional dimensions.

The study setting

India provides a paradigmatic case to illustrate poor people's political negotiations with democracy. It is, on one hand and famously, the world's largest democracy. On the other hand, and notoriously, it is also home to nearly a third of the world's population living in extreme poverty and to 40 per cent of the world's bottom billion poor.[23] It is in World Bank parlance a 'middle income country'.[24] As a member of the G20 group of nations, India is widely referred to and recognised as a Rising Power, an Emerging Market and a member of such potentially influential groupings as the BRICS, an acronym for the group of potentially high-growth economies such as Brazil, Russia, India, China and South Africa. The rural setting of my study is justified by the fact that between 70 and 85 per cent of the world's poor – howsoever defined – lived in rural areas as of 2010.[25] India's rural poor alone constitute nearly a quarter of the world's poor.[26]

The people whose political practices are discussed in this book live in eastern India, find employment in manual work and are largely drawn from the region's culturally-subordinated communities. They share much in common with poor people elsewhere. Internally differentiated on grounds of ethnicity and caste, religion, region and gender, deprivations among the poor often vary considerably,[27] making it difficult for them to engage in sustained collective action. Their livelihoods are far from assured and their lives fraught with uncertainty.[28] Their access to governments, even elected governments, is inherently uneven and variegated.[29] A large number of the people readers will meet in this book are agricultural labourers and peasants owning and cultivating small plots of arable land. Others are casual workers who migrate temporarily to work in wealthier regions of the country as construction workers, brick kiln workers, agricultural labourers, hawkers and vendors, rickshaw pullers, plumbers, masons, and domestic helps. They contribute to producing the country's food and manufactures and to subsidize the lifestyle of its burgeoning middle class by providing them with cheap labour.

It is worthwhile delineating what this book is about from what it is not. The book does not try to explore the reasons for India's poverty amidst plenty. It is not a commentary on the outcomes of the numerous anti-poverty schemes that successive governments in India and her States have promulgated from time to time. And, finally, it is not an investigation of the provenance of 'pro-poor' policy in India. These questions have been fruitfully answered by other political scientists, economists and anthropologists. My concern in this monograph is different. I want to understand the heterogeneous ways in which poor people negotiate with democracy and make meanings of it. I aim to examine the ways in which the constitution of political spaces shapes these negotiations. And, last but certainly not the least, I seek to contribute to the theorization of the entanglements between the universal and the particular while considering poor people's political practices. Readers hoping to gather heart-rending details of poverty or intimate narratives of the destitution, squalor and want that characterize poor people's daily lives will be disappointed. While people in poverty are certainly subjected to oppressive social relations, what readers will find in this book, rather, is an account of poor people's agonistic relationships with their oppressors as well as allies.

The book draws on diverse sorts of data. Much of the evidence presented in it is ethnographic,[30] but I complement this material with data from primary surveys and official data. I also mobilize the wealth of debates on social and political change in India over the last two centuries, trends in poverty and inequality, and ways of conceptualizing social stratification.

The plan of the book

In chapter 1, I introduce the conceptual, analytical and empirical themes of this study. I first outline the ways in which the terms 'poverty', 'politics' and 'the poor' are understood in this book. Next, I elaborate the agonistic approach to studying democracy that forms this book's mainstay. Following these conceptual clarifications, I engage critically with the theoretical literature that illuminates poor people's negotiations with governments and dominant classes. I then propose the analytical framework of 'political space' as co-constituted by the intersection of institutional opportunity structures and social relations of power to understand and contextualise poor people's politics. I conclude the chapter by outlining the ethnographic approach on which much of the data presented in this book draws.

Chapters 2 and 3 allow me to elaborate the political spaces that shape the politics of the poor in India. In chapter 2, I discuss the institutional opportunity structures in the context of which poor people in rural eastern India negotiate democracy. In the first part of the chapter, I direct attention to the formal, participatory and social dimension of India's democracy, based on a synthesis of the literature pertaining to its postcolonial institutional developments. I also introduce eastern India to the reader with a particular focus on political changes in postcolonial West Bengal and Bihar in the second part of the chapter. In chapter 3, I explain the social relations of power within which people in the four fieldwork localities were embedded. In doing so, I highlight the collaborations and conflicts between members of different social classes, thereby introducing the readers to some of the people whose practices make up the politics of the poor discussed in this book. The analysis of the political spaces for poor people's negotiations with democracy in Chapters 2 and 3 will set the stage for the discussions in the subsequent chapters.

In chapter 4, I analyse poor people's 'supplications' to be enumerated as living 'below the poverty line' (BPL) by the Indian government. Being enumerated as BPL entitles people to a variety of subsidies and social protection measures. The allocation of BPL cards is thus the subject of much manipulation. The negotiations over cards speak to ongoing scholarly debates over clientelism and citizenship. I steer clear from portrayals of poor people's politics as either clientelistic or of citizenship. Rather, I suggest that the supplications reveal an entanglement between the categories of clientelism and citizenship. Such supplications are, nonetheless, internally fragmented. They vary considerably across the four localities, being assertive in some localities and meek in others. In my analysis, I take care not to formulate these variations as different stages in an inexorable transition from clientelism to citizenship.

I examine my interlocutors' 'demands' for employment in a public works scheme in chapter 5. The state in India operates such works under the aegis of the Mahatma Gandhi National Rural Employment Guarantee Act (MGNREGA), providing an above-market rate wage to impoverished workers in the vicinity of their homes as a constitutional right. The works provided are valued by the poor, but couched by the state as a favour being bestowed upon the population. The negotiations over employment under the program resonate with academic debates over the persistence of moral vocabularies, hinging on idioms of care and protection on the one hand, and the emergence of juridical vocabularies concomitant on the expansion of governmental interventions on the other. However, these demands vary across localities, being more combative in some and deferential in others. As an empirical category, therefore, the 'demand' is internally disjointed, being more confident in some and reticent in others. Notwithstanding such variations, I am mindful not to slot these demands as reflective of different stages in the transition from moral vocabularies to rights-based languages of stateness.

The discussion in chapter 6 pertains to people's 'disputations' over the installation of electric poles in their locality. The installations are undertaken as part of an electrification programme undertaken by the Indian government in West Bengal under the Rajiv Gandhi Vidyutikaran Yojana. The negotiations spawned by the installations of electric poles bring to mind debates among researchers on improvement and its discontents. Even as their elected representatives exhort them to embrace the installations as an improvement in their lives, the poor insist on scrutinizing the installations in the light of their own longer-term plans. While the elected representatives accuse them on preserving their 'backward' ways of life, the poor dispute their claims to know what was good for their neighbourhood. Their disputations signal an entanglement between preserving their long-term plans and subscribing to a view of improvement espoused by the state. As with the other chapters, I am careful not to subsume their disputations under narratives of a transition from preservation to improvement.

Similarly, in chapter 7 my analysis relates to poor people's 'imaginations' of the public space as reflected in popular contentions over a temple in Bihar. An Indian government legislation declares the temple to be public property, a declaration to which the temple's trustees, privileged, and wealthy landowners of the locality turn a blind eye and a deaf ear. However, the trustees' interpretations are hotly contested by the poor who invoke the legal apparatus of the Indian government as well as draw upon myths and legends that celebrated egalitarian struggles. Their imaginations resonate with intellectual debates on tradition and modernity. However, they also defy dichotomous categorizations as reflecting either tradition or modernity, leading to my wariness towards categorizing poor people's imaginations as reflecting a stage in the transition from one to another.

The chapters in this book are assembled with a view to foreground the heterogeneities of poor people's politics. Collectively, they elaborate the manner in which variations in poor people's political practices are shaped by political spaces, the dynamic terrain constituted by the interaction of institutional opportunity structures and social relations of power. In doing so, each of the four chapters underscores the myriad ways in which poor people negotiate democracy. These negotiations exemplify the entanglements between the universal and the particular, thereby, enabling social scientists to develop an enriched account of poor people's political practices.

Each of the four chapters does four things. Each begins by contextualising the governmental intervention and public policy, which spawns the negotiations discussed therein. Empirically, they each illustrate poor people's negotiations with the politicians and political mediators who populate democratic institutions. Analytically, they each attend to the heterogeneities in their negotiations by emphasizing the variable political spaces available to the poor in the four fieldwork places. Theoretically, they each engage critically with the scholarly approaches to narrating, conceptualizing and theorizing such negotiations as reflecting either particularistic or universalistic conceptions of political life. Each chapter deploys this critical engagement to elaborate an agonistic understanding of democracy.

In the concluding chapter, I distill the key findings from the book for the meanings with which poor people imbue democracy. I first remind readers that although Liberal democracy has emerged as the hegemonic model of democratic in the closing decades of the twentieth century, liberalism and democracy are conceptually disjunctive. Thereafter, I reiterate the agonistics of poor people's negotiations as they navigate the universal and the particular. I then summarize the role of political space in shaping variations in their negotiations. I conclude by highlighting the enduring relevance of the questions raised in this book, occasioned by the widening inequalities within some of the world's emerging market economies as well as the possibilities of democratic renewal outside the confines imposed by liberalism.

Endnotes

1   Credit Suisse (2016,148) offers a succinct overview of inequalities not only across but also within countries: top 1 per cent wealth shares in the United States, China, India and Russia hovered at 42.1 per cent, 43.5 per cent, 58.4 per cent and 74.5 per cent respectively. These figures are higher than reported in 2010 (Credit Suisse, 2010, 120) when 1 per cent of the world's top 1 per cent wealthiest people owned 43.6 per cent of its wealth: the figures for China, India and the United States were, respectively, 31.7 per cent, 40.3 per cent and 34.6 per cent.

2   Poverty and inequality have a complex interface with one another. Poverty, if measured in terms of absolute deprivations, may decline even as inequalities widen. Alternatively, high incidence of poverty may well coincide with very little inequality. Of the vast literature that exists on this subject, readers may be interested in Grusky and Kanbur (2006), Birdsall and Londono (1997), Fields (2000), White and Anderson (2001) and Pikkety (2015).

3   For a useful discussion with helpful visual aids, see Roser (2016).

4   See Alkire *et al.* (2014). This figure is based on the global Multidimensional Poverty Index (MPI) developed by the Oxford Poverty and Human Development Initiative (OPHI) and the United Nations Development Program (UNDP).

5   My estimates, based on matching national MPI with Polity IV classifications. Polity IV data is publicly available online at http://www.systemicpeace.org/polity/polity4x. htm. Polity IV classifies many countries, such as Nigeria and Bangladesh, as anocracies, or countries whose governments 'combine an, often, incoherent, mix of democratic and autocratic traits and practices' (Marshall and Cole, 2009, 9). It is instructive to note that although China is not classified as a democracy, the Chinese people are able to select local governments on the basis of elections (Tsai, 2007; O'Brien, 2010). As such, the number of poor people engaging with democracy in some form or the other is well over a billion.

6   Typical of this cynicism included such scholarship produced in the immediate aftermath of World War II as Almond (1954), Almond and Verba (1965), Lipset (1960 and 1963) and Shils (1965). These writers associated poor people's political participation with tendencies towards communism as well as fascism. This trend continued right through the Cold War years, as exemplified by works such as Huntington (1968) and Verba, Nie and Kim (1978). Even after the collapse of the Union of Soviet Socialist Republics (USSR), scholars such as Ingleheart and Baker (2000), Ingleheart and Welzel (2000), Przeworski and Limongi (1996), Rosenstone and Hansen (1993) and Verba, Schlozman and Brady (1995), remained sceptical of poor people's suitability for democracy. Such cynicism was subjected to early criticism by Reuschmeyer (1992).

7   Examples of such exuberance can be found in the commentaries offered by Diamond *et al.* (1997) and Diamond (1992). This enthusiasm is shared for India by Dasgupta (1993), Krishna (2000), Yadav (1999) and the Lokniti (2008). For Africa, Bratton and van de Walle (2001) and Mattes and Bratton (2016) demonstrated similar enthusiasm. See Mainwaring (1999) for similar perspectives on Latin America. Rare examples of

sobering, but unduly pessimistic, scholarship comes from Lijphart (1996), Linz and Stepan (1996), O'Donnell (1996), Przeworskiet al. (2000) and Heller (2000).

8   Diamond (2014) provides the clearest exposition of this view. In the wake of recent events such as the Brexit vote in the United Kingdom and the election of Donald Trump in the United States, the earlier cynicism about poor people's support for democracy appear to be making a comeback.

9   See Fukuyama (2011) for a restatement of the relationship between liberal democracy and socio-economic inequality. Recent data suggests that although inequality between countries might have been contained, inequalities within countries are widening (Milanovic, 2016).

10 The cover of the twenty-fifth volume of the influential *Journal of Democracy* asks 'Is Democracy in Decline?' See Plattner (2015) for an anxious statement outlining the reasons for democracy's apparent decline. Indeed, different volumes of the *Journal of Democracy* provide a useful barometer for the changing mood in the political science community. From asserting that democracy was enjoying a global resurgence in 1991 (Diamond and Plattner, 1991) to exuding confidence that it 'reign(ed) supreme' in the ideological sphere (Diamond and Plattner, 1996) to declaring that 'We are all Tocquevilleans now' (Diamond and Plattner, 2001), the mood has been considerably more downcast since 2006.

11 Broadly speaking, universalistic ideas underscore the importance of generalized relationships of people with the political community. In the realm of political sociology, Parsons and Shils (1951) offer a clear statement. In political philosophy, Rawls' (1971) remains the most lucid exposition. A universalistic perspective of democracy was most famously the position advanced by Francis Fukuyama (1992). His latest work offers a far more sobering analysis (Fukuyama, 2014).

12 Particularistic ideals assert the primacy of the specific relationships that people inhabit and through which they make meaning of their individual and collective lives. A number of scholars have contributed to clarifying the meanings of particularism. See, for instance, Walzer (1983), Taylor (1985), MacIntyre (1988) and Young (1992). The perspective that the poor are constrained by the particularistic constraints they confront is advanced by such anthropologists as Lewis (1971).

13 Diamond and Marks (1992), Varshney (2000) and Bratten and van de Walle (1997) exemplify such hopes.

14 Kaviraj (2011) and Comaroff and Comaroff (1993) for instance are sympathetic to the particularistic claims of the poor.

15 The authors with whose works the argument in this book resonate include Javier Ayuero (2001), Asef Bayat (2011), Mathew Gutman (2002), Benedict Kerkvliet (2009), Laura McLean (2014), Kevin O'Brien and Li (2006), Steve Robins (2008) and Abu Malik Simone (2004).

16 While a number of political theorists – such as Hannah Arendt (1958), Bonnie Honig (1993) and William Connolly (1995) – subscribe to an agonistic perspective of politics, the specific account of agonism on which this book draws has been formulated by Chantal Mouffe (2000; 2005).

17 For influential elucidations of this perspective, see Skocpol (1979), Evans (1995), Migdal (1988) and Houtzager and Moore (2003).

18 The classic statements in support of this perspective include Moore Jr (1966), Wolf (1969), Thompson (1971), Scott (1985) and Escobar (1995).

19 This argument builds on, but also departs from, leads provided by such scholars as Partha Chatterjee (2004), Stuart Corbridge *et al.* (2005), James Holston (2008), Courtney Jung (2008), Achille Mbembe (2001), Mortimer Nielsen (2009), Gail Omvedt (2008) and Nandini Sundar (2011).

20 The scholarship pertaining to the macro-institutional questions of democracy are enough to fill up several large libraries. Useful overviews of the third wave of democratization are provided in Huntington (1992), Diamond, Plattner, Chu and Tien (1997), Linz and Stepan (1996). A more historical perspective is offered by Barrington Moore Jr (1966), Joel Migdal *et al.* (1994), Theda Skocpol (1979) and Charles Tilly (2007).

21 Insightful studies in this regard include Apter (1987), Coronil (1997), Gutmann (2002), Schaffer (1997), Schirmer (1998), Spencer (2007) and Tambiah (1997).

22 Excellent interventions in this vein are offered by West (2005), Yashar (2005), Michelutti (2007), Paley (2001), Nugent (2009) and Witsoe (2013).

23 See Alkire *et al.* (2013, 6) for an account of the incidence and intensity of India's poverty in comparative perspective.

24 The World Bank defines middle income countries as those with a per capita gross national income (Atlas method, current US$ prices) from US$1,026 to $12,475. Lower income countries are countries whose per capita gross national incomes are lower. Middle income countries are further classified as 'low' and 'high'. India is classified as a 'low middle income country' in World Bank parlance.

25 The International Fund for Agriculture and Development (IFAD) estimates that 70 per cent of the poor in the Global South inhabit rural areas (IFAD, 2011). Alkire *et al.* (2014) suggest that as much as 85 per cent of poor people inhabit rural areas.

26 IFAD (2011) reports that slightly over one billion rural people live under US$ 1.25 per day. Of them, over 230 million live in India, according to IFAD data available here: http://www.ruralpovertyportal.org/country/statistics/tags/india.

27 See Alkire *et al.* (2014), Krishna (2009), Vera-Sanso (2014) and Harriss-White (2005a) for nuanced accounts of the heterogeneities within the poor.

28 Exemplary ethnographies of poor people's lives in the Latin American context include Scheper-Hughes (1992) and Perlman (2007). For India, see Mendelsohn and Vicziany (1999) and Breman (1996).

29 Baviskar (1995) and Corbridge *et al.* (2005) offer eloquent commentaries on central and eastern India, as Steinberg (2008) and Horneberger (2013) do for South Africa. In the Latin American context, Stokes' (1995) ethnographic account of Peru and Caldeira's (2000) anthropological research from Sao Paulo merit attention.

30 A brief introduction to the dramatis personae about whose political practices readers will read in this book is provided in Annexure 1.

1

The Perspectives of the Study

Towards an Agonistics of Democracy

Poverty generates an intense focus on the present to the detriment of the future.

World Bank, 2015

It is always good to remind ourselves that people are not fools.

Michel de Certeau, 1983

This chapter clarifies the conceptual frameworks used in the book. I first outline the relational understandings of 'poverty' and 'the poor' to which my argument is indebted. I then pinpoint the relevance of a perspective that foregrounds politics as an ensemble of practices through which people conduct their lives. Thereafter, I introduce the agonistic approach to studying democracy which frames my argument. Following these conceptual clarifications, I offer an overview of early approaches to poor people's collective practices before engaging critically with the growing body of literature that locates poor people's negotiations within debates over universalism and particularism. Next, I propose the analytical framework of 'political space' as co-constituted by the dynamic intersection of institutional opportunity structures and social relations of power. Before concluding the chapter, I defend the ethnographic approach on which much of the data presented in this book draws.

I

Perspectives of poverty: Residualist or relational

Poverty is a fuzzy concept.[1] Sometimes, people who are clearly not poor describe themselves as living in poverty.[2] While it is not uncommon for *pundits* in the Anglo-Saxon West to label poor people as being wasteful and lazy,[3] public opinion in much of the world generally steers away from holding alleged faults in their work ethic as responsible for poor people's poverty.[4] Most commentators associate poverty with a lack of employment, educational opportunities and reliable social networks.[5] Several economists, and following them, national governments and international donors refer to poor people's limited consumption[6] of select bundles of commodities, usually stemming from low incomes.[7] Sympathetic perceptions of the poor usually relate poverty to people being malnourished[8] and ill.[9] Of late, more multidimensional approaches to poverty[10] are beginning to emphasize the ways in poverty is caused by deprivations of specific functioning, what Amartya Sen (1999) famously calls capabilities. In this vein, Table 1.1 presents a regional snapshot of the incidence of poverty, based on two enormously influential, but widely disparate measures. The presentation shows the ways in which the choice of measures influences inferences about the extent of poverty, complicating any attempt to develop a homogenous understanding of the term.

Table 1.1: Poverty headcounts: Income and multidimensional poverty indices compared

Region	Multidimensional Poverty Index (2015)	Income poverty[11] (2013)
Sub-Saharan Africa	61.1	42.7
South Asia	52.5	18.8
Middle East and North Africa	20.7	2.7 (2007)
East Asia and Pacific	7.1	7.2
Latin America and Caribbean	5.2	5.6
Europe and Central Asia	2	2.1
World	29.8	12.7

Source: For Multidimensional Poverty Index, see Alkire et al. (2015, 3). For Income poverty, see World Bank (2014, Table 2.8, Part 2), accessed http://wdi.worldbank.org/table/2.8.2.

Some scholars highlight to the ways in which poor people are adversely incorporated into the economy through informal employment. Others emphasize the influence of employment in such low-productivity sectors as agriculture being a cause of poverty. Table 1.2 depicts data from select countries on vulnerable employment alongside agricultural employment to illustrate the extent of poverty along such measures. As with Table 1.1, the key takeaway is that poverty remains a fuzzy concept with different conceptualizations yielding enormously different statistics on its prevalence.

Table 1.2: Vulnerable employment in select countries, percentage

Country name	Agricultural employment, 2011–14		Informal employment outside agriculture		
	Women	Men	Reference year	Women	Men
Argentina	0	1	2009	49.6	49.8
Brazil	18	10	2009	45.9	39.2
Egypt	24	43	2009	23.1	56.3
India	43	60	2009–10	84.7	83.3
Indonesia	36	33	2009	72.9	72.3
Mexico	19	4	2009	57.8	50.8
Pakistan	34	74	2009–10	75.7	78.7
Philippines	38	20	2008	70.2	69.9
South Africa	6	3	2010	36.8	29.5
Tanzania	64	70	2005–06	82.8	70.9
Turkey	15	32	2009	32.6	30.1
Vietnam	45	49	2009	66.8	69.4

Source: For Agricultural Employment, see World Bank (2014, Table 2.3), accessed http://wdi.worldbank.org/table/2.3. For Informal Employment outside Agriculture, see ILO (2012, Table 2), accessed http://laborsta.ilo.org/applv8/data/INFORMAL_ECONOMY/2012-06-Statistical%20update%20-%20v2.pdf.

The normative rhetoric about the poor has prompted much heart-wrenching and head-scratching about the definition of people living in poverty. The category of 'the poor' is often invoked by national governments and development agencies to identify people who suffer from certain deprivations. Such identifications form the basis of interventions by governments and others purporting to improve poor people's living conditions and socio-economic behaviour. The poor are thereby reduced to a governmental category in the Foucauldian mould, marked out so that they may be better 'governed'.[12] Poor people, more than others, are seen by activists and policymakers to be ideal subjects of such a 'government'. They also see *themselves* as ideal subjects of 'government' and actively engage with their governments to access services and resources to which they believe they are entitled. Thus, governments' standards for identifying poor people assume a great deal of importance for many people, poor and non-poor alike because these influence access to public policy in the form of social protection. Governments may not always recognize people who identify themselves as poor as such, and they may sometimes fail to identify people who face severe deprivations as poor. Nonetheless, governmental definitions of poverty and identifications of poor people matter to people, making such rationales for defining poverty important. This explains the salience given in this book to poor people's negotiations with governmental interventions. However, as we shall see, to infer from such a perspective that the state is the sole focus of their negotiations would be erroneous.

Scholars remain divided between residualist and relational analysis of poverty.[13] Those taking a 'residual' view of poverty would have us believe that poverty is a residue of the past, an anachronism in the present, the result of incomplete transition from particularism to universalism, from tradition to modernity, from backwardness to improvement, from arbitrary despotism to the rule of law, from a religious to a secularized society, from superstition to rationality, and from feudal serfdoms to capitalist democracy.[14] As societies progress, they argue, the incidence of poverty diminishes. Such a perspective primes analysts to expect that poor people's politics is a politics of welcoming modernity, improvement, the rule of law, secularization, rationality, capitalist democracy and universalism in general. This is the optimistic prognosis of institutions such as World Bank. As Table 1.3 indicates, World Bank data on poverty, based on an income-derived poverty line, suggests a steady decline in the incidence of poverty in almost every region of the globe. The concentration of poverty in certain regions such as Sub-Saharan Africa and South Asia reflects the tardiness of their transitions, it is argued.

Table 1.3: Trends in global and regional income poverty indicators, poverty line of $1.90 a day (2011 PPP)

Region	Incidence of poverty within region		Share of global poverty	
	1990	2012	1990	2012
Sub-Saharan Africa	56.8	42.7	14.7	43.4
South Asia	50.6	18.8	29.3	34.5
Middle East and North Africa	6	2.7 (2007)	0.7	0.7 (2007)
Latin America and Caribbean	17.8	5.6	4	3.8
East Asia and Pacific	60.6	7.2	50.8	16.4
Europe and Central Asia	1.9	2.1	0.4	1.1
World	37.1	12.7		

Source: World Bank (2014, Table 2.8.2), accessed http://wdi.worldbank.org/table/2.8.2.

By contrast authors taking a 'relational' view of poverty point to its dynamic nature and the ways in which contemporary economic and political institutions exacerbate, and even produce, it. Far from being a relic of the past, they argue, poverty is a product of capitalism. By alienating people from their means of production, capitalist development creates winners and losers, and the losers swell the ranks of the poor. Taking a relational view of poverty entails taking seriously the lens of oppression.[15] A relational view of poverty cautions analysts from expecting that poor people would welcome the transition to universalism and the attendant paraphernalia of capitalism, modernity, improvement, citizenship and democracy. Adhering to a relational view of poverty implies appreciating a 'relative' account of poverty which analyses not only the absolute condition of different population groups but also their relative position vis-a-vis other groups in society. This approach is based on the understanding that 'the minimum level of living regarded as acceptable by a society increases with rising national prosperity' (Abel-Smith and Townsend, 1965, 19).[16]

The stakes of adhering to a relational or residual view of poverty are high. The two approaches lead to opposite conclusions about the nature of poverty and the relationship of the poor to contemporary economic and political institutions. The 'residualist' view of poverty – popular among prominent contemporary economists as well as national governments, actors in global civil society and multilateral financial institutions – entails enormous enthusiasm about the ameliorative possibilities of democracy and associated economic and political institutions. Advocates propose different combinations of aid, trade, and policies to reduce 'social exclusion' and promote 'inclusive growth'. On the other hand, the espousal of a relational view of poverty alerts scholars and practitioners alike to the possibility that the perpetration of poverty might be valuable to members of certain social classes and that neither noble intentions nor robust policy might be sufficient to eliminate poverty. Such analysis should sober the expectations that 'residualists' pin on democracy, capitalism and the alleged inclusiveness of concomitant institutions. They compel us to take seriously the concomitance of poverty and inequality.

Table 1.4 presents a snapshot of World Bank data to support the perspective that an increase in the growth in mean consumption income per capita for the total population need not translate into similar increases in growth for those at the base of the economic hierarchy. In several economies–shaded in grey–the share of consumption/income of the bottom 10 per cent of the population *actually declined* during the period of high growth. While their absolute condition may well have improved, the socio-economic position of the bottom 10 per cent vis-à-vis the better-off sections of society worsened. The fortunes of the bottom 40 per cent of the population were similarly mixed.

A residualist perspective hinges on governmental understanding of poverty, the subject of targeted and well-planned statist interventions. As a governmental category, the normative constituency of poor people has been the target of intervention by nation-states, political parties, multilateral agencies, non-governmental organizations (NGOs) and increasingly even the corporate sector since 1990 (Wuyts, 1990). A multilateral financial institution such as the World Bank dreams of 'a world free of poverty'. World leaders, pursuing different ideological orientations, committed on 8 September 2000 at the United Nations General Assembly to halve the proportion of people living in 'extreme poverty' by endorsing the first of 10 Millennium Development Goals (MDGs). Proponents of capitalism nod toward its poverty-reducing potential: an editorial in *The Economist* recently went so far as to suggest that capitalism could 'take a bow'[17] ostensibly because of its role in the massive reduction of global poverty (defined in World Bank terms) since 1990.

However, scholars adopting a relational view see poverty as a political problem perpetrated by oppression. As a political category, poor people excite much less sympathy from states, multilateral agencies and NGOs. A content search of the World Bank's (2015) 221-page landmark report *Ending Poverty and Sharing Prosperity* does not contain the word 'oppression' or its derivatives even once. The few times the term 'exploitation' is used, the context is not the exploitation of people by other people. The term 'marginalization' and cognate terms makes more of an appearance but in rather general terms. The political dimension of poverty, which stem from the social relations of oppression to which poor people are subject, receives attention by only a few political parties, advocacy organizations and researchers across the globe. But, as we shall see, it is a matter to which many poor people themselves are attentive.

Table 1.4: Changes in distribution of consumption or income among select consumption or income groups, select countries

Country name	Baseline year	% share of consumption or income for Bottom 10%	Bottom 40%	Top 10%	Ratio of mean consumption or income per capita for bottom 40% to total population	Most recent year	% share of consumption or income for Bottom 10%	Bottom 40%	Top 10%	Ratio of mean consumption or income per capita for bottom 40% to total population	Annualized growth in mean consumption or income per capita for bottom 40%	Annualized growth in mean consumption or income per capita for total population
Argentina	2007	1.2	12.4	34.9	0.307	2013	1.6	14.6	30.6	0.363	6.4	3.1
Brazil	2007	0.9	9.9	43.6	0.242	2013	1	10.9	41.8	0.274	6.9	4.5
China	2008	1.8	14.4	31.8		2010	1.7	14.4	30.0		7.2	7.9
Ethiopia	2004	4.1	22.5	25.6	0.556	2010	3.2	20.6	27.4	0.518	-1.5	-0.1
France	2007	3.1	20.6	26.3	0.516	2012	3.1	20.4	26.8	0.51	0.2	0.4
Germany	2006	2.5	19.3	25.5	0.505	2011	3.4	21.5	32.7	0.537	1.4	0.1
Greece	2007	2.2	18.5	26.2	0.469	2012	1.7	17.3	26.7	0.428	-10	-8.4
India	2004	3.8	20.8	28.3	0.535	2011	3.5	20	30	0.5	3.2	3.7
Indonesia	2008	3.6	20	27.8		2010	3.4	18.9	28.2	0.437		
Iran	2009	2.1	15.1	31.4	0.149	2013	2.9	17.9	29.1	0.18	3.1	-1.2
Mexico	2008	1.8	13.6	38.9	0.3	2012	1.9	13.7	38.9	0.312	1.1	-0.2
Nigeria	2003	2.1	16.1	29.8	0.391	2009	2	15.1	32.7	0.36	0.1	1.1
Pakistan	2004	3.8	21.5	28.4	0.529	2010	4.2	22.8	25.6	0.575	3.8	2.7
Philippines	2006	2.3	14.7	33.9	0.375	2012	2.5	15.4	33.4	0.385	1.1	0.4
Russia	2007	2.3	15.7	32.8	0.391	2012	2.3	8.2	32.2	0.402	5.9	5.3
South Africa	2006	1	7.3	54.3	0.178	2011	0.9	7.2	51.3	0.177	4.1	4.4
Tanzania	2007	2.5	16.9	31.9	0.417	2011	3.1	18.5	31	0.461	3.5	1.6
Turkey	2007	2.2	16.8	28.2	0.418	2012	2.2	16.3	30.5	0.411	4.3	4.8
Uganda	2009	2.3	15.7	36.4	0.387	2012	2.4	16.2	33.9	0.411	3.9	2.9
United Kingdom	2007	2.5	18.7	28	0.467	2012	2.9	19.8	24.7	0.49	-1.7	-2.8
United States	2007	1.3	15.2	30.7		2013	1.7	15.4	30.2		-0.2	-0.4
Vietnam	2004	2.9	18.2	29.1	0.42	2010	2.6	17.3	30.1	0.392	6.2	7.8

Source: Calculated from World Bank (2014, Table 2.9), accessed http://wdi.worldbank.org/table/2.9. Shaded rows refer to countries where the share of consumption/incomes of the bottom 10% fell between baseline and most recent years.

Poverty as oppression

A relational view of poverty enlivens analysts to the ways in which the poor are *oppressed* by the very people, institutions and structures that produce wealth. Iris Marion Young (2005) elucidates the 'five faces of oppression': exploitation, marginalization, cultural imperialism, violence and powerlessness. Poor people inhabit and are embedded in each one of these relationships. Because the bulk of the discussions in this book is about the ways in which they negotiate these relationships, it would be useful to reflect briefly on the conceptual meanings of oppression and its 'faces'.

Marxist scholars have conceptualized exploitation as the directly-observable appropriation of the fruits of labour of one social group. They use the vocabulary of class in formulating their ideas of exploitation (Buchanan, 1982). Much of the literature on exploitation of labour relates to a context of formal employment in factories.[18] Some scholars distinguish exploitation from marginalization, to direct attention to the 'people the system of labour cannot or will not use' (Young, 2005, 53). Formulations of marginalization are important because they help analysts recognize that people may be consciously kept out of production systems and not inadvertently left out. They are not marginal to it, but marginalized (Perlman, 1976). If the exploited contribute to the production process from the 'inside', the marginalized contribute to it from the 'outside'.

The neat analytic distinctions between exploitation and marginalization blur considerably when confronted with the empirical reality of the fragmentation of labour and its dispersal across formal and informal employment in rural and urban areas throughout the world.[19] Unorganized workers, with casual contracts and precarious (often non-existent) social security – for example, construction workers, head-loaders and manual scavengers employed by public authorities – confront both exploitation as well as marginalization, as do agricultural labourers, workers in brick kilns and small-scale garment manufacturing units, and domestic helps. They stand beside hawkers, vendors, masons, plumbers, weavers, potters and others in what is often called 'self-employment' in their experience of exploitation and marginalisation. Peasants owning marginal and small plots of land face similar situations, as do people engaged in animal husbandry and other activities allied with agriculture. Pastoralists, fisher-folk and people dependent on harvesting minor forest produce also share the same general predicaments, even though their specific vulnerabilities differ. As 'self-employed' persons, they are not exploited in the domain of labour but in the domain of market and bureaucratic exchanges. Their marginalization foments their exploitation, which in turn marginalizes them even further. Furthermore, it is not uncommon for marginalized populations (such as hawkers, vendors and other street-side entrepreneurs, owners of small-scale manufacturing units and other service-providers who own their means of production, for example, barbers, plumbers and automobile mechanics) to exploit labour, thereby, resulting in the perpetuation of the exploitation-marginalization complex.

Panitch *et al.* (2001, 9) remind us that a growing number of the 'world's producers ... depend – directly or indirectly – on the sale of their labour power for their own daily reproduction.' Henry Bernstein's (2001; 2008; 2010) formulation of 'classes of labour' nicely encapsulates the interlocked relationships of exploitation and marginalization. The classes of labour refer to both wage labourers (who do not own the means of production and are exploited in the labour market) and 'self-employed' owners of precarious 'informal sector' enterprises, including agriculture and allied activities. Lerche (2013, 396) elaborates that the classes of labour include

> those who possess some means of production, but who nonetheless share with wage labourers the overall position of being exploited ... and who, indeed, may alternate between being wage workers and being small-scale petty commodity producers, seasonally or throughout their lifetimes.

However, Bernstein's (2009: 248) assumption that the 'classes of labour' are released from what he calls 'pre-capitalist social relations' to constitute a fragmented reserve army of labour understates the ways in which pre-capitalist social relationships are often mobilized under conditions of capitalism. The characters readers will meet in this book without doubt 'defy inherited assumptions of fixed and uniform notions of "workers", "farmers", "petty traders", "urban", "rural", "employed", "self-employed"' (Bernstein, 2010, 111). But they are no mere reserves of labour, impelled by circumstances to fill labour gaps. Even as they circulate between different locations and take on different occupations, they continue to identify with their villages, are subject to communal identities, and remain materially and emotionally attached to their land. They are not released from 'pre-capitalist social relationships', as Bernstein would have it. As we shall see in chapters 2 and 3, several aspects of village life, communal identities and agricultural operations are far from anachronistic residues of the past, but fashioned and reinforced by capitalist developments under colonial and postcolonial regimes.[20] Nevertheless, while I refrain from adopting Bernstein's formulation to analyse the collective identities of the labouring poor, I retain the vocabulary of *classes* in recognition of the overarching influence (though not the triumphalist dominance) of capitalist social relations. The plural (of classes) is made necessary by the diverse nature of global capitalism (Bernstein, 2010). I thus use the term labouring classes interchangeably with terms such as labouring poor, poor people and the poor to reflect the prevalence of exploitation and marginalization, two faces of oppression identified by Young.

Charles Tilly avers that the interlocked relations of exploitation and marginalization are reproduced and stabilized by mechanisms that generate, and perpetuate, 'durable inequalities'. Central to the creation of these durable inequalities is 'opportunity-hoarding', or 'confining use of a value-producing resource to members of an *ingroup*' (Tilly, 1999, 366; emphasis added). Exploitation and marginalization should therefore not be seen as individualized transactions but as unequal relations between social *groups*. After all, group membership – the need 'to belong, to identify and hence to exclude' (Gellner, 1964, 149) – is intrinsic to human life. Tilly also tells us about the processes of 'emulation' and 'adaptation' through which the privileged and the oppressed '*naturalise*'[21] these unequal social relations, thereby contributing to the maintenance of categorical inequalities. In this vein, Frances Stewart's (2002) formulation of horizontal inequality – '*the existence of severe inequalities between culturally-defined groups*' (2002, 3; emphasis in original) – is instructive for underscoring the ways in which cultural imperialism – the third face of oppression elucidated by Young – directly structures poverty and inequality. When cultural affiliation becomes a social category and when mobility across such categories is weak or limited – as is often the case with gender, race, caste, or ethnicity – the inequalities between them are durable indeed. The cultural imperialism resulting from what David Mosse (2007) accurately calls social closure has devastating consequences for poverty and inequality.

Admittedly, cultural affiliations are not as primordial as has sometimes been suggested.[22] These are often the product of governmental technologies of classifying populations and may even undergo mutations over time.[23] However, that cultural imperialism renders poverty and inequality durable is evident from a wide range of studies.[24] In this book, I subscribe to Eric Wolf's (1999, 65) advice that class and culture 'occur together and overlap in various ways'. I find it impossible, therefore, to avoid questions of cultural imperialism while discussing poverty and inequality. Indeed, cultural imperialism might serve as an important factor for the concentration of poverty among certain social groups.

The intermeshing of exploitation, marginalisation and cultural imperialism spawns social inequalities.[25] As Elizabeth Anderson has argued, social inequality refers 'not so much to the distributions of goods as to *relations between superior and inferior persons*' (Anderson, 1999, 312; my emphasis). Where inequalities assume 'categorical' terms – that is, entire categories of people are deemed unequal, inferior and imputed negative stereotypes – then social inequality is about discrimination against persons on the basis of their group (categorical) membership. Social status and associated notions of prestige, shame and humiliation are formative contributors to the experience of social inequality, and often concomitant with the experience of poverty. Tussles over social inequality are thus central to the study of poor people's lives.

Some scholars have characterized the oppression and subordination to which poor people are subjected as 'structural violence' (Farmer, 2005), a systemic exclusion of people from the benefits of membership in society. This view alerts analysts to the perspective that the poor are allowed to die – if not killed – by hunger, illness and natural disasters. Following this view, Akhil Gupta (2012) has directed attention to poverty as a form of biopolitics. Drawing on Foucauldian analytics, he suggests that it might be fruitful to analyse the experiences of poor people as being determined by the arbitrary actions of bureaucrats, bankers and others who wield authority and influence over them. The imagery of violence is vivid and not entirely inaccurate – poor people confront daily assaults on their dignity, security and life. However, perceiving poverty as structural violence – 'crime without criminals' as Farmer would have it – detracts from the classes and institutions which are responsible for perpetrating poverty. A formulation emphasizing arbitrary outcomes, rather than the class and cultural constitution of the state, does not, in the ultimate analysis, help to understand why people of specific classes and from specific cultural backgrounds are systematically impoverished and why others do not seem to care. Nevertheless, as Nancy Scheper-Hughes' (1993) sensitive portrayal of *favela* life in Brazil shows, the formulation of structural violence remains a useful reminder of the mundane ways in which violence is integrated into the lives of the poor.

A consideration of the ways in which poor people are constrained through relations of exploitation, marginalization, cultural imperialism and violence should not lead us to ignore their importance to the global political economy. Nearly three-quarters of the world's poor live in its middle income countries,[26] many of which are postcolonial states. They constitute the low-cost labour which powers economic growth and generates profit. It is this labour that produces the garments, mobiles, beverages and food consumed across the globe. It is they who provide cheap and casual services to emerging global middle classes, ranging from providing domestic help, vending vegetables, pedaling trinkets, being electricians and plumbers in homes and offices, and cleaning sewers and sweeping roads. Indeed, channels of constraints are not the only circuits through which they are incorporated in the global economy. Social entrepreneurs identify poor people are a potentially useful market for mass-produced goods and attractive credit services.[27] Politicians enthusiastically solicit and genuinely consider poor people's participation as a touchstone of their own legitimacy. In this respect, Marxist authors are correct in suggesting that the poor are subjects of global capitalism,[28] oppressed by it but also included within its ambit as labourers and producers who fuel the engines of the global political economy. I would push their argument further by insisting that the poor are also the subjects of internal colonialism,[29] a source of cheap labour and petty commodities, a market for mass-produced commodities and a field of investment for financial services and other social and cultural products. Indeed as targets of governmental and private philanthropic interventions, which claim to educate, improve and even civilize them, poor people epitomize the internal colonialism of contemporary states.

As subjects whose consent is sought through electoral mechanisms and entrepreneurial interventions, the inclusion of the poor into the global, national and political economy synchronizes with the oppression which they confront.

The concomitance of inclusion and oppression points to a very specific kind of powerlessness, the fifth face of oppression discussed by Young, that they experience. The powerlessness of the poor stems from their inability to substantively influence the agenda of the political economy of which they are a part (Bachrach and Baratz, 1960).

Even if they benefit from certain processes or interventions, people in poverty exercise very little control in formulating or shaping them. This quite specific understanding of powerlessness helps us to be wary of perceiving poor people as being either passive objects of oppression or gullible victims of false consciousness. As voters, consumers and labourers, the poor are central to contemporary political economic projects epitomized by both capitalism and democracy. Although instances of brute force and stark slavery are not unheard of in contemporary democracies, mechanisms of social control cannot indefinitely rely on these tactics without, at some point, inviting public censure. If the strategy of direct coercion is unreliable, the ability of dominant classes in middle income countries – where the majority of the world's poor live – to create consent is limited due to the restricted hegemonic capacity of governments and the historic weakness of the bourgeoisie.[30] However, while poor people participate in the economy and the polity, they are rarely able to set the agenda of public discussion. They might benefit from specific governmental practices or philanthropic interventions. Their stark destitution and desperate hunger may be ameliorated. But they have little substantive control over the formulation of agendas.

Thus, poor people live through myriad forms of oppression. Even as they suffer, it is not uncommon for them to be participants as well as perpetrators.[31] They are exploited and marginalized by those better-off than themselves, people who may themselves be poor. Poor people belonging to certain social groups may be subjected to cultural imperialism by poor and non-poor alike of other social groups. They may be victims of violence as well as its perpetrator, for example, through participating in vigilante groups. They may be incorporated into broader structures of capitalist democracy as voters and consumers. But the situation of powerlessness and the inability to substantively set the agenda of their polity mark their lives.

Politics: Contests over power, meanings and identities

If poverty is a fuzzy concept, politics is even more so. The study of politics has frequently focussed on studying 'who gets what, when and how' (Lasswell, 1936). Lasswell and Kaplan (1950, 75) suggest that politics refers to the 'shaping, distribution and exercise of power'. In this vein, politics is often studied as a contest over the distribution of resources, thereby rendering competition for political offices, which control the distribution of resources, as the subject of study (Haywood, 1998).

Marking a departure from Lasswell and Kaplan's approach, Goodin and Klingemann (1996, 7) argue for an understanding of politics as a 'constrained use of social power', a definition that allows them to accommodate the multitude of ways in which political actors manipulate, manoeuvre and modify the preferences of others. In foregrounding social power in their definition of politics, they remind us that politics signals relationships between actors inhabiting society. By emphasizing the *use* of social power, these authors take a broader perspective than its *exercise*. These approaches allow them to encompass within the ambit of politics both intentional acts as well as unintended consequences, thereby taking cognizance of the covert and overt ways through which people practice politics. However, their approach begs the question: if politics is about the (constrained) use of social power, how do people with little or limited access to power *do* politics?

Their expansive view of politics notwithstanding, the positivist framework within which Goodman and Klingermann locate their conceptualization limits a fruitful analysis of politics in many ways. Although they descriptively cover under the rubric of politics such complex workings of power as internalized norms (Lukes, 1974), the ability to prevent oppositional agendas from even being raised (Bachrach and Baratz, 1962) and hegemonic practices (Lalclau and Mouffe, 1985), Goodin and Klinermann analytically subscribe to a notion of power derived from behavioural political scientists whereby an individual may be said to exercise power over another if they are able to make them do things to their liking and which they would not have otherwise done.[32] Therefore, in their view, the use of power *encumbers* human freedom. While undoubtedly useful, this perspective on power is also limiting.

A conception of power that assumes its use to be a constraint on freedom has been challenged by scholars following the work of Michel Foucault.[33] Foucault famously departs from other theorists of power in insisting that the exercise of power need not encumber freedom. Rather, power refers to the 'conduct of conduct' instituted through dispersed disciplinary mechanisms. As an ensemble of practices, power is not always constraining, but also productive. The practice of power can be enabling rather than disabling.[34] Instead of endorsing binaries of power and freedom, Foucault's interventions enable analysts to think of the two as entangled. To buttress his argument, Foucault (1982, 790) proposes that power is a relationship of *agonism*, 'a relationship which is at the same time reciprocal incitation and struggle, less of a face-to-face confrontation which paralyses both sides than a permanent provocation.' Foucault's theories challenge political theory's uncritical reliance on liberal categories of the democratic state, freedom and intentionality (Connolly, 1987 and Honig, 1991) as well as notions of empowerment (Hindess, 1986 and Cruikshank, 1999).

Although Foucault's interventions greatly advanced the field, his emphasis on disciplinary practices has caused some disquiet among sociologists of political practice. Critically reflecting on Foucauldian analytics, de Certeau (1984, 176) comments that 'it is always good to remind ourselves that people are not fools'. The practices through which people negotiate with the imposition of disciplinary practices – the complex of adherence, autonomy and cautious engagement – constitute politics. Laclau (1994) reminds us that such practices encompass tensions over meanings as well as the tussles over identities in the context of the overarching structures that strive to maintain social order. More specifically, Rancière (2001) points to politics as the ensemble of practices associated with living in the community to which one belongs. He distinguished 'politics' from 'the police', which signals the disciplinary practices in a community. This book makes use of some of these insights, but is careful in noting that political practices straddle the distinction between state and society: therefore, I remain somewhat wary of dichotomous formulations that inhere in claims that 'society must be defended' (Foucault, 2004) or underscore the binary between police and politics (Rancière, 2009).

Indeed, there are several aspects of Foucault's work from which my understanding of power departs. Applying Foucauldian analytics becomes particularly problematic while investigating oppressive social relations wherein some people are disproportionately affected than others by the relations of power permeating society. The Foucauldian approach sheds little light on the reasons that members of certain social groups are able to appropriate disciplinary institutions while others are subjected to those very same institutions. While Foucault's approach prevents analysts from sliding into conspiracy theories about some people *intending* to keep others poor, it cannot help explain why the operation of power benefits some more than others. His approach does little to illumine the ways in which certain social classes benefit from poverty and whose interests are served by keeping people poor. That poverty arises from the presence and reproduction of oppressive social relations, intentionally perpetrated by certain social classes against others, is a perspective to which Foucault appears inattentive.

Following Foucault, I concede that power refers to an ensemble of dispersed disciplinary practices. I find especially useful his insight that the practice of power might facilitate freedom and the subject of power may not be constrained by its practices. Departing from Foucault, however, I use for the purpose of this book a formulation that considers power to be about the exercise of material, social and symbolic resources. Power is exercised by individuals to shape the values, behaviours and practices of others. The exercise of power by some agents over others may be detrimental to the latter's interests, but they may also enhance and support those interests.

Based on this understanding of power, politics refers to the variegated ensemble of practices through which people conduct their lives in the context of the disciplinary mechanisms that seek to institute order in society. Compliance with such practices as well as contesting them both constitute political practices. Such an understanding of politics encompasses struggles over meanings as well as contest over identities, rather than being centred on the acquisition of material resources. For the purpose of this book, a practice is considered political so long as it is *intended* to advance a perspective, idea or notion of social life. Such intended practices may do little to advance (what external observers may deduce to be) their practitioners' own solipsistic interests.[35] Furthermore, people's actions may result in outcomes that they themselves did not anticipate. It may be possible that people intended to 'merely' lead their lives in accordance with their collective life-plans, but their actions resulted nonetheless in interrogating extant power relations or redistributing relations of power. It is also possible that people may not consider the outcomes of their actions as favourable. The outcomes of their practices may not be the result of their intentions but other factors over which practitioners have little control. But the absence of either favourable outcomes or furtherance of interests should not obscure the intention of the practitioners of politics to advance a given perspective of social life, based on critical reflection and/or collective discussion. The practices attendant upon such intentions are integral to the study of politics.

Politics thus refers to the pastiche of practices through which people advance their points of view in society, prevent the emergence of oppositional perspectives and make public the perspectives that have been hitherto been obfuscated. Through such practices, people make meanings of their shared lives and forge collective identities while engaging with one another over the distribution of resources. Politics permeates social relations as well as the institutions responsible for maintaining the social order. It encompasses the myriad purposeful actions through which people sustain or interrogate prevailing meanings of social life and facilitate or prevent the creation of social identities. However, their purposeful actions and social practices can barely be abstracted from the institutional opportunity structures and the social relations of power within which people are embedded. Marx's reminder to his readers from over a century and a half ago that "men (sic) make history but seldom under the circumstances of their choice" is particularly apposite in this context.

Marx's insight persuades me to appreciate the entanglements between structure and agency (Marie-Smith, 1996) in the production of political subjectivities. On the one hand, we can talk about the subject in the classic socio-political sense of being subordinated to those controlling resources, influence, and authority. Contemporary subjects are 'subjected to' governmental technologies emanating from public policy interventions designed at regional, national, and even global levels. They inhabit social relations and are subject to social controls and disciplinary actions. On the other hand, we can also denote the subject as one who possesses some ability to initiate action, as their own destinies. Understood this way, they are authors of their own personal choices and collective decisions. Subjects can and do act, appropriating political ideas of others, and advancing political ideals of their own. This double meaning of the term 'subject' allows analysts to consider the ambivalent ways in which people negotiate democratic institutions and processes. Such a perspective is poignantly pertinent to this study: the poor, who are subject to multifaceted forms of oppression nonetheless, advance their ideas and interests when they can.

A politics of the poor is not necessarily pro-poor politics. The practices through which they advance their points of view in society may not result in a betterment of their individual condition as measured through social surveys and economic censuses. Indeed, such practices may even exacerbate the oppression they face because of a backlash from the members of the privileged classes. Alternatively their economic conditions might be improved as a result of governmental interventions over which they have little control. Because the poor are not a homogenous social category, their practices are often contradictory and may undermine one another. It is to investigate such poly-vocal practices that this book attempts. Because this is a book on the *politics of the poor* and not on either the politics or the economics of poverty, it is therefore less concerned with outcomes for poverty reduction, important as they are in their own right.

An agonistics of democracy

Political scientists have regarded elected institutions as the *sin qua non* of politics in democracies since Schumpeter's (1947) influential formulation.[36] Against such proceduralized views, scholars have urged for more associational, participatory, deliberative and substantive conceptions of democracy to include greater involvement of civil society, popular participation, public consultations on policy, and equality of policy outcomes as a means of deepening democracy.[37] In this book, even as I am sympathetic to critics of a proceduralized account of democracy I find pertinent David Beetham's (1999) suggestion that democracy is *at once* a form of government as well as a process. Democracy is thus not only a form of government where people hold their elected representatives accountable through periodic elections. Democracy is also a social process to assert people's equality with one another (Luckham *et al.*, 2003).[38]

Moreover, I am wary of the scholarship that conflates democracy with liberalism. Political liberalism, as enunciated by John Rawls (1971, 1999) in the context of his theorization of justice, animates much of the contemporary thinking about democracy, the concomitant ideas of free and equal persons imbued with the right to own property, and the assumption that all people

will eventually assimilate into its universal promise. For instance, Marc
Plattner makes a case for emphasizing the compact between liberalism
and democracy when he observes that 'on the whole, countries that hold
free elections are overwhelmingly more liberal than those that do not, and
countries that protect civil liberties are overwhelmingly more likely to hold
free elections than those that do not' (Plattner, 1998). Plattner's account is
instructive because it reiterates the tendency to conflate democracy with
political liberalism. Communitarian theorists, critical as they are of the primacy
accorded to liberal individualism, privilege the ideal of the community over
the individual. However, by rejecting both the universality of liberalism and
democracy, the communitarians paradoxically reaffirm the link between the
two.[39] The compact between liberalism and democracy is further underscored
through the model of deliberative democracy proposed by Jürgen Habermas
to reconcile the tension between the liberal and the communitarian view.
In the deliberative model, people engage in rational discourse to determine
the public good, thereby re-emphasizing the necessity of the links between
liberalism and democracy.

Again these views, I find Chantal Mouffe's (1996; 2000; 2007; 2009)
approach to studying democracy to be more fruitful. Mouffe insists on
directing attention to the fraught conceptual histories between liberalism
and democracy to argue that there is in fact no necessary relation between
the two. Accepting the reality of liberal democracy as the dominant model of
democracy in contemporary times, she reminds us of the distinctiveness of
the two traditions:

> On one side we have the liberal tradition constituted by the rule
> of law, the defence of human rights and the respect of individual
> liberty; on the other the democratic tradition whose main ideas
> are those of equality, identity between governing and governed
> and popular sovereignty (Mouffe, 2000, 2).

Her account reminds scholars that democracy and liberalism are
disjunctive, a perspective that is valuable to the argument I make in this book.

Another important contribution that Mouffe makes is to urge analysts to
recognize the impossibility of eliminating conflict from human life. She alerts
us that, even in contexts of free and fair elections where robust mechanisms
exist to hold elected leaders accountable, the dimension of conflict can neither

be wished away nor co-opted within electoral institutions.[40] Mouffe offers us what she calls 'an agonistic account' to conceptualize democratic processes as spaces which supply an arena for reconfiguring power relations. Proponents of the agonistic view distinguish themselves from votaries of antagonistic conflict. Antagonism is violent and involves physical liquidation of adversaries. By contrast, the perspective of agonism points us to *negotiations* over the terms on which the political community is constituted. Unlike antagonists, agonists see themselves sharing a common framework even as they are in conflict. They do not seek to liquidate one another. Rather, their practices reshape (or maintain) the social relations that connect them. Analysing people's negotiations through an agonistic optic enables me to interrogate dichotomous views of proceduralized co-option into electoral institutions on the one hand and violent conflict between antagonists on the other.

Drawing on an agonistic perspective of democracy, I investigate the heterogeneous politics of the poor. The politics discussed in this book is not therefore a politics of assimilation into liberal values constituted by juridically-defined individual rights, private property and the rule of law. At the same time, the politics of the poor is not the politics of either sustaining difference or mounting resistance. This book does not celebrate the putative march of liberal democracy. Nor does it valorize the alleged resilience of communitarian ways of life and the supposed inevitability of class struggle. Rather, it contributes to interrogating the binaries between assimilation and difference by elaborating the entanglements between the universal and the particular.

In this vein, I avoid the temptation of analysing poor people's negotiations as reflecting a teleos. Categories such as citizenship, incorporation into languages of stateness, improvement, and modernity are critically assessed in the light of the ethnographic material without assuming that they provide the endpoint for people's political practices. Side by side, that there are impulses for change is undeniable rendering the application of such categories as clientelism, moral vocabularies, preservation and tradition untenable. The material presented in the forthcoming chapters suggests that the labouring poor neither acquiesce in the primacy of electoral procedures nor do they seek to resist it. Rather, their political practices entail negotiations with the ensemble of institutions and individuals that constitute actually-existing democracies. The arguments presented here resonate with the emerging scholarship that emphasizes the complex and apparently contradictory politics of vulnerable and marginalized populations without assuming a teleos.[41] By revealing these negotiations, the agonistics of democracy illuminate the entanglements between the universal and the particular.

II

Poor people's politics: Early skeptics

Research on poor people's politics would have been scoffed at by the doyens of the social sciences. Across the ideological spectrum, authors dismissed the possibility of the poor conducting any politics at all. If during most of the nineteenth century, observers of European societies condemned poor people's public practices as mindless and without purpose, commentators in the twentieth century remained sceptical of their ability to exercise newly acquired suffrage. Several of these academic opinions were intertwined with domestic political struggles over the extension of the franchise as well as the fear among liberal theorists of totalitarian ideologies, which, according to them, found nourishment among the poor. It was only in the final quarter of the twentieth century that, based on the seminal work of such scholars as E. P. Thompson, James Scott and Ranajit Guha, academics began to appreciate the political import of poor people's practices, their ideas and perspectives.[42]

Asserting the very impossibility of people in poverty being engaged in any purposeful activity, social theorists of nineteenth-century Europe pointed to the dislocations caused by the then on-going processes of industrialization and urbanization. Liberal political theorist Herbert Spencer wrote of the poor as imbeciles, idlers and criminals who had failed to respond to the exigencies of modern social conditions (Spencer, 1881, 344–45). His writings resonated with physicist Enrico Morselli's observations that 'progress' produced both winners and losers: the struggle for existence among the latter produced 'social evils' such as misery, disease, prostitution, madness and suicide (Morselli, 1881, 363).[43] Perhaps the most cogent articulation of this position was that of Gustave Le Bon, writing in the closing years of that century. Le Bon invoked the rubric of the 'crowd' to refer to aggregations of the poor. He describes crowds as atavistic, irrational, impulsive and resonating with supposedly-inferior beings such as women, children and savages (Le Bon, 1896, 20). Participation in crowds implied a tendency to eschew any kind of reasoning and reflection: instincts, affectivities and sentiment took over the constituents of crowds and prevented them from exercising critical judgment. Although scholars writing in the twentieth century expressed less paranoia about public practices of the poor, the perspective remained influential, particularly among scholars influenced by the writings of the sociologist Emile Durkheim, that the stresses caused by industrialization and urbanization ruptured existing social networks. The resultant 'strains' on society, it was believed, led those who were unable to cope – the marginals and the underclasses – to react against the structural factors that had caused the dislocations in the first place (Smelser, 1962).[44]

It is not only Durkheim's followers who took this view. Karl Marx famously suggested that the urban poor of his time, those who experienced the most precarious livelihoods in the transitioning economies of Europe, had little potential for advancing any political or social claims.[45] As constituents of the category he labelled as the *lumpenproletariat*, they were vanguards of the counter-revolution, the 'bribed tool of reactionary intrigue' (Marx, 2010, 20) against the progressive movements of the newly emergent proletariat and their progressive de-classed bourgeois allies. Where authors have been more sympathetic, as historian E. J. Hobsbawm was to the *sans-culottes* who he argues provided the striking force of the French Revolution, they denied poor people's ability to imagine political possibilities: 'History moved dead against them', Hobsbawm approvingly observes (Hobsbawm, 1962, 85).

Noting the political practices of Europe's large peasant population during the mid-nineteenth century, Marx was as disparaging about them as he was about their urban counterparts. For him, peasants were a 'sack of potatoes' (Marx, 1852), and for this reason did not possess any political acumen. When they did participate in political activities, they tended to be conservative, as they demonstrated through their support of Louis Napoleon during the 1851 referendum.[46] Following this line of analysis, Hobsbawm famously characterized peasants as 'pre-political people who have not yet found, or only begun to find, specific language in which to express their aspirations for the world' (Hobsbawm, 1978, 2). In the contemporary politics of bourgeois-democratic states, he says, they 'tend to be election fodder, except when they demand or inhibit certain specialized political measures' (Hobsbawm, 1973, 19), he observes elsewhere.

In characterizing peasants as pre-political, Hobsbawm echoed fellow-historian Eugene Weber's claim that eighteenth-century French peasants remained 'at an archaic stage' (Weber, 1976, 20) as far as their politics was concerned. Although both Hobsbawm and Weber drew on very different intellectual traditions, it is interesting to note that their conclusions on the peasantry were similar. As for Hobsbwam, in Weber's account, any public action by the French peasantry prior to the advent of the national network of railways, roads and canals was 'pre-political'. Even to think of these as 'political' was absurd as peasant responses to economic crisis were almost always mediated through their supposedly traditional 'mentalities': (Weber, 1976, 10), or ways of life and thought. Where peasants rebelled, they were only 'shaking a fist at fate', he tells us (Weber, 1976, 277). Weber's account of peasant collective actions are replete with epithets such as 'feuds', 'raids' and 'pillage', bolstering his implicit acceptance of the metropolitan Parisian view that the rural poor 'lacked civilization' (Weber, 1976, 5).

Nonetheless, where Weber and Hobsbawm were willing to at least consider that the poor sometimes acted collectively to defend their possessions or ways of life scholars who claimed explicitly to study the 'cultures of poverty' studiously stayed away from discussing the ways in which the poor might be involved in politics. Oscar Lewis, studying urban slum settlements in the United States of America and Mexico during the 1950s, asserted that the poor acquired a poverty-perpetuating value system. This value system characterized the 'sub-culture of poverty that prevailed in the urban low-income neighborhoods that he researched. His observations led him to conclude that the poor are 'a marginal people who know only their own troubles, their own local conditions, their own neighborhood, their own way of life' (Lewis, 1998, 7).

Supporting these views but arriving at their conclusions through a different approach, were rational choice theorists of collective action (Zald and Ash, 1966; Oberschall, 1973; McCarthy and Zald, 1977). They took individual utility as their analytical point of departure. Drawing on the incentive focussed approach of economists such as Mancur Olson (1965), these authors aimed to demonstrate the logical fallacy of the view that socially isolated and rootless individuals sought to escape the situation of anomie by immersing themselves in mobs and crowds. They emphasized that, given the costs associated with collective mobilization, only people with resources could be expected to initiate or participate meaningfully in them. Accordingly, political entrepreneurs who were able to mobilize resources usually directed collective mobilizations, and people participated in them by calculating the relative costs and benefits accruing to them. As the poor, by definition, led vulnerable lives, they tended to avoid participating in collective mobilizations, unless they calculated the benefits to outweigh the costs. Given the opportunity costs associated with political mobilization, they could be anticipated to desist from engaging in any political activity unless the benefits outweighed the costs.[47]

The consensus that the poor were unable to or unwilling to participate in politics resonated with post World War II writings of US political scientists and sociologists. This period coincided with the hardening of ideological divisions, decolonization and the emergence of the Third World, and, as a consequence, a concern in the United States that Europe and the postcolonial countries needed to be saved from communism. A particular area of intellectual inquiry for US based scholars writing in the wake of the Cold War was the examination of the conditions under which democratic politics emerged and sustained. These inquiries produced a rare agreement among scholars on the right (Lipset, 1963) and the left (Moore Jr, 1966), among those enthused about the possibility of 'modernization' (Almond and Verba, 1965) or those sceptical of its prospects (Huntington, 1968) that the poor were incapable of any kind of politics, much less democratic politics. This consensus continued right through till the 1990s (Lijphart, 1997 and Przeworski et al., 2000), although voices of dissent began to be advanced by scholars studying urban labouring classes to suggest that poor people's attitudes were, in fact, more favourable to democracy than academics were willing to admit (Reuschemeyer et al., 1992).

The social historian E. P. Thompson's (1971) path-breaking intervention on the 'moral economy of the crowd' challenged several of these theses and is an important work for the purpose of the argument advanced in this book.[48] Interrogating the perspective that 'the crowd' was impulsive and motivated by greed, he mined archival data to present the variegated practices of people who participated in the food riots of the closing years of eighteenth-century England. Thompson's analysis revealed the shared solidarities, communal understandings and mutually supportive relationships shared by peasant populations who collectively reflected on the changes affecting their lives and livelihoods and took what they considered to be appropriate action.

Influenced by Thompson's framework, Ranajit Guha's (1983) seminal work on the 'elementary aspects of peasants insurgency' read the colonial archives in India against the grain and uncover the shared moralities that animated rural resistance to colonial encroachments. Guha's scholarship took to task the assumption that peasant collective action was 'pre-political' and noted the calculation of social and individual risks that peasants made prior to commencing armed collective action in eastern India. Through these actions, they defended and sustained a subaltern autonomy from the colonial state. Similarly, drawing on Thompson's leads, James Scott (1985) directed attention to the 'weapons of the weak' to argue that peasants and agricultural labourers shared common codes of practice against the depredations visited on them by wealthy and powerful people in colonial and postcolonial Malaya. Far from being the 'sack of potatoes' that earlier scholars had thought of them, peasants developed a sophisticated ensemble of practices to defend themselves against such claims without being openly confrontational: such everyday forms of resistance included feigning ignorance, foot-dragging, gossiping and the like. While there is much in this book that differs sharply from the analysis offered by these scholars, it is important to acknowledge their contribution in challenging the long-prevalent assumptions in academia about poor people's alleged inability to do politics.

The problem revisited: Negotiating the universal/ particular conundrum

A potentially interesting approach to studying poor people's negotiations is offered by scholars who argue that they appropriate 'universalizing vocabularies' advanced by states (following Corrigan and Sayer, 1985). According to these scholars, people in poverty present their claims in the name of universalistic idioms. Ideas of citizenship, liberal rights, and progress mean very concrete things to them. Such notions reflect the imbrications of people with the processes of state-making (Hansen and Stepputat, 2001). In this vein, James Holston (2008) directs attention to the 'insurgent' views of citizenship among his interlocutors in Brazil's 'autoconstructed' neighbourhoods: by highlighting their role as tax-payers and consumers, residents of 'autoconstructed' neighbourhoods deployed the language of rights and demanded to be treated as citizens. Similarly, elaborating the notion of 'critical liberalism', Courtney Jung (2008)notes the salience of the language of rights among the indigenous population in Mexico even as they protest the developmental claims being made by the state. Of a piece with this literature is O'Brien and Li's (2006)work on 'rightful resistance', which tells us of the ways in which peasants in rural China invoke the rights conferred upon them by the state to defend themselves against claims on their land by private corporations. Similarly, Comaroff and Comaroff (2009) point to the increasing use of the law by Africa's subaltern populations as a means of bettering their lives, thereby inverting the practices of 'lawfare' instituted by colonial authorities to dispossess those very same people on that continent.

In the Indian context, Nandini Sundar (2011)highlights the ways through which impoverished women in remote parts of central India insist on emphasizing their rights when confronted with oppression. Likewise, Stuart Corbridge and his colleagues (2005) note that eastern India's rural poor want to see more of the democratically-elected Indian government, rather than less of it. In these readings, people in poverty derive their ideas of membership in the political community from the universal terms offered by the state. The poor take seriously the languages of stateness, the promises of citizenship, the ideas of development and improvement advanced by the state, and the prospects of modernization.

Proponents of an alternative approach suggest that the poor appropriate the particularisms that are imposed upon them by states and dominant classes. In the view of these scholars, such appropriations are the result of poor people's systematic exclusion from the formal spaces of the polity and the economy, first by the authoritarian colonial state and thereafter by the postcolonial state and members of the privileged classes. The provenance of particularistic practices of political membership in colonial policies of indirect rule has now been well-documented.[49] Achille Mbembe (2001) avers that the manner in which colonial and postcolonial states in Africa exercised sovereignty led directly to what he calls the 'socialization of arbitrariness'. Such a normalization of arbitrary governance in turn structured the political practices of the continent's oppressed populations, compelling them to take recourse to particularistic tactics. Documenting the strategies of 'inverse governmentality' among the poor in informal urban neighbourhoods in Mozambique, Mortimer Nielsen (2009) similarly tells us that the poor mimic the practices of the housing authorities to render their unauthorized colony legible to them.

From the perspective of these authors, the poor are exposed to systematic forms of exploitation and marginalization, which are not uncommonly perpetuated by the very institutions (and people) that offer promises of citizenship, liberal rights and development. As a result, people in poverty formulate their membership in the political community in quite particularistic terms to defend themselves from the depredations of universal rules and institutions. Partha Chatterjee (2004) argues that the governmental technologies of the state in India promote exemptions rather than universal rules. By way of example, Chatterjee (2012b) refers to targeted poverty-alleviation programmes often focussed on members of specific communal or occupational groups. The poor respond accordingly by articulating quite particularistic claims, anchored in a language of seeking exceptions rather than advancing juridical notions of rights. Chatterjee goes so far as to ask whether such practices can 'be framed as a redefined norm that endorses differentiated rather than equal citizenship as the normative standard for the modern state' (2012, 24).

These two strands of scholarship provide useful leads for the present study. The first challenges the view that poor people remain impervious to universalistic ideas related to democracy, such as citizenship, stateness, improvement and development, and modernity. The second interrogates the notion that states promote universalistic ideas, suggesting the renewed relevance of such ideas as clientelism, moral vocabularies, preservation and backwardness, and tradition. Both perspectives acquaint readers to the rich tapestry of political negotiations in which the poor engage. The insights offered by their work help scholars interrogate flattened narratives that claim the mutual exclusiveness of universalistic and particularistic ideas.

Nevertheless, the analytical salience of both groups of scholars tends to underplay the entangled ways in which both universalistic and particularistic imaginations are advanced by states, especially in democracies. Elaborating the examples from India, with which this book is concerned, will substantiate this point. Stuart Corbridge and his colleagues (2005) note that poor people view the Indian state in contradictory ways as being concurrently coercive, developmental and facilitating empowerment. The universal promises of empowerment, development and rights are concomitant with particularistic practices of coercion that are disproportionately targeted toward poor people, particularly those of culturally subordinated communities. However, to conclude from this evidence, as they do, that the poor derive their ideas from the universal vocabularies of the state contradicts their own empirically rich fieldwork. Likewise, Partha Chatterjee's (2004; 2011; 2012) work highlights the ways in which democratic imaginations have assumed unprecedented salience for the mass of India's impoverished population. To conclude, then, as he does, that poor people's politics is all about 'inviting governmental authorities to declare an exception and suspend the norm in their case' (2012, 25) ignores precisely the salience of democratic imaginations for India's poor, to which he otherwise appears sensitive.

To be sure, the differences between the two approaches are many. Corbridge *et al.* highlight the ways in which India's poor hope for the universalization of the laws promulgated by the state. Chatterjee, by contrast, emphasizes the manner in which the poor call upon the state to declare them exempt them from these laws. Corbridge and his colleagues argue that poor people aspire for more of the state. Chatterjee does not deny that this is the case, but he adds, presciently, that the poor want more of the state in order to be exempt from, rather than included within, the ambit of its laws. While Corbridge and his colleagues privilege a conception of equal citizenship, Chatterjee prefers a differentiated notion of citizenship.

Despite these important disagreements, there is much that the two views share. Both narratives provide state focussed accounts of poor people's politics: the former on its universalizing vocabularies, the latter on its particularistic techniques of governmentality. In their accounts, poor people either appropriate the former or operate within the confines structured by the latter. With the substantive democratization of the state, the poor view governments as spatially and socially more accessible to them than they did in the past. Thus, while the former account examines the ways in which the poor, as citizens-in-the-making, 'see the state', the latter unambiguously analyses the politics of the poor as the 'politics of the governed'. While both accounts promise to explore state–society imbrications, they could delve more into the ways in which the poor advance their claims in society. As a result, the ways in which the universal and the particular are entangled remain understated in their works.

The contributions of the afore-mentioned scholars direct attention to poor people's politics and, in particular, to their negotiations with democracy in ways that had seemed implausible to earlier writers. However, the perspectives they offer reify, rather than undermine, the binary between the universal and the particular. Implicit in the suggestion that poor people appropriate the universal vocabularies advanced by the state is the assumption that they possess no universal ideas of their own. Such universal ideas as they might actually possess are analysed as derivatives or imitations of ideals advocated by progressive elites at the apex of the democratic state. The state leads, the people follow. Scholars who highlight the particularistic practices institutionalized by the state differ only slightly in which they critique the universalistic presumptions of states and progressive elites. In their narrative, the poor readily acquiesce in these particularistic practices and invite the state to declare further exemptions. Again, the state leads, the people follow. In both arguments, poor people are portrayed as repositories of particularistic worldviews. Either they adopt the universalisms offered by progressive elites or they strategically deploy the particularities to extract resources from states. The possibility that they might incubate universalistic ideals is not even alluded to, let alone given serious consideration.

Against these authors, Gail Omvedt (2008) urges scholars to not ignore people's social ideas – their 'theories and utopias' (2008, 27) as she puts it. Popular experiences of being subjected to exploitation, marginalization and subordination do not preclude their harbouring universalist ideals of justice, equality and dignity and insert these into the vocabularies of the state. Drawing on her notes of caution, I am wary of endorsing Corbridge and his co-authors' conclusion that poor people's politics derives from their internalization of the universalizing vocabulary of states. An appreciation of her discerning critique also distances my perspective from Chatterjee's alternative framing that poor people's politics is one of competing particularisms, reified by the state's governmentalizing technologies. Omvedt's work is a subtle yet powerful reminder of the continued salience of universalistic ideals among poor people and their attempts to advance these ideals. Seen from this perspective, the politics of the poor is not a contest between universalistic views and particularistic ideas or a competition between particularistic practices. Rather, their negotiations exemplify the entanglements between the universal and the particular.

Political spaces for negotiations: Opportunity structures and social relations

In this section, I want to elaborate the framework of political space to think analytically about the ways in which this dynamic interaction shapes people's negotiations. The leads provided by Stuart Corbridge and his colleagues, Partha Chatterjee and Gail Omvedt provide me with the conceptual apparatus to think systematically about the 'political spaces' in which people negotiate with the state and with each other. I conceptualize 'political space' as co-constituted by the dynamic interaction of institutional opportunity structures and social relations of power. Spaces are conventionally thought to constrain and contain. But political geographers have recently reminded us that spaces also indicate frontiers and horizons. If, as Doreen Massey (2005, 8) proposes that 'we recognise space as a product of interrelations; as constituted through interactions, from the immensity of the global to the intimately tiny', then political space emerges as the terrain on which the entanglements between the universal and the particular are revealed.

Scholars theorizing about opportunity structures focus on the nature of states and policy design.[50] Of particular interest to the argument in this book is the influence of the design of public policy in shaping poor people's claim making. The literature48 suggests that where governmental interventions in public policy are designed as universal in scope, poor people's negotiations over implementation is qualitatively different, as compared to a context where it is more targeted in scope. Even as implementation might be patchy, public policies intended for universal coverage are important media through which the concreteness of the state is conveyed to people. Within policies designed for universal coverage, schemes that are unconditional in scope transmit a universalistic ideal of the political community. Especially where public policy entails the introduction of social protection schemes, the design of the policy assumes even greater salience for poor people.

An important intervention in studies of democracy has been the exploration of the notion of 'postcolonial democracy', as explored by scholars such as Partha Chatterjee (2012), Sudipta Kaviraj (2000), Koelble and Lipuma (2009). They urge students of democracy to consider the possibility that trajectories of democracies in postcolonial settings may never converge with those of democracies in Europe and North America. These differences arise due to different processes of state-formation, the positioning of postcolonial states in the global economic and financial system, and the limitations of the postcolonial state in terms of domestic capacities. This book finds much merit in the theorization offered by postcolonial analysts of democracy, even as it recognizes the enormous variations that are possible within postcolonial democracies.

Perspectives that underscore the importance of the opportunities provided by the state are invaluable. They remind us of the importance of states in structuring opportunities and providing the vocabularies, which people, including people in poverty, are able to use in order to influence public policy in their favour. However, Sidney Tarrow (1998) is correct in cautioning scholars against an overwhelming dependence on state-provisioned opportunities as an explanatory variable of popular negotiations. For a public policy or institutional design to provide a political opportunity, it must be *perceived* as such by people. The scholarly approaches that focus on trajectories of democratization and state-formation, institutional design and scope of public policy tell us little about the mechanisms through which such interventions are recognized as opportunities. Recognizing these limitations, Laurence Whitehead (2003) calls upon social scientists to direct attention to the subjective identifications among poor people of the factors and groups supportive of their interests and those opposed to them. An understanding of these subjective identifications is impossible without directing attention to the going-ons in society.

The academic traditions that shed light on the societal factors of people's negotiations are quite disparate.[51] Of interest to me is the scholarship that emphasizes the importance of social relations to understanding and explaining variations in political negotiations. Such social relations are ineluctably political when they involve tussles over social meanings, collective identities and the distribution of resources in society. Given the oppressive conditions that underpin poor people's lives, I find particularly useful analytic approaches that combine class with culture in their analysis of social relations. Two variables are of specific importance in any consideration of social relations. One variable relates to the social relations of *production* between different classes. The second relates to the balance of *distribution* between the different classes. I elaborate each of these two variables by turn below. However, as will become clearer through the study, politics between classes is analytically separate from politics over the formation of classes. The social relations between classes is as much about the social relations through which people make meaning of class in the first place.

Scholars focussing on the social relations of production highlight the manner in which the configuration of class relations shapes popular negotiation between different classes. But they remain divided over the class relations that most ably challenge the power-base in the countryside. On the one hand, some scholars, such as Eric Wolf (1969) and Hamza Alavi (1973) have advanced the 'middle peasant thesis'. Briefly, their argument is that the middle peasant – farmers who own small plots of land, which they cultivate by exploiting their own or family labour – are at the forefront of challenging rural hierarchies, because of their economic autonomy from the rich peasants.[52] The activism of such 'middle peasants', opens up avenues for negotiations for the rural poor. A contrasting viewpoint is offered by Jeffrey Paige (1975) who identifies the rural poor – the landless wage earners and the sharecroppers – as the incubators of insurrectionary ideas and practices. In this vein, several scholars explicitly refer to the organization of the rural poor, especially if they share the same occupation, such as agricultural wage labour or sharecropping.[53] The obvious differences in their empirical salience notwithstanding, both perspectives illustrate the role of class relations in facilitating, or inhibiting poor people's political negotiations.

The social relations of distribution provides the second key societal variable to help and explain the differences in political negotiations. This variable calls attention to the ways in which members of classes, which gain access to and control the levers of power, are able to advance their interests in society. This they do not only through direct control over elected governments but also by shaping policy agendas. Even more importantly, they institute social norms and values that frame disciplinary mechanisms in society. In this context, Barrington Moore Jr's (1966) insight on the ways in which the balance of class power shapes political change is interesting. His argument primes analysts to expect that a strong bourgeoisie makes for democracy, while entrenched landed interests result in fascist rule. In areas where the bourgeoisie and the entrenched landed interests were both weak, peasant-led communist revolutions instituted political change. Although the Indian case spectacularly defied Moore Jr's dictum of 'no bourgeoisie no democracy', I retain in this book the more general insight that the balance of class power shapes political practices. Dietrich Rueschmeyer *et al.* (1992) highlight the varied ways in which working classes in advanced capitalist countries exercised power, with variable successes in containing the claims of the dominant classes. In similar vein, Gøsta Esping-Andersen (1990) reminds us, again based on data from the industrialised capitalist countries, that differences in the balance of class power shaped heterogenieties in negotiations over welfare regimes.

A consideration of the social relations of power helps scholars examine the different mechanisms through which people imbue policies and institutions with collective meanings. Such perspectives illuminate the contested perceptions of specific state interventions. However, by assuming the autonomy of the social domain from the state, they inhibit analysts' ability to investigate the way institutional structures *shape* social relations. They obfuscate the materiality of popular perceptions, and abstract away the institutional realities that foment people's imaginations. Recognizing these pitfalls, some scholars have sought to integrate both explanatory approaches in their scholarship. For instance, Patrick Heller (2000) emphasizes the importance of decentralized governance institutions in the Indian State of Kerala. The Left Front led State government devolved substantial resources and authority upon these institutions, leading to the facilitation of assertive claims from the rural working classes. Democratic institutions and democratic processes bolster one another. States and contentious subjectivities simultaneously influence one another in dynamic ways. Alongside, organizations of the rural working classes worked together with urban middle class civil society activist to strengtehn the participatory milieu of the state. The social relatons of power and the instututitional opportunity structures bolstered one another to produce a synergy whereby states and societies shaped one another to be more participatory than they earlier were.

Focussing attention on the same people's engagements with different kinds of policies and different people's engagements with the same policy, as I aim to do in this book, helps me understand the heterogenieties that characterize poor people's politics. As we shall see in forthcoming chapters, the people who supplicate in one instance to be exempted from rules in one instance demand the implementation of the law, the next instance. Some of the people who do the supplicating and the demanding also dispute their leaders' presumptions.

Others combine their supplications and demands with asserting their claims over the public space against the assumptions of privileged classes.

However, policies provide at best an opportunity structure. The perception that a given policy provides an *opportunity* is a social process. For instance, it is one thing for governments to institute universal adult franchise. It is quite another for people to view that suffrage as an opportunity to further their specific interests and participate in political life. The design of policy provides crucial, but necessarily partial, perspectives when it comes to explaining variation in political practices. The same policy could provoke varied responses among working classes in different regions. Labouring people inhabiting neighbouring localities and sharing the same idea of social life could perceive the same policy in very different ways, based on the class collaborations and conflicts within which they are embedded.

The *dynamic intersections* of the institutional opportunity structures and social relations of power together constitute the 'political space' in which poor people negotiate with democracy. In thinking about political spaces in such a manner, scholars are able to investigate ethnographically the minute ways in which power is negotiated (Gupta and Ferguson, 1997a). The concept of 'political space' allows me to think about the ways in which the entanglements between the universal and the particular simultaneously constrain and enable poor people's negotiations with democracy. A consideration of such entanglements alerts us against a view of political space as a terrain for action autonomous from relations of power. Political spaces are not unencumbered by the configuration of social relations and by the mechanisms through which popular claims find institutional expression. But they indicate the horizon of possibilities. In the way in which the term is used in this book, political space is not a normative concept but an analytical one. Some political spaces are more enabling for poor people than others are. Whether or not such spaces facilitate their negotiations with democracy is shaped by the specific configuration of opportunity structures and social relations of power and their dynamic interaction with one another.

III

An ethnography of everyday negotiations

The analytical utility of the spatial metaphor should not detract us from recognizing that people inhabit places, not spaces. Therefore, any analysis of political space has to be grounded in concrete 'places' (Basso, 1996 and Wolf, 2001). Places render meaning to space. They provide the terrain on which the entanglements between the universal and the particular, between state and society, and between institutional opportunities and social relations manifest. These are the locales wherein people negotiate with their polities, make meanings of democracy, advance their claims against dominant classes and elect their representatives to office. It is here that they labour, love and live.

It is in places that the agonistics of democracy manifest themselves. A study of the agonistics of democracy entails an analysis of the detailed and the contingent without, however, losing sight of the general and the structural. This methodological route requires stepping beyond the usual focus on institutions and formal procedures while studying democracy. A spatially-focused political ethnography (Baiocchi and Connor, 2008), is particularly suited to understanding the institutional and societal negotiations that are the focus of this book.

This book is based on ethnographic work in the eastern Indian States of Bihar and West Bengal to understand poor people's negotiations with democracy. These States were selected because they shared certain background similarities, enumerated below.

1. They both devolved formal and substantive responsibilities to elected local government councils called gram panchayats, making these councils the obvious loci of contentions over resources and authority.

2. Electoral politics was constituted by discourses of contestations, challenging dominant structures and a rhetoric of empowerment of the toiling masses.

3. Both States shared similar administrative and social histories, stemming from a common land tenure system.

The two States were also selected for variations *between* them (George and Bennett, 2005). The vocabulary of 'class' in West Bengal provided a sharp contrast with the language of 'caste' deployed in Bihar. Based on a review of the comparative politics literature (Kohli, 1990 and Harriss, 2003), I was led to believe that the class-centred vocabularies of West Bengal would be more enabling of poor people's politics than the caste-centered languages of Bihar. Although the nuanced findings of Corbridge et al. (2005) alerted me to the surprises in store, I had assumed prior to undertaking fieldwork that political space in West Bengal was more conducive to poor people's politics than it was in Bihar. I was mistaken.

I conducted the ethnography for this project in select gram panchayats, which form the base of local government in India. Each gram panchayat comprises between 10 and 25 electoral wards. I selected two gram panchayats within three kilometers of one another in a single block of Bihar's Araria district and another two gram panchayats within five kilometers of one another in a single block of West Bengal's Maldah district. Within the four gram panchayats, I coordinated a census of 18 wards to identify the specific wards in which I could focus my ethnographic work. Although gram panchayats were the obvious focus for any ethnography of poor people's politics, their institutional design lent importance to ward-level councilors. This was all the more so in West Bengal where ward councilors were allocated budgets for their wards. Ward-level councilors were directly elected by the population. In turn, they elected the president of the gram panchayat from among themselves, making the latter dependent on them for support. In Bihar, although ward-level councilors held no authority over budgets and were elected alongside the president of the gram panchayat, they proved to be useful mediators with the populations for their respective presidents. Thus, although I attempted to focus on specific wards, it was impossible for me to narrow my observations to the wards in which I lived.

Although the research sought to explore the 'how' of poor people's politics, I was also interested in explaining the similarities and variations across the study locations. Following the conventions of 'small-n' qualitative research in comparative political science,[54] I selected the study locations on the 'independent variable' I had initially believed might predict and explain variations. Following the thesis that political power follows economic resources and that economic autonomy enhanced political voice I had presumed that the greater the economic resources at the disposal of the poor, the more vociferously they would assert their claims. During the preliminary stage of my research, I looked particularly towards the marginal landowners as the leading fraction of the labouring poor and analysed the acreage they possessed. Table 1.5 (see next two pages) presents land-size and class-disaggregated households and acreage across the eighteen wards where the survey was conducted.

The higher the cumulative acreage under marginal landholdings, I assumed, the greater the confidence with which the poor would advance their claims. Conversely, the lower the acreage, the feebler the collective voice of the poor.[55] Based on this hypothesis, I selected Ditya (higher acreage among marginal landowners) and Rahimpur wards (lower acreage among marginal landowners) in West Bengal, the State where political scientists report that political discourse is shaped by class. In Bihar, the State where we are told that political discourse is shaped by caste, I selected Sargana Ward 1 (higher acreage among marginal landowners) and Roshanar Ward 5 (lower acreage among marginal landowners) wards for in-depth fieldwork. The populations constantly crossed ward boundaries in their quotidian economic and political lives. Landless workers in Roshanar Ward 5 laboured on the farms of large landowners in Roshanar Wards 7 and 9 just as their counterparts in Gotra Dakkhin and Hebtul worked for farmers with medium and large holdings in Rahimpur. Such fluidities reinforced my inability to limit my observations to select wards. The names of the villages and all their inhabitants have been changed to protect their identities.

As a collection of methods that entail immersion in a given place and sustained contact with their interlocutors (Willis and Trondman, 2000), ethnography provides researchers with the opportunity to gain insights into everyday practices as well as their interpretation of past events. Ethnographic methods allow researchers to develop textured accounts of people's ambivalences, anxieties and dilemmas by providing them with a window to people's observable practices as well as expressed thoughts. Fieldwork was conducted in the four wards for eight months during 2009 and 2010, followed up by three rounds of further fieldwork lasting two months each. Although fieldwork included conducting census and sample survey data, semi-structured interviews and group discussions, the most interesting and insightful accounts emerged from the stories people told me while they allowed me to 'hang out' (Rabinow, 1977 and Geertz, 1998) with them at *chai* kiosks, government offices, village squares, their homes, places of worship, and sundry other public and private spaces.

Table 1.5: Landholding patterns: Percentage number and operational agricultural area in surveyed localities

	Landless (No land)		Marginal (Less than or equal to 1 hectare)		Small (Greater than 1 hectare, but less than or equal to 2 hectares)		Medium (Greater than 2 hectares but less than or equal to 10 hectares)		Large (Greater than 10 hectares)		Households (n)
	Population	Area	Population	Area	Population	Area	Population	Area	Population	Area	
Bihar											
Roshanar Ward 5	80	0	16	45	3.73	15	0.62	14	0	0	**161**
Roshanar Ward 7	61	0	24	20	8	19	4.59	24	2.75	36	**109**
Roshanar Ward 8	74	0	23	62	1.62	14	0.81	13	0.40	11	**247**
Roshanar Ward 9	54	0	32	17	4.48	6	5	26	3.73	51	**134**
Roshanar Ward 10	68	0	27	43	1.69	14	2.26	20	1.13	23	**177**
Roshanar Ward 12	81	0	18	52	0	0	1.60	48	0	0	**188**
Sargana Ward 1	70	0	28	71	1.81	21	0.6	8	0	0	**165**
Sargana Ward 4	91	0	8	49	0	0	1.49	51	0	0	**202**

contd. ...

contd. ...

	Landless (No land)		Marginal (Less than or equal to 1 hectare)		Small (Greater than 1 hectare, but less than or equal to 2 hectares)		Medium (Greater than 2 hectares but less than or equal to 10 hectares)		Large (Greater than 10 hectares)		Households (n)
	Population	Area	Population	Area	Population	Area	Population	Area	Population	Area	
Sargana Ward 5	85	0	8	18	4.46	37	1.49	31	0.50	14	**202**
Sargana Ward 6	56	0	36	51	7.64	42	0.59	7	0	0	**144**
Sargana Ward 7	84	0	14	48	0.49	15	0.98	37	0	0	**205**
Sargana Ward 8	91	0	5	25	2.17	30	0.72	18	0.36	27	**276**
West Bengal											
Ditya	40	0	33	33	20	40	5	19	1.2	7	**326**
Gotra Dokkhin	80	0	14	49	4.95	27	1.65	23	0	0	**182**
Hebtul	75	0	14	35	7	27	4.74	37	0	0	**232**
Jalna	86	0	4.38	11	6	31	2.34	24	1.46	34	**685**
Rahimpur	75	0	9	12	11	33	1.65	8	4	46	**424**
Sindhugram	75	0	15	32	7	26	2.17	17	1.30	25	**461**

Source: Own census survey, 2009–10; all figures, except last column, as %; Figures may not add up to 100 because all figures over 0.5 per cent have been rounded to the nearest whole number.

I explained my research to my interlocutors in each of the four fieldwork places as one documenting the changes they had experienced in their lifetimes, and then following up on the insights I was offered. This appeared to me to be a safe, yet accurate, way of explaining my research project and understanding my interlocutors' political practices.[56] My presence in the fieldwork places aroused some initial anxieties and people confronted me with their misgivings. Was I a Christian missionary, they asked me in West Bengal? Did I eat beef, they wanted to know in Bihar? My being a male of the Kayasth community, a privileged caste among the Hindus, and the son of a private sector employee from Delhi, India's capital, was a matter of great interest for my interlocutors. By subjecting me to incessant scrutiny, they helped me come to terms with my own positionality, as an individual who was deeply implicated in the perpetration of the gender, class and communal hierarchies to which many among them were subordinate. On one occasion, I was offered a bribe by a bureaucrat responsible for the maintenance of official records so that I did not report the absence of some information I had requested. It took me a great deal of effort to convince the bureaucrat that I was a nonentity in the scheme of things that oiled India's administrative machinery. As a Kayasth man with some ancestral property in South Delhi studying in the United Kingdom, I was accurately marked out as a person who had benefitted from the same social, economic and political processes that oppressed many of my interlocutors.

England provided a topic of conversation for many of my interlocutors even as I arrived in the field with a primarily extractive view of the ethnographic approach. My interlocutors' interest spanned a variety of themes, ranging from that country's social norms, the role of the queen in politics, farmers' agricultural techniques and the depth of the water table, industries, and marriage and relationships.[57] Conversations about experiences in England were interspersed with conversations about experiences in India, reminiscent of the lively tradition of story-telling of which my interlocutors were proud inheritors.

The stories that constituted the politics about which I was told encompassed accounts of friendships, hostilities, rivalries, loyalties, legalities and illegalities. They offered far from a coherent narrative about my interlocutors' social relationships and political practices. I failed to unearth lurking discourses about hidden motives from them. Rather, these stories approximated a 'montage of patchy and sometimes disjunctive experiences' (Sivaramakrishnan and Agarwal, 2003, 48). A focus on stories, rather than discourse or narrative, enables ethnographers to devote attention to the production of unpredictable accounts that their interlocutors offer. The production of these accounts often depends on the recounting of specific events. After all, there is no single way in which a story can be told. As Patai (1988, 9) notes:

> Memory itself is no doubt generated and structured in specific ways by the opportunity to tell one's life story and the circumstances of the situation in which it occurs. At another moment in one's life, or faced with a different interlocutor, quite a different story, with a different emphasis, is likely to emerge.

Where I situate conflicting accounts with one another, the intention is to emphasize the tensions and strains rather than to signal a problem requiring resolution. Contrary to the advice of the founding fathers of the 'participant observation' methods (Malinowsky, 1967) I make no claims to rescue objective knowledge from the screen of subjective experience. I recognize that, at any given point of time, what I had access to was a partial truth. My resistance to smoothen tensions in the stories does not mean that I simply reproduce the stories my interlocutors told me. Rather, I attempt to forge 'links between different *knowledges* that are possible from different locations' (Gupta and Fergusson, 1997b, 39). I do this not only by situating the stories emerging from the four villages side by side but by bringing these into analytical conversations with social science research in other parts of the world. In doing so, I want to not only compare my fieldwork findings with similar findings from elsewhere but also contribute to ongoing conversations about power and politics, democracy, class relations and public policy.

Many of the characters that readers will encounter in this book found my interest in what was for them a routine matter both amusing and annoying. Indeed, the negotiations to which I direct attention focus on food, work, electricity and public presence alongside questions about dignity, equality, representation and social justice. People's discussions vis-à-vis access to state-funded welfare schemes are not only about this or that benefit. Rather, these exchanges are also negotiations over social relationships, over setting the agenda of the locality and over forging collective meanings of poverty. Even as they outlive electoral cycles and do not anticipate revolutionary fervour among the poor, such negotiations permeate the ways in which people lived. Because they indicate on-going tussles over material resources, social status, setting agendas, and meanings of collective life, I find such negotiations to be unequivocally political. To some observers, they might appear intensely mundane. However, de Certeau (1984) reminds us that it is people's everyday practices – the little manoeuvres they make within constrained spaces – that result in lasting change.[58] Whether or not such practices do actually contribute to lasting change is less important for my analysis than my interlocutors' intentions of purposeful action to live their lives in accordance with their life plans.

In this chapter, I have outlined the perspectives of the study on which this book is based. I began the first section by specifying the relational perspective of poverty that is used in this book. Thereafter, I sketched the ways in which concepts of power and politics are deployed, before introducing the agonistic perspective of democracy that informs the analysis in this book. In the second section, I first presented early perspectives undermining the very possibility of poor people's politics, echoes of which can still be found in influential perspectives today on both the Left and the Right. I then critically reviewed the theoretical approaches to studying poor people's politics in the light of the 'universal/ particular conundrum', insisting that scholars take seriously the entanglements between the two. This discussion led me to specify the institutional and societal components of 'political spaces'. In concluding this chapter, I delineated the ethnographic methods used in this study. The following two chapters will specify the institutional opportunity structures and the social relations of power within which the people whose politics are described in this book are embedded.

Endnotes

1   See the useful discussion in Stewart, Luderchi and Saith (2003).

2   A recent example comes from the astounding claim made in 2014 by the United Kingdom Independent Party (UKIP) politician Nigel Farage that he and his wife were poor. In fact, their income is estimated to be over £100,000 per annum. See http://www.independent.co.uk/news/uk/politics/poor-nigel-farage-finds-it-hard-to-get-by-on-109000-a-year-plus-expenses-9901390.html for the full news report.

3   The American TV presenter and host Rush Limbaugh is an outspoken proponent of such views. See his unhinged rant here: https://www.youtube.com/watch?v=dJhr3slNbYg.

4   A news report in the journal *Foreign Policy* suggests that views upholding moral weakness as a cause of poor people's poverty prevails in the Anglo-American sphere, unlike in most of the world, where public policies are held responsible for poverty. See report here: http://foreignpolicy.com/2014/10/22/is-laziness-the-cause-of-economic-inequality/.

5   The World Bank's pioneering *Voices of the Poor* study emphasizes several of these themes. See Narayan *et al.* (2000a), Narayan *et al.* (2000b) and Narayan and Petesch (2002).

6   See Meyer and Sullivan (2003) for a critical analysis of the relative merits of consumption data in the measurement of poverty.

7   See Ravallion, Datt and de Walle (1991) for useful introduction to the argument.

8   The International Food Policy Research Institute (IFPRI) has been computing the Global Hunger Index annually since 1990. Many of its studies are helpfully linked to discussions on poverty and inequality.

9   See Krishna (2010) for a useful discussion on health, illness and poverty.

10 The MPI, developed by the OPHI is a paradigmatic example. For details about the measure, see Alkire and Santos (2010).

11 US$ 1.90 per day, 2011 purchasing power parity or PPP.

12 Indeed, elaborating the paradoxes of contemporary citizenship, Etienne Balibar (1991) avers that contemporary regimes of governmentality have downgraded membership in the political community to the 'right' to be well governed. This paradox is aptly conveyed in the title of Partha Chatterjee's (2004) collection of essays: *The Politics of the Governed*.

13 This discussion is separate from debates on absolute poverty and relative poverty (See Roy, forthcoming).

14 This view is shared by the most influential thinkers on poverty-reduction, including Amartya Sen (1999), Jeffrey Sachs (2005), William Easterly (2006) and Paul Collier (2007). That many of these scholars differ substantially from one another does not detract from the fact that they all see poverty as a stubbornly-persistent residue of the past. In the Indian context, despite their fundamental differences on the policy frameworks needed to eradicate poverty, both Bhagwati and Panagriya (2013) and Drèze and Sen (2013) appear to adhere broadly to a residualist view of poverty.

15 This position is endorsed by Henry Bernstein (1992), Eric Olin Wright (1994), Barbara Harriss-White (2005b) and David Mosse (2007).

16 The concept of relative poverty is not without its problems, especially for countries where mass poverty is a featureof social life, as Amartya Sen (1983) lucidly points

out. However, a case is certainly to be made for taking accounts of relative poverty seriously in such rapidly growing Emerging Market economies as China and India.

17 See http://www.economist.com/news/leaders/21578665-nearly-1-billion-people-have-been-taken-out-extreme-poverty-20-years-world-should-aim.

18 For useful studies in the Western context, see Foster (1974), Stedman-Jones (1983) and Gallie (1984).

19 For excellent reviews of these debates, see Bernstein, 2008; Breman, 1996; Gooptu and Harris-White, 2001; and Veltemeyer, 2010.

20 This is not to suggest that such identities and obligations are entirely capitalist constructions.

21 Naturalizing such relationships need not entail their *internalization* by the oppressed, as theorists of 'false consciousness' (Lukes, 2011) imply, but a resigned acceptance of their present circumstance in the absence of any perceptibly better options (Scott, 1990). Indeed, as we shall see in this book, it is difficult to sustain the argument that poor people internalize in their own subordination.

22 Such appears to be the inference of scholars such as Bromley (1974), Dumont (1980) and Smith (1991).

23 This perspective is supported in the writings of such scholars as Cohen (1969), Ranger (1983), Lemarchand (1994) and Dirks (2001).

24 Important interventions in this regard are to be found in the collection of essays in Kushnick and Jennings (1999) for race and poverty in the United States. For discussions on caste and poverty in India, see Mendelsohn and Vicziany (1999) as well as Guru and Chakrabarty (2005). Much recent scholarship has sought to illuminate the connections between cultural subordination and poverty. Baulch *et al.* (2007) analyse the predominance of poverty among ethnic minorities in Vietnam. Tomovska (2010) illuminates the systemic ways in which discrimination against the Roma community in Europe perpetuates poverty in the community. Thorp and Parades (2010) apply the lens of horizontal inequalities to explore inequalities in Peru. Mustapha (2009) explores similar themes in the context of ethnic conflict in Nigeria. That poverty is bolstered by the cultural imposition of the values of the dominant classes on the labouring classes has been illustrated by Tholfsen's (1971) study on mid-Victorian England and in the context of colonial India by Gooptu (2001), Joshi (2001) and Kidambi (2011).

25 It is important to recognize that class and cultural difference need not manifest in hierarchy and inequality. But analysts of poverty need to be sensitive to the construction of difference as social inequalities (Gupta, 1991; Young, 1990).

26 See Summer (2012) and Alkire *et al.* (2014) for the empirical evidence.

27 This is the suggestion of authors who write texts with titles such as the 'fortune at the bottom of the pyramid' (Prahlad, 2009).

28 See, for instance, Harriss-White (2005b) and Panitch *et al.* (2001).

29 Variations of this argument have been advanced by Hechter (1975) and Gutirriez (2004).

30 See Kaviraj (1988) for a Gramscian elaboration of this phenomenon in India. Ranajit Guha's (1997) aptly titled *Dominance without Hegemony* lays thread-bare this argument.

31 This is a perspective to which such sensitive portrayals as in Scheper-Hughes (1993), Buur (2007), Bhatia (2005) and Kunnath (2012) direct our attention.

32 See Dahl (1957) as a paradigmatic example.

33 See useful commentaries in Foucault (1980), Gordon (1991) and Dreyfus and Rabinow (2014).

34 See collection of essays in Burchell *et al.* (1991).

35 Readers may also be interested in following the debate between James Scott and Samuel Popkin in Brocheux (1983).

36 See, for example, Huntingon (1968), Dahl (1971) and Karl (1990).

37 Cohen and Arato (1992) provide a useful associational account of democracy. See Pateman (1970) for an incisive discussion on participatory democracy. Cohen (1997) outlines a nuanced model of deliberative democracy. A substantive conception of democracy is fleshed out by Huber *et al.* (1997) and Kaldor and Vejvoda (1997).

38 Recent scholarship quite appropriately challenges the sharp distinctions that political scientists have often drawn between representative and participatory versions of democracy (Urbinati and Warren, 2008).

39 See, for example, such works as Sandel (1982), Walzer (1994), MacIntyre (1999) and Taylor (1999).

40 This advice follows from the distinction Mouffe (2007, 9) draws between what she defines as the realm of 'politics' and the realm of the 'political'. Inspired by the work of Carl Schmitt, she defines 'politics' as the ensemble of practices and institutions through which an order is created and human co-existence is organized. The 'political' on the other hand, refers to an arena of struggle where order is destabilised and ideas about politics are contested.

41 See endnote 15 of the previous chapter.

42 As with most things, academia followed in the wake of public intellectuals such as Bhim Rao Ambedkar, Franz Fanon and Paulo Freire.

43 Morselli incidentally is best known for his work on suicide.

44 That this perspective continues to wield enormous influence is evident from the coverage in the popular media during the first half of the present decade of the conflagrations from as far afield as London, Cairo and Rio. The responses of leftwing commentators to London's 2011 violence are telling. In a celebrated tract published with the *London Review of Books*, Slavoj Žižek called the boys and girls who took to the streets 'beast(s) produced by capitalist ideology' (See http://www.lrb.

co.uk/2011/08/19/slavoj-zizek/shoplifters-of-the-world-unite): the piece was titled 'Shoplifters of the World Unite'. In an apparently-sympathetic piece for the journal *Counterpunch*, David Harvey described them as 'mindless rioters'. (See http://www.counterpunch.org/2011/08/12/feral-capitalism-hits-the-streets/). Contrasting the events with hunger and bread riots of the eighteenth century, Zygmunt Bauman described them as 'riots of defective and disqualified customers' (See http://www.socialeurope.eu/2011/08/the-london-riots-on-consumerism-coming-home-to-roost/). Such comments by trendy Left Wing commentators would probably make even Durkheim blush.

45 However, based on her analysis of Marx's contribution to Rhineland's 'Wood Theft Debates' in 1842–3 Sherover (1979) suggests, based on her analysis of Marx's contribution to Rhineland's 'Wood Theft Debates', that he had considered the poor to be an 'elemental class of human society'. Their poverty, deriving from their being property-less, made them guardians of universal values of humanity and fraternity. Marx appears to have substantially modified his views on the poor and their politics in later years.

46 The referendum was held to seek voter approval of the continuation of the authority of the Emperor Louis Napoleon to formulate a Constitution for France.

47 The World Bank's World Development Report for 2015 titled Mind, Society and Behaviour is a case in point. The chapter of poverty (Chapter 4) suggests that everday life choices associated with poverty tax the mental resources of individuals. The authors continue thus: 'This cognitive tax, in turn can lead to economic decisions that perpetuate poverty.' (World Bank, 2015, 81: emphasis in original).

48 Thompson's work was by no means the first. Earlier writings that challenged derisive characterizations of the 'crowd' included that of George Rude (1964) for instance, and others who wrote 'history from below'.

49 See the excellent commentaries in Mamdani (1996), Mitchell (2002) and Mantena (2010).

50 Much of this work draws on the polity centred approaches pioneered by Charles Tilly (1978), Theda Skocpol (1979), McAdam et al. (1988) and Meyer and Staggenborg (1996). Writing about institutional opportunity structures in the context of negotiations over public policy, researchers have highlighted the explanatory potential of differences in regime type between autocracies and democracies and within democracies (Boix, 2001; Brown and Mobarak, 2009; Rothstein 2011; Gerring, Thacker and Alafro, 2012), the nature of state institutions (Huber et al., 1993; Gerring and Thacker, 2008), the organization of the bureaucracy (Tendler, 1997; Grindle, 2007) and synergies between states and societies (Evans, 1995; Migdal et al., 1994; and Houtzager and Moore, 2003).

51 Some scholars follow Talcott Parsons (1951) and investigate the role of 'pattern variables' that allegedly characterize entire social structures. Others draw on Robert Dahl's (1959) pluralist analysis to highlight the ability of interest groups to shape the

respective pitch of their negotiations. A third approach emphasizes, alongside Paul Ricoeur (1977) the importance of intersubjective frameworks – the 'structures of living together' through which people collectively make meanings of their life. The approach of this book is, as the reader might have recognized already, distant from these.

52 James Scott (1977) concurs with this view, although his reasons are different: he highlights the cultural and social autonomy, rather than economic independence, of the middle peasants to be responsible for their insurrectionary capabilities.

53 For India, see Das (1982), Hauser (1993), Banaji (1990), Lerche (2001), Tanner (1995), Pattenden (2011b) and Kunnath (2012). For Latin America, see LeGrand (1984), Assies (1987), Petras (1998), Redclift (1980) and Gill (1987).

54 These conventions are discussed in King, Keohane and Verba (1994, 124–28) and Collier and Mahoney (1996, 60).

55 I realized later that there was little to justify my assumption that the marginal landowners would make common cause with the landless. They sometimes did, just as they sometimes did not.

56 Direct questions asking my interlocutors whether they 'did' politics *aapni raajniti koren* (Bangla) or *aap rajniti karte hain* (Hindi) led to bewilderment and vigorous shaking of heads to indicate that they had nothing to do with politics, except to vote.

57 Most conversations were enthusiastic exchanges. However, enthusiasm turned to horror each time the discussions veered round to the use of toilet paper instead of water for the purpose of cleaning up after one's morning ablutions. I also noted a rapid dissipation of enthusiasm when my interlocutors discovered that one of my doctoral supervisors was an Indian Bengali woman. 'What was the need to go all the way there? You might as well have done your studies from here', was only one of many wry remarks directed my way.

58 In this vein, the notion of the 'everyday' has been used in relation to resistance (Scott, 1985), violence (Scheper-Hughes, 1992), the state (Fuller and Harriss, 2001) and politics (Kerkvliet, 2009) to elucidate the meanings that people make of the different influences on their lives.

2

Political Spaces

Institutional Opportunity Structures

The first task of the Assembly is to free India through a new constitution, to feed the starving people, and to clothe the naked masses, and to give every Indian the fullest opportunity to develop himself according to his capacity.

Jawaharlal Nehru, 1947

Political democracy cannot last unless there lies at the base of it social democracy.

Bhimrao Ambedkar, 1950

While being the world's largest electoral democracy, India contains more people in poverty than any other country in the world. Moreover, poor people – oppressed though they are – are central to India's democracy. Political parties routinely seek legitimation from them, and governments are wary of being perceived as antagonistic to their interests. This chapter synthesizes key literatures to present the opportunity structures that inhere in India's democratic institutions and which impinge upon the politics of the poor. I will first highlight three general features that India shares with other postcolonial democracies before I unpack its formal, participatory and social components (Huber and Stephens, 1996). In this context, I highlight the country's majoritarian electoral system as well as the privileging of civil and electoral rights over social and economic rights that is hard-wired into the formal component of Indian democracy. I follow up this discussion with an examination of the participatory aspect of India's democracy, through which I call attention to the advances and limits of electoral participation among India's poor. I finally discuss the social component of democracy to remind readers of the widening inequalities in India and the concentration of poverty among members of certain historically oppressed communities. A discussion of these three dimensions persuades us to appreciate contemporary India's unequal democracy.

If an overview of the formal, participatory and social dimensions of India's postcolonial democracy offers general insights into the opportunity structures available to the country's population, a consideration of the economic geography and social history of eastern India, where this study is based, helps to specify them: this is the purpose of the second section. While doing this, I signpost two points. One, I emphasize the salience of manual labour to the region's paddy-based agrarian economy. Access to manual labour is mediated through the social category of caste, making it central to any analysis of social relations in the region. However, to assert the centrality of caste is not, and this is the second point, to endorse the influential view that the region's political economy is 'semi-feudal'. Rather, it is to note, with Lerche *et al.* (2013) that the caste basis of social organization can coexist, indeed flourish, even when the relations of agrarian production may accurately be analysed as capitalist. Recognition of the capitalist nature of agrarian relations entails that I use the vocabulary of class while analysing social relations. But an appreciation that capitalist agrarian relations are conjoined to the salience of caste necessitates that I take seriously a caste-centred account of class relations.

In the third section, I offer a cursory political introduction to the two States, Bihar and West Bengal, where this study is based. A political introduction to the two States will provide readers a historical view of the institutional opportunity structures available to the poor therein. I will complement the discussion of political developments with an account of recent analysis of National Sample Survey Organisation (NSSO) data by political economists that reveals patterns in the distributions of resources. The purpose of this presentation is to underscore the multifaceted opportunities and constraints to which poor people in the two States are exposed. Such a discussion will enable readers to take cognizance of the social relations of power within which the poor are embedded and to which I direct attention in the next chapter.

I

A paradigmatic postcolonial democracy

Poor people's centrality to the collective self-image of the Indian nation perhaps owes much to the trajectory of nationalist agitation for political independence from Britain (Gooptu, 2001). Ever since Dadabhai Naoroji's *Poverty and Un-British Rule in India* was published in 1867, poverty provided an enduring trope for anti-colonial mobilization in the country. Much of the nationalist agitation for independence was anchored in the claim that colonial rule had impoverished the Indian masses, de-industrialized the country, and caused avoidable famine and health disasters.[1] It was fitting then, that when Jawaharlal Nehru, as interim Prime Minister, inaugurated, on 22 January 1947, the discussion on 'Resolution of Aims and Objectives' of India's Constituent Assembly, he urged upon members that the task before them was 'to ... feed the starving people, and to clothe the naked masses ...' (Constituent Assembly Debates, 1947). Nehru's promises, Partha Chatterjee (1994) reminds us, were emblematic of the commitments of India's postcolonial leaders, who sought to legitimize the fledgling state by promising to eradicate poverty and inequality.

India's republican constitution, adopted in 1950, instituted universal adult franchise. As Sudipto Kaviraj (2005) reminds us, India's adoption of universal suffrage predates the country's economic growth and industrial development. Such adoption is similar to the trajectories of postcolonial democracies elsewhere in Asia and Africa, the overwhelming majority of which instituted universal suffrage without reaching the levels of economic development at which point Euro-American states historically universalized the vote. While suffrage in the fledgling Euro-American democracies remained the privilege of propertied men (Mann, 1997; Dunn, 2006 and Przeworski, 2009) for several decades after representative government was first introduced in those countries, postcolonial democracies universalized the right to vote within a relatively compressed duration. While India's success at sustaining electoral democracy is remarkable, the country's espousal of universal adult suffrage makes it similar to other postcolonial democracies rather than the Euro-American ones. Indeed, because the size of the country's bourgeoisie was so tiny when universal suffrage was introduced, many observers believed India's democracy would collapse.[2]

Another feature India shares with other postcolonial democracies is the relative strength of the executive and the judiciary vis-à-vis the legislature. Riggs (1963) postulates that the sequencing of bureaucratization and democratization matters to the political process in any country. Where bureaucratization precedes democratization, as in most postcolonial democracies, elected representatives must compete with bureaucracies and judiciaries whose members are drawn from privileged backgrounds and who seek to inhibit the emergence of popular representatives. The patterns of colonial rule ensured that India's bureaucracy and judiciary were relatively well-developed before the elected legislatures, based on adult suffrage, came into being (Kaviraj, 1988; Chatterjee, 1998). The executive and the judiciary remained bastions of privilege even as legislatures became, given the exigencies wrought by universal adult suffrage, more representative of the Indian population. Christophe Jaffrelot (2003) calls this latter trend India's 'silent revolution' to indicate the progressive incorporation of India's less privileged people into the legislatures, as compared to other arms of government. Such incorporation has meant that the poor believe elected representatives, rather than the bureaucracy or the judiciary, to be socially proximate to them and are therefore likely to perceive them to be more sympathetic. At the same time, elected representatives compete with bureaucrats over asserting social and symbolic authority as well as over the control over material resources. They not only perceive the bureaucracy as a threat, but struggle to establish their pre-eminence in the public perception Their regular appeals for support to the poor is a direct outcome of this struggle.

A third defining feature of postcolonial democracies such as India refers to the bureaucratization of social identities prior to the advent of elected legislatures. Such bureaucratization is often attributed to colonial governmental technologies (Cohn, 1987). In the Indian context, scholars have suggested that colonial rule in India instituted an 'ethnographic state' obsessed with classifying and codifying its population in line with Orientalist conceptions of Indian society (Appadurai, 1988 and Dirks, 2001). Joining issue with such an interpretation,[3] Susan Bayly (1999) argues that colonial rule merely formalized processes of identity formation already underway in the period just prior to the institution of the British Raj.[4] A very large number of the newly emergent lords and kings originated from peasant backgrounds.[5] In order to enhance and maintain their legitimacy, such chieftains turned to ascetics and ritualists of the Brahman community who claimed high-caste status as well as scriptural authority. Commercial and scribal communities flourished, and espoused Brahmanic idioms to gain social legitimacy. The colonial regime sought advice from literate Brahmans on 'native' law and custom[6]. In a series of celebrated judicial cases throughout the nineteenth century, the colonial courts adjudicated on the caste status of different communities by taking recourse to the scriptural authority claimed by Brahmans.[7] By bureaucratizing social identities, the colonial regime lent legal sanctity to a hierarchy of caste identities that already enjoyed legitimacy among the Brahman communities. The formidable collusion of the colonial judicial authority with Brahmanical scriptural authority resulted in caste becoming politically salient in the decades preceding India's independence and in the country's postcolonial democracy.

Although inequality remains an important element of caste, the emergence of political parties that explicitly challenge such hierarchies has contributed to 'ethnifying' caste, offering prospects of dissolving the ritual hierarchies associated with it (Searle-Chatterjee and Sharma, 1994). Consequently, the terms 'caste' and 'community' are often used interchangeably in political parlance, as it will be in this book. Scholars and policymakers refer to three broad clusters of castes, based on the combination of social status and bureaucratic legalese.[8]

The three broad clusters of caste/communities recognised in the sociological and administrative literatures are the Scheduled Tribes and Scheduled Castes; the Other Backward Classes; and the General Castes.[9] The General Castes refer to the self-styled 'higher' or 'upper' castes, (Savarnas among the Hindus and Ashraf among the Muslims) whose members consider themselves at the apex of a hierarchical caste system. Members of such communities regard themselves as socially and ritually superior to others. They constitute some of the most privileged people in the country, in terms of wealth (Motiram and Vakulabharanam, 2013) and occupation (Deshpande, 2011), and I will mostly refer to them as 'privileged castes' in this book. At the other end of the caste spectrum are the communities designated as Scheduled Castes (SCs) and Scheduled Tribes (STs), whom political activists refer to as Dalits and Adivasis respectively. Members of these castes are condemned by others as 'untouchable' and 'primitive': Muslim converts from 'untouchable' castes, Arzals, may also be considered as part of this category. Dalits and Adivasis face widespread social discrimination with debilitating consequences for the wealth and occupations available to them (Gang et al., 2008; Teltumbde, 2001 and Guru, 2005). In between these polar categories are caste communities of 'intermediate' status, commonly referred to as Other Backward Classes (OBCs). The OBCs, (Shudras among Hindus and Ajlaf among Muslims), represent a more amorphous category. Members of communities classified as OBC tend to be better-off than members of 'untouchable' communities but worse off than those of privileged communities (Deshpande and Ramachandra, 2014). The amorphousness of the OBCs has also to do with the fact that Indian States do not follow a uniform criterion for classification and different States follow different conventions. Table 2.1 presents an overview of the relative population of the different caste clusters in 16 large Indian States.

Table 2.1: Proportion of SCs, STs, OBCs and 'Others' in select Indian States

Name of State	Total population (1)	% SC (2)	% ST (3)	% OBC (4)	% 'Others' (5)
Andhra Pradesh	84,580,777	19.8	7.1	48.4	24.8
Assam	31,205,576	9.2	14	27	49.5
Bihar	104,099,452	20.2	0.9	60.7	18.2
Chhattisgarh	25,545,198	13.7	37.5	41.8	7
Gujarat	60,439,692	11.3	16.5	43	29.2
Haryana	25,351,462	25	0.1	28.1	46.8
Jharkhand	32,988,134	19.1	20.8	31.8	28.4
Karnataka	61,095,297	18.4	6.8	41.1	33.7
Kerala	33,406,061	10.3	1.1	61.5	27
Madhya Pradesh	72,626,809	17.6	22	41.2	19.3
Maharashtra	112,374,333	13.1	8.4	27.1	51.4
Odisha	41,974,218	18.9	23.6	36.7	20.8
Punjab	27,743,338	36.7	0.1	14	49.3
Rajasthan	68,548,437	19.2	13	47.5	20.3
Tamil Nadu	72,147,030	22.8	0.8	70.7	5.7
Uttar Pradesh	199,812,341	25.8	0.8	52.5	20.9
West Bengal	91,276,115	29.2	5.2	31	35

Source: Census of India (2011, A series Table A5), accessed http://www.censusindia.gov.in/pca/ pca.aspx February 2017 for Column (1). Planning Commission (2011, Annex Table 2A.1, 253) for Columns (2), (3), (4) and (5). Readers should note that the category 'Others' include Savarna Hindus and all Muslims.

India's unequal democracy: Perspectives on formal dimensions

Most influential accounts of India's democracy tend to credit the country's formal institutions for its broad success.[10] Not only do they highlight the regularity, freedom and fairness of elections but also acclaim the progressive provisions of the Indian Constitution. Indeed, there is little doubt that routine elections provide the poor with important political opportunity structures. Likewise, the importance of guarantees of freedoms of associations and expression and guarantees against discrimination on the basis of caste, creed, sex and religion cannot be overlooked. However, there is much that demands a critical scrutiny. I note below three aspects of India's formal democracy as they impinge upon the political practices of the poor.

The first aspect to which I want to direct attention pertains to India's majoritarian electoral system. Under this system, representatives are elected to single-member constituencies based on the 'first-past-the-post' principle. Comparative political scientists tell us that majoritarian electoral systems based on the 'first-past-the-post' principle conduce to upper class–middle class coalitions (Iversen et al., 2007). Proportional representation systems, on the other hand, engender middle class–labouring class coalitions. In this vein, Sridharan (2004) suggests that India's electoral system stimulates the forging of a class coalition between the privileged and the middle classes, to the exclusion of the labouring classes.

In socially heterogeneous contexts, riven by communal contests and inequalities, electoral competition over single-member constituencies spawns fierce contests between people with unequal economic and social resources over single political offices. As Chairman of the Drafting Committee of India's Constitution, Ambedkar (2014, 348) had anticipated this situation when he argued that 'the safety of the minority[11] lies in the majority having a larger number of seats to contest. Otherwise it is sure to be overwhelmed by the majority.' These recommendations, as contemporary political scientists will recognize, inhere the substance of the 'proportional representation' principle of candidate selection. Ambedkar's proposals envisaged the explicit protection of minorities against being overwhelmed by the majority. It bears quoting him in full here:

> A candidate put up by the [social] minority cannot be successful even if the whole of the minority were solidly behind him … Even if a seat is reserved for a minority, a majority can always pick up a person belonging to the minority and … get him elected. The result is that the representative of the minority elected to the reserved seat instead of being a champion of the minority is really a slave of the majority. (Ambedkar, 2014, 347)

Ambedkar's formulations were unacceptable to the Congress Party, which inherited the reins of power from the departing colonizers. Gandhi, the foremost leader of the Congress, was particularly hostile to these views. He eventually coerced Ambedkar to withdraw his demands (Kumar, 1985 and Rodrigues, 2005). By the time Independence dawned, any idea of proportional electorates stood thoroughly discredited, evoking fears of partition, Balkanization and worse. The majoritarian electoral system, prevailing in Anglo-Saxon democracies, was adopted by the Congress with seats 'reserved' for Dalits and Adivasis. Although the bravery of the many impoverished men and women of Dalit and Adivasi communities who have battled social ostracism and cultural discrimination to assert their claims must be saluted, the fears first articulated by Ambedkar have remained.

Under the first-past-the-post principle, most candidates who win elections to become members of parliament or legislative assemblies are able to do so without having to obtain the majority of the vote. Even when successful political parties trounce their adversaries in terms of seat-shares, winning candidates are unable to gather the majority of votes. Table 2.2 reveals this phenomenon by drawing on electoral data from the national elections held in 2014, when the National Democratic Alliance (NDA), led by the Bharatiya Janata Party (BJP) swept the elections. Even in those elections, only a third of all successful candidates who went on to become members of parliament won absolute majorities in their constituencies. Elected representatives' connections to their constituencies remain tenuous as a result, because they are aware of the patchiness of their support. The majority of the populations in the constituencies cannot be assured of their legislators' sympathy for their claims. Thus, while elections provide important opportunities for people to discuss and argue about political matters, the country's electoral system prevents the transfer of those deliberations into the elected institutions.

Table 2.2: Proportion of votes secured by Members of Parliament (MPs) during the 2014 Lok Sabha elections in select States

Name of State	Total no. of MPs	MPs securing [%] of vote:					
		<35%	35–45%	45–50%	50–55%	55–60%	>60%
Andhra Pradesh	42	2	11	15	10	4	0
Assam	14	0	7	3	2	2	0
Bihar	40	5	28	3	4	0	0

Name of State	Total no. of MPs	MPs securing [%] of vote:					
		<35%	35–45%	45–50%	50–55%	55–60%	>60%
Chhattisgarh	11	0	2	4	5	0	0
Gujarat	26	0	0	0	8	11	7
Haryana	10	0	5	3	1	1	0
Jharkhand	14	0	8	3	3	0	0
Karnataka	28	1	7	5	14	1	0
Kerala	20	1	10	7	2	0	0
Madhya Pradesh	29	0	4	5	8	5	7
Maharashtra	48	0	3	13	17	12	3
Odisha	21	3	8	3	5	1	1
Punjab	13	3	7	3	0	0	0
Rajasthan	25	1	2	4	4	6	8
Tamil Nadu	39	0	19	14	6	0	0
Uttar Pradesh	80	6	38	17	12	6	1
West Bengal	42	6	23	7	6	0	0

Source: Election Commission of India (2014), Table 14, accessed http://eci.nic.in/eci_main/archiveofge2014/14%20-%20PC%20wise%20distribution%20of%20Votes%20Polled.pdf   in February 2017.

The second aspect of India's formal democracy that I want to highlight pertains to the Constitution's privileging of political and civil rights over social and economic rights. On the eve of the adoption of the Constitution, Ambedkar (1949) lamented that a commitment to political equality notwithstanding, the Indian state would 'by reason of [our] social and economic structure, continue to deny the principle of one man, one vote.' In his *Memorandum and Draft Articles on the Rights of States and Minorities,* he hoped that the purpose of the new republic would be 'to remove social, political and economic inequality by providing better opportunities to the submerged classes' (see Rao, 1967, 84). But wrangling in the Constituent Assembly over financing such an objective resulted in the hiving off of social and economic rights from civil and political rights (Jayal, 2013). Matters pertaining to economic and social justice were eventually placed in the non-justiciable Directive Principles of State Policy rather than bringing them under the purview of enforceable Fundamental Rights and Duties. The distinction between political and civil rights on the one hand, and economic, social and cultural rights on the other was thus substantiated through institutionalization in the Constitution itself. Indians could hold their state to account over political and civil rights but not over the violation of economic, social and cultural rights. Effectively, the ambit of citizenship was restricted to electoral and civil matters, bracketing out substantive social and economic rights.

Among the landmark laws promulgated by the Constitution, the one important law with a bearing on the lives of the most oppressed groups in the country pertained to the abolition of untouchability. The result of this law was the juridical liberation of millions of the people stigmatised as untouchables. Even so, the constitution-makers steered clear of abolishing caste: social relationships pivoted on caste were left untouched. Contrary to Ambedkar's proposals calling for the 'annihilation of caste', the delegates to the Constituent Assembly were content with legally eliminating only the worst forms of caste oppression. The social structures that fomented caste hierarchies such as caste endogamy, caste pride and caste associations remained intact both in letter and in spirit.

Recent efforts by the state in India appear to extend the ambit of citizenship over social and economic matters. A plethora of legislation confers upon the country's people the 'right to food', the 'right to work' and the 'right to education'. While some authors have viewed these developments as evidence of a new social compact in India (Manor, 2010), others are more sceptical. Chandhoke (2005) suggests that these rights are effectively meaningless because of limited state capacity. Jayal (2013) points to the irony of social and economic rights becoming salient in a context of unabashed embrace of what she calls 'buccaneer capitalism' by the state in India.

India's Constitution declares it to be a union of States. The division of responsibilities between the union and the States reflects the tension over political and civil rights on one hand and economic, social and cultural rights on the other. The Constitution devolved upon States many of the responsibilities for social and economic development, such as agricultural operations, natural resources, industries, trade and commerce, education and health facilities. Such a provision leaves States with flexibility in formulating policies for social and economic development. Consequently, variations across different States in terms of social and economic outcomes as well as design of public policy are very common. Central government allocates resources to States. Relations between Central and State governments often determine the extent to which allocated resources are actually disbursed, adding to the contingency and unpredictability of the implementation of programmes for economic, social and cultural rights.

The split between political and civil rights on the one hand and social and economic rights on the other is further institutionalized through legislation aimed at resuscitating three-tier Panchayati Raj Institutions (PRIs) through the Seventy-third Amendment to the Indian Constitution, enacted in 1992. With this piece of legislation, the Indian government devolved authority and responsibility for 'economic development and social justice' upon elected village-level representative institutions, the most subsidiary tier comprising nearly 250,000 gram panchayats.[12] Almost three million elected representatives populate the three tiers of the PRIs.[13] The legislation envisages that State governments endow gram panchayats with powers and responsibilities to plan and implement programmes for economic development and social justice. To that end, the legislation lists 29 items over which the panchayats can exercise their authority; these include agriculture and land improvement, poverty alleviation schemes and maintenance of an elaborate public distribution system, rural electrification, management of community assets, cultural activities, and provision of education and health services. The legislation provides for States to ensure that funds are available to panchayats for this purpose; States augment panchayat resources by authorizing them to levy taxes, by assigning taxes to them and by providing grants-in-aid as they (the States) might deem appropriate. However, the devolution of functions does not often match the devolution of the funds and functionaries necessary to perform them.[14] As a consequence, the commitment to social and economic rights appears farcical.

This point links with the third aspect of formal democracy in India to which I want to direct attention: the relationship between populations and their elected representatives. Every panchayat is constituted by several 'wards'; inhabitants of each ward elect a representative to represent their interests and concerns in the panchayat. Panchayats typically comprise between 10 and 25 such ward representatives as well as a president and a vice president. The rules for the election of the president of the panchayat differ from State to State. In some States, the president is elected directly by the population alongside the ward representative; in such States, the president and the ward representative compete with each other for the affections of their constituency. The president, rather than the ward representative, becomes the focus of the population's demands. In other States, the population elects the ward representative as their ward members. The ward representatives in turn elect the president, making him or her dependent on *their* affections rather than the population for continuation of office. This makes the ward representative, rather than the president, the focus of the population's demands. The variations that characterize the organization of elections to India's PRIs bear implications for the ways in which elected representatives relate to their constituencies.

Analysts remain divided on the relation between devolution to PRIs and democratization in India. Some critics fear that devolution empowers and emboldens local elites (Mosse, 1994). The system through which representatives are elected to the panchayat replicates the 'first-past-the-post' principle of candidate-selection followed at the national and state levels, with seats reserved for Dalits, Adivasis, women and other sections of society designated as 'weak' by the States. There are few institutional guarantees to ensure that the collective interests of historically oppressed communities are indeed represented. On the other hand, researchers more sympathetic to devolution's role in democratization suggest that the experience of being in local government is empowering for the poor (Jain, 1997). The policy of reservations for Dalits, Adivasis and women enables the election of members of these social groups to public office. Such elections raise the collective confidence of other members of these groups and broaden the participatory basis of democracy. Recent scholarship suggests that State-level processes of democratization reinforce or inhibit people's ability to participate in the public life of the panchayat.[15]

India's unequal democracy: Perspectives on participatory dimensions

The valourization of democracy in India is often bolstered by claims about the electoral participation of the poor. Based on his analysis of the National Election Survey (NES) data, Yogendra Yadav (1999, 2397) tells us that the odds ratio that the 'very poor' would vote had increased from 0.89 in 1971 to 0.93 in 1998. For the 'poor', it increased from 0.98 to 1.03 over the same period. By contrast, the odds ratio for the 'upper middle' classes declined from 1.06 to 0.96 and for the 'upper' classes from 1.38 to 0.75. At the turn of the century, it seemed that not only was democracy in India alive and well, but also that it was particularly hospitable to the country's poor. Contrary to the established theories of democracy, poor people in India were outvoting their wealthier counterparts, at least during the 1990s.

The enhanced political participation of the poor stood in some tension with the governmental categories of care and protection that had marked Prime Minister Nehru's appeals to 'feed the starving' and 'clothe the naked'. Where Nehru's approach to the question of poverty was to appropriate 'the poor' as a governmental category, his socialist opponents such as Ram Manohar Lohia insisted on constituting them as a *political* category. Lohia was particularly trenchant in his criticism of the Nehruvian regime's apathy towards poverty as well as its socio-economic factors constituted the core of his political strategy, which united disparate Socialist and conservative political parties and caused the rout of the Congress Party in the 1967 legislative elections. The incumbent party lost office in as many as nine States.

The emergence of the poor as a political category was, however, appropriated by Prime Minister Indira Gandhi's call to 'end poverty' (*garibi hatao*). Her call struck a chord with an impoverished electorate and won her rich electoral dividends. She even justified the imposition of Emergency in the name of the poor. Her apologists claimed – like many political scientists of their generation – that democracy was a luxury the poor could not afford.[16] Emergency-era schemes such as the Integrated Child Development Services (ICDS),[17] designed to support the nutritional needs of the rural poor, especially women and children, continue to this day, but they could not prevent Gandhi's humiliating defeat in 1977. Upon her reelection in 1980, she expanded[18] the coverage of the public distribution system (PDS) to hitherto-neglected rural areas to ensure the availability of subsidized food to all sections of the population, thereby seeking to protect them from market shocks. By again reducing the poor to a governmental category, Gandhi sought to contain the emergence of the poor as a political category. Nevertheless, for nearly three decades since her first calls to 'end poverty', India's poor turned up in ever-growing numbers to cast their vote.

Recent accounts, however, present a sobering picture. An analysis of NES data suggests that the participation of the 'lower' economic strata might have peaked in 1999 (Kumar, 2009). In 1999, 62 per cent of the 'lower' classes participated in elections, compared with 60 per cent of the overall sample. Two elections later (2009), 58 per cent of them did so, compared with 58.4 per cent in the overall sample. Kumar's (2009, 50) analysis also shows that this national pattern was replicated in most Indian States, with only few exceptions. Furthermore, voter turnouts among the poor in the more impoverished States of Bihar, Uttar Pradesh, Jharkhand, Madhya Pradesh, Rajasthan and Chhattisgarh tended to be lower than the all India average.[19] Sridharan's (2014) analysis of NES from 2014 General Elections shows that electoral turnout among the 'poor' was 60 per cent, compared with 67 per cent for the overall sample population. From a consideration of these analyses, it appears that poor people's electoral participation appears to be declining relative to the participation of other classes.

However, the uncertain electoral participation of the poor did not prevent them from asserting democratic claims against people who claimed superior economic and social status (Omvedt, 1993). A particularly illuminating example is provided by the ongoing politicization of questions of social dignity. Scholars generally concur that, notwithstanding its numerous shortcomings and deficiencies in redistributing resources, democracy in India has entailed a redistribution of dignity (Kaviraj, 2005 and Gupta, 2012). The politicization of social dignity has been made possible by the struggles mounted by members of India's historically oppressed communities against the dominance of the privileged castes. Although such struggles have characterized India's historical milieu for centuries, the emergence of electoral logics and mass mobilization has lent them political salience. The anti-caste movements are perhaps the most salient examples of movements that have contributed to the redistribution of social dignity. Some scholars suggest that the redistribution of dignity is facilitated by the 'silent revolution' ushered by political parties representing members of hitherto oppressed communities (Jaffrelot, 2003). Others contend that such redistribution stems from the 'egalitarian protocols' (Guru, 2005), which impoverished members of historically oppressed communities, seek to institute in society. Likewise, scholars remain divided on whether the politicization of dignity has occluded a focus from what some of them consider to be the more substantive issues of redistributing material resources (Corbridge *et al.*, 2013; Jayal, 2013) or whether it ought to be considered as emblematic of the substantive deepening of democracy (Omvedt, 2006) in the country.[20] Notwithstanding these disagreements there is general concurrence that poor people in India are not quiescent in their own oppression. While it is true that electoral participation of India's poor is declining relative to the participation of privileged classes, we need to remember that electoral participation does not constitute the sum-total of the political practices of the labouring poor. Contentions and negotiations outside of the electoral arena are an integral part of their politics.

India's unequal democracy: Perspectives on social dimensions

The poor have continued to provide a normative focus for successive governments in postcolonial India. Politically, this was evidenced as recently as the 2014 General Elections. The incumbent Congress party – which inaugurated the liberalization process in the country – claimed that its policies had pulled 150 million people out of poverty.[21] Narendra Modi, the avowedly pro-business leader of the victorious BJP, dedicated his newly-formed government to the welfare of the poor.[22] Economically, India's postcolonial democracy relies upon what Barbara Harriss-White (2003) refers to the 'India of the 88 per cent', the people she calls petty commodity producers, who are often in vulnerable employment. Importantly, Harriss-White is also sensitive to the heterogeneities within the people in vulnerable employment, and the presence of exploitative labour relationships within. If, as voters, the poor sustain India's postcolonial democracy, as petty producers and labourers they sustain its economic growth. Harriss-White distinguishes the India of the 88 per cent from the corporate India of the 12 per cent, which is depicted as the poster-boy of India's growth miracle. The 88 per cent are central to the existence and maintenance of India's middle income economy and postcolonial democracy.

The precariousness and vulnerability of the poor have coexisted with India's rapid economic growth: some might aver that such precariousness and vulnerability actually fuelled it. During the 1980s, India embarked upon a cautious process of liberalizing its economy, steps about which contemporary observers were pessimistic (Harriss, 1987 and Manor, 1987). Corbridge *et al.*, (2013, 23) note that India's gross domestic product (GDP) grew at an average annual rate of 6 per cent from 1980–81 to 2000–01 in contrast with an average of 3.7 per cent per annum from 1950–51 to 1979–80, although they take pains to emphasize the importance of the achievements of the former period in laying the foundations for the achievements during the latter period. A sustained growth of India's per capita gross national income meant that by 2007, the country was reclassified by World Bank as a 'middle income country' rather than a 'low income country'.

Eswaran *et al.*, (2009) remind us that, since 1983, the share of the Indian population engaged in agriculture has been steadily declining, although agriculture continues to provide employment to a large proportion of the Indian population: most recent estimates (Shaw, 2013) suggest that nearly 45 per cent of the Indian population derives its employment primarily from agriculture. The contribution of the manufacturing sector has similarly registered a decline, as indeed has the contribution of services. The one industry where more and more Indians are finding employment is construction, whose share of the working population employed increased from 5.6 per cent in 2004–05 to approximately 11 per cent in 2009–10. In terms of contribution to GDP, however, Eswaran suggests, it is the services sector, which outstrips all others.

The impact of these structural changes on poverty has been a matter of heated debate. But even more heated has been the debate over the measurement of poverty itself. The first official measure of poverty, adopted by the Indian government as far back as 1962, introduced the notion of 'a minimum level of living' (GoI, 1993, 8), which set the poverty line at the monthly minimum level of consumption at ₹ 20 per capita. This measure was replaced in 1973–74 by monthly income, based on the recommended 'daily calorie norm' of 2,400 calories per day for rural areas and 2,100 calories a day for urban areas. In subsequent exercises, the Planning Commission delinked consumption poverty from calorie deprivation and relied on consumer price indices to estimate poverty levels (Planning Commission, 2014 and Patnaik, 2013). It is a variation of these indices, rather than intake of the recommended calorific norms, that most studies in India use to deduce the proportion of the poor. On the basis of consumer price indices and monthly per capita expenditures, a government-appointed commission[23] estimated in

2011–12 that about 21 per cent of India's population lived 'below the poverty line'. In July 2014, another government-appointed commission rubbished these claims.[24] The new commission revised the poverty line to reflect the calorific norms required by individuals to be adequately nourished *as well as* non-food expenditures on essential and other 'behaviourally-determined' items (Planning Commission, 2014). The result of the new commission's endeavours was an upward revision of poverty estimates for India, declaring that nearly 30 per cent of the Indian population was poor. A more recent study, commissioned once again by Indian government, casts doubts on these figures, indicating that an even higher proportion of the population lives in poverty than was previously assumed. A snapshot of the contentions over the incidence of poverty in India is presented in Table 2.3. Even as India's poor live, labour and produce in oppressive conditions, scholars and policymakers are far from any agreement on the incidence of poverty in the country.

Scholars have debated not only the incidence of poverty in India,[25] but also the direction of change since India began to cautiously liberalize its economy during the 1980s. Bhalla's (2002) analysis of the consumption expenditure presented in the National Accounts Survey convinces him that India had halved its poverty by 2000. Other analysts offer more sobering conclusions. Analysis of the National Sample Survey Organisation (NSSO)'s monthly per capita consumption expenditure (MPCE) from the Consumption Expenditure Survey by Himanshu and Sen (2014) reveals that the incidence of poverty has indeed declined since India's gradual adoption of liberalization, although such reductions were highest in States where poverty headcounts were low to begin with. Using estimates on consumption from the NSSO's Employment–Unemployment Survey, the National Commission for Enterprises in the Unorganised Sector (NCEUS) also suggests that poverty rates, while substantially higher than the official projections, have been declining (Sengupta *et al.*, 2008): their broader argument is that India's economic growth has bypassed the poor. These conclusions are supported by scholars who use the Multidimensional Poverty Index (MPI) to measure access to services, which promote human capabilities – such as education, health and piped drinking water. Such scholars too argue that, although the incidence of poverty in India is higher than what the government would have us believe, it is on the wane (Alkire and Seth, 2014). To be sure, the accounts

Table 2.3: Contentions over poverty measures in select Indian States, various official measures, 2004–05 to 2015

Name of State	2004–05				2009–10			2011–12		2011–12	2015
	Sengupta measure, poor only (1)	Sengupta measure, poor and vulnerable (2)	Lakdawala measure (3)	Tendulkar measure (4)	Lakdawala measure (5)	Tendulkar measure (6)	Rangarajan measure (7)	Tendulkar measure (8)	Rangarajan measure (9)	Rangarajan measure, rural (10)	SECC income, rural (11)
Andhra Pradesh	24.9	64.6	14.8	29.9	11.1	21.1	28.1	9.2	13.7	12.7	79.5
Assam	33.5	80.2	20.4	34.4	18.8	37.9	42.5	32	40.9	42	76.9
Bihar	56.5	92.5	42	54.4	35.7	53.5	63.9	33.7	41.3	40.1	71
Chhattisgarh	56	84.5	41	49.4	37.2	48.7	53.8	39.9	47.9	49.2	90.8
Gujarat	28.4	67.4	17	31.8	9.6	23	36.4	16.6	27.4	31.4	68.7
Haryana	22	60.1	13.6	24.1	10.3	20.1	21.1	11.2	12.5	11	59
Jharkhand	59	87.5	42	45.3	33.5	39.1	52.1	37	42.4	45.9	76.6
Karnataka	35.2	75	24.3	33.4	17.8	23.6	25.2	20.9	21.9	19.8	69.1
Kerala	23.7	61	14.8	19.7	8.9	12	16	20.9	11.3	7.3	70.5
Madhya Pradesh	53.4	85.9	38.2	48.6	28.3	36.7	49.6	31.6	44.3	45.2	83.5
Maharashtra	42.4	75.4	30.6	38.1	18.1	24.5	28.8	17.4	20	22.5	70.7
Odisha	62.2	89.7	46.6	57.2	28.3	37	48.5	32.6	45.9	47.8	87.9
Punjab	13.5	47.5	8.1	20.9	5	15.9	20	8.3	11.3	7.4	57.6
Rajasthan	38.4	81.1	21.4	34.4	14.2	24.8	33.5	14.7	21.7	21.4	73.1
Tamil Nadu	37.6	72.7	22.8	28.9	12.7	17.1	27.7	11.3	22.4	24.3	78.1
Uttar Pradesh	48.3	84.4	32.7	40.9	27.5	37.7	47	29.4	39.8	38.1	71.5
West Bengal	40.4	76.6	24.7	34.3	17.7	26.7	37.4	20	29.7	30.1	82.5
All India	40.9	77.2	27.7	37.2	20.3	29.8	38.2	21.9	29.5	30.9	74.5

Sources: Column (1) and (2): Kannan and Raveendran (2011); Column (3) and (5): Panagariya and Mukim (2014, Table B5); Column (4): Planning Commission (2014, 29); Column (6): Planning Commission (2014, 30); Column (7): Planning Commission (2014, 68); Column (8): Planning Commission (2014, 31); Column (9): Planning Commission (2014, 66); Column (10): Planning Commission (2014, 68); Column (11): SECC (2011), accessed at http://secc.gov.in/ stateSummaryReport accessed in February 2017.in/.

presented by these authors emphasize different aspects of poverty and are often considerably at odds with one another. But in terms of the direction of change of poverty, they all appear to concur that poverty in India is declining, even if they disagree about the rate of decline.

Against these views are perspectives that poverty in India has been *increasing*, especially after India began to liberalize its economy. Utsa Patnaik (2013) reminds us about the calorific norms that had initially determined India's poverty line. She contends that more Indians in rural India are unable to meet the calorific norms recommended by the Indian Planning Commission required of 2,400 calories per day today than they could in 1983. Similarly, P. Sainath (2013) points to a decade of rural distress. He notes the growing rural outmigration and the flight from agriculture as evidence to bolster his argument. Indeed, figures from the Indian Census show that the proportion of agricultural labourers to total workers has increased from 26 per cent in 2001 to 30 per cent in 2011, while the proportion of cultivators has declined from 32 per cent to 25 per cent during the same period. Because agricultural labourers typically hire out their labour and depend upon cultivators for work, social scientists suggest that their conditions are more vulnerable than that of their employers.[26] An increase in the proportion of their population points to the growing pauperization of the Indian countryside, although Lerche (2013) reminds us that such pauperization affects poorer farmers more than the wealthier ones. Indeed, Map 2.1, based on a comparison of Census data of 2001 and 2011, reveals that in large swathes of the country, the increase in the proportion of agricultural labourers is coterminous with a decline in the proportion of cultivators.

Notwithstanding the acrimonious debates on the measures and incidence of poverty, there is some agreement that India is becoming more unequal. Himanshu and Sen (2014) point to growing inequality in both urban as well as rural areas. They emphasize that the ratio of average consumption expenditure between the top decile and the bottom decile has increased in both rural and urban areas. They also tell us that the ratio of average MPCE of agricultural labourers to all labourers in rural areas declined slightly between 1993–94 and 2009–10. Using a class-analytic lens, Vakulabharanam (2014) demonstrates the divergent ways in which different classes have benefitted from the political-economic changes since 1991. His research shows that the

Map 2.1: Changing proportion of cultivators and agricultural labourers between 2001 and 2011: All workers

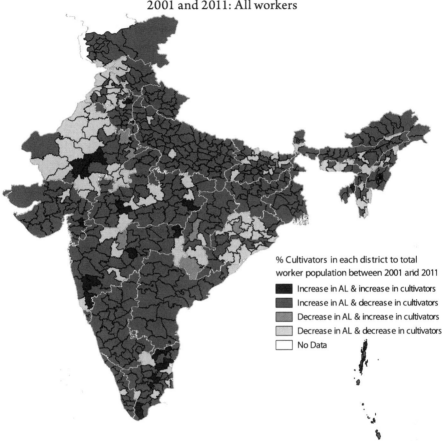

% Cultivators in each district to total worker population between 2001 and 2011

- ■ Increase in AL & increase in cultivators
- ▓ Increase in AL & decrease in cultivators
- ▒ Decrease in AL & increase in cultivators
- ░ Decrease in AL & decrease in cultivators
- □ No Data

Source: Own calculations from Census of India (2001, Primary Census Abstract, A Series) and Census of India (2011, Primary Census Abstract A Series).

increase in consumption expenditures of the urban elite between 1993–94 and 2004–05 outstripped the increase in consumption expenditures by other classes. The biggest losers, he contends, are the rural elites, followed by small peasants and agricultural labourers.[27]

The communitarian basis of poverty and inequality in India is unmistakable. Members of specific communities bear the brunt of poverty in India. Gopal Guru and Anuradha Chakravarty (2005, 136) remind us that poverty in India cannot be meaningfully understood without a consideration of the 'mutually reinforcing effects of caste and class hierarchies'. The experiences of Dalits and Adivasis, communities stigmatized by the privileged castes as 'untouchable' and 'primitive', bear testimony to these inequalities. Together, Dalits and Adivasis make up a quarter of India's population. Particularly startling is the fact that even as (consumption) poverty in India has been declining since 1993, the decline in the proportion of Dalits and Adivasis that constitute the country's poor is not as sustained. Ira Gang and her colleagues observe that, whereas poverty headcounts in India declined from 50 per cent to 42 per cent from 1993–94 to 2004–05, the share of Dalits and Adivasis to the population of the poor *increased* from 43 per cent (Gang *et al.*, 2002) to 47 per cent (Gang *et al.*, 2008). Although this proportion appears to have subsequently declined to approximately 36 per cent,[28] it is still far in excess of the proportion of these communities to the national population. Dalits, who contribute 16 per cent of the population, make up 45 per cent of the lowly-remunerated and precariously located agricultural labour population in the country (Census of India, 2011).

Not only are Dalits and Adivasis over represented among agricultural labourers, landless farmers, manual scavengers and other poorly remunerated jobs requiring them to do manual labour, they tend to be more impoverished compared to members of other communities involved in the same occupations. Sukhadeo Thorat and Amaresh Dubey (2012) point out that decline in poverty head count ratios among Adivasi agricultural labourers is slower (from 60.2 per cent to 44.7 per cent between 1993–94 and 2009–10) compared with decline in the general population (from 37.2 per cent to 21.9 per cent during the same period). The incidence of poverty among Dalit agricultural labourers (36.5 per cent in 2009–10) remains higher than among agricultural labourers as a whole (34.7 per cent) as well as among Dalits as a population group (29.6 per cent). Contrasted with this view, Panagriya and Mukhim (2015) aver that the rate of poverty reduction among Dalits and Adivasis is sharper among socially disadvantaged communities. They expect a convergence in poverty ratios across all communities. Whether their optimism will hold or not is a matter of conjecture. Suffice to say that in the present circumstances exploitation, marginalization and cultural subordination overlap with powerlessness and violence against the overwhelming majority of India's Dalits and Adivasis. Such rampant inequalities contribute to making India an unequal democracy.

Indeed, inequality is on the rampage in India. Not only are the rich getting richer, but they are doing so at a faster pace. Bannerjee and Pikkety (2005) suggest that the top 1% income shares have been ascendant since 1982-3, but their analysis stops at the turn of the century due to the lack of available data. Nevertheless, data generated by the financial services company Credit Suisse seems to buttress their point. Their data indicates that wealth shares owned by the top 1% in India have been rapidly increasing since at least 2010, when they owned 40.3% of the country's total wealth. Top 1% wealth shares catapulted to 49% in 2014, and galloped to a further 58.4% within the subsequent two years. By contrast, the bottom half of the Indian population shares a mere 2.1% of the total national wealth.

II

Eastern India: Economic geography and social history

While a consideration of the formal, participatory and social dimensions of democracy present us with a general consideration of the institutional opportunity structures available to India's poor, an appreciation of the geographic and historical factors that have shaped eastern India will enrich our contextual understanding of the region. Prescient observers note that '(a) train journey from Delhi to Kolkata takes a traveler through the global epicentre of extreme income/consumption poverty, notwithstanding common conceptions that conditions for the poor are much worse in sub-Saharan Africa than in South Asia'. (Corbridge et al., 2013, 78). Sabina Alkire and her colleagues (Alkire et al., 2015) at the OPHI report that multidimensional poverty in the eight States of eastern and central India is as acute as in the poorest 26 sub-Saharan African countries. Over 200 million of the world's poorest billion live in the populous eastern States of Bihar (77 mn), West Bengal (56 mn), Jharkhand (25 mn), Chhattisgarh (19 mn) and Odisha (28 mn).[29] A recent report by India's Planning Commission suggests that 53 of India's 100 most impoverished districts are located in the eastern part of the country (Bakshi et al., 2015). Therefore, a cursory account of the region's economic geography and social history is in order.

The geography of eastern India is arguably heterogeneous, ranging from the low-lying flood plains of Bihar, West Bengal and coastal Odisha to the highlands of Jharkhand, and forested tracts of Chhattisgarh and western Odisha. Coastal Odisha and southern Bengal are proximate to ports and long coastlines. Chhattisgarh, Jharkhand and Bihar are landlocked. Within this heterogeneity however, analysts have directed attention to the economic geography of wet paddy cultivation that marks the agrarian operations in the low-lying flood plains of the region. Andre Bèteille (1987) reminds us that arduous manual labour is characteristic of wet paddy cultivation. A key operation during the cultivation of paddy pertains to the transplantation of the rice sapling from the seed beds on which they germinate to puddled fields. Although paddy is a deep-water crop, the seeds cannot germinate if they are submerged under water. Therefore, paddy seeds are sowed on seed beds so that they may germinate under healthy conditions. They are then transplanted to fields that are submerged in at least one foot of water.

Although manual transplanters are increasingly available, the transplantation of paddy remains labour intensive across much of Asia, including in eastern India where it is the chief crop. Labourers first have to carefully pluck the newly germinated sapling from the seed bed at the edge of the paddy field. This activity requires them to stand barefoot with their bodies bent waist downwards. They must then walk with those saplings into the submerged paddy field and replant the sapling carefully at allocated spaces. This activity too requires labourers to stand with their bodies bent waist-downwards, barefoot, in at least ankle deep muddy water. Farmers opt out of such onerous operations as soon as they have enough means to employ labour. Bèteille (1987) points out that in the regions of India where wet paddy cultivation is practiced – not only in the east, but also in the south – even owners of small plots of cultivable land tend to hire labour in order to toil on the crop. The management and control of labour is therefore key to paddy cultivation. However, these factors assume a particular salience in eastern India, where colonial-era regimes of agrarian tenure enabled landlords to compel workers to labour on their fields, often on the basis of the caste into which they were born.

Nevertheless, a consideration of the official cropping data compels us to nuance this perspective and avoid crop determinism. As of 2008–09, not more than two-thirds of West Bengal's gross cropping area was under paddy cultivation. Likewise, slightly over a third of Bihar's gross cropping area was under paddy cultivation. Although the historical pre-eminence of paddy cultivation may have shaped social relations of production and distribution, it certainly does not overwhelm the agrarian operations in the two States in contemporary times. West Bengal's agricultural seasons are structured by the *aus* (spring), *aman* (summer) and *boro* (winter) paddy seasons. Details for two of the more important crops are presented in Table 2.4, wherefrom it is clear that the *aman* crop is cheaper to produce. Paddy and wheat crops provide the spine for Bihar's agricultural seasons, as is evident from Table 2.5. Wheat cultivators seem to be better-off than paddy producers.

Table 2.4: Cropping patterns in West Bengal for two principal crops, 2008–09

Attribute	Aman	Boro	Source
% of gross cropped area	43	16	Ministry of Agriculture (2009a, Area under crops for each district in West Bengal, 2008–09), accessed at http://aps.dac.gov.in/LUS/Public/Reports.aspx in February 2017
Per quintal production cost (₹)	475	602	Adhikari *et al.,* (n.d., 54)
Cost of irrigation as % of production cost	1	15	––do–––
Operational seasons Sowing Transplantation Harvest	Kharif May/June July/ August December/ January	Rabi November/ December February April/May	Field notes and observations

Table 2.5: Cropping patterns in Bihar for two principal crops, 2008–09

Attribute	Paddy	Wheat	Source
% of gross cropped area	34	29	Ministry of Agriculture (2009a, Area under crops for each district in Bihar, 2008–09), accessed at http://aps.dac.gov.in/LUS/Public/Reports.aspx in February 2017
% of crop on irrigated land	40	89	Ministry of Agriculture (2009a, Area irrigated and crops irrigated for each district in Bihar, 2008–09), accessed at http://aps.dac.gov.in/LUS/Public/Reports.aspx in February 2017
Minimum support price (per quintal)	950	1100	Ministry of Agriculture (2009b), accessed at http://eands.dacnet.nic.in/msp/MSP_4th-Sep-English.pdf in February 2017
% crop cultivators who operate marginal landholdings	75	67	Ministry of Agriculture (2011, Table 6B: Estimated irrigated and unirrigated area by size classes, all crops), accessed at http://agcensus.dacnet.nic.in/StateSizeClass.aspx in February 2017
% crop cultivators who operate small landholdings	12	16	--do---
% crop cultivators who operate semi-medium, medium and large landholdings	13	16	--do---
Operational seasons Broadcasting/ sowing Transplantation Harvest	Kharif May/ June July/ August November	Rabi November/ December - March/ April	field notes and observations

Central to the account of oppressive relations to which poor people in eastern India are subjected is legacy of colonialism. The British East India Company gained de facto control over the area of the contemporary eastern Indian States of Bihar, West Bengal and Odisha during the middle of the eighteenth century. The Company instituted the Permanent Settlement in 1793, a tenurial arrangement designed to facilitate revenue collection by creating a class of landlords who were bestowed permanent rights over allocated 'estates' so long as they met their revenue obligations. The description of the landlords as *zamindars* suggests that the Company borrowed from Mughal usage and might even have believed that they were consolidating, rather than disrupting, Mughal practice. N. K. Sinha (1968) and Bhowani Sen (1971) remind us that the Company and its successor, the British Government in India, introduced a number of improvizations, in order to facilitate efficient use of land, collection of revenue and maintenance of peace and stability for nearly a century after the original 'settlement'. The basic feature of the Permanent Settlement was, in the words of one observer, the 'relegation of cultivator-owners to the status of tenants-at-will' (Robb, 1988, 349). The occupancy rights of such cultivator-owners, the peasants who tilled the land, were dispensed. The *zamindar*, who had hitherto enjoyed only the right to collect revenue, was now vested with land ownership.

As a result of these reforms, the Settlement established a hierarchy over the land, with the colonial state at the apex. Below the state were the estate holders, the *zamindars*. The *zamindars* parcelled their estates among 'under-tenures', called *raiyats* in Bihar and *jotdars* in Bengal. As tenants, the 'under-tenures' further parcelled out their holdings to a variety of *patnidars*, or holders of tenurial rights, and *darpatnidars*, their subordinates, holding different degrees of rights over the land and its produce. At the base of this hierarchy were a variety of petty peasants and sharecroppers, with limited rights over the land. Although *zamindars* held the tenure of the estate, they were rarely involved in either the agricultural operations or their management. Agricultural operations were managed by 'under-tenure' tenants, while the actual operations were carried out by the small and marginal landholding peasants who hired labourers to complement their own family labour. Outside the pale of the settlement as it were, but central to the agricultural functions that bolstered land revenue, were a plethora of landless agricultural labourers, who toiled on the land with absolutely no rights whatsoever over it.

Scholars remain divided as to the stability of the Permanent Settlement. While Jannuzzi (1974) suggests the arrangement established a firm hierarchy of intermediaries with the *zamindars* in control over the countryside, Yang (1989) reminds us that the *zamindars* were not an undifferentiated class, with large estate holders such as the Maharaja of Darbhanga and the Raja of Burdwan jostling with landlords and smaller landholders to be recognized as tenure-holders. Ray and Ray (1975) suggest that it was not the *zamindars* but their wealthier 'under-tenures' who were the real masters of the countryside. Frankel (1989) highlights the ability of such tenants to levy cesses in flagrant violation of the legal stipulations. The limited authority of the *zamindars* notwithstanding, the Permanent Settlement was predicated on the institution of what at least one observer describes as 'landlordism':

> the concentration of economic power in the rural economy in the hands of a small number of very large landholders, often absentees, who held sway over what was often a hierarchy of tenants with varying degrees of security of tenure (Harriss, 2013, 353).

Other scholars also point to the flexibility in the system. Amit Bhaduri (1976) reminds us that the emergence of a significant market in the sub-tenurial and tenancy rights introduced the commercialization of agriculture in eastern India, as the growing number of 'under-tenures' sought to increase their surpluses without investing in the productivity of the land they did not legally hold. Their demands for surpluses, coupled with the *zamindar's* insistence on maintaining their tenurial rights, increased their revenue claims on the peasants, sharecroppers and agricultural labourers. The result was an exponential indebtedness among the peasantry. As evidence of the fluidity of society under the Permanent Settlement, Bose (1986) notes that the peasantry was increasingly differentiated. A section of wealthier feudatories took advantage of the emerging credit markets while the bulk of the smallholders who relied on credit for their agricultural operations and subsistence needs fell into debt.

However, such differentiation did not necessarily result in peasants becoming wage labourers, as the 'agrarian system permitted very many intermediate stages' (Bhaduri, 1976, 51) between holding a tenure and losing all rights over land. S. J. Patel noted, somewhat controversially, that 'before the landlord threw his tenant into the class of agricultural labourers, he tried to rack-rent him as much as possible; therefore the terms of tenancy continued to deteriorate for the cultivators in the *zamindari* region' (Patel, 1952, 67). The increasing indebtedness of peasants was mirrored in the growing indebtedness of their agricultural labourers, who needed to borrow in order to meet their basic needs of subsistence. Where peasants could mortgage their lands, the landless could only hire out their bodies. Indebted agricultural labourers were often compelled to a life of bondage that was passed on from generation to generation. The processes of commercialization and differentiation did not necessarily dilute the ties of the peasant to their land or of the landless to the bondage to which they were subjected.

The Permanent Settlement does appear to have stabilized social relations in eastern India in rather unanticipated ways. Under its terms, the share of the revenue between the *zamindar* and the state was fixed. Given this fixity, any enhanced revenues from the land would accrue to the *zamindar*. This was the theory. In practice, however, the absence of viable mechanisms for sharing the cost of land improvement inhibited any innovations that the *zamindar* might have made. Notwithstanding such inhibitions, observers point to the 'peasantization' (Bayly, 1988) of what used to be mobile pastoral communities into agrarian villages by landlords with a view to increase, however little, their revenues. The Permanent Settlement induced the sedentarization of the population. Not only did landlords settle peasants, they also recruited agricultural labourers who they hoped would serve as a cheap labour pool from which their 'under-tenures' could draw in order to maximize production. The consequent pressures on land and the attempts by landlords and their 'under-tenures' to establish and sustain social distinctions between and among themselves as well as vis-à-vis their labourers fomented processes of exclusion and subordination (O'Hanlon, 1989). In her sophisticated analysis of the transformations undergoing India during the seventeenth and eighteenth centuries, Susan Bayly (2001) argues that the insecurities faced by the newly peasantized communities attracted peasants to those teachings of devotional orders that exalted the qualities of the virtuous tiller. As the pressures on arable land grew, so too did the attempts by 'peasantized' communities to consolidate their claims of shared status and community. Nowhere was the implication of the processes of 'peasantization' to be more prominently manifested than in the realm of caste as a basis for exploitation and marginalization.

Caste relations sustained the agrarian hierarchy established by the Permanent Settlement. Caste specific preferential treatment appears to have been a key mechanism for *zamindars* and their under-tenures to create enclaves of support among peasants, sharecroppers and even agricultural labourers. Frankel (1989) points to the forced unpaid labour that stigmatized 'untouchables' were compelled to undertake in Bihar, and from which agricultural labourers of the so-called 'upper castes' were exempt. Kunnath (2012) lists, based on his readings of colonial archives, the numerous ways in which Bihar's *zamindars* assessed their 'upper caste' tenants at preferential rates. 'Upper caste' tenants were expected to pay lower rents than 'lower caste' tenants, and did not need to pay certain cesses that 'low caste' tenants were compelled to. Arild Ruud (2003) observes the ways in which Bengal's 'upper caste' *zamindars* perpetrated the differentiation among their labourers: while 'low-caste' labourers would be served on disposable banana leaves as they sat on the ground in the middle of the courtyard, 'upper caste' labourers sat on the porch eating from the same plates that the *zamindar's* family would also use. Agricultural labourers labelled as 'untouchables' were expected to cleanse the ground on which they had sat with cow-dung, even as labourers from other communities were exempt from such humiliation.

The prevalence of an agrarian structure whose relations of production 'have more in common with the classical feudalism of the master-serf type than with industrial capitalism' (Bhaduri, 1973, 120) has led observers (Prasad, 1975) to characterize eastern India as marked by semi-feudalism well after three decades of Independence. The reasons such observers advance for the 'semi-feudalism' thesis are: the continued influence of landlords in the political-economic life of the people; the persistence of such ascribed identities such as caste, ethnicity and tribe; the prevalence of sharecropping, indebtedness, bondage and limited access of peasants to the market. The empirical observations of these scholars are not off the mark for the period in which they were writing, though critics have justifiably criticized the appellation of 'semi-feudalism' to describe such conditions.

While some authors (Alavi, 1975) have suggested that 'colonial mode of production' better characterizes the political economy of colonial and postcolonial eastern India, more vociferous sceptics (Brass, 2002) argue that capitalistic economies frequently mobilize apparently 'pre-capitalist' relations of production in their service. Much recent scholarship, while appreciating the legacy of the 'landlordism' entailed in the Permanent Settlement has shed light on the emerging processes of through which capitalism has begun to permeate agrarian relations in India in general as well as eastern India in particular.[30] In this vein, scholars point to the advent of capitalist landlords who often emerge from among the ranks of the richer peasants rather those of traditional landlords. They point not only to enhanced marketable surpluses among cultivators but also to investments by richer farmers outside agriculture in usury, grain mills, dairy, trade and speculation, and construction, transport and real estate.

Their accounts serve to remind us that a consideration of the social inheritance of the Permanent Settlement in the context of a labour-intensive agronomy need not, indeed should not, detract from an understanding of the increasing salience of capitalistic relations of production. After all, as Joan Smith (1984, 64) reminds us, '(o)ur homes, the favelas, urban ghettos and working class suburbs, the Bantustans- on and on- belie the classical description of capitalism'. Simultaneously, such scholars also alert us to a historically-informed perspective that the emergence of capitalism does not follow a singular trajectory. Therefore, any study of the opportunity structures under capitalistic conditions must necessarily anchor itself in the concrete social realities in which it is embedded. This sketch of eastern India's economic geography and social history adds specificity to the general accounts of the formal participatory and social dimensions of India's unequal democracy. A more detailed analysis of the political and social change that have shaped the institutional opportunity structures in the States of Bihar and West Bengal is offered in the remainder of this chapter.

III

Bihar and West Bengal: A cursory political introduction

Fieldwork for this study was conducted in the States of Bihar and West Bengal, both located in eastern India. Both States have inherited the socio-economic arrangements associated with the Permanent Settlement. The politics of both States has been constituted by discourses of contesting social hierarchies, and a rhetoric of empowerment of the toiling masses. Whereas in Bihar, socialist parties politicized caste-based inequalities and discrimination, communist parties politicized class-based inequalities and deprivation in West Bengal. To be sure, poverty rates continue to be high in both States but themes of exploitation, injustice and denial of dignity pervade political discourse and shape, as we shall see, poor people's negotiations with democracy.

The inheritance of caste

The places that comprise the States of Bihar and West Bengal were acquired by the British East India Company following a treaty with the Mughal Emperor in 1765 and ruled as part of the grandly-titled Bengal Presidency. The introduction of the Permanent Settlement sedimented caste hierarchies in the region. But it did not create those hierarchies. Susan Bayly (1998) reminds us that, concomitant with state-formation under the Mughal Empire, revenue contractors recognized by the Emperor claimed hereditary ritual superiority over their subordinates. Several of these revenue contractors, titled *zamindars* (Hasan, 1969), were appointed by the Mughal Emperor and his governors in northern parts of Bihar. They claimed Brahman, Rajput or Pathan status. Paradigmatic was Darbhanga's revenue contractor. Appointed by the Mughal Emperor Akbar in the sixteenth century, he and his dynasts signaled their lordly pretensions by adopting grandiose titles alluding to their Brahman origins (Brass, 1974). In central and eastern Bengal, the revenue contractors appointed by the Mughals claimed ritually superior status (Ray, 1984). Although the subsequent institution of the Permanent Settlement by the colonial state resulted in widespread land transfers through auctions, the new owners of the properties were usually the officials and rich tenants of the old *zamindars* or their neighbours: land transfers, where they transpired, remained limited to families of very specific classes, who invariably claimed ritually superior Brahmanized honorifics and portrayed themselves as patrons of Brahmanic culture.

By the same token, Irfan Habib (1965) notes that the occupational divisions prevented ritually subordinated castes from holding land. The extension of the agrarian frontier, well under way prior to the advent of the British East India Company as a territorial power, required a settled agrarian population that could be made to labour on the land, especially perform the arduous manual work required for the cultivation of paddy. Revenue contractors and their wealthier tenants began to cultivate networks of contractors who could be counted on for the recruitment of labour to service the expanding zones of sedentary agriculture. The annexation of labouring groups to meet agrarian production needs led to the subordination of communities who were of pastoralist origin, such as the Bhuiyans in Bihar (Prakash, 1990) and the Bagdi, Bauri and Chandal (Bose, 1986) in Bengal. These developments, occurring just prior to the completion of colonial conquest, were fostered under British rule and its hunger for land revenue.

By the time electoral politics was introduced in the Presidency late in the twentieth century, caste identities had bureaucratized, especially among the privileged castes. Through their participation in caste associations, they strived to exert a measure of influence in public life, while simultaneously limiting competition over scarce opportunities in employment and education. The social dominance of the Brahmans, Rajputs and Pathans in Bihar (Chakravarti, 2001) and of the Brahmans, Kayasthas and Baidyas in Bengal (Bandyopadhyay, 2004) continued unabated, although other caste communities, such as the Kayasthas and Bhumihars in Bihar and Ashraf Muslims in Bengal elbowed their way into the closely knit structures of control in the two regions. That emergent caste associations did not only perform social roles became clear from the successful advocacy by Bihar's Kayastha groups pressing for the severance of Bihar from the Presidency in 1911 (Brass, 1990). Over the next two decades, caste consciousness among the privileged castes in Bengal pushed to extremities, as evidenced by their political support for the preservation of untouchability till as late as 1933, on grounds that they did not regard untouchables as possessing any innate worth (Chatterjee, 1994, 40). The most spectacular success of Bengal's tri-caste elite lay in the manner in which they neutralized the emerging alliance between Dalits and Muslims of peasant and labouring backgrounds and partitioned the province between India and Pakistan in 1947 (Bandyopadhyay, 2004) in order to safeguard their political and economic interests in its western part, which became the Indian State of West Bengal.

The aftermath of Independence

The pivotal role of caste–communal organization among the privileged castes in the founding of the two States could not but have left its imprint on subsequent developments. This was most clearly evident in the contests over the introduction and implementation of land reforms that would redistribute their vast properties to the landless. Under the Indian Constitution, agrarian reforms were listed as a State subject, gifting state based elites the autonomy to legislate on such matters. In Bihar, the privileged caste elites delayed the passage of legislation for nearly 10 years, using the influence of their caste networks in the Bihar legislative assembly (Das, 1982). The legislation, when it was eventually passed, allowed the partition of the properties and to arrange fictitious transfers, making it possible for landlords to evade land ceiling.[31] Moreover, the legislation allowed landlords to retain extensive areas of their properties and to categorize them as being used for residential or industrial purposes, in which case ceiling laws would cease to apply. West Bengal's privileged castes were no less intransigent in the wake of legislation to initiate land reforms (although they appear to have been less successful). In addition to indulging in fictitious transfers, privileged caste landholders in both States evicted tenants from their properties to prove that they were personally cultivating their fields. Although their abolition as revenue intermediaries between the cultivators and the state significantly diminished their political salience, the socio-economic dominance of the *zamindars* was not eliminated.

Nevertheless, many *zamindars*, who perceived the erosion of their socio-economic status to be imminent, began selling their properties or transferring them to their wealthy tenants in the hope of making the best of a worsening situation. Side by side, properties of Muslim landlords departing for Pakistan were occupied or purchased by tenants. Such sales and transfers marginally benefitted the rich and middle peasants who could afford to purchase land or had access to credit markets for that purpose. Approximately 10 per cent of agricultural properties passed into the hands of the rich and middle peasantry in this way (Prasad, 1979). Such transfers did little to ameliorate the condition of the insecure sharecroppers, poor peasants and landless labourers. In some cases, these transfers even exacerbated their vulnerabilities because the new peasant proprietors actively undermined the customary ties that landlords cultivated with the poor. Land hunger continued to be a major political issue, resulting in a countryside seething with discontent.

Many among the poor considered popular mobilization to be an effective means of asserting their demands, and began to organize the forcible occupations of agrarian properties held by landlords (and, in some cases, rich peasants) in violation of the ceiling laws. The electoral rout of the Congress Party in 1967 across nine States, including Bihar and West Bengal, provided a window of opportunity. In West Bengal, during the two year rule of the United Front Government (1967–69), which represented a coalition of centrist and leftist parties, landless labourers and poor peasants identified and occupied nearly 300,000 acres of such properties, according to a Communist Party of India (Marxism) Central Committee member cited by Ross Mallick (1993). The scale of such movements was much less in Bihar, where sharecroppers and landless labourers organized 'land liberation' movements in specific districts under the aegis of socialist and communist parties (Sengupta, 1982). As a political entity, the United Front government, which exercised power in Bihar (1967–68), was even more incoherent than its West Bengal counterpart, constituted as it was by a coalition of socialists and communists on the one side and the rightist Jan Sangh on the other. The relative weakness of mobilization by political parties only enhanced the attractiveness among the landless of extreme leftwing groups as the Naxalites[32].

Continuities and change in agrarian structure

Governments in both States could claim some success in redistributing surplus among the poor, although West Bengal far surpasses Bihar, and indeed every other Indian State. As Table 2.6 below shows, of the nearly five million acres of land redistributed by the postcolonial Indian state, over one million lie in West Bengal alone. Even more startling is the fact that over half of all the 'beneficiaries' (to use the official term) of the redistribution measures in India live in West Bengal. These figures are impressive from the perspective of West Bengal. But they also indicate that, on average, each 'beneficiary' in the State received approximately 0.38 acres, against the all India average of 0.90 acres. Nearly 38 per cent of all 'beneficiaries' were Dalits and another 20 per cent Adivasis, similar to the all India figure of 38 per cent and 15 per cent respectively. However, in this respect, it must be noted that the land redistribution in States such as Bihar and Uttar Pradesh (UP), limited though they might be in scale, are oriented towards Dalits. Over 60 per cent of the 'beneficiaries' of land redistribution in Bihar were Dalits, while nearly 70 per cent in UP were so. While the scale of West Bengal's reforms are noteworthy,

Table 2.6: Implementation of land ceiling laws in select Indian States, 1950–2008, area in acres

Name of State	Total area distributed	Total no. of beneficiaries	Total area distributed among SCs	Total no. of SC beneficiaries	Total area distributed among STs	Total no. of ST beneficiaries
Andhra Pradesh	597,461	531,977	229,657	213,051	120,796	85,717
Assam	545,875	445,862	86,069	43,723	58,986	42,365
Bihar	305,512	396,600	177469	239,354	24,800	31,404
Chhattisgarh	60,680	27,452	10,367	6,057	29,047	9,608
Gujarat	161,805	36,051	100,966	17,083	33,034	14,628
Haryana	101,169	29,351	43,672	12,687	–	–
Jharkhand	876	1,316	310	487	277	328
Karnataka	126,122	31,638	68,961	18,393	8,459	2,251
Kerala	76,676	165,149	27,832	68,240	9,364	9,718
Madhya Pradesh	134,188	47,058	38,906	16,045	51,305	18,383
Maharashtra	542,788	139,577	158,776	41,023	100,392	29,977
Odisha	159,384	142,616	51,109	48,704	66,303	52,934
Punjab	103,409	27,520	44,564	11,138	743	216
Rajasthan	465,517	83,617	145,547	30,340	50,501	12,047
Tamil Nadu	189,428	149,952	71,132	66,290	320	236
Uttar Pradesh	262,755	303,442	184,495	207,103	974	486
West Bengal	1,113,172	2,881,536	385,004	1,065,721	226,931	537,599
All India	4,964,995	5,457,522	1,828,826	2,111,056	783,022	848,657

Source: Ministry of Rural Development (2008, 271, accessed at http://rural.nic.in/sites/downloads/annual-report/anualreport0708_eng.pdf in February 2017).

the prioritization of the socially discriminated populations by Bihar and UP – in the teeth of continued dominance of the privileged castes – are no less remarkable.

The land reforms (limited though they were), alongside transfers and sales, intensified the processes of social change ongoing since the early twentieth century in the two States. Although the *zamindar* remained an important notable as a landlord, the importance of 'landlordism' in village life had diminished. With their diminution, the social claims to prestige and status that had hitherto been their preserve became open to access to other groups, especially the rich and middle peasants who acquired property and tilled the land. The increased social and political salience of these rich and middle peasants was among the most significant changes induced by the constitutional abolition of *zamindari* privileges.

The *zamindars* in Bengal had claimed the status of 'gentlemen', as encapsulated in their appropriation of the term *bhadralok*. Broomfield notes that early nineteenth century *bhadralok* were distinguished by such aspects of their behaviour as 'their deportment, their speech, their dress, their style of housing, their eating habits, their occupations, and their associations' (Broomfield, 1968, 5). They were supposedly men of refinement, (western) education and high status. Some scholars are keen to emphasise that *bhadralok* status was achieved, and not ascribed, although they agree that a key character of the *bhadralok* was to maintain distance from manual labour (Broomfield, 1968 and Chatterjee, 1998).

However, Dayabati Roy (2012) notes that *bhadralok*, and its obverse, *chhotolok* are often grounded in concrete caste categories, and are in fact 'ascribed'. *Bhadralok* folk disparaged those with little education or were allegedly unrefined, and were involved in manual work as *chhotolok*, or 'petty people' (Ruud, 2003). The Bengali term *chhotolok* does not encompass a homogenous social category (Ray, 1985 and Bose, 1986). Peasants who tilled the land and owned/rented property sought to distinguish themselves from both landlords as well as labourers. Although the distinctions between peasants and labourers were necessarily blurred (Chaudhuri, 1983), the two groups sought to perpetuate different lifestyles. In Bengal, peasants espoused the ideal of a model *chasi*, centered on their 'clean-caste' (but not 'upper caste') status, frugality, hard manual and dedication to their property. *Chasis* did not aspire to become *zamindars*, whose lifestyles they condemned as decadent, extravagant and vulgar. But they also sought to distance themselves from their labourers, or *majurs*, who they considered to be wayward in their dietary patterns, commensal relations, consumption of alcohol and sexual practices. The *majurs* in turn refrained from adhering to the norms to which the *chasis* adhered. Differences in their ways of life extended to ways of worship, ceremonies related to births, deaths and other life-events, diets and daily schedules, and sexual mores.

In Bihar, where opportunities for education and public sector employment were limited to a few urban pockets, a category cognate to the *bhadralok* does not appear to have emerged. Rather, Bihar's *zamindars* sought to establish themselves as *maliks*, owners of property and people (Yang, 1989). Bihar's peasants identified themselves in relation to their lands and to their households. As owners or tenants who knew their land and loved it, peasants were *kisans*. As model householders, who valued thrift and prudence, nurtured families, and scorned the opulence displayed by the *zamindars*, peasants claimed the status of *grihasth*. At the same time, the *grihasth* was not a labourer, a *majdur* (Chakravarti, 2001), who hired out their labour to work for others. The *grihasths* considered the *majdoors* to be thriftless and vagrants, without fidelity to property or family, and sexually promiscuous. The *majdurs* lived their lives in accordance with religious practices, social norms and sexual mores that were often markedly different from those of the *grihasths*. It is true that peasant leaders, such as the millenarian activist Swami Sahajanand Saraswati, sought to use the term *grihasth* in an all-encompassing way to include both *kisans* and *majdurs*, but excluded *zamindars* (Das, 1982). While such a use of the term underscored the antagonism between the landlord on the one side and the peasant and labourer on the other, it was not very successful in papering over the tensions within the latter.

With the abolition of the *zamindar* as the revenue contractor, the *bhadralok* status to which they lay exclusive claim was opened up in West Bengal. As peasants acquired land, went to school and acquired literacy, and even began to have family members with salaried jobs, the exclusive identification of 'gentlemen' with 'landlords' could no longer be taken for granted. To be sure, peasants continued to value their properties and the model of hard work and frugality, but they complemented such values with appropriating *bhadralok* status. In Bihar, *zamindari* abolition eliminated the *zamindar* as the revenue-contractor but did little to erode his claim as *malik*. As peasants owned or leased in more land, and their children accessed educational and employment opportunities provided by the State, they continued to value the status of *grihasth*. However, some scholars note the assertions of some labour-hiring peasants affiliated with socially powerful and locally dominant communities as *malik* (Chakravarti, 2001 and Kunnath, 2012). While the 'zamindar-chasi-majur' complex characterizes agrarian social relations in West Bengal, it is complicated by the *bhadralok* status claimed by *zamindars* and *chasis*. Likewise, the 'zamindar-kisan-majdur' complex, which denotes social relations in the Bihar countryside, is complicated by the competing status of *malik* and *grihasth* claimed by both the *zamindars* and *kisans*.

The socialist challenge in Bihar

The Congress Party in Bihar identified with the landlords and a few rich peasants, who had benefitted from the limited land reforms of the early postcolonial period. Such identification resulted in the party's gradual alienation from not only the poor and the landless but also the middle peasants. The middle peasants were neither affiliated with the privileged castes nor could they be stigmatized as 'untouchable'. Marginalized under Congress dominance, the middle peasants began to organize soon after independence under such forums as the Bihar Backward Classes Federation, coalescing together under the somewhat inchoate rubric of 'socially and educationally backward classes' (Galanter, 1984; and Jaffrelot, 2000), referred to in the official parlance of the time as *pichada*, or backward. These forums anticipated the OBCs as a political force. The socialist opposition to the Congress Party recognized the legitimacy of the grievances of the OBCs. Led by Ram Manohar Lohia, the socialists endorsed their demands for affirmative action in the realm of public sector employment and education, in addition to massive state intervention in the agrarian economy by way of land redistribution, crop price support system and security of tenancy. The socialist slogan during the electoral campaigns of 1967 called for provisioning 60 per cent reservations for OBCs in public sector employment and education, commensurate with their share of the State's population. Moreover, near-famine conditions prevailed in the State during the middle of the 1960s, increasing the misery of the poorer sections of the population as well as the attraction of the socialist demands. The Congress victory was routed in the 1967 legislative elections in Bihar.

Although socialist participation in the subsequent State government was tenuous and short-lived, the State's political arena emerged as a bitter tussle between the privileged caste constituencies of the Congress and the 'backward caste' constituencies of the socialists for the next two decades. Although attempts by socialist politicians such as B. P. Mandal and Karpuri Thakur to institute either affirmative action or land reforms through the 1970s were frustrated by the privileged caste supporters of Congress and the rightist Jan Sangh, they held their ground. Agricultural labourers, most of whom were Dalit, remained suspicious of both parties, and some among them appear to have initially gravitated towards armed insurrection (Sinha, 1977). By the 1980s, however, many members of armed groups accepted the possibility that electoral politics could be responsive to poor people's claims, with the result that their members among the landless labourers and poor peasants extended cautious support to the socialist-oriented Janata Dal or to the more stridently militant (but parliamentary) Communist Party of India (Marxist/Leninist-Liberation). In 1990, Lalu Prasad Yadav, the charismatic peasant leader from the Yadav community, the largest OBC community in Bihar, was elected as Chief Minister, ending the political instability of nearly three decades. Hereafter, the Congress Party was reduced to a minor player in the State's politics, often playing second fiddle to Lalu Yadav's Janata Dal.

The communist challenge in West Bengal

The Congress Party dominated West Bengal's political life after independence for nearly two decades. It was widely perceived as the party of the landlords and the industrialists. The province's partition led to the influx of six million Hindus – first the wealthier landlords of the privileged castes followed slowly, painfully, by vastly larger numbers of poorer peasants, sharecroppers and landless labourers, many of who were 'untouchables'. Relatively few Muslims went the opposite direction, but 'staying on' for them meant implied a transformation from a precarious majority to a hopelessly vulnerable minority (Chatterji, 2007). Although most Muslims on either side of the new international border were peasants, the salience of religious politics in the decades preceding the province's partition meant that their religious, rather than class–caste identity attained prominence (Chatterjee, 1998). Many of the concerns of the early postcolonial State pertained to control and rehabilitation of the incoming refugees, maintenance of law and order in the face of communal disturbances and maintaining agricultural production as well as ensuring food availability in those tumultuous days. Food shortages as well as Hindu–Muslim violence were common through the 1950s and 1960s. Land hunger and insecure tenancies remained common problems in the countryside, particularly for the middle peasants, neither privileged caste nor stigmatized as untouchable. However, no political party appeared willing to lend support to their demands.

The situation changed radically after 1964, following a split in the Communist Party of India (CPI) and the creation of the more Left Wing Communist Party of India (Marxist), or CPI(M). The CPI(M) posed an effective threat to Congress in West Bengal, leading to its considerable weakening and eventual defeat in the legislative assembly elections of 1967. The ensuing United Front coalition government was short-lived. A resurgent Congress swept the next legislative assembly elections, held in the aftermath of the 1971 Liberation of Bangladesh. Although the repression it then visited on the CPI(M) cadre was brutal, the Congress resurgence proved ephemeral. In 1977, the CPI(M) stormed to power in the State on the back of the general anti-Congress wave and formed a coalition government with its leftist allies (including the CPI from which it had earlier split) to form the Left Front Government. The result of that election brought to an end the turbulence of an entire decade. The Congress Party continued to enjoy pockets of electoral support in Muslim majority districts, based on the patronage networks anchored in narratives of security and protection its local party bosses had built up with village-level landlords. But on the whole, it was reduced to general electoral insignificance in the State.

Kisans, socialists and 'caste' politics: Bihar

The Janata governments in Bihar initiated cautious measures for empowering the poor. Some of these measures entailed public policy reforms. Recognizing the diversity among the OBCs, the Janata government in 1977 provided affirmative action in public sector employment for members of marginalized communities from among them, christening them as Extremely Backward Class (EBC). An attempt to introduce affirmative action for EBCs in the State's

Panchayati Raj Institutions (PRIs) met stout resistance from the privileged castes, who subverted the elections to these bodies for over two decades. After 1990, Lalu Yadav's government eliminated tree and toddy tax, a move that benefitted members of communities who depended on such activities for their livelihoods. Slums in Patna were regularized, and milk suppliers were allowed to establish cowsheds freely in towns and cities. 50 per cent seats were reserved for OBCs in university level decision making bodies, and Bihar University was renamed as B. R. Ambedkar University after India's foremost champion of civil rights (Chaudhury, 1999). Elections to PRIs were reintroduced in 2001.

However, as Jeffrey Witsoe (2013, 67–69) notes, Lalu Yadav's most important initiatives for 'lower' caste empowerment stemmed from political, rather than policy, strategies. One, he systematically emasculated the State bureaucracy as well as the police dominated by the privileged castes. Second, he politicized the rural poor by convening public rallies through which they developed shared solidarities cutting across caste distinctions. Third, he developed personalized networks with politicians and political mediators, *not* on the basis of their caste but on their ability to deliver him votes, thereby democratizing patronage. Although known to be sympathetic to landless labourers who forcibly occupied the properties of rich landlords (Hauser, 1993), Lalu Yadav realized that the core of the support for his own Janata Dal came from the rich and middle peasants who had benefitted from the initial bout of land sales and transfers. He was further constrained by the fact that any reforms would have to be implemented by the very same bureaucracy he sought to undermine. The dilemmas before him were unenviable. Occupations by the landless poor of the properties of entrenched landlords would certainly undermine his opponents and strengthen his middle peasant constituency politically. But providing such occupations legislative sanctity threatened to undermine the recent gains by the very same constituency. Tacit support to the 'land liberators' appears to have been his solution to this problem. Perhaps most importantly, by publicly disparaging ideas of development via slogans such as 'We want dignity, not development',[33] Lalu Yadav politicized issues of caste-based discrimination in unprecedented ways.[34]

Lalu Yadav and his wife Rabri Devi, between them, ruled Bihar from 1990 to 2005. Within a short time, his regime began to be associated with specific communities from among the OBC caste clusters, such as his own Yadav community, Ashraf Muslims and – occasionally – the Dusadh community among the Dalits. Such allegations of favouritism were not unjustified, thereby fomenting discontentment among other OBC communities, not to speak of EBCs and Dalits. Several splits in the Janata Dal later, Lalu Yadav's Rashtriya Janata Dal (RJD) was ousted during the elections of 2005 by Nitish Kumar's Janata Dal (United), supported by the Hindu Rightist Bharatiya Janata Party (BJP). Nitish Kumar stitched together a multicaste coalition comprising his own Kurmi (an OBC) community, the EBCs, and a section of the poorer Dalits, alongside the BJP's traditional privileged caste supporters in urban areas. This multi-caste coalition represented a rainbow class alliance of urban professionals and traders (the BJP's urban privileged caste supporters), rich peasants (mostly Kurmis), poor peasants and sharecroppers (EBCs) and landless labourers (Dalit communities such as the Musahars). Nitish Kumar promised 'development with social justice', a slogan that appealed to different constituencies because of its fluffiness. In power, and despite opposition from a number of his core supporters, Nitish Kumar initiated schemes directed towards ameliorating the conditions of members of such historically oppressed Dalit communities as Musahars, Doms and others. In 2007, his Government formally identified 18 of the State's 22 Dalit communities as 'Mahadalit' and sought to direct a number of schemes towards them. Such schemes included provision of homestead lands, and appointment of a para-professional (in the tradition of 'barefoot educators') in each hamlet, and provision of free radios to households and bicycles to school-going girls. The provision of such club goods enhanced his popularity among members of Mahadalit communities, even as it enraged his privileged caste supporters. Eventually, when he parted ways with BJP in September 2013, it was only the support from the Mahadalit communities on which he could count for electoral survival.

A glance at the changing composition of Bihar's legislative assembly conveys the political transformation under way in the State since the first elections under universal adult franchise in 1952. A number of observers have noted that the proportion of 'backward caste' legislators has increased significantly since the constitution of provincial assemblies in the late-colonial period.[35] From 20 per cent in 1952, their share increased to nearly 40 per cent in 2001, although recent analysis suggests that this figure might have peaked, and might even be reversed (Robins, 2009).[36] Although their share remains lower than their share in the population of the State, it nonetheless signals an increase in the political importance of the 'backward castes'. Such changes notwithstanding, it is important to remember that the share of privileged castes in the legislatures continues to outweigh their share in the population, as Table 2.7 confirms.

Table 2.7: Communal composition of the Bihar Legislative Assembly, 1952–2005

	1952	1957	1962	1967	1969	1972	1977	1980	1985	1990	1995	2000	2005
Privileged caste	46	45.9	46.2	44.8	42	42.8	40.8	36.5	38.5	34.5	21.8	23.1	30
Backward caste	19.3	18.8	23.6	26	27.9	24.9	27.7	29	25.3	34.2	43.6	35.2	34.5
Extremely backward caste	1.2	0.6	0.9	0.6	0.9	0.9	0.6	1.5	1.8	0.6	3.1	5.2	5.3
Scheduled Caste	13.9	14.7	13.2	13.5	14.1	13.8	13.8	14.5	14.8	14.8	15.1	14.8	16.9
Scheduled Tribe	10.9	11.2	9	9.2	8.8	8.9	8.5	8.6	8.9	9	8.2	8.9	–
Muslims	7.6	8.1	6.6	5.6	6	8.2	7.7	8.9	10.2	6.2	7.1	9.3	9.5

Source: Robins (2009, 101).

Poverty in Bihar

A functionalist connection between the increasingly representative character of the legislative assembly and sustained decline in poverty is neither possible to make, nor desirable. Indeed, a glance at the Monthly Per Capita Expenditure (MPCE) data collected by the NSSO and collated in Table 2.8 between 1983 and 2009–10 reveals a mixed picture. The table is limited to rural Bihar. On the one hand, the data indicates that the incidence of poverty, measured according to the Uniform Reference Period method (URP), reduced during the period. On the other hand, according to the Mixed Reference Period method of collecting data (MRP), the incidence of poverty appears to have *increased* during the years of instability transitioning from the Congress regime to Lalu Prasad Yadav's government. Nevertheless, according to both measures, the overall incidence of poverty appears to have declined quite considerably during the remainder of Lalu Yadav (and his wife's) tenure as Chief Minister. The poverty gap and the squared poverty gap, measures used by economists to understand the depth and severity of poverty, also reduced indicating a decline in both the depth and severity of poverty.[37] The extent to which poverty declined after Lalu Prasad Yadav's defeat, however, appears to be a matter of some contention. Perhaps more alarmingly, the rate of poverty reduction for Dalits under Lalu Prasad Yadav's regime is also a matter of debate, indicating that his advent may not have been an unremitting boon for members of Bihar's most oppressed communities.

Table 2.8: Rural poverty in Bihar, 1983–2010

Attribute	1983–84	1987	1993–94	2004–05	2009–10	Source
URP method						
Headcount ratio, total population	64.94	53.91	58	42.6	36.4	Panagariya and Mukim (2014, Table B1)
Headcount ratio, SC population	81.56	70.57	70.6	64.2	53	Panagariya and Mukim (2014, Table B1)
Headcount ratio, ST population	74.61	61.44	69.3	56.2	39.9	Panagariya and Mukim (2014, Table B1)
Headcount ratio, OBC population				38.5	35.8	Panagariya and Mukim (2014, Table B2)
MRP method						
Headcount ratio, total population			62.3	55.7	55.2	Himanshu and Sen (2014, 76–77, 79)

Attribute	1983–84	1987	1993–94	2004–05	2009–10	Source
Headcount ratio, SC population			76	77.6	68.1	Panagariya and Mukim (2014, Table B8)
Headcount ratio, ST population			73.3	59.3	64.4	Panagariya and Mukim (2014, Table B8)
Headcount ratio, OBC population				52.6	56.4	Panagariya and Mukim (2014, Table B9)
Poverty gap			15.9	12.7	13.4	Himanshu and Sen (2014, 76–77, 79)
Squared poverty gap			5.6	3.9	4.5	Himanshu and Sen (2014, 76–77, 79)

A disaggregation of the MPCE data, along land-size classes reveals even more fascinating details, as can be seen from Table 2.9. Using the same methodology as Vakulabharanam (2010; 2014), the economist A. P. Sreeraj calculates the class disaggregated growth rates in the MPCE for the State. An examination of this data suggests that the biggest gainers in the State during and after the 1990s are 'urban elites, whereas the biggest losers are the 'urban workers' (email communication, 19 December 2015). The gains to 'urban elites' during the previous period only intensify during this period, a trend consistent with what one sees at an all India level. In the countryside, however, the biggest gainers are the small peasants or those who own between five and 10 hectares of land and hire in labour as well as hire out their own labour. Their gains contrast not only with their losses during the previous period but also with the losses which confront small peasants at an all India level. Agricultural workers in the State too have gained, though not to the same extent as in the previous period. Nevertheless, their gains stand in sharp contrast to the losses faced by agricultural workers at an all India level. The gains of small peasants and agricultural workers also contrast with the slight losses faced by rural elites.

Table 2.9: MPCE growth rates among classes, Bihar (Base year = 2009–10)

	1983		1993–94		2009–10		Bihar ratio growth rate		All India ratio growth rate	
Class	MPCE (1)	Ratio to total (2)	MPCE (3)	Ratio to total (4)	MPCE (5)	Ratio to total (6)	1983/ 1993–94 (7)	1993–94/ 2009–10 (8)	1983/ 1993–94 (9)	1993–94/ 2009–10 (10)
Urban elite	888.9	1.45	1182.28	1.78	1519.08	2.10	22.99	31.92	11	22
Urban worker	846.04	1.38	943.99	1.42	915.98	1.27	3.17	–15.59	1	2
Rural elite	684.85	1.12	701.75	1.06	762.98	1.06	–5.25	–0.24	–5	–10
Small peasant	621.56	1.01	638.83	0.96	767.36	1.06	–4.96	9.85	–4	–4
Non-agricultural worker	569.22	0.93	613.89	0.93	661.61	0.92	–0.28	–1.02	–8	–8
Agricultural worker	440.66	0.72	499.29	0.75	562.76	0.78	4.77	2.58	–3	–7
All classes	613.32	1	663.29	1	722.80	1	–	–	–	–

Source: A. P. Sreeraj (personal communication) for columns (1) to (8) (Estimated from NSSO Unit Record Data, 1983 (round 38), 1993–94 (Round 50) and 2009–10 (Round 66). Vakulabharanam (2014) for column (9) and (10).

Data from the Indian Government's Agricultural Census on Bihar appears to corroborate the picture of the declining economic standing of rural elites. Table 2.10 below reveals that large landholdings constitute a miniscule proportion of all landholdings in terms of number as well as area operated. Furthermore, the area they control has been declining, registering a particularly sharp decline between 1995-6 and 2005-6, at the peak of Lalu Yadav's and his wife's tenure as Chief Minister. These patterns of landholdings indicate that large landowners have indeed witnessed some whittling down of influence and resources they once wielded. Side by side, also noteworthy is the overwhelming proportion of marginal landholdings and the growing number and area under this land size class.

Table 2.10: Percentage of operational landholdings in Bihar

	1995–96		2005–06		2010–11	
Land-size class	Number	Area	Number	Area	Number	Area
Marginal	80.14	36.23	89.64	53	91.06	57.44
Small	10.78	18.89	6.68	19.58	5.86	18.56
Medium (including semi-medium)	9	40.39	3.66	26.24	3.06	23.30
Large	0.2	4.4	0.02	1.18	0.02	0.71

Source: Ministry of Agricultural (2011, 38 and 40).

Bhadraloks, communists and class politics: West Bengal

The Left Front government ruled West Bengal for an uninterrupted 34 years, the longest by any political party in any Indian State. Among its earliest, and most celebrated, public policy reforms was Operation Barga, the initiative related to tenancy reforms, which many scholars have described as 'spectacular' (Kohli, 1987) and 'effective' (Nossiter, 1988). The State government claimed that 1.3 million of the State's 2.5 million sharecroppers had been registered, which bestowed on them security of tenancy and legally stipulated that they could retain 75 per cent of the share of the harvest, instead of being tenants-at-will, and able to keep only half the crop share. The Left Front's success in tenancy reforms appears to have anticipated its limits in effecting the redistribution of land among the landless poor. Mallick (1994) argues that the sharecroppers who benefitted from the tenancy reforms were middle peasant-sharecroppers (rather than the poorer peasant-sharecroppers). They were, consequently, the Left Front government's most enthusiastic supporters and blocked any serious moves by the CPI(M) to effect the redistribution of land. Indeed, he cites (Mallick, 1994, 47) a CPI(M) Central Committee member to suggest that more land was vested and redistributed by the activism of poor peasants and landless labourers during the 19 months of United Front rule than in the first 12 years of the Left Front government. The leadership of the CPI(M) and its peasant affiliate, the Kisan Sabha, continued to be dominated by privileged caste rich peasants, even as the majority of the support emanated from middle peasants of 'backward caste' Hindu and Muslim origin. Privileged caste rich peasants claimed to possess, as Arild Ruud (1994) notes, the 'qualities' traditionally associated with political authority, such as wealth, knowledge/education and ritual status. The democratic centralism of the CPI(M) prevented a quick turnover of leadership, which meant that the leadership that connected the party at the grassroots with the State-level functionaries remained bureaucratic (Tama-Lewang, 2009). The 'party-society' (Bhattacharya, 2008) that emerged in the West Bengal countryside successfully controlled law and order and managed political expectations for over three decades on the basis of the stable leadership that it cultivated. Key to this political project was their revitalization of the three-tier PRIs through which the government's agrarian reform and development programmes were implemented.

The Left Front's espousal of tenancy reforms and its abeyance of land redistribution endeared the CPI(M) to the middle peasants, especially among the sharecroppers, many among whom were labour-hiring cultivators or even capitalist farmers. Conversely, the same policies arguably distanced the party from the landless labourers, large numbers of whom were Dalit or Adivasi. Although the CPI(M)'s longstanding political activism among such communities contributed to increasing the political awareness among the labouring classes among them, these relationships were often enmeshed in sentiments of gratitude (Ruud, 1994). The party refused to politically foreground the caste specific discrimination to which Dalit agricultural labourers were subjected, although party cadre members are known to encouraged inter-caste commensality (Ruud, 2003). The CPI(M) was spectacularly insensitive in its dealings with Dalit refugee demands for rehabilitation, and did not hesitate to use violence to repress such demands (Mallick, 1994).

The continued importance of caste in structuring everyday social relationships, despite the 'extensive governmental intervention in the form of land reforms and democratic decentralization' (Bhattacharya, 2009, 59), is clear from several anthropological accounts.[38] Neither was the CPI(M)'s urban privileged caste leadership nor the rural middle peasant activists able to or willing to accept this reality. Not only that, the CPI(M) refused to acknowledge the caste specific disabilities to which the middle peasants were subjected in the fields of public sector employment and education. The CPI(M) was among the few political parties that opposed proposals in the early 1990s urging that State governments be allowed to set their own quotas for affirmative action benefiting OBCs (Bayly, 1998, 301). By the middle of the first decade of the present century, the party's inability to represent the interests of the middle peasants was hopelessly exposed through the manner in which it repressed the legitimate protests by middle and poor peasants against governmental decisions to acquire agrarian properties for industry. What followed was a steady erosion of electoral support, and the Left Front government's eventual loss in 2011 to the Trinamul Congress, which stitched together a multiclass coalition of urban professionals and industrialists on the one hand, and poor peasants on the other. In power, the Trinamul Congress has been remarkably alert to demands for affirmative action by different communities in the State, as evidenced by the recent decision to recognize nearly 87 per cent of the State's Muslims as OBC, signaling a nascent recognition of legitimate caste claims by the political representatives of that State.[39]

The espousal of class politics did little to reduce the dominance of the privileged castes in the political life of the State.[40] An analysis of the composition of the West Bengal Legislative Assembly reveals that, although the share of the privileged castes in the legislature might be declining after 1996, it remains disproportionately high. Except for a very brief period during the turbulent decade between 1967 and 1977 the proportion of 'backward castes' – among both Hindus and Muslims – has been abysmal. The 'middle peasant' support for the Left Front does not appear to have translated into increased political representation of this class, as Stephanie Tawa Lama-Rewal's (2009) careful analysis of the occupational and educational profile of the State's legislators reveals. Table 2.11 below presents the continuities and changes in the caste profile of the State's legislators.

Table 2.11: Communal composition of the West Bengal Legislative Assembly, 1952–2005

	1952	1957	1962	1967	1969	1972	1977	1982	1987	1991	1996	2001
Privileged caste	45.4	50	49.2	40	41.8	38.2	45.9	43.2	45.2	44.9	49	37.8
Backward caste	4.6	7.5	5.9	6	8.2	7.5	9.5	7.5	7.5	5.4	4.8	6.1
Scheduled Caste	19.7	20.6	22.6	21.8	20	20.4	22.1	21.4	21.4	22.4	23.1	21.1
Scheduled Tribe	5	8.3	6.7	6.8	5.7	6.1	5.8	6.1	6.1	6.5	6.8	6.5
Muslims	9.7	10.7	11.1	13.6	13.6	14.6	13.9	14.6	12.9	14.6	15	14.3
Not ascertained	15.5	2.8	4.4	11.8	10.7	13.2	2.7	7.1	6.8	6.1	1.4	14.3

Source: Tawa-Lama-Rewal (2009, 101) computed on the basis of tables from which the graph was presented.

Poverty in West Bengal

Functionalist analysts seeking linkages between the character of the West Bengal legislative assembly and poverty rates in the State are bound to be disappointed. Notwithstanding the unrepresentative character of its State legislative assembly, that the State has been successful in sustained poverty reduction since the implementation of Operation Barga is not in doubt. Table 2.12 reveals the broad concurrence among scholars and policy-analysts in this regard. The table is limited to rural West Bengal. According to both measures of counting poverty, the URP and the MRP data indicates that the incidence of poverty reduced during the period. Further, the poverty gap and the squared poverty gap have continued to reduce. The incidence of poverty among Dalits registered a sharp decline, although its extent is a matter of disagreement.

Table 2.12 : Rural poverty in West Bengal, 1983–2010

Attribute	1983–84	1987	1993–94	2004–05	2009–10	Source
URP method						
Headcount ratio, total population	63.80	48.83	41.2	28.4	19.7	Panagariya and Mukim (2014, Table B1)
Headcount ratio, SC population	73.30	58.06	46.3	28.9	21.6	Panagariya and Mukim (2014, Table B1)
Headcount ratio, ST population	76.71	63.21	62.1	42.7	22.6	Panagariya and Mukim (2014, Table B1)
Headcount ratio, OBC population				17.7	17.7	Panagariya and Mukim (2014, Table B2)
MRP method						
Headcount ratio, total population			42.4	38.3	28.8	Himanshu and Sen (2014, 76,77, 79)
Headcount ratio, SC population			48.2	37.1	31.5	Panagariya and Mukim (2014, Table B8)
Headcount ratio, ST population			66.5	54.3	32.9	Panagariya and Mukim (2014, Table B8)

Attribute	1983–84	1987	1993–94	2004–05	2009–10	Source
Headcount ratio, OBC population				28.3	26.3	Panagariya and Mukim (2014, Table B9)
Poverty gap			8.7	7.9	6	Himanshu and Sen (2014, 76,77, 79)
Squared poverty gap			2.6	2.4	1.7	Himanshu and Sen (2014, 76,77, 79)

A disaggregation of the MPCE data along land-size classes complicates the picture somewhat, as we see from Table 2.13. Using the same methodology as Vakulabharanam (2010; 2014), the economist Debolina Biswas (2012) calculates the class disaggregated growth rates in the Monthly Per Capita Expenditure (MPCE) for West Bengal. An examination of this data suggests that the biggest gainers in the State between 1993–04 and 2009–10 are the 'urban elites', as is the case elsewhere in India. 'Urban workers' manage to reverse (albeit ever so slightly) their declines of the previous period. But what is remarkable about the West Bengal context, is the unprecedented decline in the fortunes of both rural elites and agricultural workers, unlike the losses incurred by the small peasants, which were ongoing since the previous period. The losses of agricultural workers are particularly catastrophic not only in comparison with agricultural workers at the all India level, but more so in contrast to their own gains during the previous period. Non-agricultural workers appear to have been the only gainers in the countryside during this period, indicating an increased economic standing among those not involved in agriculture.

Table 2.13: MPCE growth rates among classes, West Bengal
(Base year = 2009–10)

	1983		1993–94		2009–10		West Bengal ratio growth rate		All India ratio growth rate	
Class	MPCE (1)	Ratio to total (2)	MPCE (3)	Ratio to total (4)	MPCE (5)	Ratio to total (6)	1983/ 1993– 94 (7)	1993– 94/ 2009–10 (8)	1983/ 1993– 94 (9)	1993– 94/ 2009–10 (10)
Urban elite	1455.6	1.64	1760.9	1.84	2818.3	2.64	12.13	43.10	11	22
Urban worker	1171.4	1.32	1247.9	1.30	1424.9	1.33	-1.25	2.09	1	2

Rural elite	666.2	1.01	835.01	0.99	958.4	0.90	-2.07	-9.34	-5	-10
Small peasant	708.1	1.07	799.3	0.95	864.1	0.81	-11.80	-14.61	-4	-4
Non-agricultural worker	536.3	0.81	649.1	0.67	854.6	0.80	-17.19	18.76	-8	-8
Agricultural worker	406.4	0.61	568.4	0.77	739.0	0.69	24.80	-10.08	-3	-7
All classes	885.25	1	955.03	1	1068.14	1	-	-	-	-

Source: Biswas (personal communication) for columns (1) to (4) and (7). Biswas (2012) for columns (5), (6) and (8) (Estimated from NSSO Unit Record Data: 1983 (Round 38), 1993–94 (Round 50) and 2009–10 (Round 66). Vakulabharanam (2014) for column (9) and(10).

Data from the Indian Government's Agricultural Census adds further complexity. Table 2.14 below reveals that small landholdings, which constitute nearly 13 per cent of all landowners, operate nearly a third of the total operational area. However, the table also indicates that their numbers and the area under their operations have declined slightly. Similarly, medium landholdings, which comprise about 4 per cent of all operational holdings, hold over 16 per cent of all area. Marginal landholdings continue to contribute an overwhelming, and increasing, proportion of all operational holdings in terms of number and area. These trends are of a piece with the goings-on in other Indian States. Where West Bengal appears to be unique, despite the losses the rich farmers have supposedly faced since 1983, is in terms of its large landholdings. Large landholdings comprise 0.01 per cent of all holdings, but made up 3.63 per cent of total operated area in 1995–6. By 2005–6, the area under large landholdings *increased* to 4 per cent and further to 4.2 per cent in 2009-10, indicating a degree of polarization in the State's countryside, with the higher landowning size classes tending towards consolidating their holdings.

Table 2.14: Percentage of operational landholdings in West Bengal

| | 1995–96 | | 2005–06 | | 2010–11 | |
Land-size class	Number	Area	Number	Area	Number	Area
Marginal	76.41	42.93	81.17	50.65	82.16	52.47
Small	16.81	29.06	14.38	28.87	13.76	28.26
Medium (including semi-medium)	7	24.37	4.40	16.47	4.07	15.25
Large	0.01	3.63	0.01	4.00	0.01	4.02

Source: Ministry of Agriculture (2011, 38 and 40).

Conclusion: Opportunity structures and the making of political space

As a postcolonial democracy, India's achievements are noteworthy. Free and fair elections, freedom of association and expression, and constitutional guarantees against the practice of untouchability provide important opportunities for millions of the country's poor. Nevertheless, the institutional constraints they face are manifold. A majoritarian electoral system prevents substantive coalitions between working classes and middle classes, as well as an effective say in parliaments and legislative assemblies. A disjunction between political and civil rights on the one hand and social and economic rights on the other restricts the scope of the promise of democracy. The devolution of power to three-tier PRIs remains patchy at best, and open to the possibility of being appropriated by dominant classes. Despite the important gains by the poor in recent years, inequalities have escalated. A cognizance of these limitations allows social scientists to develop a more realistic account of poor people's negotiations in the context of an unequal democracy.

The general constraints and opportunities posed by institutional structures are specified by specific historical inheritance and geographical milieu of eastern India. While constrained by the institutional structures, the region's populations have also sought to appropriate the opportunities offered by them. Majoritarian electoral systems did not prevent the emergence of political movements that either instituted pro-poor reforms (West Bengal) or constrained the forces detrimental to their interests (Bihar). The anemic consideration of social and economic rights in the Constitution has not prevented the emergence of political claims on social dignity and material equality in either of the two States. The cautious introduction of legislation on land reforms did not prevent the landless poor from asserting their claims on the agricultural properties controlled by landlords. Oppressive social relations have not remained uncontested.

By analysing the multifaceted opportunity structures that facilitate and obstruct the political practices of India's labouring poor, this chapter provided glimpses into *one* aspect of the ways in which political space is forged. In it, I noted the generalized institutional mechanisms, deeper historical inheritances, and broad processes of political change that impinge upon poor people's politics. I first analysed the different aspects of India's democracy by noting its formal, participatory and social dimensions. I then investigated the economic geography and social history of eastern India with a view to provide a more contextualized view of the opportunity structures that bolster or hinder poor people's politics in that region. I concluded with a focussed political introduction of the two States of Bihar and West Bengal, noting the ways in which these developments might have interacted with changes in poverty and inequality in those States.

The political spaces that shape the politics of the poor are constituted by the intersection of institutional opportunity structures and social relations of power. Social relations of power can scarcely be read off from institutional opportunity structures. Such relations are often contingently expressed. The following chapter outlines the social relations of power in the study localities, compelling us to embrace the unpredictable ways through which such relations are forged or interrogated. If the discussion in the present chapter has been general and broad, the analysis of the next chapter will be particular and detailed. The fine grained optic in that chapter will illuminate the precise ways through which political spaces for poor people's politics are forged, thereby complementing the wider lens deployed in this chapter. In that chapter, readers will be introduced to the men and women whose collaborative and contentious practices constitute the politics of the poor. Subsequent chapters will focus on the dynamic interaction between institutional opportunity structures and social relations of power in the four study places.

Endnotes

1   See Mitra (1951) for a comprehensive, if controversial, statement in this regard.

2   US scholar–journalist Selig Harrison claimed as early as 1960: 'The odds are wholly against the survival of freedom and ... the issue is, in fact, whether any Indian State can survive at all' (Harrison, 1960, 338). During the fourth general elections in 1967, *Times of London* journalist Neville Maxwell declared in a three-part essay titled 'India's Disintegrating Democracy', 'The great experiment of developing India within a democratic framework has failed.' Defending the Emergency imposed by Indira Gandhi (1977–79), B. K. Nehru (1977) argued that liberal democracy was a western value that was particularly unsuited to a country with the number of poor people that India had.

3   This debate is not unique to the South Asian context. A parallel debate has raged in the African context over the question of 'tribal' identity. See Mamdani (1996) and Cooper (2002).

4   The revenue demands made by the newly emergent lordships and kingdoms on regional economies based on agriculture accelerated the tendencies towards 'sedentarization' of itinerant communities as well as the 'peasantization' of pastoral groups (Bayly, 1988). The emergence of a relatively settled peasantry increased the competition for land between cultivators who coalesced around their shared communal identities (O'Hanlon, 1989). Likewise, the emergence of opportunities in trade and artisanal production exacerbated the importance of security provided by communal networks. New kingdoms needed standing armies, which enhanced the importance of shared networks that facilitated military recruitment.

5   The paradigmatic case was, as noted by Ambedkar (1946), that of the Maratha chieftain Shivaji.

6   Frykenberg (1977), Washbrook (1993) and Peabody (2001) provide excellent insights into these processes.

7   Ambedkar's (1946) lucid analysis of three cases from across India illustrates the authority wielded by literate Brahmans over the colonial judiciary.

8   These clusters cut across religious divisions and are not limited to adherents of the Hindu religion (Bayly, 1993 and Guha, 2013).

9   The appellation of 'general' castes for the self-styled 'upper' castes is ironic, given that they constitute less than 15 per cent of the Indian population, according to the 1931 Census.

10 See, for instance, the accounts offered in such influential texts as Mehta (2003), Khilnani (1997) and Kohli (1990).

11 During this intervention, Ambedkar's concerns included not only India's religious minorities, such as Muslims but also social minorities, such as Dalits.

12 This figure is based on official data obtained from: http://www.panchayat.gov.in/documents/10198/595743/USQ%201863.pdf, accessed January 2016.

13 This figure is obtained from: rural.nic.in/sites/.../10.%20Panchayati%20Raj%20Institution%20PRI.xls, accessed January 2016.

14 For details, please see: http://www.pib.nic.in/archieve/others/2012/dec/d2012121302.pdf, accessed January 2016.

15 This suggestion is advanced by Kumar (2006), Bardhan and Mookerjee (2006), Heller (2011), and Crook and Manor (1998).

16 See BK Nehru's (1979) defense of the Emergency on the pages of the *Third World Quarterly*.

17 See http://wcd.nic.in/icds.htm, accessed January 2016.

18 See http://planningcommission.nic.in/reports/peoreport/peo/peo_tpds.pdf, accessed January 2016.

19 As did, for that matter, turnouts in the more prosperous States of Delhi, Gujarat and Haryana.

20 The terms of the debates appear to be unnecessary polarized. For example, the case of Uttar Pradesh appears paradigmatic of the poverty-reduction outcomes possible under conditions of what is often derided as caste politics. The State has been governed since 1993 by political parties explicitly espousing the cause of communities stigmatized as 'lower caste' or 'untouchable' for all but four years. During that period, rural poverty rates among Dalits declined from 68.6 per cent to 53.6 per cent (Panagriya and Mukhim, 2013).

21 The star campaigner of the Congress Party Rahul Gandhi made this claim at an election speech in Ghaziabad, video available here: https://www.youtube.com/watch?v=poV13GxYI2g, accessed August 2015.

22 Video available here: https://www.youtube.com/watch?v=TyHBPO_EDOg, accessed June 2015.

23 This commission was headed by a distinguished economist S. D. Tendulkar, then chairperson of the Prime Minister's Economic Advisory Council. For detailed discussion of Tendulkar's methods and criticisms, see Himanshu and Sen (2014).

24 The newly-appointed commission was headed by distinguished economist C. Rangarajan, currently chairperson of the Prime Minister's Economic Advisory Council.

25 This debate is succinctly discussed in Deaton and Kozel (2005).

26 See, for instance, Breman (1974), Deaton and Drèze (2002) and Vakulabharanam (2014).

27 See Vakulabharnam (2010; 2014) for the detailed methodology used in the study.

28 Kunal Sen (personal communication, November 28, 2014), Professor of Development Economics and Policy, University of Manchester.

29 Suman Seth (personal communication, April 20, 2015), then Research Officer, OPHI

30 See Harriss (2013), Harriss-White (2007) and Ramachandran (2011) for general accounts of capitalist permeation in India. See Jha (2004), Rakshit (2011) and Rodgers and Rodgers (2011) for accounts specific to eastern India.

31 Official reports suggest that nearly half a million acres of ceiling-surplus land, or land that ought to have been vested and redistributed among the landless, were fictitiously transferred by landlords in the names of their wives, children, servants, tenants, agricultural labourers and even unborn grandchildren, cows, dogs and cats! (Ojha, 1977).

32 Useful resources on leftwing extremism in eastern India include Bhatia (2005), Kunnath (2012), Louis (2002) and Shah (2011).

33 The original slogan (in Hindi) was *Vikas Nahin Samman Chahiye.*

34 Other slogans such as 'Remove Bush, Save the World, Remove the [four Savarna communities], Save Bihar' excited the imagination of the rural poor: the original slogan (in Hindi) was '*Bush Hatao Duniya Bachao, Bhu-Ra-Ba-L Hatao, Bihar Bachao*'. Bhu-Ra-Ba-L is an acronym for the State's principal Hindu Savarna communities, Bhumihar, Rajput, Babhan (Brahman) and Lala (Kayasth). Such slogans emboldened the poor in their dealings with landlords.

35 See, for instance, the accounts presented in Blair (1980), Frankel (1985) and Kunnath (2012).

36 However, in November 2015, a coalition of the two Janata Dal factions won a spectacular victory in the State's legislative assembly elections. With this victory, the proportion of backward caste legislatures is now an all-time high, at 45 per cent. See analysis at: http://scroll.in/article/768130/how-the-grand-alliance-swept-bihar-18-charts-that-explain-the-electoral-verdict, accessed November 2015. Even so, this figure remains less than the share of the OBC population in the State, estimated at 61 per cent (See Table 2.1).

37 Readers interested in technical definitions of these measures may want to look up the World Bank's Poverty Manual, available here: http://siteresources.worldbank.org/PGLP/Resources/povertymanual_ch4.pdf, accessed March 2016.

38 See, for instance, Davis (1983), Ruud (1994) and Roy (2012).

39 See report here: http://twocircles.net/2012may18/mamata_includes_more_muslims_obc_covering_87_community.html.

40 This point has been reiterated by Kohli (1990), Mallik (1994) and Chatterjee (1998).

3

Political Spaces
Social Relations of Power

...the caste system is not merely a division of labour. It is also a division of labourers.

Ambedkar, 1936

Caste is congealed class.

Ram Manohar Lohia, 1964

India's poor are integral, not marginal, to its postcolonial democracy and emerging market economy. Their participation in the political and economic life of the country is mediated through the social relations of power in which they are enmeshed. Social relations of power shape the ways in which political parties seek legitimation from them during and after elections, employers recruit their labour for purposes of production and mercantile and commercial actors interact with them in market places. Such relations are constituted by the intersecting collaborations and conflicts between different social classes, of which the labouring poor are but one. This chapter introduces the four political places in which fieldwork was conducted. It does so through a discussion of the social relations of power – the web of collaborations and conflicts – within which the people of the localities are embedded. Because any discussion of social relations of power must necessarily be grounded in concrete realities, the material in this chapter underscores the detailed and the contingent unlike than the general and broad discussion of institutional opportunity structures of the previous chapter. Readers will meet the plethora of characters whose actions constitute the politics of the poor. I deploy a class-analytic framework to think through the social relations of power within which they are embedded. I first elaborate the key building blocks of class in the context of eastern India, highlighting the importance of labour relations and caste status in the constitution of class: three social classes are identified, based on a synthesis of the rich literature on the subject. I then introduce each of the four fieldwork localities by detailing the social relations of power that permeate their political economies. To understand the social relations of power, I direct specific attention to relations of production and the relations of distribution in the study localities. In the context of this chapter, the social relations of production refer to the ways in which members of the three identified social classes organize around their economic activities and deploy labour and material resources. The social relations of distribution relate to the ways in which the three social classes influence the allocation of governmental and social resources and shape the polity. The introduction to the political spaces prevailing in of each locality aims to distil for the reader the webs of class collaboration into which the poor are enmeshed and the class conflicts in which they are embroiled. But before we embark on the introductions, a brief note delineating the categories of social classes deployed in this and the subsequent chapters is in order.

Social class: Labour and caste

Erik Olin Wright (1979; 1997) counselled students long ago that 'class' is not so much about discrete grades inhering ownership of material resources, as it is about the social relations that underpin access to those resources. Recognizing the relational dimension of class has led scholars to call for the integration of culture in class analysis (Wolf, 1982) because the collusion between the two conduce to opportunity hoarding (Tilly, 1976). Pierre Bourdieu (1984) demonstrates the strong correspondence between social and cultural stratification: this correspondence is the product and manifestation of the *habitus* of individual class members. More importantly, for Bourdieu, class competition and conflict permeate the cultural field as much as they do the economic field, with high-status dominant classes deploying their 'cultural capital' as much as they deploy their 'economic capital' to shore up their dominance. In a similar vein, Paul Willis (1981) illustrates the ways in which the deprivations of social and economic resources reinforce one another. However, Willis' work also reminds us that such reinforcements are not mechanical; they are riven with negotiations, interruptions and fragmentations. Such multifaceted accounts of class remind us that relations, contradictions and struggles *between* classes are usually accompanied (or preceded) by contests *over* the meanings of class.

A consideration of classes under conditions of actually-existing capitalism leads students to eschew a polarized model of the class structure in which the ruling classes and the working classes engage in direct confrontation with one another. Bernstein (1996, 2010) suggests, for instance, that the spread of capitalist relations in agriculture have created three, rather than two, broad social classes with significant empirical overlaps, rather than neat distinctions, between them. Additional to the labour-hiring capitalists and the labour-selling working classes, his work calls attention to the category of the petty commodity producers. Harriss-White (2012) goes even further. While Bernstein's prognosis is that class differentiation will result in the *eventual* polarization between capitalists and labouring classes, Harriss-White suggests that the petty commodity producers are 'not transitional' (2012, 117). Despite their differences of opinion, both scholars alert us against accepting binary notions of a straightforward class conflict between the rich and the poor, capitalists and workers, dominant classes and labouring classes, bourgeoisie and proletariat. Their accounts remind us of the complexity of class relations and the need for inductive examination of the concrete relations between, within and over different classes.

How are such classes empirically constituted? In an agrarian economy, ownership over arable land has typically been used as a proxy for class (Sen, 1966; Thorner, 1980). In India, the easy availability of official data on the basis of acreage adds to the temptation of using land ownership as a criterion for deducing class; the landless (owning no land), marginal landowners (less than one hectare), small landowners (1–2 hectares), medium landowners (2–10 hectares) and large landowners (over 10 hectares) appear to constitute observable social classes. Decrying this obsession, Utsa Patnaik (1986) calls for a consideration of labour exploitation as a criterion for measuring class. Her formulation is in turn criticized by Sumit Guha (1993) for its assumption of identical labour days. Complicating the straightforward assumptions that class is determined by access to material resources or control over the exploitation of labour, Gopal Guru (2005) insists that caste and class be analysed conjointly in any analysis of social relations in the Indian context.

Labour

Patnaik (1986) proposes a 'labour-exploitation' criterion for a classification of class through the measurement of net exploitation of labour. The 'labour-exploitation ratio' indicates the 'extent of employing others or working for others, relative to self-employment' (Patnaik, 1986, 202). The classification she obtains is the following: landlords, rich peasants, middle peasants, small peasants, poor peasants and landless labourers. Towards the conclusion of her study, she arrives at a twofold distinction between the classes that hire *in* labour (landlords and rich peasants) and the classes that hire *out* their labour (middle peasant, small peasants, poor peasants and landless labourers): according to her the former comprise the rural well-to-do while the latter constitute the rural poor.

Patnaik's measure has been justifiably critiqued for the assumption of standardized work days (Guha, 1992). Her emphasis on net labour exploitation of labour detracts from the social dimension of labour. A labour-hiring farmer enters a contradictory relationship with their labourers, irrespective of the number of days they may hire in labour, hire out their labour or deploy their own labour. Empirically, this contradiction derives from the subjective experience of hiring in or hiring out labour in the first place rather than from the net number of days that labour-hiring farmers employ labour. Most labouring households combine all three models of employment: they hire out their labour, they hire in other people's labour and deploy their labour within their own production units. The experience of performing labour, even if it is on one's own farm, workshop or kiosk, proves to be a marker of social differentiation. A consideration of the relational dimension of class makes it impossible to deduce it from a singular application of an objectively defined labour-exploitation criterion.

VK Ramachandran (2011) suggests a broad criteria for the identification of classes in the Indian countryside by considering the ownership and control by households of the means of production, the relative use of different forms of family and hired labour, and the surplus that a household is able to generate each year. The novelty of Ramachandran's formulation is that he does not restrict his analysis to landholdings or the production process in agriculture, but includes variables that are not often associated with rural class differentiation, such as control over transportation networks, cinema houses, petrol pumps, urban real estate, contracting and usury. Based on these criteria, he suggests that there are three broad social categories: the rich landlords and capitalist farmers; the peasantry; and manual workers. Ramachandran is careful to note that these are categories, not classes, and proceeds to lay out the class differentiation *within* these categories, as they impinge upon the social relations of production in the Indian countryside.

In Ramchandran's formulation, the landlords and capitalist farmers control the best land and have access to assured surpluses. Members of neither class engage in any agricultural operations themselves but either lease out their land to tenants (as landlords do) or exclusively hire labour to do so (as capitalist farmers do). Capitalist farmers share many of the same class interests as landlords, based on their control over land as well as diversified sources of income. But their origins in peasant backgrounds differentiate them socially from the landlords. Landlords derive their incomes from ground rents and agricultural surplus while capitalist farmers rely mostly on agricultural profits. Ramachandran notes that landlords provide the main pillar of the power of the ruling classes, but then goes on to add that the wealthier among the capitalist farmers 'are also entrenched in positions of social and political dominance' (Ramachandran, 2011, 59). Ramachandran may well be right in emphasizing the shared class interests between the landlords and the capitalist farmers, but perhaps overestimates the degree of social coherence between the two classes. In doing so, he underestimates the caste differentiation between, *and within*, the traditional landlords and the capitalist farmers. Even as I adopt the terminology of landlords and capitalist farmers as Ramachandran does, I specify their caste affiliation when the context so requires.

The social category of the peasantry is similarly differentiated into socio-economic classes. Based on a range of criteria, Ramachandran (2011) classifies the peasantry as rich, middle and poor. Such a differentiation indicates that, although all classes of peasants deploy their own labour on their farms and produce for (and are subjugated by) exchange in agricultural markets, they are far from homogenous. Their market orientation makes peasants capitalist, even if they may not all benefit uniformly from their access to such markets. Rich peasants supplement their own labour by hiring in labour: while they may participate in agricultural operations on their own farms, they do not hire out their labour. Poor peasants hire out their labour in addition to farming their own plots of land so that they could meet their subsistence needs; they do not hire in labour. Middle peasants hire in as well as hire out their labour in addition to deploying their own labour on their farms; 'upper' middle peasants tend to hire in more than they hire out, while 'lower' middle peasants tend to hire out more than they hire in.[1] Ramachandran's (2011) scheme for the differentiation within this category is a useful guide to examine the contradictions within the peasantry, although it completely ignores the caste contradictions within and across the peasant classes outlined. When I use the term 'peasant' in this book, I follow Ramachandran's broad categorization, even as I note the caste affiliation of specific peasants as the case might require.

The third social category to which Ramachandran directs our attention, which he analyses as a class, is the one he calls manual workers. His use of the term stems from the empirically-informed perspective that 'it is no longer possible (nor particularly helpful) to separate a class of non-agricultural workers from the larger pool of manual workers–that is, to recognize rural farm and non-farm workers as discrete categories–in most villages' (Ramachandran, 2011, 62). The category of the 'manual worker' exceeds the term 'agricultural labourer' (Patnaik, 1986) as well as avoids the pitfalls associated with such conceptualizations as the 'agricultural proletariat' (Lenin, 1963). In this sense, the term approximates, but is not restricted to, Lerche's (1999) formulation of 'rural labour' in that it refers to any casual labourers who work at daily rates or piece rates. The use of the term also recognizes that manual workers are engaged in a diversity of non-agricultural occupations, such as animal husbandry, petty vending, domestic work and miscellaneous low-remuneration jobs in the private sector. Tailors, butchers, porters and venders with vulnerable livelihoods could well be included in the category of manual workers. A large number of 'manual workers' in eastern India find temporary, often seasonal, employment on farms in rural northwestern India as well as, increasingly, in construction sites and brick kilns across the country. Ramachandran notes presciently that manual labourers tend to be the most caste-heterogeneous class in the Indian countryside. An examination of the implications of such caste heterogeneity on the class coherence of the manual labourers lies outside the scope of his paper and which, therefore he does not elaborate, although readers will encounter this theme in the four empirical chapters of the present book. While I follow Ramachandran's usage when referring to the 'labouring classes' and to the 'labouring poor', I am careful about noting their caste affiliation as might be required given the importance of such affiliations to workers' own self-identifications and political subjectivities.

Ramachandran's account illuminates the agrarian relations in the Indian countryside, with a nod towards non-agricultural activities. One source of diversification within the rural economy lies in the growth of rural retail in India, whose owners may not derive their surpluses from the exploitation of agricultural labour. For instance, a recent study notes that rural India accounts for as much 55 per cent of private retail consumption (Kesari and Srivastava,

2012). Rural retailers tend for the most part to be shopkeepers stocking such consumables as subscriber identity module (SIM) cards, soap and shampoo, toothpaste, small bottles of aerated drinks in addition to the ubiquitous betel leaf, tobacco and limestone syrup. Wealthier retailers sell clothes, shoes, bangles and trinkets, stationary items and small plastic gift items. Almost all retailers stock mobile top-up cards. Some retailers may be landowners, with varying qualities of land, while others may well be landless.

Another source of the diversification lies in the salaried professionals who live in villages. Such individuals serve as employees of such state-run institutions as schools and hospitals, government offices and public sector banks. Specific occupations could range from being bank managers, school teachers, hospital attendants, security guards and office sweepers. Adding to the heterogeneity is the diverse social backgrounds of such professionals, both in terms of caste as well as class. Some professionals may be from landlord or capitalist farmer families of the privileged castes with several generations of education. Others may be from agricultural labour or poor peasant backgrounds, of 'untouchable' or 'low caste' communities and be the first people in their families to have attended school.

Such diversifications in the Indian rural economy compel us to integrate retailers and professionals into any scheme of classifications. Of course, as we noted above, retailers and professionals are internally heterogeneous. The key aspect of class differentiation is the hiring of labour. Some retailers and professionals exploit their own and family labour to manage their shops, clean their houses and wash their clothes. Others hire in labour for these purposes. Moreover, as with others, they are not free of caste affiliations.

Caste

Ramachandran's formulation reminds us that caste remains a crucial marker of exploitation, discrimination and marginalization in contemporary India. Caste positions facilitate, and restrict, access to mechanisms of capitalist accumulation (Harriss, 1982), agrarian investments (Lerche, 1995) as well as governmental resources (Jeffrey and Lerche, 1999; Jeffrey, 2002; and Pattenden, 2011). That this is the case is hardly surprising, given Mahmood Mamdani's (1996: 272) reminder of the "many ways in which power fragment(s) the circumstances and experiences of the oppressed." Indeed, as Bernstein (2010: 116) aptly reminds us, the circumstances of the oppressed "are not experienced self-evidently and exclusively in general but in terms of specific identities like 'urban/ rural dwellers, industrial workers/ agricultural labourers, urban craftsmen and women peasants, men/women, mental/ manual labour, young/old, black/ white, regional, national and ethnic differences, and so on,' in the list of examples given by Peter Gibbon and Michael Neocosmos (1985: 190)". Not only is caste a basis of shaping ideas of labour and status in the Indian context (Guru, 2006; Teltumbde, 2016), labour markets continue to be segmented along caste lines (Ahmed, 1998; Parry, 1999). Caste has been accurately described as 'enclosed' (Ambedkar, 1979) or 'congealed' (Lohia, 1964) class : the closures intimated by membership in caste communities lend caste inequalities a durable quality (Mosse, 2007). Caste endogamy remains widely prevalent, contributing to its enclosure and congealment (Desai and Dubey, 2010). Caste shapes not only access to social and symbolic resources but also material resources. Caste solidarities are common, as is discrimination on the basis of caste (Thorat and Newman, 2012). Violence to suppress collective claims by oppressed castes or to protect the honour of privileged caste women from purported interlopers of 'low castes' is also not uncommon. But above all, caste supremacist avowals of privileged castes indicate the cultural imperialism to which members of oppressed castes are subjected.

Caste and class exploitation interpenetrate in employers' strategies. Harriss-White and Gooptu remind us that, if

> caste, as a social institution, continues to configure the labour market and determine relations between labour and capital, then it would be too restrictive an interpretation to exclude 'caste' politics, outside the work place, as being irrelevant to the politics of labour (Gooptu and Harriss-White, 2001, 101).

Because experiences of labour rest very significantly on caste status (Rao, 2008), it is impossible to exclude caste from an analysis of class. Ambedkar's insight that the caste system signals not so much a division of labour but a "division of labourers" is particularly apposite in this context. Since contentions between classes are preceded by contentions *over* class, it follows that notions of class are inflected by assertions of caste identities.

A synthesis of the scholarship on the intersections of labour and caste leads me to operate with a three-fold classification of social class, depicted in Figure 3.1. A key feature of this three-fold schematisation is that it avoids the

Figure 3.1: A preliminary scheme for categorization of social class

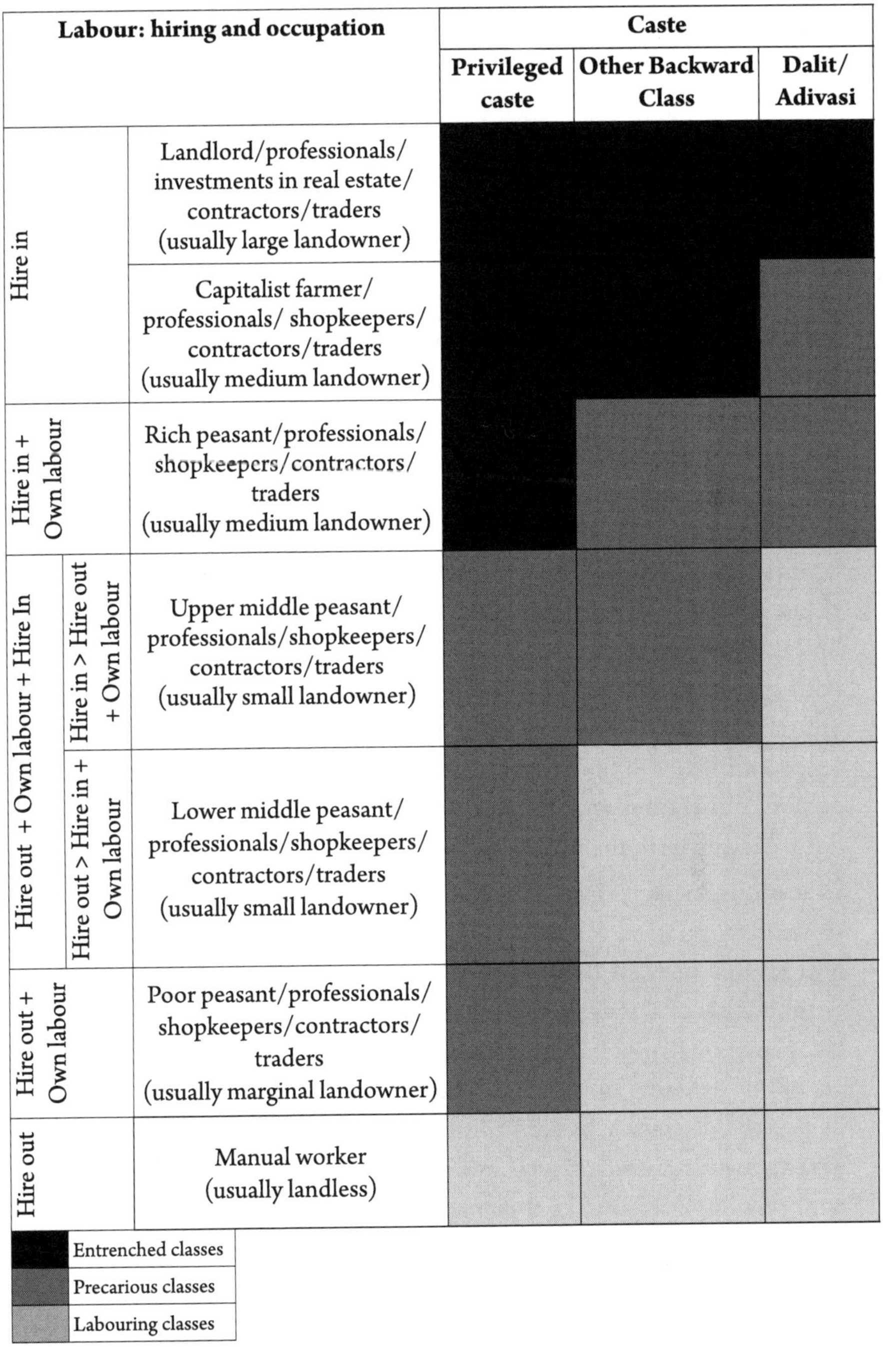

Labour: hiring and occupation			Caste		
			Privileged caste	Other Backward Class	Dalit/ Adivasi
Hire in		Landlord/professionals/ investments in real estate/ contractors/traders (usually large landowner)			
		Capitalist farmer/ professionals/ shopkeepers/ contractors/traders (usually medium landowner)			
Hire out + Own labour + Hire In	Hire in + Own labour	Rich peasant/professionals/ shopkeepers/contractors/ traders (usually medium landowner)			
	Hire out > Hire in + Own labour / Hire in > Hire out + Own labour	Upper middle peasant/ professionals/shopkeepers/ contractors/traders (usually small landowner)			
		Lower middle peasant/ professionals/shopkeepers/ contractors/traders (usually small landowner)			
	Hire out + Own labour	Poor peasant/professionals/ shopkeepers/contractors/ traders (usually marginal landowner)			
Hire out		Manual worker (usually landless)			

Entrenched classes

Precarious classes

Labouring classes

polarisation implied in accounts that pit 'dominant classes' against 'working classes'[2] and recognises, with Harriss-White (2012) that the intermediate social classes are not transitional.

Readers will appreciate that this schematisation in preliminary and has been developed with the limited objective of structuring the analysis of collaborative and contentious social relations without subscribing to such casteless categories as capitalist and proletariat, or peasant, petty commodity producer and classes of labour. These three social classes are:

1. Entrenched social classes: The classes at the apex of the regional and/ or national political economy, entrenched classes typically comprise of privileged caste status, labour-hiring families who are able to capitalize on their economic and social resources in order to sustain their position at the apex of the agrarian hierarchy. Their control over the economy enables them to hire and discipline labour to their advantage. Command over social status buttresses their economic clout. Their position in the political economy is entrenched, allowing them to stave off significant challenges to the economic and social resources at their disposal. Social mobile landlords and capitalist farmers of intermediate caste status, whose economic and social position is entrenched in the agrarian hierarchy are also included within the ambit of the entrenched classes. The entrenched classes combine their dominance in the agrarian hierarchy with investments outside of the sector, connections with the bureaucracy and family members who work as professionals in the formal sector.

2. Precarious social classes: The classes at the middle of the regional and/ or national political economy, precarious classes typically comprise rich and middle peasant families of intermediate caste status who deploy a combination of labour strategies (hire in labour, hire out labour and exploit their own or family labour) to reproduce themselves. However, middle and poor peasants of privileged caste backgrounds are also categorized as precarious classes, as are Dalit and Adivasi capitalist farmers and rich peasants who may exclusively hire in labour. Although they might command some economic resources, their social resources are inadequate to buttress their economic position. Their economic resources might allow them to hire in labour, but they are in no position to discipline labour to their own advantage: moreover, they may find themselves as hiring out their labour

as well. Their position in the political economy is precarious, dependent on the electoral success of politicians who represent their interests. Given that their socio-economic position remains vulnerable, the appellation of 'precarious classes' is applied to them.

3. Labouring social classes: The classes at the bottom of the regional and/or national political economy, labouring social classes have little control over the economy, except as manual workers who must hire out their bodies to perform manual work. Their position in the political economy is shaped by their poverty, making it imperative for them to hire out their labour if they are to survive. Their social resources are often inadequate for them to raise their economic status. Labouring classes typically comprise of manual workers of all caste groups. In addition poor and middle peasants of families of intermediate caste status or stigmatized as 'untouchable' (Dalits) and/ or 'primitive' (Adivasi) are also categorized as 'labouring classes'. The labouring social classes are the most caste-heterogeneous among the three social classes, and are- as we shall see- riven by social contradictions, primarily, but not solely, due to distinctions of caste. Needless to say, the circumstances and experiences of all labouring classes are far from being similar. Indeed, labourers of Dalit and/or Adivasi backgrounds confront what Bourgois (1988, 330) calls the "conjugated oppression" based on the subordinate position imposed upon them in the hierarchies of caste and labour.

On the one extreme, landlords and capitalist farmers of privileged caste backgrounds are categorized in this book as 'entrenched classes', to refer to their economic and social position. Likewise, landlords and capitalist farmers of intermediate caste status who exclusively hire in labour are also categorized entrenched classes. Privileged caste rich peasants who hire in labour as well as exploit their own labour are also categorized as entrenched classes. At the other extreme, manual workers who hire out labour are categorized as labouring classes, to highlight the need for them to sell their labour in order to reproduce themselves. Poor peasants and lower middle peasants of Shudra, Dalit and Adivasi backgrounds who combine hiring out of labour with exploitation of own labour are also classified as labouring classes, as are Dalit/ Adivasi middle peasants. In between these extremes lie the precarious classes, who typically combine petty commodity production with an intermediate status in the caste hierarchy.

In the rest of this chapter, I will draw on this caste-centred class-analytic framework to analyse the social relations of power prevailing in the four study localities. The four localities are the concrete places in which people live and which render meanings to political space. It is in these places that labourers argue with the peasants who hire them, sharecroppers dispute the claims of their landlords, and landlords plot against capitalist farmers, rich peasants and professionals they consider upstarts. It is here that retailers and professionals revile the attitudes of landlords and landlords gossip about everyone else. It is in places such as these that elected representatives and political mediators are subjected to claims by the poor, the precarious and the entrenched social classes. It is here that members of different social classes advance their collective perspectives as well as bicker within themselves. An examination of the social relations of power in the particular fieldwork places will provide glimpses of the political spaces within which the poor (and other social classes) are embedded. The discussion draws on a combination of census and sample surveys, ethnographic observations and 'hanginig out', and indepth interviews with the residents of the fieldwork areas.

Rahimpur: An incorporative political place

The political place I call Rahimpur is one of 23 wards in a gram panchayat in West Bengal's Maldah district. The census for this study suggested that approximately 424 households lived in it. The ward was located north of Maldah town, about 3 kilometres to the east of the National Highway that connects Kolkata with Guwahati. Several markets dotted the ward's neighbourhood. At the time of the fieldwork, the road from the highway to the market was an unpaved potholed mud path, over which motorized four-wheelers feared to tread. Public transport into the ward comprised improvised cycle carts fitted with small engines. Onto these carts men, women and children huddled together with their livestock. Such services were infrequent but predictable. During fieldwork, I lived at the local Madrasah, a site selected for me as a public place by the ward member in consultation with different politicians as well as community elders in the locality.

Table 3.1 presents Rahimpur's landholding structure in relation to its occupational diversity. The failure of successive governments in vesting ceiling-surplus land and subsequent redistribution is demonstrated by the widespread incidence of landlessness. Nearly three-fourths of Rahimpur's households was landless. Less than a tenth of the landless hired out their labour primarily to local farmers and peasants. These agricultural labourers were paid through a combination of cash and kind, primarily food grains, which they appear to have preferred.[3] Their employers were usually the small, medium and large landowners of the ward, although it was not uncommon for marginal landowners to hire workers from time to time. A large proportion of the landless relied chiefly on employment in suburbs of different north Indian cities to work in the construction sector and its ancillaries such as brick kilns. They were recruited by labour contractors on 50 day *dadon* contracts. Others worked in *chai* kiosks, eateries and shops selling knickknacks, groceries, mobile SIM cards and stationary items within the village or were tailors, butchers and petty shopkeepers. Yet others were itinerant vendors of vegetables, milk and fish. Some found employment in the transport industry, either as truck drivers or as cleaners.

Table 3.1: Land and occupation, Rahimpur, December 2009

	Agriculture	Other casual	Artisanal	Business	Salaried	Total
Landless	27	227	3	46	4	314
Marginal landowner	12	20	0	5	0	37
Small landowner	17	26	0	6	1	50
Medium landowner	3	0	0	2	2	7
Large landowner	5	0	0	5	6	16
All	64	273	3	64	13	424

Source: Own census survey; 2009–10.

It was not only the landless who complemented agricultural labour with itinerant migration or off-farm activities. Indeed, nearly one-tenth of itinerant migrants owned land up to 3 *bighas*.[4] Over two-thirds of all marginal, small and medium landowning households derived their incomes chiefly from off-farm activities. Some such households owned or rented the kiosks and eateries in the village and its environs selling SIM cards, snacks, meals, *pan* and *chai*. Others owned small provisional stores that stocked grocery items of daily and special consumption. Some also worked as peons and clerks in the local panchayat where they earned a modest, though regular, salary. Rahimpur's Anganwadi Centre, a publicly funded pre-school centre serving midday meals for children and offering a variety of medical and nutritional services to pregnant and lactating women, was managed by a local woman. The locality's High School provided employment to a few families as teachers, guards, sweepers and peons.

Rahimpur's diverse occupational structure was reflected across the landholding hierarchy. If at the base, the landless sought employment in a variety of occupations, at its apex, as many as 11 of the 16 large landowners supplemented their agricultural incomes with employment in public service and in business. Akbar Ali, the most prominent Congress politician in the locality and the person who organized my stay and at whose home I ordinarily ate my meals in Rahimpur was a labour contractor who derived more profits from the outmigration of labourers to Mumbai and Delhi than from cultivating his land. But he also leased out much of his land to sharecroppers, as we might expect of a 'capitalist landlord'. Babar Hossein, the Congress-affiliated ward member during my fieldwork was as an agent for an internationally renowned insurance provider. He recruited agricultural labourers to work his land and hired a manager to sell his product at the local agricultural market, indicating his being a 'capitalist farmer'. Both gentlemen rented their agricultural properties and derived ground rents. Abdur Rehman, another Congress politician and Akbar Ali's maternal uncle, was a registered medical practitioner. He also rented out his tractor to less wealthy agriculturalists, often of the precarious classes who could not afford to buy a tractor of their own. He leased out all of his land to sharecroppers, leaving him with adequate time to do 'social work' as he described his party activities: Abdur Rehman's reliance on a combination of rents and incomes from consultations makes him difficult to be classified.

Rahimpur's labour-hiring structure overlapped with its landholding structure, as evident from Table 3.2. Over 90 per cent of the landless and nearly 70 per cent of the marginal landowners worked as manual labourers. Manual labourers comprised 75 per cent of Rahimpur's population. They either exclusively hired out their labour, or complemented labouring for others with working on their own tiny plots of land and small-scale workshops or business units. They did not hire in any labour. By contrast, none of the 16 large landowners hired themselves out for manual labour. As many as 14 of them managed their agricultural operations either by directly recruiting workers or through sharecropping arrangements. Only two were directly involved in any kind of agrarian activity.

However, the limits to such overlaps must be noted as well. Landless and marginal landowning households hired in labour in addition to hiring out their labour: 4 per cent of all landless households and 14 per cent of marginal landowning households hired in labour. They were mostly engaged in businesses and salaried employment. Such households comprised nearly half of all the exclusively labour-hiring households. Readers will to note that nearly a tenth of all households relied exclusively on hiring in labour to meet their production or consumption needs.

Table 3.2: Labour and land, Rahimpur, December 2009

	Landless	Marginal landowner	Small landowner	Medium landowner	Large landowner	Total
Manual workers	284	26	11	0	0	321
HO>HI, also self and family labour	5	6	24	1	0	36
HI>HO, also self and family labour	2	0	6	2	0	10
HI + self and family labour, no HO	3	3	5	3	2	16
HI only, neither self/family labour, nor HO	12	2	4	1	14	35
All	314	37	50	7	16	424

Source: Own census survey, 2009–10.

Chart 3.1 reveals the overlaps between Rahimpur's labour-hiring structure and its different communities. The representation of the three communities among the manual labourers was approximately proportionate to their share of the ward's population. However, the apex of the labour-hiring hierarchy was far more homogenous than its base, with Sheikh Muslims comprising 29 of the 35 households that exclusively hired in labour and Hindus of various castes a further five. Only one Shershabadiya household was represented among such households.

Chart 3.1: Labour by caste in Rahimpur

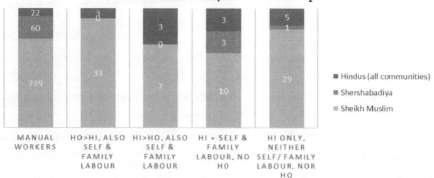

MANUAL WORKERS | HO>HI, ALSO SELF & FAMILY LABOUR | HI>HO, ALSO SELF & FAMILY LABOUR | HI + SELF & FAMILY LABOUR, NO HO | HI ONLY, NEITHER SELF/FAMILY LABOUR, NOR HO

■ Hindus (all communities)
■ Shershabadiya
▧ Sheikh Muslim

Source: Own census survey, 2009–10.

The dominance of the Sheikhs as hirers of labour was bolstered by their self-proclaimed ritual status. Rahimpur's Sheikh Muslims claimed descent from the village's Brahmans. Although such assertions were challenged by their Hindu neighbours, the Sheikhs developed elaborate origin-myths about the advent of Islam in the region being foretold by an oracle of the Hindu goddess Kali to local Brahmans during the fifteenth century. According to their legends, the Brahmans, being convinced of the doctrinal robustness of Islam, adopted that religion. The Sheikhs took pride in their 'clean-caste' origins, emphasizing the similarities, rather than the differences, between Brahmanic and Islamic rituals. They simultaneously worshipped at *dargahs*, or shrines commemorating Sufi mystics and believed in the power of talismans given by holy men. On the other hand, their Hindu neighbours, of the Bind and Napit communities (classified by the State government as SC), maintained that the Sheikhs were converts from the Rajbanshi community. Controversies over their social status notwithstanding, the institution of *shamajs* among the Sheikh earned them much social respect from neighbours and other villagers. A *shamaj* was a collective of of households presided over by a headman, locally called *sardar*. Each one of Rahimpur's Sheikh Muslim households was a member of a *shamaj*. The *shamaj* took contributions from every member-household according to their abilities and supplied resources to households who needed them. The *shamaj's* role in preventing destitution among members of the Sheikh Muslim community was especially commended. Also of importance was the *shamaj's* role in ensuring that no child of school-going age belonging to affiliated households dropped out of school due to financial reasons. Educational attainments among Sheikh Muslims in Rahimpur were higher than for members of other communities. The caste belonging of the Sheikhs bolstered their educational attainments which, in turn, maintained their dominance over labour and land.

Rahimpur's other communities did not enjoy such a compact between social status and dominance over land and labour. At 8 per cent of the population, the locality's Hindus were too few in number and dispersed across different castes to present a coherent social bloc. Moreover, the Sheikh Muslims, invoking ritual hierarchies among the Hindus, stigmatized the overwhelming majority of them as 'untouchables'. But their most vituperative prejudices appear to have been reserved for the Shershabadiyas, against whom they used epithets as *nongra* and *jhograte* to condemn, respectively, their allegedly unhygienic practices as well as putatively quarrelsome nature. The Sheikhs considered themselves more cultured and prided themselves for their syncretic practices and worship at *dargahs*. Unlike the Hanafi sect to which the Sheikh Muslims adhered, the Shershabadiyas affiliated with the Salafis and considered *dargah*-worship heretical. The Sheikhs ridiculed the Shershabadiyas' abhorrence of *dargah* worship as representing religious orthodoxy and social backwardness. Table 3.3 highlights the total marginalization of the Shershabadiyas and the Bind and Napit communities in respect of landholdings. Only one of the locality's large landowners was Shershabadiya and one was Hindu, and that too a sole member of the Brahman community.

Table 3.3: Caste and land, Rahimpur, December 2009

	Sheikh Muslim	Shershabadiya	Hindus (all castes)	Total
Landless	246	26	22	314
Marginal landowner	32	4	1	37
Small landowner	31	12	7	50
Medium landowner	6	1	0	7
Large landowner	14	1	1	16
All	323	64	37	424

Source: Own census survey, 2009–10.

Social relations of production: An entrenched–poor coalition against the precarious

Landless manual workers of Rahimpur's different communities confronted several deprivations, insecurities and vulnerabilities. They shared their general situation of oppression with a number of the small and marginal landowners whose labour was exploited by others and who also exploited labour. But while the large majority of manual workers shared their communal affiliation as Sheikhs with labour-hiring peasants, capitalist farmers and landlords, Shershabadiya, Bind and Napit workers could not because members of their communities were relatively under-represented in those categories. Rahimpur's Sheikh labourers could lay claim on communal obligations of their Sheikh employers through the *shamajs*. *Shamaj* sardars reported to me that disputes between labourers and labour-hiring peasants were among the most numerous tensions into which they got embroiled. While the *sardars* claimed that they weighed in on the side of the labourers, they also complained that labourers' employers refused to defer to their authority. The use of such mechanisms to hold employers to account, effete though they might have been, meant even less to Shershabadiyas and others, who were not affiliated with any of the four *shamajs*. Communal differences were less pronounced at the top of the labour-hiring hierarchy where Sheikh Muslims formed the overwhelming majority of the hirers of labour.

Most labour-hiring peasants who directly engaged in agricultural operations described themselves, and were described by others as, *chasis*. As peasants, they underscored their reliability, while highlighting the alleged autonomy that stemmed from their working on own plots of land. Many were proud of their family history of personal cultivation and emphasized the hard work to which they were accustomed, in order to contrast themselves with the more genteel and urbane *bhadralok*. They also emphasized their distance from labour-hiring landlords, or *zamindars,* who they referred to as the 'Big Men' or *bodolok* to refer to their entrenched privileges. A number of peasants with whom I spoke emphatically denied aspiring either to *bhadralok* or *zamindar* status, even after they or their family members had attained education. Although they did seek to reduce their personal involvement in manual work because of the arduous conditions associated with paddy cultivation, peasants took pride in being *chasi*, and hoped that their children too would take to agriculture even after attaining the highest levels of education that they could.

Nevertheless, that many impoverished *chasis* actually laboured for other *chasis* threatened the primary identity of labouring peasants as autonomous cultivators of the land. Such experience blurred the putative distinction between peasants and labourers. As labourers, *majurs* depended on other people for work. Their dependence made them unreliable in the eyes of both *chasis* and *bodolok*. *Chasis*, including labouring *chasis*, sought to maintain a social distance from the *majurs*. Social distance was relatively easy to maintain by rich peasants, but not so among middle and poor peasants. It was here that communal differences assumed salience, especially for Sheikh middle and poor peasants who sought to increase their social distance from labourers. Sheikh middle peasants who combined the use of family labour with hiring themselves out and recruiting workers asserted their identity as *chasis*. They emphasized their solidarity with richer Sheikh peasants rather than with the vulnerabilities of labourers.

Middle peasants of other communities emphasized their identities as *majurs*, as did poorer peasants and manual workers of all communities, their mutual misgivings notwithstanding. A number of my interlocutors from these classes suggested that people who lived by hiring their labour to other people (*mojuri kore khaye*) were poor, or *gorib*. They distinguished themselves from people who sustained themselves and their families through agriculture, salaried employment and business. Of course, the term *gorib* also proved notoriously slippery, as many Sheikh middle peasants insisted that anybody who had to work for other people, irrespective of whether they hired *out* more labour than they hired *in*, was poor. The collective self-identifications of being poor rendered even more complex the already blurred distinctions between peasants and labourers.

Disagreements over being poor notwithstanding, labourers and peasants emphasized their mutual distinction vis-à-vis the landlords and capitalist farmers. Such families, as Akbar Ali's, Babar Hossein's and Abdur Rehman's, were Rahimpur's *bodolok*. They also claimed *bhadralok* status, to which members of none of the other classes objected. These families maintained their social distinction from both the peasants as well as the labourers. They scorned peasants as 'thick-headed' and labourers as 'good-for-nothing'. Family members recalled with pride their origins as tenants of the *zamindar* of Muchia under the Permanent Settlement. As tenant-landlords, they told me, they were responsible for maintenance of law and order, the upholding of principles of justice and punishment, and responsibility for the welfare of the villagers. Sceptical peasants explained to me that 'welfare' meant advancing loans at exorbitant rates, provisioning of starch water meant for buffaloes to starving families, and meeting even the tiniest of infringements with brutal punishment.

In my estimation, and recognizing that alternative categorizations may be possible, Rahimpur's population could differentiated along the following social classes. The locality's landlords, capitalist farmers and rich peasants of the Sheikh community constituted the locality's entrenched classes. Middle and poor peasants of the Sheikh community, and rich peasants from the Shershabadiya and Bind/Napit communities comprised Rahimpur's precarious classes. Manual labourers of all communities, alongside poor peasants of the Shershabadiya and Bind/ Napit communities, made up the labouring classes.

Conflict and collaboration between Rahimpur's different classes were intertwined. Tensions marred the relationship between the labour-hiring peasants and the entrenched landlords/capitalist farmers. Rahimpur's entrenched classes rented their agricultural properties to precarious class sharecroppers and tenants, from whom they derived ground rents. Issues of timing and modality of paying the rent often soured relationships. The account provided by Abdul Bari, one of Akbar Ali's many sharecroppers, is typical. After each harvest, Akbar Ali insisted that Abdul Bari deliver the share of the produce on the very day he completed his tasks. At each insistence, Abdul Bari told his landlord he could not afford to. With each rejection, Akbar Ali threatened to send musclemen to confiscate the produce. At each threat, Abdul Bari dared him to do so. This cycle was enacted season after season for at least seven years, I gathered from Abdul Bari's account. What was striking for me was the repetition of the cycle as neither Abdul Bari nor Akbar Ali appeared to keen to exit what was obviously a fraught relationship.

Conflictual relations also marked the relations between the locality's labour-hiring peasants and the labouring poor, although collaboration was also common. A particularly sore point of contention between the precarious class and the labouring classes was over payment of wages. Arif Miya's narrative was typical. He told me of the manner in which peasants such as Abdul Bari routinely haggled with him and other labourers over wages. Table 3.4 reveals the extent to which wages were depressed in Rahimpur. Labourers frequently turned to members of the entrenched classes for help to overcome the shortages caused by their wage shortfalls. Daultat Bibi, a destitute widow who lived with her teenaged daughter, spoke glowingly of Akbar Ali's generosity and willingness to help whenever she needed it. Arif Miya told me of the enthusiastic support he received from Akbar Ali when he demanded the timely payment of his wages from Abdul Bari. Importantly, even as Rahimpur's poor acknowledged the entrenched classes' generosity, they did not cease to recall that their own relations with them had changed due to the activism of such precarious class activists as Abdul Bari, Noorul Islam and others. Arif Miya's metaphor was telling: '[Abdul Bari and others] tamed[5] the *bodo lok*. The roaring tigers have now become purring cats.'

Table 3.4: Agricultural wages in Rahimpur,
State-level and locality-level wages compared

Month	State-level prevailing wages (₹) (2)	Locality-specific wages (₹) (3)
January 2009	78/71 (Aman harvest)	60/58
February 2009	81/72 (Boro transplant)	45/43
April 2009	80/71 (Boro harvest)	70/65
July 2009	85/76 (Aman transplant)	50/48
January 2010	85/70 (Aman harvest)	70/68
February 2010	87/71 (Boro transplant)	50/48
April 2010	91/74 (Boro harvest)	70/68

Sources: Column 2: For January/ February/April 2009: Labour Bureau (2010, Tables 9a, 10a and 12a respectively); For July 2009: Labour Bureau (2011, Table 3a); For January/ February/April 2010: Labour Bureau (2012, Tables 9a, 10a and 12a respectively).
Columns 3: Field notes and observations. Figures on the left under each column indicate wages for men while figures on the right indicate wages for women.

Nevertheless, the social relations of production in Rahimpur were characterized by a broad coalescence of the entrenched classes and the labouring poor against the precarious classes. Precarious classes found themselves in contentious relationship with both the entrenched classes as well as the labouring poor. The labouring poor called upon the entrenched classes in their frequent tussles with the precarious classes. The entrenched classes supported the labouring poor in their wrangles with the precarious classes, often helping them out with timely assistance. The precarious classes found themselves hemmed in between both the entrenched classes as well as the labouring poor, contending against both.

Social relations of distribution: A polity shaped by entrenched classes

Table 3.5 reveals the patterns of membership in political parties among Rahimpur's population, disaggregated along land-size class. The survey instrument used for the study solicited specific information about membership in political parties but did not probe the depth of involvement in or the name or type of political party. Slightly over a quarter of the locality's households have at least one member of the family affiliated with a political party. Large and small landowners sought and obtained membership in political parties in excess of their share of the population. A perusal of the data indicates heightened political party membership at the apex and middle levels of the landholding hierarchy. The table also shows data from the sample survey to indicate that electoral participation in the gram panchayat elections remained consistent throughout the landowning hierarchy.

Table 3.5: Political participation in Rahimpur, disaggregated along land-size class, percentages

	Data from Census Survey		**Data from Sample Survey**	
	Population	**Political party membership**	**Population**	**Voting in PRI election**
Landless	74	66	75	75
Marginal landowner	9	4.72	7.46	8
Small landowner	12	19.81	11	11
Medium landowner	1.65	1.89	3.73	3.5
Large landowner	3.77	7.55	2.98	2.6
	N= 424	N= 118	N= 134	N= 112

Source: Own surveys, 2009-10.

Neither Rahimpur's landlords and capitalist farmers nor the peasants and sharecroppers could establish their electoral control over the ward. In multicornered contests, as in 2008 when candidates from other parties such as the Trinamul Congress and BJP contested elections against established

Congress and CPI(M) politicians, Congress-affiliated Babar Hossein was elected ward member by securing barely 35 per cent of the votes polled: nearly 65 per cent of the ward's electorate had rejected him. Babar Hossein succeeded the CPI(M) affiliated Henna Khan, who had herself been elected by a slim majority. Both Babar Hossein and Henna Khan followed in the footsteps of preceding ward members, who were all elected with pluralities or slim majorities, exemplifying the tenuous hold of the entrenched and the privileged classes over Rahimpur's electoral politics. Nevertheless, the entrenched classes enjoyed an edge over the precarious classes in shaping Rahimpur's polity.

The parents and grandparents of Rahimpur's peasants led extremely precarious lives as sharecroppers when the Muchia based *zamindar* and his tenants held sway during the era of the Permanent Settlement. As sharecroppers, they provided enthusiastic support to the CPI(M) when the party first emerged in the region. During my interviews with such activists as Abdul Bari, Joynal Ali and Kamruz Zaman, I could not help note the sparkle in their eyes when they recalled the tumultuous events of the time when the party first made an appearance. Their actions directly threatened the entrenched privileges held by Congress-affiliated tenant-landlord families of Akbar Ali, Babar Hossein, Abdur Rehman. The dedicated activism of the CPI(M) cadre bore fruit in 1971, when the party won the parliamentary constituency of Maldah for the first time. Brutal repression by the Congress government as well as its local supporters followed, but could not stem the growing tide of support for the CPI(M) in the district. In 1977, the CPI(M) candidate was reelected. More importantly, the CPI(M) swept to power in the State and took office as the Left Front Government in Kolkata.

A year later, in 1978, the CPI(M) won the panchayat elections and sought to vest ceiling-surplus lands. However, the tenant-landlords put up stiff resistance and frustrated their efforts. Although some properties of the Muchia based landlord were vested and redistributed among the landless, the surplus properties of his tenants in the possession of families such as Akbar Ali's and Babar Hossein's, remained in their hands, enabling them to maintain their dominance. However, the CPI(M) was more successful with introducing tenancy reforms. Sharecroppers could now keep three-quarters of the produce (against the customary two-thirds). But even more important, some of the sharecroppers told me, and something on which there was no legislation, was the shift in the responsibility for collecting the produce. The landlord was now responsible for collecting the share from the sharecropper's fields, rather than the sharecropper being responsible for delivering it to the landlord (saving them the time and effort this required, not to speak of the indignity of waiting). This change had transformed the social relations between sharecropper and landlord, making it conceivable for sharecroppers to relate to Rahimpur's landlords as social equals. Nevertheless, while the sharecroppers, most of whom were affiliated with, or were sympathetic to, the CPI(M) benefitted from the Left Front Government's tenancy reforms, the landless, who had also supported the CPI(M), remained landless. Side by side, while the political influence of the Muchia based landlord was decimated, that of his tenant-landlords, people such as Akbar Ali and Babar Hossein remained.

When Maldah reverted to Congress control in 1980, the chances of any redistribution of ceiling-surplus land vapourized. The CPI(M) remained in a position of strength in the panchayat, but it could not dislodge the Congress-affiliated landlords the way the party had done at the State level. Rahimpur's poor and middle peasants, those who had most benefitted from tenancy reforms, remained committed to the CPI(M). On the other hand, the landlords wielded effective influence over Rahimpur since the Congress Party's resurgence in Maldah in 1980 and its continued electoral sway in that constituency till date. Although Rahimpur ward oscillated between the CPI(M) and Congress after 1978, the landlords clearly set its agenda. Not only did they frustrate any programmes for land redistribution, they were able to convert the CPI(M)'s success at tenancy reforms into a major liability for the party. Congress politicians underscored the fact that the tenancy reforms enabled Rahimpur's CPI(M)-affiliated poor peasants to improve their economic conditions without any benefits to the landless poor. Moreover, the poor peasant leadership of the CPI(M) increasingly assumed a rich and middle peasant form. But their inability to redistribute land made the CPI(M)'s rich and middle peasant leadership suspect in the eyes of the landless.

The leadership of Congress remained from the very beginning in the hands of the landlords, who increasingly turned to capitalist farming. In this respect, Congress' class base was more elitist than that of the CPI(M). The landlord-capitalist farmer leadership of Congress could more successfully obfuscate its class contradictions vis-à-vis the labouring poor than the rich and middle peasant leadership of the CPI(M) could. The rich and middle peasants who headed the CPI(M) in Rahimpur were often the very same labour-hiring peasants against whose wage depressions labourers were most likely to complain. By contrast, the landlords and rich farmers who headed the Congress Party were more easily able to extend individualized assistance to labourers, even as they privately ridiculed poor people's dependence. Such assistance, at such crucial life-stages such as marriages, births and funerals, was crucial to the survival of the poor as social persons. Their personal involvement in the lives of the poor, and ability to influence the course of their lives, was enormous. These interventions allowed the entrenched classes to shape Rahimpur's polity.

The making of an incorporative political place

Several imbroglios marked the social relations of production in Rahimpur. The entrenched classes and the precarious classes contended over the timing and modalities of paying ground rent. The precarious classes and the labouring classes struggled over the payment and timeliness of wages. The shared antipathy of the labouring classes and the entrenched classes against the precarious classes resulted in their coalescing together, even if such coalescing was fractured. Collective self-identifications such as *chasi*, *majur* and *bhadralok* marked people's attempts to distinguish themselves as a class from others.

The social relations of distribution in Rahimpur were likewise marked by recurring contentions between the entrenched classes and the precarious classes. The electoral tussles between the Congress and the CPI(M) exemplified the oscillation of the panchayat between the precarious classes and the entrenched classes. Nevertheless, it was clear that the latter set the agenda for Rahimpur's polity. Their antipathy towards the precarious classes was shared by the labouring poor. The entrenched classes appropriated the very concrete contradictions between the precarious classes and the labouring poor to their own anxieties against the ascension of the precarious classes. Despite recognizing the contribution of the precarious classes to the betterment of their own social situation, the labouring classes acquiesced, albeit guardedly, in the demonization of peasants in which the landlords and the capitalist farmers indulged. The entrenched classes incorporated the labouring poor into class coalescence against the precarious classes.

The incorporation of Rahimpur's labouring poor into class coalescence with the entrenched landlords and capitalist farmers against the labour-hiring peasants marked the locality's social relations of power. Such incorporation underpinned the negotiation between and within the locality's different classes. The poor celebrated the landlords as their 'guardians' (using the English term) and reviled the peasants as their exploiters. However, poor people's support to the landlords remained cautious. They were not willing to support the marginalization of the peasants despite their very real grievances against them. The result was that the entrenched classes at best *shaped*, rather than controlled, the political place that was Rahimpur.

Sargana Ward 1: A populist political place

The political place I call Sargana gram panchayat was located in Bihar's Araria district. The panchayat comprised a total of 10 wards. The census for this study suggested that Ward 1, on which I focussed, comprised 165 households. The ward was located approximately three kilometres north of the Bhargama block headquarters. It straddled the State highway connecting Araria to Forbesganj and was served by the adjacent market. The major part of the ward lay to the highway's east. During my fieldwork, the road connecting this part of the ward to the highway was brick laid. However, the portion of the ward to the west of the highway was connected to it with nothing more than a mud path. Public transport to Bhargama block headquarters and to Raniganj town was frequent, with convenient connections to other parts of the State: autorickshaws and tempos ferried their human and avian passengers between Forbesgunj on the Nepal border and Ranigunj town while lambs and cattle accompanied their human masters on bigger buses. I lived in the eastern part of Sargana Ward 1, hosted by a Yadav mason whose wife had been a member of a women's collective convened by a Patna based NGO. While conducting fieldwork I alternated between Sargana Ward 1 and Roshanar Ward 5, located three kilometers across the highway.

Table 3.6 shows Sargana Ward 1's landholding structure in relation to its occupational diversity. Nearly 70 per cent of Sargana's population was landless. Approximately 40 per cent of the landless earned their household incomes primarily from labouring on the fields of local farmers and peasants, while a third of all households depended mainly on employment outside of the village. They travelled nearly 1000 kilometers to the west, as far as Punjab and Delhi, to work in a variety of industries ranging from agriculture to construction. Some people, such as my host, worked as masons, plumbers and labourers in the locality while others found employment in the *bazaar's* numerous eateries, kiosks peddling *chai* and *pan*, and shops retailing stationary items, low-cost garments, daily items of grocery and footwear, or offering photocopying services. Some of these establishments were owned by landless households. A few vended fruits and vegetables, milk, and trinkets and bangles. Additional to the landless, a small number of marginal landowners too complemented their agricultural labour with temporary migration to other locations in northern India. Over a quarter of all landless and marginal landowning households derived their incomes overwhelmingly from off-farm activities. Such households were involved in a range of activities including tailoring, weaving baskets, and pottery. Others owned small kiosks and eateries that sold snacks and meals or shops that retailed items of daily and special consumption. Members of two landless families of the Dhobhi community were employed as teachers in the High School, while the wife of a medium landowner of the Yadav community managed the Anganwadi Kendra.

Table 3.6: Land and occupation, Sargana Ward 1, December 2009

	Agriculture	Other casual	Artisanal	Business	Salaried	Total
Landless	45	37	10	18	2	113
Marginal landowner	39	5	3	4	0	41
Small landowner	3	0	0	1	0	4
Medium landowner	1	0	0	0	1	2
Large landowner	2	0	0	0	3	5
All	80	42	13	23	6	165

Source: Own census survey, 2009–10.

Agricultural labourers were paid through a combination of cash and kind, primarily a share of the harvest, which appear to have been their preference.[6]

Their employers were usually the small, medium and large landowners of the ward, although it was not uncommon for marginal landowners to hire in workers from time to time. Sargana's occupational profile was considerably more diverse at the base than at the apex. At the base, the landless sought employment in a variety of occupations. But at higher levels, households either depended on agriculture (two Rajput families) or on a combination of agriculture and salaried employment (two Kayasth and one Rajput family). The case of Gajen Singh, a Rajput, was typical. His family owned nearly 20 bighas[7] of land. He worked as the subeditor of a renowned Hindi language daily. Gajen Singh's mother was a prominent functionary of a national political party. They had many relatives holding bureaucratic positions in Bihar and elsewhere in the country.

That Sargana's labour-hiring structure overlapped with its landholding structure is evident from Table 3.7. 80 per cent of the landless households and nearly half of all marginal landowners worked as manual labourers. Manual labourers comprised nearly two-thirds of Sargana's population. They either exclusively hired out their labour, or complemented labouring for others with working on their own tiny plots of land and small-scale workshops or business units. They did not hire in any labour. By contrast, none of the seven medium and large landowners hired out their labour. Four of the locality's large landowners and one medium landowner managed their agricultural operations either by leasing their land to sharecroppers or by directly recruiting workers and overseeing their labour. People like Gajen Singh opted for leasing out their land. They were Sargana's capitalist landlords who combined ground rent with income from extra-agricultural sources. Others, for example, Gultu Yadav, whose wife managed Sargana's public pre-school centre, recruited agricultural labourers of the Musahar community and directly oversaw agricultural operations. Gultu Yadav could be counted among capitalist farmers who did not lease out their properties, but supplemented their incomes from the sale of their agrarian produce with earnings from holding government office. Less than a tenth of all households in Sargana depended exclusively on hiring in labour for their production or consumption activities.

Table 3.7: Labour and land, Sargana Ward 1, December 2009

	Land-less	Marginal land-owner	Small land-owner	Medium land-owner	Large land-owner	Total
Manual workers	93	22	0	0	0	104
HO>HI, also self and family labour	4	10	1	0	0	15
HI>HO, also self and family labour	10	6	1	0	0	17
HI + self and family labour, no HO	0	1	1	1	1	4
HI only, neither self/ family labour, nor HO	7	2	1	1	4	15
All	115	46	3	1	0	165

Source: Own census survey, 2009–10.

However, the limits on the overlaps between the labour-hiring structure and landholding need to be noted as well. Landless households engaged in a variety of artisanal and entrepreneurial activities apart from agricultural labour. As artisans and entrepreneurs, they often hired in more labour than they hired out. Indeed, as many as seven landless families exclusively hired in labour for their various household, artisanal and business activities: such landless households comprised nearly half the population of the exclusively labour-hiring households.

Chart 3.2 reveals the overlaps between Sargana's class structure and its several communities. Members of the Musahar community, who made up a quarter of the population, constituted 40 per cent of the locality's manual workers. On the other hand, the Kayasths, who comprised 23 per cent of the ward's population, made up a miniscule proportion of its manual labourers. No member of the Rajput community, who made up 9 per cent of the locality's population, was engaged in manual labour. The proportions of the Yadav, Kejri and Dhobhi to the total population of manual workers were commensurate with their proportion of the total population of the ward. Although the base of Sargana Ward 1's labour hierarchy reflected the communal diversity of the ward, the apex did not. Kayasths comprised the overwhelming majority of exclusively labour-hiring households, while Rajputs, Yadavs and Dhobhis comprised a smaller proportion.

Chart 3.2: Labour by caste in Sargana Ward 1

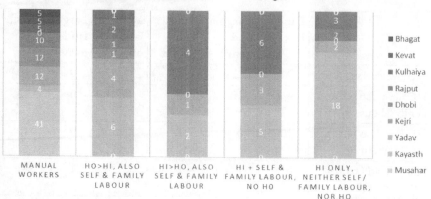

Source: Own census survey, 2009–10.

Considerable ambiguities shrouded the ritual status of the locality's Kayasth and Rajput communities. The class dominance of the Kayasth and Rajputs obtained in spite of, rather than because of, their ritual status. While members of the Kayasth community claimed 'upper caste' status on the basis of colonial era legal pronouncements, their claims were scoffed at by others who considered them as being of Shudra origin with merely superior pretensions. Even though my Kayasth interlocutors were aware of the potential bureaucratic and economic benefits that could accrue to them if they were categorized as OBC they assiduously described themselves as 'Forward Castes', the administrative appellation for Savarna communities: 'call us minority if you will, but please don't abuse us as *backward*,' a community elder sternly told me when I suggested the potential advantages of Kayasth registering themselves as OBC. Similarly, the Rajputs' claim to 'upper caste' were repudiated by others on the basis of their allegedly dubious origins, although the State government categorized them, as did others in the locality, as Forward Caste. Indeed, where members of both Rajput and Kayasth communities claimed 'clean-caste' origins, the meat eating associated with them made such claims laughable in the eyes of members of other communities.

Members of both communities more than compensated for their ritualistic ambiguities through their control over the State's bureaucracy, judiciary and police, as well as through access to educational opportunities. Every Rajput family in the ward boasted a relative in the district or higher administration. Likewise, nearly two-thirds of all Kayasth families recounted their intimate connections in the apparatus of the State. To be sure, variations between popular attitudes to members of the two communities were discernible. Members of the Rajput community possessed reputations of being violent and even cruel. Their reputations led local people to refer to them as *dabang*, an epithet for a brutally oppressive person or collective. Kayasths on the other hand were considered to be manipulative and calculating, but not violent. Despite such variations, the privileges accruing to members of both communities outstripped any ambiguities in their ritual status as well as any resource enjoyed by members of the locality's other communities. Indeed, members of other communities expressed the view that while the ritual claims of the Rajputs and Kayasths were bogus, there was no doubt that they had cornered educational and bureaucratic resources and established their dominance in society.

There was little ritual ambiguity regarding Sargana's Yadav, Koeri and Kevat communities who were socially and ritually considered Shudras, of 'low' but not 'untouchable' social status. The State government classified them under one or the other list of backward castes. Yadavs and Koeris were classified as OBC, while Kevats were designated as EBC. Where they claimed 'clean-caste' status to distinguish themselves from the so-called untouchables, they also categorically asserted their distinction from the privileged castes. On the one hand, then, members of such communities identified themselves as 'cleaner' than the so-called untouchables. On the other hand, however, they refused to attribute 'superior-caste' status to Kayasths and Rajputs. Their claims and counter-claims problematize any straightforward assumptions about the prevalence of an immutable caste hierarchy.

The advent of Lalu Prasad Yadav in the State during the 1980s enthused Sargana's Shudra communities. Particularly excited were the middle and rich peasants of the Yadav community who developed connections with Janata Dal politicians at district and State levels. Their political networks made them locally efficacious and led many among them to claim that they were the 'natural leaders' of the poor, a claim of which other backward caste communities were suspicious. The Yadavs gradually acquired reputations of being *dabang*, and were likened to the Rajputs in their social attitudes. But when

Lalu Yadav lost the elections in 2005, the social precariousness of Sargana's Yadavs was exposed. Although a quarter of Sargana's Yadavs claimed familial connections with low-level bureaucrats and policemen, such individuals were either transferred or rendered powerless in the new administration. On the other hand, the social connections, on which the Kayasths and Rajputs could continue to capitalize, made members of the latter two communities far more influential. They routinely ridiculed the Yadavs as possessing 'backward brains' and the Koeris as 'only capable of hard work'.

A further target of scorn were members of the Dhobhi community, classified by the State government as Scheduled Caste. Literacy rates among members of the Dhobhi stood at 34 per cent, ahead of the literacy rate of 22 per cent for SCs in Bihar, although behind the State average of 47 per cent.[8] Some members of the Dhobhi community had secured salaried employment in the local school on account of state-enforced protective discrimination. Against them, the Rajputs and Kayasths hurled such epithets as 'sons-in-law of the government', signaling their disdain for the Dhobhis' educational and employment attainments. The continued influence of the Rajput and Kayasth communities paradoxically bound the Shudras and Dalits together, despite their mutual disagreements and apprehensions.

The community whose members were widely regarded as the most oppressed of all were the Musahars. Some of my interlocutors located the Musahars as being 'lowest' in the caste hierarchy. Others suggested that the Musahars were not a caste at all in the sense that they did not traditionally provide a service, as the Yadavs, Koeris and Dhobhis supposedly did. Such differences of opinion notwithstanding, there was general concurrence that members of the Musahar community had been recruited, most probably through coercion, to provide forced labour for the Rajput and Kayasth landlords of the locality. Although recognized to be 'hard working', the Musahars were subject to stereotypes ranging from the putative stupidity of the men to the alleged promiscuity of the women. A 'trait' about the Musahars that evoked both admiration and contempt was their alleged obstinacy. Their purported diet of rodents was also reason for other communities, including other Dalit communities to scorn them as unclean. One of my Kayasth interlocutors reported with undisguised disgust his opinion that 'the Musahars do not even use water to clean up after their morning ablutions'. A few well meaning individuals offered the view that the Musahars needed greater care and protection by the government as they were too naïve (*bhola-bhala*), and hence trusted other people too much. Most of my Musahar interlocutors objected to such descriptions, and especially the use of terms 'low' and 'high' to describe either themselves or other communities. At the same time, they were well-aware of their collective socio-economic deprivation. Indeed, their educational attainments were extremely low, at an abysmal 7 per cent.[9] Bolstering their marginalization was their over-representation at the lower end of the landholding hierarchy. Table 3.8 reveals their marginalization by underscoring the widespread extent of landlessness among the Musahars.

Table 3.8: Caste and land, Sargana Ward 1, December 2009

	Musahar	Kayasth	Yadav	Kejri	Dhobi	Rajput	Kulhaiya	Kevat	Bhagat	Total
Landless	37	24	7	12	10	3	5	5	5	115
Marginal landowner	3	12	14	1	2	11	1	0	0	46
Small landowner	0	1	1	0	0	1	0	0	0	3
Medium landowner	0	1	0	0	0	0	0	0	0	1
Large landowner	0	0	0	0	0	0	0	0	0	0
All	41	38	22	13	13	15	6	5	5	165

Source: Own survey, 2009–10.

Social relations of production: A precarious-poor coalition against the entrenched

One of the striking aspects of Sargana Ward 1's class structure was the complete absence of Rajputs and the near absence of Kayasths from among the manual workers. Manual workers shared several uncertainties pertaining to their livelihoods with a number of the small and marginal landowners who were both exploited and exploiters in the domain of labour. To be sure, Yadav and Koeri labourers maintained commensal taboos against labourers of Kevat, Kulhaiya, Dhobhi and Musahar communities in order to maintain their distinctiveness as 'clean-caste' people. But it was not uncommon for them to help labourers from other communities with small loans for consumption or travel purposes. Furthermore, where labour hirers were either Kayasth or Rajput, the solidarity among labourers from OBC and SC communities was heightened, with Yadav and Musahar labourers often sharing the leadership of spontaneous actions against errant employers. Such actions were common because agricultural wages remained repressed, as can be gleaned from Table 3.9.

Table 3.9: Agricultural wage rates in Sargana Ward 1, State-level and locality-level wages compared

Month	State-level prevailing wages (₹) (2)	Locality-specific wages (₹) (3)
April 2009	73/67 (Wheat harvest)	45
July 2009	81/70 (Paddy transplant)	35–50
September 2009	85/76 (Jute harvest)	70
November 2009	83/78 (Paddy harvest)	45
April 2010	91/74 (Wheat harvest)	50

Source: Column 2: For April 2009: Labour Bureau (2010, Table 12a); For July/November 2009: Labour Bureau (2011, Table 3a and 7a); For April 2010: Labour Bureau (2012, Table 12a). Columns 3: Field notes and observations.

Labour-hiring peasants of the Yadav and Rajput communities who participated in agricultural operations referred to themselves, and were identified by others as, *kisans*. As peasants, they celebrated their ties to the land. Peasants affirmed the narrative of being autonomous producers of the country's food. However, while the Yadavs were proud of their family histories of personal cultivation and emphasized the hard work, which they performed, the Rajputs were less forthcoming about their peasant inheritances. Rather, they highlighted their ownership of the land and command over labourers. Labour hirers from among the Kayasths considered themselves and were considered by others as *grihasts*, or householders who managed their agricultural operations without manually labouring on their fields.

That many labour-hiring *kisans* actually laboured for wealthier *kisans* contradicted the idealized collective self-identity as independent cultivators of the land. Their experience of labouring for other peasants blurred the putative distinction between peasants and labourers, or *kisans* and *majdurs*. As labourers, *majdurs* depended on employers for work. Labourers' dependence rendered them unstable in the eyes of both *kisans* and *grihasths*. Consequently, some *kisans* sought to maintain a social distance from the *majdurs*. Kayasth and Rajput peasants who sought to increase their social distance from labourers as well as peasants of other communities found it useful to underscore their communal differences from other labourers. Kayasth families who deployed their own and family labour on the fields and/or hired out their labour claimed *grihasth* status, and sought to emulate the lifestyles of the wealthy *grihasths* from their own Kayasth community. Rajput families in similar positions asserted their status as *kisan*, but sought to distinguish themselves from *kisans* of other communities.

Labouring peasants of the Yadav and other communities accepted the blurred boundaries between being peasant and being labourers, but tended towards the locality's *majdurs*. Poor peasants and labourers of the Yadav community harboured little illusions of solidarity with rich peasants of their community. They often referred to the latter as *gaddars* to emphasize their perception of having been betrayed by the wealthy of their own community. A number of my interlocutors from these classes suggested that people who lived by hiring their labour to other people (*majduri karne wale*) were poor, or *garib aadmi*. They distinguished themselves from people who sustained themselves and their families through cultivating their own lands. The term *garib* entailed several slippages, as many middle peasants insisted that anybody who had to work for other people, irrespective of whether they hired *out* more labour than they hired *in*, was poor. Such self-identifications of being poor complicated the already blurred distinctions between peasants and labourers.

The collective self-identifications of those involved in entrepreneurial occupations added a further layer of complexity to the overlaps between labour and community in Sargana. This was especially so among labour-hiring Kayasth entrepreneurs not involved with agriculture. A number of these Kayasth families were shopkeepers and retailers who hired in manual labour to help with keeping the precincts of their business units clean or to load and offload supplies. Some among them channeled their profits to usury and were involved in political activism for parties such as the BJP. Other landless Kayasths sustained themselves through political mediation as brokers and fixers who facilitated people's access to politicians and the bureaucracy in return for a fee. Even as they claimed *grihasth* status similar to that claimed by Kayasth landowners, the humble provenance of such families (many of them had been landless or were immigrants from nearby areas) reduced their social status in the eyes of the entrenched landowning Kayasth and Rajput families.

Sargana's population could be categorized along the following social classes. The landlords, capitalist farmers and rich peasants of Sargana's Rajput and Kayasth communities made up the locality's entrenched classes. Middle and poor peasants of these communities, as well as the rich and middle peasants of the Yadav, Kevat and Dusadh communities, reviled as they were as 'low' caste or 'untouchable', comprised Sargana's precarious classes, as did labour-hiring professionals of the Dhobhi, Musahar and Dusadh communities, all stigmatized as 'untouchable'. Labourers from all communities, poor peasants of the Yadav and Kevat communities, and poor and middle peasants of the Dhobhi, Musahar and Dusadh communities made up the locality's labouring classes. While alternative categorizations might be possible, this three-way classification best enables me to explain the contentions and collaborations that marked social relations in Sargana.

Indeed, contentions and collaborations subjectivities wove together to mark the relations between Sargana's different social classes. Sargana's entrenched classes, the landlords and capitalist farmers of the Kayasth and Rajpur communities, rented their agricultural properties to precarious class sharecroppers and tenants of the Yadav, Koeri and Kevat communities. Contentions over the timing and modality of paying rents often soured relationships. Amaresh Yadav's was a typical account. He often leased in land from Gajen Singh who demanded that he deliver three-fourth of the share of the produce on the day he completed his harvest, a demand with which Amaresh Yadav refused to comply. Gajen Singh was also a slack paymaster to the agricultural labourers hired directly by him in order to work his fields. One such labourer Maturi Rishi complained that Gajen Singh constantly haggled over wages. Another sore point related to social discrimination – although public use of caste-based epithets was rare, culinary segregation was common. Gajen Singh served his Musahar labourers food on leaf plates, which could be easily disposed, preventing the slightest possibility of contact with them. By contrast, Amaresh Yadav, a gentleman of more modest means than Gajen Singh, served his labourers on metal plates, although he segregated the utensils in which Musahar labourers served. These utensils were, nonetheless, stored in his kitchen with other utensils. Although conflicts over wages were common between precarious class peasant hirers of labour and their workers, instances of discrimination were fewer. Maturi Rishi, who hired his labour to both Gajen Singh and Amaresh Yadav was unambiguous in offering his verdict. He noted that in his own frequent – and public – confrontations with Gajen Singh, Amaresh Yadav invoked egalitarian expressions and ridiculed the landlord's supremacist presumptions. Despite Amaresh Yadav being a slack paymaster himself, it was not uncommon for him to confront landlords such as Gajen Singh over non-payment of labourers' wages. Maturi Rishi also worked for a time as a construction labourer while Dharmesh Srivastava was building his shop. Dharmesh was an immigrant Kayasth, upon whom the locality's established Kayasth families looked down. Although Dharmesh Srivastava was a better paymaster than either Gajen Singh or Amaresh Yadav, what Maturi Rishi admired the most about him was his refraining from any discriminatory practice.

The labouring classes drew on the support of the precarious classes in their frequent contentions with the entrenched classes. The precarious classes cultivated the support of the labouring classes while asserting their claims against the entrenched classes. The entrenched classes found themselves confronting a coalition of the precarious classes and the labouring poor.

Social relations of distribution: A polity shaped by precarious classes

The origins of Sargana's labour-hiring agriculturalists are quite diverse. Till the abolition of the Permanent Settlement, most of the locality's agricultural property was in the hands of the Rajput *zamindar* Partap Singh. Although Partap Singh's descendants inherited some of his properties, a larger proportion was parceled out during his lifetime to different Rajput clansmen in the wake of the State government's land ceiling reforms, which threatened to vest all surplus properties. Even prior to the legislation, Kayasth professionals from Purnea and Darbhanga had descended on the locality and begun purchasing some of his properties in order to invest their surpluses. With the abolition of the Permanent Settlement, the *zamindar's* legal title over the properties became tenuous. Through the 1960s, some of his wealthier Yadav tenants, or *raiyats*, were able to make use of the reforms and take possession of the properties they had been cultivating. Partap Singh attempted to 'resume' cultivation by evicting his tenants, but he were not successful against the Yadav *raiyats*, leading to lasting resentment between the (ex)landlords and their (ex)tenants. The *raiyats* encouraged other sharecroppers to defy Partap Singh's authority, adding to the woes of the entrenched classes.

Throughout that period, Partap Singh, who now joined the Congress Party, controlled the gram panchayat as its Mukhya. In the 1978 elections, the Yadav peasants supported a rival candidate, Sarvesh Mandal, the *zamindar's* Kevat sharecropper. Sarvesh Mandal offered stiff competition to Partap Singh, although he was eventually defeated. Over the next 20 years, Partap Singh remained Mukhya because elections to all panchayats had been suspended in the State. Partap Singh appropriated the panchayat resources for his own clansmen as well as the Kayasth landlords who supported him. He awarded the dealership of PDS to his own brother Neem Singh and also appeased potential detractors from among the Rajputs and Kayasths by diverting public resources their way. But against the Yadavs and other OBCs, the entrenched classes demonstrated the greatest antipathy. Partap Singh refused to recommend names of OBC householders for any of the proliferating poverty-alleviation programmes. Partap Singh's antipathy towards the OBC contrasted with his apparent benevolence towards members of the Musahar community. He bestowed legal titles over homestead plots to select Musahar households. The hollowness of the benevolence became apparent when it was discovered that the titles were not legally tenable, placing the Musahars at the mercy of the landowners in whose name the titles were officially issued. Moreover, Partap Singh disallowed Musahars' requests that they be allowed to use loudspeakers during the commemoration of their legendary heroes Dina and Bhadri, although he allowed Rajputs and Kayasths to use similar devices during the celebration of their festivals.

With Lalu Yadav's ascension to power in Patna, some of the wealthier Yadavs became intimately associated with Janata Dal politicians, thereby compensating for their political marginalization within the panchayat. It was to them that the Musahars requesting for the use of loudspeakers turned for support. Joint petitions by Sargana's Musahars and Yadavs were instrumental in the interventions by Janata Dal politicians, which encouraged the Musahars to use loudspeakers during their commemorations. Likewise, when landless labourers of the Musahar, Dusadh and Yadav communities affiliated with the Communist Party of India (Marxist/ Leninist-Liberation) (CPI (M/L-L), a political party furthering the cause of militant parliamentary communism, began to occupy ceiling-surplus properties illegally held by the landlords, such Yadav politicians extended their tacit support to them and staved police retaliation.

However, such support was withdrawn the moment Yadav landlords holding ceiling-surplus properties were the target of the CPI(M/L-L) activists. Yadav peasants were particularly vindictive towards any trespass of their own properties, meting out such brutal punishments such as beatings, whippings and, in at least one recent case that is unlikely to have been exceptional, slashing the wrist of a nine-year old Musahar boy who a Yadav peasant alleged was stealing corn cobs from his farm. Their actions made the Yadav peasants unreliable allies from the point of view of the landless Musahar labourers, rendering the relationship between them a fraught one.

Partap Singh's control within his elected council was constantly challenged by his deputy Sarvesh Mandal. Matters came to a head after Partap Singh's death in 2000, when his son Hunny Singh inherited his mantle. Sarvesh Mandal opposed this claim on grounds that the Mukhya's post was a public position. Although Hunny Singh's claims evoked the consternation of his uncle, Neem Singh, the latter stood by him in the face of Sarvesh Mandal's challenge. The following year, when elections were held in the panchayat for the first time in 21 years, the electorate witnessed a three-cornered battle between the incumbent Mukhya Hunny Singh, the Yadav rich peasant Hiren Yadav, and the Kevat middle peasant Sarvesh Mandal. Although Hunny Singh won that election, his position was no longer as secure as his father's had once been. Not only had Hiren Yadav and Sarvesh Mandal posed to be formidable opponents, family disputes with his own uncle Neem Singh had become public.

In the 2006 elections, Sarvesh Mandal was elected Mukhya, winning nearly 45 per cent of the vote. Hiren Yadav came second, securing 29 per cent of the vote. The uncle and nephew, scions of the old *zamindar*, between them, received 27 per cent of the votes polled. In three out of 10 wards, Sargana wards 1, 4 and 5, the elected gram panchayat members confirmed their informal allegiance to Sarvesh Mandal. In three wards, successful gram panchayat members had expressed their support to Hiren Yadav, but were willing to work with Sarvesh Mandal after Hiren Yadav publicly acknowledged that he would offer his support to the new Mukhya. That left only four members of the gram panchayat, two Rajput and two Kayasth, who consistently opposed the Mukhya. As Mukhya, Sarvesh Mandal enjoyed wide, but far from absolute, support within the panchayat council and outside of it.

Table 3.10 reveals the patterns of membership in political parties among Sargana's population, disaggregated along land-size class. The census survey asked respondents about their membership in political parties although it did not probe the depth of involvement or the name or type of political party. The data suggests that nine of the 12 individuals with political party affiliations were marginal landowners, or farmers owning less than 2.5 *bighas* of land. A perusal of the data indicates that all 12 individuals were of the Savarna communities, either Rajput or Kayasth. The table also shows data from the sample survey to indicate that electoral participation remained consistent throughout the landowning hierarchy.

Table 3.10: Political participation in Sargana Ward 1, disaggregated along land-size class, percentages

	Data from Census Survey		Data from Sample Survey	
	Population	Political party membership	Population	Voting in PRI election
Landless	70	25	77	77
Marginal landowner	28	75	21	20
Small landowner	1.82	0	1.16	1.19
Medium landowner	0.61	0	1.16	1.19
Large landowner	0	0	0	0
	N= 161	N= 12	N= 86	N= 84

Source: Own surveys, 2009–10.

The making of a populist political place

Sargana's social relations of production were marked by many crisscrossing fissures and sutures. The precarious classes contested the entrenched classes' demands regarding the timing and modalities of paying ground rent. The labouring classes struggled against the precarious classes' attempts to depress and delay wages. They were also embroiled in contradictions with entrenched classes over the continuing practices of caste discrimination. The labouring classes and the precarious classes shared a common antipathy against the entrenched classes and coalesced together despite their mutual contradictions. Collective self-identifications as *majdur, kisan* and *zamindar* enabled people to forge distinct class identities.

Contests between the entrenched classes and the precarious classes characterized the social relations of distribution in Sargana. The precarious classes successfully challenged the authority of the entrenched classes in the gram panchayat as well as in six of its 10 wards. Although the entrenched classes remained in control of the remaining four wards, and were by no means subdued, the precarious classes shaped the polity in Sargana. The continued, if reduced, influence of the entrenched classes was a source of anxiety for the precarious classes. The precarious classes cultivated the support of the labouring poor, supporting selectively their claims against the entrenched classes. Their espousal of vocabularies of social equality provided the hinge on which the labouring poor could assert their own claims. Although they recognized that the precarious classes also practiced caste discrimination, the labouring classes cautiously aligned with the peasants and sharecroppers rather than larger landlords from the high status castes as the lesser of two evils. The result was a populist coalescing between the precarious classes and the labouring poor against the entrenched classes.

The ability of the poor and middle peasants, retailers and low paid professionals to coalesce with the labouring poor against landlords and capitalist farmers marked the locality's social relations of power. This populist coalescence anchored the negotiation between the locality's different classes. The poor acknowledged the peasants' role in challenging and undermining the hierarchical relationships perpetrated by entrenched landlords. However, their support to the peasants was careful because of their fear that the precarious classes sought to recreate, rather than annihilate, those hierarchies. Moreover, faultlines divided the precarious classes. The entanglements between and over classes demonstrate the overlapping contests and collaborations in the locality. As a populist political place, Sargana's polity was at best *shaped*, rather than controlled, by the precarious classes.

Ditya: A differentiated political place

The gram panchayat of which Ditya was a part comprised 15 wards in all. It was located, like Rahimpur, in West Bengal's Maldah district. According to the census conducted for this study, 326 households inhabited this ward. The ward was located north of Maldah town, approximately 15 kilometres to the east of the national highway that connects Kolkata with Guwahati. The nearest market, some three kilometres to the south, served as the bus stop for the ward's population. At the time of the fieldwork, the road from the highway to the market was severely potholed: a distance of 15 kilometres took about an hour to cover on public transport. Public transport usually meant 30 seater vans into and atop which men, women and children jostled for space with hens, goats and lambs. Services from the market to the highway were frequent though, which facilitated smooth travel to and from different locations that I needed to travel. During fieldwork, I lived alternately in the home of one of Ditya's most influential contractors and in his office in the market, a hub of gossip, business and intrigue in the locality.

Table 3.11 depicts Ditya's landholding structure in relation to its occupational diversity. The CPI(M)'s isolated success in the district in vesting ceiling-surplus land and subsequent redistribution considerably reduced the incidence of landlessness. Less than half of Ditya's population was landless. Less than a sixth of the landless hired out their labour primarily to local farmers and peasants, while a large proportion of them sought additional employment in Delhi and its suburbs to work in the construction sector. Others worked as labourers in the *chai* kiosks, eateries and shops selling trinkets, groceries and stationary items that dotted the nearby market. A few were itinerant vendors of vegetables, milk and fish, while some worked as cobblers, tailors and fishermen. It was not only the landless who complemented their agricultural labour with temporary migration or off-farm activities. Indeed, 35 per cent of itinerant migrants owned land up to 7.5 *bighas*. Off-farm activities for marginal, small and medium landowners included pig rearing, shopkeeping or working as sweepers, guards and cleaners in the local panchayat where they earned a meagre, though regular, salary. Farm labourers were paid through a combination of cash and kind, primarily food grains which they seem to have preferred. Their employers were usually the small, medium and large landowners of the ward, although it was not uncommon for marginal landowners to hire workers from time to time.

Table 3.11: Land and occupation, Ditya, December 2009

	Agriculture	Other casual	Artisanal	Business	Salaried	Total
Landless	20	89	4	15	0	131
Marginal landowner	75	26	1	3	1	108
Small landowner	42	17	0	4	2	68
Medium landowner	10	3	0	1	0	15
Large landowner	4	0	0	1	0	4
All	151	135	5	24	3	326

Source: Own census survey, 2009–10.

Ditya's diverse occupational structure was reflected across the landholding hierarchy. If at the base, the landless sought employment in a variety of occupations, at its apex, four of the five large landowners supplemented their agricultural incomes with other employment in public service and in contracting. My host, Phanindranath Sarkar, was a contractor whom friends and foes across Maldah district knew to be a shrewd businessman. His elder brother worked for the Land Revenue bureaucracy in nearby Adina town. His younger brother, Paresh Sarkar, was elected ward member between 2003 and 2008. Their cousin Shobhan Sarkar was a small-time contractor in the district. They were neighbours of Shashanka Sarkar, whose son worked as a clerk in the nearby high school, where his daughter-in-law taught.

The overlaps between Ditya's class structure and its landholding structure is evident from Table 3.12. Over 80 per cent of the landless and nearly 70 per cent of the marginal landowners worked as manual labourers. Manual labourers comprised 58 per cent of Ditya's population. They either exclusively hired out their labour, or complemented labouring for others with working on their own tiny plots of land and small-scale workshops or business units. They did not hire in any labour. By contrast, none of the four large landowners hired out their labour. Three of them managed their agricultural operations exclusively by recruiting workers, from within the village as well as from the neighbourhood: these families did not lease out their land at all. They and other labour-hiring peasants were Ditya's capitalist farmers who hired in labourers on payment of cash and in-kind wages but did not labour in any part of the production process themselves. They were not alone: Nearly 20 of the ward's 326 households relied exclusively on hired labour for their production activities.

The limits to such overlaps may also be noted. Among the locality's labour hirers, landless and marginal landowning households comprised half of all households. They operated shops where meat, fish and vegetables, and items of grocery were sold. Some established eateries in the market, where they hired local young men as waiters and older people as cooks, while they themselves managed accounts and entertained customers.

Table 3.12: Labour and land, Ditya, December 2009

	Landless	Marginal landowner	Small landowner	Medium landowner	Large landowner	Total
Manual workers	109	72	9	0	0	190
HO>HI, also self and family labour	13	26	18	1	0	58
HI>HO, also self and family labour	0	6	26	9	0	45
HI + self and family labour, no HO	0	0	0	4	1	5
HI only, neither self/ family labour, nor HO	6	4	6	1	3	20
All	131	108	68	15	4	326

Source: Own census survey, 2009–10.

Chart 3.3 reveals the overlaps between Ditya's labour-hiring structure and its different communities. Members of the Saotal community, who made up 52 per cent of the population, constituted 63 per cent of the locality's manual workers. Members of the Desiya community, at 28 per cent of the population, comprised 20 per cent of all manual workers. (with the possible exception of Pahadiyas) were over represented. The base of Ditya's class structure was socially quite heterogeneous. Unlike at the apex, where as many as 16 of the 20 families that exclusively exploited labour were Desiya. If the Desiyas were underrepresented at the base of the labour-hiring structure, they were overwhelmingly over represented at its apex.

Chart 3.3: Labour by caste in Ditya

					Moholi
					Paharia
					Sheikh
					Bind
					Saotal
					Desiya

MANUAL WORKERS | HO>HI, ALSO SELF & FAMILY LABOUR | HI>HO, ALSO SELF & FAMILY LABOUR | HI + SELF & FAMILY LABOUR, NO HO | HI ONLY, NEITHER SELF/ FAMILY LABOUR, NOR HO

Source: Own census survey, 2009–10.

The Desiya dominance of the apex of Ditya's class hierarchy appears to have little to do with the comminity's ritual status, which was rather tenuous. On the one hand, the Desiyas claimed to be 'cleaner' in comparison to communities such as Rajbanshis and Paliyas, signaling their integration into the caste hierarchy as self-styled 'clean castes'. (However, I also noted that whenever members of the Desiya community claimed 'clean-caste' status, such claims were immediately dismissed by members of Ditya's other communities.) On the other hand, informal conversations with a number of young Desiya men revealed that many households had in fact obtained SC certificates in order to access the provisions of protective discrimination instituted by the Indian government. Many of my interlocutors from the Desiya community reminded me that their rituals pertaining to key life events differed from that of the Brahmans and other self-styled 'high castes' with whom the Brahmans engaged in commensal relations. The institution of the Dashavali (or Committee of 10), headed by a *morol* (headman), provided Desiyas with platforms for deliberating communal matters without deferring to the authority of other communities such as Brahmans. The Desiyas' social precariousness was exacerbated by their relatively low literacy levels, indicating their limited access to educational facilities and public sector employment. Literacy rates for the Paliyas, with whom the Desiyas are enumerated in the Indian Census, are far lower (40 per cent in 2001) as compared to the West Bengal average (68 per cent).[10] The social precariousness of the Desiyas was, nevertheless, mitigated by the dominance within the locality enjoyed by some members of their community due to their being hirers of labour.

Such sources of mitigation were not available to members of other communities, such as the Saotals. The Saotal community is classified by the Indian government as ST in recognition of the specific forms of marginalization and vulnerabilities to which its members have historically been subjected. Literacy rates among the Saotals (43 per cent) are comparable with those of the Paliyas, although still far behind the State average.[11] Their educational backwardness, some of my interlocutors from the community reminded me, did not entail any kind of social subservience to any other community at any time in history. The Saotals were not a caste and never had been, they emphasized. The Saotals' communal institutions led by the Majhi Haram provided them with the occasion to deliberate on communal matters without deferring to anybody else. However, I could not help noting during conversations with some among my Desiya interlocutors that they stereotyped Saotals as thick-headed. 'If a truck runs over a Saotal's chicken, the Saotal will refuse the compensation and ask for the chicken back,' were among the proverbs which I heard Desiyas use to describe the alleged stupidity of the members of the Saotal community. Others tended to be patronizing and espoused the language of 'protecting' the Saotals, often from their own religious beliefs and social customs. Elders of the Desiya community publicly – and with ostensibly good intentions – downgraded Saotal practices of worship and healing. Augmenting the Saotals' social marginalization was their over-representation at the lower end of the landholding hierarchy. Table 3.13 corroborates this point by highlighting the extent to which Saotals were over represented among the landless and marginal landowners. Only one of the four large landowners in the ward was Saotal. None of the ward's other communities were represented in the 10 land-rich households of the village.

Table 3.13: Land and caste, Ditya, December 2009

	Saotal	Desiya	Bind	Sheikh	Paharia	Moholi	Total
Landless	62	28	19	7	5	7	132
Marginal landowner	75	24	0	1	3	0	105
Small landowner	28	26	1	0	12	0	68
Medium landowner	4	9	1	0	1	0	15
Large landowner	1	3	0	0	0	0	4
All	170	90	21	8	21	7	326

Source: Own census survey, 2009–10.

Social relations of production: The precarious classes against the labouring poor

Manual workers of Ditya's different communities faced several deprivations, insecurities and vulnerabilities. Table 3.14 indicates the extent to which agricultural wages were repressed in the locality. Manual workers shared their general precariousness with a number of the small and marginal landowners whose labour was exploited by others but who also exploited labour. But while Ditya's Desiya labourers could lay claim on communal obligations of their Desiya employers via the Dashavali, labourers of other communities could not. Executives of the Dashavali suggested that several deliberations they convened pertained to labour disputes between Desiya employers and Desiya labourers. In such disputes, Dashavali executives maintained that they weighed in on the side of the labourers, and compensated the employers by dipping into the committee's incomes from the mango orchards and ponds they leased in or owned. They also reported that the major heads on which they incurred expenditures over the previous three years included the organization of communal feasts, providing subsistence to impoverished and destitute Desiya families, and provisioning of electric connections to every Desiya home that wanted it. Although labourers of other communities could lay similar claims on employers from their own communities, the relative absence of Saotals and others from the higher echelons of the labour and landholding hierarchy made such claims practically redundant.

Indeed, communal differences were less pronounced at the top of the hierarchy where Desiyas form the overwhelming majority of the hirers of labour, and where Saotal employers often made common cause with Desiya employers rather than Saotal labourers. The labouring poor of Ditya's different communities shared at best ambivalent solidarities with one another that were marked by mutual mistrust and suspicion. To be sure, Desiya labourers' relations with Desiya employers were far from cordial. But Desiya labourers also sought to distance themselves from their Saotal co-workers in order to emphasize their worth to their Desiya employers. It was common, I gathered from informal conversations, for Saotal labourers to work for Desiya farmers, but not for Desiya workers to serve Saotal employers.

Table 3.14: Agricultural wages in Ditya,
State-level and locality-level wages compared

Month	State-level prevailing wages (₹) (2)	Locality-specific wages (₹) (3)
January 2009	78/71 (Aman harvest)	60
February 2009	81/72 (Boro transplant)	45
April 2009	80/71 (Boro harvest)	70
July 2009	85/76 (Aman transplant)	50
January 2010	85/70 (Aman harvest)	70
February 2010	87/71 (Boro transplant)	50
April 2010	91/74 (Boro harvest)	70

Sources: Column 2: For January/ February/ April 2009: Labour Bureau (2010, Tables 9a, 10a and 12a respectively); For July 2009: Labour Bureau (2011, Table 3a); For January/ February/ April 2010: Labour Bureau (2012, Tables 9a, 10a and 12a respectively). Columns 3: Field notes and observations.

Labour-hiring peasants who directly engaged in agricultural operations identified themselves, and were described by others as, *chasis*. They emphasized their stability, while reminding me of the autonomy they supposedly enjoyed because of working on their own plots of land. Many recalled their family history of personal cultivation, their chests swelling with pride as they did so. They highlighted the experience of toil and sweat that defined their collective identity as *chasis* and distinguished them from the gentrified *bhadralok*. A number of peasants with whom I spoke emphatically denied aspiring to *bhadralok* status, even when they or their family members had attained education. Although they did seek to reduce their personal involvement in manual work because of the arduous conditions associated with it, many of my interlocutors took pride in being *chasi*, and hoped that their children too would take to agriculture even after attaining the highest levels of education that they could.

However, many impoverished *chasis* actually toiled on the farms of other *chasis*. This experience threatened their collective self-identification as unencumbered cultivators of the land. Their labouring for other peasants blurred the putative distinction between peasants and labourers, or *chasis* and *majurs*. As labourers, *majurs* depended on peasants, entrepreneurs and artisans for work. Their dependence rendered them an unstable social collective, responding to employment opportunities. *Chasis* sought to maintain a social distance from the *majurs*. Such social distance was relatively easy to maintain at the apex of the class hierarchy, but not so among middle and poor peasants. Communal differences assumed importance, particularly for Desiya middle peasants who sought to increase their social distance from labourers of all communities. Desiya middle and poor peasants who combined the use of family labour with hiring themselves out and recruiting workers asserted their identity as *chasis* and emphasized their solidarity with peasants who mostly, if not exclusively, hired labour. Such labour-hiring peasants tended to be of the Desiya community. Precarious though the fortunes of even the most land-endowed *chasis* were, such middle Desiya peasants struggled to identify themselves with 'rich' peasants rather than with the vulnerabilities of labourers.

Middle and poor peasants of other communities underscored their collective identities as *majurs*. So did manual workers of all communities, their mutual misgivings notwithstanding. The idea of poverty as deriving from the experience of labouring for other people was pervasive among them. They distinguished themselves from people who sustained themselves and their families through agriculture, salaried employment and business. Many middle peasants insisted that anybody who had to work for other people, irrespective of whether they hired *out* more labour than they hired in, was poor. Their insistence rendered the term *gorib* very slippery. The contradictory self-identifications of being poor problematized the already ambivalent distinctions between peasants and labourers.

Despite the mutual disagreements over poverty, labourers and peasants concurred that they were both socially distinct from the three capitalist farmers who supplemented agricultural incomes with incomes from salaries and business. To be sure, such families were not described as 'Big Men' or *bodolok* as they were in Rahimpur. But their success in using their control over the panchayats to develop contacts in the district and improve their economic conditions was widely appreciated. The experience of these families illustrated the ongoing differentiation among the peasantry. Nevertheless, while these three families experienced upward economic mobility, they remained socially embedded among the Desiya peasantry. They were sensitive to the fact that the political influence which had helped them improve their economic condition derived from the social support of the Desiya rich and middle peasants. Such families emphasized their rootedness in the peasantry. While quietly expressing their embarrassment at what they considered to be anachronistic lifestyles, they balked at any suggestion that the peasantry was a burden on the economy.

The labour-hiring peasants of the Desiya community constituted the locality's precarious classes, while the capitalist farmers who increasingly relied on incomes from salaries and businesses comprised its entrenched classes. Middle and poor peasants of the Saotal community as well as the manual workers of all communities made up Ditya's labouring classes. Manual workers perceived labour-hiring peasants, artisan and entrepreneurs – precarious though their surplus and status were – as their exploiters. But, as the following section illustrates, they also possessed a shared history of solidarity.

Social relations of distribution: A polity controlled by precarious classes

Shared memories of solidarities emanated from the collective action by sharecroppers and agricultural labourers against their common oppressor, the Muchia based landlord until the 1960s. The landlord's sharecroppers were often Desiya, while the agricultural labourers on his estate were Saotal. The sharecroppers provided enthusiastic support to the CPI(M) when the party first emerged in the region under the leadership of a Desiya activist based in nearby Gajole. Shashanka Sarkar and his protégé Motaram Sarkar, then young men from marginal sharecropper families, were among the earliest to join the CPI(M). They remained unswerving supporters through the tumultuous decade from 1967 to 1977. In 1978, a year after the Left Front Government's accession to power in the State, the CPI(M) won the panchayat elections. Shashanka Sarkar was elected the Vice-President. Together, he and the President (who was resident in another ward) not only implemented the tenancy reforms but also set about vesting the *zamindar's* ceiling-surplus land, and redistributing it among the landless population. The CPI(M) was exceptionally successful in effecting the redistribution of land in a district that remained a Congress bastion throughout the 34 years of Left rule. As a result of the successful redistribution of land, the political influence of the *zamindar* and his minions in the panchayat was decimated.

Shashanka Sarkar was subsequently elected Pradhan of the panchayat, and Motaram Sarkar became the party's secretary. Although the two men continued to be directly involved in agricultural operations on their own farms, they and other CPI(M) politicians acquired properties, benefitted from tenancy reforms and improved the economic conditions of their families. From marginal sharecroppers serving exploitative landlords, CPI(M) politicians gradually became rich and middle peasants. The complete control of the CPI(M) machinery in the hands of the rich and middle peasants, primarily of the Desiya community, lent a communal complexion to the programme of land reforms. The CPI(M) leadership kept its promise of redistributing land to landless members of all communities. Further, they depicted their actions as 'thanksgiving' to the Saotals for the latter's help during the occupations. The accompanying narrative was that the Desiyas had 'led' and the Saotals had 'followed', the Desiyas had 'planned' and the Saotals had 'executed'. While my interlocutors from all communities were categorical that they were 'all in it together' (*aamra shobai ek shonge chhilam*), the division of intellectual labour was discernible. As far as the Desiya leadership of the CPI(M) could see, the redistribution of land titles was an appropriate gesture in return for the sacrifices the Saotals had made. In return, the Saotal elders were particularly warm in their appreciation of the CPI(M)'s action. During my interviews with them, they recorded their gratitude. The Majhi Haram, an elder of the Saotal community, told one of his nephews in Neechu Pada in my presence:

> Shashankada came as a deity (debota). We would have been nowhere without him. He would always ask about us, and care for us. He made sure where were not excluded [from the land redistribution]. The Desiyas have done a lot for us. We should be very grateful for all that they have done. We should help them

in whatever we can, not make their life difficult by asking for more and more.

Indeed, the CPI(M)'s Desiya leadership made assiduous attempts to enumerate Saotal and other Adivasi households eligible to receive land and implemented the legislation. They sought the support of and information from the elders of the different Adivasi communities. The support of the elders greatly facilitated the transmission of information and found favour as a model to govern the widely dispersed ward. Such support was crucial in managing discontent that arose from time to time over the allocation of targeted welfare schemes or failure of this or that programme. Many of Ditya's senior CPI(M) politicians possessed reputations of honesty and integrity. Their selection of beneficiaries in line with the official policies of targeting often created resentment because they invariably excluded many more people than they included. But the support they cultivated from among the Adivasi elders insulated them from popular anger.

The leadership of the CPI(M) remained unchallenged from 1978 till about 2003.That its formal control lay in the hands of select rich peasant families lent it a high degree of coherence. The Congress leadership, which began to register resurgence during the last decade, also drew upon the very same families for its leadership. For instance, its leading light in Ditya was CPI(M) veteran Shashanka Sarkar's half-brother Sasaram Sarkar. The contractor Phanindranath Sarkar was a Congress financier. His younger brother Paresh Sarkar was the CPI(M)-affiliated ward member from 2003 to 2008. Paresh Sarkar's father-in-law was Motaram Sarkar, the Secretary of Ditya's CPI(M), whom we met earlier. Congress leaders also sought to cultivate the support of the sons or nephews of the Saotal and other Adivasi elders to cultivate support.

The rich peasant leadership of both political parties remained socially embedded in a milieu where middle peasants exercised effective influence. The three capitalist farmer households originated in these very families. Given the influence of rich and middle peasants over both the political parties, the possibility of the labouring poor obtaining a political voice appeared remote indeed. The similarities between the two parties led one of my interlocutors from among the Desiya poor to comment, 'Their rivalry is for us. In the night they share everything, including….(expletives).' The Saotal poor were even less hopeful of their voices being heard.

Table 3.15 reveals the patterns of membership in political parties among Ditya's population, disaggregated along land-size class. The specificity of the survey instrument was focussed on information about membership in political parties and did not probe the depth of involvement or the name or type of political party they supported. The table shows that over a third of the locality's households have at least one member of the family affiliated with a political party. Medium and small landowners (those owning between 7.5 *bighas* and 30 *bighas* of land) obtained membership in political parties in excess of their share of the population. Political party membership tapered off at the lower end of the landholding hierarchy. Saotals and Desiyas were proportionately represented. The table also shows data from the sample survey to indicate that electoral participation in the gram panchayat remained consistent throughout the landowning hierarchy.

Table 3.15: Political participation in Ditya, disaggregated along land-size class, percentages

	Data from Census Survey		Data from Sample Survey	
	Population	Political party membership	Population	Voting in PRI election
Landless	40	30	42	42
Marginal landowner	33	19	31	31
Small landowner	21	41	23	22
Medium landowner	4.60	9	3.36	3.39
Large landowner	1.23	1.85	0.84	0.85
	N=326	N= 108	N= 119	N= 118

When Ditya ward was 'reserved' for a woman from among the STs during the panchayat election of 2008, the labouring poor from among the Adivasis harboured vague hopes that their voice would finally find representation in the polity. However, although rival candidates were both agricultural labourers from Adivasi communities, they were selected by the rich peasant leadership of the two political parties. The CPI(M) candidate, Shyamoli Hasda was an agricultural labourer: her husband Madan Hembrom was handpicked by Mota Sarkar as a reliable man (*Bhalo chhele*, Mota Sarkar told me). The candidate of the Congress Party, Teji Hasda was a marginal landowner. Ditya's Congress leaders identified her husband Honinh Hembrom, a cousin of Madan's, as the most pliable. Shyamoli Hasda secured 53 per cent of the votes polled, scraping the CPI(M) to victory. However, neither she nor her husband could assert their autonomy of the control exercised by Mota Sarkar and other rich peasant politicians of the CPI(M). In turn, Mota Sarkar could not assert his autonomy from the middle peasants who were so crucial to his political role. Even with a member of the labouring class elected as the ward member, Ditya's polity remained firmly under the control of the rich and middle peasants.

The making of a differentiated political place

Social relations of production in Ditya were sharply differentiated. Such differentiation framed the negotiation between and within the locality's different classes. The engagements between the classes reflected engagements over their constitution. Although the precarious classes and the entrenched classes enjoyed a compact, their relations with the labouring poor were characterized by ambiguous contradictions. Whereas labouring classes struggled with precarious classes over the payment and timeliness of wages, they noted the role of the precarious classes in dislodging the landlords. The entrenched classes lent their public support to the precarious classes in recognition of the close kinship links, although they were not averse to expressing their exasperation at what they perceived to be their kinsmen's clinging to outmoded ways of life. The labouring classes confronted a coalescence of the precarious and the entrenched classes, led by the former.

The precarious classes dominated the social relations of distribution in Ditya. They decimated the power of the entrenched classes associated with the *zamindars*. The emergent capitalist farmers willingly accepted the leadership of Desiya rich and middle peasants. Precarious class politicians in turn used their control over panchayat resources to allocate resources as they deemed appropriate. To be sure, several of their decisions were favourable to the labouring poor. But they excluded the labouring poor from the decision making process itself, leaving no one in doubt as to who set the agenda in the panchayat.

The resultant differentiation between the precarious classes and the labouring poor marked the social relations of power in Ditya. The peasants considered themselves as having liberated the locality from the thrall of the landlords. With this view, the labouring poor consented. Ditya's rich and middle peasants appropriated the levers of authority in the panchayat. This was amply demonstrated by the influence they exerted over the contestants in the 2008 panchayat elections, both of whom were agricultural labourers selected for their perceived pliability. Fault-lines among them arising out of different political party affiliations notwithstanding, the precarious classes remained tightly knit, lending stability to Ditya's polity. Their political practices illustrated the ways in which social identities inflected class politics. As a differentiated political place, Ditya's polity was *controlled*, rather than shaped, by the precarious classes.

Roshanar Ward 5: A paternalistic political place

Roshanar gram panchayat, located in Bihar's Araria district, comprised a total of 15 wards. The census for this study suggested that 161 households lived in it. The ward was located approximately five kilometres north of the block headquarters, three kilometres west of the State highway, which connects Araria to Forbesganj. It was served by a market nearly two kilometers to the east, on the highway. During the first round of fieldwork, a mud path connected the ward to the market. During subsequent visits, I noted that a tar road had been laid. Public transport comprised matadors, which plied regularly on the path, navigating the stones that littered it as best as they could. During the fieldwork, I alternated between Sargana, located three kilometers west (across the highway) and Roshanar where I lived in the house of a Kunjra Muslim peasant Kamruz Alam.

Table 3.16 illustrates Roshanar Ward 5's landholding structure in relation to its occupational diversity. Almost 80 per cent of Roshanar's population was landless. 17 per cent of the landless hired out their labour chiefly to local farmers and peasants, while a huge proportion sought additional employment outside the village. Favoured destinations included Delhi and its suburbs where they worked in the construction sector and as tailors, butchers and assistants to shopkeepers. Others found employment locally, in and around Roshanar, as plumbers, cobblers, mechanics and autorickshaw drivers. Some were itinerant hawkers selling vegetables, meat, trinkets and bangles, and toys. Additional to the landless, a tiny number of marginal landowners too complemented their agricultural labour with temporary migration. Only seven households derived their incomes entirely from off-farm activities: they included artisans such as tailors, potters and carpenters. No household in the village was involved in either business or salaried employment. Farm labourers were paid through a combination of cash and kind, mostly food grains, which seem to have been preferred. Their employers were usually the small, medium and large landowners of the ward, although it was not uncommon for marginal landowners to hire in workers. Roshanar's occupational profile was diverse at the base but narrow at the apex. At the base, the landless sought employment in a variety of occupations. But at higher levels, few households engaged in any occupation other than agriculture.

Table 3.16: Land and occupation, Roshanar Ward 5, December 2009

	Agriculture	Other casual	Artisanal	Business	Salaried	Total
Landless	22	99	6	0	0	127
Marginal landowner	14	6	1	0	0	20
Small landowner	8	0	0	0	0	8
Medium landowner	2	0	0	0	0	2
Large landowner	2	0	0	0	0	2
All	48	105	7	0	0	161

Source: Own census survey, 2009–10.

Roshanar's labour-hiring structure overlapped quite considerably with its landholding structure. Table 3.17 illustrates this overlap. Each one of the landless households and two-thirds of the marginal landowners worked as manual labourers. Manual labourers comprised 90 per cent of Roshanar's population. They either exclusively hired out their labour, or complemented labouring for others with working on their own miniscule plots of land and small-scale workshops or business units. They did not hire in any labour. By contrast, none of the four medium and large landowners hired out their labour. Further, only one large landowner, Gajdeo Mandal, managed his agricultural operations exclusively by recruiting workers, from within the village as well as from the neighbourhood. Gajdeo Mandal was Roshanar's sole capitalist farmer hiring in labourers on payment of cash and in-kind wages. Although his intimate knowledge of agricultural practices had been recognized by the State government, which conferred upon him at least one prestigious award for excelling in farming techniques, he no longer engaged in any part of the agricultural process himself.

Table 3.17: Labour and land, Roshanar Ward 5, December 2009

	Landless	Marginal landowner	Small landowner	Medium landowner	Large landowner	Total
Manual workers	127	14	2	0	0	143
HO>HI, also self and family labour	0	7	1	0	0	8
HI>HO, also self and family labour	0	0	5	0	0	5
HI + self and family labour, no HO	0	0	0	2	1	3
HI only, neither self/ family labour, nor HO	0	0	0	0	1	1
All	127	21	8	2	2	160

Source: Own census survey, 2009–10.

Chart 3.4 reveals the overlaps between Roshanar's labour-hiring structure and its different communities. Members of the Kunjra community, who made up 77 per cent of the population, constituted 80 per cent of the locality's manual workers. Members of the Gangot community, at 22 per cent of the population, comprised 20 per cent of all manual workers. Although the base of Roshanar Ward 5's class structure reflected the communal diversity of the ward, the apex was too narrow to do so. The sole family that exclusively exploited labour was Gangot, as were two of the three families which combined labour-hiring with deployment of their own family labour. While the differences between the two communities were not too stark, the presence of Gangots, rather than Kunjra, at the apex of the class hierarchy tended to tip the scales considerably in the favour of the former.

Chart 3.4: Labour by caste in Roshanar Ward 5

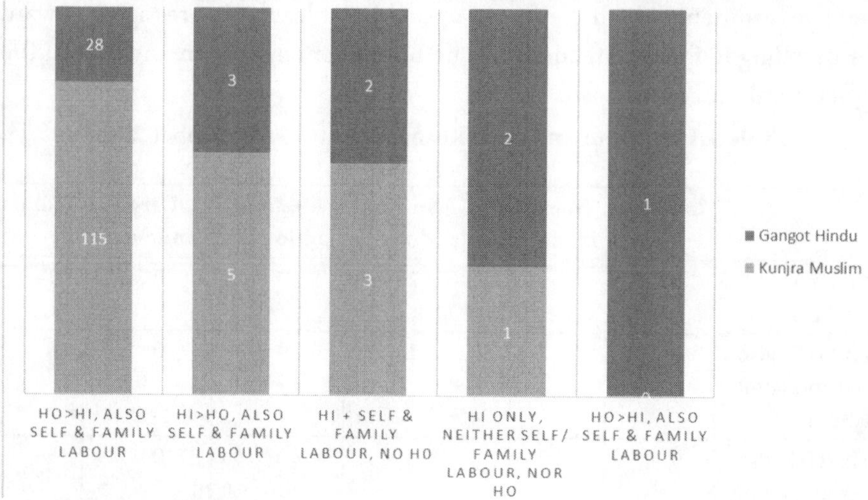

Legend:
- ■ Gangot Hindu
- ■ Kunjra Muslim

Bar labels (Gangot Hindu / Kunjra Muslim values):
- HO>HI, ALSO SELF & FAMILY LABOUR: 28 / 115
- HI>HO, ALSO SELF & FAMILY LABOUR: 3 / 5
- HI + SELF & FAMILY LABOUR, NO HO: 2 / 3
- HI ONLY, NEITHER SELF/ FAMILY LABOUR, NOR HO: 2 / 1
- HO>HI, ALSO SELF & FAMILY LABOUR: 1

Source: Own survey, 2009-10.

The dominance of the Gangots in the labour hierarchy stood at odds with their ritual status in the hierarchy of castes. Their neighbours considered them to be Shudra, citing their putative origin among the boatmen who plied across the river Ganga. The State government classified them as EBC, indicating their relatively 'low' social and educational status in comparison with other Shudra communities. However, Gangots claimed to be 'cleaner' not only in comparison to so-called 'untouchables' but also other cognate Shudra communities such as the Kevats. Such claims signalled their integration into the caste hierarchy as self-styled 'clean castes'.

Wealthy Gangots such as Gajdeo Mandal organized regular devotional gatherings called *satsangs,* to which local notables including politicians, landlords, bureaucrats, contractors, rich farmers and businessmen were invited. At these *satsangs,* Gajedeo Mandal hosted preachers of the Radhasoami sect who delivered lectures and led the collective chanting of hymns. *Satsangs* were accompanied by communal vegetarian feasts, or *bhandaras,* at which villagers of all stations were invited. Gajdeo Manda's *bhandaras* were popular among his neighbours in Roshanar Ward 5. They earned him the title of the Gangot community's *mahant,* to refer to his religious commitments. His *satsangs* and *bhandaras* did much to enhance not only Gajdeo Mandal's personal reputation but also the social status of the Gangots as a community. At the same time, the sobriquet of *mahant* did not imply that Gajdeo Mandal was a saint with an otherworldly disposition. Far from it, Gajdeo Mandal was considered the epitome of a *grihasth*, a householder who took his familial and social obligations seriously. Members of other communities accepted the Gangots' 'clean-caste' claims. Kayasth and Rajput bureaucrats at the Block level referred to Gajdeo Mandal, to 'his people' and the Gangot community in general as respectable people (*ijjatdar samaj*).

Such respectability was denied to the Kunjra Muslims. As a community associated with vegetable vending, they were disparaged as 'low-status' by the Ashraf Muslims of the surrounding regions. Inter-marriage between Ashraf and Kunjra Muslims were unheard of, and some of my Kunjra interlocutors complained that even their burial grounds were separate. Their Gangot neighbours loathed them for their dietary practices, especially their occasional consumption of meat. Gajdeo Mandal was visibly distressed during our first interview when I informed him that Kamruz Alam was hosting me. I noted that while he did not prevent his Kunjra neighbours from entering his house, the Kunjra were served *chai* in glass cups, while the rest of us (Gangots, Kayasths and Ashraf Muslims) were served in more expensive steel cups. Within a few days of acquaintance with me, Gajdeo Mandal told me, in the presence of his Gangot neighbours, that he despised the Kunjra. The word he used was *grhina*, indicating revulsion. His neighbours added that the Kunjra were 'dirty people'. Exacerbating the Kunjras' social marginalization was their over-representation at the lower end of the landholding hierarchy. Table 3.18 corroborates this point by highlighting the extent to which Kunjras were overrepresented among the landless. On the other hand, none of the large or medium-sized landowners in the ward was Kunjra.

Table 3.18: Land and caste, Roshanar Ward 5, December 2009

	Kunjra Muslim	Gangot Hindu	Total
Landless	106	22	128
Marginal landowner	16	9	25
Small landowner	4	3	7
Medium landowner	0	1	1
Large landowner	0	0	0
All	125	36	161

Source: Own census survey, 2009–10.

Social relations of production: An entrenched-precarious coalition against the poor

Manual workers of Roshanar's different caste-communities shared with one another several deprivations, insecurities and vulnerabilities. Table 3.19 provides an indication of the wages they earned for agricultural operations. Small and marginal landowners whose labour was exploited by others and who exploited labour also faced similar vulnerabilities. But Gangot labourers sought to distance themselves from Kunjra labourers in order to demonstrate their social worth to their employers. They could lay claim on communal obligations of their Gangot employers. As *mahant* of his community, Gajdeo Mandal was frequently called upon by Gangot employers and labourers to resolve disagreements over wages.

Table 3.19: Agricultural wage rates in Roshanar Ward 1, State-level and locality-level wages compared

Month	State-level prevailing wages (₹) (2)	Locality-specific wages (₹) (3)
April 2009	73/67 (Wheat harvest)	40
July 2009	81/70 (Paddy transplant)	30–35
September 2009	85/76 (Jute harvest)	60
November 2010	83/78 (Paddy harvest)	40
April 2010	91/74 (Wheat harvest)	40–50

Source: Column 2: For April 2009: Labour Bureau (2010, Table 12a); For July/November 2009: Labour Bureau (2011, Table 3a and 7a respectively); For April 2010: Labour Bureau (2012, Table 12a). Columns 3: Field notes and observations.

Gajdeo Mandal told me that on such occasions, he would try and work out a compromise that did not affect peasant's profits nor pushed the labourer to discontentment. While reminding the employers of their obligations towards their labourers, he would also ask the labourers to view their employers as their guardians. Where disputes proved to be intractable, Gajdeo Mandal's neighbours reported that their *mahant* would personally extend a small grant to the labourers to help them and to potentially reduce any ill-will they might harbour towards peasants. Kunjra labourers could potentially lay similar claims on their Kunjra employer. But few Kunjra Muslims hired labour to begin with. While Gangot labourers' relations with their Gangot employers were by no means cordial, they assiduously distanced themselves from their Kunjra co-workers. While it was common for Kunjra labourers to work for Gangot farmers, the obverse – Gangot workers serving Kunjra employers – was less so.

Most labour-hiring peasants who also took part in agricultural operations described themselves, and were described by others, as *kisans*. They highlighted their dependability. As peasants, they upheld the perspective that their working their own plots of land bolstered their autonomy. The Gangot peasants recalled with sparkles in their eyes their family history of personal cultivation. Ideas of hard work shaped their collective identity as peasants. But they consciously sought to emulate the lifestyles and practices of *grihasts* such as Gajdeo Mandal. For a number of peasants, Gajdeo Mandal provided the perfect role model of a *grihasth*. His agricultural property was well managed without him having to manually labour on his farm. His intimate knowledge of agricultural practices won him accolades from the State government. He was well connected with the members of the agricultural product marketing board. Not only that, he was educated up to senior school and took an active interest, as member of the Village Education Committee, in the educational attainments of Ward 5's children. He was widely networked in the local bureaucracy. Perhaps most importantly, he was highly regarded by the wealthiest landlords of the region. One such landlord was the Congress politician Pritam Singh, who had acquired the reputation of being *dabang*, the usual epithet for an oppressor. Pritam Singh lived in the adjacent Roshanar Ward 7 but had sharecroppers and agricultural labourers servicing him from elsewhere in Roshanar and beyond.

The aspiration among some of Roshanar's *kisans* towards becoming *grihasth* rudely clashed against the material reality of their being labourers for other *kisans*. This materiality threatened the primary identity of labouring peasants as free cultivators of the land. Their experience of labouring for other peasants blurred the putative distinction between peasants and labourers, or *kisans* and *majdurs*. As labourers, *majdurs* depended on labour-hiring peasants and farmers for work. Their dependence made them appear fickle to both *kisans* and *grihasts*. *Kisans* sought to maintain a social distance from the *majdurs*. Communal differences assumed salience for the maintenance of such distinction, especially for Gangot peasants who sought to increase their social distance from labourers. Even Gangot peasants who hired out more labour than they hired in asserted their identity as *kisans* and emphasized their solidarity with the very same peasants who exploited their labour. A large number of such labour hirers were middle peasants of the Gangot community. They in turn aspired to *grihasth* status, an aspiration that was expressed by Gangot labourers as well.

Roshanar Ward 5's few Kunjra peasants on the other hand identified with the labourers from their community. A number of my interlocutors from these classes suggested that people who lived by hiring their labour to other people (*majduri karne wale*) were poor, or *garib aadmi*. They distinguished themselves from people who sustained themselves and their families through agriculture. The term *garib* also proved notoriously slippery, as many middle peasants of the Gangot community insisted that anybody who had to hire out their labour, irrespective of whether they hired *out* more labour than they hired in, was poor. Such ideas of collective self-hood complicated the already ambivalent distinctions between peasants and labourers.

Disagreements over being poor notwithstanding, labourers and peasants concurred that *grihasth* farmers such as Gajdeo Mandal provided the role model for them. Such families were not described as landlords, who continued to be known as *zamindars*. But *grihasths* were known for their social proximity to the *zamindars*. They had also substantially improved their own economic and social status because of low interest loans extended to them by the *zamindar* in addition to what subsidized loans offered by the public sector banks. *Grihasths* such as Gajdeo Mandal developed a reputation for their ability to leverage key contacts in the bureaucracy and the judiciary to solve common problems. Although the *grihasths* did not identify with the *zamindar*, they publicly acknowledged the latter's alleged magnanimity.

Grihasth families took care to provide cheap loans to *kisans* as the occasion arose, for example to meet the costs associated with life-cycle ceremonies, purchase property or to meet health related expenditure. For this, they did not expect any repayment. Such steps made *grihasths* objects of deep gratitude of peasants, just as they themselves expressed their gratitude to the landlords. Networks of gratitude knit peasants, capitalist farmers and landlords closely together. Peasants and farmers remained beholden to landlords such as Pritam Singh, even if they did not envisage transforming into landlords themselves. Consequently, they took care to keep the landlords in good humour. Although the peasants and farmers considered themselves distinct from the landlords, they accorded him the status of their guardians. Such self-identifications among the peasants and farmers lent weight to the relative influence of Roshanar's landlords.

The landlords and farmers insisted that peasants deserved help more than labourers. Unlike labourers who 'merely' obeyed instructions, peasants took risks. The landlords and farmers further distinguished between the deserving labourer from the undeserving ones and took the former under their guardianship. Deserving labourers were hardworking, thrifty, religious, and possessed 'clean' personal habits – abstinence from alcohol, meat-eating and promiscuous sexual relationships. They were deferential and courteous, unlike undeserving labourers. Undeserving labourers were shirkers, profligate, irreligious, and indulged in drinking, meat-eating, and wanton sexual encounters. Gajdeo Mandal told me of the many deserving labourers he had helped, but maintained that he and other responsible people had a duty to discipline the callous, wayward and insolent. It was sometimes the case that labourers were more deserving of help than peasants because of their impeccable behaviour, in which case such labourers were held up as exemplars. Most of the labourers Gajdeo Mandal identified as deserving of help were Gangot. The Kunjras, whose meat-eating practices he reviled as filthy, were excluded.

Capitalist farmers such as Gajdeo Mandal, upheld family values, propagated 'clean-caste' practices and derived their income from market exchange of their agricultural produce. They also recognized landlords such as Pritam Singh as their guardians because of the financial and social support they received. This analysis suggests that people such as Pritam Singh and Gajedeo Mandal comprised Roshanar's entrenched classes and were recognized as leaders by the precarious classes. Middle and poor peasants of both Gangot and Kunjra communities constituted the locality's precarious classes. The entrenched classes appropriated to themselves the role of guardians for the locality's rich and middle peasants who they helped from time to time. Manual labourers from all communities made up Roshanar's labouring classes. The landlords, farmers and peasants sought to isolate the 'undeserving labourers' deemed unworthy of their support from the 'deserving labourers' who they considered helping. The others were absorbed in a paternalistic framework marked by shared solidarities between the entrenched and the precarious classes against the labouring poor.

Social relations of distribution: A polity controlled by entrenched classes

The humble origins of Roshanar's labour-hiring farmers and peasants were well-known. Gajdeo Mandal's father, his neighbours recounted, was a sharecropper for the-then most influential landlord of the region, Pritam Singh's father. When the land ceiling laws were finally implemented towards the end of the 1960s, the landlord began to parcel away small tracts of his land in the name of trusted people, including tenants, sharecroppers, ploughmen and bodyguards, even as he registered the huge bulk of his property in the names of his relatives and friends to evade detection. Gajdeo Mandal's father was an early beneficiary of the landlord's act of self-preservation. Gajdeo Mandal continued to be a sharecropper for the landlord's son, Pritam Singh, although he now purchased scattered plots of land the landlord's family sold in the market. Publicly and privately deferential towards Pritam Singh, Gajdeo Mandal ensured that he paid his rents on time, and was instrumental in persuading other sharecroppers to do the same. As Pritam Singh entered politics on a Congress ticket, Gajdeo Mandal became one of his most trusted advisors. That he personally kept aloof from party politics added to his aura of a perfect *grihasth*. His reputation remained untainted, despite his association with such *dabang* characters as Pritam Singh.

In 1978, elections were held in the gram panchayat, as elsewhere in Bihar. Pritam Singh was elected as Mukhya unopposed, just as his Congress-affiliated father had been. He was enthusiastically supported by his network of sharecroppers, musclemen and ploughmen, who further ensured that their economic and social dependents voted for him. Gajdeo Mandal was instrumental in drumming up support for Pritam Singh among the locality's Gangots and Kunjras. Pritam Singh continued his father's policy of appropriating panchayat resources to reward his coterie of supporters as well as the political mediators who had brokered electoral support for him. He ignored the claims of the peasants and agricultural labourers of the Kevats, Dusadh and Musahar communities. Encouraged by activists of leftwing parties such as the CPI(M/L-L), they began to oppose his political and economic dominance. One immediate consequence of Pritam Singh's targeting resources to Gajdeo Mandal and his Gangot and Kunjra neighbours was the deepening of *their* gratitude towards him. A second consequence was the growing antipathy among the radicalizing members of the oppressed communities towards the recipients of Pritam Singh's benevolence.

Through the 1980s, the Congress Party, which then ruled Bihar and to which Pritam Singh was affiliated, promulgated ordinances to extend the tenure of the State's gram panchayats. During the following decade, the Janata Dal government sought to institute protective discrimination for the OBCs in gram panchayats, a move stoutly opposed by privileged caste Mukhyas such as Pritam Singh. The Janata Dal government, in turn, remained adamant in not allowing elections to be held, until provisions for protective discrimination would be made. As a result of this deadlock, the tenure of the panchayats, and of Mukhyas such as Pritam Singh, continued to extend till elections were finally held, after a gap of 23 years, in 2001. During this time, Pritam Singh and his supporters from among the landlords and rich farmers made the most of their control over the panchayat.

However, their control was not undisputed. Many among the landless labourers of that region gravitated towards militant communism. Others secured public sector jobs thanks to the government policy of affirmative action for Dalits. Both groups of people became ever more vocal in opposing the Mukhya. Landless labourers and poor peasants in the gram panchayat had organized, sometimes successfully, land liberation movements in the panchayat from time to time. A number of them joined the CPI (M/L-L). One of their activists, a poor peasant named Hareram Mandal from the Kevat community, contested the 2001 elections against Pritam Singh. However, widespread intimidation by the landlords prevented the landless and poor peasants from actually casting their vote in Hareram Mandal's favour. Although Hareram Mandal lost that election and subsequently fell out of favour with the CPI (M/L-L) leadership, he maintained the political challenge to Pritam Singh. His wife, Susheela Mandal, contested the elections in 2006. She was successful, winning 56 per cent of the vote.

Table 3.20 reveals the patterns of membership in political parties among Roshanar Ward 5's population, disaggregated along land-size class. The census survey elicited information about respondents' membership in political parties although it did not probe the depth of involvement or the name or type of political party. Only one person in the ward was affiliated with any political party, a Kunjra Muslim who owned about 5 bighas of land. The table also shows data from the sample survey to indicate that electoral participation remained consistent throughout the landowning hierarchy.

Table 3.20: Political participation in Roshanar Ward 5, disaggregated along land-size class, percentages

	Data from Census Survey		Data from Sample Survey	
	Population	Political party membership	Population	Voting in PRI election
Landless	80	0	84	83
Marginal landowner	16	0	14	14
Small landowner	4.35	100	2.30	2.38
Medium landowner	0.62	0	0	0
Large landowner	0	0	0	0
	N=161	N= 1	N= 87	N= 84

Roshanar's labouring poor celebrated Susheela Mandal's victory as their own. But her electoral success was tempered by the fact that her council was dominated by ward representatives publicly supportive of Pritam Singh's nominees. Although Susheela Mandal had been elected the Mukhya, as many as nine of the panchayat's 15 wards elected gram panchayat members, who were beholden to Pritam Singh. Many among them, including the gram panchayat member of ward 5, were Pritam Singh's sharecroppers or laboured on his farms as agricultural workers, ploughmen or watchmen. They remained hostile towards Sushila Mandal's position as President of the panchayat. In turn, she and her husband reviled Pritam Singh's nominees as his stooges, and refused to engage them in consultations regarding the utilization of panchayat funds.

In Ward 5, Gajdeo Mandal remained unswerving in his support to Pritam Singh. When Kamruz Alam's wife Qudsiya Khatun decided to contest the elections for the post of gram panchayat member in Ward 5, Gajdeo Mandal tried to persuade her to announce her allegiance to Pritam Singh. Kamruz Alam had been one of his agricultural labourers before he had purchased his own plot of land and become an independent, even if marginal, peasant. Kamruz Alam and Qudsiya Khatun hesitated because they wanted to be autonomous of any such pressure. Gajdeo Mandal then persuaded the wife of another of his agricultural labourers, a woman named Hadisa Khatun to contest the elections. Considering her to be more pliable, and hence reliable than the wavering Kamruz and Qudsiya, he mobilized support in Hadisa's favour. Capitalist farmers (such as Gajdeo Mandal himself) as well as rich and middle peasants of both communities stood solidly behind her, as did labourers of the Gangot community and a section of Kunjra labourers. Hadisa Khatun won nearly 60 per cent of the vote, and was declared elected. Once elected, both Hadisa Khatun and her husband remained dependent on Gajdeo Mandal and the rich farmers and wealthy peasantry who had backed them. These classes in turn remained beholden to Pritam Singh. Hadisa Khatun's victory signalled the continued assertion of the entrenched classes in the ward's politics, despite the significant changes elsewhere in the panchayat. Her victory also invited the ire of the newly-elected Mukhya and her husband towards the Kunjra Muslims of Roshanar Ward 5.

The making of a paternalistic political place

The entrenched classes and the precarious classes coalesced together and sought to absorb the labouring poor in a paternalistic framework. Both the labour-hiring classes collaborated to tame potential radicalization among the labouring classes. The entrenched classes dominated the social relations of distribution in Roshanar Ward 5. The locality's rich and middle peasants willingly accepted the leadership of the capitalist farmers and landlords. The entrenched classes controlled nine of the 15 wards in the gram panchayat, a control which enabled them to effectively oppose the policies of the newly-elected Mukhya and her husband, the preferred candidate of the labouring classes. The contestations at the panchayat level did not translate into contestations at the ward level, where the entrenched classes were able to preserve their paternalistic relationships with other classes. The precarious classes publicly acknowledged the magnanimity of the entrenched classes who extended to them loans and allowed them to purchase properties at less-than-market rates.

The consequence for Roshanar Ward 5 was a paternalism that successfully mobilized the precarious classes (and sections of the labouring poor) under the leadership of the entrenched classes. Such mobilization excluded the majority of the labouring classes. They also reflected the ways in which social identities impinged upon class-formation. As a paternalistic political place, Roshanar Ward 5 was *controlled*, rather than shaped, by entrenched classes.

Conclusion: Social relations of power and the making of political space

This chapter points to the diverse ways in which political spaces are co-constituted by the dynamic interaction of opportunity structures and social relations of power. The detailed account of the social relations of power in the four political places provided in this chapter complements the generalized narrative about institutional opportunity structures of the previous chapter. I explained the contingent manner in which social relations of power are produced in the fieldwork sites by examining the interaction of the social relations of production with the social relations of distribution. Together, the two chapters provide us with a fuller picture of the political spaces available to poor people in rural eastern India, the similarities and variations one might expect, and possible factors for those variations.

In analysing the social relations of power, I applied a class-analytic framework to which the interlocked experience of labour and caste are integral. My account of the social relations of power in the four political places offered a window to understanding the ways in which entrenched classes, precarious classes and the labouring classes contended and cooperated with each other. An examination of the relations *between* classes necessitated an examination of the relations *over* classes. To that end, I underscored the heterogeneous ways in which the practices of labour intersected with the practice of caste to produce diverse class subjectivities. By noting the inchoate entanglements between landlords, peasants and labourers of different communities, I detailed the processes through which negotiations over class operated alongside negotiations between classes.

A key purpose of this chapter was to introduce the reader to the variety of collaborations and contests which permeate the lives of the labouring classes in the fieldwork locations. In an 'incorporative political place' as Rahimpur, the entrenched classes made common cause with the labouring poor, under the social leadership of the former, against the labour-hiring precarious classes. By contrast, in a 'populist political place' as Sargana, the precarious classes coalesced with the labouring poor, under the leadership of the former, against the entrenched classes. The obvious differences in the social relations of power notwithstanding, the labouring poor in both localities were enmeshed in a broad coalition with one or the other labour-hiring classes. Such a situation was reversed in Ditya and Roshanar Ward 5, where the poor confronted a class collaboration between the entrenched and the precarious classes. In a 'differentiated political place' as Ditya, the entrenched classes and the precarious classes collaborated under the leadership of the latter against the labouring poor. Entrenched and precarious classes coalesced together under the leadership of the former in the 'paternalistic political place' that constituted Roshanar, thereby excluding the poor.

Variations notwithstanding, three commonalities are discernible in all four accounts presented above. One, the collective self-identifications by people in all four localities problematize such conceptual categories as 'peasant' and 'labourers'. That such concepts are slippery indeed is evident from the contrasting ways in which these notions were invoked by peasants and labourers alike. The second commonality in the four accounts pertains to the central role of caste in the production of class identities. Each of the four accounts revealed that caste shaped the processes through which class identities were forged. A third commonality relates to the concurrently contentious and collaborative relationships between classes. The material from the four villages should caution against imageries of either class conflict or class contention. Rather, the attempt has been to unravel the complex negotiations between and within classes that mark the lives of actually-existing people in concrete political places.

The complementary accounts presented in this and the previous chapter provide us an understanding of the processes that shape the political spaces available to poor people. They allow us to contextualize the similarities and variations in poor people's political practices that we will encounter in the subsequent chapters. Those forthcoming chapters will highlight the dynamic interactions between the institutional opportunity structures and analysed in the previous chapter and the social relations of power examined in this chapter. A focus on such dynamic interactions will enable us to grasp the multifaceted ways in which the poor negotiate contemporary India's unequal democracy.

Endnotes

1   The 'upper' middle peasant class of Ramachandran's (2011) formulation appears to be proximate to Patnaik's (1986) 'middle peasant'. His 'lower' middle class seems to map on to the latter's 'small peasant'.

2   See, for instance, the research of Jeffrey (2002), Harriss (2013) and Pattenden (2014)

3   For more details, see Roy (2014a).

4   3 *bigha* equals to 1 acre in West Bengal. (Email communication, Subhasis Dey, postdoctoral scholar at University of Manchester, July 11, 2015).

5   The phrase he used was *thaanda kore diyechhe*, which literally translates into English as 'made them cold'.

6   See Roy (2014a) for further details.

7   1.25 *bighas* equals to 1 acre in and around the fieldwork locality. Local observers suggest that the size of a *bigha* in Bihar varies from region to region. Anindo Banerjee, Director- Internal Program Initiatives at the social research agency PRAXIS suggests that 1 *bigha* = 1.4805 acres in West Champaran; 0.741 acres in Gaya/Nawada; 0.874 acres in Jamui, and 0.625 acres in Patna (email communication, Anindo Banerjee, July 13, 2015).

8   Census of India (2001: Bihar Series, Table A10).

9   ibid.

10   Census of India (2001: West Bengal series, Table A10).

11   Census of India (2001: West Bengal series, Table A11).

4

From Clientelism to Citizenship?

The Politics of Supplications

We appealed to [Mukhya in Roshanar gram panchayat] *to help us. We pleaded with him today so that our children do not have to plead before anyone tomorrow.*

Shamsul Alam,
Roshanar Ward 5, 5 April 2010, c. 60, Kunjra Muslim,
marginal landowner

Institutional opportunity structures interface with social relations of power to shape political spaces. India's democracy, even as it allows inequalities to flourish, offers quite specific political spaces for the poor to negotiate their claims. Such opportunities are further shaped by the design of public policy. This chapter examines poor people's politics in the context of a narrowly targeted social policy. Where governments disburse social assistance within the framework of targeted public policy, the role of political mediators and the discretion of elected politicians, as well as bureaucrats, increases manifold. The labouring classes are compelled to supplicate before political mediators, elected representatives and myriad other politicians in order to even be enumerated for social assistance. Their supplications are further shaped by the particular relations of power in which they are embedded. The empirical material in this chapter pertains to the supplications poor people make to their politicians and political mediators in order to be classified as living 'below-poverty-line' (BPL). Enumeration as BPL enables households to claim access to BPL cards. The cards entitle their bearers to subsidies on housing, food and cooking fuel, pensions, and scholarships. Realizing the potentially exclusionary effect of targeting, the labouring classes refuse to submit quietly to their elected representative's decisions on the matter. At the same time, however, they do not reject such policy or collectively protest its implementation.

How are we to understand people's supplications in the context of our overarching interest in the meanings of democracy for people who live in poverty? The material offered in this chapter combines fieldwork with a discussion of the recent history of the Indian government's shift to targeted interventions and an analysis of the policy narrative on which the targeting policy is hinged. Fieldwork included a combination of data from surveys, elite interviews and ethnographic material. I rely on a census survey (See Annexure 2) conducted by my team of investigators in each of the study localities to highlight the arbitrariness of the targeted interventions. The survey schedule included the measures (See Annexure 3) used by the Indian state to identify BPL households as well as indices (See Annexure 4) developed by the Oxford Poverty and Human Development Initiative (OPHI) to identify the multidimensional character of poverty.[1] In addition, the surveys elicited information about the possession of BPL cards in addition to other socio-economic attributes. Therefore, the data collected through the surveys helped me to identify overlaps between the people who actually received the BPL cards, those who were eligible to receive it under the state's policy framework, and those who might be eligible under a more expansive 'multidimensional poverty index' framework for identifying the poor.

This material speaks to the prevalent scholarly approaches of conceptualizing supplications as either clientelistic or reflecting a transition to citizenship. Such readings are predicated on the universalism/particularism binary, according to which clientelism reflects particularistic practices that undermine the universalistic ideals associated with citizenship. Based on the fieldwork material, I consider the ways in which people's supplications signal the entanglements between the categories of clientelism and citizenship. In doing so, I critically review Partha Chatterjee's thesis on political society that speaks to ongoing debates on clientelism and citizenship. Although Chatterjee's thesis possesses merit, I am circumspect of its theoretical utility and instead urge readers to think about supplications not so much as working the levers of political society but as agonistic negotiations.

In Section I, I first cast a cursory glance at the burgeoning literature on clientelism and the anticipated shifts toward citizenship. I then outline the targeted policy framework that mandated the tangible identification of BPL populations in India. In Section II, I analyse my fieldwork evidence of poor people's pleas and appeals to local politicians requesting to be considered eligible for the cards. I attend to the heterogeneity of their supplications by disaggregating their experiences across the four political places where fieldwork was conducted. The supplications are combative and assertive in some, while being meek and reticent in others. I examine the possible factors that shape such variation. In Section III, I outline the theoretical issues at stake as they relate to our overarching concerns about the meanings of democracy for poor people.

This chapter, thus, does four things. One, it presents a brief history of targeted approaches to social assistance to remind us of the rather limited political space provided by social policy. Two, it documents poor people's supplications for social assistance. Three, it attends to the heterogeneities in their supplications by underscoring the variable political spaces in the four study places. Four, it engages critically with the scholarly ways of narrating such supplications as clientelistic practices, reflecting a particularistic worldview, necessarily at odds with universalistic values inhering in such formulations as citizenship.

I

Clientelism and citizenship

The scholarly literature on clientelism is enormous.[2] A succinct formulation is offered by Jonathan Fox's description of clientelism as 'a relationship based on political subordination in exchange for material rewards' (Fox, 1994, 153). The client supports and is politically subordinated to the patron. In return, the patron rewards him (or her) materially. Although recent scholarship has sought to underplay the element of subordination in the clientelistic relationship (Kitschelt and Wilkinson, 2007), there is near unanimity that contingency (Hicken, 2011) is crucial in determining whether a transaction is clientelistic or not. In this model, if a largesse extended by politicians is contingent upon support by their constituency – either now or in the future – then the transaction is deemed to be clientelistic. The argument further proceeds to suggest that the poor, whose lives are marked by a great deal of uncertainty, are constrained to seek help from politically influential and authoritative individuals for their security. Such individuals protect them and secure them resources. In return, the poor extend their support to them.

Fox's paper marks a discernible shift in analysing the mediated political transactions between those in positions of authority and influence and those without. Rather than flattening such transactions under a singular trope of clientelism, his insights allow scholars to map the changing ways in which poor people attempt to secure their basic entitlements without having to barter away their membership in the political community. Fox introduces the concept of 'semi-clientelism' to emphasize the transition away from authoritarian clientelism in Mexico to other forms of exchanges (eventually unequal in his analysis) that allow the poor to assert their membership in the political community. He reminds us that semi-clientelistic transactions are 'unenforceable deals' through which politicians try to secure the compliance of their clients by threatening to withdraw benefits (Fox, 1994, 157) rather than by actively exercising violence.

Recent scholarship has drawn attention to the shifting sands of clientelism in the contexts of political change in India. Akhil Gupta (1998) notes the shift away from patronage to brokerag. Patrons own and distribute resources as they please. Brokers, on the other hand, facilitate access to resources owned by patrons and increasingly institutions such as the state, Krishna (2011) argues that *naya netas* (emerging leaders) in rural India act as 'intermediate institutions' between the state and the population and to secure welfare benefits for the latter. *Naya netas* undertake such acts to win social prestige and influence rather than political authority or economic rents. Krishna's work resonates with the scholarship that underscores the shifts in the polities of the Indian countryside from elite-based patronage networks to broader based clientelistic relationships.[3] Such shifts are symptomatic of the widening radius of participation of people from hitherto-marginalized social and economic backgrounds. As political entrepreneurs, the *naya netas* of Krishna's conceptualization substantiate the citizenship claims of the poor by bringing them face-to-face with the institutions of governance that matter most to them. Extending this thesis, James Manor (2013) calls for a 'post-clientelistic' approach to studying local politics in India. He argues that with the institution of elected local government institutions and increased exposure to the practice of such institutions, approaches that hold clientelism central to the study of India's politics need to be discarded.

Against such optimism, however, scholars have pointed to the institutional and cultural factors that contribute to perpetrating clientelistic relations. Pattenden (2011a) details the forms of 'gatekeeping' practiced by the dominant classes to control the labouring classes' access to state resources. Williams *et al.* (2003) make a similar point about poor people's access to their entitlements under the public-funded Employment Assurance Scheme. These authors call attention to the institutional features of democratic decentralization in India, which enables members of privileged and dominant classes to perpetuate their control over other people's lives. A different argument is advanced by Piliavsky (2014), who highlights the moral economy of clientelism and the ways in which patronage is embedded in a value system wherein 'efficacy' is attributed a key role. To be sure, none of these scholars suggests that clientelistic relationships have remained untouched by the democratic claims articulated by India's poor over the last 25 years. They agree that clientelistic relationships are not immutable. However, they maintain that such changes in clientelistic relationships do not reflect a deepening of democracy in any meaningful sense.

A third approach is advanced by Partha Chatterjee who demands that our understanding of citizenship depart from the usual formulations of political equality, grounded in universal suffrage and juridical rights for all. Partha Chatterjee's (2012) suggestion that the analysis of political practices be framed 'as a redefined norm that endorses differentiated rather than equal citizenship as the normative standard for the modern state' (Chatterjee, 2012b, 24) is important in this context, although flawed in many respects. He labels the relationship on the basis of which poor people seek a negotiated settlement with their governments as the terrain of political society. Further, he distinguishes the relationship inhered in political society from the relationships inhabiting civil society where, according to him, the imaginary of the rule of law and a juridical conception of citizenship predominates. Chatterjee's argument has significant implications for the discussion on clientelism and citizenship, although it is one with which the material presented in this chapter compels me to disagree.

The institutional provenance: Targeted social provisioning

Scholars concur that clientelistic politics and targeted public policy co-produce one another (Heller, 2000; Keefer and Vlaicu, 2005; Kitschelt and Wilkinson, 2007). Targeted policies imply that welfare benefits are directed toward specific segments of the population, and justified in the name of economizing the allocation of resources rather than the promotion of social justice. Unlike universalistic policies that extend (at least in theory) to all sections of the population, targeted policies are intended to reach only 'eligible' or 'deserving' individuals or groups. Targeted social policies have been implemented in a variety of political and historical contexts (Skocpol, 1991), but have become particularly contested after the ideological shifts and the fiscal constraints of the 1970s (Mkandawire, 2005, 2). The World Bank advocated resource shifts in favour of the poor through 'a program of well-targeted transfers and safety nets' (World Bank, 1990, 3). However, this shift in policy has been accompanied by an emphasis on identifying the 'eligible poor', a process that facilitates the emergence of brokers who claim to be able to secure assistance and use it to wield enormous influence over the poor (Sen, 1995 and Rothstein, 2001). The problem is particularly acute when the targeting criteria is directed toward identifying 'eligible' individuals/households through rules and procedures that are not legislated, but implemented through executive fiat or arbitrary ordinances. The resultant unpredictability and insecurity makes local politicians, bureaucrats, and their minions all the more important in the disbursal of welfare schemes. The consequence is that the intended beneficiaries of the targeted programmes are regarded as supplicants and hence subjected to humiliating uncertainties.

Important though the discursive shifts are, one cannot deny that the implementation of targeted regimes stems from a crisis in the attempts by postcolonial states of the Global South to universalize social welfare. Part of the problem was the gap between the universalist proclamation of these governments and the actual capacity of their organization. In practice, 'universalisation was stratified and tended to apply to social groups directly linked to the nation-building project' (Mkandawire, 2005, 4). For the poor who were in practice excluded from 'universal welfare', the prescriptions associated with stabilization packages and structural adjustment policies that called for the rolling back of universal principles in favour of targeted regimes seemed to make little practical difference.

India's experience by and large conforms to this global trend. The public distribution system (PDS) was introduced in 1950 as a 'universal' programme where food was to be made available to the population at subsidized rates.

In practice, its operation was limited to urban areas of the country till the 1980s: the rural poor, who comprised the bulk of the population of the poor in India, were effectively excluded from it (Swaminathan, 2000; Kumar and Stewart, 1992). Even after the system was extended to rural areas in 1980, observers reported the exclusion of the poor from the PDS, leading some analysts (Subbarao, 1992) to call for the introduction of arrangements to specifically target them.[4]

Within two decades, the Indian government extended 'targeting' to the PDS on the specious grounds that such a policy increased efficiency of resources. A World Bank (1996) report, which recommended that only the poor, an amorphous category to begin with, be 'targeted' for subsidized food was enthusiastically received: by 1997, the government had introduced the Targeted Public Distribution System (TPDS) and began to offer subsidized food only to households that lived 'below the poverty line'. Such households were to be identified on the basis of means-tests. Households classified as living below poverty line were issued with BPL cards. BPL cards entitled their holders to purchase subsidized food and cooking fuel from PDS outlets. BPL cardholders were also entitled to housing subsidies, pensions, scholarships and other social assistance. Furthermore, the government streamlined social assistance by predicating access to all other schemes – maternity and child benefits, old age pensions – on the possession of BPL cards. For this reason, the cards were coveted objects, including by the obviously wealthy. However, the cards were narrowly targeted. Only some people, even among the poor, were eligible to receive them.

The means-tests instruments for targeting the poor eligible for social assistance have undergone at least two amendments since the introduction of the TPDS in 1997. With each change, the fortunes of several millions of the poor hang in the balance. The BPL cards spawned anxieties among the population, desperate to obtain these for themselves but unsure of the prospects. Indeed, where the poor had faced irregular supplies and corrupt retailers in the past, they now had to confront both these circumstances *and* a plethora of elected representatives and other political actors who mediated their inclusion in the BPL lists and procured BPL cards for them.

A more appropriate solution to the problem of universally prescribed social assistance not reaching the poor might have examined the possibilities of 'targeting within universalism' (Skocpol, 1991). Instead, the Indian state abandoned 'universalism' in favour of the 'targeting' approach in relation to providing social assistance. The 'reforms' in the PDS were motivated by the need for fiscal prudence rather than animated by concerns for poor people (Swaminathan, 2000). Such motivation distinguished targeting of the PDS after 1992 from other targeted approaches under programs such as the Integrated Rural Development Programs (IRDP) prior to 1992. The IRDP was undoubtedly ill-implemented (Dreze, 1990; Copestake, 1992). But that programme has to be seen against the backdrop of the Janata Party's explicit promises of eradicating poverty. Targeting under the IRDP was followed by the Congress Party *extending* the PDS into rural areas, reflecting the commitment of the Indian state to ensure that all members of the political community would have universal access to basic food security. That commitment was severely truncated during the 1990s.

Not only did the Indian state welcome the World Bank Study recommendations on reforming the PDS, in fact, it exceeded those recommendations! The Bank study, while severely indicting generalized social assistance programmes, had also warned of the high transaction costs of sustaining the targeted policy regime. It had suggested that 'leakages appear to be lowest in programs that self-select beneficiaries into the program' (Radhakrishna et al., 1997, 74).[5] The Indian government ignored this suggestion and introduced in 1997 a threefold classification of population into: the destitute; those living 'below the poverty line'; and those living 'above the poverty line'. As Table 4.1 illustrates, the 131 million households that were now classified as 'above poverty line' lost the entitlements they possessed under the universal PDS. Some of these households were indeed economically well-off and did not need the subsidies available under the PDS. But others were not. Many poor households were edged out of the list by their better connected neighbours. Several studies point to these exclusions. One study estimates that as many as 52 per cent of agricultural labour households and 61 per cent of SC households – arguably among the most impoverished groups in the country – did not possess BPL cards in 2004–05 (Swaminathan, 2008). Another study moderates the proportion of exclusions (Desai et al., 2005); however, even its authors admit that one-third of agricultural labourers, 46 per cent of Dalits and 30 per cent of Adivasis, and 41 per cent of those households at the poorest income quintile are excluded from BPL cards. A third study points out that 61 per cent of the poorest quintile was excluded from BPL cards and the benefits accruing thereof (Ram *et al*, 2009). Other field research also shows that 'targeting' social assistance to the poor has only deepened the ubiquitous uncertainties that plagued their access to services (Hirway, 2003).

Table 4.1: Number of households (in millions) categorized as BPL and Above Poverty Line (APL) in select Indian States, 2013

Name of State	Projected no. of households	No. of BPL households	Ration cards		
			BPL cards	Antyodaya Anna Yojana (AAY) cards	APL cards
Andhra Pradesh	15.82	4.06	20.51	1.58	2.99
Assam	4.49	1.83	1.20	0.70	4.087
Bihar	11.87	6.52	3.92	2.50	1.53
Chhattisgarh	4.41	1.87	1.15	0.71	2.64
Gujarat	8.75	2.12	2.37	0.81	8.31
Haryana	3.14	0.78	0.90	0.29	4.47
Jharkhand	4.35	2.39	1.47	0.91	0.51
Karnataka	9.43	3.12	8.42	1.13	3.66
Kerala	6.11	1.55	1.44	0.59	5.82
Madhya Pradesh	9.70	4.12	5.24	1.58	7.99
Maharashtra	17.72	6.53	4.58	2.46	13.95
Odisha	6.79	3.29	3.67	1.26	3.45
Punjab	3.97	0.46	0.28	0.17	5.59
Rajasthan	8.86	2.43	1.65	0.93	11.16
Tamil Nadu	13.88	4.86	17.67	1.86	–
Uttar Pradesh	26.14	10.67	6.58	4.09	33.11
West Bengal	14.52	5.17	3.91	1.48	12.98
All India	180.37	65.20	87.07	24.32	131.59

Source: Ministry of Consumer Affairs, Food and Public Distribution (2013, 59), accessed at http://dfpd.nic.in/writereaddata/images/pdf/food-grain/november-2013.pdfinFebruary 2017.

India was not alone in abandoning generalized welfare programmes during the 1980s and 1990s. Other countries that did so included Mexico, Brazil, Argentina, Nigeria, Egypt, and Pakistan. These abandonments were universally accompanied by a language of fiscal prudence, new public management, and good governance. It is difficult to pinpoint a single source for these discourses, tempting as it might to lay the blame for these at the door of multilateral financial institutions. As we have seen, India exceeded the recommendations of the World Bank study on PDS. The country's policymakers consistently ignored evidence against means-tested targeting and refused to acknowledge the 'targeting errors' (errors of including non-eligible populations and errors of excluding eligible populations) that resulted in the exclusion of millions of improverished Indians from any net of social protection (Kumar and Stewart, 1992).

Bina Fernandez (2011) suggests that targeting is a 'neoliberal technology' of governance. By unleashing it the state in India seeks to encourage the population to cease depending on it for social protection. Nikolas Rose (1999), writing about Britain, argues that with neoliberalism, the economic fates of the state and its population are no longer seen as interdependent. The state no longer accepts the responsibility for the social protection of its constituents. The effects of this neoliberal turn has been far from an abstraction for the 131 million households, many of them poor and vulnerable, who were deprived of the entitlements they possessed under the universal PDS. Such massive exclusions from social assistance in a country where the only agreement on the question of poverty is that it is widespread are nothing short of a scandal.

The massive exclusions spawned by the introduction of the Indian state's targeting regime appears to have been relatively uncontested in rural India. The apparent quiescence may partially be a reflection of the patchiness of the PDS as it prevailed before targeting was introduced. Corruption in the PDS had been widespread, and political mediators were often called upon in order to facilitate poor people's access to the universal PDS. If the aforementioned studies underscoring the exclusions from the BPL lists are correct, then, empirically, the majority of the 131 million households who lost their entitlements may well have been among the poorer people in the countryside – those with the most fragile and vulnerable livelihoods, and with uncertain access to PDS in the first place.

The newly instituted targeted regime facilitated the emergence of politicians and political mediators who secure social assistance for people unrelated directly to them. Such mediators are distinct from traditional patrons who limited favours to members of their own kinship or ethnic groups. Rather, mediators are analytically closer to brokers and fixers (Hargopal and Reddy, 1975 and Manor, 2000). Many political mediators value the opportunity to structure poor people's access to social assistance because it allows them to extend their network of supporters. They expect such support to help them meet their political ambitions. In this respect, they approximate the *naya netas* (Krishna, 2007) or *chhoto bhai neta* (Corbridge *et al.*, 2005) described in recent works. However, in the context of the BPL cards, political mediators did not only transmit information from a source to a destination: they were not merely intermediaries. Rather, they added value by offering their own analysis of that information. It was not uncommon for them to create or mobilize opinions among the population by informing them about the different provisions under which they might be eligible for the BPL cards. As conduits of information and gatekeepers of resources, they made sure that BPL cards were widely talked about.

Governmental strategies: Identifying 'below-poverty-line' populations

The institutionalization of the targeted regime required the state to not only estimate the numbers of people living in poverty but to concretely identify them so that they received the designated social assistance. Such identification was an inductive exercise quite different from the deductive exercise of estimating the proportion of people in poverty from sample surveys. The Indian state had been deducing the numbers of the poor from various sample surveys based on consumption patterns since at least 1962. But sample surveys, useful though they are to arrive at aggregate estimations of poverty ratios, cannot be used to identify poor households. Therefore, India's Planning Commission designed a 'BPL Census' schedule in order to enumerate and identify the specific households that would be eligible for social assistance. The schedule adopted through much of the first decade of the twenty-first century broadly reflected the government's attempts at collecting data about household vulnerabilities. However, and this is important, the number of households deemed eligible for BPL cards was subject to the ceiling set by the estimations of the Planning Commission's deductive exercise.

In 1999–2000, the Planning Commission deduced from its sample surveys that 65 million households in India lived below the official poverty line. It also estimated poverty rates for each of the States (GoI, 2013, 56). Thereafter, the Commission constituted an expert group to design the BPL census comprising 13 questions to be administered to every rural household. The 13 questions that constituted the BPL census schedule included a range of parameters, reflecting the emergence of a multidimensional view of poverty in official circles. These parameters included ownership of assets and durable items, sources of income, sanitation practices and literacy levels. The schedule also canvassed information on the number of meals eaten by the household for most parts of the year, the number of clothing items and the households' preference for assistance – variables that barely lent themselves to categorical answers. Each question was to be scored on a 0–4 scale, which meant that every rural household could receive a score ranging from '0' to '52'.

India's different States introduced their 'cut-off' scores and deemed households that scored less than the cut-off as BPL households as 'eligible' for social assistance. Although States were free to amend the census schedule and the scoring scheme, the number of BPL families identified by them could not exceed Planning Commission's overall estimations for each State by more than 10 per cent. Thus, if Planning Commission determined that 4.86 million households in the State of Tamil Nadu were poor, the State would have to ensure that it set the 'cut-off' such that the number of BPL households identified did not exceed the Planning Commission's estimation by more than 10 per cent (no more than 5.32 million). In short, the States were allowed flexibility *within the limits* established by the Union Government's Planning Commission.

In fact, some States were able to make significant amendments to the scoring procedure. West Bengal provides one example. It omitted two questions from the Planning Commission's survey schedule and introduced one of its own. As readers will see in Annexure 5, the State's survey schedule, instead of asking 13 questions marked on a scale of 0–4, scored 12 questions on a scale of 1–5: consequently, it set the 'cut-off' at 33 (of 60 marks), as the letter reproduced in Annexure 6 from the seniormost bureaucrat of the State to the district magistrates instructed. Others, such as Tamil Nadu, refused to abandon the universal measures promulgated in their territories. They were free to do so, but were enjoined by the Union Government to meet the costs of subsidizing the food and fuel requirements of these additional households from their own revenues.

Bihar resolutely protested the limits imposed by the Planning Commission. In 2000, the Planning Commission had estimated the BPL households in the State at 6.52 million. However, the State government, headed at that time by Lalu Yadav's Rashtriya Janata Dal, claimed that BPL households in the State exceeded 15 million. The Union Government, led by the Center-Right NDA (of which the BJP), refused to consider additional allocations for these households. As a result, the State government was left with little choice but to establish a lower cut-off than the national average, which would reduce the number of BPL households it could subsidize. Accordingly, it adopted the 'cut-off' score of 13 while most States set this at 17. A Supreme Court-appointed commission on the functioning of PDS unearthed another strategy deployed by the State government to meet the shortfall (Wadhwa Committee, 2005): the government reduced the entitlement for each BPL household so that it could reach more households with the same pot of resources. Bihar's compliance with the Union Government's directives was only partial. Like Tamil Nadu, the State government refused to imbibe the neoliberal technology of governance entailed in targeting resources. Unlike Tamil Nadu, however, it did not possess the financial resources to provide for the requirements of all BPL households it identified. Rather, the State government took the position that it was the Union Government's responsibility to provide for all its citizens. The impasse between Bihar and the union government outlasted the decade.[6]

Nationally, the decision to target resources based on the BPL survey faced fierce criticism from the outset. The People's Union for Civil Liberties (PUCL) submitted a petition to Supreme Court,[7] demanding that the provisions for limits on the number of BPL families be eliminated. The BPL survey could be operationalized only in 2006 following an interim order from the court. If civil rights activists were infuriated with the unjustified caps proposed by the union government, economists disagreed with the technical robustness of the survey methodology. In particular, they raised questions about the lack of objectivity and the possibility of arbitrariness, the assumption of substitutability among indicators, and the cardinal scoring scheme.[8]

Such criticisms notwithstanding, the entitlements of India's poor were determined by the targeting exercise for an entire decade. Although the targeting exercise was proposed by the Centre-Right BJP-led NDA, it was implemented by the Centre-Left Congress-led United Progressive Alliance (UPA). Political parties appeared to share a rare unanimity in endorsing the targeting practices of the state, producing what must go down in the annals of global history as a shameful tragedy.

Such attempts by the state in India to 'target' the population as objects of intervention allow the state to determine the fate of millions inhabiting its jurisdiction. However, the 'targeted' populations are not passive either. Their strategies differ from the ones deployed by the civil liberty activists and their criticisms are very different from those offered by social scientists. As I observed during fieldwork, the BPL exercise was a significant event in the collective life of the study localities. It was a matter of animated discussion during occasions as diverse as participating in a political rally, drinking *chai* at the neighbourhood kiosk or attending a funeral. Sitting through these discussions, I caught a glimpse of the ways in which the targets of the state's targeting exercise negotiated with politicians to make an incoherent and ill-conceived policy meaningful and favourable to their lives. They were not always hapless victims of the state's technologies of government although, as we shall see, their ability to manoeuvre the available political spaces was more limited in some localities relative to others.

Gram panchayats were tasked with identifying BPL households.[9] This administrative decision increased the social profile of the gram panchayats, whose representatives were now responsible for the classification of their constituents into those who lived 'below' the poverty line and those who lived 'above' it. These institutions now became the focus of poor people's negotiations. The requests that attended to these negotiations were framed as supplications, '*aagrah*' in Hindi and Bangla. Supplications are understood as entreaties, pleas or petitions. To supplicate is to appeal for a commodity or service that is seen to be granted as a favour. The act of supplication is associated with humility. However, the requirement of humility does not preclude assertive expressions by supplicants, as Thorner (2006) points out through her study of women's petitions during the treason trials of early-seventeenth century England. The supplication is substantively a call for generosity, sympathy, and care to be showed by the supplicated. It is an invocation of the kindness of the person to whom the supplication is addressed. No claim is made specifically defending its overarching justness. Households requesting for BPL cards or hoping to receive BPL cards described themselves as supplicants or 'nivedak' in Hindi/'abedak' in Bangla. But the form of these supplications varied across the four political places under discussion assertive and confident in some while being reticient and meek in others. Such variations were shaped by the dynamic interaction between the institutional opportunity structures and social relations of power.

In the next section, I report people's supplications from the four fieldwork localities. For each of the localities, I begin by introducing the arbitrariness ingrained in the BPL schedule and demonstrate that even were the BPL cards to be disbursed as per the schedule and without any interference, only a small proportion of all households in the localities would even be eligible to receive them. For each locality, I present data on the asset profile of the households. I further classify the household into 'BPL schedule poor' households and 'BPL schedule non-poor' based on whether (or not) households could be classified as living below the poverty line according to the BPL schedule (Roy, 2011). The questions of the BPL survey were integrated into the census questionnaire I used for the present project. Through the survey, I also attempted to count the households that might be considered 'poor' according to the OPHI formulated MPI. A descriptive comparison of households that were enumerated as 'poor' using the two approaches, one based on the BPL schedule and the other on the MPI schedule, further testifies to the BPL Schedule's arbitrary outcomes. The survey for this project was conducted approximately two years after the official BPL survey. BPL cards had only recently been distributed. Hence, the possibility that the distribution of BPL cards had facilitated any major material change by the time of the research is greatly reduced. Although I tried to make clear that the study survey had nothing to do with the official mechanisms of poverty enumeration, it is of course possible that my respondents feared that their responses may result in the cards being stripped away from them. Readers are advised to examine the tables in the ensuing discussion with these caveats in mind.

II

Assertive supplications in an incorporative political place: Rahimpur

Everyone was suspicious. How would BPL cards be disbursed? Who would decide? No one was answering these questions. So, twenty-five of us confronted (*shommukhin holam*) Joynal da and Abdur da [senior CPI(M) leaders]here [pointing to a stone platform] the village square. We told them to keep us in his thoughts.... They began giving their philosophy: Allah, Marx, Jyoti Basu....all over the place....We told them to come to the point- were they going to give us the cards or not....more stories followed...Central government ploy, State Government inefficiency, Party greatness..... We didn't want their opinions... just an answer. Joynal da is the only gentleman (*bhodrolok*) in that party. The rest are good-for-nothing.

Interview notes, Fatema Bewa, Rahimpur Village Square,
3 February 2010

The BPL survey in Rahimpur was conducted during the summer of 2007. The ward's population was justifiably suspicious that the survey would leave behind a trail of arbitrary exclusions from BPL related entitlements. The arbitrariness associated with the BPL schedule is illustrated in Table 4.2. Readers will note that only 31 per cent of all Rahimpur's households would be eligible for BPL cards, assuming a completely unbiased selection process. indices (See Annexure 4). Table 4.3 shows that even were the BPL schedule to be implemented without bias, slightly over half of all Rahimpur's households would be categorized as MPI poor but not BPL poor.

Table 4.2: Asset profile of BPL schedule poor households in Rahimpur

Attribute	BPL schedule poor %	BPL schedule non-poor %	Total (N)
Landless	41.08	58.92	314
Mud floor	32.41	67.59	361
Bicycle as only means of transport	15.61	84.39	237
Total population	31.13	68.87	424

Source: Own census survey, 2009–10.

My interlocutors in Rahimpur reported that they recognized early enough that they could not depend on the implementation of the BPL schedule to safeguard the social assistance to which they were entitled. They would need to influence their elected representatives and other politicians to secure BPL cards for their families. The institutional design of West Bengal's panchayats made the ward member, rather than the panchayat's President, the focus of people's claims. The ward member at that time and her husband were both affiliated with the CPI(M). Therefore, many of the supplications were directed toward them. However, other politicians of the CPI(M)

Table 4.3: BPL schedule poverty and multidimensional poverty in Rahimpur

Multidimensional poverty	BPL schedule poverty	
	No	Yes
No	18.39	0.94
Yes	50.47	30.18

Source: Own census survey, 2009–10.

were also the focus of people's requests. Among them was the respected Joynal Ali, one of the targets of Fatema *bewa's* ire in the quote above. He was the *sardar* of one of Rahimpur's six *shamajs* and was well-regarded even among electoral opponents for his ability to collaboratively resolve disputes. Although respect did not tantamount to reverence, and many decisions he took were subjected to scrutiny and criticism, I discerned warmth across party affiliations for his personal integrity. My interlocutors concurred that he was a particularly affable person, even if his tendency to pontificate irritated many. The ward member and Joynal Ali each owned over 80 *bighas* of arable land, to cultivate which they hired labour from neighbouring Habibpur. While they were clearly members of the entrenched classes, other CPI(M) cadres in Rahimpur, such as Habibur Rehman, Abdur Bari, and Gaurob Shil were not. They typically owned small plots (8 to 20 *bighas*) of land, which they cultivated themselves or with hired labour.

My interlocutors told me about the manner in which they discussed the ramifications of the BPL cards among themselves – as neighbours, friends, and co-workers. They sought out the individuals they knew to be helpful and considerate, as well as efficacious, and approached them in delegations of 10–15 people, to understand the enumeration exercise. I gathered that they formed such collectives rather spontaneously. People discussed the matter with each other during the many times in a day that they met one another. Typically, people who worked in fields, shops and eateries located near each other walked together to work during the day and returned together in the afternoons and in the evenings, shared their anxieties with each other about

BPL cards. On the way back home, they met other similarly-anxious men, and sometimes women. A delegation of people, formed rather contingently, walked to the residence of the politicians or political mediators they thought would be helpful. At other times, they got together in different kiosks of the village in the evenings. As neighbours, they were concerned about the fate of the enumeration exercise. In between sips of *chai*, puffs of *bidi* (leaf-rolled cigarettes) and snatches of views from the television, they deliberated over the procedure for identifying households eligible for BPL cards. (*Aamra ek shonge bichar korlam,* was a common theme I heard from my interlocutors). Politicians' preferred kiosks were well-known to everyone. It was not uncommon for groups of men and women to collectively accost a politician or political mediator they knew and enquire about the process in greater detail.

During my interviews with them, Fatema Bewa and six of her Sheikh neighbours reported that they had approached Joynal Ali to request him to help them be enumerated as BPL households. They proposed to him that they would reduce their scores to the region of 20–25 during the survey. But he is reported to have told them, 'Scores as low as this are sure to invite scrutiny. We'd all get caught out. That everyone has uniformly low scores would look ridiculous to the survey supervisors in the block.' That was when Fatema *bewa* and other members of their delegation vented their frustration on him.

Joynal Ali's party associate Abdur Bari remembered that exchange with Fatema *bewa* and her neighbours too well. He recalled that people were particularly upset at his suggestion of reporting realistic scores. But that incident was not unique at all. Joynal Ali recalled other instances vividly:

> [One householder] came and told me how I could ask them to do this. He said he was extremely poor, and couldn't afford to lose the BPL card. [A second householder] complained that I was inconsiderate. Now, you tell me, what could I do? [A group of eight householders] threatened to vote for the Congress if we didn't give them the cards....This is what the Government has done, made us [politicians] look like enemies of the people. [Ward Member] and I could do nothing. I have resolved several disputes in the past, and been confronted with many complex problems. But never have I had to deal with such hostility.[10]

The exchanges reported in Rahimpur exemplify the instability and contradictions of supplications that I referred to earlier. On the one hand, there were references to 'concern' (*chinta*). For instance, Joynal Ali reported being asked by his interlocutors time and again to 'be concerned' about them: '*amader jonno chinta korun*' (Please be concerned about us). Others asked him to take 'care' (*kheyal rakhun*) of them. The people making these requests did not only intend for care to be restricted to feeling, but also wanted their politicians to practice it in ways that would benefit them. Their requests were public. Narratives of care and protection co-existed with practices involving accusation and confrontation to make the supplications by Rahimpur's poor rather assertive. Joynal Ali was only one of many CPI(M) politicians against whom such assertive supplications were directed.

Fatema *bewa's* neighbours Arif Miya and Shefali Bibi, both Sheikh Muslim told me that they, along with 12-15 of their neighbours, approached Congress politicians Akbar Ali and Alauddin Ali. As we have seen, both Akbar Ali and Alauddin Ali were members of Rahimpur's entrenched classes. Fatema *bewa* and her neighbours found Akbar Ali and Alauddin Ali to be far more reassuring and supportive than either Joynal Ali or Abdur Bari. Arif Miya said:

> They [Akbar and Alauddin] told us not to worry. They said they would teach the *motobbors* (upstarts) of the CPI(M) a lesson. They would fight for us if necessary. They kept their promise. Joynal da tried to quieten the situation down. But Akbar Ali stuck to his point. There was some fisticuffs between Akbar Ali and Abdur Bari, but the others intervened. After that, Joynal da came to us to ask if we were fine. We told him again- you better give us the BPL cards or you see what we will do! We are *gorib manush* (poor people). He should care for us. We didn't need to go to Akbar Ali again.[11]

Neither Akbar Ali nor Alauddin Ali could remember this incident as precisely as Arif Miya and Shefali Bibi did. They told me they helped 'lots of people' (*onek loker shahajyo korlam*), and it was impossible to remember every single instance. But they did reiterate their presumption that the CPI(M) was a party of upstarts (*matobbors*), people who thought they could govern, but were plainly incapable. They insisted that the Congress Party, the party of the *bhadrolok* (gentlemen, men of social standing), was the natural party of governance, while the *matobbors* of the CPI(M) were *chhotolok* with unjustified assumptions about their abilities. Congress politicians alone were the natural *'garjian'* (the locally used word for 'guardian') of the poor and could protect them from the depredations of the *chhotolok* who controlled the CPI(M). Arif Miya not only agreed that everyone needed a *garjian*, but also added that *garjians* had responsibility to provide for those under their care. One of his employers had been Abdur Bari, the CPI(M) politician whose inability to even promise him a BPL card despite his being a CPI(M) politician revealed his limits as a *garjian*.

Poor people such as Arif Miya looked to wealthier co-villagers, members of Rahimpur's entrenched classes, as their guardians. The relationships inhered by the vocabulary of guardianship provided them with the confidence to assert their demands before the politicians they held responsible for their well being. Given their class backgrounds, more members of the entrenched classes were able to perform the role of guardians than members of the precarious classes were. A guardian's role was multifaceted. Guardians needed to have access to surpluses from which they could dip in to make resources available to those who sought their help. This often meant their own surpluses. However, successful brokers, fixers, and other political mediators could also become guardians if they could facilitate access to state resources. Indeed, perhaps the most important facet of being a guardian was to support the claims of people under their care. This facet is of immense salience in understanding the ways in which class relations impinged upon the assertive supplications of Rahimpur's poor over the disbursal of BPL cards. Poor people like Arif Miya, Shefali Bibi, Fatema *bewa*, and others did not want money from members of the entrenched classes. Instead, they wanted BPL cards, which would entitle them to valued social assistance. Fearing that the precarious classes who controlled the CPI(M), would be unable to (or unwilling to) make BPL cards available to them, they solicited help from members of the entrenched classes. They were confident that the Congress-affiliated entrenched classes would support the poor, despite their being CPI(M) voters. Their confidence enabled the labouring poor to supplicate assertively before precarious class politicians.

The entrenched classes shaped the agenda of Rahimpur's polity even when they did not politically control it. Admittedly, they could not directly control the disbursal of the BPL cards. The precarious classes did, and this made *them* the focus of the claims of the labouring classes. On the other hand, the entrenched classes knew that they would never be eligible for the BPL cards. As guardians, therefore, they supported and even provoked poor people's claims for the BPL cards. Such claims cornered the precarious class leadership of the CPI(M). The public embarrassment caused to such senior CPI(M) politicians as Joynal Ali was a matter of no small joy to his adversaries in the Congress Party: I could not miss the smirk on Akbar Ali's face each time he talked about the CPI(M) politicians' responses to popular demands. In lending their voice to such demands, members of the entrenched classes buttressed the perception among the poor of themselves as effective guardians.

Backed by their entrenched class guardians, a large number of Rahimpur's Sheikh Muslim poor were able to supplicate assertively before CPI(M) politicians while demanding BPL cards. They were able to supplement their pleas, appeals and requests with more conflictual claims. People accused precarious class politicians of being uncaring and threatened to switch electoral support to Congress. The complex of appeals and accusations, pleas and threats comprised their negotiations in Rahimpur. Even as their assertive supplications weakened the precarious classes and bolstered the entrenched classes, such negotiations enabled the labouring poor to collectively advance their social perspectives in the ward.

Assertive supplications in a populist political place: Sargana Ward 1

> They [The enumerators] asked us how we would like the government to help us. We told them we'd like to work- like they did, so we'd like some kind of training. Then we saw those mo****f***ers gave us high scores. Do we migrate for work? Oh yes we do. Every season. But my father [pointing to an elderly gentlemen resting on his cot] doesn't go, he's too weak to go, he's not ill, just too weak.... So, they gave him a '4'...They then asked why I was reporting us as separate households [face flashing in anger].... Why doesn't he take him [my father] home if he cares so much...we don't live like that. But these boys- they just did not understand. They were pandits [reference to the enumerators' Brahman caste], from the town... We had no option but to ask for a meeting [in English] with Sarvesh Mukhya [The Mukhya].

We had a meeting with him each evening for a week, just to be
sure that things were alright.

Group discussion notes, Sargana Ward 1, Musahar tola
machan (West), 7 March 2010

The BPL survey in Sargana Ward 1 was eventually rolled out in early 2008,
as in the rest of Bihar. It was not clear how the survey would sift through a
mass of impoverished population and determine households eligible to be
on the BPL list. The results of the survey conducted for this study, presented
in Table 4.4 concurred with the justified perception among the population
that the government's BPL survey would result in arbitrary exclusions.
It may be noted that only 13 per cent of all households would be eligible for BPL cards, assuming
a completely unbiased selection process. Table 4.5 shows that even were the BPL schedule to be
implemented without bias, over half of all Sargana Ward 1's households would be categorized as MPI poor
but not BPL poor.

Table 4.4: Asset profile of BPL schedule poor households in Sargana Ward 1

Attribute	BPL schedule poor %	BPL schedule non-poor %	Total (N)
Landless	18.26	81.74	115
Mud floor	14.71	85.29	136
Bicycle	3.95	96.05	76
Total population	12.73	87.27	165

Source: Own census survey, 2009–10.

The institutional design of
Bihar's gram panchayats makes the
panchayat's Mukhya, rather than the
ward member, the focus of people's
claims. Sargana's Mukhya Sarvesh
Mandal, a middle peasant of the
Kevat community who cultivated his
10 *bigha* plot through a combination
of own, family and hired labour, was
confronted regularly by supplicants
asking to be considered favourably for the BPL cards. I met Sarvesh Mandal
at his home as he reviewed the progress over the actual disbursal of the BPL
cards with his close associates, who happened to be middle and rich peasants

Table 4.5: BPL schedule poverty and multidimensional poverty in Sargana Ward 1

Multidimensional poverty	BPL schedule poverty	
	No	Yes
No	34.54	0
Yes	52.72	12.72

Source: Own census survey, 2009–10.

from the Yadav and Kevat communities, members of the locality's precarious class like him. As I broached the subject of the BPL cards during our interview, Sarvesh Mandal's composed demeanour underwent a radical change. He was visibly agitated:

> It seems the Bihar Government does not want any poor people in this State. It's ridiculous that they have set a cut-off of '13' for such a poor State. People tell me the cut-offs in other States is '17'. Is that true? [I nodded in agreement]...See, now what am I supposed to do? This has been the bitterest part of my public life. I wanted to help them....I had people come in every day. They would not understand my position...they only wanted to have their way.....
>
> Now look at the Musahars.... They are good people, but they don't know how to conduct themselves in public. They are easily excited. They talk without listening to others. They said, 'Mukhyaji, you have to help us. We elected you. Now you better look after us..... On the one hand, they were shouting at me. Can you imagine, the women came here too, and shouted at me! And the abuses they heaped on me... Even men don't say such things. On the other hand, they were asking me to look after them... I didn't know whom to talk to. If there were one or two of them, I could have a proper discussion, and we could sort this out. I tried to talk with Shyamdev Rishi [Ward representative]. But they shouted him down. They all wanted to talk to me...But what do you do with a *bheedh* (crowd)?[12]

Although broadly sympathetic to their demands, Sarvesh Mandal's account of the individuals who came to meet him invokes images of unruly and uncontrollable crowds. It diverges from the account offered by the said Musahars. My interlocutors in the ward's western hamlet, all landless labourers, emphasized that they held regular 'meetings' (in English) with the Mukhya where they tried to clarify the survey questions and the implications of the answers they had given. They reported that they tried to speak directly with him because they considered him their well-wisher. After all, in his youth, his family had been a smallholder tenant. Moreover, he – rather than the ward member – was ultimately responsible for finalizing the BPL lists. My interlocutors' accounts suggested that they were annoyed by his inability to assure them that he would help them. They exchanged angry words with him because *he* tried to dodge responsibility for helping them. Bhukhan Rishi, a 51 year-old manual worker said:

> All we wanted was for him to help us. Is this too much to ask? We voted for him, so he ought to help us. He was poor once, so he should help others who are poor. Why ignore us and talk to the Ward Member?[13]

An analysis of both accounts revealed the internally fragmented quality of the supplications. On the one hand, supplicants requested the Mukhya for 'help' (*madad*). They appealed to their Mukhya to look after them. They urged him to enumerate them as BPL population. Because of the Mukhya's impoverished origins, they considered it his obligation to help them out of poverty. These references to *madad* were intended to arouse sympathy. They expressed a contractual relation with their elected representative: he had to help them because they had elected him. Even when they asked him to 'look after us', they anchored their request in vocabularies of holding him to account for having elected him.

My interlocutors among the landless labourers of the Musahar community nodded their heads vigorously while acknowledging the help they received from others in Sargana. Maturi Rishi, Bhukhan Rishi's nephew and, like him, a manual worker told me that they often requested other manual workers such as the feisty Gunvati Yadav and her husband Narendra Yadav to accompany their delegations. The couple usually obliged and asked their friend Amaresh Yadav to join them. Amaresh Yadav owned 8–10 *bighas* of land, on which he deployed hired labour, alongside his own and family labour. Many of his labourers were hired from among the same Musahars whose case he was asked to support. Affiliated with the RJD, he had been elected the Deputy Sarpanch, vice-president of Sargana's judicial council (Nyay Panchayat) in 2006. The manual workers also sought to involve retailers such as the BJP-affiliated Dharmesh Srivastava, a Kayasth whose argumentative skills they admired greatly. Activists of the Musahar Sevak Sangh (MSS) and the CPI(M/L–L) added to their numbers and voice, while bringing them information about the ways in which people in other localities were negotiating with their elected representatives and political mediators.

Mutual acrimonies among the members of the delegations were not uncommon. The activists of the CPI (M/L–L) and the MSS were openly hostile to one another. They also shared a mutual dislike for Dharmesh Srivastava, who reciprocated their distaste. Although Maturi Rishi and his friends disliked Amaresh Yadav's partisan role in disputes between Musahar agricultural labourers and their Yadav employers in a neighbouring ward, they tolerated his presence presumably because it added to their influence. Amaresh Yadav's motivations appeared less clear to me: perhaps he hoped to cultivate goodwill among members of the numerically large Musahar community. Nonetheless, all of these individuals contributed their presence and voice to the delegations that Bhukhan Rishi, Maturi Rishi, and other manual workers took to the Mukhya.

Delegations from other hamlets also sought to meet the Mukhya and convey their concerns to him. Yadav middle peasants such as Amaresh Yadav led such delegations, in which poor peasants and landless labourers from the Yadav, Musahar and Kevat communities contributed their numbers. The Mukhya noted that his 'meetings' with the Yadav peasants were less chaotic than the one with the Musahar labourers, because only three or four people spoke. His use of the term 'meeting' to describe their interaction contrasts with the use of terms recalling images of 'crowds' to describe his discussions with the Musahars. From the accounts of my interlocutors, the delegations led by the Yadav middle peasants were the result of some planning rather than spontaneously formed. Their members were carefully recruited by the convenors although their constitution was contingent on both availability and willingness of people. Membership in such contingent delegations was fluid, and it was rarely the case that when they met again, they would comprise exactly the same people.

However, the Mukhya also reported that many supplicants approached him individually or as duos or trios. Such supplicants were usually rich peasants and farmers who would not, under most circumstances, be eligible for receiving BPL cards. He claimed that his predecessor Hunny Singh, his uncle, the postmaster Gajen Singh and scores of other entrenched class householders had approached him requesting for BPL cards. If he was correct, that would mean that the wealthiest members of Sargana's entrenched classes sought BPL cards for themselves. The Mukhya's supplicants also included poor peasants from among the Kayasth and Rajput communities, who approached the Mukhya individually and without involving members of other communities.

The Mukhya's views chimed with the accounts of manual workers and poor peasants from among the Yadav and Musahar communities. I also gathered that not one of ward's Kayasth or Rajput poor joined the delegations led by either Yadav middle peasants or Musahar labourers. While members of the labour-hiring wealthier classes clearly separated themselves from the negotiations of the labouring classes, it is evident that poor people of Kayasth and Rajput communities did not share many solidarities with those of the Yadav, Musahar and Kevat communities.

A number of individuals tried to broker BPL cards. For instance, Gunvati Yadav reported that a wealthy Yadav peasant tried to convince her and her husband that he would procure the BPL card for them, if they paid him some money for his efforts. Likewise, Maturi Rishi narrated that a landless Kayasth political mediator promised him and his neighbours that he would obtain BPL cards for them: in exchange, he demanded a sum of fees from them. Maturi Rishi also remarked that one or two literate members of his own Musahar community were following in the said mediator's footsteps and trying to emerge as political mediators in their own right. Both Gunvati Yadav and Maturi Rishi told me the names of a few people who had gained repute for their political mediation. Political mediators commonly made such offers to their poorer friends and neighbours, and their offers were often accepted. Although Gunvati Yadav and Maturi Rishi assured me that they rejected the offers made to them, they said they knew of individuals who obtained BPL cards on payment of bribes. From their accounts, it appears that a number of literate individuals from the privileged castes, and some individuals from other social backgrounds with connections in the local bureaucracy, took on political mediation as a full-time occupation. They preferred brokering discrete deals to participating in the numerous contingent delegations, which a number of their neighbours and friends joined.

Notwithstanding their confrontations with the Mukhya and expletive-laden exchanges with him, most of my interlocutors from among the labouring classes admitted that he was easier to approach and to negotiate with than his predecessor had been. His predecessor, Hunny Singh was a Rajput member of the entrenched classes. He treated the Musahars with disdain. In a remarkably frank interview with me, he condemned the PDS on the specious grounds that it made labourers lazy and unproductive. According to him, it distorted incentives and reduced their motivation to work. Subsidized food made the labouring poor insolent and allowed them to bargain for higher remuneration. Hunny Singh's views were not an isolated strand of opinion among the entrenched classes. Postmaster Gajen Singh, his cousin with whom he shared no love lost, was even more emphatic about dismantling the limited edifice of PDS that existed. They both criticized as representing a 'backward brains' the encouragement to the poor for claiming BPL cards.

By contrast, the present Mukhya was at least willing to talk to them, to hear them out, and to consider their supplications. As we have seen, the Mukhya readily admitted the justness of their claims: it was the official stipulation to hold the cut-off at 13, which was coming in the way. He rubbished his predecessor's dismissive views on social provisioning as representative of a 'feudal mind set' (*samantvadi manasikta*). As far as the Mukhya could see, the BPL cards were not the problem. That there were too few of them was. The contrast in attitudes between an elected representative from the entrenched classes and one from the precarious classes could not be more telling. Sarvesh Mandal's stance was typical of my interlocutors from the precarious classes, including his principle electoral opponent Hiren Yadav.

The precarious classes set the agenda for Sargana's polity. They depended on the labouring poor for bolstering their nascent political influence and did their best to solicit and retain their support. Both classes shared an antipathy toward the presumptions of the entrenched classes. Given the dearth in the total number of BPL cards, the interest showed by members of the entrenched classes in these resources alarmed members of the other two classes. On the one hand, their members supported the demands of the labouring poor and joined the delegations they took to their elected representative. On the other hand, their elected representative and his advisers, also members of the precarious classes, recognized the justness of these demands. The knowledge that people sympathetic to their supplications controlled the disbursal of BPL cards encouraged the labouring poor to be assertive in their supplications and to advance their claims publicly and with confidence.

Meek supplications in a differentiated political community: Ditya

> When the surveyors came, I had to make sure that my family got the card... I asked [a Saotal community elder] to help. But

he simply told me not to worry. I approached my neighbour. He knew both Mota kaka and Sasaram babu. But what was the use? They always help their own people, never us. That's the way the world is, *jaar mathaye joto tel, she aaru beshi paye* [a phrase to mean, 'those who have more, get more'].But at least I tried.

Field notes, Group discussion, Tudtudiya hamlet,

18 February 2010

If the BPL survey schedule were to be implemented in accordance with the procedures, without any distortions, then the survey for this study (data presented in Table 4.6) suggests that only 37 per cent of Ditya's population would have received the BPL cards. Assuming a completely transparent process, over 63 per cent of all Ditya's households would be excluded from the BPL list. My interlocutors recalled harbouring anxieties that many impoverished people would inevitably be excluded from the BPL lists, irrespective of how perfectly it might be implemented. Table 4.7 shows that even were the BPL schedule to be implemented without bias, nearly half of all Ditya's households would be categorized as MPI poor but not BPL poor.

Table 4.6: Asset profile of BPL schedule poor households in Ditya

Attribute	BPL schedule poor %	BPL schedule non-poor %	Total (N)
Landless	52.67	47.33	131
Mud floor	35.91	64.09	298
Bicycle	11.45	88.55	131
Total population	36.81	63.19	326

Source: Own census survey, 2009–10.

Most accounts of people's attempts at obtaining BPL cards in Ditya converged on the actions of two Desiya men. One of these was 60-something Mota Sarkar, on whom CPI(M) politics in the ward was pivoted. The other was Sasaram Sarkar, a 50-something politician. of the Congress Party who was responsible for that party's resurgence in Ditya. The BPL survey was conducted in 2007, when Mota Sarkar's CPI(M)-affiliated son-in-law was ward member. Mota Sarkar

Table 4.7: BPL schedule poverty and multidimensional poverty in Ditya

Multidimensional poverty	BPL schedule poverty	
	No	Yes
No	14.41	1.84
Yes	48.77	34.96

Source: Own census survey, 2009–10.

accompanied the surveyors on several occasions and narrated to me some of the exchanges he had with the householders who responded to the surveyor's questions.

> [One householder] said he had no fan, nothing- not even a mobile. I knew he was lying, so I told the surveyors so. He fell at my feet, and begged me to let him have the low scores. He said he was a poor man, who needed to go out of the village to seek employment. Now, I know he is poor. But I have also to ensure the rules are followed. However, I have a heart too. [Another householder] told the surveyors that he had only one set of clothes. That's rubbish- I know he received lots of clothing at his son's recent wedding. But I can't go scouting around inside everyone's rooms, can I?[14]

Mota Sarkar was uncharacteristically open about people 'falling at his feet' and appealing for help. He rarely referred to the problems of managing a difficult population or invoked images of having to deal with motley crowds and unruly mobs. Where it was common for politicians to emphasize the difficulties of 'dealing with' the masses on account of their putative unruliness, Mota Sarkar's account referred instead to people falling at his feet requesting him to help. His account fits with that of many others whom I met in Ditya, women and men who referred to having requested him for help. Sasaram Sarkar shared similar stories. Like Mota Sarkar, with whom his relations were cordial, Sasaram Sarkar recalled that many supplicants pleaded with him to help them obtain BPL cards. However, he was even less sympathetic than Mota Sarkar to the claims of his supplicants.

> So many people said they were landless…It's amazing because then you ask [pointing to the fields], 'whose land is all this?' Maybe the government should say they are acquiring the land, and offering compensation. Then we'll see how many people say they are landless![15]

Both gentlemen's accounts resonated with the stories of supplication recounted by my interlocutors from among the labouring poor. Adivasi households anticipated – quite accurately – that they were likely to be excluded from the BPL list. Many Desiyas too knew that they would be left out of BPL lists and began to make individual requests to Mota Sarkar. Although

targeted programmes had been implemented in the past, they had been tied
to specific communities. But the BPL approach pitted members of the ward's
different communities in direct competition with one another for the same
pot of resources. Mota Sarkar and other CPI(M) leaders recognized their
inability to be able to meet all claims. They requested the elders of the ward's
different Adivasi communities for help in managing expectations among 'their'
people. Although the community elders had experience of targeting resources
to households in the past for different schemes, the challenge before the
Ward's politicians was to ensure an acceptable distribution of the same pot
of resources between the Saotals and the Desiyas. The Majhi Haram of the
Saotal community in Tudtudiya hamlet described Mota Sarkar's request thus:

> Mota appealed to me (*agrah korlo*) to help out (*sahajyo korte*).
> How could I not help him? He and his kinsmen have done so
> much for us. I asked my boys (*chengra*) to not put too much
> pressure on the old man. Although they didn't like me saying
> it [long detour on how younger people refused to abide by
> 'community' rules anymore], they kept my honour.[16]

During our conversations, Mota Sarkar paid glowing tribute to the role
of the community elders in preventing the younger and more belligerent
members of their communities from making organized representations against
him and the CPI(M). These men and women convened informal delegations
requesting their community elders to confront the CPI(M) politicians but
to no avail. The result was the proliferation of individual performances of
passive supplications to which Mota Sarkar referred in his quote above. These
supplications were aimed at convincing, persuading and sometimes cajoling
him about individual claims. Reined in by community elders, the supplicants
avoided collective contentions altogether.

The political isolation of the Saotal poor was a major factor for their meek
supplications. The Saotal elders persuaded them to have faith in Mota Sarkar's
generosity. As agricultural labourers, they were in direct conflict over wages
with the very classes who controlled the agenda of Ditya's polity. Ditya's
agricultural labourers inhabited a similar class position but could more easily
invoke moral claims of ethnic solidarity while requesting the labour-hiring
precarious class politicians for inclusion into BPL lists. Although rivalries and
intrigue between the members of the labour-hiring families were common

and mapped along political party affiliations, a remarkable consensus among them emerged over treating the Saotal and Desiya labourers differently when it came to distributing the BPL cards.

Such consensus stemmed from the moral obligations that Desiya politicians felt they owed to Desiyas less wealthy than themselves. Such politicians often voiced sentiments such as 'politics is temporary, sociality is permanent' or 'party politics [in English] has its place in our head, and social obligations (*samajik dayitto*) have a place in our hearts'. Disbursing BPL cards according to the cut-offs would mean disbursing more cards for Saotal households than for Desiyas because more Adivasis would clock up higher scores if the BPL schedule were to be correctly implemented. However, disbursing more cards to Adivasis would destabilize the moral obligations they believed they owed to their poorer neighbours and friends. Mirroring their beliefs, poorer Desiyas deployed deferential gestures and vocabularies to highlight the obligation of the Desiya leaders to provide for members of their own communities. Desiya politicians affiliated with both Congress and CPI(M) politicians acceded to the legitimacy of their claims, making it unnecessary for claimants to raise the pitch. Despite fierce electoral competition, Desiya politicians were embedded in shared moral frameworks with the poor of their communities. They steered clear of any actions that might undermine those frameworks.

The institutional responsibility for identifying BPL households rested with the ward member and other ward-level politicians. In Ditya, this meant the tightly-knit Desiya labour-hiring peasants wielded considerable influence over the process. Their control over the identification of BPL households in Ditya provided them the material resources to fulfil their moral obligations. The disbursal of BPL cards was an important means of demonstrating that they 'cared' for the Desiya poor. By doing this, the Desiya farmers and labour-recruiting peasants retained the political loyalty of the Desiya poor. While their selective provisioning of social assistance increased the economic autonomy of the Desiya poor, it did not threaten the supply of labour provided by the Saotal poor to the Desiya labour-hiring peasants. The Saotal poor, worse off than the Desiya poor and less politically networked with Desiya politicians, provided a cheap and readily available reservoir of labour into which the locality's peasants, both Saotal and Desiya, could dip.

The precarious classes' control over ward level politics pit the vast majority of the poor, most of whom were Adivasi, against a largely apathetic Desiya peasantry. Affective claims emphasizing *samajik* obligations were difficult to express for the Adivasi poor. The ones upon whom the Adivasi poor could make such claims were their own community elders. But, as we have seen, Desiya politicians co-opted these elders into the institutions of governance, deferring to them over so-called community matters while retaining the levers of authority and influence over 'political affairs', including the disbursal of welfare assistance. Not only did the Adivasi elders have little say over 'political' matters such as disbursing BPL cards, they worried that the entitlements authorized by the BPL card would induce the Saotal poor to reduce their dependence on *them* for employment and subsistence. Like the Desiya peasants, they too looked at the Saotal poor as a reservoir of cheap agricultural labour into which they could tap. Therefore, they acquiesced in the targeting of BPL cards to the Desiya poor, with a few directed toward selective Adivasi households in a bid to stymie massive discontent and anger.

Without any class allies, the majority of Ditya's Adivasi poor resigned to their exclusion from being enumerated as BPL populations. Neither the Congress not the CPI(M), both led by Desiyas, evinced any interest in fomenting demands for BPL cards among them. The Adivasi elders were enveloped in a narrative of gratitude toward the Desiya peasants because of the historic role of the latter in judiciously implementing the land redistribution programmes. The Desiya poor counted on the moral obligations of the Desiya peasants and did not need to forge cross-community alliances to demand their entitlements. The Adivasi poor accepted their political isolation and took recourse to individual supplications wherever they could.

Meek supplications in a paternalistic political place: Roshanar Ward 5

> What was the government thinking? Did it not know what this would lead to? They should have known. They take our rice to make biryani [a rice and meat preparation associated with luxury] for the rich. And they do want us to eat even a simple chapatti [flattened wheat bread associated with poverty]... They reduced us to beggars. And what did they expect when the beggars were

poor Muslims and the government was run by someone [The Mukhya's husband, the de facto Mukhya] who thinks we are his enemy. We made repeated requests to him, took delegations. But he asked us to go to our guardian....

Mansoor Ali, Roshanar Ward 5, 3 April 2010

My interlocutors in Roshanar Ward 5 reported that they had worried from the onset that the implementation of the survey schedule would lead to large-scale exclusions from the BPL lists. The results of the survey for this study, presented in Table 4.8, confirm their anxieties. The table suggests that 21 per cent of all households would be eligible for BPL cards,

Table 4.8: Asset profile of BPL schedule poor households in Roshanar Ward 5

Attribute	BPL schedule poor %	BPL schedule non-poor %	Total (N)
Landless	23.44	76.56	128
Mud floor	20.30	79.70	133
Bicycle	11.25	88.75	80
Total population	20.50	79.50	161

Source: Own census survey, 2009–10.

even if one assumes a completely unbiased selection process. Table 4.9 shows that even were the BPL schedule to be implemented without bias, over three-fifths of all Roshanar's households would be categorized as MPI poor but not BPL poor.

Table 4.9: BPL schedule poverty and multidimensional poverty in Roshanar Ward 5

Multidimensional poverty	BPL schedule poverty	
	No	Yes
No	16.77	0.62
Yes	62.73	19.87

Source: Own census survey, 2009–10.

Fearing that such exclusions would affect them the most, individual Muslims tried to meet the few politicians in the locality who they hoped would take up the issue on their behalf. As the central role in the allocation of the cards was of the Mukhya, her husband Hareram Mandal was the focus of their requests. A Kevat peasant owning 3 *bighas*, Hareram Mandal and his wife drew upon the panchayat's labouring poor for electoral support. During my interview with him, he was candid about the fact that he manipulated the BPL scores of his electors because he 'knew' they came from the poorest classes. His tone changed when I asked him about the Kunjra

Muslims of Ward 5. 'Yes,' he said dismissively, 'they came here with folded hands. I asked them to go back to their *guarjian*. He could look after them.'[17]

Hareram Mandal's account of the ward's Kunjra Muslims supplicating with 'folded hands' converges with their own description of their situation as 'beggars'. 60-something Shamsul Alam, who led one of the three informal delegations to meet him over the BPL cards said, 'We tried to remind him that he was Mukhya[18] for everyone in this panchayat, not only those who voted for him. How can he say he will only provide BPL cards to his supporters?'[19] But Hareram Mandal's response to each of the delegations was the same, asking them to return to their *guarjian*. His repeated reference to their *guarjian* alluded to the fact that the ward's inhabitants voted for the candidate supported by the landlord in the previous elections. As far as he was concerned, his wife was not accountable to the population of Roshanar Ward 5 at all. Both husband and wife reviled them as stooges of the entrenched classes.

Hareram Mandal's attitude toward the population of Ward 5 contrasted sharply with his consideration of the demands from the labouring poor of other wards. During my interviews with the Mukhya, her husband and their advisers, they often expressed sentiments as 'the poor voted for us, it is our duty (*kartavya*) to provide for them'. However, the number of BPL cards available for disbursal was considerably less than the total population who scored less than '13' in the BPL survey. The Mukhya and her husband therefore prioritized the people they knew had voted for her. If she and her advisors were to provide BPL cards to those who had *not* voted for her, at the expense of those who did, it would send a conflicted message to her electors. They would see it as a violation of the political contract into which they had entered when they voted overwhelmingly for her. She and her husband were determined to use their control over the panchayat to deliver BPL cards to the labouring poor who had elected them. The poor of Ward 5 were not going to be among them.

The marginalization of Ward 5's Kunjra Muslim poor was exacerbated by the expressed inability of that Gajdeo Mandal, the rich farmer to whom most people in the ward turned to for advice. To me, Gajdeo Mandal explained that the Mukhya's avowals of enmity towards people like himself, made him personally unwilling to take up the matter of the BPL cards at all. If he saw even a faint chance of the Mukhya heeding his request, he might have considered lending his support to Shamsul Alam's delegations. But, given the Mukhya's hostility attitude, he reasoned, such a step would undermine his social status. He concluded against joining any delegation that approached the Mukhya. 'What's the point?' he asked me shrugging his shoulders and twisting his wrists as he did so.

As the wealthiest farmer in Roshanar Ward 5, Gajdeo Mandal took his responsibilities towards other members of his own Gangot community very seriously. Not only did he extend to them financial support during emergencies and key life events, he organized public feasts, to which he took care to invite all people in the locality, from the richest landlord to the poorest labourer. Gajdeo Mandal also convened devotional conclaves, at which itinerant priests delivered sermons. He frequently led negotiations with the bureaucracy over availability of seeds and fertilizers in the local market, as well as provided practical advice to his less wealthy neighbours. Gajdeo Mandal's actions won him the unstinted admiration of members of his Gangot community. Following his advice on the question of BPL cards, members of the Gangot community stayed aloof from the delegations convened by the Kunjra Muslim labourers to the Mukhya. Landowning Muslims, deeply grateful to Gajdeo Mandal for having protected their lives and properties from Hindu Rightwing mischief-mongers in the past, acquiesced with his decisions.

A conversation with Pritam Singh, the self-styled guardian of the Kunjra Muslim labourers to whom the Mukhya had asked his supplicants to return, shed further light on Gajdeo Mandal's attitudes towards BPL cards. As Pritam Singh's tenant for several decades, Gajdeo Mandal was loyal and dependable. Whereas Gajdeo Mandal emblemized authority and influence when conversing with his neighbours, I noticed that his demeanour completely transformed in Pritam Singh's presence on the two occasions that I observed them together. As Gajdeo Mandal's landlord, Pritam Singh wielded considerable influence over him. The enterprising farmer that Gajdeo Mandal was, he improved agricultural productivity on the tracts of land which Pritam Singh leased out to him. Both parties benefitted from the tenancy arrangement. Furthermore, both parties recognized that the availability of cheap and timely labour was important for agricultural outputs and consequent profits. Pritam Singh was blunt in his declaration that BPL cards made labourers lazy and unwilling to work. Because BPL cards enabled labourers to obtain cheap food, they no longer needed to work as hard as their forefathers did, he reasoned. Gajdeo

Mandal was less blatant about his disdain for BPL cards, but concurred with Pritam Singh's reasoning, as he told me in hushed tones. At the same time, he was not entirely unmindful of the fact that the BPL cards meant a lot in terms of the services to which they provided poor people access. When poor peasants and landless labourers from the Gangot community approached him for his advice, he said he had no option but to assure them that he would use his connections with the bureaucracy. But he consistently advised them against any collective action that would politicize the question of the BPL cards.

Left with no social allies, the Muslim labourers of Roshanar Ward 5 resigned to accepting that they would be discriminated against during the distribution of BPL cards. None of the locality's leading politicians supported their claims much less raise demands on their behalf. The Mukhya of the panchayat was publicly concerned about disbursing the cards to her own electors and maintaining her end of the political contract. But Ward 5's Muslim poor could count on no help at all in voicing their requests to be enumerated as BPL households. They harboured no illusions about the Mukhya's generosity. As the quote with which I started this section makes clear, my interlocutors from the Kunjra community did not think their representations would matter at all, and the President's brusque attitude to them left them with even less hope.

III

Supplications as politics

Poor people's supplications are embedded in a complex of vocabularies constituting representation and gratitude, contracts and care, and obligations and requests. Such vocabularies epitomize a crucial means of negotiating with their elected representatives and political mediators. On one hand, the poor plead for social assistance before different politicians. They make their requests for BPL cards to political mediators who possess a reputation for efficaciousness. On the other hand, they expect governments to take cognizance of their pleas and to provide them with social assistance. The supplicants know that the cards are meant to be directed to the poor and that *they* are entitled to them. They are in little doubt that the cards have been conceived of by the government and not by the mediators themselves.

The varied forms of requests, appeals, and pleas were couched in deferential language that emphasized the apparent political subordination of the supplicants. Through such supplications, they highlighted the extent to which they 'needed' the cards and emphasized that it would be good for them and their families if they were to receive it. In making these supplications, they invoked their being poor rather than referring to their status as citizens: in making such invocations, they were of course being pragmatic, as the distribution of BPL cards was contingent not on their status as citizens but on the basis of the scores obtained by individual households.

Are their supplications political? An important reason for affirming the political dimension of the supplications is their purposeful practice. The supplications are intended to advance a social perspective. These practices foment a collective self-identification among the supplicants, through which they forge shared, if contested, meanings of social life. To be sure, enumeration as a BPL household entitles people to a number of social protection schemes, ranging from subsidized food and housing to maternity benefits and old-age pensions. These are provisions that all households covet, but realize that only some will obtain. But the competition over the allocation of a limited number of BPL cards does not by itself constitute politics. Rather, what renders such supplications the subject of politics are the discussions that accompany them, and the contested meanings that are concomitant upon them.

For the labouring poor, access to social assistance schemes implies less dependence for their sustenance on local hirers of their labour. The subsidies and other assistance associated with being enumerated as BPL entitle them to minimal food and housing security as well as financial support for aged or pregnant family members. By possessing BPL cards, labouring households can access such social provisions and reduce their dependence on the labour-hiring classes. The supplications thus represent purposeful actions by the poor.

That the social perspective the poor advance brings them into tension with the social perspectives of the labour-hiring classes adds to the conflictual dimension of the politics of supplication. The labour-hiring classes are no less enthusiastic about the prospect of obtaining BPL cards for themselves. The number of subsidies and social assistance associated with the cards is a crucial motivating factor. Such provisions are important for the many precariously placed households, those who are not quite impoverished but who are not socially or economically very distinct from the poor. Another factor motivating the labour-hiring classes is to try and reduce the number of cards available to the labouring poor. If fewer poor people obtained the cards, they would have little option but to rely on their employers for their livelihoods. If the labouring classes are correct, the competition over BPL cards is no mere tussle over scarce resources, but a contest over allowing the poor to access social provisioning at all. A policy framework that targets social assistance only exacerbates this contest.

The supplications foment a number of apparently contradictory self-identifications among the poor. Even as the poor supplicate for the cards, they combine their affective vocabularies of care and concern with invocations of obligations that elected representatives bear towards their constituencies. The supplications convey to elected representatives and other political mediators that supplicants deserve help and protection. In several instances, the supplications are anchored in suggestions that it is the duty of the elected representatives to look after their electors. In other instances, people insist that their elected representatives take cognizance of them as voters. Although the supplications do not invoke any notion of entitlements, they do advance notions of care, obligation and reciprocity. The labouring classes convene contingent delegations, meet in transient collectives to confront their representatives, and publicize from time to time their concerns that the cards might be diverted to propertied families. Householders organize spontaneously before politicians and political mediators to plead that their household scores be reduced or that the official stricture be waived in their favour. At other times, they insist that the official cut-offs are too low and should be increased to accommodate more households. They keenly follow the decisions taken by their elected representatives over the formalization of the lists. Through the ensemble of such practices, poor people forge their collective identities as people needing social assistance in order to secure their livelihoods and lead dignified lives.

The arguments over enumeration as BPL reflect contrasting meanings of social life. The labouring classes interpret the BPL cards as indicative of the state's care for them. The existence of the BPL cards conveys to them that the state's functionaries *are* interested in their welfare. As far as they can see, the BPL cards constitute acts of kindness by the government toward toiling labourers. On the other hand, for many of their wealthier and more propertied neighbours, BPL cards induce laziness among the poor and corruption among the officials and elected representatives. Such individuals blatantly associate such subsidized provisioning with labour shortages and complain that governments pander to the labouring poor due to electoral exigencies instead of attending to the needs of people like themselves toiling peasants, enterprising farmers and the like. Such contests of meanings sharpen the element of antagonism between the labouring poor and the labour-hiring classes.

Nonetheless people's supplications remain embedded in the social relations of power in all the four political places. As we have seen, their negotiations with their elected representatives, political mediators and members of other classes vary across the four localities. Rahimpur's entrenched classes support the locality's labouring poor in their bid to embarrass precarious class politicians. Sargana's precarious class politicians collaborate with poor people's demands for BPL cards, even when they themselves are the focus of such demands. The labouring classes in Ditya and Roshanar find themselves isolated, as the labour-hiring classes coalesce together. People's embeddedness in the social relations of power are of course unintentional: they do not intend to confirm or challenge the social relations of power when they make their supplications. Nevertheless, what they do, as I have indicated earlier, advances a perspective of them being autonomous with respect to the labour-hiring classes. That their supplications are intended to advance a social perspective, renders these acts ineluctably political.

Beyond semi-clientelism and citizenship: The spaces of political society?

What do poor people's supplications tell us about the ways in which they negotiate democracy and the meanings they make of it? Are the pleas and requests which constitute the supplications discussed in this chapter indicative of clientelistic practices? Or are the frequent invocations of contractual vocabularies attending to the supplications representative of citizenship claims? Building on, but also departing from, Fox's (1994) framework of semi-clientelism Robert Gay (2006) analyses the overlaps between clientelism and citizenship. The president of the neighbourhood committee Gay studies in a Brazilian *favela* invites payments from several politicians for his neighbourhood in exchange of a promise to deliver votes to them. Eventually, the president double-crosses most of the politicians. Gay characterizes this process as the 'democratization of clientelism'. It is clientelistic because the votes of the neighbourhood are promised in exchange for material rewards. But it is democratizing because the provision of material rewards does not subdue the electoral autonomy of the neighbourhood's residents. The residents do not vote for every single politician who paid them: they cannot. Gay also discusses the obverse process – the 'clientelization of democracy'– to refer to a process through which the poor would 'thank' politicians and extend their gratitude to them for provisioning goods to which they were entitled by the law. Gay's account is useful in trying to think of the multifaceted encounters between poor people and democratic institutions. The supplications presented in this book inhabit these spaces at the intersection of clientelism and citizenship.

The accounts presented in this chapter reveal that poor people's supplications to local politicians and community leaders, even when marked by severe limitations, are not singularly underpinned by relations of subordination. To be sure, the supplications are couched in deferential vocabularies. But supplicants do assert their claims quite forcefully in some localities, such as in Rahimpur and Sargana. The evidence from these two localities points to the eschewal of hierarchy by the supplicants in their exchanges with their elected representatives, other politicians, and political mediators. While the cases from Ditya and Roshanar caution against generalizing these claims, even here there is little evidence that the political autonomy of the poor is truncated. Poor people openly speak about the discrimination to which they are subject. Subsequent rounds of fieldwork and telephonic conversations with select interlocutors indicate that they do not acquiesce with politicians who seek to influence their electoral behaviour: none of the elected representatives responsible for the disbursal of BPL cards is reelected. People harbour no illusions about the generosity or magnanimity of their politicians or political mediators. In the absence of hierarchical relations, it is difficult to sustain the claim that the supplications by the poor described herein are clientelistic, or even semi-clientelistic. Political subordination is nearly absent in the cases analysed in this chapter.

Kitschelt and Wilkinson (2007) suggest that clientelistic relationships persist even when political subordination is absent. To them, *contingency* in the defining feature of a clientelistic relationship. If, following Kitschelt and Wilkinson, we accept that clientelism refers to a situation where politicians' disbursal of resources to people is contingent upon the latter extending political support to the former, then the framework of clientelism may arguably be applied to the transactions in Roshanar, where the Mukhya and her husband were explicit about rewarding her voters and penalizing those who were not. However, her actions were contingent upon electoral support already extended to her, rather than in anticipation of winning more votes. In this respect, the situation in Roshanar is not very different from what obtained in Rahimpur or Sargana, where the populations demanded to be given BPL cards because they claimed to have voted for the said politicians. In much the same way, the framework of clientelism is inappropriate to apply in Ditya where the Desiya politicians were expected to provision for their Desiya brethren, irrespective of the party for which they voted.

In the absence of either subordination or contingency, clientelism appears to be an inaccurate category while discussing poor people's negotiations with democracy. If this is so, does it follow that that we discuss the negotiations presented in this chapter as incipient forms of citizenship? Much recent scholarship, following the leads provided by Margaret Somners, shows that citizenship exceeds the status conferred by the governments. Citizenship refers to 'a set of institutionally-embedded social practices' (Somers, 1993) that are constituted by and depend upon ideas and associations emphasizing membership and universal rights and obligations in a national community. Citizenship is thus a sociological rather than a juridical claim anchored in complexes of rights and obligations. The discussions in this chapter emphasize the contractual underpinnings of the pleas, which impoverished people advance vis-à-vis their politicians, and through them to the state. The delegations seek the audience of local politicians directly. When confronting politicians and political mediators, the supplicants remind them of the political support *that have already extended* to them. In Rahimpur and Sargana, people also warn their politicians of the electoral support they might direct elsewhere if their demands are not met. Although the very rationale of the targeted programme induces the understanding that not everyone will receive the cards, people do not hesitate to seek out their elected representatives, other politicians, and political mediators to collectively, if informally, press their claims. Such contractual underpinnings point to the egalitarian dimension of poor people's claims. It might be tempting then, to interpret poor people's claims as advancing citizenship claims.

Nonetheless, although the supplications are premised on contractual assumptions, there are important reasons to be circumspect about analysing them under the rubric of citizenship. For one, the supplicants *supplicate*. Although they indicate an awareness that the BPL cards are designated for the poor, they recognise the enormous discretion that lie in the hands of local politicians. They are also aware that elected representatives are subject to numerous such claims and will only be able to fulfil only a limited number. Such understandings limited the extent to which they can pressurize their representatives. People, therefore, take recourse to affective vocabularies of favour, care, and moral obligation. They avoid the juridical vocabularies of law, rights, rules, and entitlements. The supplications rarely invoke a notion of rights that they derived from their 'status' as Indian citizens. Rather, they seek to incite the sympathy of their leaders and referred to themselves as deprived (*vanchhit*) and poor (*gorib/garib*).

Another reason to be circumspect about applying the analytic lens of 'citizenship' to the cases described in this chapter stems from the imbrications of the languages of citizenship with quite specific political–economic configurations. Citizenship, Somers (1993) alerts us, results from historically precise interactions between particularist practices and universal laws that produced quite specific public spheres. Her account focuses on variations within England and the differences between the emergent public sphere in its pastoral and arable regions, due to which the rule of law became central to popular imagination in the former region, but not so in the latter. James Holston's (2008) analysis of changing political identities among the urban poor in São Paulo's *favelas* reveals that they developed a sense of citizenship through their roles as propertyowners, taxpayers, and consumers. In both these cases, citizenship emerges as a quite particular political experience that cannot simply be extrapolated to cover all situations. Indeed, the way in which citizenship as an instituted practice is implicated with notions of individual rights, private property, and payment of taxes increases my ambivalence about applying it as an optic to examine the supplications of eastern India's rural poor over the BPL cards.

Some commentators find the distinction between clientelism and citizenship overdrawn and would rather have us focus on the entanglements. They argue that the two are in fact quite compatible. Partha Chatterjee (2004) directs attention to the ways in which the poor appeal to differentiated, rather than universal, conceptions of citizenship to secure their livelihoods. To defend the meagre acquisitions that they might obtain through methods that the apparatus of the rule of law labels as 'illegal', the poor seek redress in moral, rather than juridical, terms. Through such moral claims, they request exemptions from the rule of law rather than ask for it to be applied universally. Chatterjee provides the example of the inhabitants of a squatter community in Kolkata who request, appeal, and plead before authorities to exempt them from the law and not evict them. They invoke their own poverty and ask the authorities to consider their compulsions and constraints, not in the name of the law, but in the name of the moral obligation of the state toward its poor. In doing so, they present themselves as members of a single community of refugees-turned-squatters (Chatterjee, 2004, 57). Chaterjee terms these practices as practices of political society. The arbitrariness of these practices and the results they entail is unmistakable. But such arbitrariness is preferred by the squatters, Chatterjee assures us, to the rule of law. The rule of law which Chatterjee equates to the practices of civil society is not favoured because were it to be applied, the squatters would be evicted.

Chatterjee's normative proposals for differentiated citizenship might appear to resolve the contradiction between formal political equality and substantive socio-economic inequalities that has troubled observers since at least Marx (1843). As successive scholars have shown, the 'status' of citizenship is quite compatible with economic inequality[20], citizenship 'incorporates' the working class[21], and facilitates a social truce[22] that is disadvantageous to the working class. The notion of differentiated citizenship appears to offer a way out of this conundrum. The poor seek to secure their lives and livelihoods through moral negotiations in political society. They deploy affective terms of 'agrah' and 'nibedan' to describe themselves in relation to influential politicians and political mediators. The relationships supplicants seek to forge invoke the obligations that they believe politicians owe to them. That these demands are not anchored in universalist vocabularies of the state, constitutional provisions, and government ordinances do not diminish their importance to the claims of the poor. We might follow Chatterjee to suggest that a differentiated notion of citizenship, espoused by poor people's negotiations with actors in political society, seems to provide a way of resolving the tension between political equality and socio-economic inequality.

However, critics (Baviskar and Sundar, 2008) justifiably argue that Chatterjee draws too neat a distinction between civil society and political society. Their argument chimes with Niraja Gopal Jayal's (2013) subtle criticism of the binary that scholars have often drawn between universal citizenship and group differentiated citizenship in the context of demands for affirmative action by members of India's historically oppressed communities. Indeed, writing about differentiated citizenship, Iris Marion Young (1989) reminded us long ago that egalitarian imaginations of the political community need not be difference blind. Chatterjee's endorsement of differentiated rather than equal conceptions of membership in the political community as a normative standard for governance is at odds with many of the substantive claims advanced by the inhabitants of political society. Kolkata's squatters do not want themselves and their descendants to remain squatters and be subjected of the insecurities and vulnerabilities entailed in squatting. Rather, they request not to be evicted presumably so that they can better their lives and get their children out and away from the squatter-communities.

In this chapter, as we have seen, claims expressing difference ('we are poor') do not preclude assumptions of equality vis-à-vis the politicians on whom they are focussed. Variations within and between the four villages notwithstanding, supplicants either assert their claims as equal members of the community or lament their treatment as subordinates. Even in Roshanar, where they receive the shoddiest treatment among all of my interlocutors, they resent their being 'reduced to beggars'. That their expectation of being treated as equal by the Mukhya is violated is evident from the bitterness that accompanies their narrative. Ditya's labouring classes repeat the metaphor about the wealthy becoming wealthier, but also indicate their discontent with such a situation. Where the labouring poor collaborate with either of the two labour-hiring classes, their supplications are more assertive. Nevertheless, across all four localities, despite the very concrete disparities of authority and command over resources, the form of the requests – the supplications – do not entail any acquiescence with political hierarchy. The recognition of their own actual subordination by the supplicants does not thwart their expectations that they be treated as equals by their interlocutors. Chatterjee's endorsement of differentiated membership in the political community ignores the egalitarian ideas that in fact animate popular claims. Even as I am drawn towards approaches that explore the entanglements between clientelism and citizenship, I remain skeptical of the analytical utility of the political society framework.

Agonistic supplications

If the supplications before politicians and politician mediators are exemplar neither of clientelism nor of citizenship, how are we to theorize them? How are we to understand the practices of people who inhabit the entangled spaces between the category of the client and the citizen? To answer this question, I want to emphasise the ensemble of collaborative and antagonistic perspectives to which the dramatis personae of this chapter introduce us.

My interlocutors refer to their poverty and deprivation while invoking the justness of their requests, always remarking on the fact that they are *people* (*aadmi/insaan* in Hindi, *manush* in Bangla). The refrain in all four locations, variations in the performance of supplications notwithstanding, is something like: 'We are poor people. [The elected representative] should (have) give(n) us the cards.' The sense is that politicians and political mediators *ought to* protect and help poor people, even if that makes them unpopular with the wealthy and the propertied classes. When they meet their elected representatives in their many delegations, poor people reinforce their *collective* personhood as *shob garib manush* (Bangla) or as *garib janata* (Hindi) to reiterate their commonly shared grievances and to seek collective redress. Although the delegations often comprise neighbours who might all be members of the same community, they refer less to their caste identity and more often to their social personhood. In emphasizing their social personhood, they do not ask for BPL cards to be distributed to every household in the village or to every poor household or even to every poor household of their caste. But they justify their requests by referring to themselves collectively as being poor people.

In emphasizing their poverty, my interlocutors in all four locations invoke metaphors of injustice (*anyay*) and exploitation (*atyachar* in Bangla and *shoshan* in Hindi). They anchor their supplications in vocabularies of justice (*nyaysangat* in Hindi/*nyayjyo* in Bangla). Indeed, they do not interpret their being poor to results of past deed (*karma*) and bad fortune (*kismet*). Rather, as far as they can tell, they are poor because they are exploited by farmers, industrialists, contractors, middlemen, politicians, bureaucrats, policemen, and sometimes even by other people in poverty. The government's policy of targeting social assistance only benefits the enterprising people who would easily corner these resources. The comment about the rich accruing more wealth from Ditya is particularly instructive, as is the remark about government officials pandering to the propertied from Roshanar. Variants of these views are expressed in other locations as well. A notion of inchoate antagonism against the wealthy and the propertied is discernible even in Rahimpur where the poor are incorporated in relationships of guardianship with the entrenched classes: readers will recall the satisfaction with which poor people reported at the taming of the entrenched classes.

Where the labouring classes who believe they are wrongly excluded from BPL lists express discontent, such discontent is not usually directed against other households of similar socio-economic backgrounds who do receive BPL cards. From their point of view, they lose out due to the machinations of the elected representative or other political mediators rather than to the conspiracies hatched by other poor people. Some of them point to the unfairness of the survey schedule. Or, they blame the manipulation of their wealthier neighbours who procure the BPL cards by edging out those who were more 'deserving' for the cards. For instance, in Sargana Ward 1, Maturi Rishi and his brother Shanichar Rishi, who both work as agricultural labourers, found that their names had been excluded from the list of BPL households. However, the names of their neighbours, Hansram Bhagat and Narendra Yadav, who were only slightly better off, were included. However, neither brother complained against either of these individuals for having their names included in the BPL list. But they, and almost all my interlocutors from the Musahar *tola* in Sargana Ward 1 (east), reviled their moneylender, Shalimar Singh, who succeeded in having his name included in the BPL list. Shalimar Singh was Rajput and owned several large pieces of agricultural property. He had reported himself as being landless, without any assets of his own ('even the clothes I wear are not my own,' he shamelessly told me) and had reported to the surveyors that he preferred state assistance in the form of wage labour. On the first two counts, he was not – juridically speaking – wrong: the land and the assets were indeed in his father's name. Nevertheless, almost everyone in the Musahar *tola* I spoke to pointed to him as a negative example of someone who had taken away a BPL card that should have gone to a 'poor person'.

While the claims for BPL cards do not originate from a sense that the cards constitute a right, or that they should be allocated on the basis of survey scores, the sentiment that the cards are for 'poor people' (*garib aadmi/gorib manush*) is unmistakable. These idioms of collective personhood, combined with an inchoate antagonism towards the entrenched classes, convey the coalescence of a political identity that cannot be subsumed under the rubric of either client or citizen. They are also distinct from the moral solidarities envisaged in Partha Chatterjee's (2004) formulation of political society. Chatterjee is quite correct in arguing that the poor sometimes request to be exempted from rules and laws that are likely to marginalize and exclude them further, and that in doing so, they invoke the moral obligations of the state toward its poor as well as idioms of care and kinship. But from this empirical point to make the theoretical claim that poor people's politics is a politics of differentiated membership in the political community is to ignore the egalitarian expectations that accompany their supplicating practices. My criticism of Chatterjee is not to endorse the Liberal approach of arguing that the labouring poor forge juridical solidarities derived from being recipients of the 'status' of citizenship. Indeed, the people readers have met in this chapter neither invoke notions of rights, laws, and entitlements, nor ideas of tax-paying citizens, property owners and consumers. The vocabularies through which poor people convey their supplications prevent me from imposing an exclusively juridical view of these political practices.

Rather, supplicants invoke the notion of being 'poor people' in an ambivalently conflictual relationship with wealthy and the propertied folk. A sense of antagonism against an inchoately characterized 'rich' is indeed discernible from the accounts of exploitation presented by my interlocutors. But the poor do not express any thoughts about a revolutionary overthrow of the existing order or the annihilation of propertied groups. Many among them labour on the fields and farms of wealthier peasants and farmers. They face the repression of wages, practice of social discrimination and nurturing of social hierarchy that their wealthier neighbours engage in. Others are in the debt of moneylenders or farmers, a situation about which they worry. But they do not identify a singular class enemy against whom they direct their antagonism. Thus, they neither consent with the rule of the dominant and the privileged nor conflict with it. Rather, they occupy an agonistic location whereby they strive to negotiate with democracy as best as they can.

The supplicants we have met in this chapter recognise that their poverty is the result of their oppression by the entrenched classes and/ or the precarious classes. But this recognition does not lead them to imagine the destruction of the oppressive structures to which they are subjected. Side by side, the supplicants do not quite acquiesce in their own subordination or consent to their being dominated: their frequent use of the lexes of anyay and atyachar suggest that they do not harbour any illusions that they are somehow responsible for their own poverty. Rather, the impoverished men and women whose political practices have been examined in this chapter weave collaboration with contention in their negotiations. Their supplications combine entreaties for care with heckling of politicians, though as we have seen, these combinations vary, shaped as they are by the political spaces within which the poor are embedded. The invocations of peoplehood, whose collective impoverishment is caused by the oppression of the 'rich', imbue poor people's supplications with an agonistic content.

People's supplications towards political mediators and other politicians represent a key facet of their negotiations with democracy. They realize that the targeting policy is likely to be disastrous and refuse to submit quietly to its conditions. However, they do not reject it altogether. Although their supplications are internally fragmented and vary across locations, a notion of collective personhood is discernible. Supplicants routinely invoke the notion of 'poor people' who are exploited by the rich. Such conceptualizations point us to the agonistic character of the supplications.

Conclusion

This chapter has done four things. One, it recounted the history of targeting programmes with a special reference to India. The targeted policy framework resulted in people 'supplicating' before their elected representatives, other politicians and political mediators so that they could be enumerated as eligible for assistance. Two, the chapter documented people's supplications for BPL cards. It reported the heterogeneities in people's supplications. Three, the chapter analysed these heterogeneities by directing attention to the configuration of social relations of power. Supplications are assertive in localities where the poor collaborate with either the entrenched or the precarious classes. Elsewhere, supplications are meek and reticent. Four, such variations notwithstanding, this chapter theorized supplications as intimating their agonistic negotiations which reflect the entanglements of clientelism with citizenship.

People's supplications for BPL cards do not only signal their entreaties to be enumerated as recipients of social assistance. Their actions convey the meanings with which they imbue contemporary India's unequal democracy. These meanings derive from the expectation held by the poor vis-a-vis elected institutions and the people who populate these institutions in a formal and informal capacity. Crucial to their expectations are such notions as care and concern which they ask their politicians to demonstrate. Perhaps even more important are the expectations that elected politicians would help them reduce their dependence on the dominant classes. The poor link oppression to their poverty and expect their elected politicians to blunt the oppression they confront. To be sure, popular sovereignty may not directly appear to animate poor people's claims. But the expectations is that elected politicians will listen to what they have to say. Underpinning these expectations are agonistic negotiations which combine consent with contention, thereby. These negotiations are dynamic, as will become clear in the forthcoming chapters, where we see that the very people who supplicate for BPL cards in this chapter demand employment from the state, dispute the paternalism of their self-appointed trustees and forge egalitarian imaginations of their membership in the political community.

Endnotes

1   The use of such categorical measures to enumerate poor households stands in awkward tension with the analytical approach of the book, in which I understand poverty as oppression and, hence, relational. Nevertheless, the descriptive use of such categorical measures provided me with the data to demonstrate the scale of exclusions that were spawned by the Indian government's targeted approach to identifying the poor.

2 For excellent overviews, see Piliavsky (2013) and Auyero (1999).

3 For further details, the reader may wish to consult Bailey (1960), Karanth (1987), Migdal (1988), Morris-Jones (1967), and Weiner (1989).

4 Similarly limited in its reach to the poorest segments of rural society had been India's Community Development Programme, launched in 1952, aimed at raising the standard of living of people in rural communities. By 1978, the Indian government redesigned the programme under the Integrated Rural Development Programme (IRDP) and explicitly sought to target the poor (Drèze, 1990 and Copestake, 1992).

5 As one World Bank study ironically concluded, some amount of 'leakages' was *necessary* to sustain a targeted regime and secure the support of powerful actors for it (Gelbach and Pritchett, 1997).

6 Recent developments have been more heartening. In September 2013, the Indian government instituted the Food Security Act. Under the aegis of this act, the government promises to determine the number of beneficiaries on the basis of a socio-economic census (rather than estimations by the Planning Commission). As discussed in chapter 2, the census figures show a considerably higher number of people living in poverty than the Planning Commission's estimations did. Although the policy remains a targeted one, the net is cast wider, provisioning for up to 75 per cent of the rural population and up to 50 per cent of the urban population.

7 Writ Petition (C) No. 196 of 2001.

8 Excellent discussions on these questions are to be found in Sundaram (2002), Jalan and Murugai (2007), Alkire and Seth (2008), and Planning Commission (2009).

9 Ideally, the list of BPL households had to be ratified by the gram sabha. This process was rarely followed.

10 Interview notes, Joynal Ali, c. 60, Rahimpur village square, 1 February 2010.

11 Interview notes, Arif Miya, c. 32, Rahimpur village square, 3 February 2010.

12 Interview notes, Sargana Ward 1, Mukhya's office, 3 March 2010.

13 Interview notes, Sargana Ward 1, Musahar tola machan (west), 6 March 2010.

14 Interview notes, Mota Sarkar's residence, 21 February 2010.

15 Field notes, Hanging out, Sasaram Sarkar, path connecting Ditya village with Kajhlijhopa hamlet, 19 February 2010.

16 Interview notes, the Majhi Haram, Tudtudiya Hamlet, 18 February 2010.

17 Interview notes, Hareram Mandal, Mukhya's residence, 2 April 2010.

18 Although his wife was the de jure Mukhya, people routinely referred to him as the Mukhya. Rather than reflecting gender prejudice among my interlocutors, I think there references indicated an intimate knowledge of the fact that he, rather than she, was taking the decisions.

19 Hanging out, Abdur Rehman's betel nut kiosk, 5 April 2010.

20 Marshall's (1950) work remains seminal in this regard.

21 See Dahrendorf (1959), Bendix (1964) and Lipset (1964) for the classic formulations of these sentiments.

22 Giddens' (1982) work is exemplary in this context.

5

From Moral Vocabularies to Languages of Stateness?

The Politics of Demands

We worked on the Ek Sho Deener Kaaj [100 days work scheme, a colloquial reference to NREGA] so that our children and grandchildren would never have to work on something like that. Ever.

Majhuli Moholi, 28 February 2010,
Ditya, 30, landless labourer

Democracies provide certain opportunity structures for populations within their jurisdictions to press for their claims. India's democracy, riven though it is with widening inequalities, provides quite specific political spaces for the poor to advance their demands. In the previous chapter, I noted the ways in which they negotiate with politicians and political mediators over the implementation of a narrowly-targeted social policy. In this chapter, I explore their negotiations in the context of a more broad-based social policy, one into which participants self-select themselves. Does the expansion of generalized social policy eliminate poor people's negotiations with elected representatives, other politicians and political mediators? In this chapter, I suggest that their negotiations continue despite the introduction of generalized social policy. However, the form of such negotiations is different from the supplications we encountered in the previous chapter, couched as they are in the vocabulary of 'demands'. The empirical material in this chapter refers to the labouring classes' demands for work to their elected local governments under the aegis of India's Mahatma Gandhi National Rural Employment Guarantee Act (MGNREGA, or NREGA for a shorter acronym). The stipulations of the MGNREGA entitle any member of India's rural household to apply for unskilled manual work. Such work is to be remunerated at prevailing wage rates, subject to a maximum of 100 days of work per household. The state is mandated by law to provide such work. In the event of failure, the state must pay applicants an unemployment allowance. In fact, applications for work scarcely result in the provision of work. Nevertheless, believing the programme to be useful to them, while also taking care not to antagonize influential people in their locality, applicants undertake a plethora of strategies to advance their points of view.

How are we to understand people's demands for work in the light of our concerns about the meanings people make of democracy? Do their demands appropriate the juridical vocabularies of the state, signalling their incorporation as the subject of rights? The fieldwork data on which I draw includes sample surveys, in-depth interviews with key informants (workers, politicians and bureaucrats) and ethnography. I combine these with an analysis of the policy narrative underpinning NREGA and a history of employment guarantee schemes in India. I position this material in conversation with the prevalent scholarly ways of narrating demands on the state as imbibing 'languages of stateness' and reflective of a 'transition' away from the use of moral vocabularies. Such narratives hinge on the universal/ particular dichotomy, whereby 'languages of stateness' are thought to signal universalistic ideals that inexorably erode particularistic practices. The material I present compels me to think of people's demands as exceeding the dichotomies between 'moral vocabularies' and 'languages of stateness'. I critically engage with James Ferguson's (2013) meditations on on popular claims directed at the state as 'declarations of dependence'. Although Ferguson's suggestions are important, I remain wary of their theoretical utility. Instead, I implore readers to consider demands on the state as agonistic negotiations. Such negotiations reflect neither the obstinacy of moral vocabularies nor the victory of the Liberal languages of stateness. These are also not to be conflated with poor people's declarations of dependence, I suggest. Rather, they reveal the entanglements between the two.

In Section I, I first point to key aspects of the literature on the everyday state and the moral and the juridical claims to which it is subjected. Thereafter, I situate MGNREGA in the wider literature on generalized social policy that represented a 'targeting within universalism' approach. I then provide a brief overview of public works and employment guarantee programmes in India before turning to a discussion of the key features of the MGNREGA. In Section II, I discuss the ways in which the labouring classes attempted to access employment under the MGNREGA in each of the four fieldwork locations. A disaggregated approach allows me to be attentive to the heterogeneities in their demands for work. The applications were assertive in some localities, while meek and resigned in others. In Section III, I underscore theoretical implications of these heterogeneities for our broad concerns about poor people's politics.

This chapter does four things. One, it reminds us of the provenance of the generalized approaches to social assistance in India so that we may be able to appreciate the political space provided by governmental interventions in public policy. Two, it documents poor people's demands for social assistance. Three, it is sensitive to the heterogeneities in their demands by pointing to the variable political spaces in the four fieldwork places. Four, it engages critically with the academic approaches to conceptualizing such demands as indicating the persistence of 'moral vocabularies', reflecting a particularistic worldview and one that necessarily undermines the universalistic perspectives espoused by juridical languages of stateness.

Engaging the everyday state: Languages of stateness and moral economies

Philip Abrams' (1988) seminal work heralded a significant shift in the study of the actually-existing state. Herein, he distinguishes the 'state idea' from the 'state system'. Whereas the former refers to the belief among political theorists that the state exists as a unified entity, the latter pertains to the 'palpable nexus of practice and institutional structure centered in government' (Abrams, 1988, 58). Following this lead, analysts are able to examine the variety of often contradictory ways in which the state manifests its presence in people's lives. This perspective has allowed scholars to seek quotidian understandings of the state.[1] The everyday state refers to the panoply of structures, institutions, and apparatuses that populations encounter during their routine and one-off interaction with different agencies of the government. It includes the medley of practices, procedures, operations, and representations that are institutionalized in the apparatus of the state (Hansen and Stepputat, 2001). Such institutionalizations concretize the abstract notion of the state and help people assign meanings to it. Thinking about the everyday state permits social scientists to take cognisance of the ways in which the 'language of stateness' – the state's (meta)authority to validate or invalidate other forms of authority – permeate people's daily lives.

The suggestion that states provide people with juridical vocabularies is sometimes followed up to argue that people's appropriation of such vocabularies reflects their assimilation into a juridical rights-based conception of the state. One aspect of this argument is that people imbibe the languages of states. Writing about rural eastern India, Stuart Corbridge and his colleagues (2005) refer to the manner in which the region's labouring poor absorb ideas of development and empowerment that emanate from the juridical vocabularies of the state. Courtney Jung's (2008) sensitive study of the Zapatistas in Mexico alerts us to the ways in which that country's indigenous populations appropriate the languages of rights. Mortimer Nielsen (2011), under the rubric of 'inverse governmentality', discusses the ways in which urban residents of Maputo, Mozambique, mimic the state's urban housing plans in order to claim legality for their illegal dwellings . O'Brien and Li (2006) refer to the 'rightful resistance' through which peasants in China draw upon the rights provided by the state to defend their livelihoods.

Another aspect of this argument is offered by authors who point to the more instrumental use to which the poor put the state. Fuller and Benei suggest that impoverished people engage with the state expecting that they will 'sometimes benefit from their own adequately competent manipulation of political and administrative systems' (Fuller and Benei, 2000, 25). Similarly, Akhil Gupta (2012) writes of the 'strategic opportunism' of poor people in their engagements with the everyday state, whereby the poor extract what they can from the state during their engagements. From their narratives, it would appear that the populations are incorporated in some kind of a mass patronage network of the kind that Bayart (1993) alleges to be at the heart of politics in Africa, where people's political practices focus on a clamour for state largesse.

A third aspect of this argument relates to the contradictory meanings that people assign to the state. In this vein, Jensen (2013) has recently written about the 'hope' for the state demonstrated by his interlocutors in Bosnia, the hope that the local state will help them lead 'normal' lives, without disruption of war, conflict, and shortages. Jensen's research offers a multifaceted perspective that emphasizes the simultaneous ways in which people hope 'for' and 'against' the state, indicating at least a partial assimilation into the juridical conceptualization of the state. At the same time, Jensen also reminds his readers that people harbour a suspicion 'against' the state and are wary of too intimate an association.

Indeed, the social world into which these vocabularies are introduced is not *tabula rasa*. The scholarship of an earlier generation of authors reminds us that the languages of stateness confront inherited moral frameworks that are not so easily displaced. Explaining rural conflict during the closing years of the nineteenth century England, E. P. Thompson (1971) directs attention to prevailing moral vocabularies. Such moral vocabularies were deployed by people protesting the legislative changes that privileged market-oriented forms of production and exchange. Thompson's formulation of the moral economy thesis is the basis for James Scott's (1977) theoretical framework of the moral economy of the peasant: through this framework, he directs attention to the shared communal values and idioms that animated peasants' political practices. Ranajit Guha (1983) urges historians and social scientists to take seriously subaltern views and moralities, which, he claimed, were sharply distinct from those of elites. Similarly, Arturo Escobar (1985) emphasizes the salience of collective identities that shaped protests by the popular sectors against the state. A common thread that binds this scholarship pertains to the moral econmies that characterize the lives of peasants, subalterns and other 'popular' actors.

An alternative perspective is offered by James Ferguson (2013) in a paper provocatively titled 'Declarations of dependence', a perspective which while illuminating in many respects is not without its problems. Ferguson endorses a conception of the state as a material benefactor rather than the protector of equal rights. People insist 'on being a rightful and deserving dependent of the state' (Ferguson, 2013, 237). He cautions against the labelling of these diverse understandings of membership in the political community as 'backward': it would be impoverishing, he tells us, to think that the people who seek to posit their own relations with the state in terms of dependence somehow represent a diminutive culture of democratic citizenship. Ferguson's argument has important bearings on the discussion in this chapter, although the material presented herein leads me to disagree with his conclusions.

Self-targeted social assistance

The burgeoning number of and volume of resources allocated to social assistance programmes have contributed to making the state the focus of popular claims in postcolonial states of the Global South. Such programmes assumed prominence in the aftermath of the havoc wrought by Structural Adjustment Programmes through the 1980s. Multilateral funding institutions (MFIs) were particularly worried about the social unrest that immiserization would likely foment, and proposed to supplement structural adjustment programmes with poverty reduction interventions.[2] Social assistance programmes were standard components of the numerous poverty reduction strategy papers (PRSPs) that MFIs developed in the aftermath of the crisis spawned Structural Adjustment programmes (Craig and Porter, 2003).

Barrientos (2013) suggests that social assistance programmes in the middle and low-income countries of the Global South are developmental in scope. This means that rather than being compensatory for the few as is the case in 'high-income' economies, social assistance has a protective role vis-à-vis the vast majority of the population in these countries. Indeed, the relevance of social assistance as a protective mechanism outweighs that of other interventions such as social insurance and labour market regulations. The protective role of social assistance contributes to making the languages of state even more of a 'concrete' entity in the lives of the millions of the world's poor. Where participation in public works schemes provides a key strategy of social assistance, the language of stateness is inextricably entangled with poor people's experience of work and labour.

Public works schemes are conditional upon the performance of manual labour. As such, they are exemplars of the 'targeting within universalism' approach that Skocpol (1991) commends. Such schemes are premised on the worthwhile assumption that only those who are willing to engage in manual labour would actually apply for work, thereby minimizing anxieties of 'targeting errors' and 'elite capture'. The schemes are universal in their approach (anyone can apply to work on them), but in practice exclude those unwilling to labour. They are a particularly useful means of directing social assistance to the poor in scenarios where policies such as enforcement of land and labour market reforms are politically unviable. Because they are not prima facie targeted to any section, the question of targeting exclusions does not arise. Such schemes side-step the need to identify the 'poor'. Against economic orthodoxy, Bhaduri and Marglin (1990) remind us that public works programmes might induce wage-led, rather than profit-led growth.

However, such programmes do not operate in a structural and social vacuum, parachuted down by executive fiat. Public policy interventions to increase employment, as Kalecki (1943) reminds us, result in a fundamental tension between labourers and their employers. The potential loss of labour, higher wages and increased bargaining power of workers worries employers. Where governments delink the selection of workers from means tests and allow workers to 'self-select' themselves into the programme, the worries among such employers increase manifold.

While public works programmes comprised the usual response to famines under colonial rule in Anglophone Asia and Africa, they were rarely institutionalized as a famine-*proofing* mechanism. The Indian government's institutionalization of the Employment Guarantee Scheme (EGS) in Maharashtra was perhaps the first of its kind anywhere in the world. Launched in 1971 under the Indira Gandhi-led Congress government in response to the drought that year, it was enacted into legislation by the end of that decade and continued to provide income transfers to workers. The programme helped the rural poor cope with the drought that afflicted the state through the 1970s and helped in saving lives, compared with other countries where the intensity of drought was much less (Sen, 1992). It would be worthwhile to reiterate that public works programmes complemented, rather than substituted, food-based social safety net programmes and the universalization of the PDS that was instituted in 1980. Moore and Jadhav (2006, 1286) suggest that although the immediate motivation was to ameliorate the impact of the drought that hit parts of the state, the programme was retained even after the drought passed over in order to prevent the potential likelihood of poor people being afflicted by it again. But the programme also served a broader political purpose. It helped the ruling Congress Party to outflank the potential impact of communist mobilization that the political establishment believed was about to take over the state.

Other scholars, such as Herring and Edwards (1983) and Echeverri-Gent (1988) disagree. They argue that the programme represented the political clout of the state's capitalist farmers, who were able to socialize the cost of sustaining their agricultural labourers throughout the year. Such farmers and peasants, while they had improved their agricultural techniques, found that the timing of labour availability was more crucial than ever before. After all '...labour is worth its hire only at certain times, but is critical at those times...' (Herring and Edwards, 1983, 586). However, employers did not need labourers during the slack seasons and were unable and unwilling to sustain them during these periods. The traditional system of patronage and gifts made to agricultural labourers in order to socially reproduce their labour were deemed unfeasible, given the capitalist orientation of farmers and their own precarious profits. The farmers viewed the public works programmes designed to provide employment for the rural poor over a fixed number of days through the year as a means of sustaining a pool of labour on which they could draw when they needed, but which they did not have to sustain. Such programmes would provide work to the agricultural labourers during the lean season, inducing them to stay on in the village instead of migrating to urban centres such as Mumbai. Because work would be halted during the peak season, labourers could then be deployed on the fields.

Notwithstanding their contention that the impetus for the EGS was farmer-led, rather than worker-led, both authors aver that its implementation, warts and all,[3] contributed to the radicalization of social relations in the countryside. As members of different caste groups worked together, and even drank water from the same water source, caste-based segregation was adversely impacted. In this respect, the introduction of the EGS deepened the processes fomented by Maharashtra's social movements during the 1970s, animated as they were by the emancipatory messages of the anti-caste Dalit Panthers and the Left Wing Lal Nishan Party (Omvedt, 1993).

That the state introduced such a legislation affirmed for the people, alongside the national calls for *garibi hatao*, its centrality in eliminating poverty. Anuradha Joshi draws attention to the efforts by activists to enforce the legislation using the provisions of the law. She reports demonstrators, organized under the aegis of the labour union Bandhkam ba Lakudkam Sangathana, demanding *'bheek nako, have hakkache kaam'* (not charity, we want work which is our right) and undergoing indefinite hunger strikes to demand that the government provide employment when workers asked for it (Joshi, 2010, 624). Joshi notes further that the implementation of the programme helped the labouring poor realize that structural dynamics rather than they themselves were at fault for the perpetuation of poverty.

The Indian state, in the meantime, continued to implement other employment guarantee schemes across the country. In 1989, on the eve of an election it was widely (and correctly) predicted to lose, the Congress Party merged the National Rural Employment Programme (NREP) and Rural Landless Employment Guarantee Programme (RLEGP) to implement the Jawahar Rozagar Yojana (JRY), a programme targeted at 'very poor people' (Gaiha *et al.*, 1998). In 1993, a resurgent Congress Party supplemented this scheme with yet another by the name of the Employment Assurance Scheme (EAS). The EAS aimed, like the Maharashta EGS, to be a demand-led employment generation programme (Veron *et al.*, 2003, 7). Despite its demand-led design, however, in practice it was operated as a supply-driven employment programme like the JRY (Williams *et al.*, 2003, 182), with whom it was often confused (Srivastava *et al.*, 2002, 276). Readers will recall from the discussion in the previous chapter that this was the period when universal PDS began to be wound down. Whereas hitherto the two strategies of food-based safety net programmes and cash-based public works programme had been complementary, a shift from welfare to workfare was discernible in the early 1990s.

The National Rural Employment Guarantee Act (NREGA): Neoliberal workfare or social democracy

India's Congress-led UPA government, under pressure from its Leftist allies, instituted NREGA in 2005. Scaled up to cover the rural areas of the country in 2008, the Act made it obligatory for the government to provide employment to members of any household that demands it. In 2009, following its return to power, the government no longer needed the support of its Leftist allies, and unilaterally prefixed Mahatma Gandhi's name to the Act, rechristening it as MGNREGA. NREGA was not the sole rights-based programme instituted by the state in India. The BJP-led NDA government had promulgated the Right to Education Act in 2001 as well as the more celebrated Right to Information Act (Sharma, 2014). Together, these pieces of legislation illustrate an unprecedented avowal of the language of rights by the state in India.

The NREGA builds on templates available from the relatively successful experience of the Maharashtra EGS.[4] However, while the Maharashtra EGS did not formally impose any restrictions on the number of days for which households could seek employment, NREGA, as noted earlier, limits it to 100 days a year per household. Once a person applies for employment, the panchayat is obliged to provide work within 15 days. If it is unable to, the applicant is entitled to receiving an unemployment allowance (*berozgaari bhatta*). Employment provided must be for a minimum of 14 days. Unlike in the case of the Maharashtra Act, the government is required to provide employment in the locality, irrespective of the number of applicants. Wage payments are to be made within seven days of the execution of the work. In a politically astute move, the wage component of the programme is met by the central government's funds, but the unemployment allowance component needs to be borne by the State government. This incentivizes the State government to ensure that applications for work are fulfilled within the prescribed time limit.

The rules regarding the selection of works are flexible, but clearly favouring smaller scale local-level labour-intensive projects. Unlike the EGS, which stipulated a 51:49 ratio of labour to materials, the *Operational Guidelines* of the NREGA provides for a 60:40 ratio, thereby favouring investments on labour over materials. Indeed, the wage component of the programme's annual expenditure hovered around 75 per cent in 2014 (NREGA, 2014, 20). However, where the EGS had clearly banned the use of machines, the NREGA allows the deployment of capital where it might be required and feasible, leaving the way open for contractors to crowd out labour-intensive projects. Unlike the Maharashtra EGS, where district and block-level bureaucrats had the final word on the kinds of projects to be undertaken, those decisions have been localized under the NREGA. The *Operational Guidelines* commit elected panchayats to finalize projects in consultation with gram sabhas, or popular assemblies. Although formal gram sabhas are rare, the panchayats allocate work in consultation with local notables.

Employment on an NREGA project usually entails teams of 10–20 workers carrying out earthworks toward the construction of small dams, digging pits for ponds, afforestation activities, laying non-tarred laterite roads, and the like. These works are usually carried out on public land, but limited works on privately-owned agricultural land of small and marginal farmers as well as that of Dalits and Adivasis owning larger tracts of agricultural land are also permissible. The programme's *Operational Guidelines* do not impose any seasonal conditions for the development and execution of projects, unlike under the Maharashtra Scheme, which explicitly stipulated that employment projects were to be aligned with the cropping pattern so that local agricultural labour markets would not be disrupted. Earthworks carried out under NREGA programme usually last no more than 8–10 days, assuming a team of 10 workers during a calendar year. Thus, on average, a worker may expect to be employed on 10 such earthworks projects. The application and payment cycles are repeated for each earthwork project with which the worker is employed.

That the NREGA enhances the substantive opportunities for the rural poor is clear from its provision of work during agricultural seasons. Because projects continue during these seasons, workers enjoy the option to work for NREGA project instead of for local farmers if they so choose. Where backed by timely payment of wages, the programme offers valued alternatives to the people who opt to work for the projects rather than for local farmers. Further, by apportioning a 40 per cent investment for contractors whose stakes in and aspirations for the agrarian economy were limited, the project allows for an alliance between labourers and contractors. This alliance serves as a bulwark against farmers' potential attempts to restrict the execution of projects to non-agricultural seasons, although of course contractors' incentives to corner resources are not completely eliminated.

In the backdrop of the Indian state's attempts at liberalization (Kohli, 2005; Swaminathan, 2000) and the broader espousal by it of neoliberal technologies of government (Harriss, 2011), the legislation of NREGA flummoxed many (as discussed in McCartney and Roy, 2015). Since its inception, members of between 20 million and 50 million households have received employment per year. On average, beneficiary households have received employment for far fewer than the stipulated 100 days. Nearly a million works have been taken up, on average, since the programme's inception, pertaining to water conservation, rural connectivity, land improvement and, increasingly, rural sanitation.[5] Although its introduction was unanimously supported within Parliament (Chopra, 2011), the programme's launch and subsequent continuation have been fraught with political tension. The allocations to the programme have attracted much attention from both sympathetic liberals and hostile fiscal conservatives (Drèze and Sen, 2013). Left liberal commentators have suggested that the programme heralds a new social democratic compact. Rightwing critics have derided it as an 'expensive gravy train', a 'costly joke' and a 'money-guzzler'.[6]

Given the visceral debates spawned by the programme, it would appear that with the advent of NREGA, the neoliberal project in India has stalled. The expenditure on NREGA, at almost ₹ 33,000 crores (US$ 8.8 billion) (GoI, 2013, 273), nearly 1 per cent of the GDP,[7] similar to the expenditure reported by Brazil's Bolsa Familia to that country's GDP.[8] However, some perspective is important here: Brazil's expenditure on education, health, and general subsidies to its population outstrip India's, as readers will glean from Chart 5.1 below.

Chart 5.1: Public expenditures on social sectors as percentage of GDP in Brazil and India

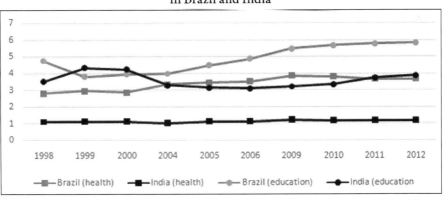

Source: World Bank Data, various years, accessed at: data.worldbank.org, accessed May 2017.

That the NREGA, alongside other social legislation, represents a departure from the targeted governmental strategies inhered in the BPL mechanism, is clear. However, to infer from this that its introduction signals a departure from neoliberal technologies of government is perhaps premature. Kalyan Sanyal (2007) argues that there need not be any contradiction between the initiation of social assistance and the espousal of neoliberal governmental projects. As the data presented in Table 5.1 shows, the employment situation in India is far from attaining its full potential. Households relying on manual labour comprise a large component of the Indian population. Marginal workers, or workers who find employment for only upto six months a year, comprise 33 per cent of the total labour force. In this context, programmes such as NREGA

Table 5.1: Labour and employment in India

Name of State	Population	Manual labour house-hold (HH) %	% workers employed for			% of marginal workers			
			6–11 months	1–5 months	No work	Total	Worked less than 3 months	Worked 3–6 months	Seeking work
Andhra Pradesh	84,580,777	58.93	37.5	0.5	3.4	21.94	1.98	13.11	6.86
Assam	31,205,576	42.58	27.7	2.3	3.1	35.53	4.34	20.02	11.16
Bihar	104,099,452	70.59	47.9	0.7	5.8	48.75	5.86	26.21	16.68
Chhattisgarh	25,545,198	52.10	56.2	1.9	2.3	41.94	5.36	22.39	14.19
Gujarat	60,439,692	43.28	22.7	0.4	0.8	21.18	1.83	15.21	4.14
Haryana	25,351,462	42.70	25.3	1.5	2.8	27.95	4.01	15.51	8.42
Jharkhand	32,988,134	51.72	45.3	6.5	2.9	58.84	8.01	29.90	20.93
Karnataka	61,095,297	32.49	30.6	0.1	1.7	19.26	1.88	13.57	3.81
Kerala	33,406,061	50.52	24	1.3	9.9	26.74	3.62	14.35	8.77
Madhya Pradesh	72,626,809	56.70	38.2	0.3	2.4	36.99	4.34	20.29	12.36
Maharashtra	112,374,333	43.85	32.7	0.5	2.1	15.12	1.62	9.36	4.13
Odisha	41,974,218	58.84	52.1	1.5	4.7	49.65	5.82	26.32	17.52
Punjab	27,743,338	48.03	17.9	0.4	5.6	20.06	2.80	10.88	6.38
Rajasthan	68,548,437	43.61	36.2	2.8	3.6	37.23	5.40	20.91	10.92
Tamil Nadu	72,147,030	65.77	22	0.2	3.6	19.03	2.10	12.23	4.71
Uttar Pradesh	199,812,341	45.79	42.2	2	4.6	40.65	5.71	22.45	12.49
West Bengal	91,276,115	58.38	28.8	0.9	3.9	37.11	4.95	17.26	14.91
All India	1,210,854,977	51.14	34.7	1.1	3.7	32.52	4.14	18.06	10.32
Sources	GoI/Census 2011	GoI/ SECC 2011	Labour Bureau (2014, Table 17/ page 100)[10]			Census of India (2011, Chapter 4, Statements 28, 46 and 43[11])			

contribute to socially-subsidizing labour so that it can be deployed at a future date. Furthermore, NREGA has to be juxtaposed against the on-going agrarian crisis (Reddy and Mishra, 2009, 28). India's expenditure on agriculture and allied services (including irrigation) was approximately ₹ 15,000 crores, or less than half the total expenditure on NREGA (Union Budget of India, 2012).[9] An appreciation of these structural features leads scholars such as Vasavi to describe the politics underlying the introduction of the NREGA as a 'palliative politics' (2012, 176).

The neoliberal character of NREGA becomes clear from a glance at its policy vocabulary, which is replete with references to workers' putative choice. Indeed, 'the exercise of choice to demand employment' lies at its core (GoI, 2008, 6). The language of choice resonates with the analytic of neoliberal subjectivity as proposed by Nikolas Rose. He suggests that ideal neoliberal subjects are 'actively responsible individuals' who seek to *fulfill themselves* within a variety of micro-moral domains' (Rose, 2006, 158). Rose's reminder that the subjects of neoliberal government are those who 'maximise their quality of life through acts of *choice*, according their life a meaning and value to the extent that it can be rationalized as the outcome of choices made or choices to be made' is instructive in this regard.

The wages earned by the workers are paid in cash, which ostensibly enhances the choices before them. But cash payments do not protect them from inflationary pressures, which adversely affect their ability to purchase food in the open market. Amartya Sen (1981) has shown, for instance, that workers who tend to be paid in grain are usually better equipped to cope with famine than those paid in cash. Moreover, cash payments contribute to forging the identity of the worker as a consumer. Vasavi (2012, 160–61) alerts us to the attempts by governments and private sector players in India to create rural consumers by underscoring the fortunes that are to be made at 'the bottom of the pyramid'.[12] The attempt here appears to be to tap into the sizable base of the rural market, comprising the millions of workers whose wage payments are now made entirely in cash. Cash payments to the millions of workers employed with the programme are essential for strengthening the market economy. Whether they provide the poor with security and dignity continues to be a matter of spirited debate between those who advocate continuing food allocations through the public distribution system (Ghosh, 2011 and Shah,

2008) and those who propose substituting it with cash payments (Kapur *et al.*, 2008; Standing, 2011).

All official documents pertaining to the programme refer to the workers as wage-seekers. The *Official Guideline on NREGA* (NREGA, 2006) is a prime example. The nomenclature of wage seeker reduces the identity of the workers from being productive social beings to individuals seeking wages. The emphasis on the wage sequesters workers from one another and seeks to convey that those who engage with the programme do so only in order to earn a wage. Espousing the vocabulary of wage seeker denies workers any collective identity. Instead, it conjures a corporatist image of the state as a huge patron with the millions of workers as its clients.

If the state seeks to co-opt NREGA workers as 'wage seekers', social activists laud NREGA for its espousal of the language of rights. They are particularly enthused about the 'Right to Work'. Although political theorist Niraja Gopal Jayal (2013, 191) welcomes this language of rights, she warns us against mistaking what are essentially welfare protections as rights. She notes that the previous two decades have seen a proliferation of the language of rights in India. Legislations in the name of social rights have gone hand in hand with the abrogation of substantive rights through violent acquisition of agricultural and urban lands by the state in the service of corporate capital (Bannerjee-Guha, 2010). The vigorous opposition to NREGA from corporate capital and fiscal conservatives should not delude analysts into believing that the programme reverses the neoliberal technology of governance that is being instituted by the Indian state. Far from being the insurrectionary piece of legislation its proponents made it out, it was the bare minimum the UPA government could do in order to keep the social peace besieged by the 'buccaneer capitalism' to which Jayal (2013) directs our attention.

The use of the term 'demand' by the state, activists as well as the rural workers themselves is of considerable interest because of the simultaneous meanings to which it lends itself. One way to think about this vocabulary is that it is a neutral 'economic' word to refer to one end of the 'demand–supply' equilibrium. In this sense, employment guarantee programmes in India have formally been demand-driven. The employment needs of unemployed rural labourers are aggregated to calculate the demand for work, which the state must then meet. A second way to think about demand is to refer to the actual practice associated with formulating a demand – the 'application' for work. Now, the application is akin to a petition, which refers to a considerably humbler exchange. It is formally a request (*avedan/nibedon*) rather than a demand, which would entail a much more assertive stance. If the first meaning of the term is economistic, the second is juridical. Both meanings offer apparently little prospects for politicization. The third meaning of the term demand is considerably more political. In this respect, to demand refers to the advancing of a social claim. When workers in Bihar collectively demanded from the block-level bureaucrat '*majdoori ki maang kar rahe hain, bheekh nahi maang rahe*', (we are demanding our wages, not [asking for] charity) this politicized meaning of the term becomes clear. Likewise, when workers in West Bengal demanded work from their ward member, they said, '*aamaader kaaj chayi, daan noye*' ([we] demand work, not [beg for] charity). The myriad meanings of the 'demand' for work will be dwelt upon in the following pages.

II

Routine demands in an incorporative political place: Rahimpur

> This programme is god-sent. We don't have to ask anyone for favours any more.
>
> Interview notes,
> Shefali Bibi, Rahimpur, 5 February 2010

I interviewed 14 members of the 32 households that had received employment under NREGA between February 2009 and January 2010. On average, they had worked approximately 25–30 days on the programme during that year. Almost each one of my interlocutors reported that employment under the aegis of the programme helped them connect with the government. 40-year old Arif Miya suggested that employment on a government-funded programme helped them increase their credibility with other people in the locality. Even as the government tried to portray the workers engaged with this project as 'wageseekers' or 'jobseekers', people like Arif Miya appear to seek social credibility through their employment with NREGA. As a worker on a publicly-financed programme, he was able to demonstrate his credit-worthiness to local retailers. Grocers were more willing to lend goods to him and others like him now, as compared with the past. He was not sure whether it was because he had more money now than in the past (he did not think so), but he could not miss this changed aspect of social life. Arif Miya's wife Shefali Bibi heard about the programme when their then ward member Henna Khan told her about it in their monthly credit association meeting, sometime in the winter of 2008. The ward member gave Shefali and Arif the job card for their household. The couple soon found out that the card made them eligible to work on public works programme for 100 days in a year (hence, *ek sho deener kaaj*). They knew they should have formally applied for the card, but figured that the ward member had managed that formality at her end. Receiving cards without formally applying for them was common practice, they said matter-of-factly, as it was more convenient than going to register for the card at the panchayat office.

The cards and the associated works appear to have been much discussed in Rahimpur in those early days when they were distributed. Many politicians offered Shefali, Arif, and others like them help with applying for work. Henna Khan and her husband Mushtaq Khan, Joynal Ali, Akbar Ali, and Babar Hossein the present ward member were among these politicians, trying to understand the mechanics of the programme themselves while also talking to others about it. Readers will recall that they were all members of the entrenched classes, farmers who hired in labour to cultivate their large agricultural properties. The political mediators who had helped Rahimpur's poor with their BPL cards also tried to contribute to a shared understanding of NREGA. There would be heated debates about this or that feature, about whether the wages were pegged too high or too low, and how this would help people's annual incomes and savings. My interlocutors agreed with one another that the programme had complex rules, but they averred that these were simpler than the employment guarantee programmes that preceded it.

The presence of several knowledgeable politicians and political mediators in the ward did not prevent Arif Miya from going to the panchayat and clarifying a few doubts he had with people he met there. Here too he met district-level politicians, leaders, and activists helping out people like him with information about the programme. He saw some people applying for cards. Others he met had already received employment under this scheme. Some of the things they said were different from what he had been told in the ward. When he got back that evening, he added to the repository of knowledge in the ward about NREGA, challenging a particular interpretation of the guidelines that had been offered by Joynal Ali the night prior. Some people filled their application for work and gave it to the ward member or her husband. For others, local politicians collected applications and deposited them at the panchayat. A minority, such as Arif Miya, felt it was safest to apply for work at the panchayat. He went with a few friends from nearby villages.

Table 5.2 presents data on demand for employment in Rahimpur, gleaned from the sample surveys conducted for this study. An overwhelming proportion of NREGA job card-holding interview respondents had applied for work at any given time. Applicants from all communities were proportionately represented in the applications. Their applications were supported by the ward member and other politicians, especially of the entrenched classes. They heaved a sigh of relief. Their relief originated in the fact that they would not have to sift through beneficiaries and risk unpopularity. Politicians of the entrenched classes assured the labouring poor that they would manage the applications. For the labouring poor, these assurances provided much needed relief from the need to follow up with bureaucrats. The labouring classes' confidence in discussing the applications made on their behalf, prospects of work and wages stemmed from such assurances by entrenched class politicians.

Table 5.2: NREGA profile, Rahimpur, 2010

	Job card	Applied for work	Received work
Total	101	92	32
Manual labourers	80	73	24

Source: Own sample survey, 2010.

However, the application filed on Arif's behalf elicited no response, and he left for his *dadon* contract a few weeks later. Shefali Bibi requested the CPI(M) politician Joynal Ali to follow up on their behalf. Arif Miya spoke with Congress politician Akbar Ali and Babar Hossein over the mobile phone, requesting them too to follow up. The politicians and other political mediators kept their word. In Arif Miya's case, I gathered from their accounts that they argued with panchayat-level functionaries and officers asking them about the status of the various applications they had filed and demanding to know why no action was being taken on applications that had been filed a while back. Eventually, Arif Miya, Shefali Bibi, and their neighbours obtained work. Although Arif Miya was not in the village when a project to rejuvenate a pond was announced, Shefali Bibi was. She worked on the project for a total number of 10 days during the *aman* sowing season (May/June) in 2009 and received the complete payment.

Labourers working under NREGA generally credited the ward's entrenched class politicians, irrespective of their party affiliations, for their employment under the programme. Such politicians and their associated political mediaries were willing to undertake the necessary leg work for it. They collected applications for employment and organized them so that panchayat functionaries could easily process them. While they may not have always been successful in securing employment for their co-villagers, my interlocutors were convinced that the politicians tried their best. They remarked that their *garjians*, the colloquial for guardian, had secured work for them. In attributing the success of receiving work to their guardian, however, they did not necessarily interpret their endeavours as evidence of generosity or magnanimity. Rather, they viewed the entrenched classes' efforts as furthering *their own* interests, which only incidentally happened to help, the labouring classes. The reasons for their cynicism are not hard to find.

Shefali Bibi told me that the pond to rejuvenate which she and her neighbours were employed was owned by the family of Akbar Ali, the Congress politician. That Joynal Ali, a CPI(M) politician might have worked closely with the panchayat to obtain employment for workers that would eventually benefit a Congress politician did not appear ironic or strange to Shefali Bibi at all. Joynal Ali and Akbar Ali may be electoral opponents, but they were both *bodo lok*, or 'big people'. Big people helped each other, she reasoned. When I asked her if she knew whether beneficiaries were allowed under the project to work on private properties of wealthy people, she shrugged her shoulders. After a pause, she asked if I knew who NREGA supervisor for Rahimpur was. I did. It was Akbar Ali's brother, who jointly owned the pond in question. He had a direct stake in the rejuvenation of the pond. In charge of the muster rolls, the document based on which workers were paid, he could manipulate the records to show that the pond was not private property, but belonged to the gram panchayat. According to Shefali Bibi, that is exactly what he did.

Akbar Ali was frank about these manipulations. He laughed off any suggestion that working on privately-owned ponds was not permissible under NREGA. As a matter of fact, the programme does allow works to be undertaken on private properties owned by SCs, STs, beneficiaries of land reforms, and recipients of BPL cards. Akbar Ali did not come under any of these categories, but insisted that all villagers benefitted from the rejuvenation of his pond. On their part, Shefali Bibi and the others who had worked on the pond reported that they had been paid the full money in a timely fashion and without having to follow up. Furthermore, the additional income reduced their economic desperation and allowed them to bargain for decent wages and working conditions vis-à-vis their employers, the labour-hiring peasants who constituted Rahimpur's precarious classes.

The enthusiasm of politicians from the entrenched classes contrasted with anxieties harboured by politicians from the precarious classes, peasants such as the CPI(M) cadre member Abdul Bari. The precarious classes' response to the programme was understandably sullen. They complained that NREGA was being used by the 'big people' for their own ends. They could not influence the entrenched class politicians – not even CPI(M) politicians such as Joynal Ali and Mushtaq Khan – to sanction works on *their* farms. Moreover, they perceived the programme to be exacerbating labour shortages by diverting agricultural labour to other ends during agricultural seasons. That the ward's labouring classes migrated to Delhi and elsewhere for employment during the agricultural seasons was bad enough. That those who remained in the village were being employed by members of the entrenched classes under the aegis of the programme to rejuvenate their own private ponds during the time-sensitive *aman* transplantation worsened the situation. Adding insult to their injury were the CPI(M)'s entrenched class politicians who obtained such employment for the labouring poor.

The suspicions of the precarious classes were not entirely unfounded. Shefali Bibi chose to work on Akbar Ali's pond rather than on Abdul Bari's fields even as he repeatedly pleaded with her and her neighbours to do so. Given the prevailing social relations of power in Rahimpur, it does appear that NREGA provided an opportunity to the entrenched classes to consolidate their class coalition with the labouring poor against the precarious classes. But it also enabled the labouring poor to demand of the labour-hiring peasants an upward

revision of agricultural wages. Table 5.3 compares agricultural wages with
NREGA wages, demonstrating the higher wages received by workers under
the programme. Such demands threatened to squeeze the limited surpluses
available to small peasants, worsening the already conflictual relations between
the precarious classes and the labouring poor.

Table 5.3: NREGA and agricultural wages rates in Rahimpur

Month	Official NREGA wage (₹) (2)	Actual NREGA wage (₹) (3)	Prevailing agricultural wages (₹) (4)
January 2009	75	60–70	60/58
February 2009	75	60–70	45/43
April 2009	75	60–70	70/65
July 2009	75	60–70	50/48
January 2010	100	70–80	70/68
February 2010	100	70–80	50/48
April 2010	100	70–80	70/68

Source: Column 2: NREGA (2012), accessed at http://nrega.nic.in/nerega_statewise.pdf in
February 2017. Columns 3 and 4: Field notes and observations.

The quiet confidence among the labouring poor that they would obtain
work was bolstered by the entrenched classes' support to NREGA. The
demands for work were routine procedures for the labourers, without them
having to organize in delegations as they did during the issue of the BPL
cards. The entrenched classes directly benefitted from NREGA when they
successfully deployed the programme's resources toward improving their
private resources. They indirectly benefitted from it because it exacerbated the
conflict between the labouring classes and the precarious classes, embarassing
the latter. The labouring poor benefitted from NREGA because it increased
their household incomes as well as creditworthiness. But more important,
their engagement with NREGA enhanced their bargaining capacity vis-à-
vis their employers, the labour-hiring peasants who comprised Rahimpur's
precarious classes. Their enhanced capacity to bargain did not adversely affect
the entrenched classes who drew on large extra-agricultural sources of income
as much as it did the middle and poor peasants, whose limited sources of
agricultural income were increasingly strained and profits suppressed. Not for

nothing did the precarious classes remain suspicious of the programme. On the other hand, it was precisely this outcome that enthused the entrenched classes and led them to support the labouring classes' demands for employment under NREGA.

Assertive demands in a populist political place: Sargana Ward 1

> The *dabang jatis* tried to eat up the NAREGA. But we didn't let them.
>
> Interview notes, Sejni Rishi, Sargana Ward 1,
> 3 March 2010

In Sargana ward 1, I interviewed members of all 17 families that had received work under NREGA between March 2009 and February 2010. On average, they had worked some 22–25 days under NREGA. Most of my interlocutors suggested that they valued the programme because it enabled them to live in the village without needing to haggle over wages with farmers and peasants who were unable or unwilling to pay at market rates. 35-year old Sejni Rishi told me that working on NREGA meant she did not have to seek employment with lecherous employers for work. However, payments for employment were far from timely and often severely truncated. Although local politicians and political mediators helped them from time to time, there was much follow up required for the payments. Nonetheless, her husband, 40-year old Maturi Rishi, endorsed her positive view of the programme. Table 5.4 presents information about demand for employment in Sargana Ward 1, gleaned from sample surveys conducted for this study in 2010.

Table 5.4: NREGA profile, Sargana Ward 1, 2010

	Job card	Applied for work	Received work
Total	31	30	17
Manual labourers	28	21	14

Source: Own sample survey, 2010.

For Maturi and my other interview interlocutors in the Sargana (West) Musahar hamlet, the sources of information about the programme were many. They did not remember when the programme was announced, but clearly recalled CPI (ML/L) politicians coming to their hamlets with forms for them to fill in so they would receive the cards. The politicians handed over the cards within a few days. In some hamlets, such as the Musahar *tola* in Bharagama (East), BJP-affiliated politicians had distributed the cards much earlier and filled in the application forms thereafter. Subsequently, politicians affiliated with the Janata Dal (United) arrived with more forms and approached those who had been undecided previously. Not one of my interlocutors knew anyone who had physically approached the panchayat and filled out applications for NREGA job cards themselves.

I had the occasion to 'hang out' with the Rozgar Sevak of Sargana gram panchayat, the official responsible for processing NREGA applications. Of the Kayasth community, he was a resident of the nearby town of Purnea. The Rozgar Sevak alleged that the enthusiasm of the locality's politicians stemmed from the opportunity to recruit supporters for their party and had nothing to do with altruistic concern. He complained that such politicians rarely spoke with him or tried to understand the supply-side constraints the bureaucracy faced. Rather, they insisted on instigating the labouring poor to demand work. As a result, Rozgar Sevaks like him were faced with demands to meet which they had little capacity. In particular, he blamed the CPI (ML/L) politicians for leading the way, compelling other politicians to compete with them. On the other hand, the CPI (ML/L) politicians wished they possessed the kind of sway the Rozgar Sevak claimed they had. A party functionary I interviewed quipped: 'If we had the kind of influence [the Rozgar Sevak] says we have, the Red Flag (*lal nishan*) would have been fluttering on the Red Fort[13] by now'.

Politicians affiliated with other political parties and political mediators unaffiliated with any party agreed that their influence over the applicants was limited. While they concurred that their pressures compelled the Rozgar Sevak to take his job seriously, they rued the fact that applicants did not always do as they asked them to. The RJD affiliated rich peasant politician Amaresh Yadav lamented applicants' refusal to desist from seeking employment during the agricultural seasons. He had tried to explain to workers not to claim work during the agricultural seasons, but without success. Their non-compliance had not deterred him and other politicians like him from helping them fill their applications for employment. But he wished that they did not work during the agricultural seasons.

Most other members of the precarious classes were supportive of the programme. The Mukhya, Sarvesh Mandal, a JD(U)affiliated middle peasant, claimed that workers' wages had increased because the introduction of NREGA intensified labour shortages. But he also insisted that the programme had benefitted Sargana's poor and allowed them to bargain for higher wages. Indeed, to this claim Table 5.5 appears to bear testimony. The Mukhya's support to the NREGA was corroborated by the accounts of the labourers working on different projects. His principal electoral opponent, the RJD-affiliated rich peasant and a kinsman of Amaresh Yadav, was more circumspect of the NREGA. He hoped that the program could be restricted to the lean agricultural seasons, but was restrained in his criticism in public. Retailers such as Dharmesh Srivastav supported the programme because he reasoned it would raise people's incomes and ability to purchase goods he sold in his shop! Teachers such as Shyam Rajak, of the Dhobhi community, were unequivocally supportive of the programme because it would allow Dalit families to cease their dependence on local farmers for work. By and large, politicians and political mediators of Sargana's precarious classes supported the implementation of the programme, even if some were more hesitant than others.

Table 5.5: NREGA and agricultural wages rates in Sargana Ward 1

Month	Official NREGA wage (₹) (2)	Actual NREGA wage (₹) (3)	Prevailing agricultural wages (₹) (4)
April 2009	89	50–60	45
July 2009	100	60–70	35–50
September 2009	100	60–70	70
November 2009	100	60–70	45
April 2010	100	70–80	50

Source: Column 2: NREGA (2012), accessed at http://nrega.nic.in/nerega_statewise.pdf in February 2017. Columns 3 and 4: Field notes and observations.

Maturi Rishi and other labourers who obtained employment under NREGA readily acknowledged the support extended by such precarious class politicians, although it is not clear that they were aware of the reservations that some of these individuals harboured. Maturi Rishi suggested that their support was helpful in understanding the programme better, and in making representations to educated professionals such as the Rozgar Sevak. But perhaps more crucial was their backing when dealing with bureaucrats such as the postmaster Gajen

Singh, a scion of the region's dominant landlord family. Gajen Singh's hatred for NREGA was almost visceral. He ranted against the NREGA, convinced that it encouraged the poor to be lazy. As postmaster, he was in-charge of the post office, the institution through which NREGA workers received their wages till 2010. Workers alleged that he wilfully truncated the wages meant for them, frequently pocketing nearly between half and three-quarters of the funds. During our conversations, Gajen Singh did not deny the charge: all he said was that since all the country's prominent politicians and bureaucrats were corrupt, was it fair to expect a small-town officer like him to not be so?

Maturi and Sejni Rishi were among the workers whose wages were reduced because of the postmaster's manipulations. Sejni Rishi and her co-workers refused to accept this reduction. They picked up a fight with Gajen Singh, which I have described elsewhere (Roy, 2014a). Not only did Gajen Singh refuse to pay them, he hurled expletives questioning Sejni Devi's fidelity to her husband. The couple and their neighbours approached several people they knew would be sympathetic to them. The CPI (ML/L) activists suggested that they file a petition with the block development officer (BDO) complaining about the delay in payments. But the Mukhya's advice was more radical. He asked them to lodge the Atrocities Act[14] against the postmaster for harassing a Dalit woman. Sejni Rishi and her neighbours reflected on this advice and decided to threaten the postmaster rather than to actually lodge a case. That, they thought, would provide them with more room to manoeuvre. They used the Mukhya's name when threatening the postmaster. Their approach worked. Gajen Singh retracted and paid up the full sum of the wages to the couple and the other co-workers.

That postmaster Gajen Singh siphoned workers' wages was common knowledge. My interlocutors recalled that on such occasions, the affected workers and their neighbours collectively approached the Mukhya to ask for his help. The Mukhya asked one of his associates to call the postmaster on his mobile phone and spoke to him. It was not uncommon for the Mukhya to accompany the workers to the post office or to the postmaster's residence to demand on their behalf that he release the full payments of the wages. When it appeared to the workers that the Mukhya was not doing enough to pressurize the postmaster, they approached his principle opponent for his help against both the postmaster *as well as* the Mukhya.

Sargana's workers sometimes found themselves in the awkward position of asserting their claims against the Mukhya. I heard from Bhukhan Rishi, Maturi's uncle that some workers unearthed the existence of a 'ghost project', a project that operated only on paper. The postmaster, the supplier of materials and the Rozgar Sevak proposed to implement a road-laying project in the name of 20 workers. They then persuaded the Mukhya, the same Mukhya who otherwise took the side of the workers, to approve the project. The deal was to share the wages of the 20 workers among the four of them. However, the Mukhya's principle opponent and other politicians got wind of it. BJP affiliated Dharmesh Srivastava let the workers, all from the Musahar *tola*, know about this. The workers were incensed. They informed their neighbours and together they trooped over to the Mukhya's residence. At the Mukhya's residence, the Mukhya confessed to being party to the deal. The delegation demanded that the workers be paid a share of the cut, or else they threatened to report the matter to the police. I am not sure exactly which of the workers were involved. Nor was it entirely clear to me what the terms of the deal were. All Bhukhan Rishi told me was that the matter was sorted out to everyone's satisfaction. Clearly, for NREGA workers, the Mukhya's general support to their demands did not imply that he could strike deals in their name with impunity. Although the workers were always less scathing in their criticism of the Mukhya than they were of the postmaster, they did not allow him to get away with stealing their share.

The assertions of Sargana's labouring poor need to be situated against the tensions between and within different classes in the gram panchayat. On the one hand, tensions entailed quarrels among members of the precarious classes, such as the Mukhya and his principle opponent, as well as between the peasants and the retailers. On the other hand, overriding these internecine squabbles was the conflict between the precarious classes and the entrenched classes. Despite their tensions with one another, neither the Mukhya nor his principle opponent sided with the postmaster. Their dislike for each other notwithstanding, neither the middle peasants nor the retailers supported the entrenched classes. The workers were certainly suspicious of the Mukhya, who showed little compunction in betraying them when it suited him. But those suspicions paled in comparison with the mutual loathing that characterized the relationship between the postmaster and the labouring poor.

The assertive practices of Sargana's labouring poor demanding for employment under NREGA stemmed from the support they received from the ward's precarious classes. The ward's precarious classes supported the labouring poor's applications for work as well as their struggles for timely and accurate wages. They were willing to openly espouse the cause of the labouring poor and to publicly confront the members of the entrenched classes who sought to sabotage the programme. Not only did the locality's rich and middle peasants of Yadav and Kevat communities make the forms available to the applicants, they pressurized Rozgar Sevaks to actually provide work. Retailers such as Dharmesh Srivastav provided advice and information to workers who struggled to obtain payments. While members of the precarious classes, such as the Mukhya, were perfectly capable of striking deals with members of the entrenched classes, their support for the labouring poor is unmistakable, as each of my interviews with NREGA workers showed. By and large, NREGA workers credited the ward's precarious class politicians with their employment under the scheme. The Mukhya's help to the workers had sustained their interest in the programme in the first place (Roy, 2014b).

Although members of the precarious classes did not directly benefit from the NREGA and were often encumbered by labourers demanding work during agricultural seasons, they realized its importance in cultivating the political support of the labouring poor. They indirectly benefitted from it when the programme increased the pressure on the rich peasants, capitalist farmers and landlords of the privileged castes. The labouring poor, on their part, benefitted from NREGA because it allowed them the opportunity to stay in the village and engage in a public works programme without being subject to the expectation of serving local elites. Work under NREGA increased the menu of livelihood options before them and contributed to increasing their incomes. An increase in their incomes enhanced their bargaining power vis-à-vis local employers – both labour-hiring peasants as well as landlords and farmers. Some respondents suggested that employment on the programme allowed them the option to select employers who they considered less likely to practice caste specific discrimination against them. Such an expansion of choices before labourers most directly affected the entrenched classes, who were most likely to publicly engage in caste discrimination. Not for nothing did they detest the programme and wanted to see it terminated.

Assertive demands in a differentiated political place: Ditya

> This thing [NREGA] was for us. They tried their best to steal it..
> Interview notes, Marangmayee Hembrom,
> Ditya, 26 February 2010

In Ditya, I was able to meet with members of 18 households whose applications for employment under NREGA had been successful. On an average, labourers had worked for 15–18 days on the programme during that year. During my discussions with them, they praised the programme for providing them opportunities for work that reduced their need to approach local employers for work.[15] Shobhan Hembrom, of the Saotal community and in his mid-50s, explained that worker under the NREGA enabled agricultural labourers such as him and his wife Marangmayee Hembrom to complement their existing livelihoods. Although their understanding of the full range of the programme's advantages was patchy at best, he recalled that they and their neighbours understood that the NREGA might increase the livelihood options available to them. They could not help noting that agricultural wages increased after the programme was introduce, even though they lagged NREGA wages. Table 5.6 depicts the gap between NREGA wages and agricultural wages.

Table 5.6: NREGA and agricultural wages rates in Ditya

Month	Official NREGA wage (₹) (2)	Actual NREGA wage (₹) (3)	Prevailing agricultural wages (₹) (4)
January 2009	75	60–70	60
February 2009	75	60–70	45
April 2009	75	60–70	70
July 2009	75	60–70	50
January 2010	100	70–80	70
February 2010	100	70–80	50
April 2010	100	70–80	70

Sources: Column 2: NREGA (2012), accessed at http://nrega.nic.in/nerega_statewise.pdf in February 2017. Columns 3 and 4: Field notes and observations.

Ironically, Shobhan and Marangmayee had no inkling of NREGA till Mota Sarkar, father-in-law of the CPI(M)-affiliated ward member came to their home and told them about it. He gave them the job card and asked them to keep it safely. Although he said that the cards would entitle them to employment in the locality, he remained vague about it. My interlocutors looked at me incredulously when I told them that they should not have received it without an application. They were emphatic that neither they nor anyone they knew had ever applied for cards. It seems that politicians from both Congress and the CPI(M) competed with each other during the initial days of the introduction of the programme to make available such documents as application forms and job cards. Because they thought the job cards were a 'free good', they were less restrained in distributing them. This factor was crucial in sustaining an enthusiasm for disbursing job cards among the politicians. By distributing the cards widely, they could claim, with some justification, that they 'cared' for everyone, not only the Desiya poor. The unlimited number of job cards allowed Ditya's Desiya politicians to transcend, rather than compromise, their particularistic moral obligations and reach out to both the Desiya poor as well as the Saotal poor. Indeed, as my survey showed, nearly every Saotal household possessed a job card, and they all acknowledged that they had received the cards from Desiya politicians without having applied for one.

Once the excitement over distributing job cards was over, however, the cardholders began to enquire about the employment opportunities associated with it. Saotal politicians elsewhere in the gram panchayat told them that 100 days of employment (or *ek sho deener kaaj*) were associated with each card. Such politicians encouraged people like Marangmayee and Shobhan, against the advice of their own community elders, to apply for employment. Saotal politicians based in the block and in Maldah town – affiliated with both the major parties – began to take interest in their applications for work, thereby inciting them against local Desiya politicians. Community organizers of Maldah based NGOs also encouraged them to apply for work. They explained to the workers the mechanics of the programme. Both offered to help workers apply for work and file their applications.

Accounts of people in the ward demanding work abounded during my fieldwork. Table 5.7 presents data on demand for employment in Ditya from the sample survey. An overwhelming proportion of my NREGA job card-holding respondents had applied for work at any given time. Given the self-targeted nature of the programme, applicants knew they would not be competing with one another for the same pool of resources. They spoke up for one another, without fearing the loss of a scarce resource. This feature of the programme brought together different individuals and groups, especially when they approached nodal points such as the panchayat office. Information was freely shared, and personal experiences with wages, works, and tactics to ensure timely payments were actively transmitted from, rather than surreptitiously emulated by, one to another without hesitation. It was not uncommon, I was told, to find 'experienced' workers helping out new applicants and following up on their applications for them. I heard no accounts of bribes having to be paid to anyone during the registration or application process.

Table 5.7: NREGA profile, Ditya, 2010

	Job card	Applied for work	Received work
Total	105	97	18
Manual labourers	42	43	7

Source: Own sample survey, 2010.

Congress politicians such as Sasaram Sarkar complemented Mota Sarkar's efforts. Like other peasant hirers of labour, both politicians worried that the programme might aggravate shortages of agricultural labour. However, drawing on their experiences of implementing the EAS during the 1990s, their conclusion was that if expectations were properly managed, the NREGA might stymie outmigration during agricultural seasons by providing incentives for labourers to remain in the village. After all, as they both told me during separate interviews, labourers left the village in search of work because they had few employment opportunities within the village. Once they left, the workers were barely concerned about the agrarian economy and were unlikely to come back just to be hired on farms. If the NREGA could be managed so as to provide employment opportunities inside the village but outside of the agrarian season, the program might be able to retain potential labour migrants and address labour shortages.

From my interviews with precarious class politicians in Ditya, it appears that both Mota Sarkar and Sasaram Sarkar attempted to reach an agreement with the labouring poor that they would support applications for employment only during the lean seasons when their own requirements for labour were minimal. According to the two politicians, the labouring poor from among the Saotals appear to have initially acceded to this demand, but later reneged on their promise. However, my interlocutors from among the Saotal labourers denied making any such promise. Whatever may have been the politicians' motivations in providing information about the NREGA they appear to have severely misjudged the seriousness with which the poor took their word. By the time Mota Sarkar, Sasaram Sarkar and others realized the full implication of the NREGA and sought to control the applications and curtail the employment offered under this programme, it was too late. Ditya's poor, both Saotal and Desiya, had begun to demand employment and actually expected to receive it and be paid the promised wages.

The NREGA programme in Ditya enjoyed support from apparently unlikely quarters. Phanindranath Sarkar, Ditya's famed contractor with investments in Maldah town and beyond, was a supplier of materials for NREGA. As he told me, with characteristic candour, more NREGA applications meant more earthworks. More earthworks meant more materials. More materials meant more deals to siphon off materials. More deals meant more profits. And more profits meant more business. 'Gold with God', as he put it during one of our numerous conversations after dinner. Phanindranath Sarkar was all praise for the programme's design and told me to ignore the ravings of his 'outdated' [in English] kinsmen who criticized the program. 'The only culture my people have is agriculture,' he declared another evening sipping his favourite Johny Walker whiskey, 'and that culture is dead.' Phanindranath Sarkar was closely associated with Maldah based NGOs whose activists fanned out in Saotal-inhabited localities to disseminate information about the NREGA. Managers of his supply-chain, residents of Maldah town, frequently provided such activists logistical support. On his instructions, they allowed these activists to use their motorcycles, offering them rides into remote hamlets. The activists were allowed to use his office space in the nearby market town of Kamra. But even Phanindranath Sarkar refused to break with his clansmen and publicly oppose their opposition to the program.

Ditya's labouring poor were caught in a bind. On the one hand, they could draw on disparate sources of support for their applications for work under NREGA. On the other hand, their actual applications for work, especially when it coincided with the agricultural seasons, brought them into conflict with the locality's labour-hiring peasant politicians, all of the Desiya community. Anxious about labour shortages and increased agricultural wages, these politicians eventually sought to sabotage the programme altogether. A commonly-used strategy was for the ward members, on the behest of politicians such as Mota

Sarkar, to truncate payments to the workers. Such antics annoyed the labouring poor of both the Saotal and the Desiya communities. Short-changed labourers did not hesitate to express their irritation. On at least two occasions, much to the consternation of NGO activists who insisted that they file petitions to complain, the cheated workers, both Saotal and Desiya, collectively thrashed their ward member. One such incident occurred in 2008, a few months prior to the panchayat elections, when the ward member, Mota Sarkar's son-in-law, arbitrarily reduced the wages paid to the workers. On that occasion, the workers of both communities beat up the ward member. They then *gheraoed* Mota Sarkar and held him hostage till the ward member produced the full payment. The care they took to not hurt the ageing Mota Sarkar while he was in their custody earned them accolades from other villagers. A year after the elections, the new ward member's husband, a Saotal, was accused of withholding payments. The workers alleged he was a stooge of the rich peasants and manhandled him. They received their payments within a week.

The assertions demonstrated by Ditya's labouring poor, despite the context of a differentiated political place where they were directly pit against the precarious classes, was made possible by the generalized policy design of NREGA. The labouring classes from among the Desiyas and the Saotals knew they were not competing against one another for a finite set of resources. Moreover, the initial tentative support of the Ward's precarious class politicians, who had hoped to use the programme to stem migration from the locality, had fomented interest among the labouring poor for very different reasons. The poor were further emboldened by the encouragement of panchayat-level political activists as well as influential contractors with a direct stake in the implementation of NREGA. That their assertions met a wall of resistance from the precarious classes should not detract from this important fact.

Quietude in a paternalistic political place

This is the Big Man's world. There is no *narega* here.

Interview notes, Mansoor Ali,
Roshanar Ward 5, 9 April 2010

Not one household in Roshanar Ward 5 reported receiving the job cards. People knew about the programme and said they would apply if only they knew what to do. The ward's residents had heard from many people about it, but no one seemed to know exactly what to do about it, whom to approach, and what the benefits were. No politician had approached them with job cards either. Needless to say, they had not applied for any work. I had initially surmised that, given the high incidence of migration among the ward's Kunjra Muslims, perhaps they were not interested in NREGA at all. My interlocutors rejected my inference and claimed that they would welcome employment with NREGA should the opportunity be extended to them. They rued the fact that such opportunities had not presented themselves.

For the ward's Muslim labourers, the absence of any politician or activist approaching them with job cards reflected the discrimination to which were routinely subjected. My interlocutors told me how they were refused loans at the local Central Bank of India, their crops were always offered lower than the Minimum Support Price, their applications for pensions or subsidized housing always took longer than others', and that, as Kunjra, they were not allowed to share their burial ground with the Sheikh Muslims of the neighbouring localities. Some of the older men also admitted that they maintained a distance from the CPI (ML/L) as they wanted to stay out of trouble. CPI (ML/L) veteran Premchand Yadav, who had come visiting his friend Mansoor Ali during an afternoon I spent with the family, surmised the problem thus in his presence:

> If the police see a Muslim with us, they simply pick him up, and brand him a terrorist. That's the end of him....As a Yadav, I have no fear: the police will think twice before laying a hand on me. Likewise with Kevats and Musahars. With *them* [looking towards Mansoor Ali], it's a different matter. That's the way the Government has kept Muslims away from our rallies and processions. Isn't that correct? [Mansoor Ali nods in agreement].[16]

The situation of Ward 5's inhabitants was worsened by the Mukhya's antipathy towards them. The Mukhya and her husband's animosity toward the ward's residents stemmed from the suspicion that they were stooges of the erstwhile Mukhya, the Congress-affiliated landlord Pritam Singh. The present Mukhya's electoral victory had been made possible by the consolidated support of the precarious classes and the labouring poor. Against threats by the entrenched classes, who looked toward Pritam Singh as the defender of their privileges, the labouring poor voted in large numbers for a Mukhya from among them. Readers will recall from chapter 3 that the inhabitants of ward 5 were an exception. Therefore, even though the Mukhya and her husband were known proponents of NREGA, and had actively encouraged their supporters in other wards to demand work, they appeared to have been indifferent to the fact that the labouring population of Ward 5 was excluded.

Roshanar's entrenched class politicians were unsympathetic to the very notion of public works for the rural poor. Gajdeo Mandal, a capitalist farmer who managed his agricultural operations entirely by hiring in labour and was well-versed with the ways of the agricultural markets, was unequivocal in pronouncing investments on programmes such as NREGA as a waste of resources. He argued with me about the sensibility of implementing such a programme at a time when the entire agrarian economy was in crisis. Rather, he suggested, the state ought to invest in agriculture on which everyone, including agricultural labourers and the urban middle class, were dependent. He reminded me, correctly, that public investment in NREGA far outstripped that on agriculture. He concluded his hour-long monologue by labelling NREGA a plot hatched by giant corporations and their urban middle class employees to destroy India's agriculture once and for all. As he told me, while sipping his *chai* on the *machan* in his courtyard, assured in the belief that he had unearthed a grand conspiracy:

> You tried to manipulate prices. It did not work.
> You tried to acquire our land for your corporations. It did not work.
> Now, you are using the agricultural labourers to fight your battles.
> [Glint in his eyes becomes prominent].
> We'll see how you succeed [clenches his fingers together to form a fist].[17]

As a member of Roshanar's tiny entrenched class, Gajdeo Mandal had no intentions either of initiating or supporting the distribution of the job cards. That he did not appear to have faced personal labour shortages made his opposition to NREGA puzzling. After all, he hired agricultural labourers for his farming operations from outside the locality. Indeed, he had a reputation of being a good employer! During my fieldwork, I overheard labourers speak warmly about his behaviour to them. He had developed the reputation of an employer who paid his labourers on time, never haggled, provided decent meals and was lax about pilferage. Nevertheless, when it came to expressing his opinion about NREGA, his hostility demonstrated a well considered antipathy towards the programme. His views were not only shared by other members of Roshanar Ward 5's entrenched classes, but also – perhaps even more so – by the labour-hiring small and medium landowners who cultivated their lands by complementing their own family and self-labour with hired labour. Most such members of the precarious classes were drawn from the same Gangot community as he was, and looked up to him as their community elder. Labour-hiring Kunjra Muslim peasant proprietors, who respected him for the protection he accorded to them from Hindu Rightist mischief mongers, concurred quietly with his bias against NREGA.

I thought that Pritam Singh might incite the labouring poor of Roshanar Ward 5 to apply for the job cards, if only to embarrass his opponent, the present Mukhya who had trounced him at the elections. But his entrenched class position made him even more unremitting than Gajdeo Mandal in his hostility against the programme. During his interview with me, on tape, he candidly admitted that if he had his way, he would abandon the programme altogether. '*Narega* will break India's spine', he asserted. Pritam Singh took credit for convincing his tenants, Gajedo Mandal and others, in Roshanar Ward 5 that NREGA was disruptive to them. He claimed it was on his advice that they realized that the programme would subvert their agricultural practices and make their labourers wealthier than them. His chest puffed out as he recounted the way in which he allegedly persuaded his tenants in Ward 5 and elsewhere in the panchayat to scuttle the programme altogether. Although I found little in my conversation with Gajdeo Mandal to corroborate his landlord's claims, it was clear to me that both entrenched classes and precarious classes saw eye to eye in their suspicion towards NREGA.

Roshanar's Mukhya perceived the implementation of NREGA to possess a number of political and social advantages. To begin with, it was as a means of rewarding her voters. The work supplied under the aegis of the programme would contribute to reducing the economic dependence of her generally impoverished electors on wealthier farmers. For these reasons, the President, her husband, and their advisers were particularly active in popularizing the programme throughout the gram panchayat. However, they assiduously stayed away from Roshanar Ward 5 and other localities where Pritam Singh's influence remained considerable. The reasons for this were not entirely clear to me although, intuitively, it might be the case that they feared that the Pritam Singh-supported gram panchayat member of Ward 5 would take credit for the program were it to be introduced in this ward.

From my interviews with Kunjra labourers, one perspective was that the entrenched and the precarious classes successfully convinced the poorer peasants and the landless labourers of the Gangot community that the NREGA would not help them very much, especially because of the widespread corruption in its implementation. Even if the labouring poor from the Gangot community might have considered the NREGA to improve the opportunities available – as they may have heard during their interactions with other labourers and people who worked on the program – they were unlikely to act against any advice offered by Gajdeo Mandal. Gajdeo Mandal had been a benefactor to many. As the community's *mahant*, Gajdeo Mandal's opinions were taken seriously. When he made his opposition to the NREGA clear, the labouring poor of his community acquiesced. Isolated, the Kunjra Muslims remained aloof from the program, convinced that their efforts would never lead to its implementation.

A conjunction of factors, leading to the effective political isolation of Roshanar Ward 5's labouring poor, was responsible for the resigned quietude among them in relation to NREGA applications. On the one hand, the Mukhya's well-publicized antipathy toward the inhabitants of the ward appeared to dim any prospects of securing employment under the aegis of the NREGA. On the other hand, the Ward's most influential people, labour-hiring farmers such as Gajdeo Mandal, perceived the programme as being against their interests. Such a perception eliminated any prospects of them raising the question of the NREGA applications even if to embarrass the incumbent Mukhya. Between the hostility of the Mukhya against them and the antipathy of the Mukhya's opponents against the NREGA, the ward's labouring classes discounted the possibility of ever securing employment under the programme. Caught between the cleft, the ward's poor appear to have concluded that they need not even bother applying for NREGA cards, for their applications would not be considered.

III

Demands as politics

The demands made by the labouring classes to local governments for employment are among their many points of contact with the state. As a juridical category, a demand refers to an application for work. As a political category, the demand pertains to the advancement of a social claim. Demands do not reflect singular communications between individuals and the state. Labourers draw on friends, neighbours, and relatives as well as local politicians and other political mediators to file applications. Acquaintances and strangers help them. At other times, activists from local NGOs support their endeavours. The demands draw on moralities of mutual support and dependence. A demand is not a solipsistic endeavour upon which individuals embark in order to secure NREGA job cards or employment for themselves alone. Rather, demands invoke mutual support and relationships.

Despite the numerous actors who mediate their access, workers understand the state to be the focus of their efforts. Through their demands for work, they seek to make themselves 'seen' by the state (to invert Scott's evocative metaphor). Their demands enable them to make a claim upon the state to provide for poor people such as themselves. They view the state as having a duty toward people in poverty and NREGA as one of the ways in which it can fulfil its obligations.

How do we understand poor people's demands in terms of the meanings they make of democracy? Are these demands political? As a purposeful practice intended to advance a social perspective, the workers' demands are ineluctably political. The demands and associated practices contribute to forging a collective identification of labour. Through such identifications, the labouring poor make meaning of their shared lives, in ambivalent conflict with the meanings forged by labour-hiring classes. That the demands impinge on the social relations of power is an important, though unintended and unanticipated, aspect of people's demands for work and wages. The labouring poor perceive the demands they make or that are made on their behalf as a sort of entitlement, a medium through which they convey their claim to the state that they deserve its protection. In claiming their entitlement, they combine formal requests with contingent collective action. The incipient sense that

NREGA is a sort of entitlement emboldens their applications in most cases, even though the results are not always favourable.

Labourers value the NREGA because it provides them the possibilities of staying on in their villages without being dependent on local hirers of labour. For not a few women labourers, the NREGA provides a more dignified space of work because it means less harassment from local employers. Other applicants view the program as an alternative to prevailing agrarian labour relations that are steeped in discrimination. It enables them to continuing to live in the village without conforming to a social hierarchy hinged on caste. To be sure, outmigration considerably enhances labourers' economic autonomy vis-à-vis local employers and reduces their dependence. Labourers who remain in the village report increased bargaining powers. But the logic of migration means that the labourer is 'absent' from the village. The alternative to being incorporated in subordinate labour relations has conventionally been to exit from the village. By contrast, employment with NREGA, albeit never more than for a paltry 15–25 days in a year, promises workers the prospect of staying on in the village without being subjected to hierarchical social relations.

An analysis of the demands for work reveals a fascinating tussle over the identity of the workers. This tussle is played out in competing meanings that are assigned to the NREGA by functionaries of the state, local elites, and the workers themselves. The operational guidelines of NREGA (NREGA, 2006) refer to workers as 'wage seekers' or 'job seekers'. It appears that as far as the policymakers who drafted the guidelines could see, the rural poor solely seek a wage. Such a view promotes the notion that NREGA is nothing more than a massive scheme to recruit clients for the government. The vocabulary of wage-seeker, formulated at the highest echelons of the Indian bureaucracy, reduces the identity of the poor as reflexive only to jobs and wages, with little recognition of the values of dignity, honour, and self-respect. In imposing the identity of the wage seekers or job seekers upon the rural poor, the operational guidelines imply that the poor ought to be grateful for what was being offered to them. This understanding of NREGA is transmitted from the elite to the vernacular tiers of the bureaucracy. The condescension displayed by the frontline bureaucracy to applicants for employment draw upon such 'elite' understandings of the labouring classes.

NREGA workers contest the solipsistic identity of 'wageseeker' and 'jobseeker', which the elite echelons of the bureaucracy sought to impose upon them. Their own descriptions of engagement with the programme invoke the idea of hard labour, or *shram*. This self-description is used to indicate the value they add to the local economy by excavating pits, building roads, and afforestation. When the workers complain about their wages not being paid on time or being truncated, they perceive it as an insult to their selves and to their labour. As not a few of my interlocutors in Sargana said in relation to delayed payments under NREGA, '*Shramik ke paseeney sookhne se pehle usko majdoori milni chahiye. Nahin to uska apamaan hota hai*'. Translated into English, this reads –'Labourers should be paid their dues before the sweat on their body dries'. Otherwise, it is an insult. The notion of work and the dignity associated with are central to the forging of their collective selves.

Such contests over the identity of the worker are conjoined with tussles over the values associated with the manual work performed by the workers. The classes hostile to NREGA offer disdainful narratives about the works undertaken under the scheme. The labouring classes' claims about their contribution to the local economy are dismissed by local bureaucrats and by the wealthier people. 'These people only dig ditches', is the scornful refrain among them. The workers on the other hand pointed to the value of the works they were undertaking. They referred to the roads they had constructed, the tanks and ponds they had rejuvenated, and the afforestation activities they had undertaken. Labourers' accounts resonate with the official data. As the Indian government's progress report on the assets created under the NREGA (Government of India, 2014, 22) tells us, over 40 per cent of all works undertaken under the aegis of the programme across the country relate to water conservation and nearly a quarter to rural sanitation. Rural roads and land development projects for farmers each comprise over a tenth of all activities. The extent of the works undertaken varies across States, as might be expected, given India's agronomic and political–economic diversity. In Bihar, projects to construct rural roads comprised 40 per cent of all NREGA projects while drought proofing (especially afforestation activities) makes up another 34 per cent. In West Bengal, drought proofing activities comprise 35 per cent of all NREGA projects and rural connectivity another 31 per cent. Such accounts negate the derisive accounts presented by the programme's antagonists.

The demands for work under NREGA are not animated by the sense of competition that marked the scramble for BPL cards. The labour-hiring classes are not so interested in securing NREGA work for themselves. But at least some among them revile the programme and remain antagonistic to it, trying where they could to reduce or completely eliminate the prospects for labourers to find employment on it. In their endeavours, they are helped by elected representatives or petty bureaucrats mandated with the task of efficiently implementing the programme but whose class solidarities shape their hostility towards it.

Indeed, the contentions among the labourers and the officials and politicians lend the political engagement with NREGA an antagonistic dimension. Such contentions are spawned by the delays or truncations of payments. They provide the context in which labourers forge class solidarities that straddle communal distinctions. Ditya's case is paradigmatic because of the manner in which the members of the Desiya and Saotal communities collaborate against the Desiya ward member suspected of siphoning funds. In Sargana too, peasants of Kevat and Yadav communities and retailers of the Kayasth communities reveal their hostility against the entrenched classes by supporting the landless labourers, a large number from the Musahar community, in their demands for employment and timely and correct wages.

Although the applications for employment and applicants' subsequent engagements with NREGA are embedded in existing relations of power in all four localities, their conflictual dimension foment incipient shifts in the relations of power. Such shifts are particularly notable in Ditya where the labouring classes of the ward's two principal communities make common cause with one another against the precarious classes. They are also observable in Sargana, where labourers force precarious class politicians to not take them for granted. Important though these marginal shifts in the social relations of power are, they are unintended. People do not demand work and wages with the intention of interrogating the social relations of power. However, the absence of the intention to interrogate prevalent power relations does not reduce the political dimension of these demands. The demands are underpinned by an intention to advance a social perspective, and that is what makes them unambiguously political.

Beyond subaltern moralities and juridical guarantees: Declarations of dependence on the everyday state?

Stuart Corbridge *et al.* (2005) enumerate three different aspects of the ways in which the state in India relates to the poor: they point to its coercive, developmental and empowerment inducing dimension. The disparate facets of the state foment contradictory responses among the poor, ranging from fear and suspicion at one end of the spectrum to enthusiasm and expectation at the other. If, on the one hand, they want to be counted as 'BPL' households or be considered for NREGA employment, on the other hand, they want to steer clear of the police or the circle officer responsible for revenue collections. Uneven as such sightings of the state by the poor are, they aver, it is these exchanges though which governed populations are transformed into rights-bearing citizens of the state. Poor people take the language of rights seriously.

The implementation of NREGA appears to have strengthened the forging of rights-bearing citizens through its broad-based scope (as opposed to the narrowly-targeted design of the BPL cards) which stipulates that anyone could 'apply' for work under this programme. Mihir Shah (2008) argues that NREGA concretizes the promise of social and economic development made by the Indian Constitution to its poorest people. This observation is persuasive indeed. The legislation pertaining to NREGA, alongside similar legislation around education and food provisioning, call to mind T. H. Marshall's (1964) account of the progressive elaboration of rights-based social citizenship. Marshall's account historicizes the evolution of the rights regime in England. He reminds us that civil rights were forged in the eighteenth century, followed by the extension of political rights in the nineteenth century. Social and economic rights were guaranteed only in the twentieth century in the aftermath of World War II. The expansion of the rights regime in India appears to be consistent with this progressive elaboration.

However, the poly-vocal experiences of applications discussed in this chapter should caution us against an uncritical acceptance of a narrative about state guarantees heralding the advent of social rights. The process of demanding work and wage do not necessarily entail applicants connecting as rights-bearing individuals with the state. As the aforementioned accounts demonstrate, politicians from competing political parties demonstrate their relevance by providing job cards to individual households even before they apply for those cards! Sometimes employment is provided in advance of the formal filing of the applications. People often do not apply for job cards or employment directly, but rather through local politicians, other political mediators, and friends and neighbours. It is not uncommon for strangers or acquaintances to provide advice or help in understanding the nuances of the programme as well as sharing workers' practical experiences, especially the delays they face when it came to securing wages.

The concrete ways through which labourers seeking employment under the NREGA actually engage with the state reveals the continued importance of political mediation in their lives. Politicians and other political mediators approach agricultural labourer households or small and marginal farmers to ask if they need or want job cards. They actively incite interest among labouring classes in the programme's specificities, much to the consternation of the bureaucrats who are responsible for implementing the programme. The broad-based design of NREGA does not eliminate political mediation as such: what it does is it reduces fears among political mediators about demand outstripping supply.

Political mediators follow up on applications for employment on workers' behalf. Their interventions often save labourers the loss of a day's wage. Narratives of politicians, friends and neighbours 'helping' (*shahajyo kora*, Bangla), 'being kind enough' (*doya korlo*, Bangla), 'looking out for us' (*dekh bhal kiya*, Hindi), and 'thinking about us' (*humaare baarey mein socha*, Hindi) permeate my interlocutors' reports about the ways in which they received employment when they did. Given their quotidian struggles with earning their livelihoods, the labouring poor welcome any such assistance with follow ups. In recounting the assistance from politicians, my interlocutors blur the distinction among politician, broker, and relative, often invoking kinship terms to refer to political mediators. The most common terms used are 'brother', 'uncle', and 'nephew'. Although admittedly the use of these vocabularies was more widespread in West Bengal than in Bihar, they were invoked in all localities.

The role of politicians becomes even more important once it was time for workers to claim their wages. Wages, as we have seen, are frequently delayed, and are sometimes severely truncated. Under such circumstances that politicians intervene on behalf of the workers and demand of the bureaucrats that full payments be made. Elected representatives sometimes make up for the delay in payments by advancing some cash to workers as soon as they complete the work so that they do not need to wait out the complete cycle through which the formal payment is made. Once the formal payments come through, the politicians pocket the entire amount. This practice is widely known and seldom criticized by the labourers. Workers are aware that their elected representatives receive more than they give. But they also acknowledge the timeliness of the support, which helps them meet their daily subsistence needs. Workers concur that the initial investment by the politicians is crucial, and the politician should be able to make some profit from such investment.

Where politicians fail to help ensure the timely payment of wages or are themselves part of the problem, it is not unheard of for workers to engage in what Naomi Hossein (2013) has called 'rude accountability'. Apparently, NGO activists in Ditya urge women workers to file a petition with the gram panchayat asking them to expedite the payments. Likewise in Bihar, cadres of the CPI (ML/L) attempt to persuade women workers to write petitions complaining of the high-handedness of the Post Master. The labourers acquiesce but not without reservations. They openly display their irritation with what they consider unnecessary politeness during the writing of petitions. As representations to the state, petitions are expected to be suffused with invocations of respect, humility, and charity. Such expectations annoy the workers. On their part, the activists who support their claims as well as the bureaucrats towards whom the claims are directed deride the workers as being uncouth. The act of writing petitions, they hope, would not only create a paper trail, but also educate the workers to shed their putative coarseness and supposedly ill-mannered comportment. Against these views, the labourers advance their claims through ways that they consider will be more effective. Underpinning these claims appears to be an inchoate notion of entitlement among India's rural poor vis-à-vis the NREGA. They 'know' that the programme is for them and that it is being implemented by the government for them.

Notwithstanding such notions of entitlement, labourers make few references to the vocabulary of rights in their demands. In West Bengal, the programme is referred to as *ek sho deener kaaj*, translated into 'Hundred Days' Work'. In Bihar, it is simply called *manarega*, the Hindified English acronym for the official title MGNREGA. During conversations with my interlocutors and listening to conversations between them, it did not occur to me that they viewed the programme as a 'right'. A contrast with labourers' view of suffrage may help illustrate this point. Whenever I would broach the question of voting and solicit their views on their electoral participation, their facial expressions turned grave. Their seriousness of purpose reflected in the direct eye contact they made with me to communicate unequivocally that voting was a right. Such seriousness was borne out of the categorical use of the term 'haq' (Urdu/Hindi) or 'adhikar' (Hindi/Bangla). While they refused to countenance any truncation of their 'right' to vote, labourers were willing to consider the possibility that they might never get paid on time and/or be paid the total amount due to them under NREGA. The split between political rights and socio-economic rights appears hard-wired into labourers' collective self-identifications.

Given the absence of a vocabulary of state-sanctioned rights, from where does the notion of entitlement vis-à-vis NREGA come? Across the four villages, despite differences in the experiences of people vis-à-vis their applications under NREGA, the refrain that the state ought to provision for its people is common. Indeed, my interlocutors say the government should have instituted a programme such as this a long time ago instead of pandering to the interests of the rich farmers and industrialists. It is the state's responsibility to look after the poor and to protect them against starvation, malnutrition, and death. The poor are not poor because they like being poor. They are poor because they were exploited by the rich, they said, invoking the lexes of *shoshan* and *atyachar*. In talking about obligations to poor people, they add that the state should help them live as human beings.

In speaking of the state's obligation to provide, my interlocutors – especially from among the Musahar, Kunjra, Saotal, and Shershabadiya communities – refer to provisioning for the poor in the past. Many of the elderly men and women recount memories of their childhood, when they were faced with dearth. In such circumstances the locality's wealthy people would take pity on them and offer them food. Back then, the 'food' ranged from the vaguely edible, such as rice starch and fodder, to what they considered lavish, which included dal and rice/*chapatti*. The terms of the provision differed. In some localities, such as Ditya and Roshanar, the rich were obliged to provide: the wealthier they were, the better they were expected to provision their subjects. The wealthy landlords controlled most aspects of life for the poor, including the responsibility to 'look after' them. Doing so was a moral obligation for them, something they were enjoined to do as part of their duty (*dharma*). In Rahimpur, the *shamajs* were obligated to levy a *zakat* on their members and to provision for the destitute using the revenues thus raised.

However, my interlocutors do not endorse the aristocratic privileges on which such provisioning were based. They are relieved when they are not dependent on the entrenched classes for assistance and disappointed when they have to approach them for help. The old ways are gone, is a common refrain in all four localities. Now, I was told, it is the obligation of the government to look after the poor, and to see to it that they didn't suffer. In this respect, NREGA is a valued intervention. In Ditya, the labouring poor find the programme an alternative livelihood option. Rahimpur's workers say that engagement with the programme enhances their credibility with local creditors. The ability to stay on in the village without having to endure caste-specific humiliations during agricultural work is an important consideration in Sargana. In all of this, the meanings assigned to NREGA scarcely invoked the juridical interpretation of NREGA as the 'right to work'.

The distinctive meanings attributed to the programme might bring to mind the analytical split that distinguishes, in Ranajit Guha's (1997) formulation,[18] 'elite' politics from 'subaltern' politics. Guha's work underscores the use of moral idioms, encapsulated by the imagery of *dharmic* dissent, in structuring protests in colonial India. The persistence of moral idioms stemmed from the inability of the colonial state to establish its hegemony over the populations it controlled. In a similar vein, it could be argued that the postcolonial state could at best establish its dominance over the population but not its hegemony: its idioms and vocabularies could not permeate the kinship and communitarian relationships in which people were embedded. In accessing NREGA, the workers initiate a number of intimate contacts with a variety of actors in their locality rather than activating a singularly solipsistic claim on the state as an applicant and a bearer of rights. They establish a claim over NREGA mediated through trusted politicians, friends, and neighbours rather than a direct command over the right to work as encapsulated in the relevant legislation.

Although workers draw connections between the obligation of the contemporary state to provide for its population with the moral duties of erstwhile notables, they are resolute in celebrating the gradual dissolution of the hierarchical social order. They offer the imageries of provisioning by the wealthy as a point of negative comparison – to indicate that times have changed now, and they no longer have to depend on, or be 'tied' to, any individual in the village. State-sanctioned social provisions reduce their dependence on wealthy individuals from privileged caste backgrounds. The employment provisioned by the state conveys to them that they are cared for by the state. Workers value social provisioning because it enables them to *rupture*, rather than sustain, a moral economy that was deeply hierarchical and predicated on the supremacy of specific social classes. To be sure, workers do not think of themselves as revolutionaries out to destroy the social hierarchy when they apply for NREGA employment. But they do advance the perspective that they value working under NREGA compared with being employed by local farmers who either ogle at them or practice caste-based discrimination.

The NREGA is of course not designed to rupture any such moral framework. Its implementation, patchy at best, cannot be held singularly responsible for any rupture that might have occurred. Nevertheless, the programme makes an important contribution to labourers' on-going attempts to lead dignified lives in their villages. Employment per worker ranges from 15–25 days per year in the three villages discussed in this chapter. In those few days, workers belie the expectations of their employers in the localities. The rich peasants, capitalist farmers and landlords expect workers, as agricultural labourers, to depend on *them* for meeting their employment needs while they live in the village. However, state-sanctioned employment provisioning under NREGA provides the rural poor with an opportunity to live in the village without depending on local farmers for employment. While variations in the social relations of power shape the ability of people to apply for work, access to the programme constitutes a key aspect of life for the poor in all the localities where it is implemented precisely because it helps them escape the moral frameworks that bind them in subordinate relations with the labour-hiring classes.[19]

A recent exploration of the ways in which the values and meanings that poor people make of the state differs from those of the elites is offered by James Ferguson (2013). Referring to poor people's interpretations of the publicly-funded Basic Income Grant (BIG) programme in South Africa, he points to a disjunction between their expectations of the state and the expectations of the privileged classes. The poor perceive the state as an entity that naturally benefits them, rather than as a protector of abstract notions of equal rights. By accessing the BIG programme, beneficiaries declare their dependence on the state as rightful and deserving claimants of its largesse. In Ferguson's (2013) analysis, relations of dependence, subordination, and contingency are as much indicative of citizenship as are Liberal notions of citizenship, anchored in the idea of equal rights.

Much of this analysis might appear applicable to the cases in this chapter, to suggest that the applications of the poor represent a 'different', and not necessarily deficient, way of claiming rights and the attention of the state. The vocabularies of care, help and protection invoked by NREGA workers as well as those who were unsuccessful in finding employment under its aegis would seem to confirm its applicability. The several ways in which people referred to the NREGA makes Ferguson's approach seem germane. His subjecting to scrutiny the Liberal normativity of the languages of stateness as underpinned by the discourse of rights is especially welcome. However, applying this framework to the cases discussed in this chapter is problematic. In demanding employment under NREGA, workers do not declare their dependence on the Indian state as wage-seekers. In fact, they emphasize their own collective identity as workers contributing to the country's growth. They invoke the obligation of the state towards them as poor people, not so much to declare their dependence on it, but to diversify their livelihood prospects and *reduce* their dependence on labour-hiring classes. In the southern African context, scholars have directed attention to the provisional character of aspirations to dependence.[20] Writing about Indonesia, Tania Murray Li (2013) suggests that labourers and poor peasants are far more likely to declare their independence from employers than their dependence. In the four places discussed in this chapter, people who worked on the programme did not aspire for themselves and their children to keep working the programme. Therefore, just as neither the juridical nor the moral economy framework is helpful, notions of declarations of dependence are not germane to thinking about the ways in which NREGA workers interpret the programme's value in their lives. Any 'declarations of dependence' on the state that might be inferred from their actions is inextricably tied to their aspirations for independence from social hierarchies.

For these reasons, I caution against analytically folding poor people's demands for work into either the narrative of accessing state-guaranteed rights or the plotline of subaltern moral solidarities and 'declarations of dependence' on the state. Taking the former approach, and emphasizing a progressive expansion of social and economic rights limit our analysis of workers' political practices to one whose end-point is accessing state-provisioned workfare. Taking the latter approach, of anchoring the political practices spawned by the programme as moral claims, or as declarations of dependence inhibits an understanding of the ways in which the labouring classes seek to interrupt, rather than maintain a hierarchical moral economy. As we have seen above, neither approach can accommodate the logics underlying the political claims of the poor vis-à-vis NREGA.

Agonistic demands

If the demands before politicians and politician mediators are exemplar neither of moral vocabularies nor of languages of stateness, how are we to theorize them? How do we understand the practices of people who appear to inhabit the overlapping spaces between expressing moral claims and languages of stateness? In responding to this question, I want to reiterate the patische of consensual and contentious perepctives to which our interlocutors in this chapter have familiarised us.

My interlocutors emphasize their hard work and contribution to the local economy while invoking the justness of their demands. They refer to their sweat and toil in reminding me that non-provision of work and delayed payments of wages are unfair. As members of contingently-formed transient collectives, they sometimes engage in direct action. Nevertheless, they also remark on the fact that they are people, poor people, who *need* work and timely wages. Variations in the performance of demands notwithstanding, a common refrain in all four localities is along these lines: 'The government should have provided us such work long ago'. When they meet their elected representatives, political mediators and other politicians, poor people reinforce their *collective* identities as labouring poor, *gorib shramik* (Bangla) or *garib majdur* (Hindi). As labourers, they are poor and see themselves as justified in demanding social assistance so that they can assert their independence from prevalent social hierarchies. The experience of applying for work, participating in the public works programme and following up to obtain wages brings workers into intimate, if ephemeral, contact with other workers. As members of the resultant transient collectives, workers learn from one another as well as pressurize their elected representatives for timely provision of work and wages.

By demanding employment under NREGA the labouring classes seek to maintain their presence in the village, without adhering to customary relations of subordination. Their demands reflect an attempt by them to lead lives that accord with *their* social perspectives. People like Sejni Rishi, Shefali Bibi, and Marangmayee Hembrom seek to assert their place in the village public on their own terms. They and their husbands refuse to conform to the social roles imposed upon them, as a pool of 'reserve labour' into which the labour-hiring classes could dip as and when they need. It is common for the hirers of labour to revile their erstwhile agricultural labourers as stepping beyond their limits (*aukat se bahar*, Hindi) and being impertinent (*ki asphorda*, Bangla). As I have pointed out elsewhere (Roy, 2014), the labourers do not *intend* to be rude or insolent to their erstwhile employers. Rather, they seek employment under NREGA to lead dignified lives as social equals. That their actions undermine prevalent meanings associated with rural living is an important consequence but not necessarily intentional.[21]

While the demands for work under the NREGA do not hark to the constitutional provisions guaranteeing work, the sentiment that the program has been designed to help 'poor people'- the garib aadmi (Hindi) or gorib manush (Bangla) is difficult to ignore. Their demands intimated collective self-identifications as impoverished labourers in an inchoate contradiction with wealthy and propertied people: such collective self-identifications render it impossible for their demands to be folded into the rubric of either moral vocabularies or languages of stateness. It is also important to distinguish these demands from the 'declarations of dependence' to which James Ferguson (2013) has directed attention. Ferguson appropriately challenges those economists who characterise popular claims invoking moral vocabularies of care and protection on the state as backward. However, from this observation to advance the theoretical claim that poor people's politics is a politics seeking dependence on powerful patrons is to ignore the egalitarian aspirations that accompany poor people's demands. This criticism of Ferguson is not to subscribe to the Liberal approach that the labouring classes assimilate the languages of stateness. Indeed, as readers would have noted, the characters we have encountered in this chapter neither invoke the constitutional status of the NREGA nor accept the identity of 'wageseeker' that the Indian government attempts to impose upon them.

An initial coalescing of diverse members of the labouring classes – landless laborers, sharecroppers and marginal-small peasants – around the program is discernible. When Arif Miya and his friends say that the NREGA is for 'people like us', or when Shanichar Rishi remarks that 'we don't have to dance to other people's tunes', they contribute to the forging of a shared labouring class identity. Thus, an incipient formation of a collective identity around shared work is unmistakable.

The contentions over the programme reveal an inchoate antagonism between labourers and the wealthier classes. Labourers frequently refer to the unjustness and oppression perpetrated by the program's saboteurs, by invoking such terms as *anyay* and *atyachar*. An antipathy towards the people who 'steal' the programme (Ditya), try to steal it (Sargana ward 1 and Rahimpur) or do not allow it to be introduced (Roshanar) is discernible. Nevertheless, they do not voice any ideas about annihilating the saboteurs or liquidating class enemies. Rather, what they repeatedly assert is their pursuit of a dignified life for themselves and their future generations. They neither consent with the saboteurs of the NREGA nor engage in conflict with them. Instead, they are located in an agonistic relationship with them. The labourers demanding work under the NREGA appreciate the causes of their poverty in the oppression and injustice to which they are subject by the entrenched and/ or precarious classes. They quite clearly do not consent to their own domination. Nevertheless, they are not led to demanding or perhaps even imagining the destruction of the oppressive structures to which they are subjected. Rather, the people whose political practices have been examined in this chapter weave collaboration with contention in their negotiations. Their demands combine appeals to be taken care of with collective assaults on politicians suspected to be unfairly withholding wages: however, we have seen that these combinations vary, shaped as they are by the political spaces within which the poor are embedded. The demands for employment inhere invocations of their labouring identities, and are anchored in narratives of collective impoverishment perpetrated by the oppression of the 'rich'. Side by side, however, in advancing their demands for employment, members of the labouring classes consent to as well as contend with the claims of the entrenched and precarious classes. This conglomeration of seemingly opposing practices infuses an agonistic content into their demands.

The demands people make on their elected representatives, political mediators and other politicians represent a crucial repertoire in their negotiations with democracy. They realise that the self-selection principle of conditional social assistance notwithstanding, their access to governmental resources are far from assured. They neither acquiesce in being denied the resources nor, however, do they plot the overthrow of those who deny them the access they seek. Although their demands differ across locations, an incipient identity around labour is discernible, anchored in the notion of 'poor people' who are exploited by the rich. Such conceptualisations signal to us the agonistic character of poor people's demands.

Conclusion

This chapter has done four things. One, it rehearsed the history of public works programmes in India. The generalized policy framework in which people self- selected themselves into the programme meant that people 'demanded' work and wages from their elected local governments. Two, the chapter documented labouring classes' negotiations as demands for employment and timely payment of wages under the aegis of the NREGA. Three, the chapter analysed these variations by directing attention to the configuration of social relations of power. Demands are confident in localities where the poor are embedded in collaborations with either the entrenched or the precarious classes. The generalized design of the programme facilitates solidarities among poor people from across communities and among poor people from the same communities across localities, leading to assertive demands in a locality such as Ditya where the poor are otherwise isolated. However, where they are ranged against a coalition of labour-hiring classes led by the entrenched class, as in Roshanar, poor people see little point in making any demand at all. Four, such heterogeneities notwithstanding, this chapter theorized poor people's demands as agonistic negotiations that reveal the entanglements between moral vocabularies and languages of stateness.

Negotiations with political mediators, elected representatives and labour-hiring classes remains an imperative for labouring classes, even in the context of broader-based social policy. However, given that people can self-select themselves into such broad-based social programmes, the nature of their negotiations changes. Members of labouring classes are able to advance collective claims, sometimes alongside labour-hiring peasants who themselves hire out their labour vis-a-vis the state. The demands are internally fragmented, shaped as they are by variations in the constitution of political places. But they do reflect incipient forms of collective self-hood. Those seeking work refer to themselves as labouring people oppressed by the wealthy and the powerful. Such conceptualizations of collective self-hood neither reflect an assimilation into the languages of stateness as propagated by the Indian government nor do they indicate an espousal of different moral vocabularies by the labouring classes. By foregrounding their collective self-identification as labouring poor in some sort of ambivalent conflict with the privileged classes, they also negotiate the meanings of democracy. By demanding work under the NREGA, the people readers have met in this chapter convey the meanings with which they imbue India's unequal democracy. These meanings are substantiated by poor people's expectations from their elected politicians and other political mediators who populate the democratic institutions. While notions of kindness and help are a crucial component of these expectations, so is the anticipation that the support from them will reduce workers' dependence on the dominant classes. Poor people express a causal connection between oppression and poverty and hope that elected politicians will intervene to reduce the oppression to which they are subject. An inchoate antagonism between the poor and the rich frames these concerns, even as such antagonism does not harden into class conflict. However, poor people's negotiations with democracy and the meanings with which they inflect democracy are both dynamic. The people demanding work and wages whom we met in this chapter were supplicants for BPL cards in the previous chapter. Some of them will be disputants in the following chapter. Others will forge egalitarian imaginations of their membership in the political community in the subsequent chapter.

Endnotes

1   Ethnographies of the state abound. Corrigan and Sayer (1985) led the way with their historical sociology of the English state. Other path-breaking, if controversial, works include Bayart's (1993) research on the state in Africa; Herzfeld's (1992) work on Greece; and Joseph and Nugent's (1994) collection on state-formation in Mexico. The anthropological perspective has been enriched by more recent research on the imaginations (Hansen and Stepputat, 2001) and affective dimensions (Stoler, 2004) that attend to statist projects. Other significant additions to the literature include Navaro-Yashin's (2002) work on secularism in Turkey, Verdery's (2004) research on post-socialist transitions in Romania, and Jensen's (2013) account of the hope for and against the state in post-conflict Sarajevo. Useful ethnographies of the state in India are provided by Fuller and Harriss (2001), Corbridge *et al.,* (2005), Gupta (2012) and Sharma and Gupta (2006).

2   See Cammack (2004), Naudet (2003), and Teichman (2016).

3   Referring to its drawbacks, Echeverri-Gent (1988) reports that the programme's officials could not properly register workers through its life. Only about a fifth of those receiving employment were agricultural labourers.

4   I base the discussion about the Maharashtra Employment Guarantee Scheme on Moore and Jadhav (2006). I base the discussions about the NREGA on McCartney and Roy (2015) as well as the *Operational Guidelines* (NREGA, 2006).

5   Data on the NREGA is freely available at the programme website: www.nrega.nic.in. Readers may also be interested in the annual reports released by the Indian government (NREGA, 2014; NREGA, 2013; NREGA, 2012 and so on).

6   These discursive onslaughts on the program have continued under the NDA regime. No less a person than Prime Minister Modi has mocked the MGNREGA in recent years (Roy, 2015).

7   India's GDP for 2012 (at current US$ prices) is estimated to have been US$ 1.86 trillion (World Bank, 2013, Table 4.2).

8   See World Bank report here: http://www.worldbank.org/en/news/opinion/2013/11/04/bolsa-familia-Brazil-quiet-revolution.

9   Expenditure on NREGA represented nearly 8 per cent of the Indian government's central plan outlay for the rural sector. By contrast, expenditure on agriculture and allied activities notched up a measly 2 per cent. Such a shift marks a very calculated departure away from public investment in agriculture.

10   Accessed at http://labourbureau.nic.in/Report%20%20Vol%201%20final.pdf in February 2017.

11   Accessed at http://www.censusindia.gov.in/2011census/PCA/PCA_Highlights/pca_highlights_file/India/Chapter-4.pdf in February 2017.

12   Authors who have promoted the notion that the 'bottom'-of-the-pyramid' should be

viewed as consumers and entrepreneurs rather than as victims and recipients of dole include Prahlad (2004), Hart (2005) and London (2008).

13 A reference to Delhi's Red Fort, from where India's Prime Minister delivers his annual Independence Day address. Interview notes, Parsvanath Jha, 7 April 2015.

14 The reference is to the Prevention of Atrocities (Act), 1989, a legislation enacted by Indian government to prosecute individuals who harass members of the SCs and STs. See http://socialjustice.nic.in/poa-act.php for details.

15 Group discussion, Tudtudiya hamlet, Neechupada, Ditya, 25 February 2010; all cited matter till the next footnote from this source.

16 Field notes, Mansoor Ali's residence, 7 April 2015.

17 Interview notes, Gajdeo Mandal, 9 April 2015.

18 Guha's formulation draws on the 'moral economy' perspective introduced by E. P. Thompson. At the heart of the moral economy thesis lies an ensemble of mutual dependence, trust, and reciprocity. In a similar vein, and following a similar lead, James Scott (1977) reminds us about the 'moral economy of the peasant' – the collection of shared values and idioms on which peasants draw in order to defend themselves against the claims of the elites. Scott's later work builds on these insights to advance the theory of 'everyday resistance', emphasizing thereby the quotidian ways in which peasants draw on their shared values and idioms to keep in abeyance the state's attempts to control them.

19 Roy (2014a) clarifies this argument.

20 See, for instance, the works of Rutherford (2001), Bolt (2010), and Bolt (2013).

21 For that reason, I argue (Roy, 2014a) that such actions must not be confused with the idea of 'everyday resistance' proposed by James Scott (1985). C. P. White (1986) contends that what is often 'resistance' (every day or otherwise) may not have been intended to be that. The label of 'resistance' is an identity imposed by elites.

6

From Backwardness to Improvement?

The Politics of Disputation

*I am poor today. Does that mean that my children should not lead
a better life tomorrow?*

Interview notes, Shekhar Shil,
15 February 2010, c. 55, marginal landowner

The preceding chapters illuminate the ways in which the intersections
in between opportunity structures and social relations of power in
contemporary India's unequal democracy constitute political spaces. Such
spaces, in turn, shape labouring classes' negotiations with other classes.
These chapters note the importance of the policy design, which further
specifies opportunity structures. Where the policy is narrowly targeted,
people 'supplicate'. Where the policy allows people to self-select themselves,
they 'demand' access, although Roshanar's case alerts us to the continuing
importance of the social relations of power. Although popular negotiations
spawned by the different policies vary considerably, they signal for us the
entangled meanings with which the poor imbue democracy. The negotiations
underpinning these entangled meanings provide a window to analyse the
entanglements between the universalistic ideas and particularistic practices
that characterize any democracy.

I continue to explore these entanglements in this chapter and the next by
shifting attention to a different kind of policy and focussing discussions on
heterogenieties in poor people's negotiations within a single political place.
The policy context is provided by an electrification programme which is
universal in scope. This programme is neither narrowly targeted to specific
localities or populations nor is access to it conditional upon performance of
any manual labour.[1] The discussions in this chapter are based on ethnographic
observations in West Bengal's Rahimpur village, an incorporative political
place where the labouring poor and the entrenched classes coalesced uneasily
against the precarious classes. The discussion in the next chapter will proceed
along somewhat similar lines, focussing on Bihar's Sargana village, a populist

political place where the labouring poor gravitated towards the precarious classes against the entrenched classes.

The material presented in this chapter enables me to analyse the ways in which Rahimpur's labouring classes dispute their elected politicians' unilateral efforts to implement an electrification program that promises to improve everyone's lives. Through their disputations, they advance their own myriad views on what improvement means to them. Side by side, I underscore disputes *among* the ward's population, from which the elected politicians and his associates could not, try as they might, extricate themselves. Many in Rahimpur were unenthused about the electrification project because they were not convinced by the location of the electric poles proposed by technicians. But rather than rejecting the electrification programme altogether, the affected people sought to negotiate the location of the elected poles with their politicians and other mediators.

How are we to understand poor people's disputations over the location of electricity poles given our broader interest in the meanings that they attribute to democracy? Do their disagreements with their elected representatives' claims to improve their material conditions reflect a resistance to improvement *tout court*? Do their disputations with their politicians' ideas of improvement suggest that they seek to preserve their ways of life? I juxtapose my ethnographic observations on disputes in Rahimpur with the scholarship that laments popular encounters with improvement schemes or development discourses as depoliticizing, destructive or worse. Simultaneously, I distance my material from teleological narratives that celebrate such schemes and discourses as heralding the transition from backwardeness to improvement. Such narratives center on the universalism/particularism binary, according to which improvement schemes signal universalistic ideals that dissolve particularistic ways of life. Proponents of improvement schemes are enthused by such impending dissolution while critics worry about the disappearance of entire ways of life and are overjoyed at any prospect of resistance. The analysis offered in this chapter hopes to contribute to the emerging literature that steps beyond such dichotomies.

After a brief overview of the discontent with the theorization of improvement and concomitant notions of development, I refer readers to the key debates over the relationship of electrification with social change.

A short introduction to the Rajiv Gandhi Grameen Vidyutikaran Scheme follows, under which Rahimpur village and nearly 475,000 of India's 600,000 villages were sought to be covered. This is the subject of Section I. In Section II, I lay out the manner in which Rahimpur's ward member assumed upon himself the role of the ward's trustee, and the ways in which his assumptions were interrogated by the ward's population. The ward's population was not a monolith however, with several of the disputations occurring between neighbours. Moreover, for members of the ward's marginalized Shershabadiya community, such disagreements appeared a luxury, for their hamlet faced a real threat of being excluded from the electrification programme. Section III offers, like in the other chapters, some theoretical reflections on the agonistic contours of poor people's disputes in respect of the improvement schemes and development discourses.

This chapter, thus, does four things. One, it emphasizes the fluid nature of political space by focussing on one locality: Rahimpur's incorporative political place. By outlining the policy context, it enables readers to appreciate the dynamic character of the opportunity structures available to the labouring poor and the ways in which they negotiate with these structures. Two, it reflects on people's disputations with their neighbours, politicians and political mediators in the context of the opportunity structures and social relations of power within which they are embedded. Three, it reminds readers of the heterogeneities in people's disputations. Four, it critically engages with approaches to theorizing such disputations as indicative of either an enchantment with narratives of improvement or resistance to these.

I

Improvement and its discontents

James Ferguson's (1994) interventions were among the earliest to alert social scientists to the depoliticization affected by improvement schemes. Based on a fascinating ethnography of the development bureaucracy in Lesotho, his work suggests that schemes for the improvement of poor people's condition often limit political challenges to governments. In this vein, Timothy Mitchell's (2002) study of bureaucratic rationalities in colonial Egypt, Achille Mbembe's (2001) discussion of the logics of colonially inflicted violence in sub-

Saharan Africa, Miguel A. Centeno's (1994) research on neoliberal Mexico' technocratic revolution and Michael Watts' (2003) analysis of development and governmentality in oil rich Nigeria elucidate the ways in which bureaucratic and governmental practices that promise to improve people's lives often constrict their political interrogations of poverty, inequality and injustice.

However, political scientists have also been alert to people's vigilance in the wake of schemes that purport to improve the human condition. James Scott (1985, 1990) reminds us that the people affected by doctrines and practices of improvement collectively reflect upon the pros and cons of such interventions. Scott researches peasants' manipulation of improvement schemes which they considered to be detrimental to their own interests. It would be a mistake, he concludes, to think that poor people remain passive victims of improvement schemes with which they do not concur. While Scott concedes that the growing power of states with 'high modern' ambitions leaves ever reducing space for people to manoeuvre, his approach encourages analysts to investigate the ways in which people undermine the scope and reach of improvement schemes when these do not suit them. The merit of his approach lies in his uncovering of the subterranean tactics deployed by peasants who avoid open confrontation with their powerful adversaries. They challenge people in authority, not openly but quietly and surreptitiously. More recent scholars have departed from his approach by suggesting that the poor do not obstinately reject improvement schemes. They suggest that poor people, in fact, seek to negotiate with such schemes so that they can influence them in their own favour (Baviskar, 1995 and Li, 2007). That they do not always succeed in influencing them should not detract from their intention to negotiate.

The relationship between democracy and improvement has remained a fraught one. Indeed, the utilitarian provenance of the notion of improvement has not infrequently entailed the justification of despotism. John Stuart Mill, acclaimed among normative political theorists for his liberal humanist views, contended that despotism was a 'legitimate mode of government in dealing with barbarians, provided the end be their improvement' (Collini, 1989, 13). Notions of improvement profoundly shaped theories about Liberalism and democracy during the nineteenth century. The period Asa Briggs (1959) has called the 'Age of Improvement' (1783–1867) was a formative one in the constitution of Liberalism in England.

Mill's philosophical concerns with improvement were intricately tied with theories of human progress and an evolutionary view of human society. He extended and built upon his father James Mill's efforts to develop a scale of civilization where different societies could be graded vis-à-vis others that were supposedly at different stages of social progress. The Senior Mill held a dichotomous view of human society: as far as he could see, there were 'rude' or 'barbarous' nations on the one side and 'civilized' nations on the other.[2] Rude societies were those where 'the ingenuity [of the population] is wasted on contemptible and mischievous objects', whereas civilized societies were ones where '*Utility* [Mill's italics] is the object of every pursuit'. Having dichotomized human society thus, Mill Senior nonetheless firmly believed that 'rude' societies could progress to civilization under the tutelage of 'civilized' societies (Mill, 1968, 105). Eventually, these led Mill and other proponents of Liberal democracy to support a 'trusteeship' model of electoral democracy, whereby people would entrust their representatives with the authority to take decisions on their behalf. Trustees were people with education, possessed technical know-how, and desired to ameliorate the lot of those less privileged than them. Those whose lot was to be improved were placed under trustees' 'tutelage' till the time they were educated and became ready to govern by themselves. This model of trusteeship and tutelage toward people whose condition was to be improved applied not only to colonized people in India or Ireland, but also toward the poor within England.[3]

Eric Stokes (1959) has documented the improvement schemes that characterized Britain's agrarian and land tenure policies in India under the terms of such tutelage, as Cowen and Shenton (1996) have done for Kenya. In similar vein, following the Second World War, the President of the United States Harry Truman set out for his country the agenda to 'embark on a bold new program for making the benefits of our scientific advances and industrial progress available for the improvement and growth of underdeveloped areas' (Truman, 1949). Truman went on to outline the ways in which what he called 'underdeveloped areas' could 'develop'.

Recounting the historical imbrication of ideas of improvement with notions of liberalism on the one hand and colonialism on the other alert us to the practices of the individuals and institutions about whom Ferguson, Mbembe, Centano, and Watt write and of whose practices they are deeply suspicious.

The post-development scholar Arturo Escobar is particularly scathing of the project of development, which he argues perpetuates the dominance of a specific idea of improvement, as propagated in post-War United States. That several of these logics of colonial governance continue to inflect postcolonial strategies of government and development justifies these authors' suspicions. While on the one hand, governments continue to mark the poor out as targets of improvement, on the other they ignore the factors that structurally perpetuate poverty and inequality.

Concomitant with such selective exercises are the stigmatization and devaluation of whole ways of life (Pigg, 1992) in the name of effecting improvement. Proponents of improvement schemes harbour contempt towards critical reflection by the intended target populations on the nature and efficiency of those schemes. A paradigmatic example of such contempt was demonstrated by India's former Finance Minister Palaniappam Chidambaram during an interview with the prominent Indian journal *Tehelka*[4] that people were 'being deceived to believe that the existing state of life is an ideal state of life and development and industrialization will make it worse'. Further in the same interview, he went on to allege that objections to improvements formed a 'conspiracy by the socially driven class to keep poor people poor.' Articulating his vision of 'a poverty-free India... where a vast majority, something like 85 per cent, will eventually live in cities,' he responded to his interlocutors' concerns about the feasibility of effecting such a transition in by posing the counter-question: 'So, shall we leave people to live in these villages?' As this book goes to press, Chidambaram was no longer India's Finance Minister, but his successor Arun Jaitley is as committed, if not more so, to his vision outlined above.[5]

Arguments such as Chidambaram's glibly ignore the structural factors which make and keep the labouring classes poor. Proponents of improvement schemes believe that people are poor because they are excluded from the benefits of development, such as roads, schools, hospitals, toilets, electricity, and markets. What such a focus occludes are the relations of exploitation, marginalization, and discrimination that generate and perpetuate poverty. The processes through which people are, or remain, impoverished involve their adverse incorporation into relations of labour and power. This is not to deny the importance of access to the sorts of infrastructure noted above. Rather, it is to highlight the importance of social relations in shaping access to such infrastructure. Many of the world's leading development and poverty research agencies recognize this when they speak of 'sustainable development goals' (UN), 'inclusive growth' (World Bank), 'multidimensional poverty' (OPHI), and 'from poverty to power' (Oxfam). To believe, as many proponents of improvement schemes do, that infrastructural interventions *in themselves* will reduce poverty is to naively ignore the attendant social contests. For example, if schools were to be used by dominant classes to indoctrinate pupils from labouring class backgrounds, their contribution to helping the labouring poor enhance their conditions of life is limited. This is precisely what the educationist Paulo Freire (1970) had in mind when he reminded his audiences that the manner in which education is imparted and the uses to which it is put – rather than the 'fact' of being able to read and write – shapes the ability of the oppressed to interrogate the relations to which they are subjected.

Schemes purporting to improve the human condition are neither the unalloyed benefit that their proponents celebrate nor the unmitigated evil that their opponents suggest. People's attitudes to such schemes are shaped by their perceptions of the associated individual and social costs. People affected by such schemes find themselves in awkward confrontation with trustees who are not only responsible for implementing the programme but also possess the authority to decide the specifics of the implementation. Trustees could be bureaucrats, activist-professionals, politicians or even exemplary individuals. Many trustees genuinely believe that the strategies and practices they propagate are in the best interests of the people. Rahimpur's ward member, with whom the ward's population negotiated over the installation of the designated electric poles, portrayed himself as one such trustee. Unfortunately for him, the ward's population shared neither the assumption of his trusteeship nor his proposals about the specific locations of the electric poles.

The social life of improvement: The case of electrification

Electrification provides a powerful narrative around which discussions on improvement of poor people's lives are structured. An impact evaluation conducted by World Bank suggests that rural electrification 'can make a major contribution to achieving several of the Millennium Development Goals' (World Bank, 2008, 141).[6] The several potential benefits accruing from rural electrification to the poor listed by it include – increased income, supporting education, improving women's quality of life, and reducing environmental harm. Among indirect benefits, the Bank suggests the poor would benefit in terms of a richer social life, reduced fertility, and entertainment. Some of these assumptions are so commonplace that there can be no question of voicing any scepticism about the benefits of electrification. It is, after all, undeniable that electrification permits more working hours, especially indoor working hours. Factories and other industrial units would be inconceivable without electrification, depriving millions of people the opportunity to earn their livelihoods. Likewise, the pumps that irrigate agricultural lands in several parts of the world are powered by electricity: their absence would very likely result in grave starvation and food insecurity. Vaccine cold chains and other life-saving equipment would be impossible to sustain without electricity, as would potable drinking water in urban areas. As an inseparable trope of improvement, the desirability – and inevitability – of electrification is unquestioned.[7]

Early accounts situating electrification in a social context tended to assume its independence of social influences. This view suggests that electrification determines cultural and political processes rather than being shaped by it: Lenin's quip that communism was Soviet power combined with electrification is instructive in this regard. The introduction of the electric grid was imbued with much promise across the ideological spectrum: Henry Ford was no less a proponent of electrification than Lenin. The Soviet animation film for children titled 'Onward to the Shining Future: Plus Electrification' provides a fascinating example of the anthropomorphic qualities with which states imbued electric poles. The film shows electric poles marching across the diverse landscapes of the Soviet Union and other East European nations to an excited musical score.[8] The English subtitles, starting approximately two minutes into this nine-minute film read:

> Through the village, one by one, power poles rise up and run
> How the wires hum with spark keen, that's a sight we've never seen
> It's a sight not seen in dreams, now the Sun in darkness gleams

A departure from such technological determinism was first suggested by Thomas Hughes (1983) in his seminal work *Networks of Power: Electrification in Western Society*. Scholars of electrification have since examined the ways in political contests and contentions have shaped the layout of electric grids (Chikowero, 2007; Rao and Lourdoswamy, 2000) in colonial societies where interlocked axes of race and class were clearly identifiable markers of property and privilege. More nuanced perspectives are offered by sociologists who call for exploring the dialogic ways in which the electrification process and socio-political relationships shape one another. David Nye (1990) argues that although electrification is a social construction, the terms on which people adopt it are socially and culturally shaped. When it was first introduced in the United States, people identified electrification with urban and modern spaces. However, in the countryside, Ronald Kline (2000) tells us, there was far from unambiguous embrace of this hallmark of modernity. Farmers analysed, selectively used and adopted it to suit their conveniences, rather than welcoming electrification with open arms.

Increasingly, scholars are wary of context-determinism. Ronen Shamir (2013) argues that context cannot be assigned a deterministic role in thinking about the imbrications of electrification and concomitant socio-political tendencies. He treats the electric grid as a 'social assemblage' because of the way it brings together apparently unrelated elements. The grid generates and affirms 'identifiable social networks' (Granovetter and McGuire, 1998, 148). Alongwith the poles and wires, the grid does not merely transmit electric currents, but also transform social and political relationships. Indeed, Nye (1990) and Kline (2000) acknowledge the impact of electrification in society when they recall that inequalities between rural and urban and rich and poor were fomented in the early decades of electrification. Similarly, Winthers (2008), following an 'anthropology of energy' approach (Wilhite, 2005), shows the ways in which men and women in a rural Tanzanian village were unevenly impacted – vis-a-vis one another and vis-a-vis inhabitants of neighbouring villages – by the electrification process. Ruiters (2009) also notes the gender differentials that were widened with the introduction of electric grids in different urban settlements of South Africa. A World Bank study admits that the share of poor people in the consumption of energy continues to remain lower than that of others (Komives *et al.*, 2005). Such arguments persuade us to be aware of the dialectical ways in which electrification shapes and is shaped by social relations and political contestation.

Nonetheless, in the policy literature, electrification projects, like other improvement schemes, are often embedded in a teleological narrative whereby their introduction is assumed to pull people out of the drudgery and misery of their lives. Such narratives assume that electrification projects will 'lift' people out of poverty. They do not specify the ways in which the vulnerability, powerlessness, and discrimination that mark poor people's lives will be addressed by electrification. Mining coal and damning rivers – the basis of electrification – is an impoverishing process seen from the point of view of those displaced. Roads may facilitate the movement of labourers hoping to secure livelihoods and reclaim their dignity in urban areas. But they also facilitate the extraction of surpluses and movements of troops in ways that may be inimical to rural residents. Any teleological belief in the efficacy of roads or electrification to poverty reduction would have to account for the existence and reproduction of the urban poor, for whom access to neither is a problem. My scepticism is to be distinguished from a postmodernist dismissal or disavowal of these interventions and a romanticization of a preservationist stance. Instead, my argument is more modest: any celebration or condemnation has to be rooted in the specific circumstances of the intervention.

The International Energy Association (IEA) estimates that 81 per cent of the world's population has access to electricity. Further, the agency tells us that 93 per cent of the world's urban population and 68 per cent of its rural population use some form of electricity, pointing to the differentials between rural and urban areas in the matter of accessing electricity. Of the 1.3 billion people in the world *without* electricity, 300 million live in India alone. Although governments and political parties in the country have sought to politicize the uneven pace and spread of electrification from time to time, the Congress-led UPA took an active interest in provisioning electricity to all rural households in the country after it came to power. After being unexpectedly swept to power in 2004, the government instituted the Rajiv Gandhi Grameen Vidyutikaran Yojana with the goal of extending electrification to all rural habitations across the country, named in the memory of India's former Prime Minister Rajiv Gandhi. The project's website informs its audience that the programme was introduced 'to electrify all un-electrified villages/habitations and to provide access to electricity to all rural households in un-electrified and electrified villages in the entire country'.[9] Almost 475,000 villages were expected to be covered under this scheme. These included over 120,000 villages with no electrification whatsoever, as well as some 352,000 villages where electrification had hitherto remained partial. Villages with no electrification were selected for initial electrification.[10] Villages with partial electrification were selected for 'intensive electrification', aiming for complete coverage of all households. Rural electricity infrastructure, ensemble of grids, towers, wires and transformers, would be improved. The scheme envisaged that the electrification of rural households would be completed by 2010.[11]

Under the aegis of the scheme, the West Bengal State Government selected the 'partially electrified' Rahimpur village for intensive electrification in February 2010.[12] The news that 35 electric poles had been allocated to this ward generated an important spark. Rahimpur already possessed a distribution transformer, which routed power to hundred-odd houses, those located around the main village square. Five electric poles catered to the needs of these households, and consequently suffered from high load. Several households sourced electric connections illegally, thereby increasing the load on the existing poles. Besides, entire hamlets, such as Dargahpada, Thakurpada and Intar Rahimpur, the hamlet inhabited by the Shershabadiyas, had no access to electricity. For the ward's Congress politicians, the scheme was an excellent opportunity to drive home their argument that their party was indeed the party committed to the welfare of the people. For them, the arrival of the poles represented one of the advantages of having a Congress government at the Center. For me, the discussion spawned by the arrival of the poles proved to be a fortuitous occasion to observe the ways in which people in Rahimpur negotiated with their politicians, political mediators and one another. By the time the poles arrived, my presence in the locality as a harmless student from faraway Oxford studying something vague such as social change had been somewhat taken for granted. I could be a 'fly on the wall' during the furious exchanges on the topic without the worry that my presence would distort people's interactions with one another and with their elected representative, the ward member Babar Hossein.

II

Trustee assumptions

When the poles arrived at Rahimpur, it had been a year since Babar Hossein had been elected ward member. In a closely fought election, he had narrowly defeated the CPI(M) affiliated Mushtaq Khan, whose wife Henna Khan, had been the ward member from 2003 to 2008. I happened to hang out with Babar and his associates at his office when he received the call on his mobile phone from the panchayat office that the poles had been allocated to Rahimpur and were on their way. Babar dismissed early suggestions by his associates that they target the poles to neighbourhoods whose inhabitants were known Congress supporters. In fact, he and his close aide Akbar Ali believed that the poles would provide him the opportunity to win over the support of people who had hitherto voted for the CPI(M). They both shared the view that the village's electrification ought to benefit everyone. As Congress politicians, they opined they were the custodians of the poles and responsible for their installations throughout the ward. Their belief appears to have stemmed from their seriously considering themselves as trustees. To be sure, they did not refer to themselves by the Bangla term for trustee, *nyasi*. But the manner in which they sought to take responsibility for all aspects related to the implementation of the electrification programme conveys their assumption of trusteeship.

Babar Hossein adored Jawaharlal Nehru, India's first Prime Minister. When he received news of the allocations, his exuberance knew no bounds.[13] In a meeting he convened at his office early the next morning, at which all his associates in the Congress Party were present, Babar Hossein spoke of the arrival of the poles as the fulfillment of Nehru's 'dream' (*shopno*) for India as well as the dream that *they,* Babar and other Congress politicians, had seen for their co-villagers. With the arrival of the electric poles, the village would be one step closer to modernity. Its condition would improve, as would the condition of its inhabitants. '*Gramer unnati hobey*' (The village will witness *unnati*, see below), he gushed. His associates agreed wholeheartedly. The gap between Rahimpur and Maldah Town would be narrowed, averred Akbar Ali. A new era would dawn. It would only be a matter of time before the sleepy village would 'become like' Maldah (*Maldah'r moton*), suggested Alaluddin Ali. For far too long, especially because of Communist 'misrule' –Babar Hossein did not fail to repeat – the village had remained a backwater. Now, finally, it would 'catch up' with Maldah (*Maldah ke dhore phelbe*). He and his colleagues admitted to the possibility of human costs attending to the generation of electricity in neighbouring Jharkhand, but – he reasoned – most of that electricity was consumed by the rich in their factories and homes. How could anyone expect poor villages in Maldah to be burdened with the guilt of displacements induced by coal mines? Did I, a person born and brought up in a metropolis, ever think of displacements each time I used my laptop, Babar Hossein asked me with his characteristic flourish.

The use of the term *unnati* is of interest because it alerts us to the focussed scope of the changes that Babar and his colleagues associate with the electrification of their village. The Samsad Bangla–English dictionary translates *unnati* into a number of English terms, including prosperity, progress, advancement, development and – of course – improvement. It is also of interest that Babar and his associates insisted on using the term *unnati* over the term *unnayan*, which is part of the official lexicon to refer to development. For example, Village Development Committees are called Gram Unnayan Samitis (that these were never formed in Rahimpur is another matter!). My interlocutors' preference for *unnati* rather than *unnayan* derived from their appreciation of the difference between the two terms and was not as absent minded as I had initially believed. The distinction between improvement and development is subtle, yet significant.[14] References to improvement entail a narrower focus than development. They point to advancements in quality of life and increased prosperity. Narratives of improvement promise betterment of lives. Development, on the other hand, refers to transformations that are often far more structural and more all-encompassing. By referring to Rahimpur's *unnati*, rather than *unnayan*, Babar Hossein and his colleagues appreciated the limited scope of the changes that electrification would anticipate. Electrification was not industrialization, as Babar Hossein reminded some of his younger and overtly enthusiastic colleagues in the party. Therefore, to expect electrification to lead to a revolutionary transformation of Rahimpur's society would be unrealistic. This narrow scope notwithstanding, Babar Hossein and his associates appeared convinced that electrification would represent a significant change in the life of the village and the villagers.

Babar decreed that the electric poles be installed in consultation with a technical team of engineers. Once erected, the poles would be connected with the transformer. A group of technicians had already completed their survey of the locality under his supervision. They knew exactly where it would be

Map 6.1: Map showing the proposed locations of electric poles in Rahimpur, 2009

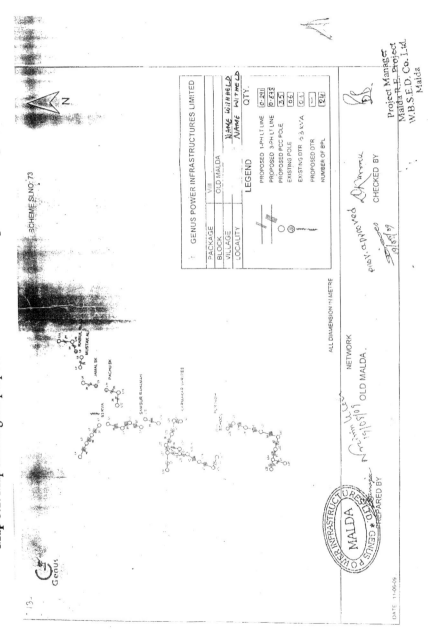

feasible to erect the poles. They then generated a map and shared with the ward member. He in turn confided its contents with only his closest associates, Akbar Ali, Abdur Rehman, and Alauddin Ali. I obtained a copy from him on condition that I would not tell anyone in Rahimpur that I possessed it. See Map 6.1. The spots marked with an 'L' (followed by a number) indicate the location of the poles. The numbers associated with each location are arbitrarily assigned. They cumulate to 35 poles. Babar made it clear to his colleagues that they were not to share these contents with anyone else, because he did not want what he considered to be unnecessary discussion on the matter. He feared that his adversaries in the CPI(M) might use the contents of the map to foment opposition to his plans. At the same time, he was confident that Rahimpur's residents, especially the ward's poorest people, would completely acquiesce in any decision he took. The possibility of isolated instances of dissent could not be ruled out. But that, he believed, would be limited to a few 'unreasonable persons'. As he mused, 'Who does not want *unnati*?'

Akbar Ali was less sanguine. He feared that the ward's population might not be as enthused as they were about the electrification project. Households could be impacted in a number of ways. Their connection to the grid via the allocated pole was only one among many considerations. The physical location of the pole might be too close to the entrance of a house, to which householders might object. Or the wires might pass too close to their windows.

As we shall see, Akbar Ali's fears were not entirely unfounded. Rahimpur's residents refused to uncritically embrace the electrification drive promoted by their elected representative, although, they were just as unwilling to uncritically reject it. Recognizing that the ramifications of installing the electric poles exceeded its technical aspects, Akbar insisted that they involve the people in their discussions. 'If there are any objections they could be made right away. Who is afraid of conflict? If there is an issue, it has to be resolved. If we hide from it today, it will 'find' us tomorrow.' Abdur Rehman and Alauddin Ali worried that consultations would lead to so much discussion and conflict that 'it would be impossible to take decisions.'[15] Eventually though, Babar Hossein and Akbar Ali compromised. They agreed to consult households directly affected by the installation of a specific pole. By convening meetings with households in a single neighbourhood, they reasoned they could avoid large-scale meetings, while at the same time, they would be able to tell critics that they had in fact consulted the public. Babar remained convinced that, consultations notwithstanding, villagers would acquiesce with his decisions.

While there was disagreement among the assembled Congress politicians about whether villagers should be consulted, there was unanimity that they were better off *not* convening a public meeting with all villagers. They were aware of provisions in the panchayat legislation for a gram sabha, an assembly of all voters in the village. But they felt it would be a waste of time. They opined that any discussions they held ought to be kept practical and manageable. Abdur Rehman worried:

> People only listen to the CPI(M) leaders during these meetings. And those fellows ask too many questions. 'Why here'? 'Why not there?' 'Who are you to decide'? And if you ask them to do it, they will say- 'Oh, you are running away.' They are able to sway poor people's opinions. That is not something we do well.

Abdur Rehman's dismissal of formal meetings appears to reflect the entrenched classes' mistrust of public forums. At these forums, they feared, the CPI(M)'s precarious class politicians would incite the village's labouring poor and manipulate them. Their reasons for avoiding meetings were to prevent such a scenario where the precarious classes and the labouring poor might make common cause against the proposals of the entrenched class leadership of the Congress. Akbar Ali's suggestion appeared to all of them to be a sensible compromise between holding public meetings and consulting no one at all.

Next morning, I was privy to discussions among the ward's CPI(M) politicians about the electric poles. The news that 35 electric poles had been allocated to Rahimpur was public knowledge by now, although Babar had successfully concealed any information about the exact location of the poles. CPI(M) politicians admitted that the arrival of the poles had allowed Babar to claim a major victory. They agreed that it would be pointless to ask too many questions about the installation of the poles. After all, they concurred, their village did need electrification. The venerable Joynal Ali warned his associates that they could not afford to be seen as against the improvement of the village. They resolved among themselves not to press for a public meeting or a gram sabha but to accept Babar's decision.[16]

Babar and his colleagues intended to walk through Rahimpur and halt at each of the 35 proposed locations. At each location, they aimed to meet with the neighbouring householders who were likely to be affected by the installation of the pole in the ways that Akbar Ali anticipated. They would secure the agreement of the households inhabiting the neighbourhood on the exact location of the pole servicing their households. Alongwith the technicians, they would mark out spots where the poles could be erected. The overriding factor was that the exact locations of each pole would be less than25 feet from the houses it serviced in line with the programme's technical guidelines. The politicians hoped that their strategy of meeting individual or small groups of householders in neighbourhoods would reduce prospects of having to deal with demands from a united populace. However, by now, Akbar Ali's anxieties were gradually creeping onto Babar Hossein. He worried that CPI(M) politicians might fuel opposition: 'They are like ghosts. We have to isolate the malevolent ones'.[17]

For that reason, he and his associates agreed, contrary to Babar Hossein's original plans, that they would begin their trek through the village with the neighbourhoods whose inhabitants were known Congress supporters and sympathizers. They would definitely not ignore the CPI(M) supporting neighbourhoods. But early successes were more likely to bolster their chances of persuading the entire population to accept their proposals. They also agreed to begin their discussions in the most impoverished neighbourhoods where they expected residents to be less confrontational about any doubts or concerns they might have. The entrenched class leadership of the Congress hoped to be able to build on their goodwill with the labouring poor to convince them to agree with their proposals.

Through that evening, the Congress politicians rehearsed their performance. Accompanied by the technicians, they would all set out in batches to Rahimpur's different localities. Babar Hossein, as ward member and President of Congress, would arrive first accompanied by the technicians. They would initiate conversations with local householders about the locations where the poles were to be erected by marking the area out. They would enquire if the householders were in agreement with the specific spots that had been marked out for the installation of the poles. Although Babar expected people to acquiesce, he asked Abdur Rehman and Alauddin Ali to follow closely behind. They would engage householders in more in-depth conversations, sense their mood, dispel doubts and reiterate the decision that had just been taken. Akbar Ali, conscious of the need to continuously affirm the party's link with existing and potential constituencies, would amble in last, partly reiterating what had already been discussed, partly encouraging people to air any lingering grievances and questions, and partly to thereby reaffirm contact and identify any other problems people faced. CPI(M) leaders were not invited to be a part of this team, and did not ask to be invited to join either. By the end of their rehearsals, the Congress team had convinced itself that a grateful village would agree with their proposals. With the exception of Akbar Ali, they expected their operation to be over in about two hours.

Disputing trustee assumptions

The next morning, and over the two subsequent days, Akbar Ali's worst fears were confirmed. The Congress politicians' proposals were disputed at each one of the proposed locations. What was expected to be a walkover took three days, and seemingly endless discussions. More than once, Babar fumed: 'Let the poles be taken away. They will never be seen again'.[18] Alauddin Ali threatened his interlocutors: 'If we return the poles to the block, *you* will be responsible'. Akbar Ali pleaded: 'This is a lifetime opportunity. Don't waste it'.[19] But Rahimpur's inhabitants remained unmoved by these persuasions. They carefully considered Babar's proposals. While they agreed that the village needed electrification, they disagreed with Babar's approach and insisted that people be *collectively* taken into confidence.

Babar and his colleagues tried to highlight the favour they were doing on the people by bringing in the poles. A term they frequently used was *upkar*, as when they declared, 'We are doing you an *upkar* by calling for the poles', or when they claimed, 'Babar has taken a lot of trouble to bring these poles in. He is doing you an *upakar*'. Their declarations were met with a range of responses. Some of their interlocutors maintained a stony silence. Others counter-argued: 'If the poles are returned, *you* are the ones who will be in trouble'. Many argued that, with legislative assembly elections just a year away (scheduled for 2011), local leaders of all parties were being instructed by the top leadership to show results. A former Congress politician Murshid Hossein was downright dismissive, 'There is no *upakaar*. You are only doing your duty. You ought to do it'. When Babar tried to counter-argue saying this was more than what they got in 32 years of CPI(M) rule, Murshid Hossein retorted, 'That is why we kicked them out'.[20] Other families remained unimpressed. They said they knew that the scheme was in the offing. Now that it had been operationalised, electrification in the village would be complete sooner rather than later. Most people interpreted Babar's demonstrations as the result of instructions issued from the Congress High Command. They insisted he was not doing them any favour. As far as they could see, he was doing his job, much as Babar and his associates tried to impress upon them the good they were doing for the village.

Rahimpur's residents were also annoyed with more practical aspects of Babar's efforts. In Masjid *pada*, one of the very first neighbourhoods that Babar and his team visited, their women interlocutors ridiculed the timing of their visit. Masjid *pada* was one of the impoverished neighbourhoods where the majority of voters were known to be Congress supporters. Shefali Bibi and Arif Miya lived here. Shefali Bibi remonstrated to her ward member that he had chosen a bad time for such discussions. At the time of Babar's visit, her husband Arif Miya was in Maldah Town, where he was working at a construction site depending on the availability of work. She explained: 'Men take these decisions. They are away at work. We don't understand these things. What is the point of talking to us?'[21] Shefali and her neighbours expressed their inability and unwillingness to commit to agreeing to Babar's proposals regarding the location of the poles. They were unsure about the nuances of the proposed arrangement. Consequently, they refused to endorse any decision without consulting their husbands. Some of the more vocal women accused Babar of conspiring to time his visit in such a way that none of the real decision-makers would be available. Babar protested that he had to keep in mind the technicians' availability – and they could possibly not be expected to come in the evening, after their working hours. Moreover, it would be dark in the evenings, which would inhibit accurate marking of most of the locations. He even invoked the notion of women's empowerment, suggesting that they were, after all, 'equal to men in all respects, and more so in household decision making'.[22] His interlocutors giggled at this remark but none of them agreed to be talked into agreement.

Babar and his associates realized the futility of continuing the persuasions and decided to revisit the sites the following day. They asked the residents of the neighbourhood to ask their husbands to be at home the following day. Shefali Bibi protested that such a request would mean the loss of a day's work and wages. If her husband stayed on till late in the morning to wait for Babar, he would lose out any opportunity at all for the entire day. And that would imply the loss of an entire day's wage. How could Babar Hossein even contemplate making a request like that? At that point, Akbar Ali intervened and assured both Shefali Bibi and Babar Hossein that he would find a way to talk with her husband and secure his agreement. From what I gathered, the matter remained unresolved till the *next* evening, primarily because Arif Miya and Akbar Ali could not agree between themselves about the potential location of the pole.

Babar and other Congress politicians' assumption that impoverished people in neighbourhoods with sympathies for their party would offer little or no opposition to their proposals were wrecked. Even more difficult challenges awaited them than their failure to convince Shefali Bibi and her neighbours to agree. The disputes spawned by Babar's proposals were of four types. People most commonly disputed the technically feasible location for the installation of the poles because the proposed locations encroached into their homesteads. The second set of challenges was to the proposed overhead route of the transmission wires that would connect the poles to the houses they were to service: the objection was that these wires would pass over the roofs of existing mud houses, or too close to their doors and windows. The third set of objections was to the installation of poles in locations where they would block the doorways through which people entered or exited their homesteads. A fourth set of oppositions arose against the technicians' proposals for installing the poles at street corners, where people feared they would obstruct the passage of vehicles. Each of these objections was advanced, supported by an appeal to the politicians to be *shotheek* (correct, fair in this case). The politicians responded, by requesting plaintiffs to be *juktipurna*, or reasonable.

Undergirding people's complaints was the argument that they should not be bullied by the powerful, frequently described as those with *khomota*. The Bangla term *khomota* was frequently used during the ensuing disputes. Hence, it deserves comment. Arild Ruud (2003) tells us that *khomota* can be translated into English to denote several meanings. One meaning has to do with authority.

Thus, it might be said that Party X attained *khomota* in the elections: this would relate to the assumption of formal authority by Party X. Or, it might be said that Person X has *khomota* to refer to the informal authority that might be wielded by him or her. In his capacity as *samaj sardar*, for instance, Joynal Ali was said to possess *khomota*. Groups possess *khomota* as well, so it might be said that Group X wields *khomota* at the State level.

A related meaning of the term has to do with command over resources. For instance, it was standard male gossip (the kind to which I was privy) to refer to other men's *khomota* (or otherwise) to 'raise' a wife, as in '*bou pala'r khomota*'. This would refer not only to the authority that men were expected to wield over their wives or to their sexual prowess (or, for that matter, to the sexual prowess of women), but also to their ability in terms of earning and providing for a family. It was also used to describe the physical or mental ability of individuals, to describe the ability of Person A to think or of Person B to walk, for instance.

Another meaning, the one that Ruud is more inclined to pursue in his study, has to do with an intentionality centred view of power. In this rendition, *khomota* refers to power, 'the capacity an individual has to mobilize others, into action or non-action, a capacity for 'getting things done' or making others agree, inspiring confidence, arousing interest or enthusiasm, or 'forcing' people' (Ruud, 2003, 65). *Khomota* then refers to the ability to mobilize consent and cooperation. It is not only possessing resources, but about dominating a relationship.

The use of the term *khomota* is often distinguished from *shakti* or *bal*, which referred to physical strength. It is also different from *probhab*, which more directly is used to refer to influence. And it is also distinct from *probhutto*, a word that is often invoked to refer to supremacy: an example might be '*amerika'r probhutto*' to describe US supremacy. The way in which my interlocutors used the term *khomota* linked it more closely with control over resources and the possession of power. Poor people, or *gorib manush*, were typically referred to as people with little or no *khomota*.

The powerful against the weak

The controversy at the spot marked L33 on Map 6.1 brought into sharp relief the tension caused by the electrification project between two neighbours.

Here, the technicians identified a spot in former Congress politician Murshid Hossein's plot as the best location for the installation of the pole. Murshid Hossein, who happened to be home when Babar Hossein and his associates arrived, was vehement that he would not give permission for the pole to be installed in his plot since that would make his property worthless. He proposed instead that the pole should be located on the boundary of his property with CPI(M) politician Joynal Ali. However, the boundaries were at the edge of a pond, where it would be technically impossible to install anything, especially something as potentially dangerous as an electric pole. Murshid Hossein then suggested that the pole be erected inside CPI(M) politician Joynal Ali's plot. His technicians told Babar Hossein that was feasible, but Babar Hossein was reluctant to approach Joynal Ali with a request for a favour. He urged Murshid Hossein to reconsider.

Congress leaders of all hues supported Babar Hossein's stance. They requested their ex-colleague, to give up his obstinacy. After all, he was an important leader and opinion-maker (even though, as they chuckled afterwards, 'no one took him very seriously anymore!').[23] If Murshid did not demonstrate a commitment to the welfare of the villagers, how would anyone else be expected to do so? Their exchanges lasted over an hour. The *azaan* announcing the noon prayers was ignored. Murshid Hossein refused to budge. The negotiations between Murshid Hossein and the Congress politicians appeared to have reached an impasse. By then, many of Murshid Hossein's neighbours realized they would be directly affected by the pole whose location was under dispute. They too joined the Congress politicians' chorus against Murshid Hossein. If he would not make sacrifices, who would, they asked him. They urged him to consider his *khomota*. As a person with a lot of *khomota*, Murshid Hossein could make some sacrifice for the benefit of the Ward's inhabitants. Murshid Hossein retorted that they ought to have this expectation from Joynal Ali. Joynal Ali possessed more *khomota* than Murshid Hossein did. Joynal Ali was, after all, *samaj sardar*. He was affiliated with the CPI(M). His daughter had a salaried job in the government school 'and was entitled to a pension'.[24] Murshid Hossein claimed correctly to have none of these privileges.

Joynal Ali was absent from the ward at that time, having been invited to attend a wedding in the neighbouring Murshidabad district. A few of his male neighbours called him on his mobile and explained the situation. A series of conversations on the mobile phone followed between Murshid Hossein and Joynal Ali, Joynal Ali and Akbar Ali, Joynal Ali and his neighbours, and Joynal Ali with Babar Ali. These conversations were interspersed with arguments between Murshid Hossein and the Congress politicians, the Congress politicians and the other residents of the neighbourhood, and Murshid Hossein and everyone else. As these exchanges progressed, approximately 40 people had gathered around the site to understand what was going on. People took sides and hotly debated Murshid Hossein's contention: yet another *azaan*, for the late afternoon prayer, was ignored. The assembled people appeared to concur that the person with greater *khomota* should acquiesce and allow work of public welfare to proceed. However, they disagreed over the manner of identifying which of the two possessed greater *khomota*, as they were both 'boro lok', Big Men and of the entrenched classes. Each owned a motorcycle. Joynal Ali owned more property. But Murshid Hossein had attended college. Joynal Ali's daughter had a permanent job with a pension. But her income was hers, not her father's (no self-respecting man would claim his daughter's salary, Akbar Ali told me, and there was not a more self-respecting man in Rahimpur than Joynal Ali, he vouched for his adversary). Joynal Ali was with the CPI(M). Murshid Hossein knew people in the bureaucracy and the police. The debate was endless. Eventually, Joynal Ali conveyed his agreement to Akbar Ali 'in the interest of the village's improvement (*gramer unnati*, Akbar Ali's report)' and offered permission for the pole to be installed on his plot.

While neither Joynal Ali nor Murshid Hossein were 'poor' in the sense I have used the term in this book, the dispute between them and its eventual resolution were closely followed by others in the village. The publicly stated expectation that the person with greater *khomota* must make the sacrifice necessary for the installation of electric poles and ushering in the 'new era' that their elected representative was promising is unmistakable. This expectation addressed the critical question about the contributions necessary for instituting improvement, and who exactly was to meet the costs. Joynal Ali's concession, rather than the ward member's persuasions, helped resolve what threatened to become an intractable problem. The manner in which the dispute among him, Murshid Hossein, their neighbours, and the Congress politicians played out during those three hours provided a point of reference for other disputants during the three days in which Rahimpur's residents argued with one another and with their elected representative and his associates over the electrification of their village.

A similar dynamic animated the dispute over the installation of the pole at the spot marked L1 on the map. This spot was located inside but close to the boundary of the homestead property owned by Ziaur Rehman, a peasant owning 3 *bighas* of land and affiliated with Congress. It was early evening when Babar Hossein and his associates arrived at this spot. Ziaur Rehman leased in about 2 *bighas* from Akbar Ali. As a tenant, Ziaur Rehman enjoyed cordial relations with his landlord. Akbar Ali persuaded him to accept the location so as to allow the electrification process to proceed peaceably. Despite the fact that its proposed location could devalue his property, Ziaur Rehman agreed. However, the plot owner's *neighbour,* the landless agricultural labourer Sarfaraz Islam argued that installing the pole at this location would mean that the wires would be routed too close to his house. They would most likely pass too near his window, making it impossible to open them outwards. Else, they might cross over his roof, making it impossible for him to increase the height of his property in the future. Like Ziaur Rehman, Sarfaraz Islam was affiliated with the Congress Party. He often laboured for Akbar Ali's tenants, including Ziaur Rehman, although he owned a tiny plot of land (less than 1 *bigha*) as well. However, Sarfaraz Islam's homestead plot included only the single-storeyed mud hut in which he lived. The land on which his house was built was public land, on which the panchayat had granted him permission. The mud hut in which he lived stood in stark contrast with Ziaur Rehman's brick house built with government subsidies. Sensing that no easy solution was forthcoming, a by-now-dishevelled Babar Hossein asked Akbar Ali to take charge while he took a break for the evening prayers. They had merely covered eight locations during the 10 hours they had spent on this matter. This realization wearied Babar Hossein even more after his exhausting exchange with Murshid Hossein.

Sarfaraz Islam's suggestion would imply shifting the pole further into Ziaur Rehman's plot. Such an action could devalue the latter's property even further. Sarfaraz Islam's suggestion derived from his claim that he possessed less *khomota* than his neighbour. An excerpt from the exchange between Sarfaraz Islam, Ziaur Rehman, and Akbar Ali is reproduced below to present the way in which the notion of *khomota* was invoked to resolve the dispute between two neighbours who both identified themselves as being poor.[25]

Ziaur Rehman (shaking his head vigorously in disagreement with Safaraz Islam's suggestion): No, this is the only place I can allow. If I place it where you suggest, it will inconvenience me. I am not very happy with the present arrangement myself. I could insist that the pole be placed outside my boundary. That is where it should be placed. But there, it will cause inconvenience to *you* even more.

Sarfaraz Islam: Look, you have more *khomota* than I have, so you should help me...Look at Joynal *da*. See how he has allowed the poles to be located in his plot. You should treat me like your younger brother, but you are treating me like your enemy... (Turning to Akbar) You, Akbar, at least you would not forget that I am a *gorib manush*. Remember, when you came to us for help. Don't forget your party is in power due to our support. We chased Musa [CPI-M politician and husband of the ex-Ward Member] away to vote for Babar because you asked me to. This is not the way to treat us! The CPI(M)'s doors are still open to us.

Ziaur Rehman (Turning to Akbar Ali): Did you hear what he said, Akbar *da*? How can you expect me to make so many concessions? I am also a *gorib manush*. He is being unreasonable (*O ajuktipurna kotha bolchhe*).

Akbar Ali (Turning to Ziaur Rehman): Look at his house. Look at yours. You have the Indira Awas Yojana. He does not even have a BPL card. You are a member of our party. He is just a day labourer. Yes, you are poor. But he is poorer. You have more *khomota* than he does. You will not lose by having the pole in your plot. But his house will be worthless if the wires go over his roof. He is our younger brother. If we don't look after him, who will?

Ziaur Rehman: Hmmmph, but this is not done. This is nonsense.

Other onlookers: Tchh.. tchh...he says you are his elder brother. Your younger brother needs your help. You should do what is just (*nyayjyo*).

Akbar Ali: Look, that is what Joynal *da* did, didn't you see. You were there, weren't you? We have to do what is just (*nyayjyo*).

Eventually, Akbar Ali prevailed over Ziaur Rehman to relent and give permission for the pole to be installed on his plot. They both drew on the precedent set by Joynal Ali just a few hours prior. Joynal Ali had accepted his neighbours' suggestions that he, as the person possessing more *khomota*, ought to compromise in his specific dispute with Murshid Hossein. Joynal Ali's decision enabled Sarfaraz Islam to make a similar claim against his better-off neighbour. Of interest is the manner in which Sarfaraz Islam invoked a relation of fictive kinship[26] to ignite the sympathy of his neighbour as well as to underscore the obligation of his neighbour to help him. By referring to himself as Ziaur Rehman's younger brother, he called attention to his own material dearth and social powerlessness. His neighbours, other onlookers, and Akbar Ali recognized the usage of the filial term 'younger brother' to indicate his appeal for support and protection. His request to his neighbour to treat him as someone to be protected rather than as enemy struck a chord with other onlookers. They asked Ziaur Rehman to reconsider his earlier stance and be more caring toward Sarfaraz Islam. The language of *khomota* merges seamlessly with the vocabulary of care and protection, mediated by the idiom of fictive kinship. Recent scholarship alerts us to the multifaceted forms of 'relatedness' (Carsten, 2000) that people forge among one another. Sarfaraz Islam invokes fictive filial relations to refer to a quite specific idiom of relatedness to underscore his own lack of *khomota*, his powerlessness, and his poverty vis-à-vis his neighbour. Akbar Ali's support for his stance indicates a recognition of this powerlessness, a lack of *khomota* as it were. His final verdict in favour of Sarfaraz Islam and against his own party associate Ziaur Rehman reflected the opinion of the onlookers and other residents of the neighbourhood that the person with less *khomota* deserved his sympathy and support.

At Nani's *chai* kiosk the following day, CPI(M) politicians supported Akbar's decision. When Akbar arrived, rather unexpectedly,[27] they were in the unusually pleasant position of actually speaking glowingly about him. I report below a fragment of the conversations between him and two of the CPI(M) politicians present in the kiosk:[28]

> Musa Khan: You did the correct thing. Every leader [English] should side with the weak against the strong. You have learnt well from us. You have imbibed our principles. You should join the CPI(M).
>
> Akbar Ali: The Congress Party has always cared for the poor. We are their *garjians*...One thing we learnt from you was never to

hold public meetings. Do you think today's disputes could be resolved through meetings? No. Resolving such disputes needs people who can reflect on right and wrong. It needs people with experience in deliberations (*bichar*). One needs to be a skilled deliberator (*bicharak*) to understand such disputes.

Abdul Bari: You are being stupid (used the slang '*gordhob das*' to describe his stupidity). You know you did nothing. You just went with the tide. If you took the side of the more powerful, everyone would have scorned you. Joynal *da* had set the precedent. How could you have done otherwise?

Musa Khan: What were those meetings that you did if not public meetings? Were they private meetings? Don't talk nonsense...

[Akbar Ali diverted the conversation to another topic]

The idiom of 'siding with the weak' provided a hinge for the exchanges between the politicians at the kiosk. That people expected politicians to defend the interest of the poor was repeatedly reinscribed through these conversations. If CPI(M) leaders attempted to take credit for the manner in which Congress politicians such as Akbar Ali conducted themselves, Congress politicians emphasized the way in which *they* had provided guardianship to the poor. The vocabulary of guardianship that Akbar Ali uses is instructive in that it resonates with the filial idiom of 'younger brother' deployed by Sarfaraz Islam. Poor people expected those with more *khomota* to be gracious toward those with less *khomota*. The interlocked vocabularies of *khomota*, the idioms of filial relatedness and the metaphors of guardianship together contributed to the repertoire deployed by the poor to resolve disputes involving themselves (Sarfaraz Islam and Ziaur Rehman) as well as their neighbours (Joynal Ali and Murshid Hossein).

In tension with these idioms emphasizing the guardianship of the entrenched classes over the poor were the conversations about contradictions between the elected representative and the residents of the locality. Differences within the people notwithstanding, they refused to uncritically accept Babar's or Akbar's requests to shelve their disputes. Not only did Rahimpur's residents insist on discussing threadbare the specific proposals advanced by the technicians, neighbours demanded the explicit involvement of their politicians in the resolution of the disputes between them that had been spawned by the electrification programme. In the process, they directly interrogated their ward member's proposals. Their disputations represented not only tussles over the location of the electric poles, but also disagreements on the role of the ward member in determining the location of the poles.

Reason against justice

An analysis of the disputes in Rahimpur directs attention to the manner in which appeals to the poor to be reasonable (*juktipurna*) conflicted with the popular perspective that justice (*nyay*) had to be done. Several meanings permeate the oft-mentioned term *jukti* and its cognates, *juktipurna* (being reasonable), *ajuktipurna* (being unreasonable), and *juktiheen* (without reason). One interpretation of the term *jukti* imbues it with a transcendental quality of thought and argumentation: there appear to be certain standards that can be applied to determine adherence to *jukti*. Adhering to these standards makes a person *juktipurna*. These standards apply to the nature and the structure of thought/argumentation. Thus, a *juktipurna* argument could be one which critically considers all aspects of a certain viewpoint: in this sense, it may be contrasted with a self-serving (or, for that matter, overtly altruistic) argument.[29] It could also refer to an argument that is presented calmly and without excitement (even if it might be entirely self-serving): in this sense, it may be distinguished from the public display of emotion and passion. In another interpretation, the term is associated with the connotation of being 'sensible', emphasizing a contingent and relative meaning. Adjudging a person as *juktipurna* would involve considering the context in which s/he was making an intervention. Babar and his colleagues appear to primarily use the transcendental quality of the term in order to coax their co-villagers to think about the greater common good of the village, although the normative connotations of being sensible and thoughtful weigh in heavily in their exhortations.

The most numerous disputes pertained to Babar Hossein's proposals to install the electric poles in people's privately-owned homestead properties. In 25 of the locations, the owners of the modest plots complained that the proposed locations encroached into a part of their property. Consequently, they feared their property's devaluation. Such devaluation would prevent them from benefitting from the anticipated spurt in real estate values that would occur when the village would become part of Maldah town, 'as it surely would', my interlocutors assured me time and again. They were 'thinking ahead',[30] said Sirajul Islam. A marginal farmer with four years of primary education, he and his family of five lived in a single-storeyed mud hut. When Babar and his associates arrived at the spot marked L22, they realized that the site was located in Sirajul Islam's homestead property. Sirajul Islam refused permission to allow the pole to be located here. Alauddin Ali and Abdur Rehman followed up and asked Sirajul Islam to be reasonable, or *juktipurna*. If everyone began to only think about themselves, how would the village's condition improve, they asked? People had to be reasonable, to think about the common good of their village and to make sacrifices. Improvements in life demanded that certain comforts be foregone, they emphasized.

Their intervention irritated their interlocutor. Sirajul Islam retorted by alleging that the Congress politicians were being unreasonable (*ajuktipurna*). How would Babar Hossein like it if he, Sirajul Islam trooped into his house with an entourage and asked him to erect electric poles on *his* plot? As others before him, Sirajul Islam turned to Akbar Ali and asked him to do what was right (*shotheek*) and just (*nyayjyo*). Eventually, Babar's team of technicians identified an alternative public spot where the pole could be erected.

The tension between reasonableness and justice haunted Babar's team throughout their negotiations with Rahimpur's people. The exchanges[31] at the spot L16 exemplified these tensions. Daulat Bibi, a destitute widow lived on the property adjacent to this location with her teenage daughter. She objected to the proposed installation as it would block the entrance into her homestead property. Babar dismissed her objection by telling her she didn't own the public space. The exchange that ensued went along these lines:

> Daulat Bibi: The door to my house opens outwards. If you erect a pole there, I won't be able to open it.
>
> Abdur Rehman: Well, get a new one made [Laughs]. Make sure it opens inwards though. Ask [her neighbour who did some carpentry]
>
> Daulat Bibi: And your father-in-law will pay for it, isn't it? I can't afford it. Do you know how much it costs? Can't you move the pole just a little bit?
>
> Abdur Rehman: Babar can't listen to everyone now, can he? Don't

you see how much he's doing for everyone? Why are you being so unreasonable?

Daulat Bibi: I am being unreasonable? I am a widow, with an unmarried daughter (breaks into sobs). You come here and mess with my space. And then you call me unreasonable. Is this fair (Turning to Babar. Babar looks away)?

Alauddin Ali: Look, we are trying to speak with you to make you understand (*bujhiye bolchhi*). Do you understand what an important thing this is? It will improve the condition of the village. You will thank us for it. If you object, you will be ruining any prospect for the village's improvement.

Daulat Bibi: It can't be more important than my moving in and out of my own house. If you erect that pole here, I will have to build a new door. I don't have any money for that (continues to sob). If my husband would have been here, he would have taught you a lesson for talking to me like that. I have always been a Congress voter. Is this the way to treat me?

Approximately four to five of Daulat Bibi's neighbours, small and medium landowners gathered at the spot hearing the commotion. They lost no time defending her.

Neighbour 1: Now, look here. You are *chengras* (lads) of this locality. You grew up here. Just because you are in a political party doesn't mean you boss around us.

Neighbour 2: You should stop behaving like *babus* (bureaucrats).

Neighbour 3: She might be a widow. But she is not alone. Don't think you can oppress (*atyachar*) her.

Neighbour 2: Let's see how you install a pole here against her wishes.

Neighbour 3: We will not let any injustice (*anyay*) happen to her.

Layered upon the oppositional construction between reasonableness and justice are tussles over meanings of reasonableness. Both Sirajul Islam and Daulat Bibi balk at Babar Hossein's characterization of them as unreasonable. They do not allow him to appropriate the mantle of reasonableness. Indeed, they aver that *Babar* and his team of technicians and politicians are unreasonable for making the kinds of demands that do upon impoverished villagers. Both repudiate his attempts at characterizing them as unreasonable persons. Such contests over the production of reasonable subjectivities pit the trustees who dream dreams for the improvement of their village against the villagers they believe to be under their tutelage. The exchanges between the self-appointed trustees and Rahimpur's villagers was not, therefore, only one over identifying the locations for installing electric poles. The exchanges represented contests over what it meant to be a reasonable person in the context of schemes designed for Rahimpur's improvement.

At the point marked L5, Shekhar Shil, a 55-year old farmer who had 1 *bigha* of land and had completed primary education, objected to the placement of the poles at the corner of the path. The technicians had proposed to install the poles at the T-point at which the mud path leading to Shekhar Shil's house intersected the laterite path that connected Rahimpur ward with the neighbouring Dokkhin Hajra ward. Shekhar Shil and his neighbours pointed out that such a location would encumber the passage of motorized vehicles. The presence of an electric pole would prevent larger vehicles from turning into the mud path or out of it. Two of his three sons attended the village school, although he himself had never studied in school. The eldest read for a degree in History at a college in Maldah Town. He and his wife cultivated the 1 *bigha* of land they owned and leased 2 *bighas* more from wealthier neighbours. They deployed their own family labour on the fields. They both expected their situation to improve over the next generation or so, especially after their sons began to earn. Although he acknowledged that his sons might not be interested in staying in the village, he anticipated that he and his wife would continue to live here, in the very same neighbourhood.[32]

> My son will have a car. He will come to visit us. And then, this pole will be standing here.... My son won't be able to drive through. He won't be able to turn his car into this path. What good will come of placing this pole in the middle of the road, at the T-point? Can the technicians not shift the pole ever so slightly?

Babar was first taken aback. He then burst into mocking laughter and told Shekhar Shil:

> In the BPL survey, you tell me you have nothing to eat. Now you are telling me that your son will have a car in 10 years. Your

son doesn't even have a moustache yet. Don't be unreasonable (*ajuktipurna*): think about the future. When your son starts earning, I will come and remove the pole from here. Don't worry.

But Shekhar Shil held his ground. By now, he was joined by three of his neighbours. All of them protested the proposed location of the pole with the same argument: what was to happen when automobiles would be commonly used for travel, when visitors would come calling, when sons and sons-in-law would buy their own cars. Babar Hossein smirked at their protests and told the technicians to take note of these 'dreams'. At this Shekhar Shil retorted:

> We are poor today. Does that mean we will remain poor tomorrow? We too have dreams... I am poor today. Does it mean that my children cannot lead a better life tomorrow? Will he not be able to buy a car tomorrow? We work hard. We save as much as we can. We do not gamble. Nor do we drink. I have dreams for my children. Are you trying to tell us that we should have no reason to dream (*amader shopno dekhar jukti ki*)? What is this injustice? (*Eta ki anyay, bolo?*)

Against Babar Hossen's exhortations asking them to be reasonable, Shekhar Shil and his neighbours, all CPI(M) supporting middle and poor peasants, posit the reasonableness of their own and their children's future. They deflect their elected representative's characterization of them as being unreasonable by emphasizing their 'reason' to dream. But they do more than that. Shekhar Shil and his neighbours invert the association that Babar tries to make between being reasonable and thinking about the future by arguing that it is *they* – Shekhar Shil and his neighbours – who are thinking about the future while Babar Hossein is only concerned about the present. They note their prospects for the future with hope. Against the mockery of their elected representative, they defend these prospects. Indeed, they subject his assumptions to scrutiny and criticism. The poor peasants interpret his demand on them to be reasonable as unjust and do not hesitate to tell him so.

Tussles over the interpretation of being reasonable remained enmeshed in the recurrent tension between being reasonable and being just. While Rahimpur's residents rejected nomenclatures labelling them as unreasonable, they were quick to point out the injustice of their politicians' claims on them. When people such as Shekhar Shil, Daulat Bibi, and Sirajul Islam invoked notions of justice, they conjoined it with vocabularies of care and protection, of siding with the weak against the strong, of defending those without *khomota* from those who possessed it. In most cases, Rahimpur's self-appointed trustees were identified as people with *khomota*. When they demanded acquiescence with their proposals from the Rahimpur's inhabitants, the latter advanced their own claims in the name of justice. By positing a vocabulary of justice against their trustees' vocabulary of reason, they were able to prevent the installation of electric poles at the sites where they believed that their current and future interests would be harmed.

Requesting improvement

Not everyone in Rahimpur worried about Babar Hossein installing electric poles against their wishes. For the village's Shershabadiya residents, the anxiety was of another nature. Babar Hossein gave little indication about allocating an electric pole to their hamlet. His accommodation of the demands made by Rahimpur's inhabitants in the main village left him with no further poles to allocate to the hamlet of the Shershabadiyas. He could always request for additional poles, but there was no telling how long it would be before his request was sanctioned, and how many months would pass before the additional poles would eventually arrive.

The Shershabadiya hamlet was located three kilometres north of the village proper and separated from it by a cluster of households that lay under the jurisdiction of the neighbouring Sindhugram ward. Called Itar Rahimpur for its rocky terrain, it was thus slightly removed from the rest of the village. One handpump serviced its 35-odd households. Not one of the households was connected to an electric transformer. When news of the installations in Rahimpur proper spread around to the hamlet, the residents wanted to know more. They approached Babar Hossein to ask him about the matter, but Babar maintained a studied silence. Babar Hossein's childhood friend Syedur Islam, who managed electoral support for Congress among the Shershabadiya community, was among the first persons to approach him when he witnessed the commotion at Murshid Hossein's plot. As soon as he found an opportunity, he asked Babar whether any poles had been allocated to the Shershabadiya hamlet. I heard Babar Hossein mumble with a faraway look and averting any eye contact that he was trying to but could not promise anything.[33] Their asides continued throughout the three days during which I accompanied Babar Hossein and his contingent as they tried to secure an endorsement of their proposals from the population. Syedur Islam's requests appear to have fallen on deaf years because Babar Hossein did not once go to the Shershabadiya hamlet during those three days. Syedur Islam's repeated requests were to ask for *unnati*, not thwart it. Like those who objected to Babar Hossein's proposals, he did not interrogate the premise of improvement. Unlike the others, however, he was offered no choice. Babar Hossein did not think it necessary to even offer the Shershabadiya hamlet a single pole.

Syedur Islam accompanied Babar's contingent throughout their walk, intently following the discussions and contributing to it as well as he could. He almost always lent his voice in support of Babar Hossein's position. In between these official discussions, the two men engaged in more personal conversations, enquiring about one another's family. They shared notes on their children's recent illnesses and marital discords. Syedur Islam was even more intimate with Akbar Ali, who invited him over for lunch each of the three days he was in Rahimpur. But on the question of the electric poles, there was a wall of silence. No commitments were forthcoming from Babar Hossein and no assurance provided by Akbar Ali. Each time Syedur Islam spoke about the poles, his interlocutors remained evasive. Their childhood friendship notwithstanding, evasive responses replaced any sort of commitment to the hamlet.

By the end of the third day, after Babar Hossein had surveyed each of the proposed locations and accommodated the demands, appeals, and requests by householders, it was abundantly clear that no electric poles would be allocated to Itar Rahimpur. Syedur Islam was visibly upset. He took Akbar Ali aside to ask him why Itar Rahimpur was being overlooked. Akbar Ali insisted that they were trying to help, a claim that Syedur Islam refused to buy. The ensuing exchange went along these lines:[34]

> Syedur Islam: We have been your most loyal voters. You know I am a Congress supporter. My father and his father have all been Congress supporters. [Repeats:] We have been your most loyal supporters. Why are you ignoring us? We also need electricity. Why are you not giving us any electricity?
>
> Akbar Ali: What can I do if there are not enough poles? Babar is trying, don't you see?

Syedur Islam: Look, I know that's not true. Don't say such nonsense.

Abdur Rehman (joking): Tell me Badiya! What do you need electricity for? So, your buffalo can sleep under the fan (Pats Syedur playfully on the shoulder).

Akbar Ali (sharp look to Abdur Rehman, then turning back to Syedur Islam): Never mind him. *Dekhi.* Let's see what happens.

Syedur Islam: You wait and see what *we'll* do. All of us will go to Babar Hossein's house and demand our share. We'll make his life miserable.... Next time he comes begging for votes, you see what we'll do.

Abdur Rehman: Who will you vote for, Badiya? The CPI(M)? You know they will eat your people alive.

Akbar Ali (after asking Abdur Rehman to shut up): Look, don't do all that drama. What happens when you spit at the sky? [Dramatic moment of silence].It falls back on you. Just be patient. We'll do something once things quieten down.

Syedur Islam's complaint that his hamlet was being ignored by the elected representatives and their technical and political associates is a sobering reminder of the ways in which Rahimpur's entrenched classes could continue to ignore some sections of the poor with impunity. While they cultivated and strengthened their incorporative relationships with the poor of the Sheikh Muslim and Hindu communities, they retained and reflected the prejudices against the Shershabadiya poor. Babar Hossein's decision to not allocate a single pole to the Intar Rahimpur, despite the residents' staunch support for Congress, is a reflection of such prejudices. Akbar Ali, who otherwise openly supported grievances against the party to be aired, insisted that his childhood friend not raise uncomfortable questions. It appears that Congress politicians took the Shershabadiyas' electoral support for granted. The question of the Shershabadiyas turning to the CPI(M) politicians did not seem to even arise. For all their talk about siding with the poor against the rich and the weak against the strong, neither Akbar Ali nor Rahimpur's CPI(M) politicians offered to the Shershabadiyas any of the support about which other poor people in the locality were confident.

Considering the vigorous ways in which the labouring poor people of

Rahimpur's Sheikh, Bind, and Napit communities disputed their elected politicians proposals, the ward's Shershabadiyas might have thought they were witnessing the theatre of the absurd. That the inhabitants of the village 'proper' were spiritedly debating locations of electric poles appeared to be a cruel joke for the 64 Shershabadiya families who realized that they were not even allotted one pole whose location they could contest! Shershabadiya men approached Babar Hossein, Akbar Ali, and Abdur Rehman hesitantly to enquire about the poles, but the standard response was the disarming *dekhi*. Syedur Islam, who appears to have been closest to Babar and his associates, could at best vent his annoyance and irritation quietly and privately. The *unnati* that Babar Hossein promised to his co-villagers in Rahimpur and which generated so much debate and negotiation in much of Rahimpur was conspicuous by the absence of even its promise in Intar Rahimpur.

III

Disputation as politics

To say that the analysis of disputes provides a window into studying the sociology of politics is to repeat a well-worn truism.[35] The analysis of disputes is no longer restricted to the domain of 'legal anthropology'[36] or the study of what Marc Galanter (1963) called 'local law-ways'. Scholars point to 'repertoires of justification' to understand the ways in which actors resolve disputes and attempt to reconcile differences among themselves.[37] On one hand, Comaroff and Roberts (1981) remind us that the 'dispute process may provide an essential key to the disclosure of the socio-cultural order at large' (1981, 249). On the other hand, Caplan (1995) suggests that analysts view disputes as configuring social relationships rather than reflecting tussles over material goods and decision making processes.

For many early observers of rural India, disputes were epiphenomena of structural or cultural inequalities.[38] Later observers emphasized the role of factions: disputes began to be analysed in terms of the opportunities they provided to factional leaders to underscore their own salience to their co-villagers.[39] However, Bernard Cohn (1965, 97) alerted us that:

> Dispute settling, norm setting and norm enforcing are situational

and every dispute or breach of norms involves a kind of social algebra on the part of the actors in the situation to see what lines of cleavage will be affected by what alliances they make.

The material presented in this chapter resonates with Cohn's warning against perceiving disputes as being determined by pre-existing relations of power. Relations of guardianship with entrenched classes do not prevent the labouring poor from disputing the decisions that politicians of these classes sought to make on their behalf. Furthermore, shared class positions do not preclude disputes within the entrenched and precarious classes. Affiliation with the Congress Party does not either stop Ziaur Rehman and Sarfaraz Islam from disputing one another's claims or inhibit Shefali Bibi from publicly reproaching Babar Hossein.

Certainly, the disputes reveal the interpretive frameworks that shaped their negotiations. Sarfaraz Islam publicly references himself as Ziaur Rehman's younger brother and hence deserving of his help. Such idioms further draw on frameworks of *khomota* that made collective sense to Rahimpur's population. But side by side, disputations among the population contribute to *amending* the interpretations of *khomota* as evidenced in the heated arguments about Murshid Hossein or Joynal Ali being more *khomotashali*.

Are these disputations political? I argue that they are for at least four reasons. One, at a basic level, the disputes are political because they entail discussions over the allocation of public resources with their elected representatives, politicians and political mediators. But they are also political – and this is the second point – because they involve the enforcement of and contestation of shared meanings of collective life. The disputants grapple with, and are generally supportive of, the notion that people with more *khomota* should make the sacrifices necessary for the village's improvement. In addition to them possessing the means to do so, it is also their obligation towards those with less *khomota* to protect them and to care for them. Three, the disputes reveal the tussles over the creation of collective identities among the disputants, especially Rahimpur's labouring poor who push back against Babar Hossein's attempts at portraying them as unreasonable people. Four, the disputes indicate a critical reflection vis-a-vis Babar Hossein's assumption that he could abrogate all decision making in the locality to himself.

Rahimpur's residents advance their social perspectives while considering the proposed locations of the electric poles. Considerations of individual gain and loss are important to the disputants even if they seldom deploy an individualistic self-interested vocabulary while objecting to Babar Hossein's proposals. Even when people talk about the value of private plots of land depreciating because of the installation of electric poles, they anchor their claims in collective terms by underscoring Babar's commitment to protect the weak. They consult with one another and reflect on his proposals without being browbeaten into agreement. People move freely with his delegation from one locality to another. They observe the discussions, learn from the arguments that have been made, contribute to it and share what they hear with others. Disputants also advise their neighbours and rehearse the questions *they* had raised. Babar Hossein repeatedly asks people of one neighbourhood to stay out of the objections raised by people in other neighbourhoods. But to no avail. Even when the outcomes of disputes have no direct bearing on their individual interests, people remain keenly interested. Although by not convening a general meeting of the ward's inhabitants, Babar Hossein and his associates are successful in staving off any united opposition to their proposals, they cannot prevent the flow of ideas and the formation of transient collectives of friends, neighbours, and other interested persons who challenge his own assumptions and opinions.

A third axis of the shared meanings forged in the wake of the disputations in Rahimpur is provided by the arguments over who possesses more or less *khomota*, and what their relative contributions to Rahimpur's improvement ought to be. The frequent appeals to support the weak against the powerful, endorsements of actions that do so, and condemnations of actions that do not, complicate the incorporative relations of power between Rahimpur's entrenched classes and the labouring poor. On the one hand the vocabulary of guardianship re-inscribes the incorporative relationships. On the other hand, direct and subtle tensions between the entrenched classes and the labouring poor are also discernible. Shefali Bibi's remonstrations and Daulat Bibi's accusations against their ward member and his associates reveal that the poor do not meekly accept decisions taken on their behalf by entrenched class politicians despite being incorporated in relations of guardianship with them. Daulat Bibi's neighbours speak up on her behalf, challenging Babar Hossein and his associates, even the endearing Akbar Ali, to dare defy the destitute woman's claims. They explicitly interrogate his presumptions. Even Syedur Islam, the Shershabadiya peasant who supplicates before his Sheikh Muslim friends, does not quietly acquiesce with Babar Hosssein's decisions. In suggesting that the powerful should protect the weak, the poor expect those with khomota to help those without, thereby pushing the limits of Rahimpur's incorporative relations of power. The labouring poor invoke the vocabulary of justice against people they otherwise acknowledge as their garjians. The series of disputes spawned by the electrification programme strains, rather than reproduces, the incorporative relations of power that marks Rahimpur.

Arguments over reasonable subjectivities provide yet another axis of the shared meanings that are forged in the wake of disputations in Rahimpur. Rahimpur's poor refuse the labels that their self-appointed trustee seeks to impose upon them. One charge frequently hurled at them by Babar Hossein and his associates is that they are unreasonable, that they are not applying their reason in their considerations of his proposals. These gentlemen accuse their co-villagers of not being sufficiently excited about the improvement that electrification is expected to bring to the ward. Babar Hossein and his colleagues allege their impoverished interlocutors of being preoccupied with their own immediate interests to think about the longer term interests of the ward. But people like Sirajul Islam, Daulat Bibi, and Shekhar Shil – and their neighbours – reject this attempt to portray them and other poor people as unreasonable. Rather, they emphasize *his* unreasonableness and question the unilateral manner in which Babar Hossein strives to secure endorsements for his proposal. The arguments over reasonable subjectivities are one important axis of the shared meanings that are forged in the wake of disputations in Rahimpur.

Through their scrutiny of Babar's proposals, Rahimpur's inhabitants interrogate his presumption of trusteeship. He and his team of technicians expect their proposals to be greeted by the ward's population with gratitude. Most of his associates in the Congress Party anticipate their decisions to be accepted by the ward's population without much discussion. They believe that all segments of the population would benefit from the installation of poles and the subsequent electrification. They think the prospects of leading improved lives (*unnat jeebon*) would excite their co-villagers into acquiescing with their proposals. He and his colleagues cannot fathom any objections to their proposals. The announcement of the electrification programme allows them not only to project their success as politicians who secure a valuable resource for the village but to present their 'dreams' and 'hopes' for their people. While I cannot attribute motivations to Babar Hossein describing his dreams and hopes for the people of Rahimpur – as he did ever so often during the three days of negotiations – his declarations do not appear to me to be mere gimmicks. His and his associates' response to people's objections indicates genuine bewilderment. Not once does he accuse his political rivals in the CPI(M) of 'manipulating' people to oppose his proposals. As a matter of fact, several objections to his proposals come from staunch Congress voters from among the labouring poor, a constituency that, as we have seen, he and other members of the Congress affiliated entrenched classes have cultivated and which constitutes the backbone of Rahimpur's incorporative political place. Their objections leave him and his associates nonplussed. Babar Hossein and his associates hope to complete the allocation of poles across the locality within a couple of hours. In fact, the entire process takes him three days. They hope to isolate disagreements and limit these to individual households that might express some disagreement among one another. Akbar Ali is more realistic in anticipating the inevitability of some sort of public deliberation. But none of the Congress politicians believe in the possibility of wide-ranging, even if uncoordinated, disputation of their views. Rahimpur's residents, on their part, dispute not only the specific location of the proposed poles, they also dispute their ward member's assumption that they could take decisions on their behalf.

To that end, Rahimpur's residents scrutinize their elected representative's proposals before endorsing them. They discuss the matter with family members, neighbours and other well-wishers as they reflect on the implications of his proposals. They voice their opinions about his proposals. Their disagreements with him do not preclude disputes within themselves. Further, where such disputes occur, the disputants reject his efforts to hurry them into compromise. As they and their neighbours seek to find common ground on which to arrive at a compromise, it becomes clear to Babar and his associates that their exhortations of *unnati* do not provide such a ground. For Rahimpur's poor, as for other members of other classes, Babar Hossein's abstract invocations of the village's *unnati* mean little when these are so divorced from their own social perspectives. Much as Babar Hossein tries to isolate the demands on him and reduce people's claims to solipsistic requests, he is only successful in one case – against the requests by members of the Shershabadiya community. That one case apart, he finds it impossible to prevent people from engaging with each other and raising collective claims. It is true that the collective discussions do not produce homogenous claims or even a demand for a generic meeting where all of Rahimpur's people congregate, raise their objections, and resolve their disputes. Nevertheless, they reflect people's insistence on scrutinizing Babar Hossein's claims of trusteeship.

Post-development? Beyond encountering, depoliticizing and resisting improvement

Rahimpur's residents remain unenthused by Babar's proposals for the installation of electric poles because they are uncertain about the ways in which these would help them advance their own future plans. They consider their household hopes as well as their collective aspirations and conclude that installation of electric poles on their homestead plots would devalue their property. People object to poles that are installed too close to doorways or when they foresee that the wires would pass too close to their windows or over rooftops preventing further construction. The disputes arise because Rahimpur's people refuse to align themselves unquestioningly to the dreams of improvement that their self-appointed trustee dreams up for them. They question his assumption of knowing the ward's problems and solutions better than they do. In doing so, they undermine his assumption of being the locality's trustee. Babar Hossein's anticipation that the ward's population would welcome his proposals with profuse gratitude is decisively dashed.

The accounts of these poly-vocal imbroligos should clarify that the disputes in Rahimpur are not a rejection of improvement as such, as Babar Hossein and his associates interpret them to be. He and his colleagues respond to objections against their proposals by denouncing their critics as being against the *unnati* (improvement) of the village. Their denunciations are disingenuous. In fact, the disputants demand to be consulted over the unfolding of the electrification scheme. While they might not appear as enthused about the prospects of *unnati* as Babar Hossein and his associates are, there is no evidence to support Babar Hossein's allegations that they are against improvement. To conclude from their ambivalence about improvement that Rahimpur's people are against it is a grave error.

The disputations in Rahimpur resonate with the scholarly debates over interpreting the espousal of improvement schemes and development discourses more generally. The population's alleged attempts at warding away the electrification programme appears to approximate general criticisms of the 'project' of development, as envisaged by post-development scholars. For instance, commenting caustically on US President Truman's project of development, Arturo Escobar writes:

> Development is the last and failed attempt to complete the Enlightenment in Asia, Africa and Latin America.

(Escobar, 1995, 221)

Escobar is not alone in expressing such criticism of what he calls the 'project' of development, by which he does not mean individual improvement schemes but the very notion of development. The contributors to the landmark *Development Dictionary*, edited by Wolfgang Sachs (1992), have subjected concepts such as development, progress and helping to critical scrutiny by focussing on the rhetorical and discursive strategies which create these concepts in the first place. Their explorations of the interplay of ideas, images, myths and languages in defining such concepts has contributed to social analysts' ability to problematize such concepts. Drawing on Foucauldian scholarship that highlights the imbrications of power and knowledge, post-development scholars force our attention to some of the unquestioned assumptions that underpin the development theme.

Ferguson's (1990) work in this field has been pioneering. Based on textual analysis of World Bank documents and a case study of the Thaba Tseka livestock and range management project in Lesotho, he examines the impact of the complex of power and knowledge that ignored history and political economy to present the country as a less developed, remote land inhabited by peasants outside of market relationships. Ferguson argues that, as a result of these entanglements between power and knowledge, development interventions 'succeed' even when they fail because their very presence enhances the capacity of central governments and international agencies to intervene in society.

In offering such analysis, Ferguson takes care to distance his argument from two then widely prevailing perspectives. The first of these perspectives, popular among Liberal modernization theorists, considers development a necessary good which ameliorates the condition of the poor and alleviated their misery. The second perspective, popular among Marxist and Dependency theorists, is that development was embedded in capitalist relationships ring-fenced by imperialism. Finding both perspectives inadequate, Ferguson suggests that even as projects purporting to improve the human condition produce unpredictable results, the *discourses* that underpin them are important fields of study. He finds naïve the Liberal theorists' belief that development interventions serve the poor. At the same time, he is sceptical of the Marxist and Dependency theorists' conviction that development interventions serve the interests of international capitalists and are intended to incorporate people into an ever-growing network of capitalism. Against both perspectives, Ferguson suggests that development interventions neither alleviate poverty nor mechanistically incorporate people into capitalist relationships. Rather, they have to navigate a 'complex set of social and cultural structures so deeply embedded and so ill-perceived that the outcome may be only a baroque and unrecognizable transformation of the original intention' (Ferguson, 1994, 17).

Unlike Escobar, Ferguson is agnostic about the outcomes of development interventions. Where Ferguson confesses that the outcomes of development interventions are shaped by the complex of social and cultural structures with which they interface, Escobar is confident that development interventions are doomed to fail. Ferguson's writings possess a nuance that Escobar's don't, although Agarwal (1996) is correct in noting that the former leaves less scope for constructive criticism than the latter does. Ferguson restricts himself to critique whereas Escobar harks to grassroots movements, local knowledge, indigenous people and popular protest for heralding a post-developmental epoch.

That Ferguson would consider development interventions as depoliticizing is intriguing. Certainly, the examples he offers flies in the face of such inference, as astutely noted by Li (1999). The villagers who constituted the target group for the World Bank programme realized that the proposed development programmes could regulate their lives in ways they deemed unacceptable. They feigned compliance, engaged in downright sabotage or merely ignored the programme. Because he turns his lens on the development bureaucracy, Ferguson is oblivious to the unforeseeable ways in which the project's target populations made meaning of programme interventions and appropriated them in creative ways. This is a gap to which James Scott's (1990) scholarship has alerted social scientists – the unpredictable ways in which people reject interventions to which they do not subscribe. States' efforts to implement improvement interventions are fragile and open to contestation. Scott's research provides a foil to Ferguson's work because it compels social analysts to take seriously popular responses to improvement schemes. To elaborate his argument, Scott formulates the notion of 'everyday resistance' to emphasize the political significance of oral exchanges, peasants' private characterizations of their superiors, pilferage, sabotage and evasions. Much of the work under this rubric focuses on 'subtle, indirect, and non-confrontational behavior' (Kerkvliet, 2009, 233) the focus of which is to avoid statist interventions at improvement and development.

The disputations discussed in this chapter might appear to resonate with the notion of 'everyday resistance' However, such an inference would be misleading. C.P. White reminds us that the notion of 'everyday resistance' focusses 'on negative manifestations of power rather than the question of how peasants can exercise positive political power' (White, 1986, 50). Indeed, Scott's conceptualization of human agency tends to focus more on the ability to adapt than to the ability to transform (Gutmann, 1993, 86). Asef Bayat argues that the notion of 'everyday resistance' restricts analytical attention to people *defending* what they have, rather than making fresh demands (Bayat, 2010, 54; italics added). There is little to be said in this framework about the ways in which people might advance their own points of view. The 'everyday resistance' paradigm tends to impose an essentialized identity on putative resistors. Resistant subjects are seen as protecting their way of life, seeking autonomy from aggrandizing elites, and evading the framework of the state. An analysis of the practices of the labouring classes in relation to the electrification programme in Rahimpur reveals that they are willing to negotiate with their elected representatives and other politicians in order to make things better for themselves, their families and their descendants.

If Escobar's contention that encounters with development immiserizes people and Ferguson's claim that development de-politicizes people presents an all-powerful view of the idea of development, Scott demonstrates the ways in which people resist schemes implemented by the government with the ostensible purpose of improving their lives. Despite the important differences in analytical salience between the works of the three authors, their scholarship shares the assumption of a hiatus separating improvement schemes from the people they purport to serve. Sketching apocalyptic account of development, Escobar condemns it in no uncertain terms. Ferguson, despite acknowledging the unpredictable outcomes of development interventions, concludes that they ultimately depoliticize people. Scott insists that peasants invariably resist governmental schemes to improve their lives. While their perspectives caution social analysts against mechanistically assuming development interventions to be a positive aspect of people's lives they have contributed to fuelling a perception that people are averse to state-initiated improvement programmes. Such a perception holds little water while thinking about the aspirations of the labouring classes.

Improvement interventions provide populations with points of popular leverage. Akhil Gupta (1995) suggests that notwithstanding the diverse failures of development programmes in India, farmers use these strategically while dealing with local elites. Pushing even further, Tania Murray Li (1999) proposes that state initiated improvement schemes be perceived as a terrain of struggle. Such struggles are constituted by banal and intimate compromises that animate relations of domination and subordination. Thinking about improvement schemes as levers of struggle and compromise helps open up conceptual spaces to envisage how ideas pertaining to development work in practice, without being led by metanarratives of capitalism, governmentality and resistance. Such strands in the scholarship enable social analysts to empirically study the meanings people associate with improvement and development without being overwhelmed by their preffered ideological predilections. The account presented in this chapter resonates with these strands of the scholarship.

Nevertheless, that many of Rahimpur's inhabitants dispute with one another rather than singularly with their elected representative makes me wary of analytical frameworks that entrench dichotomies between the state and the population. Much of the scholarship in the Foucauldian mould suffers from this problem, rendering invisible the tensions and conflicts within society. In fact, states and societies are rarely ranged against each other, as narratives of governmentality and resistance would have us believe. Rather, as the disputations over the location of electric poles in Rahimpur reveal, states and societies are enmeshed in one another. Popular disputations are embedded in these entanglements rather than being located in society against the state. For example, the Shershabadiyas' claims are ignored not only by the elected representative but found little support from members of the Sheikh, Bind and Napit communities of the ward.

In her important intervention, Baviskar (2004) urges social analysts to consider the entanglements between schemes that purport to improve the human condition and people's responses to them. She underscores the need to eschew the dichotomous lenses through which development projects and resistance to development are viewed. Based on her fine grained analysis of the gigantic Sardar Sarovar hydroelectric project implemented by the Indian government in central India, she criticizes the view that people likely to be displaced by the project eagerly await it in anticipation of the perceived benefits. But, side by side, and crucially, her ethnography also interrogates the view that the potentially displaced people are singularly against the project and want to resist it at all costs. Rather, Baviskar notes the manifold, often contradictory, perspectives among the persons who are affected by the project. In general, she notes that even as some people are pleased with the compensation while others resolutely resist the project, many occupy a middle ground. They try to engage with the project implementation in order to better understand the situation and make meaning of it. Her work enlivens us to the complexities underpinning projects of improvement and popular responses to them. In a similar vein, Gail Omvedt (1999) reminds us that people's 'refusal to be victims of development does not mean an opposition to development; they would like a share in it; and they would like it to be just and sustainable'. Drawing on her rich ethnography from Indonesia, Tania Murray Li (2009) also arrives at a similar conclusion. She insists on directing attention to the messiness of the entanglements between populations and projects that express a 'will to improve' their lives. The disputations to which I have directed attention in this chapter serve to highlight the attempts by Rahimpur's population to ensure that the electrification programme conforms to their needs and values.

The disputations spawned by the electrification programme compel me to critically consider the contention (Ferguson, 1994) that the introduction of improvement schemes de-politicizes populations. If anything, the account presented here reveals a considerable *politicization* in Rahimpur. People oppose Babar Hossein's proposals for installation of the electric poles due to a number of reasons. To be sure, none of these has to do with any ideological opposition to electrification, much less than any sort of inscrutable antipathy to *unnati*. In some instances, their opposition stems from the plan to install the poles in their property. In such instances, plot-owners such as Sirajul Islam and Ziaur Rehman worry that the monetary value of their plot would depreciate. It is pertinent to note that they anticipated their village to become part of Maldah town sooner or later. Contrary to what post-developmentalist scholars such as Escobar (1995) prime analysts to believe, Rahimpur's population are not averse to being part of that process and to benefit from it. In other instances, their rejection of Babar Hossein's plans originates in the possibility that the installations might compel them to abandon their future plans. Sarfaraz Islam's objection arises from his reckoning that he will not be able to construct a second storey if the wires passed directly over his roof. For Shekhar Shil and his neighbours, the inconvenience posed by the installations is a bone of contention. None of these objections can be reduced to objections against improvement per se. Rather, the objections are rooted in the people's consideration of their social perspectives and the future plans associated with those perspectives.

Agonistic disputations

The disputations analysed in this chapter are exemplar neither of an enchantment with the trope of improvement nor discontent with it. Under the circumstances, how are we to understand the practices of people who inhabit the overlapping spaces between accepting improvement and rejecting it? As a response to this question, I want to remind readers about the ways in which consent and contention are interspersed with one another in people's negotiations with their politicians.

Such negotiations are underpinned by references to the collective peoplehood among Rahimpur's labouring poor and to a lesser extent among the village's precarious classes. The locality's disputants reject the allegation of unreasonableness which Babar Hossein and his aides levelled against them. Rather, they insist on the reasonableness of their claims, invoking their identity as *people* who take decisions based on considerations of their individual and collective life plans. Even as they recognize their currently impoverished condition, the men and women who dispute Babar Hossein's plans insist on advancing their social perspectives and refuse to be browbeaten in the name of Rahimpur's improvement. At the same time, they are not mechanistically suspicious of the prospects offered by electrification and were keen indeed on reducing the infrastructural gap between the town and the country. Where they worry, justifiably, is in terms of the disproportionately high costs they fear they would be expected to bear. The claims and counter-claims exchanged between the population and their politicians and among different classes within the population reflect the contested attributions of reasonableness among the village's people.

Entwined with the contested idioms of reasonableness are discussions about the possession and absence of power, or *khomota*: people with less *khomota* make claims on people with more *khomota* to make the sacrifices necessary for the village's improvement. Aiding them in making such claims are vocabularies of filial relatedness and metaphors of guardianship. Through such narratives, people with limited *khomota* register their disagreement with elite expectations of them quietly falling in line with their ideas of improvement. 'Elder brothers' are called upon to make greater sacrifices than younger siblings in the cause of improvement. Guardians are requested to accommodate the requirements of installing poles so that others less privileged than them can minimize the costs to them.

Expressions of filial relatedness and guardianship do not, however, preclude poor people's rejection of the tutelage by the entrenched class politicians who spearhead the electrification program. Rahimpur's labouring poor call out such politicians over the latter's claims that they dream lofty dreams for the improvement of the locality. The assumptions of trusteeship by entrenched class politicians are not accepted without being subjected to scrutiny. Where the locality's self-proclaimed trustees try to impose their plans for electrification on the majority of the population, the latter refused to play ball. They assess, evaluate, discuss among one another, and express their assent or disagreement depending on their understandings of the ways in which the installation of the electric poles impinge on their life plans. While they do not reject the idea of the electrification program as such, they do not quietly acquiesce with it either.

Disputes are integral to people's negotiations with democracy. The universal character of public policy does not eliminate these negotiations, although it does transform the form of the negotiations. The disputants with whom we were acquainted with in this chapter were supplicants for BPL cards in Chapter 4. They demanded employment and timely wages in Chapter 5. As disputants against their elected representative in the present chapter, they are not as enamoured of their ward member's proposal for the electrification of the village as their elected representatives would like them to be. But they are willing to consider these proposals in the light of their life plans and future prospects: they do not reject the proposals outright. Rahimpur's self-appointed trustees frequently accuse their disputants of unreasonably opposing the improvement of the living conditions in the village. However, a consideration of the perspectives offered by Rahimpur's residents suggests that, unlike what the accusations levelled against them by their self-appointed trustees might suggest, they are not against improvement. What they want is for improvement scheme to be compatible with their own life plans. To assert their position, people counter their trustees' allegations on unreasonableness with invocations of justice.

Disputations vary within Rahimpur, shaped by the social class position of the disputant and the differential attitudes harboured by the entrenched classes towards them. While poor people's conflict with members of the precarious classes is overt and direct, their tensions with the members of the entrenched classes is subtle and ambiguous, reflecting the frailties of the locality's incorporative social relations. Rahimpur's poor are not homogenous, and neither are their disputations. For instance, as we have seen, Syedur Islam's desperate pleas stand in stark contrast with Daulat Bibi's assertive disputations.

The disputes over the installation of electric poles in Rahimpur reflect an aspiration to improved living conditions, but under conditions of their choice. Such projects speak to people's imaginations of a better future without necessarily enchanting them to accept whatever is offered in the name of improvement. The negotiations spawned by such hope signal the ways in which improvement schemes politicise populations rather than depoliticise them. Their negotiations also suggest that people do not seek to evade or subvert improvement schemes but seek to actively shape their implementation so that they may actually resonate with their own life plans.

The disputations analysed in this chapter signal the ambivalent conflict between the labouring poor and their entrenched class trustees. Concomitant with such conflict is the palpable tensions between those with more *khomota* and those with less. The labouring poor neither consent with their entrenched class (self-appointed) trustees nor do they engage in pitched confrontation with them. This ambivalence stems from the different, often contradictory, situations that arise from improvement schemes in general and Rahimpur's electrification program in particular. Such ambivalences signal an inchoate tension between those without *khomota* and those possessing it, as the languages of *anyay* and *atyachar* invoked time and again during people's negotiations suggests. These ambivalences intimate the agonistic dimension of poor people's negotiations in Rahimpur.

The frequent invocations of the vocabularies of *anyay* and *atyachar* by Rahimpur's disputants during their negotiations with their self-appointed entrenched class trustees reveal that they do not acquiesce in their own domination. But they do not demand the annihilation of the members of the entrenched classes. Standing outside of the binary frameworks of acquiescence and annihilation, the people we have met in this chapter intersperse collaboration with contention during their negotiations. They combine individual invocations of fictive kinship ties and obligations of those with *khomota* towards those without with collective claims that their aspirations for their and children's futures be safeguarded. The disputants make it a point to contrast their being 'reasonable people' whose legitimate grievances are threatened by the unreasonableness of those who inflict *anyay* and *atyachar* on them on a quotidian basis. But they also appeal to the kindness and reaffirm their faith in the magnanimity of their entrenched class politicians. The labouring classes thus consent to as well as contend with the actions of the entrenched classes. This complex of seemingly opposing practices inflects Rahimpur's disputations with an agonistic content.

Disputes comprise a key aspect of poor people's negotiations with democracy. They aspire to the improvement of their locality but refuse to extent their unbridled consent to the decisions of their politicians. Although their disputes are internally fragmented and are shaped by social class positions of the disputants, they signal a notion of collective peoplehood among the poor in ambivalent conflict with the entrenched classes. Such conceptualisations reiterate for us the agonistic character of their disputations.

Conclusion

This chapter did four things. One, it rehearsed a history of electrification programs with special reference to India. The universal character of the electrification program meant that poor people did not fear to dispute the decisions taken on their behalf by entrenched class politicians and their aides. Two, the chapter documented the disputations by the labouring poor, emphasizing the themes emerging from the negotiations between the politicians and the people of Rahimpur locality. Three, the chapter noted the heterogenieties in disputations by contrasting the claims made by Rahimpur's Shershabadiya community with those advanced by the locality's Sheikh Muslims and Hindus of different communities. Four, in the light of such heterogeneities, the chapter theorized the disputations in Rahimpur as evidence of agonistic negotiations.

Rahimpur's populations neither consent to the electrification program initiated by their elected politician nor do they conflict with it. Rather, they dispute the ways in which the program is sought to be implemented, insisting to have their say in the matter. The disputants frequently invoke the oppression to which they are subjected, and characterized their deprivation in terms of the lack of *khomota*, pitted against those with *khomota*. Although frequently requesting for help from their 'guardians' among the entrenched classes, the poor reject their tutelage where they consider such tutelage to be inimical to their own interests. Such negotiations indicate that they are clearly not enamoured of the trusteeship model of democracy which Rahimpur's entrenched class politicians attempt to endorse. Poor people in Rahimpur consistently reject the labels of being unreasonable that are hurled at them by their elected politicians. Further, the poor expect their elected politicians to ensure that those wielding greater social power than themselves also make the sacrifice necessary for the improvement of their collective lives. Lexes of *anyay* and *atyachar* were frequently deployed to communicate people's understanding that such disparities in social power were not natural.

Through their disputations, they signal the myriad meanings with which they imbue India's postcolonial democracy. Poor people's disputations in Rahimpur signal their skepticism vis-a-vis assimilation into projects of improvement through which they might become like the inhabitants of Maldah, Delhi or Mumbai. But they certainly do not reflect an attempt to preserve their difference. Rather, Rahimpur's labouring poor seek to advance their own social perspectives of a better life. By foregrounding their collective self-identification as poor people in ambivalent conflict with the powerful, including the self-appointed trustees of the ward, they negotiate meanings of democracy. These meanings are not only shaped by but also shape political spaces in Rahimpur, as signaled in the ambivalent conflicts that underpin the electrification program. Rather, they also shape political spaces. Such ambivalent conflict endows poor people's negotiations with an agonistic content.

Endnotes

1   Although user charges were expected to be levied upon households, these were nominal. There did not seem to be any hesitation among the population in paying for electricity as long as the services were provided.

2   See Metcalfe (1998), Pitts (2005) and Knowles (2010) for incisive commentaries on James Mill's ideas.

3   For the application of this model to India, see Mantena (2010). For the Irish context, see Kinzer (2001). The case of the English poor is the subject of discussion in Dean (1991), Hindess (2001) and Mehta (1997).

4   The interview is available here: http://archive.tehelka.com/story_main39.asp?filename=Ne310508cover_story.asp.

5   Chidambaram is a member of the Congress Party, which led the UPA government between 2004 and 2014. The UPA was trounced in the General Elections held in May 2014 by the BJP-led NDA. Jaitley is a member of the BJP.

6   Also see McDonald (2009, 17) and the references therein for the wealth of literature on these connections.

7   However, what such narratives also leave unquestioned is the human cost of electrification. Bhushan and Hazra (2008, 164) estimate that over a million people have been displaced in India between 1950 and 2000 as a result of coal mining, which generates 60 per cent of the country's electricity (CEA, 2014, 3), and which is the source of electricity in millions of homes across the country, including in Rahimpur.

8   The film is available here: http://www.youtube.com/watch?v=VvhhjayTB74. Last accessed, 6 January 2015.

9   Summary information about the scheme downloaded on 27 June 2015 from: http://www.rggvy.gov.in/rggvy/rggvyportal/rggvy_glance.html. The website also informs us that the 'scheme covers electrification of all the villages in the country except the villages under the programme of Ministry of Non-conventional Sources (MNES)

for providing electricity from non-conventional energy sources under their remote village electrification programme.'

10 Information about project coverage available here: http://www.rggvy.gov.in/rggvy/rggvyportal/dynamic/covered.html, downloaded on 27 June 2015.

11 Information accessed from the website of the Ministry of Power suggests that as of April 2015, the scheme's coverage extended to nearly 110,000 villages with no prior electricity connections and almost 320,000 villages with partial connections. Data accessed on 27 June 2015 from: http://www.rggvy.gov.in/rggvy/rggvyportal/statewisesummary.jsp/All India Status.pdf.

12 As of June 2015, the data available project website suggests that work was 'under progress'. Data available here: http://www.rggvy.gov.in/rggvy/rggvyportal/electrification-status-villages.html, downloaded on 27 June 2015.

13 I happened to be in his office when a party colleague from the Block called to inform him of this news. Hanging out, Ward Member's residence 12 February, 2010.

14 See, for example, Agarwal (1996), Pigg (1992), Gardner and Lewis (2015), Li (2007) and Sharma (2008).

15 Hanging out, ward member's residence, 12 February 2010.

16 Hanging out, Nani's Chai Kiosk, Rahimpur, 12 February 2010. All cited matter till next footnote from this source.

17 Hanging out, ward member's residence, 12 February 2010. References to 'kharab bhoot' (malevolent ghosts) abounded during this meeting between the Ward Member and his core supporters.

18 Hanging out, Rahimpur Ward, locations L11, L25 and L2, 13–15 February 2010.

19 Hanging out, Rahimpur Ward, locations L5, 13–15 February 2010.

20 Hanging out, Rahimpur Ward, location L33, 14 February 2010.

21 Hanging out, Rahimpur Ward, location L26, 13 February 2010.

22 Hanging out, Rahimpur Ward, location L26, 13 February 2010.

23 Hanging out, Rahimpur Ward member's residence, 13 February 2010.

24 Hanging out, Rahimpur Ward, location L33, 13 February 2010; all further cited material from this source.

25 Hanging out, Rahimpur Ward, location L1, 13 February 2010; all cited matter until the next footnote from this source.

26 The concept of fictive kinship has been an enduring trope in anthropological accounts. For its uses in the Indian context, see Freed (1963) and Vatuk (1969). Other prominent elaborations of the concept may be found in the works of Carlos (1973), White (2004), Howell (2009) and Jacob (2009). See Schneider (1984) for a conceptual history of the term.

27 Akbar Ali found Nani's *chai* too weak as she added more milk than the others. Her *chai* was more expensive, but Akbar Ali never indicated that to be a consideration.

Nani's *chai* was regularly patronized by Joynal Ali, Musa Khan, Jakhir Hossein, and other *bodo lok* of the locality. By contrast, the kiosk Akbar Ali patronized was owned by one of his own sharecroppers. The *chai* there was cheaper, and more 'strong'. It was the favourite of Rahimpur's labouring classes. Akbar Ali spent most of his evening hours here, much to the derision of his party associates who preferred either Nani's kiosk or others.

28 Hanging out, Rahimpur ward, Nani's *chai* kiosk, 14 February 2010, all cited matter until the next footnote from this source.

29 This resonates with Amartya Sen's (2002) elucidation of rationality as inclusive of other regarding behaviour. An important distinction is drawn in the philosophical literature between reason, rationality, and being reasonable. That distinction is unimportant for the present argument.

30 Hanging out, Rahimpur ward, location L22, 13 February 2010.

31 Hanging out, Rahimpur ward, location L16, 15 February 2010; all cited matter until the next footnote from this source.

32 Hanging out, Rahimpur ward, location L5, 15 February 2010; all cited matter until the next footnote from this source.

33 The word he used, '*dekhi*', accompanied by a long pause, is among the most effective to convey the vaguest uncertainty in the Bangla language. In English, it translates into 'Let's see'.

34 Hanging out, Rahimpur ward, Nani's *chai* kiosk, 15 February 2010; all cited matter until the next footnote from this source.

35 The reasoning and interpretations underpinning disputes has been the subject of such anthropological classics as Evans–Pritchard (1937), Barth (1987), Whyte (1997) and Bowen (2003).

36 See, for instance, Gulliver (1963), Nader (1965) and Roberts (1979).

37 'Repertoires of justification' referes to an analytic line of inquiry associated with Boltanski and Thevenot (1991) and Lamont (1992).

38 For example, see the works of Dumont (1980), Pocock (1973) and Thorner and Thorner (1962).

39 For example, see Beals and Siegel (1966).

7

From Tradition to Modernity?

The Politics of Imagination

Love, dignity, respect: no one should be deprived of these things. We may not have these in our lifetime, but we hope that our children and grandchildren do in theirs.

Jamuni Rishi, 9 April 2010, 35, Landless labourer

The conjunctions between the opportunity structures inhered in India's unequal democracy and the social relations of power form political spaces. Such spaces shape poor people's negotiations with members of other classes. Their negotiations intimate the meanings they make of democracy. In the preceding chapter, I examined these negotiations in the context of a governmental intervention which is universal in its scope. The electrification program to which I directed attention is neither targeted to a specific section of Rahimpur's population nor is it conditional upon the performance of manual labour by potential beneficiaries. The chapter noted people's negotiations with the program in the context of an incorporative political place where the labouring classes collaborated uneasily with the entrenched classes against the precarious classes. In doing so, I offered a detailed account of the ways in which their disputations with the narratives of improvement reproduce extant social relations of power, but also strain these relationships. Whereas Rahimpur's people *supplicate* before their politicians in the context of a narrowly- targeted public policy and make *demands* in the context of broader-based public policy, they are able to push the limits of these relationships against the backdrop of universal public policy. Such negotiations illustrate the ways in which universalistic ideals entangle with particularistic practices in actually-existing democracies. In the present chapter, I continue my explorations of poor people's multifaceted negotiations with democracy in the context of another universally applicable policy. However, here I focus attention on a 'populist' political space. The discussions in this chapter draw on my fieldwork in Bihar's Sargana village, where the labouring poor collaborate with the precarious classes against the entrenched classes.

The policy context is provided by the Bihar State Government's legislation declaring the public character of the State's Hindu, Buddhist and Jain temples. The legislation draws on Wakf laws that administer Muslim places of worship and guarantee their *public* character. Since the promulgation of this law, the State's temples are mandated to not only have their accounts audited by government authorities but to also involve members of the public in their administrative and financial management. The labouring classes use this opportunity to try and rupture their subordination to the entrenched classes. But in bolstering their egalitarian claims, they do not effect a clean break with their past. In fact, they appropriate many elements of their past, especially through their interpretation of religious beliefs and cultural practices.

How do we understand the imaginations that animate poor people's politics in the context of our interest in the ways in which they negotiate with democracy? Do the idioms on which they draw represent a continuity with their traditional inheritances? Alternatively, do the egalitarian ideals informing their imaginations derive from the diffusion of modern institutions, constituting colonial and postcolonial statist projects? If the latter is the case, can we infer that their imaginations are mimicries of statist projects fashioned by progressive elites in the Liberal mould? Or, might analysts consider the possibilities that poor people's contested interpretations of their traditional inheritances incubate modern social imaginations? How indeed do we understand poor people's political practices that intersect with both the legislated and the juridical processes on the one hand and the affective and social relationships on the other? How, in the context of Sargana's public sphere, do such intersections illuminate the meanings the poor attribute to democracy?

In this chapter I want to direct attention to the social imaginations that underpin labouring classes' assertions of their egalitarian claims vis-à-vis the entrenched classes. Sargana's labouring poor contested the monopoly exercised by select entrenched class families over the management of the local temple. In doing so, they negotiated the meanings of the public space in the locality. Through their negotiations, they invoked notions of a clear break with the past, even as they deployed repertoires of popular contestations honed in from previous struggles. To such ends, they engaged with the juridical process and followed up on the implementation of judicial orders, while at the same time recalling lessons of love, devotion and shared responsibilities to emphasize their affective relationships with one another. The social imagination fomented by such entanglements between the juridical and the affective made explicit references to particular categories of caste, community and religion but did so by invoking such universal notions of as justice, equality and love.

This material draws on ethnography conducted in Sargana, a populist political place in north Bihar. It speaks to the burgeoning literature that elucidates the linkages between democracy and the putative 'transitions' from tradition to modernity. On the one hand, modernization theorists, suggest that democracy and modernity are symmetrical and proceed hand in hand. On the other hand, postcolonial theorists argue that democracy and modernity are disjunctive and may even be rivals. Where modernization theorists expect to find that the symmetries between democracy and modernity facilitate the eventual flowering of a domain of civil society, postcolonial theorists offer a far more complex picture of civil society being a restricted space facing stiff competition from the domain of political society. If the politics of the poor in the modernization narrative is a politics of poor people assimilating into civil society, in the postcolonial narrative poor people's politics is about sustaining their difference through the domain of political society. A third strand of the scholarship, a 'post-postcolonial' strand if you will, highlights the limitations of both these approaches in thinking about the purported transition from tradition to modernity. In this vein, Akio Tanabe (2007) proposes the idea of the 'moral society' to underscore the continued significance of shared norms against the backdrop of political change. This chapter engages in critical conversation with all three perspectives and urges readers to consider the imaginations underpinning poor people's politics as reflecting neither the persistence of tradition nor the triumph of modernity. Rather, their imaginations signal the entanglements between the two.

In Section I, I first introduce readers to the analytic disjunctions between democracy and modernity explored in the literature. I then outline the debates over the production of modern and traditional identities in relation to the potential emergence of civil society in postcolonial contexts. The following section develops a narrative of the egalitarian social imaginations expressed by Sargana's labouring classes, supported by the precarious classes, against the hierarchical presumptions of the entrenched classes. In particular, I highlight the ways in which the affective and the juridical aspects of their imaginations are entwined. Section III concludes by reflecting on the agonistic dimension of poor people's social imaginations.

This chapter, thus, does four things. One, it directs attention to the fluid nature of 'political space' by focussing on a single location. By highlighting the policy context, it provides readers a glimpse into the dynamic character of the opportunity structures available to the labouring classes and their negotiations with the people who populate those structures. The context is the populist political place that is Sargana. Two, the chapter reflects on people's social imaginations in the context of the opportunity structures and social relations of power within which they are embedded. Three, it reminds readers of the heterogeneities that mark people's social imaginations. Four, it critically engages with scholarly approaches to conceptualizing such imaginations as indicative of the flowering of civil society, the emergence of political society and the animation of moral society.

I

The disjunctions of modernity and democracy

In elucidating the political practices of the poor (or 'governed', as he would have it), Partha Chatterjee argues that 'modernity is facing an unexpected rival in the form of democracy' (Chatterjee, 2004, 41). In his reading, poor people take recourse to moral idioms while pressing their claims, claims that violate such precepts associated with modernity as private property and the rule of law. Chatterjee's formulation usefully underscores the disjunctions between modernity and democracy. It alerts social scientists to the ways in which poor people's negotiations with democracy might contradict many of the tenets that social scientists associate with modernity.

Other scholars warn us that democracy is *internally* disjointed. James Holston (2008) reminds us about the disjunctions of democracy in Brazil when he examines the quotidian ways in which that country's urban poor are faced with contrasting experiences of the electoral and civil legal dimensions of democracy. We also know that political democracies may not be social democracies (Huber *et al.*, 1997). Electoral democracies may not even be representative (Roy, 2014c). Civil liberties may be violated with impunity in electoral democracies (Caldeira and Holston, 1999). Similarly, economic and social rights may be violated in democracies where elections are regularly held and civil liberties upheld (Jayal, 2013). Some countries, such as China, might protect economic and social rights but not civil and electoral liberties (Bell, 1999).

Such accounts outlining the disjunctions of modernity and democracy owe much to historical–sociological scholarship that painstakingly explores the specifics of regional, national and sub-national experiences. An early contribution to the interrogation of symmetrical accounts of modernization was advanced in the seminal scholarship of Barrington Moore Jr (1966). His historically-informed sociology of modernization and democratization alerted social scientists to the multiplicity of connections between modernity and democracy even in their so-called historic heartlands of western Europe and North America. Sidney Mintz (1975) argues that methods of industrial organization associated with modernity were first developed not in Manchester's textile mills but in the sugar plantations of the Caribbean. More recently, Shmuel Eisensdadt (2000) argues against the notion that any transition to modernity is uniform. He and his colleagues propose the notion of 'multiple modernities' to direct attention to plural, rather than singular, modernities.[1] Contributing to this view, Sudipto Kaviraj (2000) emphasizes the plural and often conflictual dimensions of modernity. In his formulation, democracy and modernity are not symmetrical, as normative theorists of either democracy or modernity would have us believe. Rather, they are sequential, which means some aspects of democracy may emerge independent of others. Likewise, Timothy Mitchell (2000) reminds his readers that the presentation of modernity as a phenomenon originating in Europe is the result of a specific relationship between the continent and her colonies and should not be taken for granted.

Historical and sociological perspectives on modernity as a political philosophy further bear this out. Michel Ralph-Truillot's (1995) work on the silences in the production of history in the context of the Haitian Revolution reveals that ideals of social equality were espoused by slave rebels against French colonialism without the concomitant emergence of a bourgeoisie. Haitians abolished slavery and adopted a multiracial constitution prior to the development of industrial capitalism. In the Indian context, Gopal Guru (2009) alerts his readers to the ways in which impoverished Dalits have sought to institute egalitarian protocols in society by insisting that self-styled upper castes cease to treat them as untouchables. Such claims might not be concomitant with other markers of modernity, namely the primacy accorded to the individual in social or political life, the establishment of private property, and the secularization of society. But they do point to the intimation of a social dimension of modernity.

Empirical political scientists complement these insights. Atul Kohli (2013) suggests that different Indian States exhibit different facets of modernity. He specifically contrasts the supposed economic modernity of a State such as Gujarat with what he calls political modernity in West Bengal. While economic organization in Gujarat represents modern forms of economic organization, characterized by well established commercial and industrial centres, its political organization remains shaped by communal identities anchored in supremacist ideologies. Economic modernity in Gujarat does not imply or anticipate political modernity. By contrast, political organization in West Bengal, shaped by discourses of class and interests, is modern, even as economic organization is not. Thus, political modernity in West Bengal is not concomitant with economic modernity. Reflecting on the case of Bihar, Jeffrey Witsoe (2014) discusses the disjunctions of development and democracy within that State. Calling attention as he does to the deepening in the state of 'lower caste' empowerment on the one hand and the absence of development on the other during the 15 years of Lalu Prasad Yadav's rule, Witsoe's account reiterates disjunctions between political modernity and economic modernity.

These contributions challenge longstanding Liberal claims on the putative symmetries within democracy and between democracy and modernity. Such claims were heralded by a Parsonian definition of modernity as a set of values that inscribed affective neutrality, specificity, universalism, achievement, and self-orientation[2] in society. Likewise, Anthony Giddens adds that modernization refers to a 'single overriding dynamic of transformation' (1990, 11) and is inevitable. Eugene Weber's (1976) painstaking account of the transition of 'peasant to Frenchmen' over two centuries perhaps best illustrates this perspective of modernization.

Echoing these views, Jürgen Habermas (1987) summarized modernization, the process entailing the transition to modernity, as:

A bundle of processes that are cumulative and mutually reinforcing: to the formation of capital and the mobilisation of resources; to the development of the forces of production and the increase in the productivity of labour; to the establishment of centralized political power and the formation of national identities; to the proliferation of rights of political participation, of urban forms of life, and of formal schooling; to the secularisation of values and norms.

Habermas (1985) associates modernity with the rationalization of everyday life. He relates the 'advent' of modernity with triumphal accounts of human reasoning, people's ability to critically reflect on and interrogate received wisdom as well as habits of the past. The symmetrical accounts inspired by the work of such scholars share the premise that not only is modernity synchronous with democracy, but also that both are synchronous with industrialization, capitalism, nationalism, secularization of society, rationalization of the bureaucracy, and individualization of peoplehood. Drawing on Habermas but also recognizing the limits of capitalism in inducing modernity, scholars now begin to express a 'Critical Modernist' paradigm through which they foreground the idea of emancipation as central to modernity. However, such a view of modernity is limited to struggles against capitalism and the inculcation of a scientific spirit (Peet and Hartwick, 2009), thereby excluding from its ambit popular struggles, which may neither consciously pit themselves against capitalist actors nor be explicitly anchored in a scientific worldview, and yet be emancipatory in substance.

The scholarship highlighting the disjunctions between democracy and modernity has considerably enriched our understanding of the tortuous ways in which conditions of modernity intersect with the processes through which democracy emerges. Modernity and democracy both refer to complex processes that are far from being the cumulative and mutually reinforcing bundle of processes that theorists such as Habermas would have us believe. Thinking about the disjunctions in democracy as well as in modernity compels us to take into account not only the ways in which democracy and modernity might rival one another, but also the manner in which different dimensions of democracy may be at odds with one another and various aspects of modernity may be in tension with each other.

In this vein, scholars writing about the transition from tradition to modernity pin much hope on the emergence of civil society as a space where universalism replaces particularistic ties (Silver, 1990). Liberal theorists think of civil society as a space between the state and the market which facilitates the free association of atomized individuals (Cohen and Arato, 1992) whose individual rights to privacy and private property are guaranteed. However, Partha Chatterjee (1998) suggests that civil society in postcolonial societies was quickly appropriated by the propertied classes. Poor people, by contrast, depend much more on politicians – the ensemble of elected representatives, aspirants striving for office, and fixers and brokers who mediate access to public resources – to mitigate the insecurities that characterize their day-to-day existence. Caste associations, farmers' groups and refugee organizations are more likely to be the sorts of collectives that the poor were likely to form, a cast of characters who Chatterjee designates as constituting the realm of political society. Moreover, the government is the focus of their association. In contrast to propertied Indians who occupy civil society, Chatterjee asserts, the poor are enmeshed in political society. A third strand of the scholarship highlights the limitations of both these approaches of thinking about the purported transition from tradition to modernity. Illustrative of this strand is Akio Tanabe's (2007) who proposes the notion of a 'moral society' to underscore the continued significance of shared norms against the backdropn of political change. Of course, the shared norms are not static. Rather, they reflect a reinterpretation of popular practices in the light of modern institutions of elected local governments. The practices of Sargana's labouring and precarious classes resonate with some of their observations but also- as we shall see- demonstrate crucial dissonances, compelling an interrogation of prevailing understandings of civil society, political society and moral society.

Modernity and the social imagination

The nuance in recent scholarship has considerably added to our understandings of the specific trajectories of modernity. Perspectives such as 'alternative' (Gaonkar, 1999), 'regional' (Sivaramakrishnan and Agarwal, 2003), 'parallel' (Larkin, 1997), 'local' (Piot, 1999), and 'rural' (Kumar, 2014) modernities compel scholars to take seriously the manifold manifestations of modernity. Unlike scholars who highlight the incompleteness (Habermas, 1985) or impossibility (Latour, 1993) of the modern condition, the ethnographically dense accounts of these scholars enable us to appreciate the concrete ways in which modern subjectivities are produced, without folding these understandings into teleological accounts. They have also directed attention to the unpredictable pathways of modernity and to the interruptions and reversals therein (Ferguson, 1999).

Such innovations notwithstanding, the tendency to sustain the myth of modernity's European provenance remains prevalent. Ironically, this is borne out even in the arguments advanced by authors writing in the postcolonial tradition, such as Dipesh Chakrabarty, whose case for 'provincializing Europe' concludes by urging readers that 'European thought is a gift to us all' (2008, 255). Gaonkar's (1999, 1) description is exemplary:

> Born in and of the West some centuries ago under relatively specific socio-historical conditions, modernity is now everywhere. It has arrived not suddenly but slowly, bit by bit – over the longue durée – awakened by contact; transported through commerce; administered by empires, bearing colonial inscriptions; propelled by nationalism; and now increasingly steered by global media, migration and capital.

Such views emphasizing a European origin of modernity are misplaced. The scholarship of critical historians and anthropologists bears testimony to the difficulties in perusing a Eurocentric view of the provenance of modernity. Among others, Truillot (1995)'s work suggests that the definitively modern idea of universal citizenship was first produced by Haitian slaves rather than by the French revolutionaries. This argument is developed further by Buck-Morss (2009) who traces the emergence of Enlightenment accounts of slavery and freedom to events in Haiti rather than in Europe. In fact, historians call into question the perspective that colonial rule introduced modernity of any kind. Táíwò (2009) argues that, if anything, subjugation to European colonialism *diminished* the possibilities for the emergence of modernity in Africa, rather than enhancing them.

Emphasizing modernity's multifaceted pathways, Arjun Appadurai suggests that 'the work of the imagination' (Appadurai, 1996, 3) is central to the ways in which modern subjectivities are forged. The work of the imagination is performed by the proliferating mass media and global migrants. These channels, he tells us, fuel the impetus toward modernity even further. Perspectives on imaginations informs the historian Christopher Bayly's (2004) wide-ranging account of the 'birth of the modern world', wherein he highlights the circulations of ideas among local and global actors. Bayly's account reminds readers that the provenance of modernity is far more entangled that what was once believed. The emphasis of both scholars on the mobility of people and of ideas complicates the diffusionist view of modernity made commonplace in Parsonian sociology.

Gail Omvedt's (2008) interventions push the frontiers of contemplations on modernity even further. She not only bypasses the assumption that modernity stems from contact with Europe, but also reminds us about the endogenous potentialities of modernity in different parts of the world.[3] Omvedt directs attention to the role of social radicals in India who interrogated hierarchical presumptions of caste traditions since at least the fifteenth century. She emphasizes the role of saints such as Ravidas, Kabir, Nanak and Tukaram in inciting the imagination of 'earthly utopias' among oppressed people in the South Asian countryside. Ideals of social equality were central to such imaginations, which were interrupted by colonial rule and the need for the colonizers to cultivate myriad allies in their quest for capital and security. To occlude such endogenous modernizing impulses and portray an image of modernity imported into India in the sailing vessels of colonial administrators is nothing short of a travesty of history.

Nevertheless, colonial rule continues to be credited, or disparaged depending on the standpoint of the observer, with introducing modernity in postcolonial contexts. In the Indian context, Chekuri emphasizes the 'embedding of conditions within modern governmental modes' (2007, 393) as a feature of modernity. Modernization theorists hold such mechanisms as the bureaucratic rationalization of the civil service, the introduction of the courts of law and educational institutions, investments in railways and other technological innovations, capitalistic industrialization, as well as ideas of parliamentary democracy and the exposure of the Indian population to electoral procedures as responsible for the impetus to modernity in that country. In their view, the colonial state prised open, to various degrees of success, allegedly traditional societies characterized by such collective affiliations such as caste, tribe, religion, native, and village community.[4] By contrast, postcolonial scholars insist that the identities associated with the traditions of the colonies were in fact created by the colonizers. In particular, these authors point to such modern technologies as the census, communal quotas, and the spurious theories of martial and effeminate races elaborated by colonial officials as responsible for the reification of so-called traditional identities.[5]

The importance of such identities in postcolonial democracies has been differently interpreted by the two sets of authors. As far as modernization theorists can see, the salience of such identities stemmed from the instrumental use to which enterprising politicians put the primordial loyalties that already divided populations. On the contrary, for postcolonial theorists, the significance of these identities originated in their bureaucratization by the colonial state and its technologies of governance. Modernization theorists' proposition that the political salience of identities would diminish with the deepening of modernity proved to be a mirage in postcolonial democracies. To explain what they described as the persistence of identity politics, many modernization theorists emphasized that mobilization of primordial identities for electoral support substituted for programmatic politics.[6] Postcolonial theorists' predictions that identities would only become more salient with the extension of modern technologies of government appear to have been borne out empirically in much of the postcolonial world.[7] The reason for the contemporary entrenchment of ethnic, caste, tribal and religious identities, they aver, is not that they wield primordial influence over populations, enabling political entrepreneurs to manipulate them, but that they are the product of the colonial and postcolonial state-making processes.[8]

Critics of postcolonial perspectives note correctly that the identities bureaucratized by the colonial regime built on existing, differences in society rather than being crafted anew.[9] Nuancing the postcolonial scholars' thesis but avoiding the instrumentalism inherent the work of the modernization theorists are scholars such as Simon Gikandi (1998), who argue that the social identities imposed by the colonizers were not uncritically accepted by the colonized. In fact, Gikandi's scholarship reveals, the colonized populations actively negotiated the identities sought bo be crafted by the colonial governments and tried to use them as a means of advancing their own points of view. He interrogates the assumption shared by both modernization and postcolonial theorists that the provenance of modernity lay in the colonial, and subsequently postcolonial, processes of state-formation. By applying a sociological lens, he explores the processes through which modernity incubated in the African continent as a product of negotiations between state and society in that continent. Partha Chatterjee (1997) alludes to a similar story when he refers to the story of 'our' modernity being the result of statist interventions and societal impulses in colonial and postcolonial Bengal. Such scholarship illuminates the complex ways in which ideas of modernity blossom in society without assuming that these are triggered by statist projects.

In the Indian context, notwithstanding the continued importance of caste in postcolonial times, scholars concur that its collective meanings have undergone a transformations. Fuller's summarization is apt:

> Castes are being historically constructed, or perhaps more aptly being 'deconstructed', as a vertically integrated hierarchy decays into a horizontally disconnected ethnic array ... (Fuller, 1996, 26)

However, there is little agreement on the source of such (de-)constructions. Modernization theorists suggest that the hierarchies associated with caste organization are disintegrating *because of* the diffusion of egalitarian ideals inculcated by India's democratic constitution, spearheaded as they were by Western-educated progressive elites harbouring Liberal views.[10] They believe that the Liberal notion of civil society is gradually, but inexorably, taking root among Indians. Modernization theorists interpret the dissolution of ritual hierarchies as indicative of the symmetries between democracy and modernity. Their views remain enormously influential. On the contrary, postcolonial theorists suggest that it is the bureaucratization of caste identities under the aegis of the colonial and postcolonial state that politicized these identities. It is this bureaucratization, rather than the egalitarian principles enshrined in the Constitution, which contributed to the erosion of the associated ritual hierarchies. Indeed, the egalitarian principles of the Constitution could not have achieved such a feat, because the state which was mandated to institutionalize those principles, possessed, in Sudipto Kaviraj's memorable phrase, 'feet of vernacular clay' (Kaviraj, 1984, 227). It could, therefore, do little to diffuse the Liberal ideals of equality among the population. Democracy could not be conjoined with modernity.

Ironically, both modernization theorists and postcolonial scholars share the notion that egalitarian values emanate from the progressive elites at the helm of affairs of the state and civil society. Consequently, their narratives ignore the role of the social imaginations of the labouring poor, who have followed radical saints in interrogating the hierarchical presumptions of caste traditions since at least the fifteenth century. Gail Omvedt (2008) reminds us about the legacy of popular social radicals such as Kabir, Ravidas and Dadu. Her scholarship enables analysts to shift the debate beyond the dichotomy of whether oppressed people internalize egalitarian ideas disseminated by progressive elites (as modernization theorists would have it) or remain impervious to such ideas (as postcolonial theorists prime us to believe). Omvedt's work provides us with useful leads to consider the egalitarian social imaginations harboured by the poor, and the ways in which they draw simultaneously on the juridical stipulations of the Indian state as well as their socio-cultural inheritance of religious protest to lead dignified lives.

II

Disquiet in the temple

The temple under discussion was formally called Chandrika Devi Mandir. It was dedicated to Kali, the Hindu goddess associated with time, death, and regeneration. Locally called Chandithan,[11] the temple was an endowment made in 1936 by the Raja of Champanagar. Champanagar was one of the feudatories of the Raja of Baneilli who in turn swore allegiance to the Maharaja of Darbhanga. The condition for the endowment of the Chandithan was that the temple would be a site for public worship. The total endowment comprised the site on which the temple now stands and an additional 52 *bighas* of land whose agricultural produce was to be used for the maintenance and upkeep of the temple and to provide hospitality to its devotees.

With the dissolution of the Permanent Settlement and the subsequent dismantling of the entire edifice of estate-holders and their feudatories during the 1950s, the supervision of the temple's management was transferred to the Bihar State Religious Trust Board under the terms of the Bihar Hindu Religious Trust Act, 1950. The Rajput family, which had been originally tasked wih the management of the temple, remained its trustees. However, they now were mandated by law to maintain public accounts and to audit their incomes and expenditures by a public authority. Nonetheless, for nearly five decades, the trustees flouted the provisions of the law. That situation began to change by the turn of the present century. A particular irritant to the monopoly of the trustees appears to have been Vinay Mandal, the priest appointed by the Board. Mandal had once been affiliated with the CPI (M/L–L) and was of the Kevat community. In November 2011, the trustees sacked the priest, accusing him of embezzlement. Even as the Board stood by Mandal, the trustees filed even more debilitating charges against Vinay Mandal, of possessing arms and instigating terrorism! Although the trustees succeeded in barring him from performing rituals in the temple, Vinay Mandal found overwhelming support from the locality's labouring classes, especially of the Musahar, Santhal, Yadav and Kevat communities. His friend and neighbour, Shyamdev Mandal, a Kevat peasant who owned about 3 *bighas* of land and complemented his meagre income from agriculture with casual labour earlier in Kolkata and more recently in Delhi as a rickshaw puller, filed charges of embezzlement and mismanagement on behalf of Vinay Mandal against the trustees and moved a local court to institute appropriate proceedings. The matter is presently under the consideration of the courts, and the material presented below is strictly a discussion of the perspectives and interpretations of the different contestants.

When I asked about the most important issue facing the people of his gram panchayat to the Mukhya, Sarvesh Mandal, during our interview (January 2010), he was unequivocal: the conflict, or *ladaai*, between the 'Forwards' and 'Backwards' over the management of the Chandithan loomed large over social relations in the panchayat. He explicated that the 'Forwards' were the oppressors (*dabang*) and the 'Backwards' were the oppressed (*shoshit*). The Mukhya's presentation of what at first glance appears to be a legal wrangle in terms of a *ladaai* between such dichotomous categories as Forwards and Backwards was intriguing. The closest English equivalent of the word *ladaai* is 'fight' that indicates a more physical conflict that a legal wrangle. The word is often used to discuss brawls among people, but could also refer to deeper disagreements. In referring to the conflict between Forwards and Backwards, the Mukhya refers to both senses of the conflict.

The Mukhya's use of the terms Forwards and Backwards to describe the parties to the conflict conveys his perspective that caste is its most salient axis. The terms *Forwards* and *Backwards* refer respectively to the Savarna and the Shudra communities, the self-styled 'upper castes' and the stigmatized 'backward castes'. At first glance, the Mukhya's deployment of such categories appears to derive from the governmental use of the terms to refer to the material and ritual disparities between members of different communities. The Indian government labels the communities socially stigmatized as Shudras as Other Backward Classes to signal the deprivations from which their members collectively suffer. By contrast, the *Forwards* refer to members of the historically privileged caste communities. However, during the course of the interview, it became clear to me that he invokes the dichotomy as a political rather than a governmental category. The political category provided the idiom for activists through the twentieth century to challenge the appropriation of institutional, social and material resources by the members of the Savarna communities. The Mukhya situated the conflict over the temple alongside the activism of political leaders such as R. L. Chandapuri and Ram Manohar Lohia,[12] who had politicized the caste question in Bihar during the first two decades after Independence. On further probing, the Mukhya included within the rubric of the category *Backwards* not only members of the castes enumerated as OBC but also members of Sargana's Dalit and Adivasi communities.

From the Mukhya's point of view, the oppression (*shoshan*) by the Rajput trustees of the temple precipitated the issue. The trustees refused to acknowledge the temple as a public space, as mandated under the terms of the legislation. Instead, they were intent on maintaining their domination (*varchasv*) over the temple. A particular bone of contention was their appropriation for personal use the offerings made by devotees, most of whom were impoverished men and women from the locality and its environs. Instead of utilizing these offerings for the maintenance of facilities for devotees, the trustees invested them on personal use, such as the purchase of expensive jewellery, acquisition of real estate and provision of higher education of their children. This situation was no longer acceptable to the labouring classes. In the Mukhya's words: as the government has empowered the poor, they find such behaviour among the oppressor castes (*dabang jatis*) unacceptable.

The idea that the government had empowered poor people is not confined to the Mukhya's account. I realized that this idea resonated with the palpable excitement over the conflict among my Rajput interlocutors in Sargana, some of whom were involved in the management of the temple as trustees. They resented the perceived interference of the government in their religious traditions. The Bihar Hindu Religious Trust Act, 1950 brought under the purview of the state all trusts recognized by 'Hindu Law to be religious, pious and charitable...except... a private endowment created for the worship of a family idol in which the public are not interested' (Bihar, 1951, chapter 1, section 2[1]). For my interlocutors, this clause in the Act represented a blatant attempt by the government to subvert their traditional ways of life. 'For centuries, we have upheld the social order. We have ensured stability and decency in society. How dare the government interfere with that?' one of them asked me passionately. Hunny Singh, the predecessor of the present Mukhya, was quick to identify the root of the problem. After verifying that I was not *Backward*, he told me:

> The *Backwards* control the government. In return, the government pampers the *Backwards* (*Sar pe chadha kar rakha hai*). Not only that, they talk about empowering the *harijans* (a patronising term to describe Dalits). They have both ruined the state. To top it all, they say they will protect the Pakistanis (an epithet to describe Muslims).... People raise unnecessary issues. Look at what they have done to the temple. They have raised all kinds of issues over it, threatening the peace in this village. *Arre bhai*, it's a religious place, they must respect the religiosity of the place. They must not bring politics into it.

The Mukhya and his predecessor, arch opponents, share the view that the conflict over the temple threatens the peace in the village, although they offer diametrically opposing interpretations. For the Mukhya, the issue reflects the growing assertiveness of the panchayat's oppressed people against the entrenched classes, an assertiveness that results from their being 'empowered' by the government. What he sees as 'empowerment', his predecessor derides as 'pampering'. Nonetheless, they both emphasize the role of the government in eroding the traditions of the village and threatening the domination of the privileged classes. Where the former exults in the perceived emancipatory role of the government, the latter derides it and interprets the government's role as interfering with traditional ways of life.

Such obvious differences in interpretations notwithstanding, narratives of political change are common to both my interlocutors. Both recognize the *shifts* in the constitution of government in Bihar and the challenge this posed to the social status quo. Their accounts resonate with the analysis by scholary commentators on Bihar,[13] who point to the role of political claims advanced by sections of the Shudra communities in democratizing the legislative arm of government. Side by side, researchers have also highlighted the ways in which social change and political change reinforce one another.[14] They remind us that the political mobilizations which have resulted in the democratization of the legislature are embedded in social struggles against the entrenched classes. To illustrate the salience of these social struggles to the contestations of the poor in Sargana, I report, in the following section, the perspectives of the dispute offered by my interlocutors of the labouring classes of the Kevat and Musahar communities.

Tussles over the *pablik*

At first glance, the mood among members of the Musahar community appeared to be indifferent to the matter of the temple. When I initially broached the topic among them, they seemed not to be too interested in talking about it. However, as my presence in the locality became more routine they too were more forthcoming about their insights into the matter.[15] Through conversations in the Musahar *tola* conducted over several weeks, I was able to develop an understanding of the perspective of different people on the issue. Notwithstanding the many differences of opinion among my interlocutors, it became clear to me by the end of my fieldwork that they were anything but indifferent to the question of the temple.

For many men and women in the Musahar *tola*, the monopoly of the trustees over the affairs of the temple was yet another instance of the *dabang log*, the most frequently used term for the entrenched classes, converting their economic and social resources into the dominance of the public space. Domi Rishi, an agricultural labourer in his mid-seventies, recounted the various ways in which the locality's Rajput and Kayasth landlords had in the past 'had their way' (*manmani karte the*) with people. The wrinkles on his hollowed out cheeks became even more prominent as he interspersed reflections with analysis:

> Our elders would not dare to sit on the cot when the *dabang* people passed by. Not only us, we were only labourers. Even

the tenants of the landlords, the Yadav peasants and the Kevat cowherers would spring up to attention whenever the landlord passed by. We were all in his debt, so we looked down when he addressed us, unless he asked us to look at him. We worked on his farms, so we did not speak unless we were spoken to.[16]

In this vein, Domi Rishi's neighbours reported that the trustees appropriated the offerings made to the deity housed in the temple, the incomes from the agricultural produce of the land vested with it, and other resources attached to it (such as a pond with many varieties of fish) for their own 'private' (*niji*) use. Rather than using these resources for the maintenance of the temple, they spent them for their own individual households. The jewellery offered to the deity was stored in trustees' bank lockers. The cash offerings were used to pay for the private education of the trustees' children. Moreover, the trustees did not make public the details of incomes earned by the temple by way of offerings and the sale of agricultural, horticultural, and piscicultural produce.

Members of the Musahar community viewed the appropriation of the temple's resources by the trustees, and their relatives and friends, as a continuation of their poaching of the public domain. They did not 'share' either the offerings made to the temple with other devotees or the information about the management of temple resources. While there were no restrictions on poor people's entry into the temple, what was at stake for my interlocutors was the trustees' attempt to privatize the public space and the simultaneous embezzlement of public resources. This particular infringement was only one instance of their poaching of the public space. Such poaching was facilitated by the Rajput trustees' 'enclosure' of the locality's many agricultural properties. The term used to describe such enclosement was '*kabja kar liya*' to highlight the trustees' efforts to privatize what was considered to be common spaces. The following excerpt from one of my many conversations with my interlocutors in the Musahar *tola* provides an illustration:

[Tilya Rishi, c. 45 years old, landless, construction worker]: The *dabang log* own everything: the land we till, the water we drink, the food we eat, everything…They are trying to own Ma Chandi. They want to own the very air we labour classes (*majdoor varg*) breathe.

……

[Domi Rishi, c. 75 years old, landless, agricultural labourer]: They
want to control the temple. The temple belongs to the *pablik*
[in English]. Devotees offer gifts to Ma Chandi. How can the
greedy bast***s keep the gifts we make to our mother?....[other
expletives]

.....

[Jamuni Rishi, c. 35 years old, landless, agricultural labourer]:
They think they can lord over us like they used to in the olden
days...They make us work for them, but don't even recognize us
in the market place. Look at these properties [points to the fields
owned by Rajput farmers around their hamlet, which they had
to circumvent to reach the temple]. They say it's theirs. We can't
walk across these fields to reach Ma Chandi. We have to go around
it to get to our mother. Is this fair?...love, dignity, respect – no
one should be deprived of these things....[17]

The above conversation points to the multilayered ways through which
impoverished men and women of the Musahar community make meaning of
the public domain (*pablik*) in Sargana. Three aspects of the ways in which such
meanings are made stand out in particular. First, labouring classes interpret
the contests over the public domain through the experience of economic and
social inequality between themselves and the locality's labour-hiring farmers
of the Rajput, Kayasth, and Yadav communities. In their accounts, the public
domain is an unequal space, constituted by the landlessness of the many against
the landholdings by the few. Several of the labouring families – Musahar, Kevat,
and Yadav – depend on the Rajput and Kayasth farmers and Yadav peasants
for employment and subsistence, exacerbating the inequality of this domain.
The labouring poor's oft use of the term *shoshit* to describe their own relations
with their employers is instructive, for it conveys their appreciation of the ways
in which these inequalities are constructed, rather than being natural. They
interpret such inequalities in interlocked vocabularies of caste and class: they
speak of their exploitation as being perpetrated by members of 'dominant
castes', but they refer to themselves as being of labouring classes (*majdoor varg*).
The interlocked use of caste and class vocabularies allows them to identify the
caste-basis of *their* exploitation but did not preclude cooperation with other
labouring classes of other communities.

Despite being subjected to exploitative labour relations, Sargana's poor expect egalitarian social intercourse in the public domain. In voicing these expectations, Sargana's labouring classes express the idea of a break between the 'present time' and the 'olden days' when they were subjected to a variety of social indignities. This leads me to my second point about the meanings the labouring poor assign to the public domain. Despite the persistence and reproduction of material inequalities, Sargana's labourers conceive the public domain as a normative space where resources, information, ideas, and responsibilities are shared. Even though such conceptions do not actually materialize, the labouring poor express the possibility of egalitarian social exchange. By insisting that the members of the entrenched classes 'try to' or 'think they can' – rather than concede that they *do* – control poor people's lives and livelihoods, the labouring classes convey their unwillingness to naturalize or internalize actually-existing dominance. They discursively deny the *de facto* control exerted by the entrenched classes over the temple. Furthermore, Sargana's poor insist that the offerings to the temple and the incomes from the resources at its disposal be used for the well being of the impoverished labourers and poor peasants who constitute the overwhelming majority of devotees. Resthouses *ought to be* built and devotees *should be* accorded with due hospitality. The idea of sharing resources is also linked with other spheres of life, such as the access to the paths that lie through privately owned fields. Walking on these paths through private properties provides the shortest route to the temple for the Musahar women and men in Sargana wards 5 and 6. The suggestion that not being allowed to do so was somehow 'inappropriate' (*anuchit*) drives home their emphasis that they be allowed to use what they understand as community resources.

The third point to which I want to direct attention is the affective dimension of the manner in which the locality's landless labourers and poor peasants interpret their claims. The claims on the public domain are replete with references to the relationship they perceived to possess with their deity. They imbue her with a maternal imagery to assert their *moral* claim over what is seen to be hers. The poor are as much her children as the trustees were, perhaps even more so because they actually worship her and make her offerings even as they themselves live in penury. On the one hand, their being her children implies a claim to share the resources that are offered to her. On the other hand, their relationship also brings with it a responsibility to protect her from being usurped. Such claims are not only claims borne out of the particularity of their self-perceived relationship with their deity. Rather, these claims endorse universal principles, when they suggested that 'no one should be deprived of [love, respect, dignity]'. Their emphasis on filial bonds pinpointing love, mutuality, and devotion provides affective ingredients to their concerns about inequality and social injustice, concerns that animate their attempts to constitute the public domain in Sargana.

The manual workers of Sargana's Musahar community hold their ideas of social equality, sharing resources and filial affection in common with the poor peasants and manual workers I met in the Kevat *tola* in the same gram panchayat. If anything, these ideas are even more vocally articulated here. Discussions on the matter of the temple are animated among members of the Kevat community because both Vinay Mandal, the landless labourer who raised the issue in the first place and Shyamdev Mandal, the poor peasant who filed the case on Vinay Mandal's behalf live here. Educated up to the secondary school, Shyamdev Mandal had immersed himself in the legal aspects of the case. His affiliation with the Janata Dal (United), the political party leading the government in Bihar since 2005, facilitated the social connections needed to follow up the case with lawyers at the district and State capital as well as with stringers to direct attention in the vernacular media to situation in the temple. For his neighbours in the Kevat *tola* where he lived, Mandal's efforts are a symbol of their collective effort to salvage the *pablik* character of the temple. As my interlocutors in the Kevat *tola* discussed with each other, while I struggled, unsuccessfully, between taking notes and snuffing on cannabis-infused *chillam*:

> [Nandlal Mandal, c. 45, marginal farmer, seasonal migrant and casual worker]: This is a test set by Ma Chandi. She wants him to teach the *dabang jatis* a lesson. He has to make the temple safe for the *pablik*.

> [Akhilesh Mandal, c. 60, marginal farmer]: [Vigorously disagreeing]... Actually, *he* is protecting her. She is under the control of the *dabang jatis*. If they had been more *pablik-minded* [in English], this would not be necessary.

A sudden silence descended on the group as four or five dhoti-clad men passed by the *machan* on which we were sitting. They wore a vermillion mark on their forehead. Once they were out of earshot, the gentleman next to me whispered that the passers-by were Rajput and relatives of the trustees. My interlocutors continued their conversation:

> [Basdeo Mandal, c. 50, landless agricultural labourer]: They treat our mother as if she is their private property. Why? Just because we are poor and *backward*?

> [Nandlal Mandal, c. 45]: They [the *dabang jatis*] must understand: Ma Chandi is everyone's. She is not their household deity. She is not their private property (*niji sampatti*).

> [Akhilesh Mandal, c. 60]: Yes, they must understand. The old days are gone. Did you see those Thakurs pass by? In the olden days, we would jump to our feet if any of them passed us by. Today none of us would do such a thing.[18]

Disagreements among my interlocutors notwithstanding, an unmistakable concern about safeguarding the public is evident. The trustees were not 'public-minded': they did not share the wealth of the temple with the public for their benefit. The travails of the entity the poor peasants revered as Chandi was emblematic of the way in which the trustees subordinated the public. The trustees' sense of entitlement and assumption of impunity emanated from their socio-economic dominance and their appropriation of temple resources. But people were unwilling to tolerate the trustees' hierarchical assumptions.

Akhilesh Mandal's final comment is an apt, if poignant, illustration of the differences he perceived between the present and the past. It resonates with Domi Rishi's remark noted earlier. In the past, they would stand up each time a member of the Rajput or Kayasth community passed by them. In the present time, such an expectation was unthinkable. Neither Kevat nor Musahar, nor indeed any of the communities in the village, would do that any more. The public space was one of equality. But such equality could not be taken for granted. Saragana's labouring poor forged such equality through every day practices (such as continuing to sit as self-styled social superiors walked by) that might mean little in alternative contexts.

The place of the law

In September 2009, Shyamdev Mandal formally filed a petition with the Bihar State Religious Trust Board in September 2009. His petition was drafted with some help from lawyers associated with the JD (U). In the petition, it was stated:

> Anti-social elements have forcibly encroached the temple premises...the members of a particular family of a particular caste have extended their dominance over the movable and immovable properties of the temple...They appropriate offerings made to the deity, especially on Tuesdays. On a weekly basis, these offerings include 50 goats, two buffaloes, three pigeons, 100 grams of gold, five quintals (sic) of sweets. The temple premise houses a giant banyan tree, with at least 4,000 birds and an equal number of bats. Other trees in the temple premises include a *peepul* tree, a *jamun* (black berry) and a mango tree... Nearly 10,000 fish live in the pond that is attached to the temple...At least ₹ 50,000 is earned each week... Members of the said family sell these offerings and keep the proceeds for their personal use rather than on public welfare. They have embezzled public funds for the last 75 years. (Translation by author)

The petition went on to name the seven Rajput trustees as the encroachers into the temple. It requested the Board to investigate into the alleged embezzlement of funds by the trustees. Subsequently, Shyamdev Mandal filed a petition in the name of residents of the locality (*sthaniya log*) to administratively separate the tank from the temple and explicitly declare the pond as part of the gram panchayat's common property.[19] His cousin, the Mukhya (with whom he shared no love lost) supported him and testified against the trustees (despite the fact that some of them were his political backers). His testimony that the temple was indeed a public trust and not a private property of the original trustee, had been a crucial piece of evidence in the litigants' favour.

An immediate, and tangible, outcome of the petition was an official signboard erected outside the premise of the temple. The signboard explicitly declared the temple to be public property. By April 2011, the outcome was more substantial. The Board ordered the constitution of a 20-member committee to oversee the management of the temple. The trustees were not removed from their position, but their authority over the temple's affairs was legally whittled down. Henceforward, the trustees were to report the income and expenditure of the temple to the Committee and to make available all its records to the Committee for safekeeping. The Committee was responsible for auditing the accounts – the expense for the audit was to be borne by the public exchequer. The application for demarcating the pond from the temple is still under review.

In emphasizing the public nature of the Chandithan's resources, members of Sargana's Kevats and Musahar communities appear to have appropriated vocabularies instituted by the state in Bihar under the terms of the Hindu Religious Trust Act and more specifically the Bihar State Religious Trust Board. In response to litigation initiated by Mandal, the Board declared the temple to be a public religious trust (*sarvajanik dharmik nyas*) in November 2009, just two months before the commencement of my fieldwork in the locality. A signboard outside the temple heralded the 'public' status of the temple. That the legal disputations might have contributed to the vocabulary of the *pablik* is undeniable. But the provenance of the interlingual term is quite intriguing,[20] given that the language of the courts, and of the signboard that was eventually put up, was a Sanskritized variety of Hindi (*sarvajanik*) instead of the more commonly used *pablik*. The court's ruling and the presence of the signboard could not have invented the public domain that was the subject of such passionate discussion among the labouring classes in Sargana. These instruments of the state certainly lent legitimacy and respectability to poor people's vocabularies, but it would be a conceit to claim that they could have transplanted the idea of the *pablik* onto the population from nowhere.

The Board's decisions convinced the bulk of Sargana's population that the law, at least in this case, was supportive of the claims of the 'public'. The decisions bore witness to the perspective that the law treated everyone as equal, irrespective of their economic clout or social capital. The labouring classes viewed the Board's decisions as emphatically endorsing their own ideas of the public domain, as a normative space where everyone was equal. By not discriminating in favour of the propertied trustees, the Board contributed in no small way to their appreciation of the rule of law, as a political regime that would not criminalize them and sanction impunities for the wealthy. The appreciation among Sargana's poor of the Board's then Chairman, Acharya Kunal Kishore, stood in stark contrast with the expletives used by the temple's trustees to denigrate the official. The Board's directives affirmed for Sargana's poor their social expectations of respect, dignity, and equality, against the hierarchical assumptions of the trustees. Its injunctions bolstered the social confidence of the poor, even as the trustees and their associates prepared to challenge this verdict. Many among Sargana's labouring classes viewed the laws from which the Board derived its injunctions as an example of the law being compatible with justice. *Qanoon nyaysangat tha*, they told me, to emphasize the justness of the law. The underlying sentiment among the poor as well as among the precarious classes was that the law had protected the public character of a place of worship by preventing the trustees from appropriating the public domain for their own private ends.

Side by side, my interlocutors among the labouring poor contrasted this specific instance of the consonance of the law and the principle of justice with other instances where this had *not* been so. A number of impoverished Kevat peasants cautioned me against uncritically praising the law (as I was wont to) by pointing out to the experience of the Musahars in the neighbouring ward. The 100-odd Musahars of this neighbouring ward faced eviction from their homes because the Village Education Committee (VEC) claimed that they were illegally residing on the property of the local secondary school. Their settlement was threatened by the VEC members who pressed the Bihar Public Land Encroachment Act, 1956 to evict them (Roy, 2013). My interlocutors were also critical of the legal stipulation that made it mandatory for sharecroppers to furnish paper receipts to prove their tenancy. I met some individuals from among the 30-odd Santhal families in Sargana Ward 4 who had been sharecroppers for a Kayasth farmer for over two decades. Under the Bihar Tenancy (Amendment) Act 1955, they would be registered as sharecroppers (making it difficult for their landlord to wilfully evict them) only if they could furnish rent receipts indicating that they had tilled the land and paid rents for 12 consecutive years. However, their Kayasth landlord refused to provide any rent receipts at all, making it impossible for them to prove the veracity of their claims of having tilled the land in the first place (Roy, 2014b).

Such experiences contributed to my Kevat interlocutors' wariness vis-à-vis the law even though they themselves claimed never to have violated it. In both the instances cited above involving people other than themselves, they viewed the law as being antithetical to the principles of justice. Although the directive of the Bihar State Religious Trust Board somewhat tempered this view, it could not completely replace their suspicion. An ambivalence toward 'the law' among Sargana's labouring classes was discernible. Although favourable to them in this instance, they noted the other instances when this was not so. Rather than embracing the law, they evaluated the efficacy of the law in relation to the contingent manner in which it might further the realization of their ideas of justice.

Popular protest

For the labouring poor, the normative space of the *pablik* was one of social equality, where nobody was discriminated against. My interlocutors pointed to the ways in which community resources were concentrated with a handful of families while large numbers of the population were left landless. Despite these material inequalities, Sargana's poor demanded to construct a public sphere where they would be treated with respect and dignity by others as social equals, a space where they expected civil behaviour from others, irrespective of property and privilege. Such meanings of the public were forged on the anvil of social struggles in the village, against land concentration as well as caste discrimination. Musahar landless labouers and Kevat peasants frequently referred to their historical contests with the entrenched classes over the redistribution of ceiling-surplus land. Supported by the CPI (M/L–L), the locality's landless populations had from time to time occupied (*jabran dakhal kar diya*) ceiling-surplus properties of the erstwhile *zamindars* and had redistributed properties among themselves. Vinay Mandal himself had been a card-carrying member of the party when he was younger, and his eyes sparkled when he recalled the names of the villages and the landlords whose properties he and his comrades from the CPI(M/L-L) had occupied. It was here that he met and got to know Domi Rishi. He was not alone among my interlocutors in speaking warmly of the friendships that were forged among cadres of the CPI(M/L-L) and the deep solidarities that they developed with other activists.

Cameraderie was strengthened through collaborations against caste discrimination. When members of the gram panchayat's Musahar community had begun to commemorate the valour of their mythic heroes Dina and Bhadri, their efforts were resisted by the entrenched classes.[21] Members of these classes complained that the festivities were a nuisance. However, the organizers of the festivities persisted. They were supported by a cultural organization whose members called it the Musahar Seva Sangh (MSS). Under the aegis of this body, the locality's Musahars claimed the *pablik* to be as much theirs as belonging to anybody else. MSS functionaries told me of the representations they made to Janata Dal-affiliated Yadav politicians in the locality, who promised to rein in the police so that they would not act on behalf of the entrenched classes: these politicians kept their promise. During my interviews with them, MSS functionaries recalled the sympathy they received from members of other communities. A number of Kevat peasants, including Shyamdev Mandal, had joined local Santhals and Yadavs when they supported the Musahars labourers' representations to Janata Dal politicians. Common memories of these joint representations added to the friendships among members of the locality's precarious classes and the labouring poor.

Further interviews and group discussions with Sargana's precarious and labouring classes introduced me to the popularity enjoyed by the sixteenth century saint Kabir among them. Historians suggest that Kabir lived during the sixteenth century as an itinerant preacher around the region that today comprises the eastern part of Uttar Pradesh and Bihar. He is thought to have been born to a Muslim weaver family. In popular culture, Kabir is lauded as a social radical. His teachings have been preserved by his followers in the form of couplets called *bijaks* and *ramainis*. The families following Kabir's teachings described themselves as Kabirpanthis, or members of devotional sects who follow the teachings of Kabir. I was told about 20 familes, from among the Yadavs, Kevats and Musahars, who were Kabirpanthis. Among the Kabirpanthis with whom I was introduced were Maturi Rishi's father and Akhilesh Mandal's elder brother. Maturi Rishi's father, like him, was a landless labourer, while Akhilesh Mandal's brother owned nearly a *bigha* of land, and hired out his labour to wealthier farmers and rich peasants as often as he could. As Kabirpanthis, they both wore a thread with a bead of basil (*tulsi*) wood and abstained from meat and alcohol to distinguish themselves from others.

Over several conversations with both gentlemen, I asked them the reason for their adherence to the Kabirpanth. Maturi Rishi's father said they were members because they believed in the sect's egalitarian principles and practices. Anyone who was familiar with Kabir's teachings can become priests and officiate over ceremonies. Nobody was regarded as 'high' or 'low': the absence of a vocabulary of hierarchy was particularly appealing. Although caste endogamy was prevalent (and the vocabulary of caste not entirely eschewed), notions of purity and pollution were absent. Another point of attraction for my interlocutors was that rituals attending to major life events, such as marriages, births and deaths, were simple and, therefore, less costly. For example, no dowries were expected to be given during marriages. Similarly, Kabirpanthis buried their dead, reducing the need for firewood. Such practices were stigmatized by the privileged castes, but they made up a code of practice for Kabirpanthis.

'95 per cent against 5 per cent'

A recurring leitmotif among the labouring classes when specifying the meanings of the *pablik* was the opposition between the labouring many against the previleged few. Shyamdev Mandal explicated this oppositional relationship between the 95 per cent against the 5 per cent as a *ladaai* between the dominant castes (*dabang jatis*) and the labouring class (*majdoor varg*). Like the erstwhile Mukhya whose perspectives I introduced earlier in this chapter, Shyamdev Mandal and Vinay Mandal pointed to the conflict between *Backwards* and *Forwards*. Nevertheless, they took care to remind me that there were some *Backwards* in the 'Forward camp' (in English) and some *Forwards* in the 'Backward camp'. Some Yadav politicians had supported the trustees: the foremost Yadav politician in the locality was sympathetic to the trustees' position. Mandal also suggested that members of the Dom community supported the Rajput trustees. On the other hand, the Brahman and Bhumihar cadres of the CPI (M/L–L) also supported them against the trustees. Shyamdev Mandal did not lose any opportunity to remind me that the lawyers who were fighting their case so effectively were *Forwards*! One was Bhumihar and the other was Ashraf Muslim. Nonetheless, the notion of a schism in society between the *Forwards* and the *Backwards* was a recurring feature of the political contestations in Sargana. In some usages, such as that of the ex-Mukhya, the schism was expressed in descriptive terms, as in a contest between two caste clusters. For others, such as Shyamdev Mandal, such the conflict between the *Forwards* and the *Backwards* reflected a conflict between the exploiters and the exploited.[22]

The accounts offered by Shyamdev Mandal, Domi Rishi, and others among the labouring poor suggest that the *Forward-Backward* schism reflect the cleavage within the *pablik*, with the precarious and labouring *Backward* majority being simultaneously exploited and marginalized by a privileged *Forward* minority. The entrenched classes justified their domination brazenly on the grounds of their communal supremacy. To challenge these notions of communal supremacy, the protagonists for democratizing the management of the temple insisted on constituting the Chandithan Management Committee to better reflect the communal character of the village. They assigned quotas for each community in the management committee, reminiscent of the measures for protective discrimination instituted by the Indian state. However, three important departures from the legislative procedures instituted by the Indian state were notable. One, the protagonists proposed a variant of proportional representation for selection of members. Two, they advocated deliberation rather than a secret ballot as a means of selecting members. Three, members were tasked to be delegates of their voters rather than their trustees. Let us examine these departures in slightly more detail.

The most interesting departure pertained to the assignment of communal quotas in relation to the collective deprivation (rather than absolute numbers) faced by a community. They advocated the principle that the greater the collective deprivation suffered by members of a community, the higher their share of the quota in the committee. In relating the communal quotas inversely to collective deprivations, Shyamdev Mandal, Domi Rishi and their companions relied on their own impressions rather than on any survey data. The assignment of quotas was admittedly arbitrary. Shyamdev Mandal was mindful of the arbitrariness of their decision, but suggested to me its greater compatibility with the demands of justice. They reasoned that Dalits possessed the least economic resources, inhabited the most squalid part of the village, and had faced considerable historical oppression. Therefore, their share in the committee *ought to be* the highest. Following this principle, Shyamdev Mandal in consultation with Domi Rishi, Vinay Mandal and a few other elderly men of different communities assigned 10 out of 20 (or half) positions on the newly-formed committee to the Dalit communities who comprised nearly one-third of the voters in the gram panchayat. The Kevats, the community to which Shyamdev Mandal himself belonged, were assigned six seats (30 per cent), despite comprising over 40 per cent of the total voters in the gram panchayat. The Santhals and the Yadavs were assigned two seats each. The entrenched classes decried these quotas as representing a 'partitionist' mentality. Such a mentality, they believed, stemmed from the supposedly 'backward brains' of the labouring classes.[23] The Rajputs and Kayasths, each of whom were allocated one seat, scorned the proposals. Their opposition contrasted with the support to the proposals by the overwhelming majority of the labouring poor.

The second departure from the legislative model of communal quotas related to the procedure of delegate selection. Delegates were nominated through deliberations among members of their communities, rather than through secret ballots. Nominating delegates through deliberations enabled community members to publicly exchange reasons for their choices. This process also reduced suspicions among the electors. The deliberations were far from consensual, and revealed deep disagreements between community members. But the reasons for disagreements were publicly known, thereby increasing the possibility of agreement. Interestingly, through their deliberations, members of Sargana's different communities accepted the possibility that members of other communities might be more appropriate delegates. This was particularly so among members of the panchayat's five Dalit communities. Deliberations within the different Dalit communities led members to agree upon the names of as many as nine delegates who were of the Musahar community. Recalling the deliberations within his Dhobhi community, Hridaynath Baitha, a school teacher at the Sargana High School, told me that discussants broadly agreed to the names of Dalit delegates to the Committee. The school teacher told me that the names they recommended were well-known activists of the Musahar community whose commitment to democratizing the management of the temple was exemplary. No member of his community could claim such commitment, he added. Moreover, the Musahars were worse-off than members of other Dalit communities were. Therefore, consistent with the demands for social justice, they *ought* to be given a chance to steer the committee.

Members of the Dhobhi, Dusadh and Chamar communities appeared to have unanimously supported the overwhelming Musahar representation on the management committee. Such bonhomie, however, did not extend to the Dom community, of whom the other members of the labouring classes were suspicious. The 10-odd Dom families living in the panchayat were artisans and/or pig-herders, and therefore did not share the same contradictions with labour-hiring farmers and peasants that agricultural labourers did. In turn, members of the Dom community were suspicious of the growing assertion of the Musahars. Most members of the labouring classes perceived the Doms to be lackeys of the Rajput landlords. The few Doms who had utilized affirmative action policies to obtain public sector employment were viewed as informers for the Rajput families. After all, these families had been the Doms' benefactors in a previous generation. Shyamdev Mandal scoffed at the possibility of the Doms taking an independent stand against the trustees in the event of a confrontation.

A third departure from the Indian legislative model was that delegates were responsible for soliciting the opinions of their constituencies and to then discuss them with others in the committee. The motivation for this norm, according to Shyamdev Mandal, was to ensure that committee members represented the views of the people who nominated them, rather than advanced their own views. Such a 'delegative' logic to decision making contrasts sharply with the 'trusteeship' logic with which India's representative democracy is imbued. As delegates, committee members were enjoined to consult with the people who selected them. They were not trustees who could determine the best interests of the people who nominated them. Rather, they were expected to take these constituencies into confidence. Shyamdev Mandal and his associates developed such community-specific strategies of deliberative delegate selection with the intention of democratizing the management of the temple's resources and to put them to public use in an effective and transparent manner. Wary as they were of the temple trustees' potential to interfere in the management of the affairs of the temple, these gentlemen were anxious to ensure that committee members best represented the views of the labouring classes whose deliberations nominated them to the committee rather than that they were reduced to being stooges of the trustees.

III

Imagination as politics

The labouring classes' political practices expressed their collective imagination of a social existence they hoped to inhabit in the near future. Ernesto Laclau (1990) suggests that a collective imaginary acts as a horizon on which a multiplicity of often mutually conflicting demands can be advanced. Drawing on his suggestion, Aletta Norval (2007; 2012) argues that horizons of imagination open up alternative ways of conceiving the political community. Charles Taylor's succinct formulation, the social imaginary refers to 'the ways people imagine their social existence, how they fit together with others, how things go on between them and their fellows, the expectations that are normally met, and the deeper normative notions and images that underlie these expectations' (Taylor, 2004, 23). Imaginations provide a window not so much to examine a set of abstract ideas but rather the complex of understandings that helps to make sense of the practices in a given society. In his own words, 'if the understanding makes the practice possible, it is also true that it is the practice that largely carries the understanding' (Taylor, 2004, 25).

A social imaginary involves the combination of how things are as well as how they ought to be. By drawing on Benedict Anderson's (1991) work on the imaginations that imbue nation-building processes, Taylor's insights urge scholars to take seriously the mutually-reinforcing complex of understandings and practices, the practices through which people make meanings of their world and the meanings that inform people's practices. Furthermore, Taylor deploys the category to explain the ways in which certain mutually reinforcing complex of understandings and practices emerged under specific historic conditions, rather than assuming this complex to be immutable. Although scholars distinguish between imagination, imaginary and imaginal, the analytic category of 'social imaginary' is instructive to understand the ensemble of meanings and practices that animate poor people's claims in Sargana.

Are such imaginations political? In expressing eglitarian imaginations, the labouring classes advance a social perspective. To support their claims, they invoke their putative status as 'children' of the deity whose temple they defend. As the deity's 'children', the poor demand that the resources accruing to the temple as well as the responsibilities for managing it be shared. This entails three normative claims. One claim is that the temple's resources be used not only for the welfare of the devotees in particular (a guest house, free food during their stay, arrangements for recreation), but also for the general public (a hospital). A second, related, claim is that the labouring classes be responsible for managing the temple's resources. The term they use in referring to their responsibility is *seva*, a term that evokes images of selfless service. Such responsibility would allow them to perform *seva* for their 'mother' as well as toward each other. The third claim, stemming from the first two, is that they fulfil their mutual obligations to one another. This means helping one another during times of dearth; contributing to festivities and commemorations observed by the members of different communities; supporting one another against depredations by members of the entrenched classes; and providing information about opportunities for work elsewhere. A core assumption of these shared normative claims is the idea that all people are equal. In advancing such an assumption, Sargana's poor reiterate longstanding claims against hierarchical principles that structured their social organization. They and the locality's precarious classes refuse to share the hierarchical presumptions steadfastly held by the entrenched classes. Their refusal lends them a deeply political content.

The labouring classes' commemorations of the heroics of the brothers Dina and Bhadri provide a good example of their social perspective. Even as they recognize the Musahar provenance of Dina and Bhadri, labouring classes of the Kevat, Yadav and Santhal communities claim the brothers as beacons of hope for the labouring poor everywhere. They insist that the Dina–Bhadri commemorations are not exclusively Musahar events, much as the privileged castes seek to characterize them as such. Kevats, Yadavs, and Santhals contribute logistically as well as financially to the celebrations. My interlocutors of the labouring classes of these communities are unequivocal in their admiration of Dina and Bhadri. Although they do not necessarily endorse the divinity of the brothers, as some Musahars do, they concur that the legends of the two brothers inspire them to contest the indignities they often face. Yadav men remind me about the part of the legend, which suggests that the memorial to the brothers is built by cow-herders, a reference to an occupational group associated with their own community. Musahar men and women acknowledge this facet of the legend. Indeed, they happily propagate it as evidence of the universal nature of the Dina–Bhadri legend. Members of both communities view the commemorations as one of shared solidarity.

Further evidence of the social perspective advanced by the poor through their egalitarian imaginations emanate from their frequent invocations of the popular saint Kabir. Sargana's labouring poor demonstrate particular interest in his messages of social equality. Scholars have traditionally interpreted Kabir's teachings as of continuity within 'Indic' tradition. Hazariprasad Dwivedi (1964) refers to Kabir's advent as a response to the challenge posed by Islam in the fifteenth century north India. Recent scholarship refutes this proposition, to argue that Kabir's teachings interrogated prevalent practices and prejudices (Lorenzen, 1987) within the Indic tradition. His messages represented a social revolt against caste oppression (Gokhale-Turner, 1981) and therefore a rupture from hierarchical traditions (Hawley, 2005). They were among the earliest expressions of 'autochtonous radicalism' in India (Khare, 1984). Gail Omvedt (2008) defends the view that Kabir and other radical Bhakti saints represented an egalitarian interruption of the hierarchic leitmotif of Indic tradition, rather than continuity within it.

To be sure, ambivalences abound in the connections made by adherents of Kabir and Dina–Bhadri with the Chandithan. Kabirpanthis are sceptical about the worship of idols inevitable in a temple, but symphathize with and support the claims of the activists challenging the trustees. The Musahars' affection for the valour of Dina and Bhadri makes them doubt Chandi's putative efficacy as a supreme deity, which the epithet of 'Divine Mother' (*Devi Ma*) used by her worshippers conveys. But they identify with Mandal's cause. Mandal and his Kevat neighbours frequently invoke Kabir's egalitarian teachings to highlight the injustice perpetrated by the entrenched classes against the *pablik*. Kunjra Muslims remind their interlocutors of Kabir's upbringing in a Muslim family. They and labouring classes of other communities referred to Dina and Bhadri as 'poor people's heroes' rather than as 'Musahar heroes'. During the three Dina–Bhadri commemorations which I attended, I was struck by the number of attendees from communities other than the Musahar. While attendees do not worship the two brothers in the manner that some members of the Musahar community do, the respect they harbour for the brothers is evident. I frequently heard people exchange comments with one another such as 'The brothers are heroes' and 'We need such brave people today to fight oppression'.

While the entrenched classes insist on enforcing their hierarchical views of society, the precarious classes and the labouring poor advance egalitarian perspectives of the political community. Such insistence brings them into conflict with the social perspectives of the precarious classes and the labouring poor. On the one hand, the labouring classes emphasize their affective relationships with the divinities they worship. They are proud of their traditions of worship as well as of protest. On the other hand, they do want to eliminate the social hierarchies embedded in their traditions. Although they keenly highlight their mutual obligations to one another, they do not want to sustain the hierarchical relationships of the past. 'The old days are gone,' is a frequent refrain. Despite being subjected to exploitative labour relations, Sargana's poor assert themselves as social equals. My interlocutors' continuing to sit on their *machan* when the Rajputs walk past them is an act underpinned by such egalitarian imaginations.

Beyond tradition and modernity: Civil society, political society, moral society?

The multifaceted imaginations of Sargana's labouring poor and precarious classes intimate a complex of affective relationships and juridical processes through which they advance their notions of the *pablik*. They take recourse to the legal instruments while also drawing on the thought of radical saints such as Kabir. Their popular protests are inspired by the legends of Dina and Bhadri and scaffolded by connections made in the the CPI(M/L-L). They assert their social equality vi-a-vis the locality's entrenched classes, while at the same time portray themselves as responsible for protecting their Divine Mother. They initiate contacts with politicians and political mediators while also constituting a temple management committee to oversee the administration of the temple. One way to interpret these negotiations might be to think about them as anticipating poor people's aspirations to become members of civil society. Another way to make sense of these negotiations is to suggest that the poor seek to occupy spaces in political society. A third approach to these negotiations is to interpret them through the rubric of moral society. In this section, I will carefully review these alternative approaches of interpreting the political practices discussed in the previous sections.

Let us start with the formulation of civil society. Charles Taylor (1990) explains the dual meaning of the term. On the one hand, civil society indicates a self-regulating economy, a public space organized autonomous of the state and a notion of civilization that encompasses the virtues of peaceful production, accumulation of private property, the development of the arts and sciences, and polished mores that eschew warrior ethics and country lifestyles as rustic. On the other hand, civil society refers to a society intimately engaged with political structures, despite being autonomous from it. But Taylor's concerns are limited to a specific region, leading Partha Chatterjee (1990) to suggest that civil society is a provincial concept whose application should properly be restricted to western Europe and its settler regions. Chatterjee (1998, 234) goes on to define civil society as

> Those characteristic institutions of modern associational life originating in Western societies that are based on equality, autonomy, freedom of entry and exit, contract [and] deliberative procedures of decision making.

In the classic formulation, individuals 'enter' this space by virtue of their 'status' as tax-paying, property-owning citizens, autonomous of one's class position or ascribed identities. Association is voluntary. In more contemporary formulations (Kaldor, 2003), the language of rights, especially economic, social, and cultural rights has permeated the space of civil society, rendering many of the older 'disqualifications' of property and community redundant: The vocabulary of human rights, for example, provides an important justification for the inclusion of all members of a political community, irrespective of their being tax-payers, property-owners or consumers, into the domain of civil society. Nevertheless, those included into the domain of civil society are admitted as individual members of society shorn of their communal identities.

Readers will recognize that both Taylor and Chatterjee draw on the distinction introduced by Ferdinand Tönnies (1957) between *gemeinschaft* and *gesselschaft*, to refer to two contrasting principles of social organization. Where *gemeinschaft* indicates the affective forms of social relationships permeated by kinship ties and ascribed identities, *gesselschaft* refers to voluntaristic social relations conducted without reference to such ties and identities. Much of the prevalent scholarship identifies civil society as belonging to and stemming from the socialities inherent in *gesselschaft*.

In their spirited criticism of Partha Chatterjee's formulation of political society, Stuart Corbridge et al (2013) argue that poor people do indeed engage in civil society. They emphasize the need for analysts to move beyond strict European definitions of civil society in thinking about the political practices of the poor. The authors aver that India's labouring classes increasingly imagine themselves as citizens quite capable of critiquing the state. Much of poor people's mobilization, they go on to suggest, references the vocabulary of rights. A consideration of the ethnographic material presented earlier suggests however, that the political imaginations of Saragana's poor cannot be subsumed under the promises offered by ideas of civil society. This is for three reasons. One, the locality's labouring classes assert their claims as *collective* members of society. In making these claims they make very few references to their juridical identities as citizens or individuals. Two, they make a claim to egalitarian *social* relationships, which is not restricted to the idea of solipsistic selves. Three, the *communitarian* logics of representative politics they espouse stands in contrast with what Liberal theorists would permit to the individualistic constituents of civil society.

The vocabulary of juridical rights (*adhikar/haq* in Hindi/Urdu) is only warily invoked by those agitating against the trustees' control over the management of the temple. Although the activists institute legal proceedings against the trustees for breaching the provisions of the Hindu Religious Trust Act, they justifiably approach the law with caution, as their livelihoods and security have been undermined by its application many times in the past. They are wary of using the law because more often than not, the rule of law is brought into effect against them by members of the entrenched classes. It would not be out of place to suggest, as Comaroff (2006) notes in the African context, that they have been subjected to 'lawfare', whereby the rule of law is deployed as a tool of oppression. Moreover, that entrenched classes violate the law is one part of the problem. A matter of graver concern is that they appropriate the *pablik* space. Having appropriated this space, the entrenched classes do not treat them as members of society. For Sargana's labourers and poor peasants, then, the trustees' anti-social (*asamajik*) behaviour is much more a matter of concern than their legal intransigence.

The negotiations among Sargana's labouring poor reflect their assertion of social equality (*samaj mein barabari*). Their claims for social equality exceed the conception of civil society anchored in the Liberal sanctity of individual rights, privacy, and private property. One of my landless interlocutors lamented that she could not use the shortest route from her residence to the Chandithan because she was not permitted to walk across the farmers' agricultural properties that lay in between. For her, that she should have unencumbered access to her Divine Mother is more important than the sanctity of private property, calling into question a fundamental tenet on which the notion of civil society is based. Her holding this perspective not only pits her and other members of the labouring classes against the entrenched classes, but also annoys the precarious classes who have only recently acquired property and whose hold over these properties is tenuous at best. Peasants such as Amaresh Yadav and retailers such as Dharmesh Srivastav balk at her suggestions that private properties be thrown open to public access. But she holds steadfast to her views nonetheless.

Another perspective that members of the Musahar community commonly express is their opposition to caste discrimination by the entrenched and precarious classes inside the precincts of their homes. Culinary segregation continues to be commonly practiced. Musahar labourers recount the numerous instances of discrimination they face within the homes of their employers when they are served food on different plates to their co-workers. They express their outrage even as there is little they can do in order to bring the culprits to book. The claims to social equality inhered in such accounts impinges on the privacy of their employers, thereby exceeding the claims that might be admissible under the concept of civil society.

A third area of dissonance between the account presented in this chapter and Liberal notions of civil society pertains to the logic of representation. The temple management committee constituted by the precarious and the labouring classes might be construed as emblematic of *gesselschaft*-based civil society, an association of individuals autonomous of the state and market and dedicated to a public purpose. However, members of the committee are not expected to act autonomously of their communities. Rather, the anticipation is that they will be embedded in their communities. They are called upon to be communal delegates, akin to *gemeinschft*-type social organization. Moreover, the activists who conceptualize the rules of membership in the committee formulate an informal scheme of communal quotas. Now, affirmative action for members of disadvantaged communities is not by itself inconsistent with Liberal thought, after the Rawlsian innovation inhered in the 'difference principle'.[24] What is significant about the communal quotas by the activists is the principle of delegate selection on the management committee, which is based on communal quotas. Their communal character makes it difficult for us to subsume them under the rubric of civil society.

The wave of democratization since the 1980s has led many scholars to reflect positively on the role of civil society as a bulwark against despotism (Cohen and Arato, 1992), as a means of healing or preventing strife (Alexander 2006; Ferguson, 2006 and Varshney, 2001) and as a means of economic development (Putnam *et al.*, 1993). Against such general optimism, sceptics have sought to paint a more sobering portrait. Writing about Africa, for instance, Bayart (1993) avers that civil society simply does not exist on the continent. He attributes its absence to people's inability and unwillingness to develop *gesselschaft* relationships. Endorsing the view that civil society is absent in Africa, but disagreeing with Bayart's analysis, Mamdani (1996) argues that the colonial policy of ruling through 'native' chiefs and 'customary' law prevented Africans from developing social relationships of the *gesselschaft* type. Recent critics of both views have sought to free conceptions of civil society from the constraints of *gesselschaft*-centred conceptualization, thereby including within its ambit Christian missions (Ferguson, 2006), Islamic societies (Turner, 2009) and kinship networks (Mains, 2007). Corbridge *et al* (2013) are supportive of such conceptual moves.

Colonial rule in British India was less indirect than in Africa, with colonial institutions encouraging elite Indians to absorb Liberal traditions of civil consciousness (Srivastava, 1998). The fraction of mostly wealthy Savarna Indians who did imbibe these traditions went on to establish themselves as a colonial middle class (Joshi, 2001) and blended Liberal traditions with Brahamnical values as they fashioned civic associations such as schools, libraries and organizations dedicated to social service in their own image (Watt, 2005). Such trajectories lead Partha Chatterjee (2004) to suggest that elite Indians appropriated civil society as a domain through which they could consolidate their social and cultural resources. Civil society did emerge in India, but as a bastion of the propertied classes. The labouring classes, by contrast, sought politicians and other actors in political society for support. To be sure, they did not look up to traditional authorities or customary law for succour. Rather, the associations through which different groups of poor people came together were shaped by governmental policies framed for specific sections of the population, such as SCs or OBCs, farmers and refugees.

People requesting governments for help do so neither on the basis of abstract rights nor on the basis of traditional authorities. Rather, they deploy politicized idioms of caste, religion and kinship. Occupants of political society, Chatterjee (1998, 234) tells us,

> [m]ake their claims on government, and in turn, are governed, not within the framework of stable, constitutionally defined rights and laws, but rather through temporary, contextual and unstable arrangements arrived at through direct political negotiations.[27]

Casual observers might infer that the politics discussed in this chapter is a politics of political society. After all, the constitution of the temple management committee was a consequence of popular negotiations and consequent governmental interventions. Moreover, the committee was constituted explicitly on the recognition that people's caste affiliations mattered. Poor people's politics thus appears predicated on the principle of differentiated membership in the political community. Each of these two aspects merits critical discussion in order to examine the extent to which poor people's negotiations discussed in this chapter may be analysed under the rubric of political society.

To take the first aspect, Sargana's labouring poor and precarious classes constitute the Chandithan management committee on the basis of a governmental directive. In this respect, that body is arguably not a voluntaristic association constituted by tax-paying, property-owning citizens. The state is intimately involved. People credit it with 'empowering' the population, in the Mukhya's words cited at the beginning of this chapter. The *Backward–Forward* cleavage that animates the activists' claims and the adherence to the vocabularies of caste may also be seen as evidence of the continued salience of the state's bureaucratized social identities. Even the idea of the *pablik*, that so excites Sargana's labouring and precarious classes, is arguably shaped by a governmental directive. Notwithstanding such intimate connections between governmental interventions and popular claims, it is important not to lose sight of the egalitarian imaginations that spur the political practices of Sargana's poor. Central to these imaginations is the repudiation of the hierarchical social relations sought to be preserved by the entrenched classes. The affective relationships that the locality's poor and precarious classes seek to establish are predicated on social equality, whereby the supremacist presumptions of the entrenched classes are negated. Invitations to governmental interventions are an important part of this story, but we would do well to remember that they are valued because they are perceived as an instrument of achieving egalitarian relationships in society: the perspective of political society is only of partial relevance to understand the political practices of Sargana's poor.

Second, the institution of communal quotas and their attendant mechanisms of decision making highlights communal differences among the population. Membership in the committee is not unmarked, as proponents of *gesselschaft* socialities prefer. However, the vocabularies of conflict between the *Backwards* and the *Forwards*, which underpins the fact that many of the decisions taken by Harinandan Mandal and his associates is not intended to perpetuate the social and economic differences between the two communities. Rather, caste affiliations matter because the privileged castes use caste as a device for perpetuating exclusion and exploitation. Shyamdev Mandal and other activists use the term *Backwards* to refer to all those people who face collective deprivation in society. They contest the hierarchical meanings of the *pablik* space that the Rajput trustees seek to perpetuate. Indeed, the petition focussed on the need to safeguard public funds and to enhance public welfare. Although the emphasis on the *pablik* was grounded in affective relationships with one another and with different divinities, folk heroes and saints, a shared espousal of egalitarian imaginations was discernible. The importance of poor people's egalitarian imaginations in their conceptualization of the *pablik* cautions me against appropriating these political practices under the rubric of political society.

Recent scholarship critically engages with the concept of political society without reverting to rubric of civil society. Akio Tanabe (2007) proposes that the negotiations between the institutions of the contemporary state and rural people be seen as a 'post-postcolonial transformation' of local society. His is a commentary on the manner in which the institutional reformation of the Panchayati Raj Institutions (PRIs), in particular the promulgation of affirmative action for women and Dalits and Adivasis, necessitates the articulation of a new vision of the political community. A new vision of community, he tells us, is being formulated by people to facilitate egalitarian intercaste cooperation. His interlocutors in coastal Odisha recalibrate their practical-moral relationships with each other in the context of the reforms. To do so, they negotiate that which they think to be morally desirable in the changing political-economic context. Tanabe emphasizes the ways in which people concomitantly deploy modern representative logics as well as traditional ethics of sacrifice to forge what he calls a new 'moral society'. A formulation of a new moral society along these lines allows Tanabe's interlocutors to think about the manner in which egalitarian cooperation gradually replaces hierarchical domination.

Tanabe's formulation of a moral society is a potentially interesting way to analytically consider popular imaginations. Actors in moral society reflect upon what they believe to be the proper socio-political relationships in the community. Distinguishing his formulation of 'moral society' from E. P. Thompson's notion of 'moral economy', Tanabe notes that actors in moral society legitimize or criticize political-economic practices in a sphere wider than that of the subsistence economy, which Thompson had framed as the domain of the moral economy. The 'morality' of actors in moral society is not drawn from the inherited norms and shared values structured by the subsistence economy. Tanabe also takes care to distance the sphere of 'moral society' from that of political society as well as of civil society. Actors in moral society are not the voluntaristic agents conjured by modernization theorists of civil society: the idiom of social relationships exceeds the individualistic tropes that constitute associations in civil society. At the same time, actors in moral society are also not subjects of the calculative governmentalized rationalities assumed by postcolonial theorists of political society. The sphere of moral society is, in contradistinction from both these spheres, one of dialogue, a negotiation between cultural accretions and external influences and between traditional ethos and modern values.

Tanabe's perspective enriches the literature, but is not without its problems. His account of the manner in which the sacrificial ethic of caste is reinterpreted by his interlocutors in egalitarian rather than hierarchical ways resonates quite considerably with the perspective offered by Sargana's labouring poor. The vocabularies of duty and obligation in accordance with the share of each community to the total population permeate both accounts. However, Tanabe's account appears to privilege the institutional reformation wrought by the Panchayati Raj legislations to devolve power to elected local governments, with the proviso for protective discrimination for women and Dalits, as the source of the changes in society. Moreover, the rubric of 'post-postcolonial' transition lends a foundational status to a putative postcolonial transition, which I find difficult to accept for reasons I have outlined earlier in this chapter.

The second reason for the dissonance of my account with the category of the 'moral society' as an analytical category pertains to the privileged role of the dialogic and deliberative processes in this sphere. Given that the negotiations in the sphere of moral society occur between agents with differential access to economic, social, and political resources, the labouring classes do not always find deliberation to be helpful. A vital requirement of a dialogue is the presence of both parties willing to engage in negotiations on the basis of equality, trust, reciprocity, and mutual respect. However, the entrenched classes are unwilling to recognize the precarious and labouring classes as equals: they bear a supremacist attitude vis-à-vis the Musahars, Kevat, and Santhal communities and consider it beneath their dignity to engage in a civil discourse with them. They refuse to enter into a reasoned deliberation with the people they stigmatize as 'backward', 'untouchable' and 'primitive'. Given their attitudes, the labouring classes and their precarious class allies do not expect any settlement of the dispute through deliberations. However, the poor do not embark on a path of violent conflict whereby they seek to annihilate their enemies. Rather, they alternate between periodic infringements, public meetings, appeals for bureaucratic intervention, and legal action. The complex of these heterogeneous actions points to the importance among them of agonistic practices rather than either deliberative or revolutionary ones.

The third reason for my disagreement with the formulation of 'moral society' is the normative privileging in it of a harmonious life. Although Tanabe's account of the 'moral society' explicitly recognizes that 'critical self-reflection and contestatory negotiation surround what should be the proper socio-political relationships in the community' (Tanabe, 2007, 560), the account that is subsequently presented is one where harmonious living is normatively valued. In so privileging an account of harmonious life, what is missing from the formulation are the contentions that often accompany the quest for harmony. To be sure, the labouring classes certainly value living in harmony with their neighbours and co-villagers. But their notion of a harmonious existence is deeply imbued with egalitarian ideals, conflicting with the hierarchical presumptions which permeated the notion of harmonious living among the entrenched classes. They are unwilling to live in harmony if it means compromising their dignity and honour. Quotidian struggles over land, labour, and stigmatization inform their attitudes over the temple as well as other public places. Poor people are conscious of the fact that the entrenched classes who appropriate the temple's resources and management are the very same people who have captured the arable land in the locality, who disrespect and mistreat their labourers, and who scorn their religious beliefs and collective practices. Their aspiration to social justice pit the precarious and labouring classes explicitly in opposition to the entrenched classes in the name of their caste supremacy. The split induced by this opposition in Sargana's local society between the entrenched classes on the one hand, and the precarious and labouring classes on the other, reveals the antagonism in Sargana between the *Backwards* and the *Forwards*, the oppressed and the oppressors, the poor and the rich. My interlocutors allude to such antagonisms when they invoke the 5 per cent and 95 per cent as oppositional categories. Such an explicit expression of a split in Sargana's society adds to my skepticism of frameworks that emphasize the harmonious domain of the 'moral society'.

Agonistic imaginations

The imaginations discussed in this chapter exemplify neither an attachment to tradition nor an assimilation into modernity. How then do we understand such imaginations? The account presented in this chapter suggests that collaboration interwove with antagonism in the social perspectives advanced by Sargana's labouring classes. The imaginations underpinning their practices are imbued with references to a collective peoplehood which Sargana's poor share with the locality's precarious classes, but which pits them against the entrenched classes in the ward. The cleavage revealed by the oft-cited narrative of a conflict between the Forwards and the Backwards, and between the 5% and the 95% point to a simmering social conflict. Narratives of popular protests against the corrupt practices of the temple trustees are commonly expressed, and anchored in terms of protecting and defending the Divine Mother. Such narratives are entwined with invocations (albeit cautious) of the law that mandates the public accountability of the temple's resources and decrees that the temple is a public space. Sargana's poor draw on both perspectives when they struggle with the entrenched classes over the ways in which public space is constituted.

The people whose practices have been the subject of analysis in this chapter were not singularly challenging the privileges of the entrenched classes. Readers met them as supplicants for BPL cards in chapter 4. They were demanding employment under the aegis of the NREGA in chapter 5. In this chapter, we see them imagine a social world where the trustees of the local temple cease to appropriate its resources for private gain. The universal character of the legislation governing public spaces enables them to be assertive about their claims to social equality, much like Rahimpur's disputants to whom readers were introduced in the preceding chapter. A notion of collective subjectivity that binds together the locality's precarious classes with the poor is discernible. Ideas about a split between the *Backwards* and the *Forwards*, and the accompanying narrative of the 95 per cent versus the 5 per cent provides the intellectual material from which such collective subjectivites sprout. Tensions over wages and social discrimination notwithstanding, the precarious classes freely acknowledge the ideas of social equality incubated by the labouring poor. In turn, the poor remind their interlocutors about the timely support provided by the precarious classes during their struggles. Their joint participation in popular mobilization against the entrenched classes provides them with shared historical memories on which they both draw.

Poor people's imaginations of an egalitarian public space draw on the combination of juridical vocabularies as well as affective commitments to their Divine Mother. They signal the emergence of a collective peoplehood who are embroiled in conflict with their oppressors. In their imaginations, the public space is a space of social equality unencumbered by the sanctity accorded to individual liberty, private property and social discrimination. Governmental interventions are invited to defend the public. But the eventual objective is the creation of a public space where no one social actor is allowed to impose their specific perspective as that of the entire community. Such an objective implies that dialogic and deliberative processes are not privileged. and the possibilities of conflict not wished away.

The collective self-hood of Sargana's precarious classes and the labouring poor allude to an agonistic imagination of social life among poor people in Sargana. Such agonism stems from the ambivalent conflict that characterizes the relations between Sargana's different classes. For while people in Sargana openly invoke such notions as *ladaai* to refer to conflicts between the

Backwards and the *Forwards* and between the *dabang jati* and *majdoor varg*, the labouring poor do not envisage annihilating their opponents. Little from my ethnographic material suggests that Sargana's labouring classes harboured plans to liquidate their class enemies or kill their adversaries. Even as they spoke of an ongoing *ladaai* between themselves and their oppressors, an annihilation of the latter does not seem to have been on their agenda at all.

Sargana's labouring classes refer unequivocally to the simmering conflict in their locality between themselves and their oppressors: lexes of *anyay* and *atyachar* are interspersed with vocabularies of *ladaai*. Clearly, then, they are not extend their consent to their own oppression. Neither, however, do they insist on or hope for the liquidation of their oppressors. Their primary concern is the reconfiguration of the *pablik*, the public space, so that all actors are able to live as social equals. Even as they strive to contain the domination of the entrenched classes in the public space, they do not seek to altogether expel the latter from it. Thus, the people to whose perspectives we have been introduced exceed the binaries between consent and conflict. They draw on a complex repertoire of juridical and affective claims, some of which emphasise conflict while others highlight love and duty. This complex of apparently contradictory perspectives lends an agonistic content to the imaginations of Sargana's labouring classes.

People's imaginations of an alternative social world are a key feature of their negotiations with democracy. They appreciate the ways in which their oppressors seek to dominate the public space, and attempt to reclaim it as an egalitarian arena. Nevertheless, in doing so, they do not conspire a grandiose revolutionary overthrow of the social order. Despite the internal fragmentation of their imaginations, a notion of collective personhood is evident from the narratives offered by the labouring classes. Not only is this notion of collective personhood framed as one that is subjected to oppression and exploitation, but the perspective that they may intimate a new social world is also advanced. Such conceptualisations signal the agonistic character of their imaginations.

Conclusion

This chapter did four things. One, it recounted the ways in which the Indian state's policy to create public spaces accessible to all strengthens emerging solidarities between the labouring poor and the precarious classes. Two, the chapter documented the social imaginations of the labouring classes and outlined the key issues expressed by them in their negotiations with the entrenched classes. Three, it noted the mutual suspicions that fragmented the labouring classes. And finally, given the heterogeneities, the chapter theorized poor people's politics as agonistic negotiations to direct attention to the ambivalent conflict that marked the relations between the labouring classes and their oppressors.

The labouring poor do not want to singularly conserve tradition. Neither, however, do their imaginations point to an inexorable assimilation into symmetrical tropes of modernity. Sargana's people not only advance their claims over the management of the temple, but want to engage in democratic negotiations. Notwithstanding internal contradictions, suspicions and prejudices among themselves, the locality's poor and precarious classes incubate egalitarian ideals even as they affirm – rather than discard – their belief in the efficacy of divine entities and legendary heroes. Their accounts emphasize a break with the past, a break that indicates the 'old ways' are gone.

Ambivalent conflicts underpin the egalitarian imaginations of the labouring poor, rendering them an agonistic content. Elected politicians and democratic institutions are central to their imaginations for the support expected of them in containing the dominance of the entrenched classes, and ensuring that the 'olden days' characterized by hierarchical social relations do not return. The labouring poor and their allies from among the precarious classes defend the public sphere from encroachments by the entrenched classes. In advancing their claims, the labouring poor draw on diverse sorts of idioms, ranging from their putative status as the sons and daughters of the Divine Mother to the notion that *Backwards* would no longer tolerate the supremacist assumptions of the *Forwards*. Crucial to their endeavours are an ensemble of politicians and activists who not only sympathize with their claims by also channel these to relevant judicial and political authorities. These meanings shape and are shaped by political space. The ambivalent conflicts inhered in these meanings imbue them with an agonistic content.

Endnotes

1 See collection of essays in *Daedelus*, 2000, volume 129, no. 1, (Winter). Also see the debates in Sachsenmaier *et al.* (2002).

2 These values constituted one end of Parsons' famous (or notorious) pattern variables, a set of dichotomous variables on the basis of which societies could be classified as 'traditional' or 'modern'. The variables were: being affective vs. affective neutrality, diffusion vs. specificity, particularism vs. universalism, ascription vs. achievement, and collective-orientation vs. self-orientation. One set of these dichotomies represented traditional society and the other set represented modern society. Parsons' work (1951; 1960; and 1977) provided the basis for generations of scholars, who perceived democracy as necessarily flowering from the same soil that facilitated modernity. These include, but are not limited to, Lerner (1958), Rustow (1960), Shils (1961b), Lipset (1963), Weiner (1966), Eisensdadt (1966), Parsons (1971) and Elias (1978).

3 Omvedt is one of several scholars to subscribe to this perspective of modernity. For South Asia, see Subrahmanyam (2001), Washbrook, (2009) and O'Hanlon (2014). For the African continent, see Rodney (1970), Pels (1998), Sheriff (1987) and Shaw (2003). For the Caribbean, see Mintz (1985). For the Balkan provinces of the Ottoman Empire, see Allcock (2000). For Mongolia, see Bulag (2004). Some historians, notably Blaut (1993) have advocated the heuristic of 'early modern' instead of 'medieval' or 'late pre-colonial' to study the endogenous blossoming of modernity in different parts of the world.

4 A wide range of scholarship promotes this perspective. See, for example, Weiner (2002), Rudolph and Rudolph (1987), Frankel (1989), Khilnani (1997), Guha (2007) and Mehta (2003).

5 See, for instance, the works of Cohn (1987) and Dirks (2001).

6 The scholarship of Kanchan Chandra (2002) comes to mind. From the African context, one can think of the arguments advanced by JF Bayart (1993) and Chabal and Daloz (1999).

7 This is anticipated, for instance, in the scholarship of Chatterjee (1993), Mamdani (1996) and Philpott (2000).

8 Such entrenchment of identities provides a prime example of what postcolonial theorists call the 'postcolonial predicament'. At the heart of this predicament is the perspective that 'a theory of difference that was deeply interwoven with the practices of colonial control lives on in the absence of foreign rule' (Breckenbridge and van der Veer, 1993, 11).

9 These views are elaborated in Bayly (2001), Cooper (2002) and Pollock (2001).

10 For succinct statements of the liberal view on caste, see Beteille (1999) and Gupta (2005).

11 Literally, the 'place of Chandi'. The usage of this term to describe the temple was

ubiquitous among my interlocutors from the landless labourers, and poor and middle peasants. My interlocutors from among the literate rich peasants, farmers and landlords referred to the temple as Chandisthan, reflecting their use of Sanskritized Hindi.

12 Chandapuri had famously suggested that India's independence was incomplete as long as the so-called upper castes cornered administrative and material resources (Frankel, 1989). Lohia influenced the political strategy of the fledgling Socialist party in the State by endorsing the demand for protective discrimination for the Shudra communities in proportion of their population. His slogan '*samajwadiyon ne bandhi gaanth, pichhada pawey sau mein saath*' to demand 60 per cent quota in the elite civil services for members of castes designated as OBCs was nothing short of incendiary to the privileged castes. The Mukhya cited both politicians during our conversations.

13 For example, see the works of Frankel (1989), Hauser (1993), Corbridge *et al.* (2005), Robins (2009), Roy (2013) and Witsoe (2014).

14 This perspective is elaborated in Blair (1980), Jannuzi (1974), Kunnath (2012), Mendelsohn and Vicziany (1998) and Prasad (1975).

15 My endeavours were helped by the fact that the more articulate members of the community evaluated me as being sympathetic despite my Savarna Kayasth identity to their perspective that the temple in question was a public space rather than the private property of the Rajput trustees who were appropriating it as such.

16 Interview, Domi Rishi, 10 April 2010, Sargana Ward 1 Musahar Tola (West) *machan*.

17 Hanging out, 9 April 2010, Sargana Ward 5 (School Tola) *machan*.

18 Hanging out, 5 April 2010, Sargana Ward 6, *machan* under the banyan tree, outside the Chandithan.

19 Common property in administrative parlance is referred to as *gairmajarua aam* land and is usually demarcated for public purpose by the gram panchayat. *Gairmajarua aam* properties are to be distinguished from *gairmajarua khas* lands, which refer to properties expropriated from the estate-holders and are allocated to beneficiaries of land reforms.

20 This is a question to which Kaviraj (2011) directs some attention in his article 'Filth and the Public Sphere'.

21 I have discussed these events in detail elsewhere (Roy, 2015; Roy, 2016).

22 Indeed, some observers go a step further by directing attention to the cultural imperialism perpetrated by the *Forwards* over the *Backwards*. Author and politician Prem Kumar Mani, who began his political career with the CPI (ML/L) and then went on to be renowned (or reviled, depending on the commentator) as a Janata Dal intellectual, sums up this perspective in his exposition of the Hindu myth pertaining to Durga. Durga is widely worshipped as a goddess. Her mythical battle against the buffalo-demon Mahishasura is recalled each year for about a fortnight during the autumn. Mahishasur's subjugation in the myth is reinscribed in the minds of worshippers through vivid iconography, with Durga usually depicted as standing tall

and driving her spear through her adversary's heart. In most mythical narrations of the tale, Durga is portrayed as being created by the gods to destroy the evil unleashed on earth by the ravaging demon. Inverting this traditional script, Mani portrays Mahishasura as the noble chieftain of buffalo herders, suggesting his origins in the Yadav community. He then proceeds to offer a sketch of Durga not as a goddess but as a warrior fighting on behalf of the Forward Savarnas to vanquish, and eventually kill, the chieftain of the Backwards. Mani argues that rather than being a goddess, Durga is a perpetrator of a cultural imperialism of the Savarna communities against the Shudra and Dalit communities. He concludes by provoking readers to reconsider their worship of Durga, who was responsible for the decimation of such vast numbers of Dalits and Shudras in the first place. Although Mani draws uncritically on colonial categories of knowledge, the schism to which he refers resonates with the Forward–Backward conflicts, which worried my interlocutors in Sargana so much.

The original piece was written in Hindi under the title 'Kiski Puja Kar Rahe Hain Bahujan' (Who are the Bahujans, a collective term that refers to both Dalits and Shudras) for a magazine called Yadav Shakti in 2011. It was subsequently republished in the bilingual journal Forward Press. I was unable to access back issues of the journal, but found several references to the article in news items (for example, 'Fight for Mahishasura on JNU Campus', Telegraph, 1 November 2011). A cached copy of the article is available here: https://groups.google.com/forum/#!topic/dalit-movement-association-/j5o2P1DcZzo (last accessed, 1 July 2015).

23 This obnoxious term to refer to the social ideas of members of the Shudra and Dalit communities was repeated by my Kayasth and Rajput interlocutors too many times.

24 The Difference Principle permits a divergence from strict equality so long as the inequalities in question would make the least advantaged in society materially better off than they would be under strict equality (Rawls, 1993, 6).

25 Ironically, Chatterjee's formulation of political society paradoxically renders it devoid of any political content. The sole purpose of actors in political society appears to be to represent their claims to the government, to get those claims accepted as legitimate if only for themselves, and to seek exceptions to the law as may be appropriate to their interests. The conception of political society may perhaps more appropriately be rechristened 'governmental society', given the fact that governments narrowly, rather than politics more broadly, appears to be the focus of this conceptual device. Nevertheless, because the term is widely used, and derives from a well established corpus of literature, it would be appropriate to retain its use in Chatterjee's sense.

CONCLUSION

The Politics of the Poor

Agonistic Negotiations with Democracy

> For the poor the economic is the spiritual. You cannot make any
> other appeal to those starving millions. It will fall flat on them.
> But you take food to them and they will regard you as their God.
> They are incapable of any other thought.
>
> Mohandas Karamchand Gandhi, 1927

> Men (sic) make their own history, but they do not make it as they
> please; they do not make it under self-selected circumstances,
> but under circumstances existing already, given and transmitted
> from the past.
>
> Karl Marx, 1852

To say that 'democracy' is a hotly contested concept[1] is to parrot a cliché. Democracy realists (Przeworski, 1991) warn us of overloading the term with too many meanings. The proliferation of definitions of democracy with adjectives[2] and characteristics[3] of all sorts has led scholars to articulate legitimate anxieties about stretching the concept of democracy to such an extent as to render it analytically meaningless. Against minimalist and maximalist views, and advocating somewhat of a middle-range perspective, Terry Lyn Karl (1990) suggests that democracy be conceived of an institutional arrangement in which competitive elections are complemented by mechanisms to hold elected representatives accountable to the rule of law. Reiterating this view, Marc Plattner (1998) makes a case for emphasizing the compact between liberalism and democracy.

Chantal Mouffe disagrees. She directs attention to the fraught conceptual histories between liberalism and democracy to support her argument that there is in fact no necessary relation between the two (Mouffe, 2000). In similar vein, David Beetham suggests that democracy refers at once to 'control by citizens over their collective affairs, and equality between citizens in the exercise of that control' (Beetham, 1999, 3).[4] Likewise, Huber et al., (1997) suggest equal participation in public affairs as one of the characteristics of substantive democracy. The collapse of the so-called 'people's democracies' and the concomitant ascendance of Liberal democracy during the 1990s not only provided a favourable intellectual climate for the flourishing of liberal rights, but also made Liberal democracy susceptible to egalitarian claims (Schmitter, 1994). Based on these somewhat contradictory insights, we have a fragmentary conceptualization of democracy that include rather disparate characteristics: competitive elections, the guarantee of civil liberties and individual rights, protection of private property and establishment of the rule of law on the one hand, and equal participation of people in the affairs that matter to them on the other.

A further layer of complexity is added by Mouffe's (1996, 2000, 2007, 2009), contention that democracy refers to a political community wherein no one social agent is allowed to represent the totality of society. Drawing on the agonistic account of politics to which she subscribes, Mouffe sketches an agonistic view of democracy. In her view, a democratic political community is one wherein no single substantive idea of the common good prevails. It bears citing her in full:

> For democracy to exist, no social agent should be able to claim any mastery of the foundation of society. This signifies that the relation between the social agents becomes more democratic only insofar as they accept the particularity and the limitation of their claims; that is only insofar as they recognize their mutual relations as one from which power is ineradicable. The democratic society cannot be conceived any more as a society that would have realized the dream of a perfect harmony in social relations. Its democratic character can be given only by the fact that no limited social actor can attribute to herself the representation of the totality.
>
> (Mouffe, 1996, 247–48)

Because Mouffe insists that any account of democratic politics must take cognizance of power relations, she is suspicious of deliberative accounts of democracy that emphasize the desirability and possibility of disputing parties arriving at a reasoned consensus. Deliberative accounts underscore the discursive ways in which people express their views and opinions, seeking to convince others of the reasonableness of their propositions (Cohen, 1997, 75). Proponents of deliberative democracy accounts highlight the ways in which deliberators might be willing to amend their own proposals in recognition of the reasonableness of others' claims. The focus of deliberation is to ensure that 'political decisions are decided according to the exchange of reasons and arguments (broadly conceived and defined) that appeal to shared objectives... or values' (Fung, 2005, 401). Recent advocates of deliberative democracy concede that the problem of actually-existing background inequalities inhibits an equitable exchange of reason. But they free accounts of deliberative democracy from the mandate to generate a rational consensus and argues that the *process* of deliberation may in fact be a trigger to reduce some of those background inequalities (Cohen and Rogers, 2003, 245). It is possible, as Cohen (1997) suggests, that consensus eludes deliberators and that they resort to more conventional ways of aggregating preferences. But this does not undermine the value of exchanging reasons and providing justification in the decision making process. Furthermore, deliberation need not be guided by a substantive idea of the good life (Cohen, 1997, 81). However, Mouffe, justifiably, remains unconvinced. She has little patience for accounts of politics that wish away relations of inequality and power, and ignore the concreteness of conflict in social life. Her realist account of politics is based on the premise that relations of power cannot be eliminated, but can be contested within an agonistic framework.

In this concluding chapter, I want to dwell on the ways in which an agonistic perspective on politics enables us to think through the universalist/particularist conundrum. These meditations will help us grapple with the concerns laid out at the outset of this monograph: what does political life mean for the world's billion-plus poor who live in democracies, members of the labouring classes who confront deprivations and disparities while at the same time are promised a say in governing their polities. I first direct attention to the agonistics of the negotiations that have been elaborated in previous chapters. I then reiterate the political dimension of poor people's negotiations. Lastly, I summarize the importance of political space in shaping the form and substance of the negotiations undertaken by the labouring classes. In the epilogue, I remind us of the continuing relevance of these concerns, as inequalities in some of the world's most economically dynamic democracies increase, and the contradictions between liberalism and democracy stand further exposed.

Agonistics

Adopting an agonistic perspective is key to appreciating the politics of the poor. An agonistic perspective is valuable in in overcoming the theoretical impasse between universalism and particularism. On the one hand, it allows us to think beyond assimilationist perspectives which suggest that people seek to imbibe universalistic values of citizenship, stateness, improvement and modernity. On the other hand, it helps to avoid remaining confined within the perspective of difference which suggests that people attempt to preserve their particularistic values through expressing moral claims in political society, declaring their dependence on powerful patrons, and resisting improvement schemes. Against the dichotomies implied in the debates between universalists and particularists, an agonistic perspective provides us with the opportunity to analyse people's *negotiations* with democracy, allowing to us to step beyond the binaries inhered in such tropes as citizenship and clientelism, languages of stateness and moral vocabularies, improvement and preservation, and modernity and tradition. It allows us to examine the ambivalence, heterogeneity, and poly-vocality of these negotiations without pigeonholing these under the rubric of either assimilation or difference. Deploying an agonistic lens to study poor people's political practices helps analysts to understand the *grounds* on which they advance their social perspectives. Unlike either a deliberative or a pluralistic lens, an agonistic optic enables observers to examine the power relationships into which the labouring poor are embedded. It is also useful in understanding the ways in which they alter (albeit marginally) the social relations of power. An agonistic perspective is also productive in comparison with 'postmodern' lenses because it does not valourize unmitigated difference and, in fact, seeks to uncover contests over *common* ground. It helps me think about people's negotiations over the terms on which they assert their membership in the political community. The agonistic view of politics is thus invaluable in overcoming the binary between universalism and particularism that continues to dominate the social sciences.

An agonistic approach to politics enables researchers to straddle the binary between consent and contention. On the one hand, adopting an agonistic approach to politics allows us to recognise the generative potential of conflict in social life: we appreciate the ways in which social contradictions are crucial to the formation of people's collective, albeit fragmented, identities.

On the other hand, deploying an agonistic approach to politics persuades us beyond considering such contradictions to necessarily manifest in acts of violence, where members of social groups in conflict with one another strive to liquidate or annihilate one another. Agonists exist in a state of 'permanent provocation' vis-a-vis one another. Class collaboration enmeshes with class conflict, as the accounts offered in this book suggest. Their political practices can neither be analysed as of assimilation into universalism nor be interpreted as of particularist difference. By enabling researchers to consider the empirical entanglements of theoretical binaries, an agonistic perspective permits them to consider the ambivalences and heterogeneities that underpin poor people's politics.

Each of the book's four empirical chapters reflected on these empirical entanglements. Chapter 4 explored poor people's supplications. In it, I argued against characterizing such supplications as examples of either clientelism or citizenship. Rather, I proposed that the supplications could conceptually be located at the cusp of clientelism and citizenship. Similarly, poor people's demands for employment under the NREGA were the subject of chapter 5. I argued that their demands could neither be analysed solely as exemplars of moral vocabularies nor as imbibing the languages of the state. Again, such applications were more fruitfully located at the interval of moral vocabularies and languages of stateness. In chapter 6, I offered an analysis of disputations over an electrification project and suggested that these disputations provided for a further example of the entanglements that mark poor people's political practices. The disputations could neither be reduced to impulses for the preservations of extant lifestyles nor the inexorable urge for improvement. Rather, it is at the margins of preservation and improvement that I located their disputations. Likewise, the discussions in chapter 7 alerted me to the difficulties of folding up poor people's imaginations as reflecting either traditional norms or modern ideas. Instead, I situated the imaginations at the interstices of tradition and modernity. Adopting an agonistic perspective provided me with helpful leads to examine the entanglements between the universal and the particular.

Not only does the agonistic view of politics used in this book help overcoming false binaries, it also contributes to eschewing teleology. Even as proponents of the agonistic approach reflect on the conditions that facilitate and underpin human emancipation, they are critical of attempts to fix a final destination, a focal point, at which all societies and people must inevitably converge in order to achieve emancipation. However, disavowal of telos does not imply an endorsement of relativism, the approach that anything goes. Against both teleological determinism as well as relativism scholars sympathetic to agonistic views of politics formulate the notion of 'political horizon' to refer to an imaginary that animates people's aspirations. For example, Aletta Norval (2007) invokes the idea of a political horizon to intimate the inchoate sense that 'things can be better' without subscribing to a teleological view of politics. I find the idea of a political horizon particularly evocative because of its inherently unfixed character. There is no specific pathway toward a horizon. The idea of a horizon suggests an open space rather than a narrow pre-destined pathway. But its instability and open endedness, and concomitantly shifting character, does not mean that 'anything goes'. In fact, a horizon recognizes people's aspirations that 'things might be better' without pigeonholing these aspirations for change into such rubrics as modernization, citizenship, stateness and improvement. It is to such open-ended horizons that the people we met in this book seem to point when they talk about the better future they envisage for their children. An agonistic approach to people's everyday negotiations helps me take note of such horizons.

Heterogeneities

That the politics of the poor is a politics of agonistic negotiations is the most important message of this book. Such negotiations refer to provisional transactions between transient collectives of poor people on the one hand and politicians, bureaucrats and members of the dominant classes on the other. These transactions are neither formal nor official nor are they conducted by organizations of the poor on the basis of their shared class or communal identities. Rather, they occur – as I note below – at the boundaries of what some scholars have called formal politics and everyday politics. A second key message of this book is that these negotiations are heterogeneous.

What makes such heterogeneous negotiations political? One response to this question might be that the ubiquitous influence of the state in shaping people's lives makes any action they take vis-à-vis the state a political act. Or, one might say that any competition over material resources – BPL cards, NREGA work, electric poles and management of temple resources – is a political act. While this is not inaccurate, I would like to remind readers that politics refers to the ensemble of practices through which people conduct their lives in the context of the disciplinary mechanisms that attempt to institute order in society. Compliance with such mechanisms as well as contesting these both constitute political practices. Politics thus encompasses struggles over meanings as well as contests over identities, rather than being centered on the acquisition of material resources. Seen in this light, the negotiations that have been discussed in this book are political, but not only because they involve claims on the state or contests over governmental resources.

The negotiations discussed in this book are political also because they are animated by poor people's professed intention to advance their social perspectives. Advancing their social perspective sometimes, but not always, brings them into conflict with the dominant classes. The labouring classes seek to be autonomous of dependent social relations, to assert their collective self-identities as workers and as reasonable persons, to contest the presumptions of social superiority by entrenched classes, and to reconstitute the public space as egalitarian. But they also appeal to the care and kindness of their proclaimed guardians, invoke idioms of relationships that emphasize dependence at least in the short term, and look to the state, democratic institutions and elected politicians as protectors against the entrenched and/or precarious classes. In advancing their perspectives, the poor engage in political negotiations on an almost daily basis.

Intention does not always translate into outcomes. Roshanar's labouring poor may hope to obtain BPL cards so that their children may not need to depend on labour-hiring peasants, but find that their access to BPL cards depends on the elected representatives' whims: however, this fact does not reduce the political dimension of their supplications. The labouring poor in Ditya apply for employment under the NREGA so that they can withdraw from exploitative labour relations, but are frustrated by the machinations of the precarious classes: nevertheless, the political dimension of their applications has to be acknowledged. In Rahimpur, the labouring classes are largely successful in persuading their elected representative to install electric poles as per their convenience: had they not been successful, then too their disputations of their elected representatives' assumptions would have been ineluctably political. The imaginations of Sargana's labouring classes against the entrenched classes' appropriation of public spaces are ongoing: irrespective of the eventual outcome, the political dimension of their imagination cannot be ignored.

The empirical chapters discussed the political dimension of each of these distinct forms of negotiations in greater detail.

In chapter 4, I examined poor people's supplications – located analytically at the cusp of clientelism and citizenship – as a series of political acts. Through their supplications, the inhabitants of the study villages extended their claim to be included in their localities' list of BPL households. Their supplications were political not only because they signalled a contest over scarce resources. The political dimension of the supplications stemmed from the labouring classes' conviction that possessing them would relieve them of dependent economic relations. The supplications spawned contentions among the populations. Such struggles pointed to the emergence of struggles over class, for the solidarities that emerged from the contentions indicated for the labouring poor who they could count on and to what extent. The supplications and the responses to them revealed the ways in which communal distinctions within the labouring classes could be mobilized to include as well as to exclude people from the BPL lists.

My exploration of poor people's demands – situated analytically at the boundaries of moral vocabularies and languages of stateness – in chapter 5 allowed me to dwell on the political dimension underpinning their practices. Such applications were political not simply because they entailed claims on resources. Rather, poor people's applications were politicized on account of the applicant's beliefs that employment under the NREGA would enable them to withdraw from exploitative economic hierarchies. More importantly, their experiences of work contributed to the forging of their collective self-identities as labourers, against the government's attempt to label them as 'beneficiaries' and 'wage-seekers'. The ensuing contentions over timely payment of wages fomented new solidarities among labourers as well as an awareness of the social and political actors favourable to them and inimical to them. Such contentions also conveyed the ways in which communal distinctions within the labouring classes could be mobilized to incite inclusions and bolster exclusions from NREGA employment.

The political dimension of poor people's disputations – analytically viewed at the margins of preservation and improvement – over electrification in Rahimpur were the subject of discussion in chapter 6. Their disputations were, on the surface, about the location of electric poles, entailing arguments between neighbours and among the people and their elected representatives. But a careful examination of the disputations revealed the other issues at stake. One such issue pertained to the identification of the people endowed with greater *khomota* who could be called upon to make the compromises necessary for Rahimpur's improvement. Another issue that riled Rahimpur's populations was their ward member's assumption of being a trustee for the entire village and his consequent dismissal of any objection to his plans. The third issue of dispute stemmed from the rejection by Rahimpur's inhabitants of the charge that they were 'unreasonable persons', a charge hurled at them by their ward member. These tussles made Rahimpur's disputations a very political matter. However, readers will recall that Rahimpur's Shershabadiya population were excluded from the ward member's plans for the village, an exclusion fortified by the complete absence of any collective solidarity in their favour by their co-villagers.

The focus in chapter 7 was on the imaginations – analytically situated at the interstices of tradition and modernity – over a temple in Sargana. On the face of it, the contest was over the temple's resources, which were being illegally siphoned away by its Rajput trustees. But a scrutiny of the contestations illuminated the other matters at stake, adding to the political dimension of the contestations. Not only did the labouring classes involve politicians and the courts, they also interrogated the presumptions of social superiority held by the locality's Savarna landlords, farmers and rich peasants. Their actions sought to, and contributed to, democratize the management of the temple under question. They interrogated the trustees' claims over the temple by underscoring its *pablik* nature. In their bid to democratize the management of the temple's affairs, they established communal quotas that would enhance the representativeness of the management committee and make the committee members accountable to their constituencies rather than to the entrenched classes. The attendant imaginations sharpened the contradictions between the *Backwards* and *Forwards*, while enhancing the solidarities among the plethora of Sargana's oppressed communities.

An emerging body of scholarship[5] suggests that the negotiations described in this book span diverse spatial locations, across continents and across rural and urban regions. Such scholarship foregrounds the ensemble of provisional transactions which people deploy in order to navigate the dominating practices to which they are subjected. Researchers writing in this vein focus on people who confront precariousness in their quotidian lives and the ways in which they attempt to transfigure the vulnerabilities of their existence into some sort of possibility for their and their children's future. A useful starting point is Ben Kirkvliet's insightful formulation of everyday politics. Everyday politics, he suggests, 'involves people embracing, complying with, adjusting and contesting norms and rules regarding authority over, production of, or allocation of resources and doing so in quiet, mundane, and subtle expressions and acts that are rarely organized or direct' (Kerkvliet, 2009: 232). Kerkvliet's account underscores the ways in which Vietnamese peasants negotiated with the collectivization program of their government, eventually undermining it altogether. Their negotiations bear remarkable similarity with peasant negotiations with state-led collectivization programs in Bulgaria (Creed, 1998), Romania (Kideckel, 1977) and Hungary (Rev, 1987).

Kerkvliet distinguishes everyday politics from other types of politics, such as official politics and advocacy politics. Official politics lies within the domain of authorities in organizations. Governments are a significant component of such organizations, but by no means the only one. Universities, religious institutions, political parties, non-governmental organizations, social movement and revolutionary organizations are all sites of official politics. The key point to note is that the individuals involved in official politics hold authoritative positions. Advocacy politics lies outside the domain of authorities but involves a direct and concerted focus on them. Advocacy politics could be about supporting people in authority or criticising them. Kerkvliet also introduces a preliminary typology of everyday politics: support, compliance, modifications and evasions, and resistance.

The resonances of the material presented in this book with Kerkvliet's typology of everyday politics are illuminating. The supplications spawned by the institution of targeted identification of households eligible for BPL cards appear to map onto the dimension of 'compliance'. The demands fomented by the implementation of a generalized workfare program may resemble the dimension of 'support'. Similarly, the disputations over implementing a universal program of electrification, albeit in the context of an incorporative political place, seems to map onto the dimension of 'modifications'. Likewise, the imaginations incited by the introduction of universally applicable legislation declaring the local temple as public property approximates the dimension of 'struggle'. As I have noted throughout, the configuration of political space bears on the specific outcome of everyday politics.

However, the messiness of political negotiations can scarcely be contained in the neat typologies offered by Kerkvliet. The analysis offered in this book emphasizes the heterogeneities entailed within people's supplications, demands, disputes and imaginations. The four types of everyday politics outlined by Kerkvliet are combined by poor people in each of the localities. Moreover, by organizing in transient collectives, they also articulate everyday politics with advocacy politics and try to influence the working of official politics. We have noted that, while poor people did not regard their actions as political, they did not shy away from confronting their elected representatives or asserting their presence in public vis-à-vis members of the dominant classes.

Nevertheless, Kerkvliet's in an important reminder that the quotidian forms of politics described in this book are generalizable across the globe. Indeed, such forms of politics are not restricted to rural areas. The heterogeneities of popular negotiations analysed in this book reflect increasing scholarly research on political practices of vulnerable and marginalized populations in cities. For example, Asef Bayat (2011) elucidates the ways in which millions of people across cities in West Asia and North Africa quietly encroach into urban spaces in order to make a living. Bayat's work explores the practices of the urban poor in both authoritarian (Egypt) as well as democratic (Iran) contexts. Their encroachments are deemed illegal by their governments, rendering their situation all the more precarious. Bayat terms these encroachments as social non-movements, 'the collective actions of noncollective actors' (Bayat, 2011, 14). Social nonmovements encompass shared but fragmented practices that are hardly guided by a recognisable ideology, leadership or organization.

Similarly, AbdouMalik Simone's (2004) research emphasizes the ways in which precariously positioned people in urban Africa operate outside of formal institutional structures in order to seek and maintain their everyday sustenance. This work draws on observations from Senegal (Dakar), Cameroon (Douala) and South Africa (Pretoria). Noting the 'crisis of sociality' (Simone, 2005, 517) confronted by people in many African cities, he reminds us of the possibilities offered by such crisis in the creation of new collaborations and sensibilities among people. Simone's emphasis on the provisional networks through which urban Africans procure basic goods and services is highly relevant to the material presented in this book. His more recent research on urban life in South-East Asia (with a focus on Jakarta) reiterates the 'heterogeneous composite of ways of life, histories of settlement, economic activities, and contestations that engineer complex circulations of resources and opportunities, equilibrate access to experience, information and authority, and cut across clear-cut designations of social standing'. (Simone, 2015: S16).

In his incisive writings on poor people's politics in urban Argentina, Javier Ayuero (2001) notes the affective networks into which their practices are inserted. Charting the lives of men and women living and labouring in Buenos Aires' impoverished settlements, Ayuero insists on foregrounding the ambivalent ways in which poor people make sense of the political opportunities and threats they face. The way in which he navigates tempting conceptual binaries is exemplary, uncovering for his readers the complex web of practices enacted by his interlocutors.

Other useful interventions on poor people's politics are offered by scholars working on agrarian change in China. Kevin O'Brien and Lianjiang Li (2006) underscore the ways in which the rural poor in China work the political system through intricate negotiations with bureaucrats and other local officials. O'Brien and Li are particularly attentive to the ways in which their interlocutors combine the language of rights with the practices of resistance in their negotiations. They thereby eschew the false binaries of cooption and resistance that plagues much of the scholarship on poor people's politics. Their empirical descriptions of rural politics to which *both* compliance and protest are integral are relevant to my research. Similarly, Kathy Walker (2008) highlights the ways in which socialist legacy as well as older ideologies together inform the coalescence of shared political strategies among the country's peasantry.

A similarly ambiguous character of popular politics is documented by Matthew Gutmann (2002) in his fascinating study of Mexico. Gutmann sets for himself the task of describing the twists and turns experienced by residents of a neighbourhood in Mexico City as they engaged with politics. Gutmann teases out the entanglements between defiance and compliance among his interlocutors. Defiance and compliance underlie one another. Indeed, the starting point of his analysis is the huge proportion of abstentions in Mexico's electoral politics as well as the lack of involvement among people in the country's various social movements. Due to these factors, poor people's 'political views and activities are seldom remarked upon in detail in academic studies or the media. Yet they are anything but unremarkable' (Gutmann, 2002, 216). The study takes the reader on a journey through the political lives of the *los de abajo* (the 'underdogs') in a neighbourhood in the city, directing attention to the multiple meanings of democracy held and made by them. Even so, Gutmann recognizes that such fragmentations and ambivalences are inevitably nested within opportunity structures and relations of dominance.

Laura McLean's (2014) study on political participation in Ghana also contributes to blurring the boundaries between such alleged dichotomies as clientelism and citizenship. Based on her analysis of popular orientations towards claim making and political identities, the nature of political transactions, mechanisms of accountability, and notions of rights and duties, McLean demonstrates the intricate ways in which the vocabularies associated with clientelism are entangled with the idioms associated with citizenship. McLean (2014) argues that such entanglements reflect the existence of hybrid political cultures among rural Ghanians. As she notes, her informants 'were neither perfect citizens nor clients but articulated their own conception of everyday politics' (McLean, 2014, 114). Although my analytical conclusions are different from those reached by McLean (particularly in relation to her formulation of hybridity), there is much empirical resonance between the cases described by her and the ones examined in this book.

Another persuasive case for incorporating the simultaneous aspirations of people for and against the state is provided by Steff Jansen (2013). Drawing on a fascinating ethography of schools in middle-income suburbs of post-conflict Sarajevo, he proposes 'gridding' as an analytical tool to examine people's simultaneous aspirations for and against the state in their pursuit of what they perceived to be normal life. Drawing on his observations around schooling and its temporal calibration of routines, Jansen argues that people may sometimes wish to evade the state and remain illegible to its readings but they might also yearn and even clamour to be incorporated into what he calls 'griddings of improvement'. His work closes with the following call to his fellow-anthropologists: 'Rather than preposition anthropology within hope against the great beast of the state, I suggest we be prepared to replicate our interlocutors' hopes for as well as against the state' (Jensen, 2013, 20).

Reflecting on popular politics after the dismantling of Apartheid rule in South Africa, Steve Robins (2008) presents a nuanced account of emergent political life in the country. Critiquing both Mamdani (1996) and Chatterjee (2004) for subscribing to dichotomous accounts of political subjectivities, he points to the messy forms of life in the postcolony, replete with complexities and ambiguities of all sorts. Insisting that contemporary political practice in South Africa adopts idioms associated with both subject hood and citizenship, Robins (2008) advises against a singular interpretation of rights activism. The growing importance of the vocabulary of rights, he argues, does not result in the diminution of cultural tropes in political life, as modernization theorists might prime us to believe. Rather, rights-based mobilizations are coeval with cultural mobilizations.

Scholars who appreciate that the study of politics is the study of the use, exercise, distribution, reproduction and transformation of societal power recognize also that several of these processes take place outside the realm of, or at the interstices of, what has often been called 'formal politics' or the institutional realm of politics. The work of the above referenced scholars have enriched the repertoires of analyses available to social scientists interested in the study of politics, even as they interrogate the conventional focus of students of politics on institutions of the state. This is not, importantly, to suggest that institutions do not matter: they very clearly do, as the analyses of these scholars as well as the material presented in the present book argues. Rather, it is to emphasize the importance of the ways in which the interactions between institutional opportunity structures and social relations of power *interact* to produce the political spaces that shape the negotiations of the labouring classes.

Political spaces for poor people's negotiations

That poor people's negotiations are shaped by the political spaces available to them is a third key message of this book. In chapter 1, I offered an understanding of political space as constituted by the dynamic interaction of political opportunity structures and the social relations of power. In turn, political opportunity structures and social relations of power are both products of the interaction of discrete variables. On the one hand, political opportunity structures are co-produced by the nature of institutions and the design of state interventions in the form of public policy. On the other hand, the social relations of power are the result of the interaction of the social relations of production as well as the social relations of distribution.

The role of political opportunity structures was illustrated in chapter 2 as well as across the four empirical chapters. In chapter 2, I outlined the ways in which India's unequal democracy impinges upon poor people's politics. I particularly noted the implications of India's majoritarian electoral procedures, the institutionalized split between civil and political rights on the one side and social and economic rights on the other, and the concentration of poverty in certain communities in order to illustrate the opportunity structures, which the labouring poor avail during their negotiations. Eastern India's specific economic geography and social history have contributed to making caste a central axis of political discourse and, consequently, the political opportunity structure.

In chapter 3, by sketching the social relations of power in the concrete political places where this study was conducted, I underscored the variety of configurations in which the labouring poor were enmeshed. In an 'incorporative political place' such as Rahimpur, the landlords and rich farmers who constituted its entrenched classes found common cause with the locality's labouring poor because of their mutual contradictions against the precarious classes comprising labour-hiring rich and middle peasant sharecroppers. The entrenched classes shaped Rahimpur's polity, and generally supported the locality's manual workers in their claims against the precarious classes. By doing this, the entrenched classes undermined the ability of the precarious classes to sustainably threaten their dominance over the ward's social life. By contrast, in a 'populist political place' such as Sargana, the labour-hiring middle and poor peasants comprising its precarious classes made common cause with the labouring poor against the landlords and rich peasants who constituted the locality's entrenched classes. Despite bitter conflict over wages, they shared a common antipathy towards the social hierarchies that the entrenched classes sought to perpetrate. The precarious classes shaped Sargana's polity, and generally backed the locality's labouring classes against the entrenched classes thereby contributing to the erosion of the latter's dominance in the social life of the locality.

The discussions in chapter 3 also introduced us to political places where the social configurations weighed against the labouring classes. Ditya's 'differentiated political place' witnessed a full-blown antagonism between the labouring classes on the one hand and the precarious peasants and their handful of entrenched class kinsmen on the other. The precarious classes controlled Ditya's polity and sought to utilize their control in order to sustain their dominance over the locality's social life as well as the supply of labour for their agrarian operations. In Roshanar, the entrenched classes succeeded in making the locality a 'paternalistic political place' by solidly supporting the precarious classes against the claims of the labouring poor. The entrenched classes controlled Roshanar's polity and mobilized the precarious classes to maintain their dominance.

The subsequent chapters demonstrated the heterogeneous ways in which the dynamic interaction between social relations of power and the design of statist interventions shaped poor people's negotiations with democracy. In chapter 4, we noted that the institution of a narrowly-targeted public policy spawned *supplications* among the labouring poor in all the four political places where the study was conducted. Poor people perceived the targeted interventions as providing limited opportunities for them to advance their claims. But, crucially, the supplications varied across the localities, influenced by the specific social relations of power operating in each. Where the labouring poor could count on support from either the entrenched or the precarious classes, their supplications were assertive. Where, however, the labouring poor could not count on such support, their supplications were meek and reticent.

However, the political practices of the same labouring population differed with the institution of a broad-based public policy that was predicated upon self-targeting, the subject of discussion in chapter 5. The new policy, which made resource transfers conditional upon the performance of manual labour in state-sanctioned public works programme, encouraged *demands* for employment from the labouring poor in three of the four study locations. The poor perceived this program as providing a greater opportunity for them to make their claims. Again, however, the applications varied across the locations, shaped by the prevailing social relations of power. In an incorporative political place such as Rahimpur, where the labouring poor were enmeshed in collaboration with the entrenched classes, their applications were routine, despite the opposition of the precarious classes. However, in a populist political place such as in Sargana, the labouring poor aligned with precarious classes. Here the entrenched classes opposed their applications. Therefore, their applications were assertively made as they could not be sure that adhering to routine procedures would be efficacious, but they could be sure that their voices would be heard because of the support they received from the precarious classes. The most important variations were evident from an analysis of the applications submitted by Ditya's labouring classes. Despite being pitted against the dominance of the precarious classes, the introduction of a broad-based programme, unencumbered by narrow targeting, fomented assertiveness among the locality's labouring class applicants. However, the introduction of such a policy failed to be perceived as an opportunity in a locality where the majority of the labouring poor were isolated by the paternalistic machinations of the entrenched classes.

The subsequent two chapters further explored poor people's political negotiations in political places where the social configurations of power enmeshed them in supportive relations with either of the labour-hiring classes. Chapter 6 investigated their negotiations in the context of a universal public policy which would provide complete electrification coverage to Rahimpur, an incorporative political place where the labouring poor and the entrenched classes coalesced against the precarious classes. Chapter 7 undertook similar investigations in Sargana, where the labouring poor coalesced with the precarious classes against the entrenched classes. The context of the investigations was provided by a universal policy that declared the local temple as a public place which all members of the community could access, whose records they could scrutinize and to whose management they could contribute.

The discussion in chapter 6 of disputations within Rahimpur's population and between them and their elected representatives signalled both the labouring poor's discontent with the trusteeship assumptions of their entrenched class politicians as well as their abiding invocation of the obligation of the powerful to protect the weak. A governmental technology privileging universal electrification ignited disputations among the labouring populations against the very entrenched classes whom they described as their guardians, but the vocabularies on which the disputations hinged continued to express notions of care and protection.

The imaginations discussed in chapter 7 between Sargana's labouring and precarious classes against the appropriations of the entrenched classes revealed to us the fault lines that marked the locality's social landscape. The labouring poor and their precarious class supporters claimed the temple as a *pablik* space, and hinged it with other ongoing contentions in the locality against the oppression perpetrated by the privileged caste landlords and rich farmers. The passage of a legislation emphasizing universal access to the temple as a public property emboldened the labouring poor, and precarious labour-hiring peasants, to invoke affective relationships as well as notions of social justice and equality while advancing their claims to the temple and to other public spaces in Sargana. Althoug such mutual solidarities did not entail that real conflicts over wages and social status between members of these classes were smoothed over, they did solidify the *Backward-Forward* split that characterized Sargana's political place.

The similarities and differences between the two cases merit brief comment. That the labouring poor were enmeshed in collaborative relationships with either of the two dominant classes made it possible for them to assert their claims. To be sure, the labouring classes were plagued by internal suspicions and mistrusts, as evidenced by the exclusions of Shershabadiyas in Rahimpur and Doms in Sargana. But the universal nature of the governmental interventions augmented the ability of the majority of the labouring classes to advance their assertions. In both cases, class collaboration enabled them to advance their social claims at least vis-a-vis the classes against whom they were allied. However, where the labouring poor were incorporated into class coalitions with the entrenched classes, as in Rahimpur, their vocabularies continued to be permeated with notions of care and protection, notwithstanding the fact that the introduction of universal public policy augmented their assertiveness. By contrast, where the labouring poor were conjoined with the precarious classes in a populist coalition, as in Sargana, their vocabularies expressed ideas of social justice, equality and dignity to which the introduction of universal public policy further contributed. While the design and implementation of public policy was critical in shaping poor people's negotiations, the social relations of power influenced their political practices in fundamental ways.

Epilogue

As oppressed people, the political practices of the poor defy dichotomous classifications as being about either clientelism or citizenship; either derived from moral vocabularies or inspired by languages of stateness; either centred on preservation or aspiring to improvement; and either harking back to traditional ideas or emulating modern views. The characters readers have met in this book neither restrict themselves to the electoral authorization of their representatives, nor do they seek a revolutionary overthrow of the system. They neither aspire assimilation into the 'universal' ideas associated with democracy nor do they strive to maintain their difference owing to their 'particular' vulnerabilities. Rather, the material in this book suggests that labouring poor who inhabit democracies, especially unequal democracies such as contemporary India, draw on a complex of different strategies in order to advance their social perspectives. The agonisitc negotiations that constitute their political practices are located at the interstices of these analytical categories. The agonism entailed in their negotiations lends an ambivalence towards democracy.

Liberal democracy has come to assume the 'hegemonic model of democracy (Santos, 2005, 9). Recognizing such hegemonic tendencies should not obfuscate the perspective that, as a political science concept and as a political regime, the emergence of Liberal democracy has facilitated the coalescing of quite contrasting traditions (Mouffe, 2007). The liberal tradition is predicated on the rule of law, individual rights and the sanctity of private property. The democratic tradition relies on the tradition of popular sovereignty. The fusing together of these quite contrasting traditions is the result of contingent historical and political-economic factors, thereby rendering the hegemony of Liberal democracy vulnerable. The growing support for right-wing populism in countries as diverse as the USA, UK, Brazil, Turkey and India bear out the vulnerabilities of the Liberal model of democracy. However, to assume that it is the labouring classes who are driving these processes may not be accurate in every context.[6] Indeed, the material presented in this book suggests that labouring classes in an increasingly unequal democracy such as India take seriously democratic notions pertaining to social justice, equality and dignity, even if they appear considerably less enthused by liberal ideas pertaining to protection of individual liberties and safeguard of private property.

These contradictions assume importance in a world of ever-widening inequalities. As Branco Milanovic (2016) demonstrates, recent years have witnessed the widening of inequalities *within* countries rather than between them. Table 8.1 provides a snapshot of the growing inequalities within select countries across the globe, including some of the world's fastest growing economies. It directs attention to the changes in the share of the bottom 10 per cent in the consumption or income of their respective countries. A glance at the table suggests a *decline* in this share across a number of emerging market democracies, including India, Indonesia, Nigeria, South Africa, Turkey and Vietnam. This trend points to the awkward fact that, even as Liberal democracy assumed the hegemonic model of democracy, inequalities within several of these countries have widened in somewhat unprecedented ways. Even as more people might move 'above' the $1.90 a day poverty line established by the World Bank, their share in the consumption and/or income in their respective countries appears to have declined. Data contrasting the wealth shares of the top 1% and bottom half of the world's population is even more damning. Credit Suisse (2016, 148) reports that as of 2016 the top 1% of the world's population own over half its wealth, the bottom half share 0.2% of it. That wealth inequalities have worsened in less than a decade may be gleaned from a comparison with Credit Suisse's (2010, 120) report for 2010. In that year, the top 1% owned 43% of the world's wealth, while the bottom half owned 1.6% of it. The share of wealth for the world's bottom half shrunk from a minuscule 1.6% to a micro-minuscule 0.2% in less than a decade. The emergence and consolidation of democracy offers people the opportunity to participate in the affairs of the polity: the very same polity presides over widening inequalities. This apparently contradictory impulse, the institutionalized of democracy on the one side and yawning inequalities between the bottom and top tiers of the socio-economic hierarchy constitutes a fundamental aspect of political life across the contemporary world. Such contradictory impulses enhance the agonistic content of the political practices of those at the lower echelons of the socio-economic hierarchy, those who, on the one hand, are offered

Table 8.1: Changes in distribution of consumption or income among consumption or income groups, select countries

Country name	Baseline year	% share of consumption or income for						Most recent year	% share of consumption or income for					
		Bottom 10%	Next 30%	Third 20%	Fourth 20%	Next 10%	Top 10%		Bottom 10%	Next 30%	Third 20%	Fourth 20%	Next 10%	Top 10%
Argentina	2007	1.2	11.2	14	22	16.7	34.9	2012	1.6	13	15.1	23	16.7	30.6
Brazil	2007	0.9	9	11.6	19	15.9	43.6	2013	1	9.9	12.4	19.3	15.6	41.8
China	2008	1.8	12.6	15	22.7	16.1	31.8	2010	1.7	12.7	15.3	23.2	17.1	30
Ethiopia	2004	4.1	18.4	16.9	21.4	13.6	25.6	2010	3.2	17.4	16.3	21.3	14.4	27.4
France	2007	3.1	17.5	16.5	21.9	14.7	26.3	2012	3.1	17.3	16.5	21.8	14.5	26.8
Germany	2006	2.5	16.8	16.9	22.5	15.8	25.5	2011	3.4	18.1	17.2	22.7	14.9	23.7
Greece	2007	2.2	16.3	16.7	22.7	15.9	26.2	2012	1.7	15.6	17.4	23.3	15.3	26.7
India	2004	3.8	17	15.8	21	14.1	28.3	2011	3.5	16.5	15.2	20.5	14.3	30
Indonesia	2008	3.6	16.4	15.9	21.5	14.8	27.8	2010	3.4	15.5	15.6	21.8	15.5	28.2
Iran	2009	2.1	13	14	22.2	17.3	31.4	2013	2.9	15	15.6	22	15.4	29.1
Mexico	2008	1.8	11.8	12.9	19.5	15.1	38.9	2012	1.9	11.8	12.8	19.5	15.1	38.9
Nigeria	2003	2.1	14	15.4	22.5	16.2	29.8	2009	2	13.1	14.4	21.6	16.2	32.7
Pakistan	2004	3.8	17.7	15.9	21	13.2	28.4	2010	4.2	18.6	16.5	21.3	13.8	25.6
Philippines	2006	2.3	12.4	13.5	21.3	16.6	33.9	2012	2.5	12.9	13.8	21.2	16.2	33.4
Russia	2007	2.3	13.4	14.2	21.2	16.1	32.8	2012	2.3	5.9	14.5	21.2	23.9	32.2
South Africa	2006	1	6.3	7.5	14.2	16.7	54.3	2011	0.9	6.3	8	15.9	17.6	51.3
Tanzania	2007	2.5	14.4	14.7	21.7	14.8	31.9	2011	3.1	15.4	15	20.7	14.8	31
Turkey	2007	2.2	14.6	15.9	22.7	16.4	28.2	2012	2.2	14.1	15.1	22	16.1	30.5
Uganda	2009	2.3	13.4	13.5	19.6	14.8	36.4	2012	2.4	13.8	14	20.4	15.5	33.9
United Kingdom	2007	2.5	16.2	16.2	22	15.1	28	2012	2.9	16.9	17	23.1	15.4	24.7
United States	2007	1.3	13.9	15.6	22.6	15.9	30.7	2013	1.7	13.7	15.4	22.7	16.3	30.2
Vietnam	2004	2.9	15.3	15.1	21.7	15.9	29.1	2010	2.6	14.7	14	20.7	17.9	30.1

Source: Calculated from World Bank (2014, Table 2.9), accessed http://wdi.worldbank.org/table/2.9, January 2017.

unprecedented opportunities to participate in the life of their polity and, on the other hand, confront ever-widening inequalities.

Such contradictions and the attendant ambivalences shape the lives of the people readers have met in this book, people such as Shamsul Alam, Majhuli Moholi, Shekhar Shil and Jamuni Rishi for whom democracy provides unprecedented opportunities to advance their social claims but does not eliminate the social and economic inequalities within which they are embedded. Like millions of other impoverished inhabitants of democracies, these men and women combine guarded consent with inchoate conflict as they negotiate democracy. Neither do their negotiations seek assimilation into universalistic precepts nor do they inscrutably hold on to their particularistic identities. People such as Fatema Bewa, Marangmayee Hembrom, Shanichar Rishi and Mansoor Ali are democrats without necessarily subscribing to liberal values that sanctify individualism, private property and the rule of law. Their negotiations illustrate the wide-ranging possibilities of, and threats to, democratic politics. Their supplications, demands, disputations and imaginations reveal the many nuances of negotiations with the practices and meanings of democracy. The agonistics that underpin their negotiations compel us to guard against singularly triumphalist celebrations around the purported march of democracy or mournful lamentations about its alleged demise. The politics of the poor demonstrates the intricate ways through which democracies could be rejuvenated (though also undermined) by agonistic negotiations. It is time analysts of democracy did so as well.

Endnotes

1   The idea of 'essentially contested concepts' was formulated by WB Gallie (1956): see Williams (2003) for a discussion drawing from African cases.

2   This was the subject of discussion in an influential text by Collier and Levitsky (1997).

3   The allusion here is to the formulation of 'democracy with Chinese characteristics' by Bell (2000).

4   Huber *et al.,* (1997) suggest equal participation in public affairs as one of the characteristics of substantive democracy.

5   See Baiocchi and Connor (2008) for a useful overview of political ethnographies that make similar claims.

6   For instance, a slew of commentaries in the aftermath of Donald Trump's election in November 2016 suggested that the White working classes supported his candidature over Hilary Clinton's: see, for instance, Catherine Rampell, Washington Post, December 22, 2016 and Nate Cohn, New York Times, November 9, 2016 for a sample of such offerings.

The Dramatis Personae, 2009–10

Names have been changed to protect the identities of my interlocutors

Rahimpur	
Abdur Bari	CPI(M) cadre and long-time activist of the party. Joined the party as a teenager despite parental opposition and threat of religious sanction. Ardent admirer of former Chief Minister Jyoti Basu, particularly his instruction that his body was to be donated for scientific research rather than be cremated according to traditional rites. 57 years old. Male. Illiterate. Owns some land and leases in land from Akbar Ali. Deploys own and family labour and also hires in labour. Sheikh Muslim
Abdur Rehman	Congress Secretary at the Panchayat level. His first cousin is Akbar's mother. Akbar's best friend in the locality. Humyun openly makes fun of Abdur Rehman's appetite and privately wishes he was more sophisticated about taking favors from those he helped. His father is one of the locality's four *Shamaj sardars*. Abdur practices medicine in his spare time. 47 years old. Male. Completed Secondary education. Owns land, which he cultivates using hired labor and machinery. Hires machinery out when not using it. Sheikh Muslim.
Abdul Bari	CPI(M) cadre. Articulate defender of the CPI(M)'s policies in the State. 59 years old. Male. Completed primary education. Leases in land from Akbar Ali. Hires in labour to complement own and family labour. Sheikh Muslim.

Akbar Ali	Congress strategist, showman and organizer- all rolled into one. Friends and foes alike credit him with revitalizing the party in the locality from a moribund organization that used to be run by so-called criminal elements. Engineered the Congress victory despite stiff competition from one of the *shamaj* sardars. Is extremely mild-mannered, seeks to resolve conflicts through deliberations and consensus (but does not avoid conflictual discussions). Is easily the most influential Congress politician in the locality. Despite his influence, he holds no formal position in the party machinery and has been struggling to get the full-time public sector job of the Night Watchman in the local School. Has worked in the construction industry as labor supervisor and labor contractor. But suffered huge losses when the laborers he committed to a project absconded. 40 years old. Male. Completed Secondary education. Owns considerable amount of land and several ponds. Hires labor to cultivate them. Deploys machinery which he borrows from Abdur Rehman and Alauddin Ali (see below). Sheikh Muslim.
Alauddin Ali	Member of the Village Education Committee. His father, Akbar's father and Babar's father are all brothers. Alauddin was closer to Babar than he was to Akbar, and shared a deep friendship with Chandra Mahato (a Hindu Saotal) from neighboring Sindhugram, who was the Secretary of the VEC. Akbar felt that both Chandra and Alauddin were conspiring to keep him out of the job of the Night Watchman, since they wanted that job for one of Chandra's own cousins. Like Abdur, Alauddin is a private medical practitioner as well. 45 years old. Male. Completed primary education. Owns land, which he cultivates using hired labor and machinery. Hires machinery out when not using it. Sheikh Muslim.

Arif Miya	41 years old. Male. Illiterate. Owns no land. Works as agricultural labourer on the farms of peasants such as Abdul Bari, Noorul Islam, Abdur Bari and others. Combines agricultural labour with work in nearby Maldah town as well as elsewhere in India where he migrates with his wife for short periods in search of employment. Mostly works in the construction sector as a casual labourer when in northwestern India. Sometimes works as a head-loader in Maldah town.Enthusiastic worker on the NREGA project whenever he gets a chance. Sheikh Muslim
Babar Hossein	Elected Ward Member. Eloquent speaker and very well-cultivated persona. Akbar's first cousin (their fathers are brothers). In addition to his duties as elected representative, Babar sells mutual funds to customers in Maldah town and practices medicine, much to Akbar's chagrin who believes he should devote more time to his responsibilities as an elected representative. Avoids conflict and delegates their resolution to Akbar. 38 years old. Male. Completed Secondary education. Owns land, though not as much as his cousin. Sheikh Muslim.
Daulat bibi	64 years old. Female. Illiterate. Owns no land. Lives with her unmarried daughter who sometimes works as a domestic help in the houses of wealthier neighbours. She was widowed when her daughter was less than two years old. Sheikh Muslim.
Fatema Bewa	55 years old. Female. Completed primary school. Lives with two sons and their families. Sonscombine agricultural work in the village with employment as construction workers in Delhi and elsewhere in northern India. She works on the farms of her propertied neighbours, but has had to reduce her workload due to illness. Widowed three years ago. Sheikh Muslim.
Gaurob Shil	CPI(M) cadre. 51 years old. Male. Completed primary education. Owns some land and leases in some land. Cultivates using own labour although also hires in labour. Napit Hindu.

Hennah Khan	Rahimpur ward member, 2003–08. CPI(M) cadre.
	53 years old. Female. Completed primary education. Owns considerable amount of land, some of which is leased out to peasants. Sheikh Muslim.
Joynal Ali	CPI(M) strategist and chief organizer in the locality. Widely regarded for his role in the development of the party's mass base in the locality (perceived to be a remarkable feat, given the party's puzzling association with the Hindu community). One of the locality's four *Shamaj sardars*. As *sardar*, he has to transcend his party affiliations. Generally seeks a consensual resolution to problems, but does not shy away from facing conflict where it arises.
	54 years old. Male. Illiterate (and regrets it deeply. Was aghast when I told him my wife left her job as a University Lecturer to live with me after marriage). Owns land and cultivates it using hired labor. Sheikh Muslim.
Murshid Hossein	Erstwhile leader of the Congress Party. Currently, exploring avenues for social activism outside of political parties.
	71 years old. Male. Completed secondary education. Owns some land.
Mushtaq Khan	Hennah Khan's husband. CPI(M) cadre. Although his wife was ward member, he was widely believed to be wielding *de facto* authority in the Panchayat. Nevertheless, he was always referred to as the Ward Member's husband rather than as the Ward Member (which is common practice in India for men whose wives hold positions in the Panchayat). Lost the Panchayat election in 2008 to Babar Hossein.
	61 years old. Male. Completed primary education. Owns considerable amount of land, some of which is leased out to peasants. Sheikh Muslim.
Sarfaraz Islam	39 years old. Male. Illiterate. Owns no land. Works as agricultural labourer on the farms of small peasants such as Ziaur Rehman, Shekhar Shil and Syedur Islam. Works primarily in Rahimpur and its environs, and sometimes ferries passengers on rickshaw in Maldah. Sheikh Muslim.

Shefali Bibi	35 years old. Female. Illiterate. Owns no land. Works as agricultural labourer on the farms of peasants such as Abdul Bari, Noorul Islam, Abdur Bari and others. Combines agricultural labour with work elsewhere in India where she migrates with her husband for short periods in search of employment. Mostly works in the construction sector as a casual labourer. Enthusiastic worker on the NREGA project whenever he gets a chance. Sheikh Muslim.
Shekhar Shil	48 years old. Male. Completed primary education. Owns no land but leases in some land. Cultivates using own labour although also hires in labour. Napit Hindu.
Sirajul Islam	43 years old. Male. Left primary education incomplete. Owns some land, which he cultivates using his own and family labour. Complements his income from agriculture by vending vegetables in Rahimpur and its environs sometimes. Sheikh Muslim.
Syedur Islam	Congress organizer in Intar Rahimpur. The sole contact of the party in the village. Childhood friends with Akbar, Alauddin and Babar. Frank and brutally honest, and known for his mercurial temperament. 41 years old. Male. Illiterate. Owns land and cultivates it using hired labor. Shershabadiya Muslim.
Ziaur Rehman	Congress functionary in Rahimpur. 51 years old. Male. Completed primary education. Owns some land and cultivates it using hired labour. Sometimes leases in land which he cultivates using hired labour. Also leases out land at times. Sheikh Muslim.
Sargana Ward 1	
Akhilesh Mandal	62 years old. Male. Illiterate. Owns some land and cultivates it using his own and family labour. Sometimes leases in land which he cultivates using his own and family labour. Kevat Hindu.

Amaresh Yadav	RJD activist and committed to whichever electoral alliance Lalu Prasad Yadav stitches. Deputy Sarpanch (a judicial rather than political role) of Sargana Panchayat. Resident of Sargana Ward 5, but is influential throughout the Panchayat for his deliberative skills and shrewd political acumen. However, in a dispute between a local Yadav landlord and his Musahar tenants, he brought about a 'compromise' by successfully persuading (coercing through non-violent means?) the latter to withdraw their case. 39 years old. Male. Illiterate. Owns considerable amount of land, which he cultivates with hired labor and machinery. Yadav Hindu.
Basdeo Mandal	52 years old. Male. Illiterate. Owns no land. Hires out his labour to work as agricultural labourer for peasants such as Amaresh Yadav and Gajdeo Mandal as well as landlords as Gajen Singh and Hunny Singh. Kevat Hindu.
Bhukhan Rishi	51 years old. Male. Illiterate. Owns no land. Hires out his labour to work as agricultural labourer for peasants such as Amaresh Yadav as well as landlords as Gajen Singh. Combines agricultural labourer with employment in the construction sector in northwestern India. Musahar Hindu.
Dharmesh Srivastav	A political mediator. Affiliated with the BJP. His friendship with Amaresh Yadav is legendary, despite differences in caste and political party affiliation. Plays an important role in local affairs. Has a reputation for taking issues relating to poor families and individuals, in doing which he has often gone against the interests of individuals from his own caste/ economic background. Harbors political ambitions. 39 years old. Male. Owns some land, which he cultivates with hired labor. Owns a photocopy machine, which is his chief sources of income. Kayasth Hindu, but unrelated to the established Kayasth families in Sargana.

Domi Rishi	Veteran of the CPI(M/L- L) and the land liberation movements of the 1970s and the 1980s. Continues to be well respected, and at the center of several local contentions, including the contentions over the management of the Chandithan. Lives in Sargana Ward 5. 75 years old. Male. Illiterate. Owns some land, which he cultivates using his own and his family's labour. Musahar Hindu.
Gajen Singh	Post Master of Sargana. Responsible for disbursing NREGS wages, on which he frequently reneged. His mother is a block-level functionary of the BJP. Also a stringer for a widely-read Hindi daily. 40 years old. Owns considerable land. Hires labor and machines. Rajput Hindu.
Gunvati Yadav	Husband of the Anganwadi Worker, the government-appointed officer in charge of the ICDS pre-school center in Sargana. 45 years old. Completed secondary education. Owns some land, which he cultivates using hired labour. Substantial proportion of household income derives from his wife's salaried job at the ICDS center. Yadav Hindu.
Gunavati Yadav	Owner, along with her husband Narendra Yadav (See below), of a small plot of homestead land in Sargana Ward 1(East). Spiritedly defended her piece of property against encroachment by a more powerful neighbor. 40 years old. Female. Studied upto primary School. Stays in the village and works in people's homes to supplement her husband's earnings. Yadav Hindu.
Hunny Singh	Mukhya of Sargana Panchayat from 2000 to 2005. Was unsympathetic to the cause of the Musahar families who allegedly occupied the School property in Sargana Ward 5. 35 years old. Male. Owns considerable amount of land, which he cultivates with the help of hired labor. Rajput.

Jamuni Rishi	36 years old. Female. Owns no land. She and her family members work as agricultural laborers for landlords in the locality such as Gajen Singh. Musahar Hindu.
Tilya Rishi	CPI(M/L- L) activist, resident of Sargana Ward 5. Has been involved in the struggle over the management of the Chandithan.
	45 yeard old. Female. Owns no land. She and her family members work as agricultural laborers for peasants in the locality. Musahar Hindu.
Maturi Rishi	40 years old. Male. Illiterate. Owns no land. Hires out his labour to work as agricultural labourer for peasants such as Amaresh Yadav as well as landlords as Gajen Singh. Combines agricultural labourer with employment in the construction sector in northwestern India. Musahar Hindu.
Nandlal Mandal	47 years old. Male. Owns some land, which he cultivates using his own and family labour. Combines agricultural work with employment in the construction sector in northwestern India. Kevat Hindu.
Narendra Yadav	Owns a small plot of land in Sargana Ward 1 (East), where he lives with his family. Social superiors have called them 'upstarts' for this purchase. With help from friends Dharmesh Srivastav and Amaresh Yadav, they successfully defended the property from encroachment by more powerful neighbours.
	43 years old. Illiterate. Works as a farm hand in Punjab for most times of the year. Yadav Hindu.
Neem Singh	Hunny Singh's uncle. Dealer of the Public Distribution System in Sargana. Contested his nephew's bid for Mukhya in 2000, but lost the election badly. Elected Mukhya in 2011 (after the present research was complete).
	51 years old. Completed secondary education. Owns substantial properties in and around Sargana. Hires labour as well as uses machinery for agricultural operations. Rajput Hindu.

Parsvanath Jha	CPI(ML) activist and Secretary of the Agricultural Laborers Association. Has a reputation for his organizational skills. Has a regular presence at the Block Development Office where he helps people file applications for such things as pensions, NREGA employment and BPL cards.
	25 years old. Male. Completed primary education. Owns no land, but does not hire out his labour to anyone either in the village or outside. Brahman Hindu.
Sarvesh Mandal	Mukhya of Sargana Panchayat since 2005. Affiliated with the JD(U). Sympathetic to the demands staged by members of different marginalized communities for fear of alienating them all at once.
	62 years old. Male. Illiterate. Owns some land and hired labor to work on it. Kevat Hindu.
Sejni Rishi	35 years old. Female. Illiterate. Owns no land. She and her family members work as agricultural laborers for landlords in the locality such as Gajen Singh. Mushar Hindu.
Shyamdev Mandal	JD(U) activist. Has been at the forefront of mobilising popular support for Vinay Mandal. Raised funds for the legal battle with the Rajput trustees. Leveraged the support of district-level JD(U) politicians to help with legal aid.
	39 years old. Male. Completed primary education. Owns some land, which he cultivates using his own and family labour. Also hires in labour sometimes. Often, leases in land from Gajdeo Mandal, which he then cultivates with hired labour. Kevat Hindu.
Shyamdev Rishi	Elected Ward Member of Sargana Ward 1. Resides in Sargana Ward 1 (East) hamlet. Is perceived to be a stooge of the landowning families in the locality. Several of my interlocutors from among the Musahar community referred to him as 'khachhar' (dull) who had been elected because the privileged castes wanted him.
	40 years old. Male. Illiterate. Landless. Casual worker, worked as a mason or brick-layer in Rajasthan, Haryana and Delhi till he was elected Ward Member. Musahar Hindu.

Vinay Mandal	One of the members of the 'temple management committee'. Challenged the Chandithan trustees over the use of financial resources, and has been fighting a continuous legal battle to ensure that the financial transactions are known to the public. Was jailed briefly (between 2013 and 2014, after the completion of this study) for allegedly possessing firearms. 58 years old. Owns no land. Completed secondary education. Kevat. Trained as a priest under the aegis of the Bihar State Religious Trust Board. Kevat Hindu.
Ditya	
Madan Hembrom	Husband of the formally-elected Ward Member Shyamoli Hasda of the village and member of the local CPI(M) cadre. 32 years old. Male. Has completed primary education. Owns some land on which he uses his and his family's labor. Saotal Hindu.
Majhi Haram	The title of the community elder of the Saotal community. I was not sure about the appropriateness of enquiring about his personal name. Close personal friend of Shashanka Sarkar. Participant in the land liberation movements of the 1960s alongside the CPI(M) cadre. 63 years old. Male. Illiterate. Owns some land on which he used his and his family's labor. Saotal, Hindu.
Majhuli Moholi	The *Majhi Haram*'s daughter-in-law. She is particularly outspoken about the problems in the ward and the discrimination faced by Saotal children in the local schools and health center. Born in Gajol, a few kilometers north of the present location. 46 years old. Female. Has completed primary education. Owns no land in her name. Works on the farms of peasants based in a nearby ward. Saotal Hindu.

Marangmayee Hembrom	50 years old. Female. Illiterate. Owns no land. Works as agricultural labourer on the farms of local peasants including Motaram Sarkar. Combines agricultural labour with work in the construction sector in northwestern India, where she migrates for shirt durations every year with her husband Shobhan Sarkar. Saotal Hindu.
Motaram Sarkar	CPI(M) strategist and activist since 1969. His father was the *modol* (community headman) of the Desiya community in Ditya. Was Secretary of the Gram Unnayan Samiti in the previous dispensation (2003-08), when his son-in-law was Ward Member. 61 years old. Male. Completed primary school. Owns land in Ditya, which he cultivates using own and hired labor. Desiya Hindu.
Paresh Sarkar	Elected Ward Member of Ditya from 2003 to 2008. Affiliated with the CPI(M). Youngest brother of Tularam Sarkar. Has since been in the political wilderness due to several personal indiscretions. Despite his personal connections (younger brother of Phanindranath Sarkar and son-in-law of Motaram Sarkar), he has been yet unsuccessful in rehabilitating himself with the local CPI(M) leadership. 41 years old. Male. Completed Senior Secondary School. Owns some land, which he cultivates using hired labor. Desiya Hindu.
Phanindranath Sarkar	A shrewd contractor. His adversaries call him "British" for his perceived ability to make the best use of people and situations around him. Was a CPI(M) sympathizer, supporter and beneficiary of contracts. Switched allegiances after the CPI(M) lost power. Elder brother to Paresh Sarkar. Has taken responsibility for educating his nephews in what he calls the 'best English-speaking institutions in Maldah'. 45 years old. Male. Completed primary school. Owns land in Ditya as well as a house in Maldah town. Desiya Hindu.

Sasaram Sarkar	Congress boss in Ditya. Shashanka Sarkar's half-brother (their father married twice). Feels that Shashanka Sarkar cornered everything in the family and locality, from affections to resources, runs deep. Began life in the CPI(M). Fell out with his brother over his stance on building a local temple as well as the appointment of the former's son to a position he had coveted. Joined the Congress Party, and responsible for laying the ground-work for its unprecedented performance in the recent elections. Extremely religious and believes that the local Panchayat ought to support any religious activity. 58 years old. Male. Illiterate. Owns some land, which he cultivates using hired labour. Desiya Hindu.
Shashanka Sarkar	The "Grand Old Man" of the village. The first 'convert' in the locality to the CPI(M) cause. Known for his passionate commitment to the movement and to the cause of the poor. Was elected to the post of the Upa-Pradhan in 1978, and has held various offices at the Panchayat, Block and District levels till his stroke in 2002. Revered by friends, supporters and opponents alike, including Congress strong man Abdul Qadir. He subscribes to the philosophy propagated by the guru Anukool Chandra that all prophets are to be equally revered. A reluctant supporter of the cause of building a temple in Ditya. 67 years old. Male. Has completed primary education. Owns some land. Managed to get his son a public sector job in the local school, following which he earned some disrepute. Desiya Hindu.
Shobhan Hembrom	54 years old. Female. Illiterate. Owns no land. Works as agricultural labourer on the farms of local peasants including Motaram Sarkar. Combines agricultural labour with work in the construction sector in northwestern India, where she works with his wife Marangmayee Hembrom. Saotal Hindu.

Shyamoli Hasda	Elected Ward Member since 2008. An activist of the CPI(M). Is outspoken, but allows her husband to represent her at meetings in the Gram Panchayat and the Block Office, since, as she says, its an all-male affair anyway. However, is not ignorant about the goings-on in the locality. The couple live in a small home, which- like other dwellings in the Saotal localities- have no electricity. 30 years old. Female. Illiterate. Owns no land in her name. Saotal Hindu.
Roshanar Ward 5	
Sushila Mandal	Elected Mukhya of Roshanar Panchayat in 2005. Although most of the decisions are taken and representations made by her husband Hareram Mandal (See below), she is not entirely unaware of events around her. 48 years old. Illiterate. Owns no land in her name. Kevat Hindu.
Gajdeo Mandal	Widely acclaimed as the *mahant/ madal* (community headman) of his Gangot community. A shrewd politician, who was affiliated with the Congress closely till the electoral rout of Congress strongman Pritam Singh (see below). He is currently courted by the RJD and the BJP. Recognized as a mentor by many upcoming politicians. Personal antagonism towards the husband of the elected Mukhya Hareram Mandal runs very deep. Was known to be sympathetic to the insecurities of local Muslims. His role in saving Muslims in the aftermath of communal violence through the 1980s and 1990s is hailed by Muslims in the locality. However, he says he is beginning to 'hate them', largely because of their dietary practices. 58 years old. Completed primary education. Owns land and hires labor to cultivate it. Expert farmer, who has been awarded prizes that recognize agricultural productivity. Gangot Hindu.

Hareram Mandal	Husband of the elected Mukhya. Given the institutional arrangements, he exercises a great deal of influence in the Ward's politics and allocations than the Ward Member does. Was affiliated with the CPI(ML) since 1978 till he decided to contest elections independently, defeating Congress Party strongman Pritam Singh. Prior to that election, Pritam Singh had allegedly declared that every hand that rose in favor of Hareram Mandal would be slashed. With their victory, naturally, the couple were elated. Hareram Mukhya reciprocates Gajdeo Mandal's hatred and considers him Pritam Singh's stooge. 54 years old. Illiterate. Owns some land which he cultivates with his family labor. Kevat Hindu.
Hadisa Khatun	Elected the Ward Member in 2005. Although politically active, the institutional arrangements do not facilitate her decisions to be enforced. A protégé of Gajdeo Mandal, who, it is said by locals, propped her up to rally the locality's Muslims against Hareram Mandal, she was very articulate (at least to me) about her roles and responsibilities. However, she was unable to put any of her plans for her ward into action given Hareram Mandal's obstructive role. 39 years old. Illiterate. Landless. Husband works as a mason in Punjab. Kunjra Muslim.
Kamruz Alam	Political mediator affiliated with the Congress. Another protégé of Gajdeo Mandal's, but fell out recently with him over the latter's insistence on not reconciling with Hareram Mandal. His wife Qudsiya Khatun contested the election against Hadisa, but lost. Although both men spoke of each other fondly in the past tense, the little interaction I witnessed was cold and formal. 36 years old. Completed primary education. Own some land, which he cultivates with his own labor. Kunjra Muslim.

Pritam Singh	Roshanar's Mukhya between 1985 and 2006. Congress politician who claims to be in the 'inner circle' with Rahul Gandhi. Staunch opponent of the NREGS in the locality.
	75 years old. Completed secondary education. Own considerable amount of land, which he cultivates with machinery and hired labor. Rajput Hindu.
Mansoor Ali	An erstwhile cadre of the CPI(ML) and considers himself a disciple of Premchand Yadav. Once a good friend of Hareram Mandal when they were both in the Party. Fell out with him because the latter accused him unfairly of being Pritam Singh's stooge.
	38 years old. Male. Works as a tailor in Gurgaon for eight months a year. Illiterate. Owns no land. Kunjra Muslim.
Premchand Yadav	One of the few leaders of the CPI(M/L-L) for whom everyone in Roshanar and its environs conveyed immense respect. While many people scoffed at his predictions of a communist revolution, friends and foes alike spoke highly of his commitment to the emancipation of the poor. Appalled to hear that I had not read the entire corpus of literature produced by Marx, Engels, Lenin and other authors of the Marxist pantheon.
	64 years old. Male. Completed secondary education. Owned a small plot of land which he cultivated with his own, family and hired labour. He also leased in as well as leased out some land.
	Late in 2016, he and a comrade of the Musahar community were brutally murdered over a land dispute in a nearby location. The local media blames RJD-affiliated criminals. Investigations are ongoing. Yadav Atheist.
Shamsul Alam	61 years old. Male. Butcher who also owns a small plot of agricultural land. He cultivates the farm using his own and family labour but hires one young man in to assist him in his shop. Kunjra Muslim.

The Census Survey

The survey was conducted in two phases. In the first phase, census data was collected from nearly 4,500 households in 18 wards of the two states. The survey response structure elicited nominal responses. However, the codes were treated ordinally. Based on the analysis of this data, in-depth interviews were conducted with 500 households in four purposively selected localities. Probability samples for West Bengal were generated at 7.3 per cent error level and 90 per cent confidence levels. Probability samples for Bihar were generated at 6 per cent error level and 90 per cent confidence levels. In the survey, the response structure elicited nominal as well as open-ended responses. The codes were treated nominally and categorically. The data was analysed using the STATA software package.

The survey data

The survey instrument included each of the 13 questions (12 in the case of West Bengal) mandated in the Planning Commission's survey schedule. It also included the MPI that were at that time being developed by the OPHDI for the UNDP Human Development Report (Alkire and Santos, 2010). In addition, it also drew on the questions framed for the BPL survey proposed by Mehrotra and Mander (2009) and the Destitution Questionnaire developed by the Right to Food campaign in India (RTF, 2002). The survey schedule specifically asked whether the respondent household possessed a BPL card or not. The survey instrument was administered in the local dialect.

The survey response coding structure followed the cardinal response variables used by the Planning Commission's BPL survey. This harmonization facilitated the calculation and- subsequently- the assignment of a score to each surveyed household in accordance with the guidance issued by the Commission. The response variables for questions not corresponding with those on the official BPL survey, but drawing on the MPI were coded using the dichotomous variables (0/1) used by that index. Where the questions were such that they corresponded to both methodologies, the response format followed the cardinal treatment accorded to the data by the Planning Commission, since it was easier to dichotomize cardinal data.

Recruitment and training of investigators

The investigators were recruited from among a pool of NGO workers. In both States, my local NGO contacts recruited them on the basis of previous work experience, familiarity with local dialect, and ability and willingness to work in rural areas for extended periods of time. In West Bengal, the researchers were based out of Maldah Town and commuted daily to the field localities using public transport or their own vehicles. In Bihar, they were residents of the neighbouring gram panchayat.

The training imparted to the investigators emphasized not only the interview techniques but also the accurate coding of responses, since that would directly impact the scores obtained by the household during this exercise. The fact that each household would be 'scored' was not shared with the investigators, in order to prevent possible manipulations of the data. The training proceeded in two steps. I undertook a day-long training with 'senior surveyors' (two in Bihar and one in West Bengal) in Hindi/ Bangla. These 'senior surveyors', now trained the other surveyors (seventeen in West Bengal and twenty-four in Bihar) in the local dialect. I was present throughout the training period in order to monitor the training and, further, to respond to any concerns or requests for clarifications. The investigators undertook a limited number of 'mock interviews' with individuals in neighbouring localities (not the ones identified for this study). The limited number of mock interviews reflected an important constraint (borne out by limitations of time and money).

Survey coverage

Following the standard sociological approach in India, individuals habitually partaking food cooked in the same *chulha* (stove) were considered to be members of a single household. On the survey response sheet, each household was assigned a unique alphanumeric code, based on the locality where the household was located, the code assigned to the investigator who carried out the interview, and the chronological order in which the household had been interviewed. This coding ensured subsequent anonymity and data protection. It was sometimes the case that a homestead was empty when the investigators approached it to collect data. In such circumstances, they asked the neighbours the whereabouts of the individuals dwelling in those homesteads. Such individuals were 'surveyed' during subsequent visits by the investigators.

It is possible that a few households were not covered in the survey on account of having migrated from the locality during the period when the survey was conducted. No information on these households could be collected. Furthermore, it was impossible to compare the household list (either of the census or the one conducted by the State Government for the BPL exercise) given the ongoing nuclearization of families in most localities, a trend they share with other rural and urban localities throughout the country.

Data quality

The survey was very closely monitored by the trainer-surveyors as well as by me. I was based out of the localities where the surveys were conducted. The localities in Bihar lay within a five kilometer radius of my base, so I could easily walk to or hitch a ride to the localities even as the surveys were being conducted. This enabled me to verify if the investigators were doing their job diligently and to meet with randomly selected individuals who had been interviewed in order to informally cross-verify what kind of questions were being asked. In West Bengal, too, I was based out of the localities where the survey was undertaken. These settlements were denser, but also scattered across a wider area. Hence, I had to rely mostly on hitchhiking with villagers as they went about their daily business. In both states, monitoring was particularly intense the first two days, when the surveyors were unfamiliar with both the survey schedule and my monitoring techniques. I found several discrepancies in those two days. Consequently, over 50 forms in both states had to be discarded. The survey in Bihar was completed in 16 days. In West Bengal it took 21 days to complete them.

Even as the importance of communicating in the local dialect was emphasized during the training, my monitoring visits were used as a mechanism to ensure that the survey interviews were carried out in local dialects: Thaiti in Araria and Desiya and Santhali among the Desiyas and Santhals in Maldah. It is possible that a few discrepancies between the written language of the questionnaire and the local dialect in which it was administered crept in. This is a criticism that I am aware can be levelled against me.

The data collected was subjected to three different levels of checks. The first was a 'peer review', under which each completed survey form was randomly allocated among the investigators (with care taken to ensure that forms were not allocated to those who filled them). Basic logical errors were identified, and the interviews were redone where necessary. Priority was accorded to ensuring that the data collected was accurate, and logical inconsistencies arising out of investigators' negligence were reduced. Each checked form was then 'endorsed' by the senior surveyors, who 'back-checked' or cross-verified with the respondents 20 per cent of the forms of each of the investigators. Post their endorsement, it was expected that their remained no logical inconsistencies. Finally, I picked up completed forms randomly to check for logical errors. If I noted that over 20 per cent of the forms submitted by a given investigator suffered from logical inconsistencies, all the forms completed by them were subjected to my personal scrutiny. Each form for which errors were unearthed was re-administered.

I recognize, following Scott (1990), that no degree of surveillance is ever complete. The ways in which field investigators undermine the most rigorous monitoring techniques is an interesting ethnographic study by itself. It needs to be recognized that this exercise too is based on the extent to which logical inconsistencies could be exposed. For supervisors, it was easy to focus on ensuring that data collected on the response forms were amenable to data entry, rather than verifying its accuracy. Given the limited resources at my disposal (resources which would have enabled me to institutionalize supervisory arrangements), this is a possibility I cannot deny since I was unable to ensure that each form was cross-verified.

Data entry

Data collected from both districts was entered into 'excel' program by staff of an NGO contact in Maldah. I recognize that the use of the Access program would have considerably reduced errors. This choice was made given the constraints on available resources and capacities available with me. I recognize that this could be argued to be an important limitation, as the possibilities of errors increase. However, the possibilities for errors were reduced by organizing the data operators in pairs for this exercise. This composition was designed to reduce the possibilities of error likely to occur were individual data entry operators to work through the maze of questionnaires.

The data operators comprised three teams of young men and women who had received extensive formal education. The Maldah data was entered from 21 December to 25 December2009. The men had also acted as investigators, and were thus intimately familiar with the survey instrument. This concentration of skills and expertise facilitated the relatively smooth data entry process in the state. The decision to deploy this team to enter the Araria data (from 21 January to 27 January2010) was motivated by the following factors: the familiarity of the Maldah data operators with the questionnaire (recall that the Maldah data was collected prior to the Araria data), their understanding of written Hindi and the use of the Arabic numeral (rather than the Devnagari numeral) for the response variables together made it easier for them to enter the data.

Given the limitations of data presentation and analysis in the 'excel' program, the data was transferred to the STATA package. This was a crucial phase, as it would determine the subsequent analysis of the data, which in turn would impact the arguments that I make. Following the transfer into stata, the data was cleaned using basic checks: observations with spurious data were abandoned. With this exercise, there remained 4,520 observations across the 18 localities of the two states. These observations formed the basis for the analysis presented in the rest of this chapter.

Scoring of surveyed households

Each response was scored, using the scheme outlined by the Planning Commission. The scores were generated using the appropriate commands in the stata package. Based on these scores as well as the state-mandated 'cut-offs', I classified the households as 'BPL schedule poor' or otherwise. Thus, if a household in the Bihar households obtained a score less than 13 (of a total possible score of 52), they were categorized as 'BPL schedule poor', whereas if they scored 13 and over, they were categorized as 'Non-BPL schedule poor'. Likewise, for West Bengal, households were categorized as 'BPL schedule poor' if they obtained a score less than or equal to 33 (of a total possible score of 60), and as 'Non-BPL schedule poor' otherwise.

Household categories

The next and final step in the categorization of the households was to classify the households as MPI poor and non-MPI poor. The profiles of the MPI poor have already been presented in chapter 2. The MPI poor households were then categorized into four groups, on the basis of the scores they obtained, and their actual possession of BPL cards. Table 1.1A presents a schematic representation of these four groups. Households located in Quadrant A were MPI poor households that scored higher than the state-mandated cutoffs noted above but, at the same time, did not hold BPL cards. Households located in Quadrant C were those MPI poor households that scored less than the state-mandated cutoffs and possessed BPL cards. Both these groups of households supported the contention that the rules of allocating BPL cards were indeed being followed. However, the households located in Quadrants B and D subverted this contention. Households located in Quadrant B were those MPI poor households that obtained scores higher than the state-mandated cutoffs (and, therefore, were not eligible for the BPL card), yet they reported possessing BPL cards. The converse situation held for the households located in Quadrant D. These MPI poor households obtained scores less than the state-mandated cutoffs, yet they reported not possessing BPL cards. This classification was done for the general survey population as well.

Table A2.1: Classification of households on the basis of BPL scores and BPL cardholding status

		Household classification on the basis of scores obtained	
		(Non-BPL schedule poor[2]) (0)	(BPL schedule poor[3]) (1)
BPL cardholding status	Non-BPL cardholder (0)	(A)	(D)
	BPL cardholder (1)	(B)	(C)

---

2 Households obtaining scores higher thans-mandated cut-offs.
3 Households obtaining scores less than/ equal to state-mandated cut-offs.

Table A2.2: BPL card distribution among BPL schedule poor households, inclusions and exclusions

Ward	BPL schedule poor and BPL cardholder	BPL schedule poor but not BPL cardholder	BPL cardholder but not BPL schedule poor	Neither BPL schedule poor nor BPL cardholder	Total population
Rahimpur	11.79	19.33	25	43.86	424
Sargana Ward 1	9.09	3.63	41.21	46.06	165
Ditya	12.88	23.92	16.87	46.31	326
Roshanar Ward 5	5.59	14.90	17.39	62.11	161

Source: Own census survey, 2009–10.

The Multidimensional Poverty Index

Following Alkire and Foster (2011), I use the concept of the MPI to encapsulate the diverse manifestations of poverty. The MPI uses ten indicators to measure three critical dimensions of poverty at the household level: education, health and living standard. The three dimensions are equally weighted, although the weightage assigned to the indicators varies. To elaborate:

1. The dimension of 'education' comprises the following indicators, each weighted equally at 1/6

    a. Years of schooling: The household was considered deprived if no household member completed five years of schooling.

    b. School attendance: The household was considered deprived if any child aged 6–14 was not attending school.

2. The dimension of 'health' comprises the following indicators, each weighted equally at one-sixth.

    a. Child mortality: The household was considered deprived if any child aged five years or less had died in the family within the last five years.

    b. Nutrition: The household was considered deprived if anyone in the household reported that there were times when they ate fewer meals than usual or when they reported not knowing in the morning whether they would be able to afford a meal in the evening.

3. The dimension of 'standard of living' comprises the following indicators, each weighted equally at one-eighteenth.

    a. Electricity: The household was considered deprived if it had no legal access to electricity.

    b. Drinking water: The household was considered deprived if it did not have access to safe drinking water.

    c. Sanitation: The household was considered deprived if it did not have their own improved sanitation.

d. Flooring: The household was considered deprived if the house it inhabited had a dirt, sand or dung floor.

e. Fuel: The household was considered deprived if it used wood, charcoal or dung for cooking.

f. Assets: The household was considered deprived if it did not own more than one of: radio, TV, telephone, motorized vehicle, or refrigerator.

A household was identified as 'multi-dimensionally poor', or MPI Poor, if it was deprived in at least one dimension, or in a combination of indicators that added up to at least one dimension.

(see http://www.ophi.org.uk/wp-content/uploads/OPHI-MPI-Brief.pdf for further details).

Table A3.1: BPL card distribution among MPI poor households, inclusions and exclusions

Ward	MPI poor and BPL cardholder	MPI poor but not BPL cardholder	BPL cardholder but not MPI poor	Neither MPI poor nor BPL cardholder	Total population
Rahimpur	29.24	51.41	7.54	11.79	424
Sargana Ward 1	32.72	32.72	17.57	16.96	165
Ditya	27.30	56.44	2.45	13.80	326
Roshanar Ward 5	19.87	62.73	3.10	14.28	161

Source: Own census survey, 2009–10.

Annexure 4

Schedule for BPL Census 2002

3.20   Schedule for BPL Census 2002

Name of Head of Household:
House Number and Name, if any:
Name of Village: Total Score   :
Name of Gram Panchayat:
Name of Block: Sub-category:
Name of District:

A. Profile of the household:
(a) Educational status

Sl. No.	Name	Age(in years)	Sex: Male(M)/ Female(F)	Relation to head of household	Educational status * (use code S)

S : Illiterate ~   1   Passed Class V ~   2   Passed Class VIII ~   3
   Passed Class X ~ 4   Passed Class XII ~ 5   Graduate and above ~ 6

(b) Average Monthly Income of the household in Rupees * (Only one column, which is the most appropriate, to be ticked (√))

Less than 250	250-499	500-1499	1500- 2500	More than 2500

(c) Type of operational holding of land * (Only one column, which is the most appropriate, to be ticked (√))

Owner	tenant	Both owner and tenant	None

Whether owns land for construction of IAY house (Yes/No)?
(d) Drinking Water Facility * (Only one column, which is the most appropriate, to be ticked (√).
   Only one row (either 'for plain areas' or 'for hilly areas') to be used).

(for plain areas)	No source of drinking water within distance of 1.6 kilometre	source of drinking water at a distance of 1.00 – 1.59 kilometre	source of drinking water at a distance of 0.50 – .99 kilometre	source of drinking water within a distance of less than 0.50 kilometre	source available within the house
(for hilly areas)	no source of drinking water within elevation of 100 metres	source of drinking water within elevation of 50 – 100 metres	source of drinking water at elevation of less than 50 metres	source available within the house	

(c) Social Group of the household * (Only one column to be ticked (√))

ST	SC	OBC	Others

* Not to be included in the Total Score

B. Identification and Sub-categorisation of Poor

(Only one column, which is the most appropriate, to be ticked (√) against items at Sl. Nos. 1 to 13)

Sl. No.	Characteristic	Scores				
		0	1	2	3	4
1.	Size group of operational holding of land.	Nil	Less than 1 ha. of un-irrigated land (or less than 0.5 ha. of irrigated land)	1 ha. – 2 ha. of un-irrigated land (or 0.5-1.0 ha. of irrigated land)	2 ha. – 5 ha. of un-irrigated land (or 1.0- 2.5 ha. of irrigated land)	More than 5 ha. of un-irrigated land (or 2.5- ha. of irrigated land)
2.	Type of house	Houseless	Kutcha	Semi-pucca	Pucca	Urban type
3.	Average Availability of normal wear clothing(per person in pieces)	Less than 2	2 or more, but less than 4	4 or more, but less than 6	6 or more, but less than 10	10 or more
4.	Food Security	Less than one square meal per day for major part of the year	Normally, one square meal per day, but less than one square meal occasionally	One square meal per day throughout the year	Two square meals per day, with occasional shortage	Enough food throughout the year
5.	Sanitation	Open defecation	Group latrine with **irregular** water supply	Group latrine with **regular** water supply	Clean group latrine with regular water supply and regular sweeper	Private latrine

6.	Ownership of consumer durables: **Do you own** (tick (√)) -TV -electric fan -kitchen appliances like pressure cooker - radio	Nil	Any one	Two items only	Any three or all items	All items and/or Ownership of any one of the following: -Computer - Telephone - Refrigerator - Colour TV -electric kitchen appliances -expensive furniture -LMV*/ LCV@ -Tractor -mechanized two-wheeler/ three-wheeler -Power Tiller -Combined thresher/ harvester [@ 4-wheeled mechanized vehicle]
7.	Literacy status of the highest literate adult	Illiterate	Upto primary (Class V)	Completed secondary (Passed Class X)	Graduate/ Professional Diploma	Post Graduate/ Professional Graduate
8.	Status of the Household Labour Force	Bonded Labour	Female & Child Labour	Only adult females & no child labour	Adult males only	Others
9.	Means of livelihood	Casual labour	Subsistence cultivation	Artisan	Salary	Others
10	Status of children(5-14 years) [any child]	Not going to School* and working	Going to School* and working			Going to School* and NOT working

11.	Type of indebtedness	For daily consumption purposes from informal sources	For production purpose from informal sources	For other purpose from informal sources	Borrowing only from Institutional Agencies	No indebtedness and possess assets
12.	Reason for migration from household	Casual work	Seasonal employment	Other forms of livelihood	Non-migrant	Other purposes
13.	Preference of Assistance	Wage Employment/ PDS(Targeted Public Distribution System)	Self Employment	Training and Skill Upgradation	Housing	Loan/ Subsidy more than Rs. one lakh or No assistance needed

@ including Non Formal Education

Note. The Total Score for a household will vary between 0 and 52

Schedule for BPL Census 2002
West Bengal

বিশেষ সংসদ সভা

জুলাই আগষ্ট মাস ব্যাপী প্রত্যেক গ্রাম সংসদে বিশেষ বিশেষ সভা অনুষ্ঠিত হবে। উক্ত গ্রাম সংসদ সভায় সংশোধিত বি.পি.এল তালিকা নিয়ে আলোচনা হবে। সংসদ সভায় সম্পূর্ণ সার্ভে তালিকা, ৩৩ নম্বর পাত্তিয়া পর্যন্ত বি.পি.এল তালিকা সংসদ ভিত্তিক এর প্রস্তাবিত IAY তালিকা এবং ৬৫ বৎসরের উর্ধ্বে বি.পি.এল অন্তর্ভুক্ত নয়ছ নাগরিকদের তালিকা সামাজিক সুরক্ষা প্রকল্পে উপকারভোগী চিহ্নিত করার জন্য পেশ করা হবে। সংসদ সভায় আলোচনা সাপেক্ষে যে তালিকাগুলি প্রস্তুত করতে হবে :-

(১) IAY এর সম্ভাব্য তালিকা (Suggested list) থেকে স্থায়ী অপেক্ষমান তালিকা : (Permanent waiting list)

(ক) তপশীলি জাতি ও উপজাতিভুক্ত পরিবার

তপশীলি জাতি/উপজাতিভুক্ত পরিবারের তালিকা

পরিবারের ক্রমাঙ্ক	পরিবারের প্রধানের নাম	পরিবারের পূর্ণবয়স্কা মহিলা নাম যার নামে ইন্দিরা আবাস যোজনার সুবিধা দেওয়া যেতে পারে	সামাজিক অবস্থান (তপশীলি জাতি/ উপজাতি)	মোট প্রাপ্ত নম্বর (ক্রমবর্ধমান মান অনুসারে)

(খ) সংখ্যালঘু সম্প্রদায়ভুক্ত পরিবার

সংখ্যালঘু সম্প্রদায়ভুক্ত পরিবারের তালিকা

পরিবারের ক্রমাঙ্ক	পরিবারের প্রধানের নাম	পরিবারের পূর্ণবয়স্কা মহিলা নাম যার নামে ইন্দিরা আবাস যোজনার সুবিধা দেওয়া যেতে পারে	মোট প্রাপ্ত নম্বর (ক্রমবর্ধমান মান অনুসারে)

(গ) অন্যান্য ও সাধারণ পরিবার

অন্যান্য পরিবারের তালিকা

পরিবারের ক্রমাঙ্ক	পরিবারের প্রধানের নাম	পরিবারের পূর্ণবয়স্কা মহিলা নাম যার নামে ইন্দিরা আবাস যোজনার সুবিধা দেওয়া যেতে পারে	মোট প্রাপ্ত নম্বর (ক্রমবর্ধমান মান অনুসারে)

IAY সম্ভাব্য তালিকার মধ্যে যারা অযোগ্য বলে সংসদ সভায় বিবেচিত হবেন তাদের জন্য পৃথক তালিকা প্রস্তুত করতে হবে।

(২) সামাজিক সুরক্ষার জন্য বি.পি.এল তালিকাভুক্ত পরিবারের ৬৫ বা তদুর্ধ্ব বৃদ্ধ / বৃদ্ধাদের তালিকা ঃ

(ক) বর্তমানে বার্ধক্যভাতা বা অনুরূপ যোজনায় উপভোগ নন।

(খ) বর্তমানে উপভোক্তা কিন্তু বি.পি.এল তালিকার অন্তর্ভুক্ত নন।

(গ) বর্তমানে উপভোক্ত এবং বি পি এল তালিকার অন্তর্ভুক্ত।

উক্ত তালিকার মধ্যে যারা সামাজিক সুরক্ষা প্রকল্পের যোগ্য নন এমন ব্যক্তিদের তালিকা প্রস্তুত করতে হবে।

বিশেষভাবে উল্লেখযোগ্য যে কোন দরিদ্র পরিবার যদি কোন কারণে ৩৩ এর বেশী নম্বরের ভিত্তিতে বি.পি.এল তালিকার বাইরে থাকেন সেক্ষেত্রে নিম্নোক্ত তালিকার কোন কোন নির্দিষ্ট পয়েন্টে তার নম্বর বেশী (ভুল) আছে তা উল্লেখ করে সাদা কাগজে আবেদন করতে পারেন। অনুরূপভাবে যদি কোন পরিবার ৩৩ এর নীচে নম্বর থাকার সত্ত্বেও বি.পি.এল এর সুবিধা পাবার যোগ্য নন বলে মনে হয় সেক্ষেত্রে সেই ব্যক্তি নিজে বা অন্য কেউ আবেদন করে তার নাম কোন কোন নাম যদি সার্ভে লিস্টেও না থাকে তবে তিনি নতুনভাবে সার্ভের জন্য আবেদন করতে পারেন। পয়েন্টে বেশী হবে তা জানাতে পারেন।

* বিশেষভাবে মনে রাখতে হবে, নির্দিষ্ট ঘরে আবেদন করলেই এবিষয়ে সঠিক তদন্ত করা সম্ভব হবে।
* সমস্ত আবেদনেই সংসদের নং / নাম এবং -র উল্লেখ থাকতে হবে।

আবেদনগুলি গ্রাম পঞ্চায়েতে জমা দিতে হবে। জমা নেওয়ার সময় গ্রাম পঞ্চায়েতের নির্দিষ্ট কর্মী আবেদনগুলি পরীক্ষা করে জমা নেবেন।

* উপরতন কর্তৃপক্ষের নির্দেশ অনুযায়ী আবেদনগুলি তদন্ত সাপেক্ষ বি. পি. এল. তালিকা সংশোধিত হবে।

সে বিষয়গুলির ভিত্তিতে ১ থেকে ৫ নম্বর দেওয়া হয়েছে তা নিম্নরূপ ঃ-

P (1) পরিবারের মোট জমির পরিমাণ (নথিভুক্ত বর্গাদার হিসাবে চাষ করা জমির পরিমাণ সহ)

১। জমি নাই
২। ১ একরের কম (সেচসেচিত) অথবা ২ একরের কম (অসেচ)
৩। ১ একর থেকে ২ একর (সেচসেচিত) অথবা ২ একর থেকে ৪ একর (অসেচ)
৪। ২ একর থেকে ৪ একর (সেচসেচিত) অথবা ৪ একর থেকে ৮ একর (অসেচ)
৫। ৪ একরের বেশী (সেচসেচিত) অথবা ৮ একরের বেশী (অসেচ)

P (2) বাসগৃহের প্রকৃতি ও গঠন

১। নিজস্ব বাড়ি নেই, অন্যের আশ্রয়ে বা অনুমতি ছাড়া থাকেন
২। একটিমাত্র বাসযোগ্য ঘর সহ কাঁচা বাড়ী
৩। দুই বা তার বেশী বাসযোগ্য ঘর সহ কাঁচা বাড়ী
৪। আংশিক পাকা
৫। পাকা

P (3) গড় পড়তা পরিচ্ছদের সংখ্যা (প্রতি সদস্য পিছু সংখ্যা)

১। ২ এর কম
২। ২ থেকে ৪ কিন্তু কোন শীত বস্ত্র নাই
৩। ২ থেকে ৪ শীতবস্ত্র সহ
৪। ৪ বা তার বেশী কিন্তু ৬ এর কম
৫। ৬ এর বেশী

P (4) খাদ্যের জোগান

১। বছরের অধিকাংশ সময়ে দিতে একবারের কম পেট ভরে খেতে পান
২। সাধারণত দিনে একবার পেট ভরে খেতে পান কিন্তু কখনো কখনো পান না।
৩। দিনে দুবার পেট ভরে খেতে পান কিন্তু বছরের কোন কোন সময় পান না
৪। সারা বৎসর দিনে দুবার পেট ভরে খেতে পান

P (5) ভোগ্য পণ্যের মালিকানা : পরিবারে কি আছে; সাইকেল, রেডিও, সাদা কালো টিভি, বৈদ্যুতিক পাখা, প্রেসার কুকার

১। কিছু নাই

২। যে কোন একটি

৩। যে কোন দুটি

৪। যে কোন তিনটি

৫। উপরিল্লিখিত সব কটি পণ্য বা নীচের যে কোন একটি কম্পিউটার, টেলিফোন, ফ্রিজ, রঙিন টিভি, র‍্যার বৈদ্যুতিক সরঞ্জাম দামী দবাবপত্র, ভারী ট্রাক, হাল্কা ট্রাক, ভারী বা হাল্কা মোটরগাড়ী ট্রাক্টর, মোটরসাইকেল, স্কুটার, অটো রিক্সা, টেম্পো, পাওয়ার টিলার, পেষাই মেসিন, র‍্যার গ্যাসের সংযোগ, পাম্প সেট, অন্যান্য।

P (6) শিক্ষার মান (পরিবারের সর্বাধিক শিক্ষিত ব্যক্তির)

১। নিরক্ষর

২। সাক্ষর স্তর থেকে পঞ্চম শ্রেণী (শুধুমাত্র নাম সই করলেই তাকে সাক্ষর বলা হবে না, পড়তে ও লিখতে পারেন এমন ব্যক্তিকেই সাক্ষর বলা হবে।)

৩। পঞ্চম শ্রেণীর ঊর্ধ্বে দশম শ্রেণী পর্যন্ত

৪। দশম শ্রেণীর ঊর্ধ্বে স্নাতক স্তর পর্যন্ত

৫। স্নাতকোত্তর

P (7) পরিবারের শ্রমভিত্তিক অবস্থান

১। সদস্যরা সবাই অক্ষম / বৃদ্ধ বৃদ্ধা, শিশু পরিশ্রম করে নিয়মিত উপার্জন করার কেউ নেই।

২। শিশু শ্রমিক আছে।

৩। প্রাপ্ত বয়স্ক মহিলা শ্রমিক আছে। কিন্তু প্রাপ্ত বয়স্ক পুরুষ শ্রমিক নাই।

৪। প্রাপ্ত বয়স্ক পুরুষ শ্রমিক আছে

৫। অন্যান্য (টেবিলে বসে কাজ, ব্যান্সা, পড়ানো নার্স না অন্যান্য (পেশাগত কাজ)

P (8) জীবনধারণের উপায়

১। দিনমজুর / কৃষি শ্রমিক / অন্যান্য শ্রমিক যারা কায়িক শ্রম করেন / উপার্জন না

২। কৃষি এবং নিজের মাঠে কাজ করেন

৩। স্বনিয়োজিত / গ্রামীণ কারুশিল্পী (আর্টিসান) /হকার/ইত্যাদি যারা অন্য কাউকে নিয়োজিত করেন না।

৪। অসংগঠিত ক্ষেত্রে নিয়মিত মজুরীভিত্তিক চাকরী

৫। অন্যান্য, যথা সংগঠিত ক্ষেত্রে চাকরী, ডাক্তার, উকিল, নিজস্ব ব্যবসা ইত্যাদি।

(9) ৯-১৪ বৎসরের সন্তানদের শিক্ষার অবস্থান (সন্তানদের মধ্যে সবচেয়ে খারাপ অবস্থানে সে আছে তার মান দিতে হবে)

১। কোনদিন স্কুলে যায় না।

২। স্কুলছুট এবং নিজ বাড়ীর বাইরে অন্যে বাড়ী কাজ করে।

৩। স্কুল ছুট এবং নিজ বাড়িতে কাজ করে।

৪। স্কুলছুট এবং কোন বিশেস কাজে যুক্ত নয়।

৫। কেউ স্কুল ছুট নয়।

-১৪ বৎসরের মধ্যে কোন সন্তান না থাকলে পরিবারের সর্বকনিষ্ঠ সদস্যের ১৪ বৎসর বয়সে যে অবস্থান ছিল সেই মান দিতে হবে।)

P (10) ঋণের ধরণ

১। দৈনন্দিন জীবন ধারণের প্রয়োজনে কোন পরিচিত ব্যক্তির কাছে ঋণ।

২। উৎপাদন ভিত্তিক প্রয়োজনে পরিচিত ব্যক্তির কাছে ঋণ।

৩। উৎপাদন বা অন্য কোন প্রয়োজন কোন প্রতিষ্ঠান বা পরিচিত ব্যক্তির আছে ঋণ।

৪। শুধুমাত্র কোন প্রতিষ্ঠান থেকে নেওয়া ঋণ।

৫। কোন ঋণ।

P (11) পরিবারের প্রধান উপার্জনকারীর উপার্জনের জন্য গ্রামের বাইরে গমনের কারণ -

১। মরসুমী কায়িক পরিশ্রমের কাজ

২। অস্থায়ী কায়িক পরিশ্রমের কাজ

৩। অসংগঠিত ক্ষেত্রে কাজের জন্য

৪। সংগঠিত ক্ষেত্রে কাজের জন্য

৫। কোনটিই নয়

P (12) বিশেষ ধরনের দুঃস্থতা / পরিবার

১। সহায় সম্বলহীন বৃদ্ধ/বৃদ্ধা (পরিবারে উপার্জনক্ষম কেউ নাই)

২। কোন সামাজিক বা সরকারী সাহায্য পান না এরকম স্থায়ী প্রতিবন্ধী

৩। পরিবারের প্রধান উপার্জনকারী মহিলা

৪। পরিবারের কোন একজন সদস্য দুরারোগ্য ব্যাধিতে আক্রান্ত হওয়ায় চিকিৎসা সংক্রান্ত ব্যয় পারিবারিক আয়ের থেকে বেশী

৫। কোনটিই নয়।

সংসদ সভায় বি.পি.এল. তালিকা সহ সম্পূর্ণ সার্ভে লিস্ট প্রকাশিত হচ্ছে। আপনি দেখে নিন আপনার নম্বরগুলো সঠিক দেওয়া হয়েছে কিনা ?

BPL Cutoff List for West Bengal

Government of West Bengal
Panchayats and Rural Development Department

Jessop Building, 63 Netaji Subhash Road, 1st Floor, Kolkata 700001

Memo No: 3070-RD (SGSY))/ 20M-6/2005 (Pt-I)   **Date :03/05/2007**

From :   Dr M. N. Roy, IAS
           Principal Secretary to the Government of West Bengal

To: The District Magistrates – All.

Subject: **Publication of BPL list (Guideline -3)**

Ref: **This Department No. 76/JS(DG)/007/SGSY/20-M-6/2005 dated 2nd April, 2007 and No 079/JS(DG)/2007/ SGSY/20-M-6/2005 datd 4th April, 2007**

Sir / Madam,

In continuation of this department's guidelines quoted under reference I am directed to state hereunder the procedures to be adopted for identifying actual beneficiaries, who will come under the purview of different programmes targeted towards the B.P.L families. It has been decided in consultation with the Food and Supplies Department, Government of West Bengal that the cut off score for ascertaining the BPL families will be 33. In tea garden areas, the cut-off score will be 37 and in closed Tea gardens, all worker families will be treated as BPL families. It has further been decided that in respect of those Mouzas which have been totally washed away due to erosion of river the cut off marks for determining the BPL families of those areas will be reviewed after receiving relevant information from the districts.

2. In respect of IAY, the list of eligible families will be generated by running pre-defined queries (Total Score<=33 and P2=1). The permanent wait list for IAY beneficiaries will be generated from this list of eligible families after

consideration of the Gram Sansad as per the following guidelines. The list will be taken up for consideration family-wise starting from the lowest score. Those whose names appear in the list but the Gram Sansad considers that the family is not eligible because (i) it has already received benefit under IAY/ PMGY (GA)/ SGRY (IBS) for construction of new house, (ii) there is factual mistake in the scores under one or more categories which will make the family ineligible (iii) the condition of the family has changed for the better, (iv) the family has left the area permanently etc., those should be clearly mentioned and a list of such persons showing the reasons for not considering their case for each family to be separately prepared & sent to the Gram Panchayat. The list of other eligible persons, i.e., those excluding the ineligible families, will form the Permanent Wait List. This list should be segregated in three categories: - i) those belonging to SC or ST, ii) those belonging to Minorities, iii) the rest belonging to general categories. The Gram Panchayat will compile the data for each category and will forward the same to the BDO concerned. The complete data-base with names of the head of the family appearing in the Permanent Wait List along with the name of one adult female members of those families, who will be the recipient of the fund under IAY, have to be maintained at the Block-level (in case there is no adult women member in a family that should be clearly mentioned). The BDO will be the custodian of the data-base, which will have Gram Panchayat and Samsad-wise priority list of families under each category who will get benefit under IAY. In case some of them do not have any homestead land of their own the same information may also be compiled in due course. The BDO should forward the numbers of eligible families category-wise (their names should be readily available if demanded) to the Zilla Parishad. A format for preparation of the lists is enclosed herewith. The names of the head of the households, which will be included in the Permanent Wait List of IAY should be written in the external walls of the Gram Panchayat so that every one knows which families will get the benefit of IAY in due course.

There could be some families whose scores are higher than 33 but the condition of the house is of category P2=1 or there is gross mistake in scores of the family. They cannot be considered directly for inclusion in the Permanent Wait List. They may submit any factual mistake in their objective status in respect of the twelve indicators, which may be considered, not immediately, but in due course depending on numbers of such application received. The list of families whose houses have to be shifted within the current year for construction of roads under PMGSY or the houses which have been totally destroyed by any natural calamity after the survey and the loss of the family will be such that its status will come down to BPL category their list and scores are to be separately forwarded to the Zilla Parishad via the Gram Panchayat and the Panchayat Samiti. The Gram Samsad will be required to endorse this list-also. Such families may be separately considered for extending benefit under IAY only as a special case and they will not be considered for getting benefit under other schemes targeted to the BPL families. However, such families, like any one else, may always submit application to the Gram Panchayat to report their change of objective status for verification in due course.

The entire process should be completed by the middle of June so that the Zilla Parishad may fix the Gram Panchayat-wise quota of IAY for each category based on certain objective criteria and release fund to the Gram Panchayats by the and June 2007. Also, the Zilla Parishad will not release fund to the Gram Panchayats till the Permanent Wait Lists are published and information on category-wise numbers of families in the said list is received from the Gram Panchayats.

3 The Gram Samsad should also identify all persons with age 65 years or more and belonging to BPL families for giving coverage under suitable social security scheme. For that purpose the list of all such persons from BPL families are to be prepared starting from the lowest to the highest score (33). Most of them ar already covered under any pension scheme. (such as NOAPS, old age pension scheme of Women & Child Development & Social Welfare or other departments, pension scheme for tribal people etc) or under Annapurna Yojana (AY). The list of all aged persons mentioning who are already covered (the name of the scheme to be specifically mentioned in each case) should be prepared by the Gram Panchayat with feedback from the Gram Samsad / Gram Unnayan Samity (GUS). The second list of all eligible persons not covered under any scheme has to be prepared in order of their scores (lowest score to be at the top). A third list of aged persons who are not in the BPL category as per present survey but getting benefit under any of the said social security schemes should also be prepared by the Gram Panchayat with feedback from the Gram Samsad / GUS. They will continue to receive the existing benefit

until instruction is issued otherwise by the State Government. Formats for the said lists are enclosed herewith. In case there are persons in BPL families who are considered ineligible for receiving social assistance because of certain reasons, the same should also be compiled by the Gram Panchayat and communicated to the Block Office. In all the lists social categories (SC/ST/ Minority/others) of the persons are to be mentioned. All the lists, prepared for each Samsad, are to be forwarded to the Block Office by the Gram Panchayat for entering the details in the data-base. A list of persons who are eligible to receive social assistance in the form of pension or free rice under AY and yet not covered should be prepared by the BDO and forwarded to the District Panchayats and Rural Development Officer for compiling district figures. The list of existing AY beneficiaries and their scores should also be forwarded by the BDO to the District Panchayats and Rural Development Officer for consideration if some of them could be covered under pension scheme, which provides higher quantum of benefit, in lieu of coverage under AY.

For municipal areas the task of the Gram Panchayat will be performed by the Municipality concerned. In respect of Kolkata Corporation the list will be directly submitted to the Commissioner Panchayats and Rural Development. In respect of other Corporations the list will be submitted directly to the District Panchayats and Rural Development Officer concerned. This exercise should be completed by the middle of June so that coverage under NOAPS and AY may be increased immediately thereafter. Before forwarding the list by the Gram Panchayat/ Municipality to the authority concerned it must be ensured that the total no. of existing beneficiaries, now classified as those belonging to BPL and those not under that category taken together matches the existing no of beneficiaries. Those who appeared in the list of existing beneficiaries and are dead by now should also be reconciled in this opportunity.

The Panchayat bodies will be required to incur expenditure for acquisition and compiling several data as mentioned. Such expenditure may be incurred out of fund made available as grants from the 12th Finance Commission. The District Magistrates may work out the rates for various activities related to acquisition and compilation of data. Support of Gram Unnayan Samiti may be obtained for that purpose.

All concerned are requested to give utmost-importance to early compilation of the list as correctly as possible for both the categories of programmes so that there is no unnecessary delay in extending benefit of the said programmes to the deserving persons. A format showing the synoptic information to be compiled is also enclosed herewith for better monitoring. District Magistrates are also requested to closely monitor the progress for both timely completion of the task and maintaining quality of the data.

Yours faithfully,

Sd/-

(M. N. Roy)

Principal Secretary to the

Govt. of West Bengal.

No: 3070/1(32)-RD(SGSY))/20M-6/2005 (Pt-I)   Date :03/05/2007

Copy forwarded for information and necessary action to :

1. The Sabhadhipati, Zilla Parishad / Mahakuma Parishad – All.

2. The Additional Chief Secretary, Food & Supplies Department, Govt. of West Bengal, Khadya Bhavan, 11A Mirza Ghalib Street, Kolkata – 700 087.

3. The Principal Secretary, Municipal Affairs Department, Govt. of West Bengal, Writers' Buildings, Kolkata – 700 001.

4. The Commissioner, Presidency / Burdwan / Jalpaiguri Division.

5. The Principal Secretary, Darjeeling Gorkha Hill Council, Darjeeling.

6. The Director, State Institute of Panchayat & Rural Development, Kalyani, Nadia.

7. The Principal, Extension Training Centre, Burdwan / Coochbehar / Raiganj / Paschim Medinipur.

8. Private Secretary to the Minister-in-Charge, Panchayat & Rural Development Department, Govt. of West Bengal, Writers' Buildings, Kolkata – 700 001.

9. Private Secretary to the Minister-of-State, Panchayat & Rural Development Department, Govt. of West Bengal, Jessop Building, 63 N.S. Road, Kolkata – 700 001.

Principal Secretary to the

Govt. of West Bengal.

Permanent wait list of IAY based on Rural Household Survey, 2005

District Name   Block Name

Gram Panchayat Name   Gram Sansad

Gramer Naam (Village Name)

List for SC/ST

House Hold ID	Name of head of household	Name of the adult Woman Member of the Household in whose name IAY benefit may be given	Social Status (SC/ST/)	Total Score (In ascending order
A	B	C	D	E

List for Minorities

House Hold ID	Name of head of household	Name of the adult Woman Member of the Household in whose name IAY benefit may be given	Total Score (In ascending order
A	B	C	E

List for others

House Hold ID	Name of head of household	Name of the adult Woman Member of the Household in whose name IAY benefit may be given	Total Score (In ascending order
A	B	C	E

Schedule of Existing beneficiaries of Social Security Schemes (Pension or Annapurna Yojana) who are covered under BPL list prepared on the basis of Rural Household Survey, 2005
(List-I as mentioned in para 3 of Guideline-3)

District Name   Block Name

Gram Panchayat Name   Gram Sansad

Gramer Naam (Village Name)

House Hold ID	Name of head of house-hold	Total Score (In ascending order)	Social Status (SC/ST/ Minority)	Name of the person exceeding 65 years of age	A G E	Relation-ship with head of the Household	Name of the social security scheme under which the family is presently covered
A	B	C	D	E	F		G

- Column A, B and C will have to be adopted from the BPL list prepared on the basis of Rural Household Survey, 2005
- Column D is to be filled up on the basis of local information

Schedule of Eligible beneficiaries of Social Security Schemes who are not covered under any Pension Scheme or Annapurna Yojana
(List-II as mentioned in para 3 of Guideline-3)

District Name   Block Name

Gram Panchayat Name   Gram Sansad

Gramer Naam (Village Name)

Name of the person exceeding 65 years of age	Name of head of household	Social Status (SC/ST/ Minority)	Age	Relationship with head of Household	House-hold ID	Score
A	B	C	D	E	F	G

- Column A to E is to be prepared by the Gram Panchayat and to be sent to BDO;
- At the Block level Column F and G is to be identified from the databased by running query on name of head of the household;
- The member information is to be entered to capture all information on old age persons

Schedule of beneficiaries of Social Security Schemes who are not included in BPL list prepared on the basis of Rural Household Survey, 2005

(List-III as mentioned in para 3 of Guideline-3)

District Name   Block Name

Gram Panchayat Name   Gram Sansad

Gramer Naam (Village Name)

Name of the person exceeding 65 years of age	Name of head of household	Social Status (SC/ST/Minority)	Age	Relationship with head of the Household	Name of the pension scheme or AY under which the member is covered	Score
A	B	D	E	F	G	H

* to be filled in at Block level

Synoptic Information

Table – A

Name of the Gram Pan-chayat	No. of San-sad	No. of BPL fami-lies	No. of fami-lies who may be consid-ered for IAY	Social status of those families				No. of aged persons yet to be covered under social security schemes	Social Status			
				SC	ST	Minor-ities	Oth-ers		SC	ST	Mi-nor-ities	Oth-ers

Bibliography

Abrams, P. 1988. 'Notes on the Difficulty of Studying the State', *Journal of Historical Sociology* 1: 58–89.

Acemoglu, D. and J. Robinson. 2012. *Why Nations Fail: The Origins of Power, Prosperity and Poverty*. London: Profile.

Adhikari, A. and K. Bhatia. 2010. 'NREGA Wage Payments: Can we Bank on the Banks?' *Economic and Political Weekly* 45 (1): 30–37.

Adhikari, B., M. K. Bag, M. K. Bhowmick and C. Kundu. n.d. 'Status Paper on Rice in West Bengal'. Available at: http://www.rkmp.co.in/sites/default/files/ris/rice-state-wise/ Status%20Paper%20on%20Rice%20in%20West%20Bengal.pdf, accessed in December 2013.

Agarwal, A. 1996. 'Poststructuralist Approaches to Development: Some Critical Reflections', *Peace and Change* 21 (4): 464–77.

Agarwala, R. 2013. *Informal Labour, Formal Politics and Dignified Discontent in India*. Cambridge: Cambridge University Press.

Ahmed, S. 1998. 'Occupational Segregation and Caste-based Discrimination in India', in *Labour Market Segmentation in India*, edited by M. Shah, 67–92. Mumbai: Himalaya.

Ahn, P. S. 2008. 'Organising as a Catalyst for Promoting Decent Work in the Informal Economy in South Asia', *Indian Journal of Labor Economics* 51 (4): 1015–25.

Alavi, H. 1973. 'Peasant Classes and Primordial Loyalties', *Journal of Peasant Studies* 1 (1): 23–62.

———. 1975. *Dependence, Autonomy and the Articulation of Power*. Montreal: Centre for Developing Area Studies.

Alexander, J. 2006. *The Civil Sphere*. New York: Oxford University Press.

Alexander, J., J. McGregor and T. O. Ranger. 2000. *Violence and Memory: One Hundred Years in the 'Dark Forests' of Matabeleland, Zimbabwe*. Portsmouth, NH and Oxford: Heinemann and James Currey.

Alkire, S., A. Conconi, S. Seth and A. Vaz. 2014. 'Global Multidimensional Poverty Index 2014', Oxford Poverty and Human Development Initiative Briefing 20.

Alkire, S. and M. E. Santos. 2010. 'Multidimensional Poverty Index', *Research Brief*. Oxford: Oxford Poverty and Human Development Initiative.

Alkire, S. and S. Set. 2014. 'Multidimensional Poverty Reduction in India between 1999 and 2006: Where and How?' *World Development* 72: 93–108.

Alkire, S. and S. Seth. 2008. 'Multidimensional Poverty and BPL Measures in India: A Comparison of Methods, *OPHI Working Papers* No. 15. Oxford: Oxford University.

Alkire, S., C. Jindra, G. R. Aguilar, S. Seth and A. Vaz. 2015. *Global Multidimensional Poverty Index 2015*. Oxford: Oxford Poverty and Human Development Initiative.

Alkire, S., J. M. Roche and A. Sumner. 2013. 'Where do the World's Multidimensionally Poor People Live?' Available at: http://papers.ssrn.com/sol3/papers.cfm?abstract_id=2292915.

Alkire, S., M. Chatterjee, A. Conconi, S. Seth and A. Vaz. 2014. 'Global Multidimensional Poverty Index', *Research Brief*. Oxford: OPHI.

Allcock, J. 2004. *Explaining Yugoslavia*. Columbia: Columbia University Press.

Almond, G. A. 1954. *The Appeals of Communism*. Princeton: Princeton University Press.

Almond, G. and J. Coleman. 1960. *The Politics of the Developing Areas*. Princeton: Princeton University Press.

Almond, G. and S. Verba. 1963. *The Civic Culture: Political Attitudes and Democracy in Five Nations*. Princeton: Princeton University Press.

———. 1965. *The Civic Culture: Political Attitudes and Democracy in Five Nations*, Boston: Little, Brown.

Alvarez, M. J. A. Cheibub and F. Limongi. 1996. 'Classifying Political Regimes', *Studies in Comparative International Development* 31 (2): 3–36.

Ambedkar, B. R. 1946. *Who were the Shudras?* Bombay: Government of Maharashtra.

———. 1949. *Constituent Assembly Debates Volume X1, Part 1*. Available at: http://parliamentofindia.nic.in/ls/debates/vol11p11.htm. Delhi: Government of India

———. 1979. 'Castes in India: Their Mechanism, Genesis and Development', in *Dr. Babasaheb Ambedkar: Writings and Speeches Volume 1*, edited by B. R. Ambedkar, 3–22. Bombay: Government of Maharashtra.

———. 2014. *Dr. BR Ambedkar Writings and Speeches, Volume 5*. Delhi: Dr. Ambedkar Foundation.

Amin, S. 1995. *Event, Metaphor, Memory: Chauri Chaura 1922–1992*. Delhi: Oxford University Press.

Anderson, B. 1991. *Imagined Communities: Reflections on the Origins and Spread of Nationalism*. London: Verso.

Anderson, E. S. 1999. 'What Is the Point of Equality?' *Ethics* 109 (2): 287–337.

Apter, D. 1965. *The Politics of Modernization*. Chicago and London: The University of Chicago Press.

———. 1987. 'Things Fell Apart? Yoruba Responses to the 1983 Elections in Ondo State, Nigeria', *Journal of Modern African Studies* 25 (3): 489–503.

Appadurai, A. 1988. 'Putting Hierarchy in its Place', *Cultural Anthropology* 3 (1): 36–49.

———. 1996 *Modernity at Large*. Minneapolis: Minneapolis University Press.

Assies, W. 1987. 'The Agrarian Question in Peru: Some Observations on the Roads of Capital'. *The Journal of Peasant Studies* 14 (4): 500–32.

Austen-Smith, D. 2000. 'Redistributing Income under Proportional Representation', *Journal of Political Economy* 108 (6): 1235–69.

Avritzer, L. 2002. *Democracy and the Public Space in Latin America*. Princeton: Princeton University Press.

Auyero, J. 1999. 'From the Client's Point of View: How Poor People Perceive and Evaluate Political Clientelism', *Theory and Society* 28 (2): 297–334.

Bachrach, P. and M. Baratz. 1962. 'Two Faces of Power', *American Political Science Review* 56 (04): 947–52.

———. 1963. 'Decisions and Non-decisions: An Analytical Framework', *American Political Science Review* 57 (3): 632–42.

———. 1970. *Power and Poverty: Theory and Practice*. London: Oxford University Press.

Bagchi, A. K. 1982. *The Political Economy of Underdevelopment*. Cambridge: Cambridge University Press.

Bailey, F. G. 1960. *Tribe, Caste, and Nation: A Study of Political Activity and Political Change in Highland Orissa*. Manchester, UK: Manchester University Press.

———. 1969. *Strategies and Spoils: A Social Anthropology of Politics*. Oxford: Basil Blackwell.

Bajpai, N. J., R. A. Sachs and H. Kjurana. 2004. 'Global Services Sourcing: Issue of Cost and Quality', *CGSD Working Paper* 16.

Bakshi, S., A. Chawla and M. Shah. 2015. 'Regional Disparities in India: A Moving Frontier', *Economic and Political Weekly* 50 (1): 44–52.

Balibar, E. 1991. 'Citizen Subject', in *Who Comes After the Subject?* edited by E. Cadava, P. Connor and J. L. Nancy, 33–57. New York: Routledge.

Banaji, J. 1990. 'Illusions about the Peasantry: Karl Kautsky and the Agrarian Question', *The Journal of Peasant Studies* 17 (2): 288–307.

Bandopadhyay, D. 2009. 'Lost Opportunity in Bihar', *Economic and Political Weekly* 44 (47): 12–14.

Bandyopadhyay, S. 2004. *Caste, Culture and Hegemony: Social Dominance in Colonial Bengal*. New Delhi, London: Sage Publications.

Banerjee, K. 2012. 'Rights in Theory and Practice: A Case Study of the NREGA', *India: Social Development Report 2010*. Delhi: Oxford University Press.

Banerjee, K. and P. Saha. 2010. 'The NREGA, the Maoists and the Developmental Woes of the Indian State', *Economic and Political Weekly* 45 (28): 42–48.

Banerjee-Guha, S. 2010. *Accumulation by Dispossession: Transformative Cities in the New Global Order*. Delhi: Sage Publications.

Bardhan, P. 1984. *The Political Economy of Development in India*. Oxford: Oxford University Press.

Bardhan, P. and D. Mookherjee. 2006. 'Decentralisation and Accountability in Infrastructure Delivery in Developing Countries', *The Economic Journal* 116 (508): 101–27.

———. 2007. 'Decentralisation in West Bengal: Origins, Functioning and Impact', in *Decentralization and Local Governments in Developing Countries: A Comparative Perspective*, edited by P. Bardhan and D. Mookerjee, 203–22. New Delhi: Oxford University Press.

Barrientos, A. and D. Hulme. 2008. *Social Protection for the Poor and the Poorest: Concepts, Policies and Politics*. London: Palgrave.

Barrientos, A. 2013. *Social Assistance in Developing Countries*. Cambridge: Cambridge University Press.

Barth, F. 1987. *Cosmologies in the Making: A Generative Approach to Cultural Variation in Inner New Guinea*. Cambridge: Cambridge University Press.

Basso, K. H. 1996. *Wisdom Sits in Places: Landscape and Language among the Western Apache*. UNM Press.

Baulch, B., T. T. K. Chuyen, D. Haughton and J. Haughton. 2007. 'Ethnic Minority Development in Vietnam', *Journal of Development Studies* 43 (7): 1151–76.

Baviskar, A. 2004. *In the Belly of the River: Tribal Conflicts over Development in the Narmada Valley*. Delhi: Oxford University Press.

Baviskar, A. and N. Sundar. 2008. 'Democracy versus Economic Transition in India: Comment on Partha Chatterjee's "Democracy and Economic Transition in India"', *Economic and Political Weekly* 43 (46): 87–89

Bayart, J. F. 1993. *The State in Africa: The Politics of the Belly*, translated by M. Harper, C. Harrison and E. Harrison. New York: Longman.

Bayat, A. 2000. 'From "Dangerous Classes" to "Quiet Rebels": Politics of the Urban Subaltern in the Global South', *International Sociology* 15 (3): 533–57.

———. 2010. *Life as Politics: How Ordinary People Change the Middle East*. Stanford: Stanford University Press.

———. 2013. 'The Arab Spring and its Surprises', *Development and Change* 44 (3): 587–601.

Bayly, C. 1988. *Indian Society and the Making of the British Empire*. Cambridge: Cambridge University Press.

———. 2004. *The Birth of the Modern World, 1780-1914*. Oxford: Oxford University Press.

Bayly, S. 1989. *Saints, Goddesses and Kings: Muslims and Christians in South Indian Society, 1700-1900*. Cambridge: Cambridge University Press.

———. 1993. 'History and the Fundamentalists: India after the Ayodhya Crisis', *Bulletin of the American Academy of Arts and Sciences*: 7–26.

————. 1999. *Caste, Society and Politics in India from the Eighteenth Century to the Modern Age*. Cambridge: Cambridge University Press.

Beals, A. R. and B. Siegel. 1966. *Divisiveness and Social Conflict*. Stanford, CA: Stanford University Press.

Beetham, D. 1999. *Democracy and Human Rights*. Cambridge: Polity Press.

Beiner, R. 1995. 'Introduction: Why Citizenship Constitutes a Theoretical Problem in the Late Decade of the Twentieth Century', in *Theorising Citizenship*, edited by R. Beiner, 1–28. Albany: State University of New York Press.

Bell, D. A. 1999. 'Democracy with Chinese Characteristics: A Political Proposal for a Post-communist Era', *Philosophy East and West* 49 (4): 451–93.

————. 2000. *East Meets West: Human Rights and Democracy in East Asia*. Princeton: Princeton University Press.

Bendix, R. 1964. 'The Age of Ideology: Persistent and Changing', *Ideology and Discontent*: 294–327.

Berg, E., S. Bhattacharyya, R. Durgam and M. Ramachandra. 2012. 'Can Rural Public Works Affect Agricultural Wages? Evidence from India', *CSAE Working Paper* WPS/2012–05. Oxford: University of Oxford.

Bernstein, H. 1992. 'Poverty and the Poor', in *Rural Livelihoods: Crises and Responses*, edited by B. Crow and H. Johnson, 13–26. Oxford: Oxford University Press and Open University.

————. 1996. *The Agrarian Question in South Africa*. London: Frank Cass.

————. 1996. *Agrarian Questions: Essays in Appreciation of T.J. Byres*. London: Cass.

————. 2001. '"The Peasantry" in Global Capitalism: Who, Where and Why?' *Socialist Register*: 25–51.

————. 2007. 'Capital and Labour from Centre to Margins', paper presented at the 'Living on the Margins Conference', Stellenbosch, 26–28 March.

————. 2008. 'Agrarian Change in a Globalising World: (Final) Farewells to the Peasantry?' paper presented at *Journal of Agrarian Change* workshop on 'Agrarian Change: Lineages and Prospects', School of Oriental and African Studies (SOAS), University of London, 1–2 May.

————. 2010. *Class Dynamics of Agrarian Change*. Sterling, V.A.: Kumarian Press.

Beteille, A. 1987. *Essays in Comparative Sociology*. Delhi: Oxford University Press.

————. 1997. 'Caste in Contemporary India', in *Caste Today*, edited by C. J. Fuller, 150–79. Delhi: Oxford University Press.

————. 1999. 'Citizenship, State and Civil Society', *Economic and Political Weekly* 34 (36): 2588–91.

Bhaduri, A. 1973. 'A Study in Agricultural Backwardness under Semi-Feudalism', *The Economic Journal*: 120–37.

————. 1976. "The Evolution of Land Relations in Eastern India under British Rule', *Indian Economic and Social History Review* 13 (1): 45–53.

Bhaduri, A. and S. Marglin. 1990. 'Unemployment and the Real Wage: The Economic Basis for Contesting Political Ideologies', *Cambridge Journal of Economics* 14: 375–93.

Bhalla, S. 2002. *Imagine There's No Country: Poverty, Inequality and Growth in the Era of Globalisation*. Washington D.C.: Institute of International Economics.

Bhagwati, J. and A. Panagriya. 2013. *Why Growth Matters: How Economic Growth in India Reduced Poverty and the Lessons for other Developing Countries*. New York: Public Affairs.

Bhatia, B. 2005. 'The Naxalite Movement in Central Bihar', *Economic and Political Weekly* 40 (15): 1536–49.

Bhatia, B and J. Dreze. 2006. 'Employment Guarantee in Jharkhand: Ground Realities', *Economic and Political Weekly*: 3198–202.

Bhattacharyya, D. 2009. 'Of Controls and Factions: The Changing "Party-society" in Rural West Bengal', *Economic and Political Weekly* 44 (9): 59–69.

Bhushan, C. and Z. Hazra. 2008. *Rich Lands, Poor People: Is Sustainable Mining Possible?* Delhi: Center for Science.

Bihar, 1951. *The Bihar Hindu Religious Trusts Act, 1950*. Patna: Eastern Book Depot.

Birdsall, N. and J. Londono. 1997. 'Asset Inequality Matters: An Assessment of the World Bank's Approach to Poverty Reduction', *American Economic Review* 87: 32–37.

Biswas, D. 2012. 'Inequality in West Bengal, Post 1991: A Class-wise Analysis', M. Phil thesis. Hyderabad: University of Hyderabad.

Blair, H. 1980. 'Rising Kulaks and Backward Classes in Bihar: Social Change in the Late 1970s', *Economic and Political Weekly* 15 (2): 64–74.

Blaut, J. 1993. *The Coloniser's Model of the World: Geographical Diffusion and Eurocentric History*. New York/ London: The Guildford Press.

Bolt, M. 2010. 'Camaraderie and its Discontents: Class Consciousness, Ethnicity and Divergent Masculinities among Zimbabwean Migrant Farmworkers in Southern Africa', *Journal of Southern African Studies* 36 (2): 377–93.

————. 2013. 'Producing Permanence: Employment, Domesticity and the Flexible Future on a South African Border Farm', *Economy and Society* 42 (2): 197–225.

Boltanski, L. and L. Thevenot. 1991. *On Justification: Economies of Worth*, edited by C. Porter. Princeton NJ: Princeton University Press.

Borras Jr, S. 2009. 'Agrarian Change and Peasant Studies: Changes, Continuities and Challenges –An Introduction', *Journal of Peasant Studies* 36 (1): 5–31.

Bose, S. 1986. *Agrarian Bengal: Economy, Social Structure and Politics, 1919-1947*. Cambridge: Cambridge University Press.

Bourdieu, P. 1977. *Outline of a Theory of Practice*. Cambridge: Cambridge University Press.

Bowen, J. 2003. *Islam, Law and Equality in Indonesia: An Anthropology of Public Reasoning*. Cambridge: Cambridge University Press.

Brady, H. and D. Collier. 2004. *Rethinking Social Inquiry: Diverse Tools, Shared Standards*. New York: Rowman and Littlefield.

Brass, P. 1974. *Language, Religion and Politics in North India*. Cambridge: Cambridge University Press.

———. 1990. *The Politics of India since Independence*. Cambridge: Cambridge University Press.

Brass, T. 1995. 'Introduction: The New Farmers' Movement in India', in *New Farmers' Movement in India*, edited by T Brass, 3–26. London: Frank Cass.

———. 2002. 'Rural Labour in Agrarian Transitions: The Semi-Feudal Thesis Revisited', *Journal of Contemporary Asia*, 32 (4): 456–73.

Bratton, M. and N. van de Walle. 1997. *Democratic Experiments in Africa: Regime Transitions in Comparative Perspective*. Cambridge: Cambridge University Press.

———. 2001. *African Economies and the Politics of Permanent Crisis, 1979-1999*. Cambridge: Cambridge University Press.

Breckenbridge, C. and P. van der Veer. 1993. 'Orientalism and the Postcolonial Predicament', in *Orientalism and the Postcolonial Predicament: Perspectives on South Asia*, edited by C. Breckenbridge and P. van der Veer, 1–19. Philadelphia: University of Pennsylvania Press.

Breman, J. 1974. *Patronage and Exploitation: Changing Agrarian Relations in South Gujarat*. Berkeley: University of California Press.

———. 1996. *Footloose Labour: Working in India's Informal Economy*. Cambridge: Cambridge University Press.

———. 2007. *The Poverty Regime in Village India*. New Delhi: Oxford University Press.

Briggs, A. 1959. *The Age of Improvement*. Harlow: Pearson.

Brocheux, P. 1983. 'Moral Economy or Political Economy? The Peasants are Always Rational', *The Journal of Asian Studies* 42 (4): 791–803.

Bromley, Y. 1974. *Soviet Ethnology and Anthropology Today*. The Hague: Mouton.

Broomfield, J. H. 1968. *Elite Conflict in Plural Society: Twentieth Century Bengal*. Berkeley: University of California Press.

Buchanan, A. 1982. *Marx and Justice: The Radical Critique of Liberalism*. Totowa, NJ: Rowman and Little.

Buck-Morss, S. 2009. *Hegel, Haiti and Universal History*. Pittsburgh: University of Pittsburgh Press.

Bulag, U. 2004. 'Mongolian Modernity and Hybridity', *Minpaku Anthropology Newsletter* 19.

Burchell, G., C. Gordon and P. Miller. 1991. *The Foucault Effect: Studies in Governmentality*. Chicago: University of Chicago Press.

Byres, T. J., K. Kapadia and J. Lerche. 2013. *Rural Labour Relations in India*. London: Frank Cass.

Caldeira, T. 2000. *City of Walls: Crime, Segregation and Citizenship in Sao Paulo*. Berkeley: University of California Press.

Caldeira, T. P. and J. Holston. 1999. 'Democracy and Violence in Brazil', *Comparative Studies in Society and History* 41 (4): 691–729.

Cammack, P. 2004. 'What the World Bank Means by Poverty Reduction, and Why it Matters', *New Political Economy* 9 (2): 189–211.

Caplan, P. 1995. *Understanding Disputes: The Politics of Argument*. Michigan: Berg.

Carlos, M. 1973. 'Fictive Kinship and Modernization in Mexico: A Comparative Analysis', *Anthropological Quarterly* 46 (2): 75–91.

Carsten, J. 2000. *Cultures of Relatedness: New Approaches to the Study of Kinship*, Cambridge: Cambridge University Press.

Carswell, G. and G. de Neve. 2014. 'MGNREGA in Tamil Nadu: A Story of Success and Transformation?' *Journal of Agrarian Change* 14 (4): 564–85.

Castoriadis, C. 1987. *The Imagery Institution of Society*. Cambridge, MA: MIT Press.

Cavell, S. 1989. *Conditions Handsome and Unhandsome: The Constitution of Emersonian Perfectionism*. Chicago: University of Chicago Press.

Centeno, M. 1994. *Democracy within Reason: Technocratic Revolution in Mexico*. University Park: Pennsylvania State University Press.

Central Electricity Authority. 2014. *Executive Summary: Power Sector*. Delhi: Government of India.

Chabal, P. and J. P. Daloz. 1999. *Africa Works: Disorder as Political Instrument*. Oxford: James Currey.

Chakravarti. A. 2001. *Social Power and Everyday Class Relations: Agrarian Transformations in North Bihar*. Delhi, London and Thousand Oaks: Sage Publications.

Chakrabarty, D. 1989. *Rethinking Working Class History: Bengal 1890–1940*. Princeton: Princeton University Press.

———. 2002. *Habitations of Modernity: Essays in the Wake of Subaltern Studies*. Delhi: Permanent Black.

———. 2004. 'Of Garbage, Modernity and the Citizen's Gaze', in *Habitations of Modernity*, edited by D. Chakrabarty, 65–79. Ranikhet: Permanent Black.

———. 2008. *Provincializing Europe: Postcolonial Thought and Historical Difference*. Princeton, NJ: Princeton University Press.

————. 2013. 'Subaltern Studies in Retrospect and Reminiscence', *Economic and Political Weekly* 48 (12): 23–27.

Chakravarti, A. 1986. 'The Unfinished Task of the Santhal Bataidars in Purnea District, 1938–42', *Economic and Political Weekly* 21 (42): 1847–65.

————. 1986. 'The Unfinished Struggle of Santhal Bataidars in Purnea District, 1938–42', *Economic and Political Weekly* 21 (43): 1847–65.

————. 2001. 'Caste and Agrarian Class: A View from Rural Bihar', *Economic and Political Weekly* 36 (17): 1449–62.

Chand, R. and S. K. Srivastava. 2014. 'Changes in the Rural Labor Market and their Implications for Agriculture', *Economic and Political Weekly* 49 (10): 47–54.

Chandhoke, N. 2005. 'Governance and Pluralisation of the State', *Economic and Political Weekly* 38 (28).

Chandra, K. 2004. *Why Ethnic Parties Succeed: Patronage and Ethnic Headcounts in India.* Cambridge: Cambridge University Press.

Chatterjee, P. 1990. 'A Response to Charles Taylor's "Modes of Civil Society"', *Public Culture.* Fall: 119–32.

————. 1993. *The Nation and its Fragments.* Princeton: Princeton University Press.

————. 1994. 'Development Planning and the Indian State', in *The State and Development Planning in India,* edited by T. J. Byres. Delhi: Oxford University Press.

————. 1997. *Our Modernity.* Dakar: CODESRIA/ SEPHIS.

————. 1998. *Wages of Freedom: Fifty Years of the Indian Nation State.* Delhi: Oxford University Press.

————. 2004. *The Politics of the Governed: Reflections on Popular Politics in most of the World.* New York: Columbia University Press.

————. 2008. 'Democracy and Economic Transformation in India', *Economic and Political Weekly* 43 (6): 53–62.

————. 2011. 'The Debate over Political Society', in *Reframing Democracy and Agency in India: Interrogating Political Society,* edited by A. Gudavarthy. Delhi: Anthem Press.

————. 2012a. 'After Subaltern Studies', *Economic and Political Weekly* 47 (35): 44–9.

————. 2012b. *Lineages of Political Society.* Ranikhet: Permanent Black.

————. 2013. 'Subaltern Studies and Capital', *Economic and Political Weekly* 43 (37): 69–75.

Chatterji, J. 1994. *Bengal Divided: Hindu Communalism and Partition, 1932-1947.* Cambridge: Cambridge University Press.

————. 2007. *The Spoils of Partition: Bengal and India, 1947-1967.* Cambridge: Cambridge University Press.

Chaudhary, S. N. 1999. *Power Dependence Relations: Struggle for Hegemony in Rural Bihar.* New Delhi: Har-Anand Publications.

Chaudhuri, P. 1983. *The Refugees in West Bengal: A Study of the Growth and Distribution of Refugee Settlements within the CMD*. Calcutta: Centre for Studies in Social Sciences.

Chekuri, C. 2007. 'Writing Politics Back into History', *History and Theory* 46 (3): 384–95.

Chibber, V. 2013. *Postcolonial Theory and the Spectre of Capital*. London: Verso.

Chikowero, M. 2007. 'Subalternating Currents: Electrification and Power Politics in Bulawayo, Colonial Zimbabwe, 1894–1939', *Journal of Southern African Studies* 33 (2): 287–306.

Chopra, D. 2011. 'Interactions of Power in the Making and Shaping of Policy', *Contemporary South Asia* 19 (2): 153–71.

Clifford, J. 1986. 'Introduction: Partial Truths', in *Writing Culture: The Poetics and Politics of Ethnography*, edited by J. Clifford, G. E. Marcus, 1–26. California: University of California Press.

Cohen, A. 1969. *Custom and Politics in Urban Africa*. Berkeley: University of California Press.

Cohen, J. 1997. 'Deliberation and Democratic Legitimacy', in *Deliberative Democracy: Essays in Reason and Politics*, edited by J. Bohman and W. Rehg, 67–91. Cambridge, MA and London: The MIT Press.

Cohen, J. and J. Rogers. 2003. 'Power and Reason', in *Deepening Democracy: Institutional Innovations in Empowered Participatory Governance*, edited by A. Fung and E.O. Wright, 237–58. London: Verso.

Cohen, J. and A. Arato. 1992. *Civil Society and Political Theory*. Cambridge, MA: MIT Press.

Cohn, B. 1965. 'Anthropological Notes on Dispute and Law in India', *American Anthropologist* 67 (6): 82–122.

Cohn, B. S. 1987. *An Anthropologist among the Historians and Other Essays*. Delhi and Oxford: Oxford University Press.

Collier, P. 2007. *The Bottom Billion: Why the Poorest Countries are Failing and What can be done about it*. Oxford: Oxford University Press.

Collier, D. and R. Adcock. 1999. 'Democracy and Dichotomies: A Pragmatic Approach to Choices about Concepts', *Annual Review of Political Science* 2: 537–65.

Collier, D. and S. Levitsky. 1997. 'Democracy with Adjectives: Conceptual Innovation in Comparative Research', *World Politics* 49 (03): 430–51.

Collier, D. and J. Mahoney. 1996. 'Insights and Pitfalls: Selection Bias in Qualitative Research', *World Politics* 49 (01): 56–91.

Collini, S. 1989. *JS Mill: 'On Liberty' and Other Writings*. Cambridge: Cambridge University Press.

Comaroff, J. and J. Comaroff. 1993. *Modernity and its Malcontents: Ritual and Power in Postcolonial Africa*. Chicago: University of Chicago Press.

————. 1999. *Civil Society and the Political Imagination in Africa: Critical Perspectives*. Chicago: University of Chicago Press.

————. 2006. 'Law and Disorder in the Postcolony: An Introduction', in *Law and Disorder in the Postcolony*, edited by J. Comaroff and J. Comaroff, 1–56. Chicago: University of Chicago Press.

————. 2009. *Ethnicity, Inc.* Illinois, Chicago: University of Chicago Press.

Comaroff, J. and S. Roberts. 1981. *Rules and Processes: The Cultural Context of Dispute in an African Context*. Chicago: University of Chicago.

Connolly, W. 1987. *Politics and Ambiguity*. Madison: University of Wisconsin Press.

Constituent Assemblies Debates. 1947.

Cooper, F. 2002. *Africa since 1940: The Past of the Present*. Cambridge: Cambridge University Press.

Copestake, J. 1992. 'The Integrated Rural Development Programme: Performance during the Sixth Plan, Policy Responses and Proposals for Reform', in *Poverty in India. Bombay: Research and Policy*, edited by B. Harriss, S. Guhan and R. H. Cassen, 209–30. Oxford University Press.

Coronil, F. 1997. *The Magical State: Nature, Money and Modernity in Venezuela*. Chicago: University of Chicago Press.

Corbridge, S. 2007. 'The (Im)possibility of Development Studies', *Economy and Society* 36 (2): 179–211.

Corbridge, S. and J. Harriss. 2000. *Reinventing India: Liberalization, Hindu Nationalism and Popular Democracy*. Malden, MA: Polity Press.

Corbridge, S., G. Willams, M. Srivastava and R. Veron. 2005. *Seeing the State: Governance and Governmentality in India*. Cambridge: Cambridge University Press.

Corbridge, S., J. Harriss, and C. Jeffrey. 2013. *India Today: Economy, Politics and Society*. Cambridge: Polity.

Corrigan, P. and D. Sayer. 1985. *The Great Arch: English State Formation as Cultural Revolution*. Oxford: Blackwell.

Cowen, M. and R. Shenton. 1996. *Doctrines of Development*. London; New York: Routledge.

Craig, D. and Porter, D. 2003. 'Poverty Reduction Strategy Papers: A New Convergence', *World Development* 31 (1): 53–69.

Credit Suisse. 2015. *Global Wealth Report*. Available at: https://publications.credit-suisse. com/tasks/render/file/?fileID=F2425415-DCA7-80B8-EAD989AF9341D47E.

Creed, G. W. 1998. *Domesticating Revolution: From Socialist Reform to Ambivalent Transition in a Bulgarian Village*. University Park PA: The Pennsylvania State University Press.

Crook, R. and J. Manor. 1998. *Democracy and Decentralisation in South Asia and West Africa: Participation, Accountability and Performance.* Cambridge: Cambridge University Press.

Cruikshank, B. 1999. *The Will to Empower: Democratic Citizens and Other Subjects.* Ithaca, NY: Cornell University Press.

Dahl, R. A. 1957. 'The Concept of Power', *Systems Research and Behavioral Science* 2 (3): 201–15.

———. 1959. 'Business and Politics: A Critical Appraisal of Political Science', *American Political Science Review* 53 (1): 1–34.

———. 1971. *Polyarchy: Participation and Opposition.* New Haven: Yale University Press.

Dahrendorf, R. 1959. *Class and Conflict in Industrial Society.* London: Routledge and Kegan Paul.

Das, A. 1982. 'Peasants and Peasant Organisations: The Kisan Sabha in Bihar', in *Agrarian Movements in India: Studies on 20th Century Bihar,* edited by A. Das, 40–87. London: Frank Cass.

———. 1982. 'Introduction', in *Agrarian Movements in India: Studies on 20th Century Bihar* edited by A. N. Das, 1–5. New Delhi: Routledge.

Dasgupta, P. 1993. *An Inquiry into Well-Being and Destitution.* Oxford: Clarendon Press.

Davis, M. 1983. *Rank and Rivalry.* Cambridge: Cambridge University Press.

Dean, M. 1991. *The Consitution of Poverty: Towards a Genealogy of Liberal Governance.* London: Routledge.

Deaton, A. and J. Dreze. 2002. 'Poverty and Inequality in India: A Re-examination', *Economic and Political Weekly*: 3729–48.

De Certeau, M. 1984. *The Practice of Everyday Life.* Berkeley and London: University of California Press.

Desai, S. and A. Dubey. 2010. 'Caste in 21st Century India: Competing Narratives', *Economic and Political Weekly* 46 (11): 40–49.

Desai, S., R. Vanneman and National Council of Applied Economic Research, New Delhi. 2005. India Human Development Survey (IHDS), ICPSR22626-v8. Ann Arbor, MI: Inter-university Consortium for Political and Social Research [distributor], 2010-06-29. Available at: http://doi.org/10.3886/ICPSR22626.v8.

Deshpande, A. and K. Newman. 2010. 'Where the Path Leads: The Role of Caste in Post-University Employment Expectations', in *Blocked by Caste: Economic Discrimination in Modern India,* edited by S. Thorat and K. Newman, 88–122. New Delhi: Oxford University Press.

Devereux, S. 2002. 'From Workfare to Fair Work: The Contribution of Public Works and Other Labour-based Infrastructure Programmes to Poverty Alleviation', *Issues in Employment and Poverty Discussion Paper* 5. Geneva: ILO.

Diamond, L. 1992. 'Rethinking Civil Society: Towards Democratic Consolidation', *Journal of Democracy* 5 (3): 4–17.

———. 2015. 'Facing upto the Democratic Recession', *Journal of Democracy* 26 (1): 141–55.

———. 1992. *Globalisation of Democracy: Trends, Types Causes, and Prospects.* Abuja: Centre for Democratic Studies.

Diamond, L. and G. Marks. 1992. *Reexamining Democracy: Essays in Honour of Seymour Martin Lipset.* Newbury Park, London: Sage.

Diamond, L., M. F. Platttner, Y. Chu and H. Tien (eds). 1997. *Consolidating the Third World Democracies: Themes and Perspectives.* Baltimore: Johns Hopkins University Press.

Dirks, N. 2001. *Castes of Mind: Colonialism and the Making of Modern India.* Princeton: Princeton University Press.

Djurfeldt, G., V. Athreya, N. Jayakumar, S. Lindberg, A. Rajagopal and R. Vidyasagar. 2008. 'Agrarian Change and Social Mobility in Tamil Nadu', *Economic and Political Weekly* 43 (45): 50–61.

Dollar, D. and A. Kray. 2001. 'Growth is Good for the Poor', *World Bank Policy Research Department Working Paper* No. 2587. Washington, DC: World Bank.

Dreyfus, H. L. and P. Rabinow. 2014. *Michel Foucault: Beyond Structuralism and Hermeneutics* (2nd edition). Chicago: University of Chicago Press.

Drèze, J. 1990. 'Poverty in India and the IRDP Delusion', *Economic and Political Weekly* 39 (29): 195–104.

———. 2011. 'The Battle for Employment Guarantee', in *Battle for Employment Guarantee*, edited by R. Khera. Delhi: Oxford University Press.

Drèze, J. and A. Sen. 2013. *An Uncertain Glory: India and its Contradictions.* Princeton: Princeton University Press.

Drèze, J. and C. Oldiges. 2011. 'Employment Guarantee: The Official Picture', in *The Battle for Employment Guarantee,* edited by R. Khera, 21–39. Oxford University Press, New Delhi.

Drèze, J. and R. Khera. 2008. 'From Accounts to Accountability', *The Hindu,* 6 December.

———. 2009. 'The Battle for Employment Guarantee', *Frontline* 26 (1): 3–16.

Dumont, L. 1980. *Homo Hierarchicus: The Caste System and its Implications.* Chicago: University of Chicago Press.

Dunn, J. 2006. *Setting the People Free: The Story of Democracy.* London: Atlantic.

Dutta, P., R. Murgai, M. Ravallion and D. van de Walle. 2012. 'Does India's Employment Guarantee Scheme Guarantee Employment?' *Economic and Political Weekly* 47 (16): 55–64.

Easterly, B. 2006. *The White Man's Burden: Why the West's Efforts to Aid the Rest Have Done so Much Ill and so Little Good*. New York: Penguin Press.

Echeverri-Gent, J. 1988. 'Guaranteed Employment in an Indian State: The Maharashtra Experience', *Asian Survey* 28 (12): 1294–310.

Eisensdadt, S. 1966. *Modernisation: Protest and Social Change*. Englewood Cliffs, NJ: Prentice-Hall.

———. 2000. 'Multiple Modernities', *Daedalus* 129 (1): 1–29.

Election Commission of India. 2014. Parliamentary Constituency-wise Votes Polled. New Delhi: Government of India.

Elias, N. 1978. *The Civilizing Process*. Oxford: Basil Blackwell.

Engberg-Pedersen, L. and N. Webster. 2002. 'Introduction to Political Space', in *In the Name of the Poor: Contesting Political Space for Poverty Reduction*, edited by N. Webster and L. Engberg-Pedersen, 30–51. London and New York: Zed Books.

Englund, H. and J. Leach. 2000. 'Ethnography and the Metanarratives of Modernity', *Current Anthropology* 41 (2): 225–45.

Escobar, A. 1995. *Encountering Development: The Making and Unmaking of the Third World*. Princeton: Princeton University Press.

Esping-Andersen, G. 1990. *The Three Worlds of Welfare Capitalism*. Princeton, N.J.: Princeton University Press.

Eswaran, M., A. Kotwal, B. Ramaswami and W. Wadhwa. 2009. 'Sectoral Labour Flows and Agricultural Wages in India, 1983-2004: Has Growth Trickled Down?' *Economic and Political Weekly* 44 (2): 46–55.

Evans, P. 1995. *Embedded Autonomy: States and Industrial Transformation*. Princeton, N.J.: Princeton University Press.

Evans-Pritchard, E. E. 1937. *Witchcraft, Oracles and Magic among the Azande*. Oxford: Clarendon Press.

Farmer, P. 2005. *Pathologies of Power: Health, Human Rights and the New War on the Poor*. Berkeley: University of California Press.

Ferguson, J. 1994. *The Anti-politics Machine: 'Development', Depoliticization and Bureaucratic Power in Lesotho*. Minneapolis: University of Minnesota Press.

———. 1999. *Expectations of Modernity: Myths and Meanings of Urban Life on the Zambian Copperbelt*. Berkeley: University of California Press.

———. 2006. *Global Shadows: Africa in the Neoliberal World Order*. Durham, N.C. and London: Duke University Press.

———. 2013. 'Declarations of Dependence', *Journal of Royal Anthropological Institute* 19 (2): 223–42.

Fernandez, B. 2010. 'Poor Practices: Contestations around 'Below Poverty Line' Status in India', *Third World Quarterly* 31 (3): 415–30.

Fields, G. 2000. *Distribution and Development: A New Look at the Developing World*. Massachusetts: MIT Press.

Foster, J. 1974. *Class Struggle and the Industrial Revolution: Early Industrial Capitalism in Three English Towns*. London: Weidenfield and Nicolson.

Foucault, M. 1980. *Power/Knowledge: Selected Interviews and Other Writings, 1972-1977*. Ed. C. Gordon. London: Pantheon Books.

———. 1982. 'The Subject and Power', *Critical Inquiry*: 777–95.

———. 2004. *Society Must be Defended: Lectures at the College de France*. London: Penguin.

Fox. J. 1994. 'The Difficult Transition from Clientelism to Citizenship: Lessons from Mexico', *World Politics* 46 (2): 151–84.

———. 2007. *Accountability Politics: Power and Voice in Rural Mexico*. Oxford: Oxford University Press.

Frankel, F. 1989. 'Caste, Land and Dominance in Bihar: Breakdown of the Brahmanical Social Order', in *Dominance and State Power in Modern India: Decline of a Social Order*, edited by F Frankel and MSA Rao, 46–132. Oxford: Oxford University Press.

Freed, S. 1963. 'Fictive Kinship in a North Indian Village'. *Ethnology*, 2 (1): 86-103.

Freedom House. 2011. *Freedom in the World Report 2010*. Washington DC: Freedom House.

Freire, P. 1970. *Pedagogy of the Oppressed*, translated by Myra Bergman Ramos. New York: Seabury Press.

Frykenberg, R. E. 1977. 'Company Circari in the Carnatic, c. 1799-1859: The Inner Logic of Political Systems in India', *Realm and Region in Traditional India*: 117–64.

Fukuyama, F. 1989. 'The End of History?' *The National Interest*: 3–18.

———. 1992. *The End of History and the Last Man*. New York: Free Press.

———. 2014. *Political Order and Political Decay: From the Industrial Revolution to the Globalisation of Democracy*. New York: Farar, Strauss and Giroux.

Fuller, C. (ed). 1996. 'Introduction' to *Caste Today*. New Delhi: Oxford University Press.

Fuller, C. J. (ed). 1996. *Caste Today*. Delhi: Oxford University Press.

Fuller, C. J. and V. Bénéï (eds). 2000. *The Everday State and Society in Modern India*. New Delhi: Social Science Press.

Fuller, C. and J. Harriss. 2001. 'For an Anthropology of the Modern Indian State', in *The Everyday State and Society in Modern India*, edited by C. Fuller and V. Benei, 1–30. London: Hurst Publications.

Fung, A. 2005. 'Deliberation before the Revolution: Towards an Ethics of Deliberative Democracy in an Unjust World', *Political Theory* 33 (3): 397–419.

Gaiha, R. 2005. 'Does the Employment Guarantee Scheme Benefit the Rural Poor in India? Some Recent Evidence', *Asian Survey* 45 (6): 949–69.

Gaiha, R., P. Kaushik and V. Kulkarni. 1998. 'Jawahar Rozgar Yojana, Panchayats and the Poor in India', *Asian Survey* 38 (10): 928–49.

Galanter, M. 1963. 'Law and Caste in Modern India', *Asian Survey* 3 (11): 544–59.

———. 1984. *Competing Equalities: Law and the Backward Classes in India*. Berkeley: University of California Press.

Gallie, D. 1984. *Social Inequality and Class Radicalism in Britain and France*. Cambridge: University Press.

Gallie, W. B. 1956. 'Essentially Contested Concepts', *Proceedings of the Aristotlean Society* 56: 167–98.

Gaonkar, D. P. 1999. 'On Alternative Modernities', *Public Culture* 11 (1): 1–18.

Gang, I. N., K. Sen and M-S. Yun. 2002. 'Caste, Ethnicity and Poverty in Rural India', *IZA Discussion Paper 629*.

———. 2008. 'Poverty in Rural India: Caste and Tribe', *Review of Income and Wealth* 54 (1): 50–70.

Gardner, K. and D. Lewis. 2015. *Anthropology and Development: Challenges for the Twenty-first Century*. London: Pluto Press.

Gay, R. 2006. 'The Even More Difficult Transition from Clientelism to Citizenship: Lessons from Brazil', in *Out of the Shadows*, edited by P. Fernandez-Kelly and J. Shefner. University Park, PA.: Pennsylvania State University Press.

Geertz, C. 1998. *The Interpretation of Cultures: Selected Essays*. New York: Basic Books.

Gelbach, Jonah and Lant Pritchett, 1997, 'Redistribution in a Political Economy: Leakier Can be Better', mimeo. World Bank, Washington DC.

George, A. and A. Bennett. 2005. *Case Studies and Theory Development in the Social Sciences*. Cambridge, MA and London: The MIT Press.

Geschiere, P. 1997. *The Modernity of Witchcraft: Politics and the Occult in Postcolonial Africa*. Charlottesville and London: University Press of Virginia.

Gellner, E. 1964. *Thought and Change*. Chicago: University of Chicago Press

Ghosh, J. 2011. 'Dealing with "The Poor"', *Development and Change* 42 (3): 849–58.

Giddens, A. 1982. *Sociology: A Brief but Critical Introduction*. London: Macmillan.

———. 1990. *The Consequences of Modernity*. Cambridge: Polity.

Gikandi, S. 1996. *Maps of Englishness: Writing Identity in the Culture of Colonialism*. New York: Columbia University Press.

———. 1998. 'African Subjects and the Colonial Project', 'Introduction' to H. Mukasa's *Uganda's Katikiro in England*. Manchester and New York: Manchester University Press.

———. 2002. 'Reason, Modernity and the African Crisis', in *African Modernities:*

Entangled Meanings in Current Debate, edited by J-G Deustch, P. Probst and H. Schmidt, 135–57. Oxford: James Currey.

———. 2011. *Slavery and the Culture of Taste*. Princeton, N.J.: Princeton University Press.

Gill, L. 1987. *Peasants, Entrepreneurs, and Social Change*. Boulder, Co. and London: Westview Press.

Goffman, E. 1974. *Stigma: Notes on the Management of Spoiled Identities*. New York: J. Aronson.

Gokhale-Turner, J. B. 1981. 'Bhakti or Vidroha', in *Tradition and Modernity in Bhakti Movements*, edited by J. Lele. Leiden: Brill.

Goodin, R. and H. Klingemann. 1996. *A New Handbook of Political Science*. Oxford: Oxford University Press.

Goodwin, J., J. Jasper and F. Polletta. 2001. *Passionate Politics: Emotions and Social Movements*. Chicago: University of Chicago Press.

Gooptu, N. 2001. *The Politics of the Urban Poor in Early Twentieth Century India*. Cambridge: Cambridge University Press.

Gooptu, N. and B. Harriss-White. 2001. 'Mapping India's World of Unorganised Labour', *Socialist Register* 37: 89–118.

Gordon, C. 1991. 'Governmental Rationality: An Introduction', in *The Foucault Effect: Studies in Governmentality, with Two Lectures and an Interview with Michel Foucault*, edited by G. Burchell, C. Gordon and P. Miller. Chicago: University of Chicago Press.

Government of West Bengal. 2007. *Human Development Report Maldah*. Available at: http://www.undp.org/content/dam/india/docs/hdr_malda_2006_full_report. pdf.

Granovetter, M. and P. McGuire. 1998. 'The Making of an Industry: Electricity in the United States', *The Sociological Review* 46 (S1): 147–73.

Grindle, M. S. 2007. *Going Local: Decentralisation, Democratisation and the Promise of Good Governance*. Princeton, N.J.: Princeton University Press.

Guha, Ramachandra. 2007. *India after Gandhi: The History of the World's Largest Democracy*. London: Macmillan.

Guha, Ranajit. 1963. *Rule of Property in Bengal: An Essay on the Idea of Permanent Settlement*. Paris: Mouton.

———. 1982. 'On Some Aspects of the Historiography of Colonial India', in *Subaltern Studies I: Writings on South Asian History and Society*, edited by R. Guha. Delhi: Oxford University Press.

———. 1983. *Elementary Aspects of Peasant Insurgency in Colonial India*. Delhi: Oxford University Press.

——. 1988. 'The Prose of Counter-insurgency', in *Selected Subaltern Studies*, edited by R. Guha and G. Chakravorty-Spivak, 45–86. Delhi: Oxford University Press.

——. 1997. *Dominance without Hegemony: History and Power in Colonial India*. Cambridge MA and London: Harvard University Press.

Guha, S. 1996. 'Time and Money: The Meaning and Measurement of Labour in Indian Agriculture', in *The Meanings of Agriculture*, edited by P. Robb, 251–61. Delhi: Oxford University Press.

——. 2013. *Beyond Caste: Identity and Power in South Asia, Past and Present*. Leiden: E.J. Brill.

Gulliver, P. H. 1963. *Social Control in an African Society: A Study of the Arusha, Agricultural Masai of Northern Tanganyika*. Boston: Boston University Press.

Gupta, A. 1995. 'Blurred Boundaries: The Discourse of Corruption, the Culture of Politics, and the Imagined State', *American Ethnologist* 22 (2): 375–402.

——. 1998. *Postcolonial Developments: Agriculture in the Making of Modern India*. Durham, N.C.; London: Duke University Press.

——. 2012. *Red Tape: Bureaucracy, Structural Violence and Poverty in India*. Durham: Duke University Press.

Gupta, A. and J. Fergusson. 1997a. 'Beyond "Culture": Space, Identity and the Politics of Difference', in *Culture, Power, Place: Explorations in Critical Anthropology*, edited by A. Gupta and J. Fergusson. Durham: Duke University Press.

——. 1997b. 'Discipline and Practice: "The Field" as Site, Method and Location in Anthropology', in *Anthropological Locations: Boundaries and Grounds of a Field Science*, edited by A. Gupta and J. Fergusson, 1–46. Berkeley: University of California Press.

Gupta, D. 1991. *Social Stratification*. Delhi: Oxford University Press.

——. 2005. 'Whither the Indian Village: Culture and Agriculture in Rural India', *Economic and Political Weekly* 40 (8): 751–58.

——. 2005a. 'Caste and Politics: Identity over System', *Annual Review of Anthropology* 21: 409–27.

Guru, G. 2005. *Atrophy in Dalit Politics*. Mumbai: Vikas Adhyayan Kendra.

Guru, G. 2009. 'Rejection of Rejection', in *Humiliation: Claims And Context*, edited by G Guru. New York: Oxford University Press.

Guru, G. and A. Chakravarty. 2005. 'Who are the Country's Poor? Social Movement Politics and Dalit Poverty', in *Social Movements in India: Poverty, Power and Politics*, edited by R. Ray and M. Katzenstein, 135–60. Lanham: Rowman and Littlefield Publishers.

Gutiérrez, R. A. 2004. 'Internal Colonialism: An American Theory of Race', *Du Bois Review* 1 (2): 281–95.

Gutmann, M. 1993. 'A Critique of the Theory of Everyday Forms of Resistance', *Latin American Perspectives* 20 (20): 74–92.

———. 2002. *The Romance of Democracy: Compliant Defiance in Contemporary Mexico*. Berkeley: University of California Press.

Habermas, J. 1987. *The Philosophical Discourse of Modernity: Twelve Lectures*. Cambridge, Mass: MIT Press.

———. 1996. 'Three Normative Models of Democracy', in *Democracy and Difference: Contesting the Boundaries of the Political*, S. Benhabib, 21–30. Princeton NJ: Princeton University Press.

Habib, I. 1963. *The Agrarian System of Mughal India: (1556-1707)*. Bombay and New York: Asia Publishing House.

Hacking, I. 1995. *Rewriting the Soul: Multiple Personality and the Sciences of Memory*. Princeton: Princeton University Press.

Hansen, T. B. 1996. 'Inside the Romanticist Episteme', *Social Scientist*: 59–79.

Hansen, T. B. and F. Stepputat. 2001a. 'Introduction', in *States of imagination: Ethnographic Explorations of the Postcolonial State*, edited by T. B. Hansen and F. Stepputat, 1–14. Durham: Duke University Press.

———. (eds). 2001b. *States of Imagination: Ethnographic Explorations of the Postcolonial State*. Durham: Duke University Press.

Harriss, J. 1982. *Capitalism and Peasant Farming: Agrarian Structure and Ideology in Northern Tamil Nadu*. Bombay: Oxford University Press.

———. 1987a. 'Capitalism and Peasant Production: the Green Revolution in India', *Peasant and Peasant Societies*: 227–46.

———. 1987b. 'The State in Retreat? Why Has India Experienced such Half-hearted 'Liberalisation' in the 1980s?', *IDS Bulletin* 18 (4): 31–38.

———. 2003. 'Do Political Regimes Matter? Poverty Reduction and Regime Differences across India', in *Changing Paths: International Development and the New Politics of Inclusion*, edited by P Houtzager and M Moore, 204–32. Ann Arbor: University of Michigan Press.

———. 2007. 'Bringing Politics Back into Poverty Analysis: Why Understanding Social Relations Matters More for Policy on Chronic Poverty than Measurement', *CPRC Working Paper* 77. Available at: http://www.chronicpoverty.org/uploads/publication_files/WP77_Harriss.pdf.

———. 2011. 'How Far Have India's Economic Reforms Been "Guided by Compassion and Justice"? Social Policy in the Neoliberal Era', in *Understanding India's New Political Economy: A Great Transformation?*, edited by S. Ruparelia, S. Reddy, J. Harriss and S. Corbridge, 127–40. Delhi: Routledge.

———. 2013. 'Does Landlordism Still Matter?' *Journal of Agrarian Change* 13 (3): 351–64.

Harriss-White, B. 2003. *India Working: Essays on Society and Economy*. Cambridge: Cambridge University Press.

———. 2005a. 'Destitution and the Poverty of its Politics: With Special Reference to South Asia', *World Development* 33 (6): 881–91.

———. 2005b. 'Poverty and Capitalism', *Economic and Political Weekly* 41 (13): 1241–46.

———. 2008. *Rural Commercial Capital. Agricultural Markets in West Bengal*. New Delhi: Oxford University Press.

———. 2012. 'Capitalism and the Common Man: Peasants and Petty Production in Africa and South Asia', *Agrarian South: Journal of Political Economy* 1 (2): 109–60.

Harris, J. R. and M. P. Todaro. 1970. 'Migration, Unemployment and Development: a Two-Sector Analysis', *The American Economic Review*: 126–42.

Hart, G. 1991. 'Engendering Everyday Resistance: Gender, Patronage and Production Politics in Rural Malaysia', *Journal of Peasant Studies* 19 (1): 93–121.

Hart, S. 2005. *Capitalism at the Crossroads: The Unlimited Business Opportunities in Solving the World's Most Difficult Problems*. Upper Saddle River, NJ: Wharton School Publications.

Hasan, N. 1969. 'Zamindars under the Mughals', in *Land Control and Social Structure in Indian History*, edited by R. Frykenberg, 17–31. Madison: University of Wisconsin Press.

Hauser, W. 1993. 'Violence, Agrarian Radicalism and Electoral Politics: Reflections on the Indian People's Front', *Journal of Peasant Studies* 33 (1): 89–123.

Hawley, J.S. 2005. *Three Bhakti Voices: Mirabai, Surdas and Kabir in Their Times and Ours*. Delhi; Oxford: Oxford University Press.

Haywood, C. 1998. 'De-facing Power', *Polity* 31 (1): 1–22.

Hechter, M. 1975. *Internal Colonialism: The Celtic Fringe in British National Development, 1536-1966*. California: University of California Press.

Heller, P. 1996. 'Social Capital as a Product of Class Mobilization and State Intervention: Industrial Workers in Kerala, India', *World Development* 24 (6): 1055–71.

———. 2000. 'Degrees of Democracy: Some Comparative Lessons from India', *World Politics* 52 (4): 484–519.

———. 2011. 'Making Citizens from Below and Above: The Prospects and Challenges of Decentralisation in India', in *Understanding India's New Political Economy: A Great Transformation?* edited by S. Ruparelia, S. Reddy, J. Harriss and S. Corbridge, 157–171. London: Routledge.

Herring, R. and R. Edwards. 1983. 'Guaranteeing Employment to the Rural Poor: Social Functions and Class Interests in the Employment Guarantee Scheme in Western India', *World Development* 11 (7): 575–92.

Herzfeld, M. 1992. *The Social Production of Indifference: Exploring the Symbolic Roots of Western Bureaucracy*. New York, Oxford: Berg.

———. 1995. 'It Takes One to Know One: Collective Resentment and Mutual Recognition among Greeks in Local and Global Contexts', in *Counterworks: Managing the Diversity of Knowledge*, edited by R. Farndon. London: Routledge.

Hicken, A. 2011. 'Clientelism', *Annual Review of Political Science* 14: 289–310.

Hickey S. and A. du Toit. 2007. 'Adverse Incorporation, Social Exclusion and Chronic Poverty', *CPRC Working Paper* 81. Manchester: CPRC.

Himanshu, and K. Sen.2014. 'Measurement, Patterns and Determinants of Poverty in India', in *Persistence of Poverty in India: Productions and Reproductions*, edited by J. Parry and N. Gooptu, 67–98. Delhi: Social Sciences Press.

Hindess, B. 2001. 'The Liberal Government of Unfreedom', *Alternatives: Global, Local, Political* 26 (2): 93–111.

Hirway, I. 2000. 'Dynamics of Development in Gujarat: Some Issues', *Economic and Political Weekly*: 3106–20.

———. 2003. 'Identification of BPL Households for Poverty Alleviation Programmes', *Economic and Political Weekly* 38 (45): 4803–08.

Hobsbawm, E. 1959. *Primitive Rebels: Studies in Archaic Forms of Social Movement in the 19th and 20th Centuries*. London: WW Norton.

———. 1962. *The Age of Revolution: Europe, 1789-1848*. London: Weidenfield and Nicholson.

———. 1973. 'Peasants and Politics', *Journal of Peasant Studies* 1 (1): 3–22.

———. 1978. *Primitive Rebels: Studies in Archaic Forms of Social Movement in the Nineteenth and Twentieth Centuries*. Manchester: Manchester University Press.

———. 2010. *Age of Revolution: 1789-1848*. New York: Vintage Books.

Holston, J. 2008. *Insurgent Citizenship: Disjunctions of Democracy and Modernity in Brazil*. Princeton and Oxford: Princeton University Press.

Honig, B. 1991. 'Declarations of Independence: Arendt and Derrida on the Problem of Founding a Republic', *American Political Science Review* 85 (1): 97–113.

Horneberger, J. 2013. *Policing and Human Rights. The Meaning of Violence and Justice in the Everyday Policing of Johannesburg*. London: Routledge.

Hossein, N. 2013. 'Rude Accountability and the Unreformed State: Informal Pressure on Frontline Bureaucrats in Bangladesh', *IDS Working Paper* 319.

Houtzager, P. and M. Moore. 2003. *Changing Paths: International Development and the New Politics of Inclusion*. Ann Arbor: University of Michigan Press.

Howell, S. 2009. 'Adoption of the Unrelated Child: Some Challenges to the Anthropological Study of Kinship', *Annual Review of Anthropology* 38: 149–66.

Huber, E., D. Rueschemeyer and J. D. Stephens. 1997. 'The Paradoxes of Contemporary

Democracy: Formal, Participatory and Social Dimensions', *Comparative Politics* 29 (3): 323–42.

Hughes, T. P. 1983. *Networks of Power: Electrification in Western Society, 1880-1930*. Baltimore: Johns Hopkins University Press.

Huntington, S. 1968. *Political Order in Changing Societies*. New Haven: Yale University Press.

———. 1992. *Democratization in the Late Twentieth Century*. Norman: University of Oklahoma Press.

Inglehart, R. and C. Welzel. 2003. 'Political Culture and Democracy: Analyzing Crosslevel Linkages', *Comparative Politics* 36 (1): 61–79.

———. 2005. *Modernization, Cultural Change and Democracy: The Human Development Sequence*. Cambridge: Cambridge University Press.

Inglehart, R. and W. E. Baker. 2000. 'Modernization, Cultural Change and the Persistence of Traditional Values', *American Sociological Review* 65 (1): 19–51.

Institute of Applied Manpower Research. 2011. *India Human Development Report 2010: Towards Social Inclusion*. New Delhi: Government of India.

International Fund for Agricultural Development (IFAD). 2011. *Rural Poverty Report*. Rome: IFAD.

International Labour Organisation. 2012. *Statistical Update on Employment in the Informal Economy*. Geneva: International Labour Organisation.

Iversen, T. and D. Soskice. 2006. 'Electoral Institutions and the Politics of Coalitions: Why Some Democracies Redistribute More than Others', *American Political Science Review* 100 (2): 165–81.

Jacob, M. 2009. 'The Shared History: Unknotting Fictive Kinship and Legal Process', *Law and Society Review* 43 (1): 95–126.

Jaffrelot, C. 2003. *India's Silent Revolution: The Rise of the Lower Castes in North India*. New York: Columbia University Press.

Jain, S. P. 1997. 'The Gram Sabha: Gateway to Grassroots Democracy', *Journal of Rural Development* 16 (4): 557–73.

Jalan, J. and Murgai, R. 2007. 'An Effective "Targeting Shortcut"? An Assessment of the 2002 Below Poverty Line Census Method', Mimeo. New Delhi: World Bank.

Jansen, S. 2014. 'Hope for/ against the State: Gridding in a Besieged Sarajevo Suburb', *Ethnos* 79 (2): 238–60.

Jannuzi, F. 1974. *Agrarian Crisis in India: The Case of Bihar*. Austin: University of Texas Press.

Jaoul, N. 2009. 'Naxalism in Bihar: From Bullet to Ballot', in *Armed Militias of South Asia:*

Fundamentalists, Maoists and Separatists, edited by L Gayer and C Jafferelot, 21–43. New York: Columbia University Press.

———. 2011. 'Manju Devi's Martyrdom: Marxist-Leninist Politics and the Rural Poor in Rural Bihar', *Contributions to Indian Sociology* 45 (3): 347–71.

———. 2016. 'Beyond Citizenship: Adivasi and Dalit Political Pathways in India', *FOCAAL: Journal of Global and Historical Anthropolog* 76: 3–14.

Jayadev, A., S. Motiram and V. Vakulabharnam. 2011. 'Patterns of Wealth Disparities in India', in *The Great Transformation? Understanding India's New Political Economy*, edited by S. Ruparelia, S. Reddy, J. Harriss and S. Corbridge. London and New York: Routledge.

Jayal, N. 1999. *Democracy and the State: Welfare, Secularism and Development in Contemporary India.* Delhi: Oxford University Press.

———. 2001. *Democracy and the State.* New Delhi: Oxford University Press.

———. 2011. 'The Transformation of Citizenship in India in the 1990s and Beyond', in *Understanding India's New Political Economy: A Great Transformation?* edited by S. Ruparelia, S. Reddy, J. Harriss and S. Corbridge. Delhi: Routledge.

———. 2013.*Citizenship and Its Discontents: an Indian History.* Cambridge, M.A.; London: Harvard University Press.

Jeffrey, C. 2000. 'Democratisation without Representation? The Power and Political Strategies of a Rural Elite in North India', *Political Geography* 19 (8): 1013–36.

Jeffrey, C. and J. Lerche. 2000. 'Stating the Difference: State, Discourse and Class Reproduction in Uttar Pradesh, India', *Development and Change* 31 (4): 857–87.

Jessop, R. 1982. *The Capitalist State.* London: Martin Robertson.

Jha, P. 2004. 'Continuity and Change: Some Observations on the Landscape of Agricultural Labourers in North Bihar', *Journal of Agrarian Change* 4 (4): 509–31.

Jha, R., R. Gaiha, S. Shankar and M. Pandey. 2010. 'Targeting Accuracy of the NREG: Evidence from Madhya Pradesh and Tamilnadu', *ASARC Working Paper* 2010/19. Canberra: Australian National University.

Jha, R., S. Bhattacharyya and R. Gaiha. 2010. 'Social Safety Nets and Nutrient Deprivation: An Analysis of the National Rural Employment Guarantee Program and the Public Distribution System in India', *Journal of Asian Economics* 22 (2): 189–201.

Jodhka, S. 2012. 'Introduction: Modernity, Identity and Citizenship – Dipankar Gupta and the Sociology of India', in *Interrogating India's Modernity: Democracy, Identity and Citizenship,* edited by S Jodhka. Delhi: Oxford University Press.

Jones, M., R. Jones and M. Woods. 2004. *An Introduction to Political Geography: Space, Place and Politics.* London: Routledge

Joseph, G. and D. Nugent (eds). 1994. *Everyday Forms of State-formation: Revolution and the Negotiation of Rule in Modern Mexico.* Durham: Duke University Press.

Joshi, A. 2010. 'Do Rights Work? Law, Activism and the Employment Guarantee Scheme', *World Development* 38 (4): 620–30.

Joshi, S. 2001. *Fractured Modernity: Making of a Middle Class in Colonial North India.* Delhi: Oxford University Press.

———. 2010. *The Middle Class in Colonial India.* New Delhi; Oxford: Oxford University Press.

Joshi, H. and S. Kumar. 2010. *Asserting Voices: Changing Culture, Identity and Livelihood of the Musahars in the Gangetic Plains.* Delhi: Deshkal Publications.

Jung, C. 2008. *The Moral Force of Indigenous Politics: Critical Liberalism and the Zapatistas.* New York; Cambridge: Cambridge University Press.

Kaldor, M. 2003. *Global Civil Society: An Answer to War.* Cambridge: Polity Press.

Kaldor, M. and I. Vejvoda. 1997. 'Democratisation in Central and East European Countries', *International Affairs* 73 (1): 59–82.

Kalecki, M. 1943. *Essays in Economic Dynamics.* London: G. Allen and Unwin.

Kannan, K. P. and G. Raveendran. 2011. 'India's Common People: The Regional Profile', *Economic and Political Weekly* 46 (38): 60–73.

Kapur, D., P. Mukhopadhyay and A. Subramanian. 2008. 'The Case for Direct Cash Transfers to the Poor', *Economic and Political Weekly*: 37–43.

Karanth, G. K. 1987. 'New Technology and Traditional Rural Institutions: Case of 'Jajmani' Relations in Karnataka', *Economic and Political Weekly* 43 (15): 37–40.

Karl, T. L. 1990. 'Dilemmas of Democratisation in Latin America', *Comparative Politics* 23 (1): 1–21.

Kaviraj, S. 1984. 'On the Crisis of Political Institutions in India', *Contributions to Indian Sociology* 18 (2): 223–43.

———. 1988. 'A Critique of the Passive Revolution', *Economic and Political Weekly* 23 (45/47): 2429–33, 2436–41 and 2443–44.

———. 2000. 'Modernity and Politics in India', *Daedelus* 129 (1): 137–62.

———. 2005. 'An Outline of a Revisionist Theory of Modernity', *European Journal of Sociology* 46 (3): 497–526.

———. 2011. 'Filth and the Public Sphere: Concepts and Practices about Space in Calcutta', in *The Enchantment of Democracy and India*, edited by S. Kaviraj, 238–73. Ranikhet: Permanent Black.

Keefer, P. and R. Vlaicu. 2005. *Democracy, Credibility, and Clientelism*, volume 3472. Washington, D.C.: World Bank Publications.

Kerkvliet, B. 2009. 'Everyday Politics in Peasant Studies (and Ours)', *The Journal of Peasant Studies* 36 (1): 227–43.

Kesari, D. and A. K. Srivastava. 2012. 'Retailing in Rural India: An Overview of Markets and Opportunities', *South Asian Academic Research Journals* 2 (4): 215–32.

Khare, R. S. 1984. *The Untouchable as Himself: Ideology, Identity and Pragmatism among the Lucknow Chamars*. Cambridge: Cambridge University Press.

Khera, R. and N. Nayak. 2011. 'Women Workers and Perceptions of the NREGA', in *Battle for Employment Guarantee*, edited by R. Khera, 81–104. Delhi: Oxford University Press.

Khera, R. 2011. *The Battle for Employment Guarantee*. Delhi: Oxford University Press.

Khilnani, S. 1997. *The Idea of India*. London: Hamish Hamilton.

Kidambi, S. 2011. 'From "Social Reform" to "Social Service": Indian Civic Activism and the Civilising Mission in Colonial Bombay', in *Colonial and Postcolonial South Asia: From Improvement to Development*, edited by C. A. Watt and A.R. Lopez, 217–39. London: Anthem.

Kideckel, D. A. 1977. 'The Dialectic of Rural Development: Cooperative Farm Goals and Family Strategies in a Romanian Commune', *Journal of Rural Cooperation* 5 (1): 43–61.

King, G., R. O. Keohane and S. Verba. 1994. *Designing Social Inquiry: Scientific Inference in Qualitative Research*. Princeton, NJ: Princeton University Press.

Kline, R. 2000. *Consumers in the Country: Technology and Social Change in Rural America*. Baltimore: Johns Hopkins University Press.

Kinzer, B. 2001. *England's Disgrace: J.S. Mill and the Irish Question*. Toronto: University of Toronto Press.

Kitschelt, H. and S. I. Wilkinson. 2007. 'Citizen-Politician Linkages: An Introduction', in *Patrons, Clients and Policies: Patterns of Democratic Accountability and Political Competition*, edited by H. Kitschelt and S. I. Wilkinson, 1–50. Cambridge: Cambridge University Press.

Knowles, A. 2010. 'Conjecturing Rudeness: James Mill's Utilitarian Philosophy of History and the British Civilizing Mission', in *Civilising Missions in Colonial and Postcolonial South Asia: From Improvement to Development*, edited by C. A. Watt and M. Mann. London: Anthem Press.

Koehler, G. 2011. 'Transformative Social Protection: Reflections on South Asian Policy Experience', *IDS Bulletin* 42 (6): 96–103.

Kohli, A. 1987. *The State and Poverty in India*. Cambridge: Cambridge University Press.

———. 1989. *Democracy and Discontent: India's Growing Crisis of Governability*. Cambridge: Cambridge University Press.

———. 1990. 'From Elite Activism to Democratic Consolidation: The Rise of Reform Communism in West Bengal', in *Dominance and State Power in Modern India: Decline of a Social Order*, edited by F. Frankel and M. S. A. Rao, volume II. Delhi: Oxford University Press.

————. 2006a. 'Politics of Economic Growth in India, 1980-2005: Part 1, the 1980s', *Economic and Political Weekly* 41 (13): 1251–65.

————. 2006b. 'Politics of Economic Growth in India, 1980-2005: Part 2, the 1990s and Beyond', *Economic and Political Weekly* 41 (14): 1361–70.

————. 2009. *Democracy and Development: From Socialism to Pro-Business*. Oxford: Oxford University Press.

————. 2012. *Poverty amid Plenty in the New India*. Cambridge: Cambridge University Press.

Komives, K. 2005. *Water, Electricity and the Poor: Who Benefits from Utility Subsidies?* Washington, D.C.: World Bank.

Komives, K., V. Foster, J. Halpern, Q. Wodon and R. Abdullah. 2005. *Water, Electricity and the Poor: Who Benefits from Utility Subsidies?* Washington, D.C.: World Bank.

Krishna, A. 2007. 'Politics in the Middle: Mediation Relationships between Citizens and the State in Rural North India', in *Patrons, Clients and Policies: Patterns of Democratic Accountability and Political Competition*, edited by H. Kitschelt and S. Wilkinson, 141–59. Cambridge: Cambridge University Press.

————. 2008. 'Introduction: Poor People and Democracy', in *Poverty, Participation and Democracy*, edited by A. Krishna, 1–27. Cambridge: Cambridge Unviersity Press.

————. 2009. 'Why Don't 'the Poor' Make Common Cause? The Importance of Subgroups', *Journal of Development Studies* 45 (6): 1–19.

————. 2010. *One Illness Away: Why People Become Poor and How they Escape Poverty*. New York: Oxford University Press.

————. 2011. 'Gaining Access to Public Services and the Democratic State in India: Institutions in the Middle', *Studies in Comparative International Development* 46 (1): 98–117.

Kulynych, J. 1997. 'Performing Politics: *Foucault, Habermas* and Postmodern Participation', *Polity* 30 (2): 315–46.

Kumar, A. 2006. 'Culture, Development and the Cultural Capital of Farce: The Musahar Community in Bihar', *Economic and Political Weekly* 41 (40): 4281–90.

————. 2010. 'Understanding Lohia's Political Sociology: Intersectionality of Caste, Class, Gender and Language', *Economic and Political Weekly* 45 (40): 64–70.

Kumar, G. 2006. *Local Democracy in India: Interpreting Decenralisation*. London, Thousand Oaks, Delhi: Sage Publications.

Kumar, G. and F. Stewart. 1992. 'Tackling Malnutrition: What Can Targeted Nutritional Interventions Achieve?' in *Poverty in India: Research and Policy*, edited by B. Harriss-White, S. Guhan and R. Cassen. Delhi: Oxford University Press.

Kumar, K. 2014. 'Rurality, Modernity, and Education', *Economic and Political Weekly* 49 (22).

Kumar, R. 1985. 'Gandhi, Ambedkar and the Poona Pact, 1932', *South Asia: Journal of South Asian Studies* 1–2: 87–101.

Kumar, S. 2009. 'Patterns of Political Participation: Trends and Perspectives', *Economic and Political Weekly* 44 (39): 47–51.

Kumar, S., M. Alam and D. Joshi. 2008. 'Caste Dynamics and Political Processes in Bihar', *Journal of Indian Political Economy* 20 (1 and 2): 1–32.

Kunnath, G. 2012. *Rebels from the Mud Houses: Dalits and the Making of the Maoist Revolution in Bihar*. Delhi: Social Sciences Press.

Kushnick, L. and J. Jennings (eds). 1999. *A New Introduction to Poverty: The Role of Race, Power and Politics*. New York: New York University Press.

Kuznets, S. 1955. *Economic Growth: Brazil, India, Japan*. Durham, N.C.: Duke University Press.

Labour Bureau. 2010. *Wage Rates in Rural India: 2009–10*. New Delhi: Government of India

———. 2011. *Wage Rates in Rural India: 2010–11*. New Delhi: Government of India.

———. 2012. *Wage Rates in Rural India: 2011–12*. New Delhi: Government of India.

———. 2014. *Employment Unemployment Survey*, Volume 1. New Delhi: Government of India.

Laclau, E. and C. Mouffe. 1985. *Hegemony and Socialist Strategy: Towards a Radical Democratic Politics*. London and New York: Verso.

Laclau, E (ed). 1994. *The Making of Political Identities*. London: Verso.

Laclau, E. 1990. *New Reflections on the Revolution of Our Time*. London: Verso.

———. 1992. 'Universalism, Particularism, and the Question of Identity', *October*: 83–90.

———. 2005. *On Populist Reason*. London: Verso.

Laidlow, J. 2002. 'For an Anthropology of Ethics and Freedom', *Journal of the Royal Anthropological Institute* 8 (2): 311–32.

Lama-Rewal, S. T. 2009. 'Local Democracy and Access to Health Services in Delhi: Preliminary Remarks', in *Indian Health Landscapes under Globalization*, edited by A. Vaguet, 351–70. New Delhi: Manohar Publishers and Distributors.

Lamont, M. 1992. *Money, Morals, and Manners: The Culture of the French and American Upper-Middle Class*. Chicago: University of Chicago Press.

Larkin, B. 1997. 'Indian Films and Nigerian Lovers: Media and the Creation of Parallel Modernities', *Africa: Journal of the International African Institute* 67 (3): 406–40.

Lasswell, H. 1936. *Politics: Who Gets What, When, How*. New York: Whittleseye House

Lasswell, H. and A. Kaplan. 1950. *Power and Society: A Framework for Political Enquiry*. New Haven: Yale University Press.

Latour, B. 1993. *We Have Never Been Modern*, translated by C. Porter. Cambridge MA: Harvard University Press.

———. 2005. *Reassembling the Social: An Introduction to Actor-Network Theory*. Oxford; New York: Oxford University Press.

Lazar, S. 2004. 'Personalist Politics, Clientelism and Citizenship: Local Elections in El Alto', Bolivia, *Bulletin of Latin American Research* 23 (2): 228–43.

LeGrand, C. 1984. 'Colombian Transformations: Peasants and Wage-Labourers in the Santa Marta Banana Zone', *The Journal of Peasant Studies* 11 (4): 178–200.

Lemarchand, R. 1994. 'Managing Transition Anarchies: Rwanda, Burundi, and South Africa in Comparative Perspective', *The Journal of Modern African Studies* 32 (4): 581–604.

Lenin, V. I. 1963. *Selected Works*. Moscow: Progress Publishers.

Lerche, J. 1999. 'Politics of the Poor: Agriculture Labourers and Political Transformations in North India', *Journal of Peasant Studies* 26 (2/3): 182–241.

———. 2001. 'Dimensions of Dominance: Class and State in Uttar Pradesh', in *The Everyday State and Society in Modern India*, edited by C. J. Fuller and V. Bénéï, 91–114. Delhi: Social Science Press.

———. 2010. 'From "Rural Labor" to "Classes of Labor": Class Fragmentation, Caste and Class Struggle at the Bottom of the Indian Labour Hierarchy', in *The Comparative Political Economy of Development: Africa and South Asia*, edited by B. Harriss-White and J. Heyer, 64–85. London: Routledge.

———. 2013. 'The Agrarian Question in Neoliberal India: Agrarian Transition Bypassed?' *Journal of Agrarian Change* 13 (3): 382–404.

Lerner, M. 1958. *The Passing of Traditional Society: Modernizing the Middle East*. London: Collier-Macmillan Limited.

Levien, M. 2012. 'The Land Question: Special Economic Zones and the Political Economy of Dispossession in India', *Journal of Peasant Studies* 39 (3–4): 933–69.

Lewis, O. 1959. *Five Families: Mexican Case Studies in the Culture of Poverty*. New York: Souvenir Press.

———. 1964. *The Children of Sanchez: Autobiography of a Mexican Family*. London: Penguin books.

———. 1998. 'The Culture of Poverty', *Society* 35 (2): 7–9.

Li, T. M. 1999. *Transforming the Indonesian Uplands: Marginality, Power and Production*. Amsterdam: Harwood.

———. 2007. *The Will to Improve: Governmentality, Development, and the Practice of Politics*. Durham: Duke University Press.

———. 2013. 'Insistently Seeking Social Incorporation: Comment', *Journal of Royal Anthropological Institute*. 19: 252–53.

Lieten, G. and R. Srivastava. 1999. *Unequal Partners: Power Relations, Devolution and Development in Uttar Pradesh*. New Delhi: Sage.

Lijphart, A. 1996. 'The Puzzle of Indian Democracy: A Consociational Interpretation', *American Political Science Review* 90 (2): 258–68.

Linz, J. J. and A. Stepan. 1996. *Problems of Democratic Transition and Consolidation: Southern Europe, South America and Post-Communist Europe*. Baltimore: Johns Hopkins University Press.

Lipset, S.M. 1959. 'Some Social Requisites of Democracy: Economic Development and Political Legitimacy', *American Political Science Review* 53 (1): 69–105.

———. 1960. *Political Man*. London: Heinemann.

———. 1963. *The First New Nation. The United States in Historical and Comparative Perspective*. Garden City, NY: Anchor Books.

———. 1964. *The First Nation: The United States in Historical and Comparative Perspective*. London: Heinemann.

Lohia, R. 1964. *The Caste System*. Hyderabad, India: Navahind.

London, T. 2008. 'The Base of the Pyramid Perspective: A New Approach to Poverty Alleviation', *Academy of Management Proceedings* 1: 1–6.

Lorenzen, D. 1987. 'Traditions of Non-Caste Hinduism: The Kabir-panth', *Contributions to Indian Sociology* 21 (2): 263–83.

Louis, P. 2002. *People Power: The Naxalite Movement in Central Bihar*. Delhi: Wordsmiths.

Luckham, R., A. M. Goetz, and M. Kaldor. 2003. 'Democratic Institutions and Democratic Politics', in *Can Democracy be Designed: the Politics of Institutional Choice in Conflict-Torn Societies*, edited by B. Sunil and R, Luckham, 14–59. *London: Zed Books*.

Lukes, S. 1974. *Power: A Radical View*. London: Palgrave Macmillan.

MacIntyre, A. 1988. *Whose Justice? Which Rationality?* Notre Dame: Notre Dame University Press.

———. 1999. *Dependent Rational Animals: Why Human Beings Need the Virtues*. Chicago: Open Court.

MacLean, L. 2014. 'Citizen or Client?: An Analysis of Everyday Politics in Ghana', *African Studies Quarterly*, 15 (1): 93–124.

Mains, D. 2007. 'Neoliberal Times: Progress, Boredom, and Shame Among Young Men in Urban Ethiopia', *American Ethnologist* 34 (4): 659–73.

Mainwaring, S. 1999. *Rethinking Party Systems in the Third Wave of Democratization: the Case of Brazil*. Stanford, California: Stanford University Press.

Malinowski, B. 1967. *A Diary in the Strict Sense of the Term*. Stanford, CA: Stanford University Press.

Mallick, R. 1993. *Development Policy of a Communist Government: West Bengal since 1977*. Cambridge: Cambridge University Press.

———. 1994. *Indian Communism*. Delhi: Oxford University Press.

Mamdani, M. 1996. *Citizen and Subject: Contemporary Africa and the Legacy of Late Colonialism*. Princeton, NJ: Princeton University Press.

Mann, M. 1997. 'Has Globalisation Ended the Rise and Rise of the Nation-State?' *Review of International Political Economy* 4 (3): 472–96.

Manor, J. 1987. 'Tried, Then Abandoned: Economic Liberalization in India', *IDS Bulletin* 18 (4): 39–44.

———. 2000. 'Small-Time Political Fixers in India's States: Towel over Armpit', *Asian Survey*: 816–35.

———. 2010. 'Beyond Clientelism: Digvijay Singh's Participatory, Pro-Poor Strategy in Madhya Pradesh', in *Power and Influence in India: Bosses, Lords and Captains*, edited by P. Price and A. Ruud, 193–213. London: Routledge.

———. 2013. 'Post-Clientelistic Initiatives', in *Democratisation in the Global South: The Importance of Transformative Politics*, edited by K. Stokke and O. Tornquist, 243–53. London: Palgrave Macmillan,.

Mantena, K. 2010. *Alibis of Empire: Henry Maine and the Ends of Liberal Imperialism*. Ranikhet: Permanent Black.

Marcus, G. E. and M. M. Fischer. 1999. *Anthropology as Cultural Critique: An Experimental Moment in the Human Sciences*. Chicago: University of Chicago Press.

Marshall, T. H. 1964. *Class, Citizenship and Social Development*. New York.

Marshall M. G. and B. R. Cole. 2009. *Global Report 2009: Conflict, Governance and State Fragility*. Vienna: Center for Systemic Peace. Available at: http://www.systemicpeace.org/vlibrary/GlobalReport2009.pdf, accessed on 11 March 2013.

Marx, K. 1844. *On the Jewish Question*. Available at: www.marxists.org/archive/marx/works/1844/jewish-question, accessed in June, 2015.

———. 1848. *Manifesto of the Communist Party*. Available at: https://www.marxists.org/archive/marx/works/1848/communist-manifesto/, accessed in September 2013.

———. 1852. *Eighteenth Brumaire of Louis Bonaparte*. Available at: https://www.marxists.org/archive/marx/works/download/pdf/18th-Brumaire.pdf, accessed in October 2013.

Massey, D. 2005. *For Space*. Los Angeles, London, New Delhi, Singapore, Washington DC: Sage Publications.

Mathew, S. and M. Moore. 2011. 'State Incapacity by Design: Understanding the Bihar Story', *Working Paper* No. 366. Institute of Development Studies.

Mbembe, A. 2001. *On the Postcolony*. Berkeley, Los Angeles and London: University of California Press.

McCarthy, J. and M. Zald. 1987. 'Resource Mobilisation and Social Movements: A Partial Theory', *American Journal of Sociology* 82: 1212–41.

McCartney, M and I. Roy. 2016. 'A Consensus Unravels: NREGA and the Paradox of Rules-based Welfare in India', *European Journal of Development Research* 28: 588–604.

Meagher, K. and Lindell, I. 2013. 'ASR Forum: Engaging with African Informal Economies: Social Inclusion or Adverse Incorporation?' *African Studies Review* 56 (03): 57–76.

Mehta, P. 2003. *The Burden of Democracy*. Delhi: Penguin.

Mehta, U. 1997. 'Liberal Strategies of Exclusion', in *Tensions of Empire: Colonial Cultures in a Bourgeois World*, edited by F. Cooper and A. L. Stoler, 59–86. Berkeley, Los Angeles, London: University of California Press.

Menon, N. 2004. *Recovering Subversion: Feminist Politics beyond the Law*. Delhi: Permanent Black.

Mendelsohn, O. and M. Vicziany. 1998. *The Untouchables: Subordination, Poverty and the State in Modern India*. Cambridge: Cambridge University Press.

Meyer, B. and J. Sullivan. 2003. 'Measuring the Well-Being of the Poor Using Income and Consumption', *Journal of Human Resources* 38 (S): 1180–1220.

Michelutti, L. 2007. 'The Vernacularization of Democracy: Political Participation and Popular Politics in North India', *Journal of the Royal Anthropological Institute* 13 (3): 639–56.

———. 2008. 'The *Vernacularisation of Democracy*: Politics, Caste and Religion in India. London: Routledge.

Migdal, J. 1988. *Strong Societies and Weak States: State-Society Relations and State Capabilities in the Third World*. Princeton: Princeton University Press.

Migdal, J., A. Kohli and V. Shue (eds). 1994. *State Power and Social Forces: Domination and Transformation in the Third World*. New York: Cambridge University Press.

Milanovic, B. 2016. *Global Inequality: A New Approach for the Age of Globalisation*. Belknap Press: Harvard.

Mill, J. 1968. *The History of British India*. New York: Chelsea House.

Ministry of Agriculture. 2009a. *Web-based Land Use Statistics Information System*. New Delhi: Government of India.

———. 2009b. *Minimum Support Prices*. New Delhi: Government of India.

———. 2011. *Agricultural Census 2010–11: All India report on number and area of operational holdings*. Delhi: Government of India.

Ministry of Consumer Affairs. 2013. *Foodgrain Bulletin*. New Delhi: Government of India.

Ministry of Rural Development. 2008. *Annual Report, 2007–2008*. New Delhi: Government of India.

———. 2011. *Socio-Economic Caste Census*. New Delhi: Government of India.

Mintz, S. 1974. *Caribbean Transformations*. Chicago: Aldine.

———. 1985. *Sweetness and Power: The Place of Sugar in Modern History*. New York: Viking.

Mishra, D. K. 2008. 'Structural Inequalities and Interlinked Transactions in Agrarian Markets: Results of a Field Survey', in *Reforming Indian Agriculture towards Employment Generation and Poverty Reduction*, edited by S. K. Bhaumik, 231–68. New Delhi: SAGE Publications.

Mitchell, T. 2002. *Rule of Experts: Egypt, Techno-Politics, Modernity*. Berkeley: University of California Press.

Mkandawire, T. 2005. *Targeting and Universalism in Poverty Reduction*. Geneva: United Nations Research Institute for Social Development.

Moore Jr, B. 1966. *Social Origins of Dictatorship and Democracy: Lord and Peasant in the Making of the Modern World*. Harmondsworth: Penguin.

Moore, M. and V. Jadhav. 2006. 'The Politics and Bureaucratics of Rural Public Works: Maharashtra's Employment Guaranteed Scheme', *Journal of Development Studies* 42 (8): 1271–1300.

Morris-Jones, W. H. 1987. *The Government and Politics of India*. Huntingdon: Eothen Press.

Morselli, H, 1883. *Suicide: An Essay on Comparative Moral Statistics*. London: Keagan Paul, Trench, and Co.

Mosse, D. 1994. 'Authority, Gender and Knowledge: Theoretical Reflections on the Practice of Participatory Rural Appraisal', *Development and Change* 25 (3): 497–526.

———. 2007. *Power and Durability of Poverty: A Critical Exploration of the Links Between Culture, Marginality and Chronic Poverty*. Manchester: Chronic Poverty Research Centre.

———. 2010. 'A Relational Approach to Durable Poverty, Inequality and Power', *Journal of Development Studies* 46 (7): 1156–78.

Motiram, S. and V. Vakulabharanam. 2013. 'Indian Inequality: Patterns and Changes, 1993-2010', in *India Development Report*, edited by S. Mahendra Dev. New Delhi: Oxford University Press.

Mouffe, C. 1992. *The Dimensions of Radical Democracy: Pluralism, Citizenship, Community*. London; New York: Verso.

———. 1993. *The Return of the Political*. London: Verso.

———. 1996. 'Democracy, Power and the "Political"', in *Democracy and Difference*, edited by S. Benhabib, 245–55. Princeton: Princeton University Press.

———. 1999. 'Deliberative Democracy or Agonistic Pluralism', *Social Research* 66 (3): 745–58.

————. 2000. *The Democratic Paradox*. London: Verso.

————. 2007. *On the Political*. London and New York: Routledge.

————. 2009. 'Democracy in a Multipolar World', *Journal of International Studies* 37 (3): 549–61.

Mouzelis, N. 1985. 'On the Concept of Populism: Populist and Clientelist Modes of Incorporation in Semiperipheral Polities', *Politics & Society* 14 (3): 329–48.

Mukul. 1999. 'The Untouchable Present: Everyday Life of Musahars in North Bihar', *Economic and Political Weekly* 34 (49): 3465–69.

Mustapha, A.R. 2009. 'Institutionalising Ethnic Representation: How Effective is Affirmative Action in Nigeria?' *Journal of International Development* 21 (4): 561–76.

Nader, L. 1965. 'The Anthropological Study of Law'. *American Anthropologist* 67 (6): 3–30.

Nandy, A. 1987. *Traditions, Tyranny, and Utopia: Essays in the Politics of Awareness*. Delhi: Oxford University Press.

————. 1995. *The Savage Freud and other Essays in Possible and Retrievable Selves*. Delhi: Oxford University Press.

Narayan, B. 2007. *The Making of the Dalit Public in North India: Uttar Pradesh 1950 – Present*. Delhi: Oxford University Press.

————. 2009. *Fascinating Hindutva: Saffron Politics and Dalit Mobilisation*. New Delhi: Sage Publications.

Narayan, D., R. Patel, K. Schafft, A. Rademacher and S. Koch-Schulte. 2000a. *Voices of the Poor: Can Anyone Hear Us?* New York, NY: Oxford University Press.

Narayan, D., R. Chambers, M. Shah and P. Petesch. 2000b. *Voices of the Poor: Crying out for Change*. New York: Oxford University Press.

Narayan, D. and P. Petesch. 2002. *Voices of the Poor: From Many Lands*. New York: Oxford University Press.

National Commission for Enterprises in the Unorganised Sector. 2008. *Report of Conditions of Work and Promotion of Livelihoods in the Unorganised Sector*. Delhi: Academic Foundation.

Naudet, J. D. 2003. 'Debt Relief or Aid Reform?' in *New International Poverty Reduction Strategies*, edited by J. P Cling, M. Razafindrakato and F. Rouband, 219–38. London: Routledge.

Navaro-Yashin, Y. 2002. *Faces of the State: Secularism and Public Life in Turkey*. Princeton: Princeton University Press.

Nayyar, D. 2013. *Catch Up: Developing Countries in the World Economy*. Oxford: Oxford University Press.

Nehru, B. K. 1979. 'Western Democracy and the Third World', *Third World Quarterly* 1 (2): 53–70.

Nicholas, R. 1965. 'Factions: A Comparative Analysis', in *Political Systems and the Distribution of Power*, edited by M. Banton. London: Tavistock Publications.

Nielsen, M. 2011. 'Inverse Governmentality: The Paradoxical Production of Peri-Urban Planning in Maputo, Mozambique', *Critique of Anthropology* 31 (4): 329–58.

Norval, A. J. 1996. *Deconstructing Apartheid Discourse*. London: Verso.

———. 2007. *Aversive Democracy: Inheritance and Originality in the Democratic Tradition.* Cambridge: Cambridge University Press.

———. 2012. '"Writing a Name in the Sky": Ranciere, Cavell and the Possibility of Egalitarian Inscription', *American Political Science Review* 106 (4): 810–26.

Nossiter, T.J. 1988. *Marxist State Governments in India*. London: Printer Publishers.

National Rural Employment Guarantee Act. 2006. *The National Rural Employment Guarantee Action 2005 (NREGA): Operational Guidelines*. New Delhi: Government of India.

———. 2012. *Mahatma Gandhi National Rural Employment Guarantee Act, 2005: Report to the People*. New Delhi: Government of India.

———. 2013. *Mahatma Gandhi National Rural Employment Guarantee Act, 2005: Report to the People*. New Delhi: Government of India.

———. 2014. *Mahatma Gandhi National Rural Employment Guarantee Act, 2005: Report to the People*. New Delhi: Government of India.

Nugent, D. 1994. 'Building the State, Making the Nation: The Bases and Limits of State Centralization in "Modern" Peru', *American Anthropologist* 96 (2): 333–69.

———. 2009. 'Democracy Otherwise: Struggles Over Popular Rule in the Northern Peruvian Andes', in *Democracy: Anthropological Perspectives*, edited by J. Paley, 21–62. Santa Fe, NM: School of American Research.

Nye, D. 1990. *Electrifying America: Social Means of a New Technology, 1880-1940*; Cambridge, Mass and London: MIT Press.

Oberschall, A. 1973. *Social Conflict and Social Movements*. Englewood Cliffs, N.J.: Prentice Hall.

O'Brien, K. 2010. 'Introduction: Understanding China's Grassroots Elections', in *Grassroots Elections in China*, edited by K. O'Brien and S. Zhao, xi–xvi. London and New York: Routledge.

O'Brien, K. and L. Li. 2006. *Rightful Resistance in Rural China*. New York: Cambridge University Press. O'Donnell, G. 1993. 'On the State, Democratisation and Some Conceptual Problems: A Latin American View with Glances at Some Postcommunist Countries', *World Development* 21 (8): 1355–59.

O'Donnell, G.A. 1996. 'Illusions about Consolidation', *Journal of Democracy* 7 (2): 34–51.

O'Hanlon, R. 1988. 'Recovering the Subject: Subaltern Studies and Histories of Resistance in Colonial South Asia', *Modern Asian Studies* 22 (1): 189–224.

———. 1989. 'Cultures of Rule, Communities of Resistance: Gender Discourse and Tradition in Recent South Asian Historiographies', *Social Analysis* 25: 94–114.

———. 2014. *At the Edges of Empire: Essays in the Social and Intellectual History of India.* New Delhi: Permanent Black.

Ojha, G. 1977. *Land Problems and Land Reforms.* New Delhi: Sultan Chand & Sons.

Olson, M. 1965. *The Logic of Collective Action.* Cambridge, Mass.: Harvard University Press.

Omvedt, G. 1993. *Reinventing Revolution: New Socialist Movements and the Socialist Tradition in India.* London: M.E. Sharpe.

———. 1994. *Dalits and the Democratic Revolution: Dr. Ambedkar and the Dalit Movement in Colonial India.* New Delhi: Sage Publications.

———. 1999. *An Open Letter to Arundhati Roy.* Available at http://www.narmada.org/ debates/gail/gail.open.letter.html, accessed in June 2012.

———. 2006. *Dalit Visions: The Anti-Caste Movement and the Construction of an Indian Identity.* New Delhi: Orient Longman.

———. 2008. *Seeking Begumpura: The Social Vision of Anti-caste Intellectuals.* Delhi: Navayana Publications.

OPHI. 2011. *Multidimensional Poverty Index: India Country Briefing.* Oxford: Queen Elizabeth House.

———. 2013. *Multidimensional Poverty Index: India Country Briefing.* Oxford: Queen Elizabeth House.

Oxfam. 2016. *An Economy of the 1%.* Available at: http://policy-practice.oxfam.org.uk/ publications/an-economy-for-the-1-how-privilege-and-power-in-the-economy-drive-extreme-inequ-592643.

Paige, J. 1975. *Agrarian Revolution: Social Movements and Export Agriculture in the Underdeveloped World.* New York: The Free Press.

Painter, J. and A. Jeffrey. 2009. *Political Geography: An Introduction to Space and Power.* London: Sage.

Paley, J. 2001. *Marketing Democracy: Power and Social Movements in Post-dictatorship Chile.* Berkeley: University of California Press.

Panagariya, A. and M. Mukim. 2014. 'A Comprehensive Analysis of Poverty in India'. *World Bank Policy Research Working Paper 6714.*

Panitch, L., C. Leys, G. Albo and D. Coates. 2001. 'Preface to Issue on Working Classes: Global Realities', *Socialist Register* 37: vii– xi.

Pankaj, A. and R. Tankha. 2010. 'Empowerment Effects of the NREGS on Women Workers: A Study in Four States', *Economic and Political Weekly* 45 (30): 45–55.

Parry, J. 2000a. 'Lords of Labour: Working and Shirking in Bhilai', *Contributions to Indian Sociology* 33 (1 and 2): 107–40.

———. 2000b. 'The "Crisis of Corruption" and "The Idea of India": A Worm's Eye View', in *The Morals of Legitimacy: Between Agency and System*, edited by I. Pardo. Oxford: Berghahn Books.

Parsons, T and E. Shils. 1951. *Toward a General Theory of Action*. Cambridge, Mass: Harvard University Press.

———. 1959. *Structure and Process in Modern Societies*. New York: Free Press of Glencoe Inc.

———. 1960. *Structure and Process in Modern Society*. London: Frank Cass.

———. 1971. *The System of Modern Societies*. Englewood Cliffs: Prentice-Hall.

———. 1977. *Social Systems and the Evolution of Action Theory*. New York: Free Press and London: Collier Macmillan.

Patai, D. 1988. *Brazilian Women Speak: Contemporary Life Stories*. London and New Brunswick: Rutgers University Press.

Patel, S. 1952. *Agricultural Labourers in Modern India and Pakistan*. Bombay: Current Book House.

Pateman, C. 1970. *Participation and Democratic Theory*. Cambridge: Cambridge University Press.

Patnaik, U. 1986. *The Agrarian Question and the Development of Capitalism in India*. Delhi: Oxford University Press.

———. 2013. 'Updating Poverty Estimates and Comparing Official Figures: Poverty Trends in India 2004–05 to 2009–10', *Economic and Political Weekly* 48 (40): 43–58.

Pattenden, J. 2011a. 'Gatekeeping as Accumulation and Domination: Evidence from South India', *Journal of Agrarian Change* 11 (2): 164–94.

———. 2011b. 'Social Protection and Class Relations: Evidence from Scheduled Caste Women's Associations in Rural South India', *Development and Change* 42 (2): 469–98.

Peabody, N. 2001. 'Cents, Sense, Census: Human Inventories in Late Precolonial and Early Colonial India', *Comparative Studies in Society and History* 43 (4): 819–50.

Peet, R. and Hartwick, E. 2009. *Theories of Development: Contentions, Arguments, Alternatives*. New York: Guildford.

Pels, P. 1998. 'The Magic of Africa: Reflections on a Western Commonplace', *African Studies Review* 41 (3): 193–209.

Perlman, J. 1976. *The Myth of Marginality: Urban Poverty and Politics in Rio de Janeiro*. Berkeley: University of California Press.

Persson, T. and G. E. Tabellini. 2003. *Do Electoral Cycles Differ Across Political Systems?* Innocenzo Gasparini Institute for Economic Research.

Petras, J. 1998. 'The Political and Social Basis of Regional Variation in Land Occupations in Brazil', *Journal of Peasant Studies* 25 (4): 124–33.

Pigg, S. 1992. 'Inventing Social Categories through Place: Social Representations and Development in Nepal', *Comparative Studies in Society and History* 34 (3): 491–513.

Pikkety, T. 2015. *The Economics of Inequality*. Harvard, MA: Harvard University Press.

Piliavsky, A. (eds.) 2014. *Patronage as Politics in South Asia*. Cambridge: Cambridge University Press.

Piot, C. 1999. *Remotely Global: Village Modernity in West Africa*. Chicago: Chicago University Press.

Pitts, J. 2005. *A Turn to Empire: The Rise of Imperial Liberalism in Britain and France*. Oxford: Princeton University Press.

Piven, F. F. and R. Cloward. 1971. *Regulating the Poor: The Functions of Public Welfare*. London: Tavistock Publications.

Planning Commission. 2001. *India Human Development Report 2001*. New Delhi: Government of India.

———. 2009. *Report of the Expert Group to Review the Methodology of Poverty*. New Delhi: Government of India.

———. 2011. *India Human Development Report: Towards Social Inclusion*. New Delhi: Government of India.

———. 2014. *Report of the Expert Group to Review the Methodology for the Measurement of Poverty*. New Delhi: Government of India.

Plattner, M. 2015. 'Is Democracy in Decline', *Journal of Democracy* 26 (1): 5–10.

Pocock, D. 1973. *Mind, Body and Wealth: A Study of Belief and Practice in an Indian Village*. The Hague: John Wiley and Sons.

Pollock, S. 1993. 'Deep Orientalism? Notes on Sanskrit and Power beyond the Raj', in *Orientalism and the Postcolonial Predicament: Perspectives from South Asia*, edited by C. A. Breckenbridge and P. van de Veer, 76–133. Philadelphia: University of Pennsylvania.

Potter, J. 2009. 'Discourse Analysis as a Way of Analysing Naturally Occurring Talk', in *Qualitative Research*, edited by D. Silverman, 200–21. New Delhi, London: Thousand Oaks.

Prahalad, C. K. 2005. *The Fortune at the Bottom of the Pyramid: Eradicating Poverty through Profits*. Wharton: Wharton Business School.

Prakash, G. 1990. *Bonded Histories: Geneologies of Labour Servitude*. Cambridge: Cambridge University Press.

———. 1994. 'Subaltern Studies as Postcolonial Criticism', *American Historical Review* 99 (5): 1475–90.

Prasad, P. H. 1975. 'Agrarian Unrest and Economic Change in Rural Bihar: The Three Cases', *Economic and Political Weekly* 10 (24): 931–37.

———. 1979. 'Caste and Class in Bihar', *Economic and Political Weekly* 14 (7and 8): 481–4.

Przeworski, A. 1991. *Democracy and the Market: Political and Economic Reforms in Eastern Europe and Latin America*. Cambridge: Cambridge University Press.

———. 2009. 'Conquered or Granted? A History of Suffrage Extensions', *British Journal of Political Science* 39 (02): 291–321.

Przeworski, A. and F. Limongi. 1997. 'Modernisation: Theories and Facts', *World Politics* 49 (2): 155–83.

Przeworski, A., M. E. Alvarez, J. A. Cheibub and F. Lemongi. 2000. *Democracy and Development: Political Institutions and Well-being in the World 1950–2000*. New York: Cambridge University Press.

Putnam, R. D. 1993. 'The Prosperous Community: Social Capital and Public Life', *The American Prospect* 13.

Putnam, R., R. Leonardi and R. Nanetti. 1993. *Making Democracy Work: Civic Traditions in Modern Italy*. Princeton, NJ: Princeton University Press.

Rabinow, P. 1977. *Reflections on Fieldwork in Morocco*. Berkeley: University of California Press.

Radhakrishna, R., K. Subbarao, S. Indrakant and C. Ravi. 1997. *India's Public Distribution System: A National and International Perspective*. Washington DC: World Bank.

Rakshit, S. 2011. 'Capital Intensification, Productivity and Exchange – A Class Based Analysis of Agriculture in West Bengal in the Current Millennium', *Journal of Agrarian Change* 11 (4): 505–35.

Ram, F., S. K. Mohanty and U. Ram. 2009. 'Understanding the Distribution of BPL Cards: All-India and Selected States', *Economic and Political Weekly* 46 (7): 66–71.

Ramchandran, V. K. 2011. 'The State of Agrarian Relations in India Today', *The Marxist* 27 (1–2): 51–89.

Ramchandran, V. K., V. Rawal, and M. Swaminathan (eds). 2010. *Socio-Economic Surveys of Three Villages in Andhra Pradesh: A Study of Agrarian Relations*. New Delhi: Tulika Books.

Rancière, J. 1992. 'Politics, Identification and Subjectivization', *The Identity in Question* 61: 58–64.

———. 1999. *Disagreement: Politics and Philosophy*. Minneapolis: University of Minnesota Press.

———. 2000. 'Dissenting Words: A Conversation with Jacques Rancière (Interview by D Panagia)', *Diacritics* 30 (2): 113–26.

————. 2001. 'Ten Theses on Politics', in *Theory & Event* 5 (3), translated by D. Panagia. Available at: http://muse.jhu.edu/journals/theory_and_event/v005/5.3ranciere. html.

————. 2004. 'Introducing Disagreement', *Angelaki: Journal of Theoretical Economics* 9 (3): 3–9.

————. 2009. *The Emancipated Spectator*. London: Verso.

Ranger, T. 1983. 'The Invention of Tradition in Colonial Africa', in *The Invention of Tradition*, edited by E. Hobsbawm and T. Ranger, 211–62. Cambridge: Canto.

Rao, S. and J. Lourdosamy. 2000. 'Colonialism and the Development of Electricity: The Case of Madras Presidency, 1900-1947', *Science, Technology and Society* 15 (1): 27–54.

Ravallion, M., G. Datt and D. van de Walle. 1991. 'Quantifying Absolute Poverty in the Developing World', *Review of Income and Wealth* 37: 345–61.

Rawal, V. 2008. 'Ownership Holdings of Land in Rural India: Putting the Record Straight', *Economic and Political Weekly*: 43–67.

Rawls, J. 1971. *A Theory of Justice*. Cambridge, Mass: Belknap Press.

————. 1993. *Political Liberalism*. New York: Columbia University Press.

————. 1997. 'The Idea of Public Reason Revisited', *The University of Chicago Law Review* 64 (3): 765–807.

————. 1999. *Collected Papers*. New Delhi: Oxford University Press.

Ray, R. and M. Katzenstein (eds). 2005. *Social Movements in India: Poverty, Power, and Politics*. Rowman & Littlefield Publishers.Ray, R. K. 1984. *Social Conflict and Political Unrest in Bengal: 1875-1927*. Delhi: Oxford University Press.

Ray, R. 1979. *Change in Bengal Agrarian Society*, c. 1760-1850. Delhi: Manohar.

Ray, R. K. 1985. *Social Conflict and Political Unrest in Bengal 1875-1927*. Delhi: Oxford University Press.

Ray, R. K. and R. Ray. 1975. 'Zamindars and Jotedars: A Study of Rural Politics in Bengal', *Modern Asian Studies* 9 (1): 81–102.

Redclift, M. 1980. 'Agrarian Populism in Mexico—the Via Campesina', *The Journal of Peasant Studies* 7 (4): 492–502.

Reddy, D. N. and S. Mishra. 2009. 'Agriculture in the Reforms Regime', in *Agrarian Crisis in India*, edited by D. N. Reddy and S. Mishra, 3–43. New Delhi: Oxford University Press.

Reddy, G. R. and G. Hargopal. 1985. 'The Pyraveekar: The "Fixer" in Rural India', *Asian Survey* 25 (11): 1148–62.

Registrar General of India. 2001. Census of India. New Delhi: Government of India.

————. 2011. Census of India. New Delhi: Government of India.

Rev, I. 1987. 'The Advantages of being Atomised: How Hungarian Peasants Coped with Collectivisation', *Dissent* 34 (3): 335–50.

Ribot, C. and N. Peluso. 2003. 'A Theory of Access', *Rural Sociology* 68 (2): 153–81.

Richards, J. F. 1995. *The Mughal Empire*. Cambridge; New York: Cambridge University Press.

Richardson, H. 1997. *Practical Reasoning about Final Ends*. Cambridge: Cambridge University Press.

Ricoeur, P. 1977. 'Toward a Hermeneutic of the Idea of Revelation', *Harvard Theological Review* 70 (1–2): 1–37.

Riggs, F. W. 1963. 'Bureaucrats and Political Development: A Pradoxical View', in *Bureaucracy and Political Development*, edited by J. LaPalombara, 120–167. Princeton: Princeton University Press.

Rios, M. 2010. 'Claiming Latino Space: Cultural Insurgency in the Public Realm', in *Insurgent Public Space: Guerilla Urbanism and the Remaking of Contemporary Cities*, edited by J. Hou. Routledge: Oxford and New York.

Robb, P. 1988. 'Law and Agrarian Society in In India: The Case of Bihar and the Nineteenth Century Tenancy Debate', *Modern Asian Studies* 22 (2): 319–54.

Roberts, S. 1979. *Order and Dispute: An Introduction to Legal Anthropology*. London: Penguin.

Robin, C. 2009. 'Bihar: The New Stronghold of OBC Politics', in *Rise of the Plebians? The Changing Face of Indian Legislative Assemblies*, edited by C. Jaffrelot and S. Kumar. New Delhi: Routledge.

Robins, S. 2008. *From Revolution to Rights in South Africa: Social Movements, NGOs and Popular Politics After Apartheid*. Woodbridge: James Currey.

Rodgers, G. and J. Rodgers. 2011. 'Inclusive Development? Migration, Governance and Social Change in Rural Bihar', *Economic and Political Weekly* 46 (23): 43–50.

Rodney, W. 1970. *A History of the Upper Guinea Coast 1545 to 1800*. Oxford: Oxford University Press.

Rodrigues, V. 2009. 'Untouchability, Filth and the Public Domain', in *Humiliation: Claims and Context*, edited by Gopal Guru, 108–23. New Delhi: Oxford University Press.

Rogowski, Ronald and Mark Andreas Kayser. 'Majoritarian Electoral Systems and Consumer Power: Price-level Evidence from the OECD Countries', *American Journal of Political Science* (2002): 526–39.

Rose, N. 1999. *Powers of Freedom: Reframing Political Thought*. Cambridge: Cambridge University Press.

———. 2006. 'Governing "Advanced" Liberal Democracies', in *The Anthropology of the State: A Reader*, edited by A. Sharma and A. Gupta, 144–62. Oxford: Blackwell.

Roseberry, W. 1994. 'Hegemony and the Language of Contention', in *Everyday Forms of State-formation: Revolution and the Negotiation of Rule in Mexico*, edited by G. Joseph and D. Nugent, 355–66. Durham, NC: Duke University Press.

Rosenstone, S. and J. M. Hansen. 1993. *Mobilization, participation and democracy in America*. New York: Macmillan; Toronto: Maxwell Macmillan Canada; Oxford: Maxwell Macmillan International.

Roser, M. 2016. *Democracy*. Published online at OurWorldInData.org. Available at: https://ourworldindata.org/democracy/(Online Resource), accessed in May 2017.

Rothstein, B. 2001. 'The Universal Welfare State as a Social Dilemma', *Rationality and Society* 13 (2): 213–33.

Rostow, W. W. 1960. *The Stages of Economic Growth: A Non-Communist Manifesto*. Cambridge: Cambridge University Press.

Roy, D. 2012. 'Caste and Power: An Ethnography in West Bengal, India', *Modern Asian Studies* 46 (4): 947–74.

Roy, I. 2011. 'New Lists for Old: (Re-)constructing the Poor in the BPL Census', *Economic and Political Weekly* 46 (22): 82–91.

———. 2013. 'Development as Dignity: Contentious Politics and Social Equality in Rural Bihar', *Oxford Development Studies* 41 (4): 517–36.

———. 2014a. 'Reserved Labor, Unreserved Politics: Dignified Encroachments under India's NREGA', *Journal of Peasant Studies* 41 (4): 517–48.

———. 2014b. 'Flaunted Transcripts, Taunted Elites: Interrogating Domination in Bihar', in *Poverty in India*, edited by J. Parry and N. Gooptu. New Delhi: Social Sciences Press.

———. 2014c. 'Our Unrepresentative Representative Democracy', *The Hindu Center for Politics and Public Policy*. 28 April.

———. 2015. 'Utopia in Crisis? Subaltern Imaginations in Contemporary Bihar', *Journal of Contemporary Asia* 45 (4): 640–59.

———. 2016. 'Equality against Hierarchy: Imagining Modernity in Subaltern India', *Contributions to Indian Sociology* 50 (1): 80–107.

Rudolph, L. and S. H. Rudolph. 1967. *The Modernity of Tradition*. Chicago, IL: University of Chicago Press.

———. 1987. *In Pursuit of Lakshmi: The Political Economy of the Indian State*. Chicago: University of Chicago Press.

Rueschemeyer, D., E. Huber and J. D. Stephens. 1992. *Capitalist Development and Democracy*. Chicago, IL:: University of Chicago Press.

Ruiters, G. 2009. 'Free Basic Electricity in South Africa: A Strategy for Helping or Containing the Poor?' in *Electric Capitalism*, edited by D. McDonald, 248–63. London: Earthscan.

Rutherford, B. 2001. *Working on the Margins: Black Workers White Farmers in Zimbabwe.* New York: Zed Books.

Ruud, A. E. 1994. 'Land and Power: The Marxist Conquest of Rural Bengal', *Modern Asian Studies* 28 (2): 357–80.

———. 2003. *Poetics of Village Politics: The Making of West Bengal's Rural Communism.* Delhi: Oxford University Press.

Sabates-Wheeler, R. and S. Devereux. 2007. 'Social Protection for Transformation', *IDS Bulletin* 38 (3): 23–8.

Sachs, J. 2005. *The End of Poverty: How We Can Make it Happen in our Lifetime.* London: Penguin.

———. 2006. *The End of Poverty: Economic Possibilities of Our Time.* New York: Penguin Press.

Sachs, W. 1992. *The Development Dictionary: A Guide to Knowledge as Power.* London: Zed Books.

Sachsenmaier, D. and S. N. Eisenstadt (eds). 2002. *Reflections on Multiple Modernities. European, Chinese and Other Interpretations.* Leiden; Boston: Brill.

Sainath, P. 2011. 'Census Findings Point to a Decade of Rural Distress', *The Hindu,* Chennai edition. September 25.

Samaddar, R. 2007. *The Materiality of Politics II: Subject Position in Politics.* London, New York and Delhi: Anthem Press.

———. 2010. *Emergence of the Political Subject.* New Delhi and Thousand Oaks: Sage Publications.

Sandel, M. 1982. *Liberalism and the Limits of Justice.* Cambridge: Cambridge University Pres.

de Sousa Santos, B. 2009. 'Reinventing Social Emancipation: Towards New Manifestos', in *Democratizing Democracy: Beyond the Liberal Democratic Canon,* edited by B. de Sousa Santos and E. Sader, 1–9. London: Verso.

Sanyal, K. 2007. *Rethinking Capitalist Development: Primitive Accumulation, Governmentality and Post-Colonial Capitalism.* London: Routledge.

Sarkar, S. 1993. 'The Fascism of the Sangh Parivar', *Economic and Political Weekly* 28 (5): 163–64.

Sayer, D. 1994. 'Everyday Forms of State-formation: Some Dissident Remarks on "Hegemony"', in *Everyday Forms of State-formation: Revolution and the Negotiation of Rule in Mexico,* edited by G. Joseph and D. Nugent, 367–78. Durham, NC: Duke University Press.

Schaffer, F. C. 1997. 'Political Concepts and the Study of Democracy: The Case of Demokraasi in Senegal', *PoLAR: Political Legal Anthropological Review* 20 (1): 40–49.

Scheper-Hughes, N. 1993. *Death Without Weeping: The Violence of Everyday Life in Brazil.* Berkeley: University of California Press.

Schirmer, J. 1998. *The Guatemalan Military Project: A Violence Called Democracy.* Philadelphia: University of Pennsylvania Press.

Schmitter, P. C. 1994. 'Dangers and Dilemmas of Democracy', *Journal of Democracy* 5 (2): 57–74.

Schneider, D. 1984. *A Critique of the Study of Kinship.* Ann Arbor, Michigan: University of Michigan Press.

Schumpeter, J. 1947. *Capitalism, Socialism and Democracy.* New York: Harper.

Scott, J.C. 1977. *The Moral Economy of the Peasant: Rebellion and Subsistence in Southeast Asia.* New Haven; London: Yale University Press.

———. 1985. *Weapons of the Weak: Everyday Forms of Peasant Resistance.* New Haven: Yale University Press.

———. 1990. *Hidden Transcripts: Domination and the Arts of Resistance.* New Haven and London: Yale University Press.

———. 1998. *Seeing Like a State: How Certain Schemes to Improve the Human Condition Have Failed.* New Haven; London: Yale University Press.

———. 2011. *The Art of Not being Governed.* New Haven: Yale University Press.

Searle-Chatterjee, M. and U. Sharma (eds). 1994. *Contextualising Caste: Post-Dumontian Approaches.* Oxford: Blackwell.

Searle-Chatterjee, M. 2003. 'Caste, Religion and Other Identities', in *Contextualising Caste: Post–Dumontian Approaches,* edited by M. Searle-Chatterjee and U. Sharma. New Delhi: Rawat.

Sen, A. K. 1966. 'Peasants and Dualism with or without Dualism', *The Journal of Political Economy* 74 (5): 425–50.

———. 1981. *Poverty and Famines.* Oxford: Oxford University Press.

———. 1992. *Inequality Reexamined.* New York: Russell Sage Foundation; Oxford: Clarendon Press.

Sen, A. 1995. 'The Political Economy of Targeting', in *Public Spending and the Poor. Theory and Evidence,* edited by D. van de Walle and K. Nead, World Bank, 11–24. Baltimore, USA: The John Hopkins University Press.

———. 1999. *Development as Freedom.* Delhi: Oxford University Press.

———. 2002. *Rationality and Freedom.* Cambridge, Mass and London: Bellknap.

Sen, B. 1962. *Evolution of Agrarian Relations in India.* Delhi: People's Publishing House.

Shah, M. 2008. 'Structures of Power in Indian Society: A Response', *Economic and Political Weekly* 43 (46): 78–83.

Shamir, R. 2013. *Current Flow: the Electrification of Palestine.* Stanford, California: Stanford University Press.

Sharma, A. and A. Gupta (eds). 2006. *The Anthropology of the State: A Reader.* Oxford: Blackwell

———. 1961a. 'Political Development in New States', *Comparative Studies in History and Society* (Spring-Summer): 265–292, 379–411.

———. 1961b. *The Intellectual between Tradition and Modernity: The Indian Situation.* The Hague: Mouton.

Sharma, P. 2014. *Democracy and Transparency in the Indian State: The Making of the Right to Information Act.* Abingdon and New York: Routledge.

Shaw, A. 2013. 'Employment Trends in India: An Overview of NSSO's 68th Round', *Economic and Political Weekly* 48 (42): 23–25.

Shaw, R. 2003. 'Robert Kaplan and "Juju Journalism" in Sierra Leone's Rebel War: The Primitivizing of an African Conflict', in *Magic and Modernity: Interfaces of Revelation and Concealment*, edited by Birgit Meyer and Peter Pels, 81–102. Stanford: Stanford University Press.

Sheriff, A. 1987. *Slaves, Spices and Ivory in Zanzibar.* Oxford: James Currey.

Sherover, E. 1979. 'The Virtue of Poverty: Marx's Transformation of Hegel's Concept of the Poor', *Canadian Journal of Political and Social Theory* 3 (1): 53–66.

Shils, E. 1965. *Political Development in the New States.* The Hague: Mouton.

Sikor, T. and C. Lund. 2009. 'Access and Property: A Question of Power and Authority', *Development and Change* 40 (1): 1–22.

Simone, A. 2010. *City Life from Jakarta to Dakar: Movements at the Crossroads.* London: Routledge.

Singh, B. 2011. 'Agonistic Intimacy and Moral Aspiration in Popular Hinduism: A Study in the Political Theology of the Neighbour', *American Ethnologist* 38 (3): 430–50.

Singh, S. 2005. 'Limits to Power', *Economic and Political Weekly* 40 (29): 3167–75.

Sivaramakrishnan, K. and A. Agarwal. 2003. 'Regional Modernities in Stories and Practices of Development', in *Regional Modernities: The Cultural Politics of Development in India*, edited by K. Sivaramakrishnan and A. Agarwal, 1–61. Stanford: Stanford University Press.

Skocpol, T. 1979. *States and Social Revolutions: A Comparative Analysis of France, Russia and China.* Cambridge: Cambridge University Press.

———. 1991. 'Targeting within Universalism: Politically Viable Policies to Combat Poverty in the United States', in *The Urban Underclass*, edited by C. Jencks and P. Petersen, 437–59. Washington, D.C.: Brookings Institution.

Small, M. L., D. Harding and M. Lamont. 2010. 'Reconsidering Culture and Poverty', *The Annals of the American Academy of Political and Social Science* 629 (1): 6–27.

Smelser, N. 1962. *Theory of Collective Behaviour.* New York: Free Press; London: Collier-Macmillan.

Smith, A. D. 1991. *National Identity*. Rio and Las Vegas: University of Nevada Press.

Smith, A. M. 1996. *Laclau and Mouffe: The Radical Democratic Imaginary*. London: Routledge.

Somers, M. R. 1993. 'Citizenship and the Place of the Public Sphere: Law, Community, and Political Culture in the Transition to Democracy', *American sociological review* 58 (5): 587–620.

Spencer, J. 1997. 'Post-colonialism and the Political Imagination', *Journal of the Royal Anthropological Institute* 3: 1–19.

———. 2007. *Anthropology, Politics and the State: Democracy and Violence in South Asia*. Cambridge and New York: Cambridge University Press.

Spivak, G.C. 1988. 'Can the Subaltern Speak?' in *Marxism and the Interpretation of Culture*, edited by C. Nelson and L. Grossberg, 66–111. Urbana/Chicago: University of Illinois Press.

———. 1992. *Interview with Gayatri Chakravorty Spivak: New Nation Writers Conference in South Africa (Interviewer Leon de Kock)*. Ariel: A Review of International English Literature.

Sridharan, E. 2004. 'Electoral Coalitions in 2004 General Elections: Theory and Evidence', *Economic and Political Weekly* 39 (51): 5418–25.

———. 2014. 'Class Voting in the 2014 Lok Sabha Elections: The Growing Size and Importance of the Middle Classes', *Economic and Political Weekly* 49 (39): 72–76.

Srivastava, S. 1998. *Constructing Post-Colonial India: National Character and the Doon School*. London: Routledge.

Stedman-Jones, G. 1983. *Languages of Class: Studies in English Working Class History*. Cambridge: Cambridge University Press.

Steinberg, J. 2008. *Thin Blue: The Unwritten Rules of Policing South Africa*. Johannesburg: Jonathan Ball.

Subrahmanyam, S. 2001. *Penumbral Visions: Making Polities in Early Modern South India*. Delhi/Ann Arbor: Oxford University Press/University of Michigan Press.

Sundar, N. 2011. 'The Rule of Law and Citizenship in India: Post-colonial Dilemmas', *Citizenship Studies* 15 (3–4): 419–32.

Sundaram, K. and S. Tendulkar. 2002. *The Working Poor in India: Employment-Poverty Linkages and Employment Policy Options*. Geneva: Recovery and Reconstruction Department; International Labour Office.

Stewart, F. 2002. *Horizontal Inequalities: a Neglected Dimension of Development*. Helsinki: United Nations University, World Institute for Development Economics Research.

Stewart, F., C. Laderchi and R. Saith. 2003. 'Does it Matter that We Do Not Agree on the Definition of Poverty? A Comparison of Four Approaches', *Oxford Development Studies* 31 (3): 243–74.

Stokes, E. 1959. *The English Utilitarians and India*. Oxford: Clarendon Press.

Stokes, S. 1995. *Cultures in Conflict: Social Movements and the State in Peru*. Berkeley: University of California Press.

Subrahmaniam, A. 2009. *Shorelines: Space and Rights in South Asia*. Stanford, California: Stanford University Press.

Sundar, N. 2007. *Subalterns and Sovereigns: An Anthropological History of Bastar*. Delhi: Oxford University Press.

Swaminathan, M. 2000. *Weakening Welfare: The Public Distribution of Food in India*. New Delhi: Left Word.

Tambiah, S. 1997. *Levelling Crowds: Ethnonationalist Conflicts and Collective Violence in South Asia*. Berkeley: University of California Press.

Tanabe, A. 2007. 'Toward Vernacular Democracy: Moral Society and Post-Postcolonial Transformation in Rural Orissa, India', *American Ethnologist* 34 (3): 558–74.

Tanner, C. L. 1995. 'Class, Caste and Gender in Collective Action: Agricultural Labour Unions in Two Indian Villages', *The Journal of Peasant Studies* 22 (4): 672–98.

Tarrow, S. 1998. 'Fishnets, Internets, and Catnets: Globalization and Transnational Collective Action', in *Challenging Authority: The Historical Study of Contentious Politics*, edited by M.P. Hannagan, L. P. Moch and W. P. Te Brake, 228–44. Minneapolis: University of Minnesota Press.

Tawa-Lama Rewal, S. 2009. *The Resilient Bhadralok: A Profile of the West Bengal MLAs. in Rise of the Plebians? The Changing Face of Indian Legislative Assemblies*, 369–91. Delhi: Routledge.

Taylor, C. 1985. *Philosophy and the Human Sciences: Philosophical Papers 2*. Cambridge: Cambridge University Press.

———. 1987. 'Interpretation and the Sciences of Man', in *Interpretive Social Science: A Second Look*, edited by C. Taylor, 33–81. Berkeley: University of California Press.

———. 1990. 'Modes of Civil Society', *Public Culture* 3 (1): 95–118.

———. 1999. *A Catholic Modernity? Charles Taylor's Marianist Award Lecture, with responses by William M. Shea, Rosemary lulling Haughton, George Marsden, Jean Bethke Elshtain*. New York: Oxford University Press.

———. 2004. *Modern Social Imaginaries*. Durham: Duke University Press.

Teichman, J. 2016. *The Politics of Inclusive Development: Policy, State Capacity and Coalition Building*. Basingstoke: Palgrave Macmillan.

Teltumbde, A. 2001. *Globalisation and the Dalits*. Nagpur: Sanket Prakashan.

Teltumbde, A. 2009. 'Reservations within Reservations: A Solution', *Economic and Political Weekly* 44 (41/42): 16–18.

Thompson, E. P. 1971. 'The Moral Economy of the English Crows in the Eighteenth Century', *Past and Present* 50 (1): 76–36.

Thorat, S. and K. S. Neuman. 2012. *Blocked by Caste: Economic Discrimination in Modern India*. Oxford: Oxford University Press.

Thorat, S. and A. Dubey. 2012. 'Has growth been socially inclusive during 1993-94–2009-10?' *Economic and Political Weekly* 47 (10): 43–53.

Thorner, D. 1980. *The Shaping of Modern India*. New Delhi: Allied Publishers.Thorner, D. and A. Thorner. 1962. *Land and Labour in India*. Delhi: Asia Publishing House.

Tilly, C. 1975. 'Reflections on the History of European State-Making', in *The Formation of National States in Western Europe*, edited by C. Tilly and G. Ardant. Princeton: Princeton University Press.

———. 1976. 'Major Forms of Collective Action in Western Europe 1500–1975', *Theory and Society* 3 (3): 365–75.

———. 1978. *From Mobilization to Revolution*. New York: McGraw-Hill.

———. 1999. *Durable Inequality*. Berkeley: University of California Press.

———. 2007. *Democratization*. Cambridge: Cambridge University Press.

Tomovska. I. 2010. 'Poverty, Discrimination and the Roma: A Human Security Issue', *Human Security Perspectives* 7 (1): 63–82.

Tönnies, F. 1955. *Community and Association: (Gemeinschaft und Gesellschaft)*. London: Routledge & Paul.

———. 1957. *Community and Society: Gemeinschaft und Gesselschaft*, translated and edited by C. Loomis. East Lansing: The Michigan State University Press.

Truillot, M. R. 1995. *Silencing the Past: Power and the Production of History*. Boston: Boston University Press.

Tsai, L. 2007. *Accountability without Democracy: Solidary Groups and Public Goods Provision in Rural China*. New York; Cambridge: Cambridge University Press.

Tully, J. 2007. *Strange Multiplicity: Constitutionalism in an Age of Diversity*. Cambridge: Cambridge University Press.

Union Budget of India. 2012. *Expenditure Budget Volume 1, 2011-2012: Central Plan Outlay by Heads of Development (Statement 13)*. Delhi: Government of India.

Vakulabharanam, V. 2010. 'Does Class Matter? Class Structure and Worsening Inequality in India', *Economic and Political Weekly* 45 (29): 67–76.

———. 2014. 'Rising Inequality in India: The Role of Class and Global Capitalist Dynamics', paper presented at conference on 'Religious Pluralism, Cultural Differences, Social and Institutional Stability: What Can We Learn from India'. Rome: University Di Roma, Dipartimento Di Scienze Politiche, 9–10 June 2014.

van Manen, M. 1990. *Researching Lived Experience: Human Science for an Action Sensitive Pedagogy*. Albany, New York: State University of New York Press.

Vanaik, A. 2008. 'CAG Report on NREGA: Fact and Fiction', *Economic and Political Weekly* 43 (25): 39–45.

Varshney, A. 2000. 'Is India Becoming More Democratic?' *Journal of Asian Studies* 59 (1): 3–25.

Vasavi, A. 2012. *Shadow Spaces: Suicides and the Predicament of Rural India*. Delhi: Three Essays Collective.

Vatuk, S. 1969. 'Reference, Address, and Fictive Kinship in Urban North India', *Ethnology* 8 (3): 255–72.

Veltmeyer, H. 2010. *Imperialism, Crisis and Class Struggle: The Enduring Verities and Contemporary Face of Capitalism*. Leiden: Brill.

Vera-Sanso, P., A. Barrientos, L. Damodaran, K. Gilhooly, A. Goulding, C. Hennessy, and N. Walford. 2014. 'Participation and Social Connectivity', *The New Science of Ageing*.

Verba, S., K. Schlozman, and H. E. Brady. 1995. *Voice and Equality: Civic Voluntarism in American Politics*. Cambridge, MA: Harvard University Press.

Verdery, K. 1996. *What was Socialism, and What Comes Next?* Princeton: Princeton University Press.

Véron, R., S. Corbridge, G. Williams, and M Srivastava. 2003. 'The Everyday State and Political Society in Eastern India: Structuring Access to the Employment Assurance Scheme', *Journal of Development Studies* 39 (5): 1–28.

———. 2003. 'Decentralised Corruption or Corrupt Decentralisation? Community Monitoring of Poverty Alleviation Schemes in Eastern India', *World Development* 34 (11): 1922–41.

von Benda-Beckmann, F., K.von Benda-Beckmann and K. Wiber. 2006. ,The Properties of Property', in *Changing Properties of Property,* edited by F. von Benda-Beckmann, K. von Benda-Beckmann, and K. Wiber,1–39. New York: Bergahn.

Wadhwa Committee. 2005. *Central Vigilance Committee on Public Distribution System Report on the State of Bihar*. Delhi: Government of India.

Walzer, M. 1983. *Spheres of Justice*. Oxford: Blackwell.

Wampler, B. 2008. 'When does Participatory Democracy Deepen the Quality of Democracy', *Comparative Politics* 41 (1): 61–81.

Washbrook, D. 1993. 'Land and labour in Late Eighteenth-Century South India: the Golden Age of the Pariah?' in *Dalit Movements and the Meanings of Labour in India,* edited by P. Robb, 68–86. Delhi: Oxford University Press.

Watts, M. 2003. 'Development and Governmentality', *Singapore Journal of Tropical Geography* 24 (1): 6–34.

West, H. 2005. *Kupilikula: Governance and the Invisible Realm in Mozambique*. Chicago: Chicago University Press.

White, C. P. 1986. 'Everyday Resistance, Socialist Revolution and Rural Development: The Case of Vietnam', *Journal of Peasant Studies* 13 (2): 49–63.

White, H. and E. Anderson. 2001. 'Growth Versus Distribution: Does the Pattern of Growth Matter?', *Development Policy Review* 19: 267–89.

White, J. B. 2004. *Money Makes Us Relatives: Women's Labour in Urban Turkey*. New York: Routledge.

White, L. 2001. 'True Stories: Narrative, Event, History and Blood in the Lake Victoria Basin', in *African Words, African Voices: Critical Practices in Oral History*, edited by L. White, S. Miescher and D. W. Cohen, 281–304. Bloomington, Indiana: Indiana University Press.

Whitehead, L. and G. Gray-Molina. 2003. 'Political Capabilities over the Long Run', in *Changing Paths: International Development and the New Politics of Inclusion*, edited by P. Houtzager and M. Moore, 32–57. Ann Arbor: University of Michigan Press.

Whyte, S. 1997. *Questioning Misfortune: The Pragmatics of Uncertainty in Eastern Uganda*. New York: Cambridge University Press.

Williams, G. 2004. 'Towards a Repoliticization of Participatory Development: Political Capabilities and Spaces of Empowerment', in *Participation: From Tyranny to Transformation*, edited by S. Hicky and G. Mohan, 92–107. London: Zed Books.

Williams, G., R. Veron, S. Corbridge and M. Srivastava. 2003b. 'Participation and Power: Poor People's Engagement with India's Employment Assurance Scheme', *Development and Change* 34 (10): 163–92.

Williams, R. 1988. *Keywords: A Vocabulary of Culture and Society*. London: Fontana Press.

Willis, P. 1981. *Learning to Labour: How Working Class Kids Get Working Class Jobs*. New York: Columbia University Press.

Willis, P. and M. Trondman. 2000. 'Manifesto for "Ethnography"', *Ethnography* 1 (1): 5–16.

Witsoe, J. 2011a. 'Corruption as Power: Caste and the Political Imagination of the Postcolonial State', *American Ethnologist* 38 (1): 73–85.

———. 2011b. 'Rethinking Postcolonial Democracy: An Examination of the Politics of Lower-Caste Empowerment in North India', *American Anthropologist* 113 (4): 619–31.

———. 2012. 'Everyday Corruption and the Mediation of the Political Mediation of the Indian State', *Economic and Political Weekly* 47 (6): 47–54.

———. 2013. *Democracy against Development: Lower-Caste Politics and Political Modernity in Postcolonial India*. Chicago: University of Chicago Press.

Wolf, E. 1969. *Peasant Wars of the Twentieth Century*. New York: Harper and Row.

Wolf, E. 1999. *Envisioning Power: Ideologies of Dominance and Crisis.* Chicago: University of Chicago Press.

———. 2001. *Pathways of Power: Building on Anthropology of the Modern World.* Berkeley: University of California Press.

Wood, G. 2003. 'Staying Secure, Staying Poor: The "Faustian Bargain"', *World Development* 31 (3): 455–71.

Wood, G. and I. Gough. 2006. 'A Comparative Welfare Regime Approach to Global Social Policy', *World Development* 34 (10): 1696–1712.

World Bank. 1990. *World Development Report 1990.* Oxford: Oxford University Press.

———. 2008. *The Welfare Impact of Rural Electrification: A Reassessment of Costs and Benefits.* Washington DC: World Bank.

———. 2014. *World Development Indicators.* Washington DC: World Bank.

Wright, E. 1994. *Interrogating Inequality: Essays on Class Analysis, Socialism and Marxism.* London; New York: Verso.

Wuyts, M. 2011. 'The Working Poor: A Macro-perspective'. Valedictory address. The Hague: Institute of Social Studies. Available at: http://www.iss.nl/fileadmin/ASSETS/iss/Documents/Academic_publications/MarcWwuyts_valedictory.pdf.

Yadav, Y. 1999. 'Electoral Politics in the Time of Change: India's Third Electoral System, 1989–99', *Economic and Political Weekly* 34 (34/35): 2393–99.

———. 2010. 'On Remembering Lohia', *Economic and Political Weekly* 45 (40): 46–50.

Yang, A. 1989. *The Limited Raj: Agrarian Relations in Colonial India, Saran District, 1793–1920.* Berkeley, Los Angeles, London: University of California Press.

Yankah, K. 2001. 'Nana Ampadu and the Sung-tale Metaphor', in *African Words, African Voices: Critical Practices in Oral History*, edited by L. White, S. Miescher, and D. W. Cohen, 65–84. Bloomington, Indiana: Indiana University Press.

Yashar, D. 2005. *Contesting Citizenship in Latin America: The Rise of Indigenous Movements and the Postliberal Challenge.* Cambridge: Cambridge University Press.

Young, I. 1989. *Justice and the Politics of Difference.* Princeton: Princeton University Press.

———. 1990. *Justice and the Politics of Difference.* Princeton: Princeton University Press.

———. 2005. 'The Five Faces of Oppression', in *Oppression, Privilege and Resistance: Theoretical Perspectives on Racism, Sexism and Heterosexism*, edited by L. Heldke and P. O'Connor, 37–63. McGraw-Hill Humanities Social.

Yugandhar, B. N. and K. G. Iyer. 1993. *Land Reforms in India. Volume 1 (Bihar). Institutional Constraints.* Delhi; London; Thousand Oaks: Sage.

Zakaria, F. 1997. 'The Rise of Illiberal Democracy', *Foreign Affairs* 76 (6): 22–43.

Zald, M. N. and R. Ash. 1966. 'Social Movement Organizations: Growth, Decay and Change', *Social Forces*: 327–41.

Zelliott, E. 2001. *From Untouchable to Dalit: Essays on the Ambedkar Movement*. New Delhi: Manohar.

Index